Assumptions

poems

Marilyn Hacker

YEST

Marina Makarova

THE LONG APPROACH

poems by

Maxine Kumin

Something to Say

illiam Carlos Williams on Younger Poets

EDITED BY JAMES E. B. BRESLIN

Dictionary of Literary Biography
Yearbook: 1985

Dictionary of Literary Biography

Dictionary of Literary Biography
Yearbook: 1985

Edited by
Jean W. Ross

A Bruccoli Clark Book
Gale Research Company • Book Tower • Detroit, Michigan 48226

Manufactured by Edwards Brothers, Inc.
Ann Arbor, Michigan
Printed in the United States of America

Contents

Obituaries

Plan of the Series

. . . Almost the most prodigious asset of a country, and perhaps its most precious possession, is its native literary product—when that product is fine and noble and enduring.

Mark Twain*

The advisory board, the editors, and the publisher of the *Dictionary of Literary Biography* are joined in endorsing Mark Twain's declaration. The literature of a nation provides an inexhaustible resource of permanent worth. It is our expectation that this endeavor will make literature and its creators better understood and more accessible to students and the literate public, while satisfying the standards of teachers and scholars.

To meet these requirements, *literary biography* has been construed in terms of the author's achievement. The most important thing about a writer is his writing. Accordingly, the entries in *DLB* are career biographies, tracing the development of the author's canon and the evolution of his reputation.

The publication plan for *DLB* resulted from two years of preparation. The project was proposed to Bruccoli Clark by Frederick G. Ruffner, president of the Gale Research Company, in November 1975. After specimen entries were prepared and typeset, an advisory board was formed to refine the entry format and develop the series rationale. In meetings held during 1976, the publisher, series editors, and advisory board approved the scheme for a comprehensive biographical dictionary of persons who contributed to North American literature. Editorial work on the first volume began in January 1977, and it was published in 1978.

In order to make *DLB* more than a reference tool and to compile volumes that individually have claim to status as literary history, it was decided to organize volumes by topic or period or genre. Each of these freestanding volumes provides a biographical-bibliographical guide and overview for a particular area of literature. We are convinced that this organization—as opposed to a single alphabet method—constitutes a valuable innovation in the presentation of reference material. The volume plan necessarily requires many decisions for the placement and treatment of authors who might properly be included in two or three volumes. In some instances a major figure will be included in separate volumes, but with different entries emphasizing the aspect of his career appropriate to each volume. Ernest Hemingway, for example, is represented in *American Writers in Paris, 1920-1939* by an entry focusing on his expatriate apprenticeship; he is also in *American Novelists, 1910-1945* with an entry surveying his entire career. Each volume includes a cumulative index of subject authors. The final *DLB* volume will be a comprehensive index to the entire series.

With volume ten in 1982 it was decided to enlarge the scope of *DLB* beyond the literature of the United States. By the end of 1985 twenty-one volumes treating British literature had been published, and volumes for Commonwealth and Modern European literature were in progress. The series has been further augmented by the *DLB Yearbooks* (since 1981) which update published entries and add new entries to keep the *DLB* current with contemporary activity. There have also been occasional *DLB Documentary Series* volumes which provide biographical and critical background source materials for figures whose work is judged to have particular interest for students. One of these companion volumes is entirely devoted to Tennessee Williams.

The purpose of *DLB* is not only to provide reliable information in a convenient format but also to place the figures in the larger perspective of literary history and to offer appraisals of their accomplishments by qualified scholars.

We define literature as the *intellectual commerce of a nation:* not merely as belles lettres, but as that ample and complex process by which ideas are generated, shaped, and transmitted. *DLB* entries are not limited to "creative writers" but extend to other figures who in this time and in this way influenced the mind of a people. Thus the series encompasses historians, journalists, publishers, and screenwriters. By this means readers of *DLB* may be aided to perceive literature not as cult scripture in the keeping of cultural high priests, but as at the center of a nation's life.

---

*From an unpublished section of Mark Twain's autobiography, copyright © by the Mark Twain Company.

DLB includes the major writers appropriate to each volume and those standing in the ranks immediately behind them. Scholarly and critical counsel has been sought in deciding which minor figures to include and how full their entries should be. Wherever possible, useful references will be made to figures who do not warrant separate entries.

Each *DLB* volume has a volume editor responsible for planning the volume, selecting the figures for inclusion, and assigning the entries. Volume editors are also responsible for preparing, where appropriate, appendices surveying the major periodicals and literary and intellectual movements for their volumes, as well as lists of further readings. Work on the series as a whole is coordinated at the Bruccoli Clark editorial center in Columbia, South Carolina, where the editorial staff is responsible for the accuracy of the published volumes.

One feature that distinguishes *DLB* is the illustration policy—its concern with the iconography of literature. Just as an author is influenced by his surroundings, so is the reader's understanding of the author enhanced by a knowledge of his environment. Therefore *DLB* volumes include not only drawings, paintings, and photographs of authors, often depicting them at various stages in their careers, but also illustrations of their families and places where they lived. Title pages are regularly reproduced in facsimile along with dust jackets for modern authors. The dust jackets are a special feature of *DLB* because they often document better than anything else the way in which an author's work was launched in its own time. Specimens of the writers' manuscripts are included when feasible.

A supplement to *DLB*—tentatively titled *A Guide, Chronology, and Glossary for American Literature*—will outline the history of literature in North America and trace the influences that shaped it. This volume will provide a framework for the study of American literature by means of chronological tables, literary affiliation charts, glossarial entries, and concise surveys of the major movements. It has been planned to stand on its own as a vade mecum, providing a ready-reference guide to the study of American literature as well as a companion to the *DLB* volumes for American literature.

Samuel Johnson rightly decreed that "The chief glory of every people arises from its authors." The purpose of the *Dictionary of Literary Biography* is to compile literary history in the surest way available to us—by accurate and comprehensive treatment of the lives and work of those who contributed to it.

The *DLB* Advisory Board

Foreword

The *Dictionary of Literary Biography Yearbook* is guided by the same principles that have provided the basic rationale for the entire *DLB* series: 1) the literature of a nation represents an inexhaustible resource of permanent worth; 2) the surest way to trace the outlines of literary history is by a comprehensive treatment of the lives and works of those who contributed to it; and 3) the greatest service the series can provide is to make literary achievement better understood and more accessible to students and the literate public, while serving the needs of scholars. In keeping with those principles, the *Yearbook* has been planned to augment *DLB* by reflecting the vitality of contemporary literature and summarizing current literary activity. The librarian, scholar, or student attempting to stay informed of literary developments is faced with an endless task. The purpose of *DLB Yearbook* is to serve these readers while at the same time enlarging the scope of *DLB*.

DLB Yearbook is divided into four sections: articles about the past year's literary events or topics; obituaries and tributes; updates of published *DLB* entries; and new author entries. The articles section features essays which discuss the year's work in literary biography, fiction, poetry, and drama. The *Yearbook* also endeavors to cover major awards and prizes. This volume covers the 1985 Nobel Prize in Literature (including the Nobel Lecture and an excerpt from prizewinner Claude Simon's work) and the new Ritz Paris Hemingway Award. Each year a literary research archive is described; the 1985 *Yearbook*'s subject is the John Carter Brown Library. In "Biographical Documents," the *Yearbook* presents the Bobbs-Merrill questionnaires of four writers, including Vladimir Nabokov. Literary topics of current interest are explored: in this *Yearbook* there are reports on the *Adventures of Huckleberry Finn* centennial and a new edition of *Huck Finn;* symposia on the current popularity of mystery fiction and the status of Ernest Hemingway; and a history of *Contempo*. A special feature of the first section is an interview with a distinguished practicing biographer—this year William Manchester—and an article on The Spirit That Moves Us Press is the second in a series on small presses.

The death of a literary figure prompts an assessment of his achievement and reputation. The Obituaries section marks the passing of four authors in 1985.

The third section, Updated Entries, is designed to supplement the *DLB* series with current information about the literary activities of authors who have entries in previously published *DLB* volumes. An Updated Entry takes as its point of departure an already published *DLB* entry, augmenting primary and secondary bibliographical information, providing descriptions and assessments of new works, and, when necessary, reassessing an author's reputation. The form of entry is similar to that in the standard *DLB* series, and an Updated Entry is preceded by a reference to the *DLB* volume in which the basic entry on the subject appears. Readers seeking information about an author's entire career should consult the basic entry along with the Updated Entry for complete biographical and bibliographical information.

The fourth section is devoted to New Entries on figures not previously included in *DLB*. These entries follow the established format for the series: emphasis is placed on biography and summaries of the critical reception of the author's works; primary bibliographies precede each entry, and a list of references follows the entry.

Each *Yearbook* includes a list of literary prizes and awards, a necrology, and a checklist of books about literary history and biography published during the year.

From the outset, the *DLB* series has undertaken to compile literary history as it is revealed in the lives and works of authors. The *Yearbook* supports that commitment, providing a useful and necessary current record. The march of literature does not halt.

Acknowledgments

This book was produced by BC Research. Karen L. Rood is senior editor for the *Dictionary of Literary Biography* series.

Art supervisor is Patricia M. Flanagan. Copyediting supervisor is Patricia Coate. Production coordinator is Kimberly Casey. Typesetting supervisor is Laura Ingram. The production staff includes Rowena Betts, David R. Bowdler, Joseph Matthew Bruccoli, Deborah Cavanaugh, Kathleen M. Flanagan, Joyce Fowler, Ellen Hassell, Pamela Haynes, Judith K. Ingle, Beatrice McClain, Judith E. McCray, Mary Scott Sims, Joycelyn R. Smith, and Lucia Tarbox. Joseph Caldwell, photography editor, and James Adam Sutton did photographic copy work for the volume.

Walter W. Ross did the library research with the assistance of the staff at the Thomas Cooper Library of the University of South Carolina: Lynn Barron, Daniel Boice, Connie Crider, Kathy Eckman, Michael Freeman, Gary Geer, David L. Haggard, Jens Holley, Marcia Martin, Dana Rabon, Jean Rhyne, Jan Squire, Ellen Tillett, and Virginia Weathers. Valuable help was given also by staff members of the Richland County Public Library in Columbia, South Carolina.

Special thanks are due to the French Embassy in Washington, D.C., and the Swedish Academy; to the Lilly Library, Indiana University, for documents from the Bobbs-Merrill Papers; to Penguin Books Ltd; to the Steinbeck Research Center, San José State University; and to the Virginia Quarterly Review Records, University Archives, University of Virginia Library, to quote from their Editorial Papers.

Dictionary of Literary Biography Yearbook: 1985

Dictionary of Literary Biography

The 1985 Nobel Prize In Literature

CLAUDE SIMON
(1913-)

The 1985 Nobel Prize in Literature was awarded to Claude Simon, "who in his novels combines the poet's and painter's creativeness with a deepened awareness of time in the depiction of the human condition." The press release from the Swedish Academy noted that his "narrative art may appear as a representation of something that lives within us, whether we will it or not, whether we understand it or not, whether we believe it or not— something hopeful, in spite of all cruelty and absurdity which for that writer seem to characterize our condition and which is so perceptively, penetratingly, and abundantly reproduced in his novels."

Simon is associated with the *nouveau roman* school of French writers whose novels are not developed as connected or realistic narratives—instead juxtaposing seemingly unrelated events. He has commented, "I have discovered that everything means nothing and that ultimately there is nothing to say."

Simon's first novel, *Le Tricheur*, appeared in 1945. Since then he has published thirteen novels: *La Corde raide*, 1947; *Gulliver*, 1952; *Le Sacre du printemps*, 1954; *Le Vent*, 1957 (*The Wind*, New York: Braziller, 1959); *L'Herbe*, 1958 (*The Grass*, New York: Braziller, 1960); *La Route des Flandres*, 1960 (*The Flanders Road*, New York: Braziller, 1961); *Le Palace*, 1962 (*The Palace*, New York: Braziller, 1963); *Histoire*, 1967 (*Histoire*, New York: Braziller, 1968); *La Bataille de Pharsale*, 1969 (*The Battle of Pharsalus*, New York: Braziller, 1971); *Les Corps conducteurs*, 1971 (*Conducting Bodies*, New York: Viking, 1974); *Triptyque*, 1973 (*Triptych*, New York: Viking, 1976); *Leçon de choses*, 1975 (*The World About Us*, Princeton: Ontario Review Press, 1983); and *Les Géorgiques*, 1981.

NOBEL LECTURE 1985
Delivered by Claude Simon

Translated by James T. Day
University of South Carolina

Ladies and Gentlemen:

On the feelings of a prize-winner chosen by the Swedish Academy, there is no more appropriate comment than the one provided by one of my "Nobel colleagues," as we are called in a letter that Dr. André Lwoff was so kind as to send me:

"Since inquiry is a game," he wrote in his expression of thanks, "it matters little, at least in theory, whether one wins or loses. But intellectuals" (and I would say writers as well) "intellectuals, then, have certain traits in common with children. Like them they enjoy winning and like them they enjoy being rewarded"; to which André Lwoff added: "Deep down inside, every intellectual" (every writer, I would say again) "desires to be recognized."

And, if I try to analyze the many facets of this satisfaction, which in some ways is childlike, I would say that a certain pride is involved and that, beyond me personally, what attracts attention is the country that is mine for better or worse, a country where it should be known that, despite this "worse," there exists a kind of obstinate spirit of protest that is denigrated, made fun of, sometimes even hypocritically persecuted; a certain life of the mind which, in itself, with no other purpose or reason than merely to exist, makes this country one of the places where, unaffected by the inertia or sometimes even the hostility of various powers, some of today's most threatened values still survive.

Claude Simon (courtesy of the Swedish Academy)

Next, in addressing the members of your Academy, I would like to say that, if I express to them how appreciative I am of their choice, it is not just out of devotion to ritual or mere respect for the rules of courtesy.

Indeed, it does not seem to be by chance that this institution is located and deliberates in Sweden, and in Stockholm in particular; that is, more or less in the geographic center or, in other words, at the crossroads of this Scandinavia which is so small with respect to the number of its inhabitants but which, with respect to its culture, its traditions, its civility, its appetite for knowledge and its laws, is so large that ultimately it makes up a kind of privileged and exemplary islet on the edge of the hard world of violence in which we live.

So it is not by chance that the first translations of my latest work, *Les Géorgiques* (*The Georgics*), appeared in Norwegian, in Swedish, and in Danish; and again it is not by chance that, just last winter, on the shelves of a bookstore in a tiny hamlet lost amid forests and lakes, another translation could be found, this one in the Finnish language, whereas (to speak of only one of the monstrous giants that

severed hand fastened to the wall in the background of that portrait painted in grisaille hanging between the whatnot and the piano so that I could so to speak see him twice: the first time in flesh and blood (in that suit which, though it was merely dark and not black, was for me—perhaps by reason of its ceremonial aspect contrasting with the habitual informality of his clothes—the garb, the very uniform of reliction), sitting on that out-of-the-way couch where he usually remained, at the back of the salon, behind the shadowy old queens, and the second in the form of that great-grandfather portrayed standing in front of an easel, holding a mahlstick in his right hand a little in front of his body, at waist height, the other hand resting on his hip, parting the romantic gray frock-coat to reveal an embroidered waistcoat and putty-colored trousers, fixing the artist painting him (perhaps himself in a mirror) with a severe, pensive gaze under the romantic hair falling to his collar, while behind him (on the portion of the wall between his body and the inclined riser of the easel) you could see one of those plaster heads with a heavy chin and bulging blind eyes, hanging alongside the hand severed at the wrist and whose look of an anatomical specimen with its plaster veins, its plaster tendons, its plaster nails, gave the subject of the portrait an ambiguous character, as if he were holding at the end of his bent arm not an inoffensive mahlstick but some scientific and coldly cruel instrument like a scalpel or a lancet

Excerpt from Histoire *(1967), winner of the Médicis Prize*

crush us with their bulk) upon the announcement of this last Nobel choice, the *New York Times* questioned American critics in vain, and the media of my country were rushing around looking for information on this practically unknown author, while the popular press, for lack of critical accounts of my works, was publishing the most fanciful news about my activities as a writer or about my life—

when they were not deploring your decision as a national catastrophe for France.

Of course, I am neither presumptuous enough nor even foolish enough to be unaware that in the areas of art or literature any choice is questionable and, to a certain extent, arbitrary; and I am the first to consider that several other writers here and there in the world and in France, for whom I have the greatest respect, could easily have been chosen or perhaps should have been chosen instead of me.

If I have alluded to the sometimes indignant astonishment echoed in the press (or even frightened astonishment: a widely circulated French weekly asked whether the Soviet K.G.B. might not have infiltrated your Academy!), I do not want people to think I have done so in a petty spirit of gloating or easy triumph, but because these protests, this indignation, this very fright, were expressed in terms that are the best possible illustration of the problems which, in the areas of literature and art, pit conservative forces against others that I would not call "progressive" (in art, this word has no meaning) but "advancing," shedding light on the progressively widening gap we have heard so much about between living art and the broad public that is kept fearful and in a state of retardation by the powers that be, whose greatest fear is change.

Let us put aside the complaints that have been expressed about my being a "difficult," "boring," "unreadable," or "muddled" author, simply recalling that the same reproaches have been formulated with respect to any artist who has ever so slightly disturbed ingrained habits and the established order, and we should wonder at the fact that the grandchildren of those who saw the impressionist paintings as formless (that is, unreadable) daubings now interminably stand in line in exhibits or museums to go and "admire"(?) [*sic*] the works of these same daubers.

Let us also put aside the insinuation that certain agents of a political police might be sitting in your midst and might dictate your choice, although it is not without interest to note in passing that even today, in some circles, the Soviet Union remains the symbol of formidable forces of destabilization, with which it is actually flattering for a mere writer to see himself associated, for the selfish and vain gratuitousness of what is called "art for art's sake" has been denounced so often that for me it is no small reward to see my writings, which had no other ambition than to rise to this level, ranked among

the instruments of revolutionary and destabilizing action.

What I think is more interesting to deal with and deserves our attention is the issue of other judgments formulated about my work, which, given their nature and the vocabulary they use, shed light not upon a misunderstanding that might exist between the upholders of a certain tradition and what I would call living literature, but upon what seems like a veritable reversal (or, rather, an inversion) of the situation, for each of the terms used in a pejorative sense is actually used most judiciously, except that, contrary to the intentions of the critic, these terms have positive value in my eyes.

I shall come back to the criticism that my novels have "neither a beginning nor an end," which is quite correct, but first I would like to dwell on two naturally or rather logically associated adjectives which are damning and which immediately show where the problem is: I mean those that criticize my works as being the product of effort that is "laborious" and thus of necessity "artificial."

The dictionary gives the following definition of this last word: "made with art," and also, "that which is the product of human activity and not of nature," which is such a relevant definition that it could be accepted, but for the fact that, paradoxically, the associated connotations, commonly bearing a pejorative meaning, upon examination turn out to be most instructive—for if "artificial," as the dictionary adds, also describes something "factitious, fabricated, false, imitated, invented, fake," it immediately comes to mind that art, which above all is something invented and also factitious (from the Latin *facere*, "to make") and therefore fabricated (a word which should have its loftiness restored), is above all an imitation (which quite obviously presupposes falsity). But it is still necessary to qualify the nature of this imitation, for art is self-generating, so to speak, through imitation of itself: just as it is not the desire to reproduce nature which makes the painter but rather fascination with the museum, it is the desire to write, stimulated by fascination with the thing written, that makes the writer; while nature is limited, as Oscar Wilde wittily put it, merely "to imitate art. . . ."

And it is indeed a language of artisans which, for centuries before, during, and after the Renaissance, was characteristic of the greatest writers or musicians, sometimes treated like servants, doing commissioned works and speaking of them (I'm thinking of Johann Sebastian Bach, of Nicolas Poussin. . .) as works executed most laboriously and conscientiously. How then are we to explain that today, for certain critics, the notions of labor, of work, have fallen into such discredit that to say about a writer that he experiences difficulty in writing strikes them as the ultimate put-down? It might not be a bad idea to pause and consider this issue, which points to much broader horizons than mere outbursts of strong feeling.

"A common practice or any item," writes Marx in the first chapter of *Capital,* "has value only to the extent that human work is materialized in it." And such indeed is the labor-oriented origin of any value. Although I am neither a philosopher nor a sociologist, I feel troubled to observe that it is during the nineteenth century, parallel to the development of mechanization and all-out industrialization, that we encounter the rise of a certain guilty conscience and at the same time a devaluation of the notion of work (this work of transformation that is so badly rewarded): the writer is then dispossessed of the fruit of his efforts in favor of what some have called "inspiration," which makes him a simple intermediary, the mouthpiece serving some vague supernatural power, such that in contrast to his former status of paid servant or conscientious artisan, the writer now sees his personhood as simply denied: he is no more than a transcriber, or the translator of a book already written somewhere, a kind of decoding machine designed to render deciphered messages that are dictated to it from a mysterious nether world.

You can see the strategy, which is both elitist and annihilating: honored in this role of enraptured Delphic figure or oracle and yet being really nothing, the writer still belongs to an elite caste to which no one can hope to gain admittance through his merit or work. Quite the contrary, work, as formerly was the case for members of the nobility, is considered ignominious, degrading. The term that will be used to judge a creative work will quite naturally be a religious term, "grace," this grace which, as everyone knows, cannot be acquired through any virtue or even spiritual practice.

As the privileged depositary or holder, through the effect of this grace, of a body of knowledge ("Do you *have* something to say?" asked Sartre—in other words, "What knowledge do you *possess*?"), and so as a depositary even before writing about knowledge denied to ordinary mortals, the writer finds he is assigned the mission of informing them about it, and so the novel quite naturally will take on picturesque form in which religious instruction is provided, that of the parable or the fable. If the writer's personhood is overlooked (he must

"efface himself" behind his characters), so is his work, as well as its product, the writing itself: "The best style is the one that goes unnoticed," it is customary to write, recalling the famous statement that a novel is only "a mirror held up to the roadway": a uniform plane surface, with no rough spots, with nothing else behind a thin plate of polished metal than these virtual images which it reflects one after the other, indifferently, objectively—in other words: "the world as if I were not there to put it into words," according to Baudelaire's statement giving an ironic definition of "realism."

"In awarding Claude Simon the Nobel Prize, did they mean to confirm the rumor that the novel was finally dead?" a critic inquires. He does not yet seem to have noticed that if by "novel" he means the literary model that blossomed during the nineteenth century, it is indeed quite dead, despite the fact than in train stations and elsewhere people will keep on buying and selling thousands of amusing or scary adventure stories with optimistic or gloomy endings, and with titles heralding revealed truths, such as *La condition humaine* (*Man's Fate*), *L'espoir* (*Man's Hope*), or *Les chemins de la liberté* (*The Paths of Freedom*)...

What I think is more interesting is the observation that, even though two giants such as Proust and Joyce blazed completely new trails, all they did was to sanction a slow evolution during which the so-called realist novel slowly died of its own accord.

"I was trying," wrote Marcel Proust, "to find beauty where I had never imagined it to be: in the most commonplace things, in the hidden vitality of still-life paintings." And with another perspective, in an article entitled "On Literary Evolution," published in Leningrad in 1927, the Russian essayist Tynianov wrote: "On the whole, descriptions of nature in older novels, which from the standpoint of a certain literary system, might seem to have merely the secondary function of providing a transition or of slowing the pace (and thus one overlooks them), should be considered as a principal component, for it might be the case that the fable is no more than the motivation, the pretext for accumulating static descriptions." To my eyes this text, which seems prophetic in some respects, invites several comments.

First of all, let us observe that the first meaning of the word "fable" according to the dictionary is as follows: "Short narrative from which one draws a moral." An objection immediately comes to mind: as a matter of fact, the actual process of the fable's fabrication is exactly the reverse of this scheme—for indeed, it is the narrative that is drawn from the moral. For the fable writer, first there is a moral—"Might makes right," or "Every flatterer lives at the expense of the person who pays him heed"—and only after that can there be the story, which he invents to provide a picturesque demonstration, to illustrate the maxim, the precept or the thesis which the author intends in this way to make more striking.

This is the tradition which in France, from the short tales called *fabliaux* in the Middle Ages, to the fable writers and the comedies of manners or of character in the seventeenth century, then to the philosophical tale of the eighteenth century, led to the so-called realist novel of the nineteenth century, which aspired to didactic power: "You and a few other fine souls, as fine as yours," wrote Balzac, "will understand my thinking by reading *La maison Nucingen* and *César Birotteau* together. In this contrast, is there not an entire lesson about society?"

Boldly innovative in its time (a fact forgotten by his belated epigones who, a century and a half later, propose him as an example), sustained by a certain "frenzy of writing" and a certain penchant for excess that raised him above and beyond his intentions, the Balzacian novel later degenerated and gave rise to works which retained only the purely demonstrative aspect.

With this kind of perspective, any description appears not only superfluous but, as Tynianov stresses, unwelcome, since it attaches itself like a parasite to the action, slows it down, only delaying the moment when the reader is finally to discover the meaning of the story: "When I come upon a description in a novel, I skip the page," Henri de Montherlant used to say, and, in the *Second manifeste du surréalisme* (*Second Surrealist Manifesto*), André Breton (who was otherwise unlike Montherlant in every respect), declaring that the description of Raskolnikov's room bored him to death, exclaimed in a rage: "What right does an author have to dump his postcards on us?"

As social or psychological types "in action," simplified to the point of caricature (at least in a certain French tradition: "Harpagon is just a miser," observed Strindberg in his preface to *Miss Julie*. "He could have been at once an excellent town magistrate, an excellent paterfamilias or anything else; no, he is just a miser!"), the characters of the traditional novel are involved in a series of adventures, a succession of chain reactions supposedly brought about by a relentless cause and effect

mechanism which gradually leads them to the kind of ending that has been termed "the logical consummation of the novel," and which demonstrates the cogency of the author's message and expresses what his reader is to think about the men and women in society or History.

The problem is that these events, supposedly part of a causal chain, merely depend upon the fancy of the person who relates them and whose whims determine which characters meet or don't meet, like or dislike one another, live or die; and if these events are indeed possible, they also might just as well not have happened. As Conrad stresses in his preface to *The Nigger of the Narcissus*, the author appeals only to our willingness to believe, for, with regard to the "logic" of character-types or of situations, one could debate about them endlessly: while Henri Martineau, an eminent Stendhal scholar, assures us that Julien Sorel is predestined right from the beginning of *Le rouge et le noir* (*The Red and the Black*) to fire the critical pistol shot at Madame de Rênal, Emile Faguet on the other hand finds this ending "more artificial than is permissible. . . ."

This is very likely one of the reasons for the paradoxical fact that right from its very beginning the realist novel was already working toward its own destruction. Indeed, everything seems to suggest that these authors, in becoming aware of the weakness of the device to which they resort in getting their didactic message across (a device based entirely on the principle of causality), these authors had vaguely felt the need to give their fables greater substance in order to make them more convincing. Before that, in the novel or the philosophical tale, whether it be *La princesse de Clèves, Candide, Les liaisons dangereuses*, or even *La nouvelle Héloïse*, written by the nature-lover Rousseau, description is practically nonexistent and appears only in the form of unvarying stereotypes: all pretty women invariably have complexions "like lilies and roses," they are "fine-figured," old women are "hideous," shady spots are "cool," deserts "horrible" and so on. With Balzac (and here is perhaps where his genius lies), we see the appearance of long, detailed descriptions of places or characters, and in the course of the century these descriptions will not only become increasingly numerous but, instead of being confined to the beginning of the narrative or the first appearance of the character, they will be parceled out, added to the action in greater or smaller doses, and in the end they will be somewhat like a Trojan horse, simply overwhelming the fable that they were supposed to flesh out: if the tragic

*Dust jacket for the American edition of Claude Simon's
tenth novel*

stood rather than seen." A tree, a mountain, a stream, or rocks are designated by pictographic *signs*. "However, a new requirement is gradually felt, and this is to cause the spectator to witness, so to speak, the event . . . which is supposed to be the object of his meditation," and so what we finally have is the advent of naturalism, of which Giotto is one of the first artisans, with its evolution continuing until the time when, as Gombrich says, "the naturalist background scenery, previously conceived according to conceptions of medieval art for illustrating proverbs and inculcating moral lessons, this scenery which filled in the space devoid of characters and action . . . in a way devours the foregrounds in the sixteenth century, until the goal is achieved with specialists such as Joachim Patinir, such that what the painter creates is no longer relevant because of some association with an important subject, but because like music it reflects the very harmony of the universe."

After a slow evolution, the function of the painter ended up being reversed, in a way, and knowledge, or rather meaning, passed from one side of his activity to another, at first preceding and initiating it, and then finally resulting from this activity itself, which now no longer expresses meaning but produces it.

The same has been true of literature, and today it seems legitimate to claim for the novel (or to require of it) a more reliable kind of credibility than the ever debatable variety that can be attributed to a fictitious work, a credibility to be conferred upon the text by the pertinence of the relations between its parts, which will no longer be put into order or sequence according to a causal scheme that is outside the literary work, such as the psychosocial type of causality that is the rule in the traditional "realist" novel, but according to an intrinsic causality, in the sense that any event, now described and not related, will follow or precede any other only according to their individual characteristics.

If I cannot accept the idea of this deus ex machina which makes it too easy for the characters in a story to meet or not to meet, on the other hand I find it entirely believable, *because it is in the perceivable order of things*, that Proust should suddenly be transported from the courtyard of the Guermantes' mansion to the porch of San Marco in Venice by the sensation of two paving stones under his foot, or that Molly Bloom should indulge in erotic fantasies inspired by the thought of the juicy fruit that she intends to buy the next day in the market,

end of Julien Sorel by the guillotine, that of Emma Bovary poisoned by arsenic, or that of Anna Karenina throwing herself under a train may seem to be the logical culmination of their adventures and the illustration of the moral, on the other hand no moral can be drawn from the demise of Albertine whom Proust causes to disappear (one might be tempted to say, "whom he gets rid of ") through a commonplace horse-riding accident.

There would seem to be an interesting parallel to be drawn between the evolution that took place in the novel during the nineteenth century and that of painting, which began much earlier: "The end (the goal) of Christian art," wrote Ernest Gombrich, "is to give the holy figure and especially biblical History a convincing and moving place in the eyes of the spectator." Initially conceived by the Byzantines as an instrument of edification and used for didactic ends, "the event is related through use of clear and simple hieroglyphs that make it under-

or again that Faulkner's unfortunate Benjy should cry out in pain when he hears golf players yell the word "caddie," and I find all that believable because between these things, these reminiscences, these sensations, there exists an obvious community of characteristics, or in other words a certain harmony which, in these examples, is the result of associations, of assonances, but which can also result, as in painting or music, from contrasts, oppositions, or dissonances.

And with this we begin to catch sight of an answer to the eternal questions: "Why do you write? What do you have to say?"

"If . . . people ask," wrote Paul Valéry, "if people worry (and it happens, sometimes rather spiritedly) about what I meant to say . . . , I reply that I did not mean *to say* but that I meant *to do* and that it is this intention *to do* that *meant* what *I said*." I could go over the terms of this answer point by point: if the range of the writer's motivations is extensive, perhaps the need for recognition mentioned by André Lwoff is not the most futile one, for it first necessitates being recognized by oneself, which implies a "doing" (I do—I produce—therefore I am), whether it is a matter of building a bridge, a ship, of "doing" a harvest or of composing a quartet. And, to remain within the confines of writing, we should recall that "to do" in Greek is "poiein," which is the origin of the word *poem*, about the nature of which we should perhaps inquire, for, if you agree to concede a certain freedom to what in colloquial language is customarily called the poet, why is it that the prose writer is refused this freedom and instead is only assigned the mission to be a teller of fables, with no other consideration on the nature of this language he is supposed to use as a mere vehicle? Doesn't this overlook the fact that, as Mallarmé put it, "each time there is an effort for style, there is versification" and overlook the question raised by Flaubert in a letter to George Sand: "How does it happen that there is a necessary relation between the precise word choice and the musical word choice?"

Now I am an old man, and as with many inhabitants of our old Europe, the first part of my life was quite eventful: I witnessed a revolution, I went to war in unusually deadly conditions (I belonged to one of those regiments that commanders coldly sacrifice in the advance and of which, after a week, there remains practically nothing), I was taken prisoner, I knew hunger and physical labor to the point of exhaustion, I escaped, I was seri-ously ill, several times on the brink of violent or natural death, I mingled with all kinds of people, with priests and also with people who burned churches, with peace-loving middle-class citizens and also with anarchists, with philosophers and with illiterates, I shared my bread with lawbreakers, and I traveled all over the world . . . and yet, at age seventy-two, I have still never discovered any meaning to it all, unless it might be that, as I think Barthes said after Shakespeare, "if the world has a meaning, it is that there is no meaning"—except that it exists.

As you can see, I have nothing to say, in the Sartrian sense of this expression. For that matter, if some important social or historic or sacred truth has ever been revealed to me, it would have seemed highly odd to me to expose it by means of an invented piece of fiction instead of a rational treatise in philosophy, sociology, or theology.

What is there "to do," then, to get back to Valéry's word, and this leads straight to the following question: to do with what?

Well, when I find myself in front of a blank page, I'm faced with two things: on the one hand the murky mixture of emotions, memories, and images that are inside me, and on the other there is language, the words I am going to look for to express them, the syntax with which they are going to be arranged and within which they will more or less crystallize.

And right off there is a first observation: one never writes down (or describes) something that happened before the activity of the writing, but rather what happens (in every sense of the term) in the course of this activity, in its *present*, and what results—not from the conflict between the very vague initial project and language, but on the contrary from a symbiosis between the two which, at least with me, causes the result to be infinitely more rich than the intention.

This phenomenon of the present of writing is experienced by Stendhal when he sets out in his autobiography *La vie de Henry Brulard* (*The Life of Henry Brulard*) to tell about going through the Saint Bernard pass with Napoleon's army. While he is striving to produce the most truthful account possible, he says, he suddenly realizes that he might be describing some engraving that depicts this event, an engraving he has seen since then and which, he writes, "has been substituted (in him) for reality." If he had gone further with his reflection—for it is easy to imagine the number of things depicted in this engraving: cannon, wagons, soldiers, horses, glaciers, rocks, etc., of which the mere listing would have taken up several pages, whereas Stendhal's account occupies only one—he would have realized, then, that he was not even describing this engraving but rather an image which was just then taking shape inside him and which was being substituted for the engraving he imagined he was describing.

More or less consciously, according to the imperfections of his perception and then of his memory, the writer subjectively selects, chooses, eliminates, but also valorizes among some hundred or thousand aspects of a scene: how far are we from the impartial mirror held up to the roadway and to which this same Stendhal aspired.

If there was ever a break, a radical change in the history of art, it was when painters, soon followed by writers, stopped pretending to represent the visible world but only the impressions they received from it.

"A man in good health," wrote Tolstoy, "thinks fluently, feels and remembers an incalculable number of things at once." This remark should be compared to what Flaubert said about Emma Bovary: "Everything inside her in the way of reminiscences, images, and combinations was going off at the same time, and all at once, like the thousand pieces in a fireworks display. She could make out clearly, in separate scenes, Leon, Lheureux's office, their distant room together, a landscape, unknown faces."

If Flaubert speaks in this way of a sick woman, overcome by a kind of delirium, Tolstoy goes farther and generalizes when he says: "a man in good health." They are in agreement on the observation that all these reminiscences, all these emotions, and all these thoughts come up at the same time, all at once, but Flaubert states that for him it is a matter of "separate scenes," or in other words of fragments, and that the manner in which they come to us is in "combinations."

Now you can see the weak point in the timid proposition of Tynianov, who, although he judged that the traditional type of novel was outmoded, was unable to conceive for the future anything but a novel where the fable would only be the pretext for an "accumulation" of "static" descriptions.

Here indeed lies one of the paradoxes of writing: the description of what one might call an apparently static "interior scene," whose main feature is that nothing in it is either far or near, turns out not to be static at all but rather dynamic: the writer, forced by the linear configuration of language to list the components of this scene one after another (which already amounts to making a preferential

choice, a subjective valorization of certain components in relation to others), just as he begins to write a word on the paper, has immediate contact with this prodigious mass, this prodigious network of relations established in and by language, which, as it has been said, "already speaks before we do" by means of what are called its rhetorical "figures" or tropes—the metonymies and metaphores among which not a one is the result of chance since they are actually an integral part of the knowledge man has gradually acquired of the world and of things.

And if, following Shklovsky, we agree to define the "literacy act" as "the transfer of an object from its everyday perception to the sphere of a new perception," how would a writer seek to reveal the mechanisms that produce in him the association of this "incalculable number" of apparently "separate" "scenes" which make him a sentient being, and inside of whom, in his wisdom and logic, innumerable transfers or shifts of meaning are already suggested? Words, according to Lacan, are not just "signs" but clusters of meanings or even, as I wrote in my short preface to *Orion aveugle* (*Blind Orion*), intersections of meanings, such that merely by its vocabulary language already offers the possibility of "combinations" in an "incalculable number." And thanks to this, the "adventure of a story" upon which a writer embarks at his own risk appears in the end more reliable than those more or less arbitrary stories offered up to us by the naturalist novel with a self-confidence that is all the more arrogant in that it is well aware of the fragility and the quite debatable value of its means.

So—to show instead of to demonstrate, to produce instead of to reproduce, to discover instead of to express. Just like painting, the novel no longer proposes to draw its relevance from some association with an important subject, but from the fact that it strives to reflect, like music, a certain harmony. In asking "What is 'realism'?" Roman Jacobson points out that it is customary to judge the realism of a novel not by referring to "reality" itself (a single object with a thousand aspects) but to a literary genre which developed in the last century. One forgets that the characters in these narratives have no other reality than that of the writing which engenders them: how then could this writing "efface itself" behind a story and events that exist only through it? In fact, just like painting when it took as a pretext some biblical, mythological, or historical scene (who can seriously believe in the "reality" of some *Crucifixion* or *Suzanne in Her Bath* or *Rape of the Sabine Women*?), what writing recounts for us, even with the most naturalist of writers, is its own adventure and its own magic. If this adventure is of no account, if this magic is not involved, then a novel, whatever in other respects its didactic or moral pretensions may be, is of no account as well.

Now and then people are eager to speak, and with authority, about the function and duties of a writer. Someone a few years ago even went so far as to declare, somewhat demagogically and in a statement that contains its own contradiction, that "in the face of the death of a little child in Biafra, no book is of any consequence." Indeed, if this death, unlike that of a baby monkey, is an intolerable scandal, it is because this child is a baby human, that is, a being endowed with a mind and a conscience, even if only embryonic, capable later, if it were to survive, of thinking and talking about its suffering, of reading about the suffering of others, of being affected by it and, with a bit of luck, of writing about it.

At the end of the Enlightenment and before the myth of "realism" was forged, Novalis expressed with amazing lucidity the apparent paradox that "it is the same with language as with mathematical formulas: they make up a self-sufficient world for their own sake; they interact exclusively among themselves, expressing nothing else than their own marvelous nature, and the result is that they are so expressive that in them, precisely, is reflected the strange interplay of the relations between things."

It is in seeking out this interplay that one might be able to conceive of an involvement with writing which, each time it changes ever so little the relation that man maintains with the world through his language, contributes in its modest way to changing the world. The path followed will then be quite different, as one can well imagine, from that of the novelist who, starting with a "beginning," arrives at an "end." This other path, cleared with great effort by an explorer in an unknown region (getting lost, retracing his steps, guided—or deceived—by the resemblance of certain places that are in fact different or, on the other hand, by the different aspects of a single place), this path often cuts back, returns to crossroads already traversed, and it can even happen (which is the most logical thing) that at the end of this investigation in the present of images and emotions where none is closer or farther than another (for words possess the prodigious power to draw together for comparison things which, without them, would remain scattered in the time of clocks and in measurable space), it can happen that one is brought back to the point of departure, but richer for having indicated a few directions, laid down a few footbridges, for having perhaps arrived, through an unrelenting investigation of detail, with no pretension of having said everything, at this "common ground" where everyone can recognize a small part—or a large part—of himself.

And so there can be no other ending than the exhaustion of the traveler exploring this inexhaustible landscape, contemplating the approximate map that he has drawn, and only half sure that in his movement he has done his best to obey certain impulses, certain inner forces. Nothing is sure and there are no other guarantees than those mentioned by Novalis and then Flaubert: a harmony, a certain music. Looking for these, the writer advances laboriously, gropes like a blind person, runs unto dead ends, gets bogged down, takes off again—and, if one absolutely insists on drawing a lesson from his course, it should be said that we are always moving forward on quicksand.

Thank you for your attention.

Huck at 100
How Old Is *Huckleberry Finn?*

Louis J. Budd
Duke University

Seeing that Mark Twain took care to send bound copies to the Copyright Office of the Library of Congress, which received them by 3 December 1884, it may sound simpleminded to ask, how old is *Adventures of Huckleberry Finn?* But his masterpiece grew so famous that any fine point about its history has fascinated scholars and collectors. Today they may read the title of this essay as a promise to settle the question of whether its centennial fell in 1984 or 1985.

Because the Congress of the United States still

Frontispiece for the first American edition of Adventures of Huckleberry Finn

had not agreed to international reciprocity and because the British steadily bought his books, Twain was eager to protect his copyrights in both Great Britain and Canada, which could be done only by first publication there. Canadian pirates had especially irritated him and had, in fact, cut substantially into royalties on his previous books. So he worked hard at "simultaning," at having the foreign and domestic editions of *Huckleberry Finn* issued on the same day.

However, always erratic about details, Twain currently had more projects going as a lecturer, businessman, and speculator than anybody should have hoped to carry off smoothly. Furthermore, he was still publishing by "subscription," that is, his books were sold door-to-door by agents who struggled for advance orders with the help of a prospectus, a booklet that displayed sample pages and other promotional materials. For months Twain insisted on holding back *Huckleberry Finn* until it had sold 40,000 copies. That decision was entirely his to enforce because he had just set up his own firm, Charles L. Webster and Company, named after and managed by a young, inexperienced nephew. More specifically, he was also aiming for the Christmas trade. A crucial problem among many others was that transatlantic messages took longer than today, and manuscripts had to travel by ship. Nevertheless, Twain did arrange for Chatto and Windus of London to publish the novel on 10 December 1884 while he spent that day in Canada in order to establish his copyright there more firmly.

At home, the repair of a damaged illustration (which now seemed indecent) in the first printing of 30,000 held up availability. The Mark Twain Project, based in the Bancroft Library of the University of California, Berkeley, decided that the operative publication came on 18 February 1885 and has acted accordingly. So *Huckleberry Finn* has enjoyed two centennials.

Eagerness to celebrate them was so strong that most well-wishers settled for 1984. The media, al-

12

ways eager to get anywhere first, rose above the qualms of scholars. In fact, on New Year's Day of that year the lead editorial in the *New York Times* began: "If you are already weary of 1984 and all that, think back, to 1884. Politically, it was nothing special. A woman . . . ran for President for the first time; she didn't make it. But it was an epochal year for American culture, producing an extraordinary work by a writer who called himself Mark Twain." Next, on 30 April 1984 the *Times* ran a feature story about Hannibal that quickly brought up the "100th anniversary of the publication of 'The Adventures of Huckleberry Finn,' a vernacular volume of 19th-century teen-age mischief and misadventure, along with serious social satire, that has enriched the lives of millions of readers. Its publication forever changed the course of American literature and the life of this Mississippi River city." Meanwhile, the *Los Angeles Times* of 15 January had printed " 'Huck Finn' Still Young at 100 Years/Twain's Masterpiece Speaks to the Present" by Naomi Bliven, who began with, " 'Huckleberry Finn' is 100 years old this month, but it reads brand-new."

Dozens of similar feature stories appeared in other newspapers and magazines. (Many of them used *The* at the head of Twain's title, though most scholars will not.) Perhaps inspired by either *Times,* Jonathan Yardley's feature for the *Washington Post* of 7 May 1984—"Thanks, Huck Finn: Theme Parks for His Centennial"—declared that "we must not lose sight" of *Huckleberry Finn* as "an important part of the common experience of generations of American readers." Surely a few from the living generation scolded Yardley for stating that the British edition had been published in May 1884. *American Heritage* had an obligatory spread in its June/July issue that furnished a useful, accurate chronology of the critical history of *Huckleberry Finn.*

As another early sign, on 6 February 1984 the *Durham* (N.C.) *Morning Herald,* adapting a release from the Duke University News Service, printed a story headed "Huck Finn: After 100 Years, The Boy Is Still Misunderstood." At least two North Carolina papers reprinted it as "Huck Finn A Century Old." An accompanying cartoon ("Huckleberry Finn Looking Good For His Age") presents a barefoot boy in overalls (not historically accurate) who carries a fishing pole; he exclaims, "Land Sakes! A hunnert years!" But weightier publications have also shown alertness. *America: History and Life* used the frontispiece of *Huckleberry Finn* as its cover illustration throughout 1984.

Scholarly conferences need at least a year of

Mark Twain, about 1878

foresight, and the essays for them take longer to write than a news story. Yet some alert literary historian arranged to have Henry Nash Smith, dean of Twain critics, deliver his long essay "The Publication of *Huckleberry Finn*: A Centennial Retrospect" in November 1983 for a meeting of the American Academy of Arts and Sciences. Well before 1984, Pennsylvania State University started to organize its conference "American Comedy: A Celebration of One Hundred Years of *Huckleberry Finn*." With Hamlin Hill as the keynoter it came off during 26-28 April 1984, even getting a one-sentence salute in *USA Today* as well as a long report in the faraway *Los Angeles Times* of 29 April, which was distinctly more respectful than quizzical about the group of seventy-five devotees. Besides Hill, at least nine critics dealt entirely or substantially with the honored novel. In response to a growing problem, one panel was devoted to its career in the "public schools."

On 9-12 August 1984 the Charles Dickens Project marked the "centenary of the publication of *Huckleberry Finn* in England" with a conference at the University of California, Santa Cruz. Leslie Fiedler was the keynoter. Though only one paper centered on *Huckleberry Finn*, the entire conference moved to the Berkeley campus to browse a Twain exhibit, hold a session on editing, and hear an address by J. Hillis Miller: "Picture and Text in Dickens and Twain." Funded by the Pennsylvania Humanities Council, Shippensburg University hosted a conference on 3-5 October 1984 that, besides four other discussions of Twain's masterpiece, heard lectures on "The American Literary Scene in 1884" (Larzer Ziff), "One Hundred Years of *Huckleberry Finn*" (Leslie Fiedler), and "*Huckleberry Finn* and the First Amendment" (Nat Hentoff). That conference ended with another panel on its career in the secondary schools.

The Program Committee for the 1984 meeting of the Modern Language Association approved a panel of three papers especially focused on the centennial by distinguished critics—James M. Cox, John C. Gerber, and Jay Martin. Appropriately, the University of Missouri held a major conference at Columbia in April 1985, when its press released a volume of twenty-five original essays about *Huckleberry Finn*, backed up with a checklist of previous criticism. Along with the Hartford (Connecticut) Public Library, the Mark Twain Memorial arranged a series of three lectures by David E. E. Sloane and exhibits as well as other talks. Along with the National Geographic Society, it mounted in Explorers Hall in Washington, D.C., an exhibit entitled "Mark Twain and *Huck Finn:* Joy-flags and Milestones," which started traveling to other cities in the fall of 1985. In Hannibal, from May to November, Henry Sweets, director of the Mark Twain Home and Museum, helped organize many events for a 150th Birthday Celebration lasting from May to November; it included a week-long Mark Twain Sesquicentennial Writers' Conference in June. At Elmira, a Mark Twain Festival Summer was followed with a series of visits in the fall by five distinguished scholars. Almost belatedly, Siena College decided to plan a "major conference on 'Mark Twain and His America' " to be held 12-13 December in Loudonville, New York. Before then, the United States Postal Service issued an appropriate aerogram in Hannibal on Twain's birthday, 30 November.

There were several projects solely for print. Naturally, the *Mark Twain Journal* lifted its banner high. The editor, Thomas A. Tenney, devoted its Fall 1984 issue to "Black Writers on *Adventures of Huckleberry Finn:* One Hundred Years Later." Just

as naturally, the United States Information Agency, wanting to project our most inviting images, distributed abroad a collection of appropriate essays (*Huck Finn among the Critics: A Centennial Selection*) edited by M. Thomas Inge. A commercial edition, with two added essays, has followed at home. More generally, *Studies in American Fiction* had a Mark Twain issue in the fall of 1985. Though not planned with the centennial in mind, *New Essays on "Adventures of Huckleberry Finn,"* which contains a long introduction by Louis J. Budd and four substantial essays from established critics, was published in late 1985 by Cambridge University Press.

For the October 1984 number of *American Studies International* Carl Dolmetsch had ready "*Huck Finn*'s First Century: A Bibliographical Survey" while sighing that the "ink will not be dry before another profusion of books and articles that one would wish to include here will render this undertaking something less than *au courant.*"

Dolmetsch's letter inviting comment by scholars and critics stated that he had found over 2,000 items, making it clear again that *Huckleberry Finn* "holds the distinction of being the single most-written about work in the history of American fiction." Many articles and books that otherwise would ignore Twain stretch to include *Huckleberry Finn* while those focused on him follow it as far as their own purposes will tolerate. It figures in two books on Twain published during 1984: Everett Emerson's *The Authentic Mark Twain: A Literary Biography of Samuel L. Clemens* (University of Pennsylvania Press) and *The Mythologizing of Mark Twain* (University of Alabama Press), eight new essays edited by Sara deSaussure Davis and Philip D. Beidler. Of course, as in any noncentennial year or years, many academics, freelancers, and journalists will take up *Huckleberry Finn*, briefly or in loving detail. Justin Kaplan found himself in steady demand. At the popular level the centennial evoked the two ultimate accolades: an article in *Reader's Digest* (February 1985), and in *People* (25 February) a sketch of Huck as ostensibly a real person.

If asked, "How old is Huck Finn?" Twain experts would answer that Twain helps out the reader once: Huck writes that Buck Grangerford "looked about as old as me—thirteen or fourteen or along there, though he was a little bigger than me." They may go on to warn that Huck has slipped past a major problem, more keenly felt during the past twenty years than before. It lay dormant partly because Twain covered it up so gracefully. On the first or even the second delighted time through Huck's adventures, few readers recognize that his

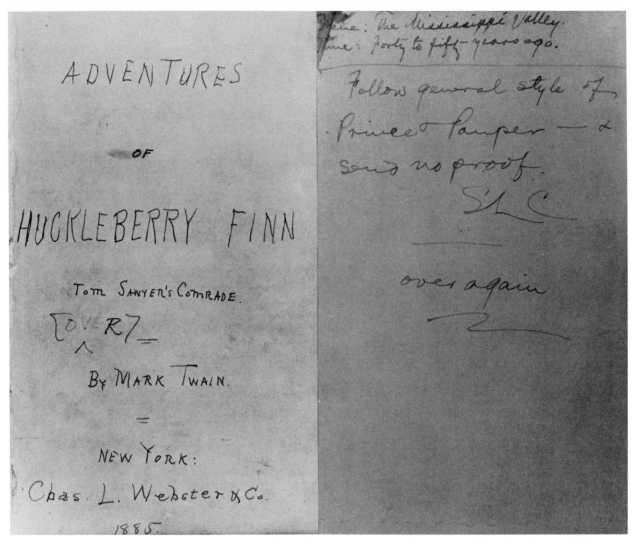

Mark Twain's title page and note to the printer for the manuscript of Huckleberry Finn *(Buffalo and Erie County Public Library)*

functional age is muddier than the river. Often he's the teenager the *New York Times* editorial recalled: skeptical, canny, resourceful, and quietly tough, confirming our notion that life had forced him to grow up ahead of his birthdays. But in the next chapter or even paragraph he turns mentally smaller than a boy of fourteen or even thirteen ought to be in any century. He can sound downright childlike, solemnly echoing Pap's excuses for stealing produce and chickens or reporting that Uncle Silas Phelps "never charged nothing for his preaching, and it was worth it, too." This naiveté helps us believe that Huck, who has roamed at will in a river town, knows little about sex and cares less.

Though pressure for civil rights rather than sexual frankness uncovered Twain's waffling, it

had literally been showing since the rise of Hollywood. Actually, any illustrated edition of the novel should force an egalitarian reader to wonder about the interplay of Huck and Jim. But when they emote from a movie (or television) screen, everybody should catch on to Twain's game. If the director makes Jim, who has a wife and children, hold to a firmly paternal tone, then Huck shrinks toward just a child who does not understand the seriousness of deciding, "All right, then, I'll *go* to hell!" Yet if Huck is bossing an adult—the choice Hollywood made, inevitably, up through the 1960s—then Jim dwindles to a dumb, helpless, grateful darky. In a musical during the 1970s loosely based on the plot, the two approach nearer the same age. But for a Huck that old, his comment about Uncle Silas and his other deadpan comedy would have to function as archly ironic, out of character for the warmhearted boy we admire.

It's not important to know whether Ralph Ellison saw a movie version of *Huckleberry Finn*. He needed only his honed sensitivity to object in 1958 that "Jim's friendship for Huck comes across as that of a boy for another boy rather than as the friendship of an adult for a junior." (That *Times* editorial says that Jim is Huck's "pal.") Once Ellison's point is made, who can forget it or deny it? Often, though not always (remember Twain's craftiness), the boy dominates this man old enough to be his father and on occasion shrewder than either of the white Finns.

The problem now keeps growing starker because of the novel's always rising status. Without mention of the centennial, Frederick Woodward and Donnarae MacCann, in their impressively documented "*Huckleberry Finn* and the Traditions of Blackface Minstrelsy" published in *Interracial Books for Children Bulletin*, decided that Jim plays the comic subordinate to a boy who is clearly his inferior in both intelligence and know-how. As another sign of concern among teachers, the summer 1984 workshop of the Virginia Center for the Liberal Arts, which is designed to let high school and college faculty learn from each other's approach, held a session on "The Pedagogical Adventures of *Huckleberry Finn*." Its most specific concern was the effect that Jim has on the racial attitudes of ninth graders.

Huckleberry Finn has occasionally been threatened by bannings ever since it first appeared. After World War II they have usually come from within the black community, as recently as July 1984 in Waukegan, Illinois. In 1982 a black administrator, John H. Wallace, joined a campaign to strike it from the required reading list at the Mark Twain Intermediate School in Fairfax County, Virginia. Defeated, he soon announced a text that uses *slave* wherever Huck wrote *nigger*. Ironically, the proposed bannings add a tang of the forbidden to a book that could start sounding like a Victorian period piece in our times of practically no taboos on vocabulary. More important, each indictment enlivens the defense. Typically, with "Morality and *Huckleberry Finn*" for the March/April 1984 issue of the *Humanist*, June Edwards confronted the three main lines of attack in order to conclude that the novel itself "was a powerful attack against prejudice and the narrow-minded religious and social strictures of the 1800s. One hundred years later, it still pricks our conscience." William McLinn, who impersonates Twain convincingly while using only

authentic quotations and who ran for President in 1984 under the slogan "Forget the Lemons—Vote for Clemens," has been resurrecting him as a firm if wry advocate for social justice.

But some citizens have agreed with John H. Wallace, who actively promotes his "adapted" edition and helps the charge of racism to persist. On 4 February 1985 that charge was validated in the public mind as a problem when Ted Koppel's "Nightline" focused a half-hour of ABC television time upon it. Wallace was matched against Nat Hentoff and the actor playing Jim for a stage version in Chicago. Meshach Taylor, the actor, and Wallace had in fact already debated the point at a public discussion arranged by the Goodman Theater itself.

Since that "Nightline" debate, no lengthy salute to the centennial has ignored racism. Angus Paul's carefully prepared article for the *Chronicle of Higher Education*, 15 February, acknowledged the "controversy" in his subtitle. In *Newsweek* of 18 February, George Will's "Huck at a Hundred" chided those who cannot see "which side Twain was on." After a Yale Ph.D. hotly denied in the *New York Times* that Twain was ever a racist, the responses led her to an unpublished letter about his helping support a black student through the Yale Law School. That letter, with her commentary, as in the *New York Times* of 14 March, got surprisingly wide coverage, amplified by appreciative editorials. Of course it entered into the *Christian Science Monitor*'s tribute on 15 March: "At 100, Huck Finn Is Still Causing Trouble." Meanwhile, Christopher Hitchens sided with Hentoff against Wallace for the *Times Literary Supplement* of 8 March. But no one, evidently, has decided to cite President Ronald Reagan's opinion, given after reading from the novel before the National Association for Independent Schools, that it teaches a "hatred of bigotry" (*Washington Post*, 1 March 1985). Though a generous segment of the "MacNeil-Lehrer News Hour" (28 May) focused on the charge of racism, the authorities appealed to were Wallace, high school teachers in Missouri, and students in New York City.

Complicating the debate over racist language and attitudes, Huck's age has changed in a way that Twain did not expect. Though no idea about *Huckleberry Finn* stands above challenge now, there's sound reason to argue that it was conceived and written as a boy's book, that is, an adventure story in which the main character stays unshakably pre-adult in mental age as well as appeal. An editorial introducing the Woodward and MacCann article rates it as "perhaps the most widely assigned novel for school children in the U.S." But the more clearly it graduates into a "classic" among mature critics, the more reluctant they are to consider Huck as a permanent boy. Christopher Clausen, who thinks that it was "written, illustrated, and marketed for children," decides that the "highest compliment a children's book can receive is for critics to say that it isn't for children at all."

At the least they should agree that Huck's story was planned as a sequel to *The Adventures of Tom Sawyer* (1876). The surface facts are plain: its title, subtitle (*Tom Sawyer's Comrade*), and opening words ("You don't know about me, without you have read a book by the name of 'The Adventures of Tom Sawyer' "). In 1885 many reviews, whether favorable or not, discussed the two novels together. Sometimes not quite consciously, many a critic has continued to do so right down to the present. The oddest case may be George Santayana. Tirelessly working to get famous names associated with the (then) *Mark Twain Quarterly*, Cyril Clemens approached him and next sent a copy of *Huckleberry Finn* because he had confessed to never having read any of Twain's "principal" books. Then Santayana responded with an essay on it that drifted without evident awareness into saying almost as much, admiringly, about *Tom Sawyer*.

True believers in *Huckleberry Finn* do not care to ponder the cases of joint identity or the combined editions of the two novels. In 1884 Twain had in fact considered such a volume himself. I have come across thirteen of those editions since his copyright lapsed, and *Books in Print* currently lists four, the latest (1979) with an introduction by James Dickey. Invariably and sensibly, *Tom Sawyer* has stood first in all of them, including Italian, German, and Russian translations.

The dominant effect from this pairing is to hold *Huckleberry Finn* toward the genre of a boy's book or, perhaps, a book for juveniles if closer distinctions are demanded. To be sure, complications usually develop where Twain is involved. Lately the pairing has had the countereffect of encouraging dark interpretations for *Tom Sawyer*. They praise an almost mature Tom for a creative triumph over, or else a searing indictment against, a crass society; or—at the other extreme—they belabor him for joining adult conformity, which had smugly tolerated his mischief as sure to fizzle out. A few critics find *Tom Sawyer* more portentous than *Huckleberry Finn*, giving the literary historian a sense of déjà vu. Twain had consistently made Huck look up to Tom during all their adventures. In 1926 nobody objected noticeably when a sculptor who recreated

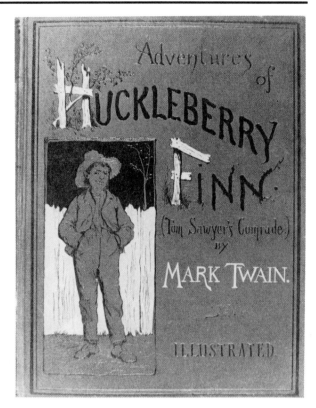

Cover for the first American edition of Huckleberry Finn *(1885)*

the boys for Hannibal intended to show that "Huck, of the easy-going nature, is holding on to Tom, urging him to stay home and live on the hill. Tom, who was in fact Mark Twain as a youth, is going out into the world to seek fame and fortune."

That statue would be projected very differently now, though not from a firm base in Twain's opinions. He was slow to say—even after being prompted—that *Huckleberry Finn* had reached a class by itself among his works. Instead, he could insist until the end of his life that his favorite book was *The Innocents Abroad* or *The Prince and the Pauper* or—especially—*Personal Recollections of Joan of Arc*. By the time he died, however, he could have guessed the choice of posterity. When that choice became clear is debatable because critics always try to be individualists. But it looked like a good bet by 1920, firmed to a sure thing during the 1930s with the support of Bernard DeVoto, and for many academics rose beyond respectable doubt after the reverential essays by Lionel Trilling in 1948 and T. S. Eliot in 1950. In *An American Procession* (1984), Alfred Kazin could reduce Twain's books to *Tom Sawyer*, which he finds duller the longer he thinks about it, and *Huckleberry Finn*, which continues to improve under close analysis. Intriguingly, Kazin was moved to add a questionable footnote: "Though it is impossible to imagine Tom Sawyer as anything but a boy, Mark Twain's sassy brat, imagination in America has often indulged itself in the fantasy of Huck Finn grown old and not a bit less derelict as he haunts contemporary scenes of progress."

In careful discourse *favorite* and *best* are not synonyms, but the difference has dwindled for *Huckleberry Finn* because it is now almost unanimously accepted as a masterpiece, indeed as a classic. It is institutionalized in the curriculum (even in the Basic Program of Liberal Education for Adults at the University of Chicago), the lists of major novels posted at city libraries, the sets of Great Books (American or world), and the web of allusions among people who talk about belles lettres as part of their job or social image. Though many girls also enjoy *Huckleberry Finn*, the impressionistic consensus holds that the audience for it, as for Twain's humor overall, is still heavily male, whatever the age group.

If *Huckleberry Finn* were to rank as a classic for adults, it had to be understood as exploring fundamental issues. A few novels have earned the status of "serious" literature by working through an unmistakable child as the narrating mind. But that is a sophisticated technique, which demands readers tautly alert to implied rather than surface meaning. Huck wanders so close to the threshold of maturity, crossing it occasionally by action more than ideas, that an inviting interpretation perceives him as learning throughout his adventures until he soon becomes distinctly older than Buck Grangerford, becomes an adolescent instead of the "boy" referred to in Twain's private letters.

Besides Jim's regression into a comic darky, that is why many modern critics have felt betrayed by the late chapters that diminish Huck to Tom's sidekick again and to such gags as having the butter hidden under his hat come melting down his forehead and starting a flurry about "brain fever." That is also why they infer solemn motives for Huck when, having agreed to join Tom in searching next for "howling adventures among the Indians," he decides to "light out for the Territory ahead of the rest." Currently, that's why his flight from decent Aunt Sally's offer to adopt him is admired as a knowing rejection of a corrupt and corrupting society. Far from thinking themselves rejected, most grownup readers in Twain's day saw a "boys will be boys" level of wild play or, in other words, saw the same Huck who, grumbling mildly, romped

with Tom Sawyer's Gang in the second chapter. They were not surprised to find that same Huck narrating *Tom Sawyer Abroad* (1894) and *Tom Sawyer, Detective* (1896).

No other novel now satisfies so many age groups as *Huckleberry Finn*. Even for non-English majors, a college course on the masterpieces of fiction ignored *Little Women, Treasure Island,* or *The Wind in the Willows* as outgrown by the students. On the other hand, the shelf of literature recommended to please the adolescent ignores *Moby-Dick, Middlemarch,* or *Madame Bovary*. James M. Cox has stated the current situation best:

> The triumph of Mark Twain's art is, as everybody knows, *Adventures of Huckleberry Finn*. And the first thing to emphasize . . . is that it is for everyone—for children, for young adults, for the middle-aged, and for the old. And the further we live into its meaning the deeper and more pervasive its humor becomes. Its capacity to meet us throughout our lives makes it a book for everybody, whether educated or uneducated, rich or poor, sophisticated or plain, and reminds us that Mark Twain was, for all his expressed attitudes to the contrary, one of the most democratic writers in the world.

Huckleberry Finn entered a new phase during the fall of 1985. Doubleday published a version edited by Charles Neider, who took back the raftsmen's passage from *Life on the Mississippi* yet cut over 9,000 words from the painful comedy surrounding Jim at the Phelps farm. With a Hamlin Hill introduction, Harper and Row reissued a mass-market facsimile of the first edition, thus returning the Kemble illustrations to high visibility. The University of California Press has had brisk sales for a handsome volume with woodcuts by our own contemporary Barry Moser and with a text based on the painstaking collation by the Mark Twain Project. Later in 1985 the California Press added that text to its Mark Twain Library while also restoring the raftsmen's passage and reproducing all the original drawings. Soon to follow is a volume that lays out the cruxes of the text, such as the changes Twain made in the manuscript or the Mark Twain Project has found a need to make in the printings of 1884-1885. Critics will ponder and then debate the implications raised by this surely definitive text.

But the most important effect of these various editions may come from the original illustrations. The earliest visible Huck may surprise his more ponderous disciples because he's clearly a boy, looking small and immature even for the age he claims. Perhaps the first illustrator failed to comprehend the novel, but Twain, after some grumbling and coaching, ended up enthusiastic about his drawings. Among new tangential factors, it is too early to judge the lasting influence of *Big River* and its songs by Roger Miller, which opened on Broadway in the spring of 1985 to mostly favorable reviews and later won seven Tony awards. More important for literary approaches, a multi-hour version of *Huckleberry Finn* will be screened in 1986 as a miniseries on PBS. It creates Tom and Huck as unmistakably boyish, not even adolescent, in body and mind. Another intriguing imponderable is David Carkeet's novel, *I Been There Before.* Though it mostly plays with the idea that Twain trod our earth again in 1985-1986 (and will reappear with future visits by Halley's comet) the charming evocation of his personality and voices will surely inspire some of Carkeet's uninitiated readers to go on to *Huckleberry Finn*, and in a highly receptive mood.

Given the intrinsic genius of *Huckleberry Finn*, along with the disagreements it keeps causing, Huck seems sure to last for at least another hundred years as a famous character, poignant and suggestive like a figure on Keats's Grecian urn. But a high-culture comparison is not the most appropriate level to end on. When William J. Bennett, as chairman of the National Endowment for the Humanities, invited some educators, scholars, and writers to list the ten books that every high school student should read, he found that a loose consensus included *Huckleberry Finn* along with Shakespeare's great tragedies. But the list also included parts of the Bible, the Declaration of Independence, and the Gettysburg Address. Though much translated into many languages, *Huckleberry Finn* has established itself at home as more than a literary masterpiece; it has become a basic text for the society that is proud to claim first rights to it.

COMMENTS FROM AUTHORS AND SCHOLARS ON THEIR FIRST READING OF *HUCK FINN*

VANCE BOURJAILY

I don't think people had decided *Huck Finn* was a classic when I first read it. If they had, nobody told me. I was a kid, and a reading fool, and about all I might have had to say was that I liked it just as well as I liked *Tom Sawyer.* I'm pretty sure I read both books twice, but that goes for *Penrod* and *Two Years Before the Mast,* too.

Maybe ten years later I became aware that Hemingway, among others, thought *Adventures of Huckleberry Finn* something better than a book for boys, which caused me to think about giving it an adult reading. And after about ten more years, I did, except I quit when that miserable Sawyer kid came into it. Boy, had he changed for the worse. By then I could mumble phrases like "vernacular poetry" and "sustained irony" as well as most, but I like to think I didn't do it very often.

Now another ten or fifteen years have passed, and it feels as if I may get restless for one more ride down the river with Huck and Jim, a call on the Wilkses, a glimpse of Pappy, a sigh of relief when we get rid of the Duke and the Dauphin (after a grin at the way they talk), and some worry over the Grangerfords. The book must have influenced me, but I haven't any way of knowing how.

STANLEY BRODWIN

In his essay "Rider Haggard," Henry Miller, contemplating the effect this great adventure writer had on his childhood imagination, remarks, "More than ever do I believe that at a certain age it becomes imperative to reread the books of childhood and youth. Else we may go to the grave not knowing who we are and why we lived."

Now it would be nice to say—even if a bit sentimental—that I read *Huckleberry Finn* in my youth and that it had a lasting poetic and intellectual impact on my adult life. But such, alas, was not the case, although *King Solomon's Mines* (also published, as fate would have it, in 1885), did so affect me (it may be irrelevant but Twain apparently disliked Haggard's work). To be sure, the "myth" of Mark Twain was part of my childhood education growing up in Brooklyn, New York, during the late 1930s and early 1940s. I had seen the Jackie Coogan and Mickey Rooney movie versions of *Huckleberry Finn*, as well as the films of *Tom Sawyer* and *The Prince and the Pauper.* And then there was Fredric March in *The Adventures of Mark Twain* (1944), a film that gave American audiences a golden and heroic image of the great humorist and author of "children's" books. Looking back, I do recall that we read the fence-painting scene of *Tom Sawyer*, which I much enjoyed, in the sixth or seventh grade; but that was all. Taken all together, it was Tom and not Huck with whom I identified, and no teacher or friend—even in high school—

ever suggested that I read The Great American Novel.

As luck would have it (or "providence," as Twain might ironically comment), I first read *Huckleberry Finn* as a college student in England (where—another irony—the book was first published in 1884). Having served in the United States Navy for four years during the Korean War, I was then in my early twenties, and with the help of the G.I. Bill, studying English literature at King's College, Durham University. The year was 1955, and apart from the popularity among my peers of such nineteenth-century writers as Poe, Whitman, Hawthorne, and moderns such as London, Hemingway, Frost, Lewis, Steinbeck, Fitzgerald, and Faulkner (James and Eliot were *Anglo*-Americans), I might as well have been living—literarily—in 1855, as far as many of my fellow students of literature were concerned. No doubt my perceptions about this, looking backward, are exaggerated, but not too much, I think. My professors, of course, knew and admired American literature, but then, no courses were available in the subject. Fortunately, things have changed in this regard over the years, but in those days I found myself constantly on the defensive, constantly embarrassed by the jibes of the wisest of my fellow students about the lack of *great* literary masterpieces produced in my homeland. *Moby-Dick?* Yes, some grudgingly admitted, that was a great book—but about a whale! for heaven's sake. Twain? Well, there was *Tom Sawyer;* that was a good book they had read in childhood. That most of Twain's work was in fact widely read in Britain and that he had received an honorary degree from Oxford, along with Kipling, in 1907, they did not know; neither did I. *Huckleberry Finn?* Also a child's book, but strange, unreadable, farce in dialect. But I was challenged, and so with some trepidation and no critical help, I got my Everyman's Library copy and read.

Perhaps not read; like Huck and Jim watching the river and days flowing by after escaping from the feud, I might say I *swum* through the book. It seemed to me the most natural and spontaneous narrative I had ever encountered, a narrative which had me laughing out loud and in some state of wonder and surprise by its poetic realism. In this way the book liberated my emotions and as true comedy should (as the medieval and renaissance critics on humor averred), left me feeling joyous—spiritually "healthy." And there is no doubt that the book's language was the key to this experience (and still is). What Emerson had said of Montaigne's style was true for Mark Twain: his words

were visceral; cut them and they would bleed. That is what overwhelmed me at my first reading of *Huckleberry Finn:* its living, visceral quality. It seemed to make all the other classic prose writers I had been reading in college appear pale and contrived, regardless of how brilliant their rhetorical devices and metaphor. Not long after I discovered that so many other critics and readers had experienced the same responses in varying degrees (always a sobering lesson for students) that I realized my reaction was little more than a grand cliché. But I felt good about that; it affirmed my perceptions and gave me a community with whom I could share the book's beauty.

This does not mean that Twain's savage cuts at human nature and "sivilization" eluded me; no. But it was clear that Huck's discourse, his *persona*, consistently qualified the underlying (and direct) horrors he encountered, exposing and then transcending them in episode after episode. What struck me forcibly was the way Twain transmuted potential tragedy into affirmative comedy or at least into a form of acceptable justice. Behind the flow of events in the narrative there was also the absurd logic of adventure itself—the essential if not primary mode which embodies the book's comic vision. That is why, on my first reading, the infamous ending never bothered me. I never skipped a line and enjoyed it immensely because it all seemed an organic part of comic adventuring. I never for a moment believed anything fatal could happen to Huck, Jim, or Tom; each was playing his role in the total exploration of freedom (and slavery) through adventure. And it was perfectly natural—even necessary—that the book should end with the promise of "lighting out" for more discovery.

All this was a strange and exhilarating experience to convey to the unconverted, the doubters. But I proselytized energetically and was finally allowed to lecture to the august student English Society on the book's comedy of the "wisdom of the ignorant." I am glad to report some converts came into the fold. Others just shook their heads and said, "Just another clever boy's book." But I am often advised that compassion for undergraduates is a necessary and possibly saving virtue—I do not know. In any case, I knew one obvious fact: *Huckleberry Finn* was an *American* epic masterpiece that could not be duplicated in any other culture; it was a book both intrinsically and extrinsically sui generis. It told me some powerful truths about my own national culture and history and, on even a profounder level, revealed to me as much about paradise lost, nature, and moral struggle as ever did Milton or Wordsworth. Necessarily there was much about the book's moral tensions (especially regarding Jim) and structure that I could not grasp then and still struggle with today. Yet what remains undiminished is the liberating comic spirit of *Huckleberry Finn*, Adamic in all its challenging insights into innocence and the ways of "providence."

VIC DOYNO

In Miss Chase's seventh grade class there were always right answers—until we read *Adventures of Huckleberry Finn*. Miss Chase had a firm belief in right answers and a devotion to utterly boring questions. But I remember that there were more silences, more furrows in her forehead when we read *Huck*. By some divine mistake, Miss Chase was in deeper water than she liked, and we loved it. Honestly, that was not a good reason to read parts of the book twice, but I did take some pleasure in tripping her up, or, at least, making her seem to ignore or skip my questions.

The previous summer I had been reading *Silver Chief, Dog of the North* as well as several Tom Lea westerns, and I became devoted to Saroyan's *Human Comedy* and then to *My Name is Aram*. But *Huck* seemed and sounded different, although I could not explain it then. That was probably about the time when my friends and I began the change from checkers to a primitive chess. The girls' mothers in our circle had not yet compelled the seventh grade PTA to subsidize a dancing school or telephoned the boys' mothers into inflicting that embarrassment upon us.

So *Huck* came into my life at a fortunate time, and several motives came together to lead me to put energy into the book. For one, my parents were intermittent Catholics, tearing apart an Irish-Italian marriage, rehearsing for their divorce. When I, a public school student, attended the Catholic Sunday school, I was told once a week to believe "truths" that would choke a hippopotamus. But everything remained tranquil at the surface. The nun would ask for rote recitation of answers, and, when I asked a question, she would walk silently, as if deep in thought, down the aisle behind me. I learned right there to fear and dislike being hit on the back of the head for asking questions. My reading of *Huck* coincided, then, with a time when my mind demanded and developed privacy.

The local Texaco station where I went for bicycle-tire air employed a kind, gentle, patient black man. Al was at least ten years older than the owner and did most of the work. He would move deliberately, slowly, and he explained how to fix flats, gears, chains, and wobbles. Now I would probably cringe for his behavior that was not then Toming, but I wish to believe that his actions were sincere. When Al said he was worried about fires in his neighborhood in South Chicago, I asked idiotically why he didn't save money and move his family to a safer neighborhood. He calmly answered that it wasn't quite so easy as that. Later I learned how right he was.

Huck validated some of what I knew seemed to speak of doubts and unknowns that twisted me. But I know that I first read for plot—hurrying to see what would happen next. I remember that the thought of being around dead bodies and of digging up a coffin sped up my reading. I think I was not originally aware that the King and Duke were scoundrels; my reading pace was fast, and my attitude was what I would now call middle-school nonjudgmental. Because of this rapid pace, the frequent suspense parts seemed to blur together. I cannot now remember any sense of outrage about the Phelps's farm part and the return of Tom to the novel. I think I felt some reassurance of familiarity when Tom reappeared.

Hearing voices different from my own was both easy and okay. I did not then know that Jim or anyone else spoke "dialect." I remember later during a high school lecture writing "dialect" and then being a bit surprised to find it there.

Much of what I read as a child was not really, fully, understood. The reading was itself a private, nonjudgmental world. Serious things occurred— in rapid succession—and I could hold the book in my hand and enter that world or leave that world, unharmed, as I wished. (I learned with *Huck* in my hand that my parents vehemently forbade reading at the dinner table.) *Huck* and I found each other, and it happened when I was ready, willing, unable, but eager.

Perhaps the book offers, at first, simply a good fast story that a boy can easily identify with and absorb. But, once read, *Huck* can offer psychological validation for some children and, later, a common reconstitutive mythic version of the past that is both private and sharable. It is not that we must make our individual past congruent with *Huck*, but we know that the congruent parts will be easily understood. Probably the book does not have that peculiar magic for girls, but I hope there is some text available to women that is equally cherished, equally engaging, equally rewarding at all ages.

IRVIN FAUST

Do I remember when I first read *Huck Finn?* Sure. It was in high school. And "literature" was supposed to be fancy stuff: *Silas Marner.* Shakespeare. Tennyson. Sinclair Lewis, who was so terribly serious. Along comes this thing called a *classic,* and it's written all funny and unfancy and the way people talk—or talked—and nobody had to push me through it; I pushed myself. *Zipped* through it.

I can't honestly say that I consciously changed my precious writing style because of *Huck* (I didn't even know I wanted to be a writer), but I'm quite certain that it and Twain seeped into the well and in later years I dropped the bucket into that well and came up with a respect for and concern with the colloquial and the everyday bric-a-brac of life as the backbone of "literature."

HERBERT GOLD

First, as a boy in Lakewood, a suburb of Cleveland, Ohio, that French city—"La Terre de la Princesse de Cleves," as my cousin in Paris thought it— I was Tom Sawyer. I read the books at about the age Tom and Huck were. Soon I learned to be Huck, and camped out, and embezzled alcohol with friends, all of us using our fathers' stocks. We assigned roles and played parts in this river story— played them on the Cuyahoga River, amid ailanthus trees and smoldering rubber tires. Later I thought I was Nigger Jim; never took the part of Becky Thatcher.

Yes, the freedom of Huck Finn was infectious. I learned from it directly—also from Henry Miller, Vladimir Nabokov, Dostoyevski, Homer, Shakespeare, Bert Lahr, William Saroyan, too, only some of whom learned from Mark Twain.

Probably lighting out for the territory ahead is the great impulse in American literature.

JAN B. GORDON

My first exposure to *Huck Finn,* like that of many other people (if they would only admit it) was by way of a classic comic book, at I think the age of seven or eight. Beyond the age of classical abridgment, I remember being given a volume as a birthday present by a black domestic who raised me in the gentle hills of East Texas. That was later, maybe at age thirteen or fourteen. She was in those days a rarity, an educated Southern Negro married to a retired army officer. Looking back on my high school diet of "texts"—*Ivanhoe* and *The Last of the Mohicans,* I now perceive of Irene's birthday gift as one of gentle subversion. If eighteenth-century French domestics read to their charges from Perrault's *Contes* as a way of forming a secret alliance of the underprivileged (children and domestic help), perhaps my Southern domestic guardian was doing the same for her upper-middle-class, suburban captive. I am grateful.

NAT HENTOFF

My first memory of *Huck Finn* is less important to me than the second time I read the book— about five years ago. I was looking for a book to figure in a novel for young readers about censorship—which turned out to be *The Day They Came to Arrest the Book* (Dell).

Huck turned out to be the most multiply evocative and provocative book for that purpose, but what really struck me—reading it some forty years after I'd first read it as a teenager—was how perennially powerful a novel it is. The most thoroughly American novel I know and therefore the most universal (for universality comes from earned particular experience).

Among so many other constant illuminations in the book, the dawning in Huck of what it is to be truly grownup on the inside—that is, what it is to be Jim—is one of the ceaselessly satisfying experiences in all of literature.

JAY MARTIN

I did not read *Huckleberry Finn* as a child, nor have I ever read it in a class, under a teacher. I read it first when I had to teach it at Yale, in a course on "Expressions of the American Experience," in the Rinehart edition, with an introduction by Lionel Trilling, one of my former undergraduate teachers. My first impression was that it was interesting to read—but much more interesting to talk about, and to write about. I have to confess, therefore, that I have talked about it and even written about it more times than I have read it. It's the best book I know on the creative imagination. I could talk about it every day for a year.

DAVID SEWELL

I must have been seven or eight years old when I first encountered Mark Twain. My parents had a boxed set of *Tom Sawyer* and *Huckleberry Finn,* and I'm sure that I discovered the novels on my own while exploring the bookshelves. As I recall, I liked the latter less than the former—as the academy has been trying to tell the world for some time, *Huck Finn* is not a children's book. I must have been more interested in the Rockwell illustrations than the text, since I can remember clearly my reactions to several—Jim and the hairball, especially, which struck me as strange and mysterious. But the part of the novel that made the biggest impression on me was the "NOTICE" on the obverse of the title page: "Persons attempting to find a motive in this narrative will be prosecuted; persons attempting to find a moral in it will be banished; persons attempting to find a plot in it will be shot." I had no idea what it all meant, but it worried me a good deal.

HENRY NASH SMITH

I think I must have come upon *Adventures of Huckleberry Finn* first when I was perhaps eleven or twelve years old. I recall being somewhat repelled by the disillusioned tone of the book and the illustrations (in contrast with the more up-beat tone of *The Adventures of Tom Sawyer,* which I had just finished reading). In short, it was too old a book, too mature in tone for me at that time.

THOMAS A. TENNEY

Huckleberry Finn was one of the first "real" books I read, after a horse story and then *Tom Sawyer.* Pap Finn shocked me: I couldn't imagine a brutal parent like that, one who couldn't read and used books for gun-wadding. To a boy of seven or eight Huck seemed pretty grown up. I trusted Jim, and couldn't understand a white society that treated him that way. After the enthralling trip down river the Phelps Farm chapters struck me as silly; I saw little point in them.

A New Edition of *Huck Finn*

Victor Fischer
Mark Twain Project, University of California

When typesetting of *Adventures of Huckleberry Finn* began, during the summer of 1884, Mark Twain had completed his revision of the book. He wanted the text accurately transmitted into print, but was impatient with the proofreading and irritated at the printers' errors. "My days are given up to cursings—both loud & deep—for I am reading the H. Finn proofs," he wrote to his friend W. D. Howells. "Most of this proof," he told his publisher, Charles L. Webster, "was clean & beautiful, & a pleasure to read; but the rest of it was read by that blind idiot whom I have cursed so much, & is a disgraceful mess." Soon after, he added, "If all the proofs had been as well read [by the printer's proofreader] as the first 2 or 3 chapters were, I should

not have needed to see the revises at all. On the contrary it was the worst & silliest proof-reading I have ever seen. It was never read by copy at all—not a single galley of it." In a fury, he wrote Howells again: "I am sending you these infernal Huck Finn proofs—but the very last vestige of my patience has gone to the devil, & I cannot bear the sight of another slip of them. My hair turns white with rage, at sight of the mere outside of the package." Partly because of this fit of temper, the author never read portions of the text in galley proof, and may have only skimmed them in a perfunctory way in page proof. The first edition did contain a number of printer's errors, as well as mistakes traceable to earlier transcription error or to Mark Twain's own

Dust jacket for the new Mark Twain Library edition of
Adventures of Huckleberry Finn

tion of error that Mark Twain himself was unable to stop—means that one has to first determine what that intention might have been and what opportunities the author had for fulfilling it. The editor must minutely reconstruct the history of composition and revision, the means by which and the documents through which the text was transmitted. In order to accomplish this, he must rationalize the textual and historical evidence, accounting for each detail and making coherent the seemingly random documents available for study. The result of this endeavor is not only a text that may significantly differ from any text heretofore published, but almost always a revised literary history. The process has produced "differences" in the present text and a revised history of *Huck Finn*.

Mark Twain's care in selecting an artist and his involvement in overseeing the illustrations make clear that E. W. Kemble's drawings are an essential component of the text. "*That* is the man I want to try," Clemens insisted to his publisher in 1884 when offered other illustrators. Although he was disappointed with Kemble's first drawings and asked for changes, he called later drawings "most rattling good" and claimed that he "*knew* Kemble had it *in* him." For the first time (drawing mainly from a recent acquisition of Webster company materials in the Jean Webster McKinney Collection in the Vassar College Rare Book Room) we were able to base our reproductions of thirty of these illustrations on the artist's original drawings, and more than one hundred others on a set of proofs pulled from the first picture plates, restoring detail lost even in the first edition.

carelessness (for instance, his mistaken "Bessie" for "Becky" Thatcher).

The University of California Press (in cooperation with the University of Iowa) has just published, as part of an ongoing series of Mark Twain's works edited by members of the Mark Twain Project, a new text of Mark Twain's *Adventures of Huckleberry Finn*. This text appears in two editions edited by Walter Blair and Victor Fischer—the Mark Twain Works or "scholarly" edition (1986), and the Mark Twain Library or "popular, trade" edition (1985). Questions one might ask of these new California editions are: How does this "new" text differ from the others? What does the editorial work have to offer? What are its limits? To begin to answer these questions, it will be helpful to quickly characterize the work of the Project.

The commitment to "edit" Mark Twain's texts to accord with the author's intention—thereby ridding them of the editorial interference and accre-

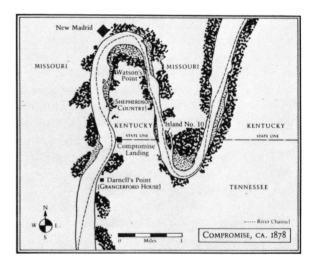

One of the maps included in the Mark Twain Library edition charting Huck's raft trip down the Mississippi

Kemble's drawings and the notation upon them also provided the key to a revised chronology of the transmission and revision of the text. Although only an incomplete manuscript of the novel remains in existence (at the Buffalo and Erie County Public Library), the page references Kemble jotted onto his drawings, in conjunction with Clemens's own references to various copies of the text, enabled us to determine that there had been three typescripts made (one of them never proofread by Clemens). Although none of these typescripts remains in existence, the identification of one of them with Mark Twain's Elmira typist—Harry M. Clarke, who was prone to eyeskips when copying—makes it likely that an eyeskip from "they was" to "they was" in the manuscript line below was responsible for omitting in the first and all later editions the second phrase in Huck's description of the men on the *Walter Scott:* "I could tell where they was, and how close they was, by the whisky they'd been having" (chapter 12, restored in this edition).

Using Mark Twain's manuscript as our basic text results in a number of such "retentions" (which will appear to be "restorations" to a reader familiar with texts based on the first or later editions). For instance, readers may have been puzzled that when Huck rows the skiff over to a ferryboat to ask for help (chapter 13), he seems to get onto the deck of the ferryboat as if by magic. This effect was probably the consequence of another of Harry Clarke's errors, overlooking two sentences now restored to the text: "Everything was dead still, nobody stirring. I floated in under the stern, made fast, and clumb aboard."

Resting solely on documentary evidence, this edition has made a longer restoration, reintegrating the sixteen-page "raftsmen's passage"—where Huck visits a lumber-raft to find out how far he and Jim are from Cairo—into chapter 16. This passage had been previously published in *Life on the Mississippi* as an extract from *Huckleberry Finn.* Charles L. Webster, charged with selling *Tom Sawyer* and *Huck Finn* as a matched set, proposed dropping the "raftsmen's passage" from the latter in order to equalize the length of the two books. Clemens acceded: the passage was removed from printer's copy, Kemble prepared no illustrations for it, and the author seems never to have complained about its omission. Nonetheless, we restore the passage because the evidence shows that Clemens intended to publish it in *Huckleberry Finn* and evidently changed his mind *only* to accommodate his publisher's convenience.

Establishing the text often raises the question: What did Mark Twain do or fail to do? Preparing the annotation as often requires that the editor ask: What did Mark Twain know? For instance, we discovered that the text shows much more reliance on and faithfulness to the real geography of the river than was heretofore known. In dealing with this fact, we had to determine a rationale for distinguishing the "real" from the "fictional." Critical studies of *Huck*'s geography have often attempted to compare average travel time of a river raft with the distance between points A and B on the Mississippi River of the novel. The inevitable result has been the frustrating conclusion that Mark Twain's identification of fictional points A and B with actual places must be in error: so many days of travel would have taken Huck far beyond Compromise, Kentucky (where the Grangerford-Shepherdson episode is set), and, later, far beyond Napoleon, Arkansas (the model for "Bricksville"). Similarly, although Mark Twain asserts in his autobiography that he set the Phelps farm in Arkansas, Huck and Jim's travel time on the raft would "really" put it in Louisiana. But if one imagines the farm in Louisiana, the Duke's attempt to mislead Huck by sending him down the "road to Lafayette" (that is, Lafayette County, Arkansas) is puzzling or incomprehensible. The assumption that Mark Twain adapted *travel time* to suit his narrative purposes solved the editorial problem: it became clear that the geographical references in the text do in fact follow a historically and geographically correct pattern, and it became possible to identify the real places that Mark Twain had fictionalized. Huck's journey could then be charted, making a graphic understanding of Mark Twain's dependence on and deviation from actual geography possible.

An aim, therefore, in the annotation, is to recreate for a modern reader what Mark Twain knew, or intended his readers to know. To appreciate the book, it is not necessary to know that when Jim grabs pap's whiskey jug and begins to "pour it down" his throat, he is following the recommended nineteenth-century treatment for snakebite (*Gunn's New Family Physician*, 1867, says "give the patient *all* the Whisky he can drink. From a quart to a gallon should be drunk in six or eight hours"); or that when Huck and Jim and the thieves move around the "texas" of the steamboat *Walter Scott* they follow in extraordinarily accurate detail the structure of a mid-nineteenth-century steamboat known to Clemens from his experience as a Mississippi River pilot; or that when the Child of Calamity says "Whoo-oop! bow your neck and spread," he is ech-

400   EXPLANATORY NOTES

137.27–35   a woman in a slim black dress . . . Never See Thee More Alas."|
Although new to Huck, this picture would have been familiar to any
middle-class reader. It includes the "stock elements" of standard nineteenth-century mourning pictures: "the weeping willow, tombstone,
and pensive mourner leaning on the monument. Even the style of dress
common in mourning pictures is accurately reproduced" by Huck's
description (Strickland, 228). Huck's allusion to this woman's "very
wee black slippers, like a chisel" echoes Mark Twain's previous characterization of illustrations in *Godey's Lady's Book*: "each five-foot
woman with a two-inch wedge sticking from under her dress and letting-
on to be half of her foot" (*Life on the Mississippi*, chapter 38). See the
illustrations.

Left: Mourning print, by D. W. Kellogg and Company, lithographers (Hartford,
ca. 1835); the purchaser of the print wrote the name and death date of the
deceased on the tombstone. From the collection of Professor Barton Levi St.
Armand. *Right*: Mourning print, by William S. Pendleton, lithographer (Boston, ca. 1836), with a handwritten inscription on the tombstone. Courtesy of
The Harry T. Peters "America on Stone" Lithography Collection, Smithsonian
Institution, Washington, D.C.

Annotation containing reproductions of two typical nineteenth-century mourning prints, from the Mark Twain Library edition

oing one of Hannibal's "prominent and very intemperate ne'er do wells," recalled from Clemens's childhood; or that the subjects of Emmeline Grangerford's drawings and poems were not unique to her but were the subjects of a genre of art and poetry familiar to almost any middle-class reader of the mid-nineteenth-century (see the illustration). Yet such information teaches us much about Mark Twain's methods of transforming experience into fiction and illuminates his artistry.

The text and explanatory notes appear in both the Mark Twain Library and Mark Twain Works edition. The Works edition includes, in addition, fuller editorial accounts of the history of composition, transmission of the text, and the principles upon which the present text was established. Appendixes reproducing documentary material, such as Mark Twain's working notes, and the textual apparatus (which shows in detail Mark Twain's revisions in the manuscript and on proof) complete the Works version.

Biographical Documents II

"Publishers have no sense of their own literary history," is the dismayed complaint of one scholar. They seem to discard more literary material than they preserve; and many notable publishing archives have disappeared. Impressive evidence of the usable treasures that may be found in publishers' files is provided by these autobiographical documents from the Bobbs-Merrill Papers at the Lilly Library, Indiana University.

Picture probably to follow

BOBBS-MERRILL GENERAL QUESTIONNAIRE

Filling out questionnaires is undoubtedly dull business so we ask you to bear with us in submitting this one to you. If it were not for the fact that there is a direct relationship between the information you give us and the sale of your book we would not bother you at all. Since there is a connection, we bother you with this "sign on the dotted line" request.

Name and pseudonym: Name: Vladimir Nabokoff. Pseudonym: V.Sirin.

Date of birth: ~~33.4.00~~ *April 23, 1899.*

Place of birth: St. Petersburg, Russia.

Present address: Pension "Les Hespérides", Menton, A.M., France.

Notable ancestors or members of family: My first ancestor, as far as I know, was a Tartar chieftain, Nabok, in the XIV cebtury. On my paternal grandmothers side the line of the Barons von Korff goes back to the Crusades. One of my mother's grandfathers was the first President of the Academy of Medecine and the other a self-made merchant, one of those industrial pioneers who added to the Russian Empire's culture and wealth. My paternal grandfather was Minister of Justice under two Tzars. My father was a famous Liberal politician, Member of the first Duma, editor of a great newspaper and an authority on Criminal Law.

Education:

     Tenishev School, St.Petersburg, and Trinity College, Cambridge University, England, where at first I studied zoology, but then changed my mind and graduated in Foreign Languages.

First experiences in writing: As a child I loved writing imaginary stories using a w h i t e pencil which being invisible on paper afforded magical possibilities. At 13, when a cousin of mine suggested that we should each write a poem and see who did it better, I chose a volume of verse in the library and discreetly copied out a couple of pretty stanzas. My cousin's amazement at my proficiency stung my pride prompting me to try whether I could not surprise him with something of my own making. So I retired to the smallest room in the house and there composed my first poem. It fell rather flat.

List of books, plays, etc.:

Novels: "Mashenka" (1926), "King, Queen, Knave", "Luzhin's Defence",   "The Exploit", ~~"Camera Obscura"~~, "Despair", "Invitation to a   Beheading", "The Gift" (in preparation).
Collections of short stories: "The Return of Tchorb", "Perfection" (in   preparation).

The present untitled volume

VLADIMIR NABOKOV

- 2 -

Stories and articles in following magazines: "Annales Contemporaines", "Rul",
"Dernières Nouvelles" and several other Russian émigré periodicals.
In French: "Nouvelle Revue Française", "Mesures", "Oeuvres Libres", "Mois";
In English: "Lovat Dickson's Magazine", "The Quarter".
In German: "Vossische Zeitung", "Berliner Tageblatt", "Kölnische Zeitung".

Single or married to whom:

      To the former Miss Véra Slonim.

Children:

      Son Dmitri, 3 years old.

Occupation other than writing:

      None.

Other personal experiences I consider remarkable or unusual: The mysterious fact of my having managed
somehow to smuggle out of Russia, which I hastily left at the tender age
of 19, a sufficient amount of word material to write my books in exile
amid a babble of foreign tongues.

→ Think he means at in the formal definition of "mode of expression peculiar to an author".

Idiosyncracies, if any:

    The squeak of cotton wool, the touch of satin.

Personal preferences:

    Hot sun, bathing, first cigarette before breakfast, writing in bed,
    boxing-matches.

Personal dislikes:

    Books with a Message. Studs. Dictators. East wind. Oysters. Wireless
    sets; voluble conversation about same.

Superstitions: Once, in London, I dreamt of a green wall and the very next
day I was introduced to a person whose name turned out to be Greenwall. I
never met him again, nor did that meeting in any way effect the course of my
existence; but several years later I picked up a book from a stall and its
title was: Dreams and their Meaning by

The vocation I was advised to follow: A.Greenwall.

    The one I followed.

- 3 -

World War service. Army, Navy, Red Cross, etc.: I was too young for the War. Sometimes I can imagine myself going to a small informal war in a warm hilly place, just for a lark, as I should go big game hunting - say. But on the whole, war, especially the popular international kind, seems to me a pastime for solemn fools and slaves.

Clubs, fraternities, organizations, etc.:

I dislike clubs, I hate organizations and I loathe fraternities.

Hobbies, collections, etc.:

The study and collecting of butterflies and moths.

Favorite outdoor sports:

I played football up to 1933, keeping goal; was sometimes brilliant and always unsound. I also played a good deal of tennis,
Favorite indoor sports: Chess and especially the composing of chess-problems some of which I have published. I was the first Russian to compose a cross-word puzzle, inventing, too, its Russian name which has now entered the language so thoroughly that people laugh when I say it is the child of my brain.
Favorite book and why:
The book I shall write some day. Also: "Eugene Oneguin", "Hamlet", "Madame Bovary", "The Shropshire Lad". Generally speaking, I like books that are well written - I don't mind what they are about.

Favorite author and why:

Don't know - I prefer books to authors.

Vladimir Nabokoff-Sirin

19 -XI- 37

Menton

Dr. C. P. Snow

BOBBS-MERRILL AUTHORS' QUESTIONNAIRE

This is our own "Who's Who and Why," because the regular "Who's Who" is most inadequate. The questionnaire when you fill it out is almost invaluable to the publicity department in preparing special news stories about your books, your life and your favorite breakfast food.

Please sign on the dotted lines and return to THE BOBBS-MERRILL COMPANY, INDIANAPOLIS, INDIANA, U. S. A.

*****

Name and pseudonym: SNOW   CHARLES PERCY

Date of birth: Oct 15   1905

Place of birth: Leicester, Eng.

Present address: Christ's College, Cambridge.

Notable ancestors or members of family:

None (except a great-grandfather who is reputed to have been hanged for smuggling)

Education:

Alderman Newton's School, Leicester
University College, Leicester
Christ's College, Cambridge (College of Milton and Darwin)

First attempt at writing:

Years ago: interrupted by minutiae necessities of scientific cases; returned seriously in 1931

List of books, plays, etc.:

Death Under Sail   1932 (Heinemann Eng. and Doubleday Doran U.SA)
New Lives for Old   1933 (Gollancz — not published in U.S.A.)
The Search   1934 (Gollancz and Bobbs-Merrill)

C. P. SNOW

-2-

Stories and articles in following magazines:

Pictorial Review.

Have not had time for much work at short stuff so far; but are now in touch with Nash's London, and shall probably write for them during next year.

Single or married to whom:

Single

Children:

None

Occupation other than writing:

Fellow of Christ's College, Cambridge
University Demonstrator in Physical Chemistry

Personal experiences I consider remarkable or unusual:

A good many, but reserved for future use.

Idiosyncracies, if any:

Too many, my friends say

Personal preferences:

Personal dislikes:

Superstitions: *None*

My aim in life: *like above, completely revealed in 'The Search'.*

The vocation I was advised to follow:

I don't think I have ever been advised in these things. I always had a definite idea.

-3-

World War service. Army, Navy, Red Cross, etc.:

Clubs, fraternities, sororities, organizations, etc.:

Hobbies, collections, etc.:

Favorite outdoor sports:

Cricket; tennis

Favorite indoor sports:

Table tennis, at which I am poor.

Favorite book and why:

Recherche du Temps Perdu
Proust A la Recherche du Temps Perdu
Karamazov
Dostoevski Brothers Karamazov
} I don't know which I like the better

Favorite author and why:

One of the two above: because they deepen one's human knowledge and so positively enrich life.

How I happened to write that book:

There was very little happening about it. It had to be done, and I enjoyed doing it.

Any other information not particularly specified:

Bobbs-Merrill Mss.
Manuscripts Department, Lilly Library
Indiana University, Bloomington, Indiana

BOBBS-MERRILL AUTHORS' QUESTIONNAIRE

This is our own "Who's Who and Why," because the regular "Who's Who" is most inadequate. The questionnaire when you fill it out is almost invaluable to the publicity department in preparing special news stories about your books, your life and your favorite breakfast food.

Please sign on the dotted lines and return to THE BOBBS-MERRILL COMPANY, INDIANAPOLIS, INDIANA, U.S.A.

******

Name and pseudonym:　　Meredith Nicholson (Nick)

Date of birth:　　December 9, 1866 (J. Milton's Birthday)

Place of birth:　　Crawfordsville, Indiana

Present address:　　Indianapolis,

Notable ancestors or members of family:　　All honest-to-God Americans, soldiers of the Revolution, and all other wars; my father and all his fathers were farmers.

Education:　　Attended Fourth Ward School; 1/2 year high school. Anything beyond this I just picked up. See article of some time ago in Good Housekeeping. I was keen about languages and took a whack at Latin, Greek, French and Italian at various times.

First attempt at writing:　　At about 16 or 17 began to write, verses and prose

List of books, plays, etc.:　　See "Who's Who." A vast amount of stuff not in books—short stories, essays, articles and addresses on many subjects.

MEREDITH NICHOLSON

- 2 -

Stories and articles in following magazines:
....   Too much trouble.

Single or married to whom:
.... Eugenie C. Kountze of Omaha, Neb.
                                    Graduate of Vassar.

Children:
.... M. N. Jr. Elizabeth and Charles L.

Occupation other than writing:
.... Nothing else for 30 years. Was newspaper
                                    man and in coal business. Have taken some
part in politics, been a candidate for office; have refused appointments(from
President Wilson); have been trustee of State Insane Hospital, jury commissioner;
was once foreman of grand jury, U. S. Court.
    Personal experiences I consider remarkable or unusual:
....

Idiosyncrasies, if any:
....

Personal preferences:
....   Too many to note; but generally broad minded,
                            and practise loving my enemies religiously.

Personal dislikes:
....

Superstitions: Thousands, as I had an Irish great grandmother.

My aim in life: What do you think?

The vocation I was advised to follow: Druggist, printer, minister, burglar.
                                          I did become a stenographer at 17
                                          and was a good performer.

- 3 -

World War Service. Army, Navy, Red Cross, etc.:

Killed the Kaiser daily
with my typewriter; Wrote and spoke for the cause.

Clubs, fraternities, sororities, organizations, etc.:

Phi Gamma Delta.
Phi Beta Kappa—with Wabash College. M. A. Butler College; M. A. & Litt. D.
Wabash College.

Hobbies, collections, etc.:

Favorite outdoor sports:

Walking. Played golf until it ruined my health
and disposition.

Favorite indoor sports:

Favorite book and why:

Favorite author and why:

I have 216 favorite authors; they include
Thackeray, Isaiah, Job, St. Paul, Emerson, Laurence Sterne, Chaucer,
Bill Nye and Robert Herrick.

How I happened to write that book:

Any other information not particularly specified:

I've used my own
experience in much that I have written—particularly in "A Hoosier Chronicle"
(novel) and there's a lot of me—religious experiences, political ideas,
etc. in my essays.

I established myself as a prophet (unrecognized) by a
poem, "In Ether Spaces", in about 1889, that forecast the radio.

BOBBS-MERRILL AUTHORS' QUESTIONNAIRE

This is our own "Who's Who and Why", because the regular
"Who's Who" is most inadequate. The questionnaire when you fill
it out is almost invaluable to the publicity department in preparing
special news stories about your books, your life and your favorite
breakfast food.

Please sign on the dotted lines and return to THE BOBBS-MERRILL
COMPANY, INDIANAPOLIS, INDIANA, U. S. A.

****

Name and pseudonym: *Talbot Mundy*

Date of birth: *April 23rd 1879*

Place of birth: *London. England*

Present address: *Point Loma . Cal*

Notable ancestors or members of family: *Adam, Eve, Noah, William the Conqueror, John of Gaunt, a lady named Jones and my parents.*

Education: *The gardener. A governess who had false teeth. Several excellent dogs, particularly a coal-black retriever named Duchess. A school at Guildford where an inferiority complex was regarded as righteousness and yelling was the medium of instruction — a caning was the method of stirring affection. Rugby. The*

First attempt at writing: *wide world, including a Chinaman and several niggers.*

Home to my mother for money. Best fiction I ever did.

List of books, plays, etc.: *See Bobbs-Merrill's list.*

TALBOT MUNDY

2

Stories and articles in following magazines: Satevepost.

Adventure. The Letter ever since
it first appeared. Everybody's.

Single or married to whom:

To a lady from Connecticut.

Children:

A stepson and four pups by an
sheep-dog out of an airedale.

Occupation other than writing:

Trying to write. Have also been a
Government Official.

Personal experiences I consider remarkable or unusual: Am the
official, hereditary, lord-high rain-
maker to the Kakkamega Kavirondo tribe.
I once shook hands with the Prince of Wales
and I once had a rhinoceros in my bedroom for
a week

Idiosyncracies, if any: Two fingers missing from
my right hand, which spoils my aim at
the typewriter keys.

Personal preferences:

Chesterfields. Matches with the bullets inside.
Arthur S. Hoffman, Lowry Trimble and my own wife.

Personal dislikes: most other people's wives and
baked beans. Also dressing on the salad.

Superstitions: A belief that most difficulties resolve
themselves if let, that nearly everybody is a lot
better inside than he looks from the outside, and that
photos don't matter.

My aim in life:

To avoid what most people seem to regard
as a good time, so that I may more fully enjoy the
wonderful time I do have.

The vocation I was advised to follow: The Church — The
sure haven for incompetents. But the
world was saved in time.

3

World War service. Army, Navy, Red Cross, etc.: *Boer War. Three*
African campaigns.

Clubs, fraternities, sororities, organizations, etc.: *None.*

Hobbies, collections, etc.: *Books.*

Favorite outdoor sports: *Sailing.*

Favorite indoor sports: *Books*

Favorite book and why: *H. P. Blavatsky's Isis Unveiled.*
Because it de-bunks the whole darned
universe, myself included.
Favorite author and why:
H. P. Blavatsky. See above

Any other information not particularly specified: *Six feet one inch.*
Bald on top. Several false teeth. A
mortgage. A hatred of public speaking
and notoriety but an enormous interest
in people, whom I enjoy almost as much as
I do rocks and trees. A conviction that
Mexico is moving upward into the sunshine.
A loathing for politics. A peculiar belief
that publishers are people.

Talbot Mundy

Taylor-Made Shakespeare?
Or Is "Shall I Die?" the Long-Lost Text
of Bottom's Dream?

John F. Andrews

As 1985 drew to a close the burning question among students of the English Renaissance was whether or not the Shakespeare canon had been enlarged by its first new entry since the seventeenth century.

In mid-November, while checking manuscript references in the Bodleian Library at Oxford, a young American named Gary L. Taylor happened upon a poem attributed to Shakespeare in a manuscript miscellany apparently dating from the 1630s. Although other scholars of Elizabethan literature had examined Rawlinson Poetic Manuscript 160 in the past, and at least two Bodleian cataloguers (Falconer Madan in 1895 and Margaret Crum in 1969) had noted the attribution to Shakespeare of an untitled lyric beginning "Shall I die," no one before had ever seen any reason to make a fuss over the poem, and hence no one had reprinted or discussed it. For many a researcher, this would have suggested that the poem was probably nothing more than another contemporary work erroneously ascribed or deliberately misascribed to Shakespeare. But Gary Taylor is not just another researcher.

During his seven years as Joint General Editor of the new Oxford edition of Shakespeare's complete works, Taylor has moved increasingly to the vanguard of the current effort to demand a fresh look at all the poems and plays. In 1983 he appeared in print as one of the principals behind *The Division of the Kingdom*, a collection of essays in support of coeditor Michael Warren's 1976 thesis that *King Lear* can no longer be approached as a single, conflated text (as it has been presented to readers in virtually every edition since the eighteenth century) but must now be viewed instead as two separate texts: an early version of the play published in the 1608 First Quarto, and a later, revised version published in the 1623 First Folio. Warren and Taylor's views about *King Lear* will be reflected in the two-text edition of Shakespeare's tragedy to be included in the forthcoming Oxford complete works. Meanwhile, in another departure from editorial tradition, Taylor announced in a 1984 paper at Stratford's International Shakespeare Conference that the Oxford edition of *Henry IV, Part 1* will restore Sir John Oldcastle to the role the dramatist had originally written for him, even though Falstaff will continue to be the name the same character bears in the Oxford texts for *Henry IV, Part 2*, *Henry V*, and *The Merry Wives of Windsor*.

In light of this background, one is hardly surprised to learn that the Oxford Shakespeare will

A portrait of Shakespeare engraved by Martin Droeshout for the title page of the 1623 First Folio (Folger Shakespeare Library)

probably also be the first collection of the playwright's works to contain the Bodleian poem that Gary Taylor declared to be by Shakespeare in a 24 November 1985 front-page story in the *New York Times.*

According to the *Times* report, Taylor believes "Shall I die?" to be a "technical exercise" from the years (1593-1595) when Shakespeare was writing such plays as *Romeo and Juliet, A Midsummer Night's Dream,* and *Love's Labor's Lost.* It was during this period in his career that the playwright published his two long narrative poems, "Venus and Adonis" (1593) and "The Rape of Lucrece" (1594), and many scholars believe that it was also at this time that he wrote most if not all of his sonnets.

Taylor has analyzed the vocabulary of "Shall I die?" with particular attention to its rhyming words, and he finds strong parallels with Shakespeare generally and with the works of Shakespeare's early period in particular. Together with the other evidence he presented in a 15 December article in the *New York Times Book Review,* these parallels persuade Taylor that the poem is much more likely to have been written by Shakespeare than by, say, Spenser, and is much more likely to have been written prior to 1596 than subsequent to that date. Among other things, Taylor analyzes "Shall I die?" for the frequency with which it employs rare words, including several words or word forms not previously recorded in the *Oxford English Dictionary.* On the basis of this analysis, he concludes that the lyric parallels Shakespeare's other works not only in its use of rare words characteristic of Shakespeare but also in its use of words that appear nowhere else in the canon. "Paradoxically," he says, "if a poem of any length does not contain words that Shakespeare never used elsewhere, then that poem cannot be by Shakespeare."

Taylor makes no extravagant claims for the literary merit of "Shall I die?" "It's not *Hamlet,*" he admits. But he thinks it considerably better than do many of the lyric's outspoken detractors. He describes "Shall I die?" as "a kind of verbal obstacle course in which one of every three syllables is a rhyme." If "the effort to rhyme distorts the syntax and weakens the sense in places," Taylor says, we must remember that "Shakespeare's rhymed poetry is often awkward and much of the rhyme in the plays was once dismissed as spurious because it is awkward." A poem as "artificial" as "Shall I die?" was probably "as admirable to Elizbethan critical taste as it seems perverse to ours."

If "Shall I die?" is in fact a lyric by Shake-

speare, it is at the very least an anomaly, with its unusual structure (nine ten-line stanzas with an *abcdecfghg* rhyme scheme, the end-rhyming third and sixth lines only half the length of the trochaic tetrameters used elsewhere in each stanza), its rapid-fire delivery of internal rhymes ("Yet I must vent my lust"), its uneven rhythms ("If she scorn, I mourn"), its crabbed phrasing ("Thin lips red, fancy's fed/With all sweets when he meets"), and its frequent banality ("If she scorn I mourn,/I retire to despair, joying never"). Taylor explains it as "a kind of virtuoso piece, a kind of early Mozart" composition. The University of Maryland's S. Schoenbaum agrees. In a 24 November *New York Times* sidebar, Schoenbaum classifies "Shall I die?" as one of Shakespeare's occasional poems. "It is artificial in the largest sense of the word," he says. "It is extremely ingenious in its rhyme scheme, it has seductive qualities, ironies, a mixture of moods, the rich complexities that you don't often find in this period. And it's different—who else could have written it if not Shakespeare?"

Other readers have been less generous in their appraisals. According to the 24 November *New York Times,* scholar and publisher Robert Giroux regards the poem as at best "adolescent." "If it is Shakespeare's," he is quoted as saying, "I can see why he never published it." Similar sentiments are expressed in the 9 December story about "Shall I die?" in *Time* magazine. The University of Chicago's David Bevington describes Taylor's find as "a really bad poem, a piece of doggerel." Princeton's Alvin Kernan confesses that the poem "does not sound much like Shakespeare to me." And Columbia's Frank Kermode says, "True, Shakespeare wrote some bad poems, but the way this one is bad is not similar in any fashion to the way Shakespeare was bad." Meanwhile, writing in the 22 December issue of the *New York Times Book Review,* Anthony Burgess invokes "the subtle testimony of the ear" to argue that "Mr. Taylor's poetic discovery" is not Shakespeare but "the work of an Elizabethan songwriter, a man who has either devised a lyric to be set to music or, with no such intention, is nevertheless haunted by the sound of song."

Gary Taylor has insisted that his case for the authenticity of "Shall I die?" be tested, not on the basis of the lyric's poetic quality (a criterion by which "much of Shakespeare's work would be relegated to the foot of the page"), but on the strength of the internal and external evidence he has marshaled in support of the Rawlinson manuscript's attribution to Shakespeare. Such a position was

The Poem

1

Shall I die? Shall I fly
Lovers' baits and deceits,
         sorrow breeding?
Shall I tend? Shall I send?
Shall I sue, and not rue
         my proceeding?
In all duty her beauty
Binds me her servant for ever.
If she scorn, I mourn,
I retire to despair, joying never.

2

Yet I must vent my lust.
And explain inward pain
         by my love breeding.
If she smiles, she exiles
All my moan; if she frown,
         all my hopes deceiving—
Suspicious doubt, O keep out,
For thou art my tormentor.
Fly away, pack away;
I will love, for hope bids me venture.

3

'Twere abuse to accuse
My fair love, ere I prove
         her affection.
Therefore try! Her reply
Gives thee joy—or annoy,
         or affliction.
Yet howe'er, I will bear
Her pleasure with patience, for beauty
Sure [will] not seem to blot
Her deserts, wronging him doth her duty.

4

In a dream it did seem—
But alas, dreams do pass
         as do shadows—
I did walk, I did talk
With my love, with my dove,
         through fair meadows.
Still we passed till at last
We sat to repose us for our pleasure.
Being set, lips met,
Arms twined, and did bind my heart's treasure.

5

Gentle wind sport did find
Wantonly to make fly
         her gold tresses,
As they shook I did look,
But her fair did impair

all my senses.
As amazed, I gazed
On more than a mortal complexion.
[Them] that love can prove
Such force in beauty's inflection.

6

Next her hair, forehead fair,
Smooth and high; next doth lie,
         without wrinkle,
Her fair brows; under those
Star-like eyes win love's prize
         when they twinkle.
In her cheeks who seeks
Shall find there displayed beauty's banner;
Oh admiring desiring
Breeds, as I look still upon her.

7

Thin lips red, fancy's fed
With all sweets when he meets,
         and is granted
There to trade, and is made
Happy, sure, to endure
         still undaunted.
Pretty chin doth win
Of all [the world] commendations;
Fairest neck, no speck;
All her parts merit high admirations.

8

A pretty bare, past compare,
Parts those plots which besots
         still asunder.
It is meet naught but sweet
Should come near that so rare
         'tis a wonder.
No mishap, no scape
Inferior to nature's perfection;
No blot, no spot:
She's beauty's queen in election.

9

Whilst I dreamt, I, exempt
[From] all care, seemed to share
         pleasures in plenty;
But awake, care take—
For I find to my mind
         pleasures scanty.
Therefore I will try
To compass my heart's chief contenting.
To delay, some say,
In such a case causeth repenting.

Poem from the Rawlinson Poetic Manuscript 160 that Gary Taylor attributes to Shakespeare

bound to attract challengers, and several scholars have already entered the lists with arguments to counter those advanced by Taylor.

In the 20 December issue of London's *Times Literary Supplement (TLS)*, for example, Robin Robbins raises fundamental questions about Taylor's methods of literary detection. He points out, among other things, that Taylor appears to be guilty of the "salmons in both" fallacy, the assumption that because two literary samples are similar to one another in certain respects, they are similar in all essential respects and for the same reasons. In response to Taylor's list of phrases and rhyme pairs paralleling "Shall I die?" to other works by Shakespeare, Robbins offers an equally persuasive list of parallels from the poetry of Edmund Spenser, Samuel Daniel, Michael Drayton, and Sir Philip Sidney. And in response to Taylor's claim that the parallels he has identified establish a prima facie case for Shakespeare's authorship, Robbins notes that there could be other explanations for such parallels even if they more closely resembled Shakespeare's works than those of any of his contemporaries, particularly if the manuscript in question is late enough for its compiler to have included works by poets consciously or unconsciously imitating Shakespeare's stylistic characteristics.

In the 27 December issue of *TLS*, I. A. Shapiro of the University of Birmingham carries Robbins's arguments a step further. "If it could be claimed that the poem's vocabulary and other characteristics could be paralleled *only*, or even almost only, in Shakespeare's acknowledged works," says Shapiro, "then we would have to weigh seriously the ascription" in the Rawlinson manuscript. "But such a claim will immediately be laughed at by anyone familiar with the verse and drama of 1580-1660." Shapiro demonstrates that two of the words

---

Another Unititled Anapestic Canter
Conjecturally (though unreliably)
attributed to Taylor the Water-Scholar

1
Shall I say that, today,
What I took from a book
            in the Bodley
Is the work of a jerk?
Or would Will, with his quill,
            write thus oddly?
There's his name—can I claim
That this sounds like a genuine poem?
      Like a shot! And why not?
I'm an editor, aren't I? I'll show 'em!

2
Not a portion of caution
I'll use, but my views
            I'll state proudly—
And I guess that the press
Will turn out, if I shout
            very loudly,
I'll add fame to my name,
And the glory will bring much enjoyment—
      And just *think* how the stink
That I'll raise will help get me employment!

3
I'll concede that the screed
(If it *is* really his)
            is his oddest,
But I'll huff and I'll puff
(With a touch—though not *much*—
            that sounds modest),
And I'll muster such bluster
That soon with my brass I'll surround it.
      I've got clout—who can doubt
That it's genuine? (Given who found it.)

4
There'll be those who oppose:
Who will say that I may
            be too hasty.
But the name of the game
Is the fame that I'll claim—
            and that's tasty!
Wait and see? Not for me:
When you're job-hunting, caution's a drawback.
      No, my word must be heard—
And the burden of proof is on *your* back!

                              Chr. Marlowe

(Several illegible stanzas here omitted)

Parody of the poem in question, posted at the Duke University English Department

Taylor identifies as Shakespearean "neologisms" (because they had not been recorded prior to 1596 in the *OED*) can be found earlier than the presumed date for "Shall I die?" in poems by Marlowe and Spenser, and he says that a thorough survey of the extant literature of the period would also eliminate a good number of additional words and usages now regarded as having been first employed by Shakespeare. Like Robbins, Shapiro suggests that much of Taylor's argument is either naive or circular.

Meanwhile, though he professes himself to be uninterested in "taking sides in the debate on the authorship of 'Shall I die?' " Peter Beal cast further doubt on Taylor's claims in a letter published in the 3 January 1986 *TLS*. Taylor asks us to base much of our confidence in the Rawlinson attribution for "Shall I die?" on the assurance that "fifty other poems in the manuscript are attributed to specific authors; none of those other attributions are demonstrably wrong, most are demonstrably right, and only two ambiguous initials are even dubious." Like Robbins, Beal points out that in fact one of the Rawlinson poems, "Sir Walter Raleigh's Pilgrimage," has "long been rejected from the Raleigh canon," and that several others, including one ascription to Donne, are either "suspect" or uncertain. He goes on to note that there are a number of reasons, quite apart from any transcriber's "motives," for poems to get misascribed in manuscript miscellanies. Among his suggestions for "Shall I die?" is the possibility that the lyric was a song "introduced in some early-seventeenth-century stage performances of one of Shakespeare's plays. . . . This would account for its association with Shakespeare whether he were actually the author or not."

So where does this leave us? Do we credit the Rawlinson manuscript's attribution of "Shall I die?" to Shakespeare, or do we align ourselves with those who either reject the poem as unworthy of the playwright or insist that it is necessary to have more evidence before we can adjudicate the issue? And how do we respond to a later development in the case, the 25 December announcement in the *New York Times* that Stephen Parks, curator of pre-1800 manuscripts at the Beinecke Rare Book and Manuscript Library, has turned up another manuscript copy of "Shall I die?" Since the Yale copy of the poem is unattributed, Parks contends that its existence constitutes yet another "challenge to Mr. Taylor to prove that what he has is a poem by Shakespeare."

In the original *New York Times* article about the discovery of "Shall I die?" Gary Taylor and his Oxford colleague Stanley Wells were said to believe that "the burden of proof is now with anyone who wants to cast doubt on the attribution." In Taylor's words, "All the evidence says this poem belongs to Shakespeare's canon and, unless somebody can dislodge it, it will stay there." Similar sentiments were expressed by their American colleague S. Schoenbaum: "It's authentic until proved otherwise." At the moment, the only thing that appears certain is that not everyone is prepared to accept that formulation of the situation.

COMMENTS FROM OTHER SCHOLARS AND POETS

RONALD BERMAN

It will be hard to prove or disprove that Shakespeare wrote the untitled poem. Anything is possible. But the main point is probably that the poem is so bad that if Shakespeare wrote it he rarely returned to its example. There were many quite terrible verses done in England in the sixteenth century. Many schoolboys were copying the "catalogs" of female beauty which were then in vogue, or just going out of vogue. These catalogues, like this poem, began with praising the hair of the beloved, then proceeded south to adore the brow, cheeks, nose, lips, teeth, neck, etc. Sometimes, as in the case of John Donne, these poems became explicit and satirical. But in any case, even if Shakespeare did write this imitative and mindless poem, he lived to recant in other more significant work like the mockery of catalogs in *The Comedy of Errors* (III, ii, 100 ff.) and Sonnet 130. So, the poem is either not Shakespeare's, which accounts for its badness, or it is, and was stylistically rejected by him when he learned to write well.

PETER DAVISON

It seems to me extremely unlikely that whoever wrote this jejune piece of Euphuism could be the author of Shakespeare's plays and poems. The metrics are not Shakespeare's, the rhythms are not Shakespeare's. The ear is not Shakespeare's, even at his worst.

GEORGE L. GECKLE

Is "Shall I die? Shall I fly ...?" by Shakespeare? That is the question. Gary Taylor's attribution (*New York Times Book Review*, 15 December 1985) is based upon a great deal of argument about the so-called verbal parallels between words, phrases, and images in the manuscript poem and Shakespeare's acknowledged plays and poems. Such internal evidence is open to much interpretation; i. e., it is subjective. Taylor argues that unless another poet is identified whose works provide better verbal parallels we must accept his argument. Given the nature of poetic convention and imitation in Shakespeare's time, Taylor's argument is not a strong one, as Anthony Burgess has already demonstrated in his contention that the poem was more likely written by a songwriter named "Anonymous" (*New York Times Book Review*, 22 December 1985).

But is there external evidence to support Taylor's claim? Ay, but there's the real rub. The poem was attributed to Shakespeare *by an anonymous scribe* in the seventeenth-century manuscript in which Taylor found it at the Bodleian Library at Oxford. Although Taylor at first believed that no other copy existed, one came to light at the end of December 1985 in the Beinecke Rare Book and Manuscript Library at Yale University. This copy is unattributed. The external evidence, therefore, is insufficient; i.e., we lack real objective proof that Shakespeare wrote the poem.

Until someone finds better factual evidence that attributes the poem to Shakespeare, I do not think that scholars should accept Taylor's arguments. As it stands now, the case for or against Shakespeare's authorship is basically conjectural. Those who want to believe for whatever reasons that Shakespeare is the author will find stylistic evidence to support their claims. Those who do not want to believe will also find reasons.

As for me, I do not believe that Shakespeare wrote "Shall I die? Shall I fly ...?" Why? Because I think that it is a conventional, trite Elizabethan poem, the kind found in such miscellanies as *The Paradise of Dainty Devices*, *A Gorgeous Gallery of Gallant Inventions*, and such other repositories of bad (and sometimes very good) Elizabethan poetry. If Shakespeare *did* write the poem in question, then I would like to believe that it was intended as a parody, perhaps in the vein of Orlando's poems in *As You Like It*. But it is more likely that, as Burgess has argued, the author was "Anonymous."

O. B. HARDINSON, JR.

Nowhere does the genius of great authors show itself more clearly than in their habit of interring the klinkers that they inevitably produced from time to time. If "Shall I die" was written by Shakespeare, he showed his genius by answering the question: "Yes." It is sad that this drab little poem has been dug up. *Requiescat in pace.*

ANTHONY HECHT

It seems to me highly doubtful that Gary Taylor's "discovery," the poem beginning "Shall I die? Shall I fly," was written by Shakespeare; and if it was, it adds nothing whatsoever to his stature. It is a work of very little merit; it is distinctly inferior not only to all the songs (for this is very evidently a song) in Shakespeare's plays, but also to the song texts of almost all of his contemporaries, both playwrights and song writers. It is guilty of clumsy and inept prosody, musical tediousness, and the fatal error of going on too long.

The musical settings of verse, even in the painstaking Elizabethan period, could sometimes accommodate and smooth over a few metrical deficiencies, but in this case it would have been impossible. For starters, the poem shifts back and forth between anapestic (or possibly cretic) feet, and dactylic feet with catalectic closures. Purely as rhythm these are badly assorted, bouncy, and suitable at best for lighthearted frolics like 'Lustily, lustily, lustily let us sail forth. . . ." It is emphatically not a rhythm suitable to a love poem, unless in the spirit of parody. Secondly, the musical setting would presumably have been identical for all stanzas, and so the corresponding lines of each stanza would have to be accommodated to the same musical phrases. This would mean that lines three and six of stanza one ("sorrow breeding," "my proceeding?") would have to fit the same musical text as the same two lines in the next stanza ("by my love breeding," "all my hopes deceiving"). I do not know a single poet of the period guilty of that kind of slovenliness. The whole text abounds in such metrical and musical discrepancies, and seems to me throughout conspicuous for its clumsiness. This was a great age of English composers: Pilkington, Lawes, Gibbons, Morley, Farneby, Byrd, Dowland, Campion, Cavendish and Wilbye, to name a few. These composers were expert at setting texts, but my guess is that they wouldn't have touched this one with a ten-foot pole.

WILLIAM HEYEN

The truth is (since time and space avail not, as his best friend in heaven says [best friend, but still testy about Willy's "art language"]) that William Shakespeare cannot remember if he wrote the deft and shallow poem only recently found and attributed to him. The controversy, in fact, is part of human nature's unfolding revelation for him, and he's thinking of writing a comedy whose main character is a scholar who discovers in a never-before-opened amphora in a British Museum vault a manuscript he believes to be in the hand of Jesus of Nazareth. Christ himself will likely appear to the scholar in his cell in the Tower of London into which he has been thrown for heretical insanity, but may not save him, and will Himself not be able to remember if the manuscript in question is His. Nor will He care. He knows He spoke much more incisively and poetically elsewhere, and believes Himself to be adequately on record. Our scholar will lecture Jesus, will insist that the authorship of the manuscript matters. Jesus will listen patiently, but will not be able to understand, no matter how hard he tries.

DANIEL HOFFMAN

We are told by Mr. Gary Taylor that attribution in an anonymous commonplace book and the appearance in the text of many words a concordance locates also in Shakespeare's voluminous works makes an unbeatable case for authorship.

In foggy waters one must navigate as did the Maine lobsterman, by the taste of the brine. Better immerse the text in Shakespeare's canon and taste it: Does it blend well with the various surrounding seas, or is it a puddle of oil on the swell?

A conclusion, instantaneously reached, is that this extended piece of jingling balderdash is not by the author of Shakespeare's plays, songs, sonnets, and poems. Someone has suggested in the *New York Times Book Review* that W. S. might have run up these feeble rhymes as a spoof, but even a middling poet would have known to terminate the send-up after a dozen lines. To drag it on shows that whoever pulled his ear to find so many rhymes was a poetaster.

Has anyone computerized a concordance to the writings of the Earl of Oxford?

X. J. KENNEDY

Read for its sense alone, the poem may seem a vacuous lump of piffle unworthy of the Bard, but if read for the pleasure of its meter and rhyme, it appears a reasonably dexterous technical exercise: deserving of low praise, perhaps, yet not to be spat upon. Shakespeare wrote many a hey-nonny-nonny song that says nothing much, and to write as a musician who for fun scrapes out a piece on his fiddle (rather than to write as a thinker who delineates an idea or a dramatist who portrays a character, as one might expect him to do) would be, I think, entirely like him. Viewed soberly, the poem is a mere string of forgettable conventions; but taken lightly, it has a pretty fair tune to it.

MAYNARD MACK

The authorship of this rather dreary little poem is not a matter about which one can speak with comfortable assurance, and I find it troubling that it is now presented to the world with more confidence than present evidence justifies.

Conceivably, the work is Shakespeare's. If so, it belongs to an apprentice period of which we have no other example so hackneyed in theme, imagery, and diction. More likely, it is not Shakespeare's but the work of any of "the mob of gentlemen who wrote with ease" throughout the period. That it has Shakespeare's name attached to it in the Bodley manuscript proves nothing save that someone, well-informed, or ill-informed, or uninformed, attributed it to him. It is a matter of record that such manuscript collections, from the sixteenth century down through the eighteenth, contain and help perpetuate misattributions along with textual misreadings. In the Yale manuscript, the poem remains anonymous. This proves nothing either, but it does argue that the poem was not in those times universally known to be by Shakespeare.

So far, the arguments put forward for the attribution do not convince. Particularly unfortunate is the notion that recognizably *un*-Shakespearean usages in the poem guarantee its authenticity. On this principle, not even the Bodleian will be able to house all the poems and plays assignable to Shakespeare's pen.

JOHN FREDERICK NIMS

My own researches, achieved by the use of stiff twin compasses, stewed mandrakes, and a sundial, confirm that this poem is a product of the prolific quill of Willibald Skilmer (1563-1615), putative forbear of Joe E. Skilmer. No other Elizabethan had the *unbeschreibliche Schrecklichkeit* (as Schiller called it) to produce an opus of this yucky ilk.

[John Frederick Nims, "The Greatest English Lyric?—A New Reading of Joe E. Skilmer's 'Threse,'" *Studies in Bibliography*, 20 (1967): 1-14. *Editor.*]

A. L. ROWSE

There is no likelihood that this long-winded, repetitive poem is by Shakespeare. It is obviously a song—and all Shakespeare's songs are short and pithy.

He was so famous a writer in his own day that people—especially publishers—would not have missed anything that he wrote. Quite the contrary: they published in *The Passionate Pilgrimage* poems under Shakespeare's name that we know definitely were written *not* by him, but by others.

Those who would like to think that this rambling song is by him say that it *might* be an early work. But we know what Shakespeare's early work was like from his early poems, "A Lover's Complaint" and "Venus and Adonis." And they are quite different.

This long song is obviously a piece of madrigal verse, just like a dozen such pieces in *The Oxford Book of Madrigal Verse*. They mostly begin like that—the best-known, "Shall I come, sweet love, to thee?" None of them by Shakespeare.

Computors are useful *machines*, not judges of poetry. To be a good judge of poetry you need to be, not just an academic nor museum-minded, but a practicing poet who is also a scholar. As I am.

STEPHEN SANDY

It could, possibly, be an example of Shakespeare's rural juvenilia, but reading "Shall I Die?" the mind's ear does not hear Shakespeare, rather a follower of Wither or some other.

THEODORE WEISS

One is tempted to believe that the same poem, whatever its merits, written by Shakespeare and by some lesser poet, would be different for each and much more meaningful in Shakespeare's case; for it would reverberate within the mighty network of his other oeuvre. But when the poem is as indifferent as the one now being attributed to Shakespeare, its attribution hardly seems—except for scholars—to matter. Something that does not add to his work may not subtract from it, but it little enhances it. Of course our best poet should be respected as having it in him to write a bad, not to say the worst poem. Shakespeare, if the poem is his, was certainly entitled to an occasional nod. But when he sank into a deep sleep scored mainly by raspy snoring?

RICHARD WILBUR

If the attribution were certain, it would interest us to know that Shakespeare was at some point capable of such an overwrought jingle. But as it is, I can't feel that the poem adds much to our knowledge or pleasure.

GEORGE W. WILLIAMS

The parallels that Mr. Taylor draws between the Bodley poem and the canon of Shakespeare's works cluster around the period 1593-1595, the years of the nondramatic poem. If the parallels are valid, the poem would have been produced when Shakespeare was between twenty-nine and thirty-one years of age. The poem would not, therefore, have been a youthful piece; it would have been the work of an accomplished poet, a man of mature power and beyond hesitant experimentation. When James Joyce published *A Portrait of the Artist as a Young Man*, he included in it a poem he had written when he was seventeen or eighteen. It is a brilliant tour de force, a villanelle of extraordinary poetic contrivance. The technicalities of this form are as demanding as are those of the Bodley poem, yet we never feel that Joyce is not absolute master of their severe limitations. Had Shakespeare at thirty decided to indulge—uncharacteristically—in such a poetic scheme as this one, he would have been in command of it. The author of these lines is imprisoned in his form; Shakespeare, like Joyce, would have been able to find within the confines of the form the very means of liberating his zest and imagination.

Shakespeare never sought rhyme for its own sake in the fashion of this poem, nor did he indulge (so far as we have record) in the mannered artificiality of such pieces. But if he had ever—perhaps as a game—engaged in the production of such a disciplined exercise, Shakespeare would have brought to the work lightness, flair, sprightliness, and joy. None of these attributes is here. The facility that we find in his use of form in, for example, the sonnet in which Romeo and Juliet first speak together is entirely absent in this poem.

MARGARET YORKE

I feel that if this is a poem by Shakespeare—and I accept the deductions made by scholars such as Gary Taylor and Stanley Wells—then because it is so inexpressibly bad it must be a real piece of juvenilia, written at a much earlier age than suggested. I have no such reservations about Edmund Ironside, an extract from which I have recently read, and would instinctively attribute that to William Shakespeare; it has the right feel about it.

A Selection of Published Responses

Peter Beal, Letter, *Times Literary Supplement*, 3 January 1986, p. 13;

Beal, Letter, *Times Literary Supplement*, 24 January 1986;

Paul K. Benedict, Letter, *New York Times Book Review*, 19 January 1986, p. 25;

M. C. Bradbrook, Letter, *Times Literary Supplement*, 31 January 1986, p. 115;

Anthony Burgess, "Is It Really Shakespeare," *New York Times Book Review*, 22 December 1985, p. 3;

Thomas Clayton, Letter, *Times Literary Supplement*, 31 January 1986, p. 115;

Philip Edwards, Letter, *Times Literary Supplement*, 19 January 1986, p. 37;

Charles M. Fair, "The Maid Replies to W. S.," Poem, *New York Times Book Review*, 19 January 1986, p. 25;

Donald W. Foster, Letter, *New York Times Book Review*, 19 January 1986, p. 4;

Foster, Letter, *Times Literary Supplement*, 24 January 1986, pp. 87-88;

Otto Friedrich, " 'Shall I Die? Shall I Fly . . . ,' " *Time* (9 December 1985): 76;

Sally M. Gall, Letter, *New York Times Book Review*, 19 January 1986, p. 25;

Roma Gill and Graham Matthews, Letter, *Times Literary Supplement*, 10 January 1986, p. 37;

Robert Giroux, Letter, *New York Times Book Review*, 19 January 1986, pp. 4, 24;

Charles Hamilton, Letter, *New York Times*, 8 December 1985;

Shirley Strum Kenny, Letter, *New York Times Book Review*, 19 January 1986, p. 24;

Edwin McDowell, "Copy of Disputed Poem Found at Yale," *New York Times*, 25 December 1985, p. 23;

Thomas H. Pendleton, Letter, *New York Times Book Review*, 19 January 1986, p. 24;

Anne Ridler, Letter, *Times Literary Supplement*, 10 January 1986, p. 37;

Robin Robbins, ". . . And the Counter Arguments," *Times Literary Supplement*, 20 December 1985, pp. 1449-1450;

A. L. Rowse, Letter, *New York Times*, 8 December 1985, p. E26;

I. A. Shapiro, Letter, *Times Literary Supplement*, 27 December 1985, pp. 1481, 1492;

Eric Sheen and Jeremy Maule, Letter, *Times Literary Supplement*, 17 January 1986, p. 61;

John J. Soldo, Letter, *New York Times*, 8 December 1985, p. E26;

Gary Taylor, "A New Shakespeare Poem? The Evidence. . . ," *Times Literary Supplement*, 20 December 1985, pp. 1447-1448;

Taylor, Letter, *New York Times*, 9 February 1986;

Taylor, "Shakespeare's New Poem: A Scholar's Clues and Conclusions," *New York Times Book Review*, 15 December 1985, pp. 11-14;

Taylor, " 'Shall I die?' Immortalized," *Times Literary Supplement*, 31 January 1986, pp. 123-124;

Taylor, "The Shakespeare Revolution," *London Sunday Times*, 15 December 1985, p. 33;

Jo Thomas, "Critics Say Poem Isn't Shakespeare," *New York Times*, 6 December 1985, p. C36;

"Too bard to be true," Poem, *Economist*, 3 November 1985, p. 61;

Ira Wallach, Letter, *New York Times Book Review*, 19 January 1986, p. 25;

Stanley Wells, Letter, *Times Literary Supplement*, 10 January 1986, p. 37;

Roger Woddis, Poem, "A Word from Will," *Punch*, 8 January 1986.

Parisian Theater, Fall 1984:
Toward a New Baroque

William Mould
University of South Carolina

The Fall 1984 theatrical season in Paris was busy, varied, alternately exciting and distressing—exactly what one might expect in one of the world's most active centers of theater. It is always difficult in such profusion to discover general tendencies, threads which when pulled together will form a coherent pattern. Nonetheless, the plays chosen for production and the way in which they were presented showed a strong taste for the extravagance, illusion, theatricality, and violent contrast which characterize the baroque style. The baroque dominated much of seventeenth-century European art, and can be found in the powerful movement and emotion of Bernini's sculpture (*St. Theresa in Ecstasy, David*); in the bulk, expanse, and sweeping wings of the palace of Versailles; in the illusion and theatricality fostered by Versailles's Hall of Mirrors; in the startling contrast between light and shadow (*chiaroscuro*) which characterizes Georges de la Tour's paintings. Strong emotions, vast panoramas, and convoluted forms run through the art, music, and literature of the age. Many of the same characteristics prevailed in the theatrical productions of 1984 Paris.

Theater is itself an exercise in illusion, but some plays and modes of production stress the aspect of illusion obsessively. One of the most frequent devices is the play-within-a-play. Most often a feature of the text itself, it is occasionally inserted by a director to stress the difficulty of locating reality in a world where nothing is what it seems. The great success of the Fall 1984 season was Giorgio Strehler's production of Corneille's *Comic Illusion* (1636) at the Odéon (now the Theatre of Europe). From the choice of text to the lighting, from the set decoration to the casting, the baroque spirit dominated the production. The play, one of Corneille's most difficult to produce, is also perhaps his most baroque. Its convoluted structure involves the quest of a father for his son; he visits the grotto of a magician, who shows him scenes from his son's life. These events involve love affairs, incarceration, and murder. After witnessing his son's

Cover of program for L'illusion, *showing the director's use of light contrast and mirroring to blur the line between illusion and reality*

"death," the father discovers that much of what he has seen and accepted as representing reality is actually part of a play; his son has become an actor. We have, then, Corneille's play; within it is the series of scenes presented to the father and depicting the son's life; within that lies another play, the one being performed by the son's theatrical troupe. In addition, most of the characters within these plays are themselves misrepresenting reality at times:

Matamore, the braggart soldier, builds for himself a life full of heroism he never possessed; the son lies about his love to at least two women; one woman pretends to love an older man so that she can be near her true lover. In addition, Strehler chose to take the illusions a few steps further by having the same actors play more than one character; most important was the decision to cast the same actor as the magician and the Matamore—two very opposite roles, one a menacing mystic, the other an egregious fool who somehow manages to capture our sympathy. Another character simply did not exist in Strehler's production—Matamore's page; he was presented by Matamore's throwing his voice, imitating a servant, and then answering. Finally, Strehler chose to keep the father before us throughout the entire production; he was seated on a bench in the center aisle just in front of the first row of spectators. This served to underline the theatricality of the series of illusions being presented.

Other productions also relied on the play-within-a-play device. An adaptation of Kafka's *Starving Artist,* performed by the Box Theater of Jerusalem at the Centre Pompidou as part of the Kafka Centennial, placed the play within a circus whose Ringmaster promised a performance by the artist, and then began to lead the show. Each of the few performers played more than one role in a series of plays-within-plays. Although less complex than the Chinese-box system of Corneille's *Illusion,* this play also stressed the illusionary quality of life and the difficulty of distinguishing reality from imagination. Another Kafka-based play, *Dreams,* was a series of nightmares based on Kafka's essays, fiction, and correspondence. The company acted plays-within-plays, both in series and within each other. The audience was soon unable to distinguish the level of reality at any given moment, and the device was used to draw the spectators into a hallucinatory vortex where reason held little function and the id was paramount. The world of dreams was presented in such a fashion that it appeared more "real" than everyday life.

I Love Corneille told the story of Corneille's life through a series of vignettes. A contemporary troupe, having just finished a mediocre production of Corneille's classical tragedy, *Cinna,* engaged in a postshow discussion of the play and its author. They put on period costumes and presented the author's life. A twelve-piece orchestra emerged from a large chest, and the play-within-a-play was made up of snippets from other plays by Corneille, as well as works by Racine, Molière, and Thomas

Page from the program for Dreams, *a play based on Kafka's writings*

Corneille. For about fifteen minutes, the troupe performed a farcical commedia del l'arte version of *Two Precious Ladies Ridiculed,* much as it might have been done by Molière's company.

Molière's *Jealous Fool* was presented as a play-within-a-play. Here director Richard Colinet had imagined a company of ambulant Italian actors performing the play as a farewell to the great comic actor Scaramouche before he left France. So, before the "play" actually began, the actors were heard loudly arguing backstage in Italian. Throughout the play, the performers broke character to assume their Italian-actor roles, commenting on the play, its characters, and its action.

This important emphasis on illusion within the theater has a variety of complicated effects on the spectators. On the one hand, it removes them from direct involvement in a production, thus achieving some of the distance between performers and audience so dear to Strehler, among others.

This distancing effect, based on the dramatic theories of Bertolt Brecht, removes the spectator from involvement with onstage events, substituting intellectual and aesthetic appreciation for emotional identification with the dramatic characters and events.

Closely tied to the effect of illusion is that of theatricality. Here again, the audience is reminded that it is present at a spectacle, that before them are actors, not "people," and that the situations are not real. One of the most common devices for stressing theatricality is the use of actors as actors; that is, showing the moments when the actor assumes or leaves the character being portrayed. This is done by inventing a preshow entertainment, as in *The Jealous Fool* or the early plays of Ariane Mnouchkine's Theatre of the Sun (most notably *1789* and *1793*), where the performers donned costume and makeup in full view of the audience entering the theater. When an actor assumes more than one role without trying to hide the device from the audience, theatricality is strong; this was evident in *The Illusion*, where fourteen roles were played by seven actors, and in *I Love Corneille*, with an even wider distribution (sixty roles for ten actors).

Even plays appealing to the Parisian equivalent of a Broadway audience toyed with strong theatricality. Most notable was Jean-Claude Drouot's production of *Kean*. A tremendous popular success, the production made few concessions to facile understanding, and employed many of the same devices seen in the more intellectual theaters. The play itself concerns the English actor Edmund Kean and his struggle to assert his own reality in a society which wants to see in him only an entertainer. Not only do he and several other characters "live" scenes where they are masking real situations or emotions, thus "playacting" in real life, but there is a lengthy scene from a production of *Othello* in which Kean departs from his role to harangue the Prince of Wales and other "spectators" who are seated among the actual audience. He addresses the entire audience:

> . . . there is no one on stage. No one. Or perhaps just an actor playing Kean in *Othello*. Wait! I'm going to make a confession to you: I don't really exist, I just pretend to.

The device of the play-within-a-play, of the actor assuming and rejecting his character and his art, could hardly be more powerfully presented. The effect on the audience was electrifying and clearly gave the play an impact beyond the mere story it told.

In "Characters in Exile," an article which appeared in *Le Monde* on 29 September 1984, Bernard Dort laments the tendency to show actors as actors; he points to it as an increasingly common device and feels that it destroys the "incarnation" essential to the theatrical experience. He sees the actor and director rejecting the whole concept of a character in order to stress the process of the theatrical game. The audience is expected to enjoy the spectacle of actors at their work, developing their art, more than the straightforward development of characters in conflict.

Most of the plays which purport to be large frescoes, often biographical in nature, indulge in multiple roles for a few actors. Aside from *Corneille*, there was the vast (four and one-half hours) *The Red Scarf* presented by Antoine Vitez at the Chaillot Palace. Operatic in form, the work depicts the struggle of individuals within the context of a Marxist revolution. The scope covers more than thirty sites, a long period of time, and includes ninety-nine characters; all are portrayed by eighteen actors/musicians. Similarly, all the performers held multiple roles in *The Life and Death of Pier Paolo Pasolini* (written by Michel Azama, directed by and starring Jean Menaud), a biographical drama presented at the Tourtour Theatre in the Marais. Only three performers portrayed a dozen characters in Pasolini's life. In all of these plays, it is fair to say that the multiplication of roles and the emphasis on the actor's artistic function served to heighten the theatricality of a production and to make the spectator aware that the play meant something beyond the mere story it told. In this sense, the device of stressing the actor's function lends greater power to the production by widening its implications, and by actually prohibiting the audience from perceiving the action of the play as an isolated phenomenon.

One of the most striking characteristics of the baroque is the predilection for the extreme, the extravagant. In the past season, the grotesque was a common production element. Jérôme Savary's production of *La Périchole* at the Mogador Theatre was roundly criticized for the extravagant exaggeration of costuming, makeup, and general production values. Savary pointed out that grotesque exaggeration was precisely what he was striving for, here to establish a contrast between the exploited peasants and the decadent aristocracy. His courtiers wore enormous wigs, tailcoats decorated with gigantic feathers, and makeup which gave unnatural colors and features to their faces. They pranced, trotted, and pirouetted through the second half of the program like creatures from Hieronymus Bosch's bizarre painting of Hell in *The Garden of Earthly Delights.* Their gestures were vast; the props and sets were gaudy, gigantic, and obviously unrealistic. The effect was to make Savary's sociopolitical point in the midst of the untrammeled gaiety of Offenbach's operetta. Similarly, Savary's *Cyrano de Bergerac,* while considerably closer to the Romantic heroism of Rostand's original, presented a De Guiche who was effeminate, camp, and grotesque. Here the effect was perhaps less fortunate, for the interpretation undercut the Count's brutality and menace, making him simply a figure of fun. Jean-Louis Barrault directed Victor Hugo's *Angelo, Tyrant of Padua* at his Rond-Point Theatre on the Champs-Elysées. The costuming was lavish and the set pieces, while few, were opulent. The text itself is a curious choice, for it is full of extreme emotions and unlikely situations. The intensely convoluted plot could certainly be characterized as baroque, although the characters fall more into the Romantic mold one would expect from Hugo. Another Hugo play, *Lucrezia Borgia,* directed by Patrick Baty at the Cité Universitaire, demonstrated a choice of text which emphasized the extravagant and outlandish. Although the sets were so stark as almost not to be there at all, the unusual and extreme characters, especially Lucrezia herself and her husband, and the number of fatal situations the characters throw themselves into, seem to push far beyond the usual limits of Romantic inspiration. In this centenary celebration of Victor Hugo's death, it is worth noting that the plays chosen for production were not the well-known *Hernani* or *Ruy Blas,* but obscure works full of extravagant sentiments, characters, and situations. Much the same observation might be made about other anniversaries celebrated that year. Corneille, dead three hundred years, was honored by *The Palace Gallery, The Illusion,* and the biographical *I Love Corneille.* Of the "great" plays, only an unfortunate *Cinna,* left over from the preceding season at the Comédie Française, and a street production of *Horace* by an amateur group were to be seen—there was not a single version of his greatest masterpiece, *The Cid.* Diderot, whose bicentenary was being celebrated, was represented by productions based on his essays and dialogues (*The Actor's Paradox* and *D'Alembert's Dream*), but not by a single one of his important melodramas.

Finally, a strong desire to imitate the style of the commedia del l'arte led a number of produc-

tions into extraordinary extravagance, usually in the style of presentation more than in visual elements. This was particularly true of some Marivaux productions, such as *The Disguised Prince* and *The False Maid.* Unfortunately, in both cases the commedia style was at such strong variance with the text that neither production succeeded. Ill-advised as the style choice may have been, it nonetheless indicates an interest in exaggeration as a keystone of production. The commedia style was also apparent, but to much better effect, in *I Love Corneille* and *The Jealous Fool.*

One need hardly observe that almost every piece by Fernando Arrabal is grounded in the grotesque; such was the case of his latest play, *Lovesong of a Weightlifter,* directed by Albert Delpy at the Lucernaire. Along with the bizarre premise—that a weightlifter will be assassinated as he tries to break the world record—is presented the weightlifter's beloved Phyllis, disguised as a castrato masseur. Here, extravagant characters, situation, and production combine for a remarkably baroque presentation.

One result of an exaggerated presentation is an intense contrast between the conflicting elements of a play. Often these contrasts are between character types which are inherently antipathetic. Of course, some level of confrontation is essential to any drama, but the violent hostility in *The Red Scarf,* in *The Life and Death of Pier Paolo Pasolini,* in the Hugo plays, and in many others stressed the strong emotions of extreme character confrontation. Quite often, these confrontations took the form of battles between warring ideologies, and the characters were almost stripped of their individuality as they expressed polarized points of view; such was the case, for example, in *Pasolini,* where the title character asserts that he is "everyone's opponent, a heretic, an absolute scoundrel, the minority figure of all minorities." At other times, the contrast is strongest between the styles of speech of certain characters. In *The Red Scarf,* two characters are paddling a canoe through the sea: one, a peasant, speaks an earthy, vulgar language, while his intellectual companion answers in Marxist-Leninist jargon; the contrast is highly amusing.

The characters in Arrabal's *Lovesong of a Weightlifter* speak in strongly contrasting styles; the weightlifter speaks spiritually and lyrically of love, God, Providence, and his beloved Phyllis. Phyllis's language is coarse, earthy, and highly sexual. The contrast is all the more striking since it is a great hulk of a weightlifter speaking poetically, and a wisp of a girl talking like an oversexed hoodlum.

A similar sort of contrast was often emphasized by the lighting effects of many productions. Across Paris, the *chiaroscuro* of baroque painters seems to have provided the guide for the lighting plots and designs. Again, Strehler's *Illusion* provides a fine example. While Corneille's text does indicate that much of the action takes place in the evening, Strehler chose to light the entire production in a melancholy half-light, where the brightest star is the moon and not the sun, and where magic, mist, and mistaken identities can flourish. As Annie Richard comments in the program, "black illusion, white illusion. The alternation of light and shadow will mark the play's rhythm like baroque paintings where a shaft of light creates zones of different lighting."

Bob Wilson's production of Gavin Bryars's *Medea* was formed visually almost entirely by lighting effects. Using over 400 lighting instruments, focused to a centimeter, Wilson strove to light the performer, not the space occupied. Strong contrasts between light and dark dominated almost the

THEATRE DE LA BASTILLE DU 11 SEPTEMBRE AU 6 OCTOBRE 1984 A 21 H

Costume sketch for the lead character in Andromache

entire production. He himself noted the importance of lighting: "prepare the lighting for each scene: the places and the quality of light, in sum the atmosphere and meaning of the scene." Similar lighting effects were evident in *The Starving Artist, Dreams,* both Hugo plays, *The Red Scarf,* and a violent production of *Andromache.*

Bob Wilson's *Medea* held the audience largely through violent contrasts, not only in lighting but in production style. Most of the production was in a strongly hieratic, classical style, formal and controlled—in sharp conflict with the material itself, one of the most highly charged emotional tragedies in Western tradition. Most of the text is in modern Greek, with a few passages in French and occasional moments in English; this language choice increased the sense of distance the spectator felt from the chilling story being told. In the midst of the presentation, dominated as it was by classical costumes and formalized presentation, Wilson presented the dramatic climax of the story, the murder of Medea's two sons, in a totally different mode. The curtain opened to reveal a stage bare except for a long metal conference table and a number of folding chairs occupied by most of the performers. The actors, dressed in contemporary street clothes, introduced themselves by their real names, and in their native tongues. They commented casually on the murder, reading newspaper articles from the current press which described horrors similar to *Medea*'s. The effect was powerful, stressing the universality of Medea's tragedy across time and place. It was also an aesthetic shock to the audience, which responded with both applause and catcalls.

The violence usually associated with the baroque was particularly evident that season. The simple choice of texts such as *Lucrezia Borgia, Medea,* and several versions of the Orestes legend lent itself to the depiction or evocation of considerable violence, often of an unnatural kind (Orestes kills his mother; Medea murders her sons; Lucrezia poisons several people, including her son). In addition, elements of violence were injected into works where one might not expect them. At the Comédie Française, in a production of *The Misanthrope* which had a number of other baroque elements as well (the set decoration included portions of enormous baroque paintings in vast gilt frames, and the lighting was high in chiaroscuro effects), Célimène's salon had splashes of blood on the marble floor. An intriguing *Andromache* was structured, according to director Jean-Claude Buchard in a personal interview, 27 September 1984, in order to emphasize the violence of the relationships and the actions, to

Program cover showing the highly baroque stage setting for The Misanthrope

LE MISANTHROPE

Nº 131/132, 25 FRANCS

bring the horror of the conflict powerfully to the audience. The baroque red of violence dominated the set of *The Red Scarf*, and even lighthearted comedies like Corneille's *Palace Gallery* were often infused with violence, brutality, and horror.

Very few of the plays were presented in a static form. Bob Wilson's *Medea* was remarkable in that it took a baroque subject and treated it statically, undercutting easy appeals to emotion at every opportunity. Wilson's actors moved very little, and in those movements they resembled ancient Greek temple friezes or urn decorations; for the most part, they assumed tightly specified positions and held them for an extraordinary length of time. Most of the plays, however, were full of movement. *Andromache*, for example, kept all the characters on stage throughout the entire five acts, and kept them frequently in motion, even when they were not part of a scene. The commedia insertions into the staging of Marivaux and Corneille frequently pushed productions toward frantic and apparently pointless activity. The Hugo plays were both infused with a good deal more activity than called for in the text, and much of this movement was in curved, baroque sweeps across the playing area.

There is a particular aspect of set decoration which was widespread and indicative of the baroque: the use of mirrors. Mirrors are unusual in set decoration, for they are notoriously difficult to light without either throwing light directly in the eyes of the audience and blinding them, or else tilting the glass so that it shows scenes from the wings of the stage area. Despite these difficulties, they were an important part of the set decoration for *The Misanthrope*, with three jagged mirrors set in a plaster wall downstage center. They also appeared in a splendid version of Molière's *Don Juan* at the Bouffes du Nord, where a full-length mirror hung on the stage left wall; it was used from time to time by Don Juan to check his appearance, but its principal function appeared at the close of the play, when the Statue took Don Juan by the hand and flung him directly into the mirror, which shattered under the impact, killing him with the shards of glass. The mirror was obviously more than a simple device for stage tricks and underlined the falsity of appearances which were the basis for Don Juan's success, and the uncertainty of the world and its favors, since Don Juan dies by the instrument of appearances through which he has lived. In *The Disguised Prince*, a whole series of mirrors was set facing the audience. Almost the only set pieces in *I Love Corneille* were a set of several dressing-room mirrors, again directly facing the public.

But once again, it is Strehler's *Illusion* which carried the device furthest.

The Illusion's set consisted of huge boulders forming the magician's grotto; they closed in or opened up from the top and two sides, depending on the nature of the scene being presented. There was a backdrop behind a scrim, representing a castle in the moonlight. But the most striking scenic element was the reflection of actors and action thrown at the audience from various directions. The stage floor represented highly polished black marble, with a gloss so intense that all actors and gestures were reflected in it. At one point, the magician gazed into the floor as into a crystal ball. Behind the scrim was reflecting material which also reflected the onstage action. As a result, the effect of illusion was multiplied, and the characters could observe themselves in action, much like the courtiers in Versailles's Hall of Mirrors. With the lighting kept low and soft, everything seemed to occur in a haze, with the misty irreality of a dream state.

Underlying the surface production values of many of the season's plays was a metaphysical disquiet, a seeking for solid answers to troubling questions. Characteristically baroque, this search rarely produced satisfying results, and the spectator was left puzzled, disturbed, and possessed by an intellectual anguish. *The Red Scarf* raised all sorts of difficult questions about political action and the place of the individual in a revolutionary society, but its answers simply stressed the inadequacy of any responses presented. *The Life and Death of Pier Paolo Pasolini* was a profoundly antiauthoritarian play, attacking and annihilating all the usual standards of society, but it proposed no neat solution to the problems it raised. Even *La Périchole*, that joyous explosion of fun, showed that the only way to solve the social and political difficulties in which the hero and heroine found themselves was to place them in a carriage which mounted into the clouds amidst the enthusiastic cheers of the crowd. The two Kafka plays probed at the subconscious, uncovering dreadful sentiments and crimes of passion, but gave no ray of hope for improvement. And yet, these were not plays of despair; the search is obviously worthwhile, and can become, as for the father in *The Illusion*, its own justification. As noted in the program, "We recognize in this play the topsy-turvy world so often presented in the ballets and festivals of the Baroque period. Here, what is crazy is true, and what appears logical is absurd. We enter a world where paradox is a fundamental law."

The season was remarkably empty of major

classical or Romantic works. A triumphant *Bérénice* at the Comédie Francaise, a very successful *Cyrano de Bergerac* at the Mogador, a valiantly new *Andromache* at the Bastille Theater; for the rest, even when celebrating the anniversaries of Hugo, Diderot, or Corneille, the works presented were atypical and often heavily baroque. Diderot's *Actor's Paradox* was presented in a very highly charged atmosphere, with disguises, violence, and enormous volume. *D'Alembert's Dream*, while calmer in its style, stressed death and the impossibility of knowing anything certainly—an odd conclusion from the progenitor of the *Encyclopedia!*

Needless to say, many of the characteristics that can be identified as baroque are not unique to that style; violence is a commonplace in much Romantic theater, and almost a requirement in the modern. Any good play needs strong contrasts, and they are to be found in works of every age and style. The delight in illusion is a theatrical commonplace; Pirandello cannot be called baroque for having made it the center of his work. Furthermore, there are a number of important aspects of the baroque which were not particularly noticeable

in the season. The curve was rarely present; most sets were angular, although actors often swept across the stage in large, baroque, curved movements. There was not much emphasis, despite *The Illusion* and Arrabal's *Lovesong*, on ritual, magic, or mysticism. Characters were not presented as types (except in the stereotypes of the commedia del l'arte), and there was no stage equivalent of Bernini's bust of Louis XIV as the typical monarch. Baroque optimism was lacking, especially in the important area of seeking answers to profound problems. And most notably, one saw little of the baroque hero, the individual who became the Great Condé on the battlefield, or the Cid on stage. The protagonists of these plays—one hesitates to call most of them heroes—are shown in an unpleasant, often distasteful or revolting light. This is as true of older plays as of newer ones. Clindor, the long-sought son of *The Illusion*, is revealed as a deceptive and ultimately shallow young man who survives by his ability to deceive those around him. Lucrezia Borgia is hardly more admirable than Medea, and her son is weak, indecisive, and unheroic.

Despite these differences, it is not unreason-

Set left, representing Rome, of split stage for Bérénice *at the Comédie Française*

able to detect a strong baroque current in the 1984 season. What are the implications? The baroque is a period of questioning, of disquiet, but also of grandeur. In the past, such periods have led to times of certainty, of refinement, of grace. At the same time, the baroque has also preceded periods of stark, empty formalism, void of creativity. The dearth of current playwrights in Paris would make one tend to lean to the latter prediction, but the vitality of directing and acting and the quality of production values give reason to hope that the current baroque period may open into a handsome age of theatrical creativity.

1985: The Year of the Mystery
A Symposium

A clear publishing trend in 1985 was the comeback of mystery and detective fiction—as distinguished from spy fiction. The resurgence of the American hard-boiled movement has been particularly strong. It is impossible to establish sharp boundaries for the kinds of writing that qualify for inclusion in this revival. The crime or criminal novel, which does not have a detective hero, is thriving; George V. Higgins is one of its most distinguished practitioners. Publishers who recently published only the occasional mystery novel are busily launching new lines. Hammett, Chandler, and Ross Macdonald have become sanctified. Elmore Leonard and Robert B. Parker are best-sellers. Contenders like Gerald Petievich have entered the field. Critical journals, newsletters, and fanzines are proliferating. Specialist book dealers are multiplying, and rare-book prices are escalating. The success of the Mysterious Press and the *New Black Mask* testifies to the appetite of a new audience for this material—or perhaps it is the old audience—as well as to the talent pool of writers. Even the activities of the sillies who attend detective parties and mystery jaunts provide additional evidence that the genre is flourishing after at least a decade of being smothered by science fiction.

DLB Yearbook invited writers and "professional" readers to comment on the staying power of mystery-detective fiction. The observations from Britain are particularly welcome because "thrillers" (i.e., suspense stories) have enjoyed enduring respect and loyal readership there.

WHY I WRITE MYSTERIES: NIGHT AND DAY

Michael Collins (Dennis Lynds)

I decide to lie. I write mysteries to reach a larger audience. Because it is a wonderfully flexible form in which one can write about almost anything. As a way to reach the ordinary reader who would never look at my "literary" work.

But, no, I'll tell the truth.

I did it for money.

There—I write mysteries to make money.

And realize that is not the truth either.

It is what I told myself at the time. The excuse I gave myself for turning away, even briefly, from the mainstream. But it was a lie, too.

Why not historical novels? I'd always been a history buff. Why not those fat soap opera best-sellers? Horror stories? Romances? Bodice-rippers? The big espionage novels that make so much money? Steamy family sagas? Bedroom and boardroom and backroom melodramas? Westerns? Science fiction? The thick fictionalized biographies that do so well? Nonfiction?

Why not go on with mainstream novels?

So a simple question—Why do I write mysteries?—is suddenly not so simple. Not even to me. Reasons and causes are hidden.

Why mysteries? Why any genre?

Those are not at all the same question.

The answer lies in two facts specific to me: I was a writer long before I was a mystery writer; and I don't write mysteries, I write detective novels that contain mysteries.

The elder Henry James once wrote a notable passage to his sons William and Henry: "Every man who has reached even his intellectual teens begins to suspect that life is not farce; that it is not genteel comedy even; that it flowers and fructifies on the contrary out of the profoundest tragic depths of the essential dearth in which its subject's roots are plunged. The natural inheritance of everyone who is capable of spiritual life is an unsubdued forest where the wolf howls and the obscene bird of night chatters."

I began to write in the army, continued in college, published poetry and stories in the smaller literary magazines. After college I published stories in the larger literary quarterlies, and two main-stream novels. By 1960 I felt established enough

on the edges of literature to quit my editorial job and work on my fourth novel full time.

That fourth novel was unpublished. It was a bad novel.

Worse, it was not a novel I *wanted* to write. It was dead—on the page, and inside me.

It was written in a way I no longer wanted to write. It was not a novel that could deal with my obscene bird of night, the wolf that howls out of the dearth in my roots. I could not write a novel that dealt with that dark bird, the metaphysical, the night, with the vision and tools I had found up until then.

I needed a new way of writing, of seeing, of painting that obscene bird. I could grope toward that in short stories, but not yet in the novel. I could not write novels the way I had written the first four and deal with my bird of night. That was going to take time and searching. And while I searched, how was I to live?

I was almost forty years old. Young enough for a writer, but far too old to become a doctor, or

Michael Collins (Grace Moceri)

lawyer, or insurance executive, or advertising man, or whaler, or civil servant, or roustabout, or any of the traditional answers to how to live while learning to write the way you wanted to write. Much too late to marry a rich woman, and I had no wealthy uncles to murder. I could have gone back to being an editor, a journalist, but I was a novelist, and I wanted to stay a novelist.

All thinking people, artists or otherwise, have two sets of deep concerns; of questions and glimpsed insights. Call them the ethical and the metaphysical; the social and the transcendental; the mind and the soul; the day and the night. Part of a whole, yes; but separate, too.

There were other birds, other beasts, to wonder about, to understand, to question. The ethical not the metaphysical. The mind not the soul. The social not the transcendental. The day not the night. I had many ideas, questions, stories to write that dealt not with the obscene bird or the internal wolf, but with very external wolves and the vultures of broad daylight. The way man lives not so much with himself as with other men. Obviously, man is a unit. Psychology is part of day and night. But art is not life, art can be only partial, and in art there is a matter of emphasis. Man is, in the end, alone with his obscene bird, but along the way he lives with many other men and he must deal with that too.

This brought me to the detective novel.

Many writers take up the mystery novel because they love it; they are fans, afficionados. This is especially true today, and, I think, unfortunate. It leads to repetition, imitation, concentration on the externals, the form not the content. The bath counts not the baby. The frame not the picture. The genre turns into charades and parlor games, train rides and cruises and weekends that have nothing to do with writing.

I came to the mystery from the opposite direction: not as a fan, a lover of the form, but as a novelist. And not to the mystery, except in passing, but to the detective novel. The American detective novel.

But why, specifically, the detective novel?

Of all the forms of popular literature the detective story is one of the only two honest forms, true to real life, capable of being used to write serious novels. The other is science fiction. All the rest are, in varying degrees, lies—soap opera bestsellers, mammoth spy novels, melodramas, romances, puzzle mysteries, historical sagas, westerns, novelized biographies, gargantuan novelized histories, horror stories. They are not true to life as it is, was, or ever will be.

The American detective novel is. In a letter that commented on my novel *Freak*, Professor J. Chesley Taylor of Washington State University wrote, "Strangely enough, detective fiction is one of the forms best suited to making observations about the nature of man and of society."

Carroll John Daly, Raoul Whitfield, others, helped develop the American detective novel, but it was Hammett and Chandler who defined and vitalized it, gave it a reason, a purpose. They did not reject the fictional detective as seeker and thinker, but put him to work in the real world, brought the real world into the mystery novel, both factually and philosophically. There are metaphysical questions in Hammett—the Flitcraft story in *The Maltese Falcon*—but essentially what he and Chandler did was to create a form almost perfectly suited to asking the ethical, the social questions they wanted to deal with, the human actions, beliefs, dreams, and violences.

So, I began to write detective novels because they were a perfect form for what I wanted to do while continuing to search for the way to deal with the chattering of my obscene night bird.

I had stories I wanted to write about this violent society of ours, a society where in any given year there are 10,000 murders in comparison to some eight to forty in any other civilized nation. About the social, economic, psychological pressures that create such a horror. About what pushes people, sometimes quite ordinary people, over the edge into violence and crime. What kind of society are we, and what made us whatever we are?

The American detective novel gave me the best tool I could find to do this, and I used it, and, eighteen years later, I am still using it.

And over these years I found other reasons for why I use it, why I need it. Other answers.

All writers are, after all, detectives. They ask questions, seek what answers they can find in the world and in themselves. In the real world of the American detective novel there are few solutions. The case ends, the world goes on little changed, and the detective goes out to ask more questions, seek more partial answers. And like detectives, writers do not seek solutions; solutions are not the province of art. Only questions and partial answers and, perhaps, some hopes.

The detective novel reveals what has happened rather than shows what is happening. In essence it eliminates the easy suspense—the how, when, where, what, and even who of the journalist—allowing a writer to concentrate on the only really important question: *why*.

The detective novel is built around an observer, a questioner, a searcher. One who watches the events and tries to understand. He is a man whose work is the questioning of the human mind and the human heart. He is, in essence, a writer. Detective and writer are one and the same.

That, then, is it?

Almost.

Art struggles to bring order out of chaos. What began as a split in my needs as a writer seems to be coming back together. Ethical and metaphysical, night and day, mainstream and detective are merging. The social and ethical is surfacing in my short stories, and in my last detective novels I find myself grappling with that obscene bird of night, the howling wolf inside. (Not always to the delight of my agent, or publishers, or even readers, I'm afraid.)

A novel has its own merit, its own reasons. Others categorize; not authors. I have worked for eighteen years with a form of artistic expression called the American detective novel I found good for my purposes. No other explanation is really necessary.

COMMENTS FROM OTHER WRITERS

ISAAC ASIMOV

I write mysteries merely because I enjoy doing so. But then I also enjoy writing science fiction, fantasy, and nonfiction of all kinds.

I just enjoy writing, that's all, and I have published 339 books in consequence—so far.

MICHAEL AVALLONE

I have been a mystery fan ever since I wondered why the game of baseball was played at a place called the Polo Grounds, why James Butler Hickok was called Wild Bill, and just why in God's name blondes were supposed to have more fun than brunettes. I rather think the long-standing love affair between readers and that peculiar genre of fiction called the mystery story is something like that. And with splendid fellows like Sherlock Holmes, C. Auguste Dupin, Ellery Queen, and their disparate and just as distinguished descen-

dants such as the Private Eyes, the Official Police, and the Gifted Amateurs à la Trent and Nick Charles following up on the game called Whodunit the reading public responded for basically the same reasons. A problem is posed; it's hairy, scary, and clever; and by book's end, the killer and the solution have been found. Also, we are transported out of our daily humdrum lives to less dull environs where wonderment, excitement, thrills, and just plain fun abound like the animals on a game preserve. What more is there to say? Mysteries will always be fun and nobody is ever going to stop reading them come hell or atom bomb. And that is end game for me and my colleagues who still practice the grand sport of writing them.

Stanley Ellin

STANLEY ELLIN

I write mysteries because criminality is not only a subject of fascination to a host of readers but to myself, and because for at least a generation now there are virtually no restrictions imposed by the genre on the writer in the choice of theme and treatment.

WILLIAM CAMPBELL GAULT

When I first started writing for the pulps back in the 1930s, sports were my genre. But the sports magazines would go in and out of business, so I added mysteries. When the entire pulp field began to decline early in 1951 or 1952, science fiction seemed to be the best-paying market and I switched to that.

When it was no longer possible to make a living on short stories in that period, I turned to books. In 1952 I wrote a mystery novel titled *Don't Cry For Me*. It won the first-novel Edgar from Mystery Writers of America. That same year I wrote a racing sports juvenile book called *Thunder Road*. *Don't Cry For Me* went into paperback reprint and foreign sales; the original hardcover edition was out of print in two years. *Thunder Road* stayed in print until 1978 and there were two separate paperback reprints of that. I continued turning out novels in both genres until 1962. But the hard law of economics convinced me then that the juvenile field was the best choice if I intended to avoid welfare.

After thirty-three consecutive juvenile sports books put out by Dutton, they decided my sales were dwindling, and they dumped me. I then sold two of my next five juveniles, both to Dodd, Mead. Two out of five is a good batting average in baseball, a bad average in writing. I went back to mysteries, using a title *The Bad Samaritan* that I had offered Ross Macdonald but he didn't use.

Samaritan sold to Raven House, as did my next three. They then decided, after publishing two of my novels, to drop the mystery line. So I kept the advances and sold the other two to Walker. Which gives me four mysteries in print since my return to the field and my fifth, *The Chicano War*, has just been purchased by Walker and will come out in the spring of 1986.

And that is my sad story; the one mainstream novel I attempted has never seen print and doesn't deserve to. But at seventy-five, with a new book coming out, it is possible that fate or fortune or God has treated me better than I deserve.

This I will admit: young adult (what an ugly phrase) sports paid me at least ten times as much as my mysteries, but mysteries are more fun. And now, with Social Security, I can have more fun. I will never quit while I'm vertical.

MICHAEL GILBERT

Any author who is honest, if asked why he writes, will say "for money." This was certainly so in my case when I started in the Hungry '30s—as an unpaid articles clerk in a law office.

If the question, more particularly, is why I chose to write crime novels, the answers are more complex.

I did take some expert advice from a public librarian in North London. He said that he could not tell me what sort of books most people bought—but he knew well what they read: books about love, crime, and cowboys. Choices one and three being outside my scope, I plumped for number two.

Perhaps more seriously I think that the first book(s) anyone writes reflect the reading he enjoys most. In the '30s it was the golden age of the whodunit. Sayers, Christie, Marsh, Allingham. I had read and enjoyed them all. And I thought, if they, being women, can pull it off, so can I, dammit.

JOSEPH HANSEN

The mystery novel is simply a means of retelling the most ancient of myths—that of the triumph of light over darkness, of order over chaos. Since God acted the detective in the Cain and Abel story—"Thy brother's blood cries to me from the ground"—the murder mystery has gripped man's imagination and held him in thrall. We are shocked and moved by murder because death is the ultimate mystery of life. And we are caught by the confusion surrounding killer and victim because we have a deeply human need for the scrambled fragments of lies and truth to be sorted out and pieced together into a coherent whole.

So when we question whether the mystery novel has a future, we really need only think for a moment about how lengthy has been its past to know the answer. In the creation myth, "the world was without form and void." In the mystery novel nothing makes much sense at first, either; nothing has a recognizable shape. But by the time the writer finishes the story and we sigh and close the book, sun and moon are giving their reassuring light once more, and the blue planet Earth is rolling again in its accustomed orbit.

I set out long ago to write truthfully about life as I saw it, and after a time I realized that one sure way to grip and hold a reader's attention was by telling him again the old, old story—and I began to write mystery novels. A good many writers of powerful talent and depth of understanding had chosen the mystery form before me to help broaden and deepen my knowledge of the world around me and my place in it, and to enlarge my compassion toward my fellowmen.

I hoped, and still hope, to do as well as they.

H. R. F. KEATING

Corkscrewing right down, I find I write mysteries for the same reason that I write, occasionally, a straight novel: because some aspect of life has bugged me and I feel, presumptuously maybe, that I can say something true about it through that test-bench of truths, fiction. But why mysteries? I think, just because it happened that way. Long ago I used to believe I had nothing to say although I had an urge to write. I harbored the misconception, too,

H. R. F. Keating (©Jerry Bauer)

that the mystery "said nothing," so I began with one. When eventually I got published I found, of course, that the mystery could say almost as much as the straight novel, and perhaps get what it had to say into more heads through being entertainment all the way. Then, after a while again, Inspector Ghote entered my world, a window to open whenever I want on almost any scene I want, hopefully never to depart again.

Joseph Hansen (Robert Munman)

PETER LOVESEY

Why do I write mysteries? The urge runs deep. As a boy, I wanted to be a conjurer, an actor, or a long-distance runner. I did a little of each without spectacular success. As a mystery writer, I'm indulging those early impulses. To write a satisfying mystery, you need something that passes for magic; a sharp eye for character; and stamina.

The traditional English mystery was snuffed out and laid to rest in 1944 by Raymond Chandler in *The Simple Art of Murder*. He categorized the English as "the best dull writers in the world." I think we're less dull now, more likely to surprise, innovate, and entertain.

GERALD PETIEVICH

I favor the mystery genre because of the mythical quality inherent in the form. Mysteries are larger than life. The Detective begins his search to avenge the most heinous of crimes, the taking of a human life. Empowered and protected by the magic of his badge and gun, he is able to move through all the strata of society in his quest. And the Detective always solves the murder by means of supernatural powers: namely his mystical, learned ability to cull truth from that mixture of fact and prevarication, of good and evil, that is life.

GEORGE SIMS

I find it difficult to explain why I write mysteries as my reasons stem from my subconscious. Graham Greene said that authors do not choose their books, the books choose them. This is certainly true of me. An idea comes into my head unprompted by me and gradually, usually over quite a long period, this develops into a rough plan for a book without any conscious effort on my part. So much of my writing is done before I even sit down at the typewriter. For this reason I am not a professional writer as I cannot write to order and am immune to suggestions as to how I could become a more popular writer.

I am fascinated by mysteries in life—did Starr Faithfull kill herself?—and the difficulties inherent in untangling any that stem back into the past. I take the existentialist, rather bleak view of the universe that it is a mystery which cannot be understood by man. Henry James made the Prince say

Peter Lovesey (Philip Lovesey)

in *The Golden Bowl* that "everything is terrible in the heart of man." I believe that we have no certainties of any kind and, as Conrad said, what we wear are the masks of illusion. My subconscious prompts me to write about those masks and the terror.

JOHN WAINWRIGHT

Mysteries, of course, have been with us since men used cave drawings in an attempt to influence hunting prowess. Since the Gordian Knot, through the witch-hunting era, and up to the present day. Science fiction writing is merely one branch of mystery writing; an attempt to solve the greatest mystery of all . . . what of the future?

The crime novel is merely one aspect of mystery writing.

As a personal opinion, I think the whodunit has just about run its course. There is a limit to the number of hidden clues and red herrings available, and the great exponents—Agatha Christie, Ellery Queen, Rex Stout, Dorothy L. Sayers, etc.—pushed the so-called "English Detective Story" to its absolute limit.

Chandler and Hammett added a new dimension and, albeit not knowingly, changed the whodunit into the whydunit. In the United Kingdom a disillusioned policeman called Maurice Proctor wrote what was perhaps the first "police procedural" in an attack of sour grapes at an unwanted transfer; no doubt he was more surprised than anybody when it turned him from a copper into a successful novelist. In the United States Evan Hunter, writing as Ed McBain, culled the experiences of his pals in the New York Police Department and set a new pattern with his 87th Precinct stories.

For myself, I read a fistful of badly written detective stories, figured I could do better . . . and did. And if that sounds particularly arrogant, it isn't meant to be. They really *were* abominable detective stories, published at a time when pure rubbish was being accepted for publication.

Of necessity (but for a different reason) I followed in the footsteps of Maurice Proctor. Twenty years in police uniform had shown me just about

Stuart Woods (Charles M. Rafshoon)

everything. All I had to do was "remember," change it around a little, and learn the knack of storytelling.

A quarter of a century on, I am now the proud father of about eighty crime novels. Most of them police procedurals, all of them (to some degree) whydunits. All the footprints in the flower beds have been found. All the stray pieces of cotton have been plucked from who-would-have-believed-it culprits. There is no new way of committing murder in a locked room.

The whydunit seems to have come of age. Rightly so, because its scope is wider and its fascination is greater. It also makes for better writing, with three-dimensional characters.

This, of course, is both odd and illogical. The motive (the "why?") is of little importance in English, and American, criminal law. Proof of identity, plus means and opportunity, is all that is necessary. The motive merely forms a backup to the evidence. If this was not so, the "motiveless" crime would remain undetected.

But, to the writer, the motive equates with the mind, and the working of the mind is the final mystery. Unlike the disguise or the alibi, it is a mystery with infinite answers and a never-ending series of permutations.

Which, in turn, brings me to my conclusion, that the mystery story will continue to dominate popular literature. As the reader becomes more sophisticated, the twists and turns of the criminal mind will become more fascinating. The form will change. The manner of telling will change. Eventually, Joseph Wambaugh will become as dated and as old-fashioned as Edgar Allan Poe. But mystery writing, in some form or another, will continue.

STUART WOODS

I didn't know I wrote mysteries until *Chiefs* won the Edgar Allan Poe award from the Mystery Writers of America, but I was glad they found it to be mysterious. Every novel must harbor some mystery of plot or character or mood, else why should anyone wish to read it? The end of every good story is a mystery, and while along the way the reader may be moved to laughter or tears, be taught something, or come to admire the author's philosophy or way with words, it is mystery that will transport through a book.

WHY I READ MYSTERIES

RAY B. BROWNE

People read mysteries for various reasons. One I think is of the utmost importance, and speaks to the near-necessity of our having some kind of fiction of violence and death around us at all times—Western, detective, horror, or whatever.

There seems to be an anthropological, primitive necessity of our vicariously witnessing death ritualistically. It is all the better if we can do this vicariously and in art rather than in person. Vicariously and in art the ritual of death becomes both a memorial to death and a celebration of triumph over death that is to come in our own cases. We feel that in witnessing the death of others, we have escaped death at least for the time being. Folklore is rife with testimonials of people who assume that death has a quota, a certain number of needed candidates every period (day-week-month), and once that quota is filled, then the living need not worry until the next "order" is made. Thus mystery fiction is a comforter to the living.

Another important reason that mystery fiction is read widely, or at least the reason I read it, is for its humanities, its humanitarianism. In the midst of death some detective fiction holds out a warm comforting human hand and heart which says that life triumphs over death through love, through comradeship. I read detective fiction in order to see how much of this feeling exists in literature and how it is developed.

IRVIN FAUST

I. The good ones are extremely well written and well researched. Simenon, Chandler, Stout, Steve Dobyns (a poet) are the equal of or superior to most "serious" writers. They know their locales and the history of people and places and have the knack of transmitting that knowledge to the reader.

II. Quality mysteries impart a sense of continuity and tradition that is most important in this crazy world. Perhaps the essential ingredient in this context is that they have a beginning, a middle, and an end.

III. The best central characters are old, de-

pendable *friends:* Maigret, Marlowe, Wolfe, et al. . . . You *care* about good friends.

IV. Supporting characters are splendidly drawn by the pros. They are also *necessary.* Archie, Gutman, Dobyns's Saratoga crowd, etc. make the wheels turn.

V. I am tired of the knock that mysteries are all "formula." Hemingway and Faulkner were also "formula." When formula bombs, it bombs; when it works, it works. The gentlemen mentioned bombed and worked. Simenon, Chandler, Hammett, and some others have a terrific batting average. Most mystery writers—as with a number of "serious" writers—have written one or two good books. That's an achievement for *anyone.*

DAVID GEHERIN

Why do I read mysteries? Mainly because of the hero, I think. My favorite type of mystery is the private-eye tale, probably because I find the character of the tough-yet-vulnerable detective, who battles against a hostile world armed with little more than a personal code of honor, a steely sense of justice, and a better-than-average supply of wit, immensely appealing. I also enjoy the vivid atmosphere, the pungent portrayal of specific place and time, that is a standard feature of these novels, plus their usual array of colorful secondary characters. Also, I'm a sucker for the clever wisecracks and colorful metaphors that are characteristic of the genre. Although most private-eye novels are simply variations on a common type, in the hands of skillful writers I find those variations endlessly enjoyable.

JOAN KAHN

After years of reading mystery (which I prefer to call suspense) novels, I think the good writers are as good as anyone else writing—excepting the genius here or there—and the average suspense novel reader is more intelligent than the average nonsuspense novel reader.

It's a *good* field to be working in—even after forty years.

OTTO PENZLER

At the simplest, most elemental, and yet most significant level, I read mysteries because I like good stories with interesting people who say interesting things in an interesting way. I liked fairy tales as a kid, and I like adult fairy tales, i.e., mysteries, today.

At a secondary level, one which I never suspected until many years and perhaps thousands of volumes had passed, I guess I like mysteries for political and social and philosophical reasons. The quintessential mystery story is a basic struggle between Good and Evil, and Good is invariably triumphant over Evil in a mystery story. That is a comfort in a world in which reality intrudes mightily and it seems less and less certain that the forces of Evil will be defeated. That's not the way it ought to be: truth and justice should always rule, and the last bastion of that concept seems to be the mystery. I fear for the mystery, sometimes, as the lines seem to be cracking even there. It is unusual for the cops to be virtuous nowadays, and our CIA guys are portrayed as even more venal than their KGB guys, or at best indistinguishable. Perhaps it is the lack of a moral viewpoint by so many of today's authors, even the most talented ones, that has driven so many readers back to the work of an earlier time. Nonetheless, as long as the great books stay in print, as long as Sherlock Holmes and The Shadow and the thousands of great crime fighters continue to fight on our side, I will continue to read and respect mystery fiction.

WILLIAM TARG

For as long as I can remember, I've been hooked by storytellers. From Scheherazade to Sherlock Holmes, the writer with something up his sleeve and a juicy puzzle to be solved in the end has been my meat. In my early teens I discovered the special magic of crime fiction. I think I started by discovering the Nancy Drew books. A great leap took place, then, for I encountered Edgar Allan Poe, our one authentic literary genius. I devoured his marvelous detective stories—the first in our literature—and reread them many times over the years.

Dashiell Hammett, Rex Stout, Ellery Queen, Raymond Chandler, Erle Stanley Gardner, Ross Macdonald, Agatha Christie, Simenon, and countless other masters of the genre attracted me, and for a time I collected their first editions. I developed a passion and possessive feeling for their books.

For a period, as reprint editor of World Publishing Company, I was obliged to seek out and publish about a dozen detective novels each month. This task enabled me to read at least a book a day for several years. Being paid for reading mysteries! Who could ask for more?

In recent years there seemed to me a decline in the publishing of "police novels." I don't know why. The homogenized romantic novel may have taken its place; novels of sex and violence, non-novels and stories that aimed at disclosure of sexual pathology, novels in which authors were preoccupied with their own neuroses—these seemed to have replaced the crime novel for a while. While Conan Doyle and Agatha Christie continued to delight new readers, fewer new books were being published. And those that did manage to see publication offered modest returns to their authors. Pulp romances, which are still inundating the shelves in bookshops, seemed to have taken over the popular fiction market.

Today, for reasons I can't discern, a renaissance is occurring; detective stories are being rediscovered and many publishers are again seeking out and publishing these books. The paperback publishers are reissuing the old favorites—and they are being avidly bought again.

Perhaps the greatest of all crime novels is Dostoyevski's *Crime and Punishment*. No writer, to my knowledge, has written anything to equal that book. I reread it recently and it is still an astonishing story. *Story* is the operative word. Most novels today fail to provide character in depth and the cat-and-mouse interaction—the suspense and story values, the essentials, that attract and entertain the reader. A good mystery (and the skill with which the author spins out its resolution) is foolproof fare for the hungry story addict, young and old. Where the writer is able to involve the reader from page one—as is true in good crime novels—he will find an audience. Perhaps the TV viewer is again searching for pure story rather than car crashes and inordinate gun play. Perhaps not; I don't know. But there is something irresistible and wondrous in a perfectly constructed and literate crime story: it will always prevail.

As a professional book editor for some forty-five years, I've had some rewarding experiences with crime fiction. I was recently asked if I ever had the good luck to publish a *great* crime novel—a novel that would endure as a classic. While the book that came to mind was not a "police novel," it is, I think, the outstanding novel of crime of our century, Mario Puzo's *The Godfather*. I derived much pleasure in editing and publishing this novel at Putnam's in 1969. I think it has outsold all other

American crime novels, which gives me a special satisfaction. Like Dostoyevski's *Crime and Punishment*, Puzo's novel, with its great narrative power, has not been equaled in its genre.

To the very young newcomer to mystery fiction, I would recommend Poe's *Murders in the Rue Morgue*, which embodies the essence of the word *ratiocination*.

ROBIN WINKS

I read mystery and detective fiction for the same reason I read history: because the material is, as history must be, interesting, significant, and true. Most readers would agree that it is interesting—that is, mystery and detective literature entertains, beguiles, puzzles. I find it significant, for it reveals much about popular culture, about what a society fears, about how technology, the law, social rebellion, poverty, and any number of significant historical subjects work. The real question then is, can such literature also be true? I think so, for the best of it is true to life. The worst is beneath contempt, but then so is the worst material that passes for history. To these three high-minded reasons for reading such fiction I add a somewhat less pompous fourth: often detective, spy, thriller, mystery fiction (for I find it pointless to separate these types, as they are part of a continuum about guilt, responsibility, blame) provides vicarious travel to well-used locales. I admire a writer who integrates crime and motivation with a sense of place, of social setting, and I deplore those writers—usually of fat best-sellers—who under the pretense of being an artist either alter the landscape, the geography, the map of London, Berlin, or Lubbock to suit the needs of their plot, or who simply do not bother with research (or limit their research to looking street names up in an atlas). Crimes take place in a particular locale, and I am interested to see how that locale is realized by the author.

In short, I read this fiction because it is fun.

The Ritz Paris Hemingway Award

James Nagel
Northeastern University

Ernest Hemingway first became familiar with the Ritz Hotel in Paris during the early 1920s when he and a coterie of aspiring writers living on the Left Bank would journey across the river to the Place Vendôme to drink at the American Bar on the first floor of the hotel. He soon became a regular, familiar with the bartender, Georges, whom he regarded as a friend. Two decades later, when German forces were leaving Paris, Hemingway was part of a group that liberated the Ritz Hotel, which had been used as German headquarters in Paris. This symbolic gesture was much appreciated by Charles Ritz, son of the founder, Cesar, and he and Hemingway eventually became friends, fishing and dining together on a regular basis. Hemingway stayed in Room 31 at the Ritz throughout the duration of the war.

In commemoration of this association the hotel initiated the Ritz Paris Hemingway Award, an annual prize of $50,000 for the best novel published in English coupled with awards of $100,000 to organizations dealing with the preservation of the environment, education, and disadvantaged children.

The impetus for this award grew out of conversations involving Mohamed Al-Fayed, the owner of the Ritz; His Majesty Hassanal Bolkiah, the Sultan of Brunei Darussalam; and the American journalist Pierre Salinger, former press secretary to President John F. Kennedy. In due course Al-Fayed agreed to host the Award ceremony at the Ritz; the Sultan became the official patron for the first year of the award; and Salinger was appointed spokesman for the prize and president of the Jury. In the following months the rules and procedures for the prize were developed along with committees to participate in the selection process.

The Board of Directors for the prize consists

Award Jury President Pierre Salinger, left, introducing winner Mario Vargas Llosa, right (photo by Gwen L. Nagel)

of Al-Fayed, Jack Hemingway, Patrick Hemingway, and Robert Woodrum, Executive Director of the award. A list was constructed that included several hundred people internationally involved in the modern novel; this group served as an initial nominating committee for the prize-winning work. These nominations were then given to a Selection Committee consisting of James Nagel (Northeastern University), as Chairman, Linda Wagner (Michigan State University), Yoshinobu Hakutani (Kent State University), Melvin J. Friedman (University of Wisconsin-Milwaukee), and Henry Louis Gates, Jr. (Yale University). A short list of nominated novels was then passed on to the Jury for final action.

In 1985 the Jury was comprised of Lucien Bodard (who was awarded the Prix Goncourt for his *Anne-Marie* in 1981), Michael Burke (former president of CBS), James Dickey (a leading poet who has also published a novel, *Deliverance*), Jean d'Ormesson (Chairman of the International Council for Philosophy and Human Sciences at UNESCO), Lady Antonia Fraser (author of books on British history), Philippe Labro (a writer for *Paris Match* and the author of the best-selling novel *Des bateaux dans la nuit*), Pierre Salinger, William Styron (awarded the Pulitzer Prize for *The Confessions of Nat Turner*), Peter Viertel (a novelist whose latest book is *American Skin*), and William Walton (a long-time friend of Hemingway and the author of *The Evidence of Washington, D.C.*).

The initial announcement of the inception of the award took place at the Ritz Hotel on 11 January 1985. Salinger explained the background of the prize to journalists from virtually every major newspaper in the world. Jack Hemingway then discussed the relationship of his father with the Ritz and expressed the support of the Hemingway family for this new literary prize. The High Commissioner for Brunei Darussalam, Pengiran Jaya, read a statement from His Majesty Hassanal Bolkiah regarding the award. The Sultan expressed his belief that great fiction captures the truth about humanity and that Ernest Hemingway was able to portray reality in simple language that continues to be admired throughout the world. He said fur-

THE RITZ PARIS HEMINGWAY AWARD

STATEMENT BY HIS MAJESTY SIR MUDA HASSANAL BOLKIAH
THE SULTAN OF BRUNEI DARUSSALAM ON THE OCCASION OF
THE INAUGURATION OF THE RITZ PARIS HEMINGWAY AWARD.

A wise man once said, "If you would understand your own age, read the works of fiction produced in it. People in disguise speak freely."

It is because we agree with that observation that we have established the Ritz Paris Hemingway Award: we believe that great fiction speaks the real truth about humanity -- and we want to encourage the telling of that truth.

Great fiction helps us understand ourselves. And great fiction, moreover, has the power to break down barriers of language, nationality, politics and culture -- and speaking to the feelings that we humans all share.

An art that works so powerfully to help us understand ourselves and others deserves to be encouraged. And so we have created this award: to salute, to celebrate and to honor those artists who produce great fiction.

We choose to do this in the name of Ernest Hemingway, one of our century's greatest authors and personalities because he exemplifies many of the qualities that we seek to honor.

He was, first of all, truly an international figure. He was an American but his career and life spanned the entire globe.

Second, he was a man who lived to the hilt -- whose life, like his fiction, was a work of courage and imagination.

Third, Hemingway managed to write about subtle and complicated events in a style of remarkable simplicity and directness: a style which has influenced writers of all languages.

By honoring his name and achievements, we hope to inspire other writers to stretch themselves and their talents as Hemingway did his: to address not a narrow audience, but all of humanity.

It is also most fitting that this award be associated with the Hotel Ritz, the world's finest hotel. The Ritz, and its staff, were both home and family for Hemingway. The Ritz, like Hemingway, is the best. It's name stands for quality and excellence around the world. Like Ernest Hemingway, the Ritz Paris sets the standard for all others to follow.

Brunei Darussalam has, we believe, much to contribute to the world. We have been blessed with rich deposits of oil and natural gas: resources which create one kind of wealth. But we are fully aware that the ultimate resource is the human intellect -- and the ultimate forms of wealth are human knowledge and understanding.

TELEPHONE 212-765-4710 · TELEX 6711286 RITZNY · 75 ROCKEFELLER PLAZA SUITE 1809, NY, NY 10019

Inaugural statement for the Ritz Paris Hemingway Award

I was very happy to act as a member of the jury for the Paris Ritz Hemingway Award. The selection of Mario Vargas Llosa seemed to me particularly appropriate as his high reputation in South America—fully justified in my opinion—has not spread as yet to Europe. I believe this award may bring his work to the attention of people who will appreciate his unique mixture of narrative and imagination.

Statement from Lady Antonia Fraser

The Ritz Paris Hemingway Award is the most prestigious prize for a novel in the world today. The members of the jury were particularly pleased to give the first award to Mario Vargas Llosa for his book *The War of the End of the World*. It is a powerful novel, a fresco of life in Brazil at the end of the last century. The characters are real and dramatic. We hope that in the future the winners of the Ritz Paris Hemingway Award will equal the high standard of our first winner.

Statement from Pierre Salinger

ther that the people of his country "are fully aware that the ultimate resource is the human intellect—and the ultimate forms of wealth are human knowledge and understanding." He concluded that the purpose of this annual award is to celebrate the association of Hemingway with the Ritz Hotel and to promote literary excellence in the novel throughout the world.

The next major development in the 1985 prize was the announcement of three finalists for the award for the novel. The Selection Committee met in Boston on 9 February and chose three novels from those nominated, and the names of those books were released to the press on 15 February. The three finalists were *The Unbearable Lightness of Being*, by the Czechoslovakian novelist and playwright Milan Kundera, now a French citizen; *The War of the End of the World*, by Peruvian writer Mario

Vargas Llosa; and *Wild Berries*, by Yevgeny Yevtushenko, one of Russia's foremost writers.

The final development in the first year of the award was a two-day event in Paris. On 28 March the Jury met at the Ritz to select the winner of the award for the novel. In an extended session they chose Vargas Llosa's *The War of the End of the World* to receive the $50,000 prize. The announcement of this award was made the following morning at a press conference at the Ritz, at which time Jack and Patrick Hemingway also released the list of winners of the organization prizes: $25,000 to the Franco-American Foundation in Paris to establish a Tocqueville Scholarship to be given to a French citizen to study American literature in the United States; $25,000 to The National Bureau of Handicapped Students in London to provide financial support for severely handicapped students; $15,000 to Rheedlen in New York City to provide scholarships and equipment to aid disadvantaged students; $10,000 to Gallaudet College in Wash-

Dust jacket for Mario Vargas Llosa's award-winning novel

ington for scholarships for deaf students pursuing a career in writing or communications; and $25,000 to establish a program to allow disadvantaged children to participate in conservation programs at The Nature Conservancy in Idaho. These awards were chosen by the Board of Directors.

The first year of the annual Ritz Paris Hemingway Award was concluded that evening with a dinner at the hotel attended by over two hundred guests, including Madame Claude Pompidou, U.S. Ambassador Evan Galbraith, and Baroness Guy de Rothchild. Representing the Hemingway family were Mr. and Mrs. Patrick Hemingway, Mr. and Mrs. Jack Hemingway, and Hemingway's granddaughters Margaux, Mariel, and Muffet. Actress Catherine Deneuve presented a golden quill to Vargas Llosa to commemorate the event. He responded with remarks about his admiration for Hemingway, whom he had seen at a bullfight in Madrid, and discussed the courage and loneliness of the art of writing fiction. "You are totally cut off from the rest of the world," he said, "submerged in your obsessions and memories. When the book is finished, you don't know what its life will be." It

was later revealed that Vargas Llosa donated his $50,000 prize to an orphanage in his native Peru.

MARIO VARGAS LLOSA'S ACCEPTANCE SPEECH

Thank you very much. I am extremely grateful to the members of the jury for having granted me the Ritz Paris Hemingway Award. It is a great honor for me. I am also extremely grateful to all those who, in one way or another, helped me to become a writer. Writing, as all writers know, is a solitary occupation. It is often difficult and anxiety-provoking. You are working by yourself, surrounded only by your obsessions, and you don't know what the outcome is going to be after so many months or years of work. Then, once the book is finished, you don't know what is to become of it once it begins to take on a life of its own, so to speak. Therefore, when a writer like me receives the recognition of the readers he is trying to reach through his books, he feels it is recompense for his efforts—and what a special recompense it is. I feel very grateful. Thank you.

Hemingway: Twenty-Five Years Later

Nearly a quarter of a century after they interrupted the baseball games to announce Ernest Hemingway's death he seems more alive than on that July day. In 1985 two major Hemingway biographies were published by Jeffrey Meyers and Peter Griffin; a volume of his *Toronto Star* journalism appeared; critical studies were produced as though by binary fission; and publication of a buried novel, *The Garden of Eden*, is scheduled for 1986. No other American writer has generated the interest—cutting across classes of readership—that Hemingway's words and legend continue to command.

In anticipation of the twenty-fifth anniversary of Hemingway's corporeal death, the *DLB Yearbook* invited assessments of his stature from writers and critics. Their responses demonstrate that he still has the power to generate argument.

CARLOS BAKER

He lives in his work, which is what he wanted to do most of all.

JOHN BARKHAM

A quarter-century after his death Ernest Hemingway has not only survived normal posthumous neglect but continues to speak to a later generation as the most stylistically distinctive American novelist of his time.

BRIGID BROPHY

A culture that should have learnt better from Ambrose Bierce, Henry James, Scott Fitzgerald and Dashiell Hammett let itself be conned by Ernest Hemingway.

He took up slushy romances and he re-wrote their content in baby syntax like this and he pretended that tormenting and killing animals who are no threat to you was a brave and somehow a mystical thing to do and he perhaps supposed that pretending was the same as imagination and he also pretended that it was laudable to read with your finger running along beneath the line and after a while that pretense became true of him and he misread the first three letters of his own surname and he thought that they said "he-man."

His chum Gertrude Stein was three times the writer as well as twice the man.

MALCOLM COWLEY

Hemingway holds a secure place in American literature in spite of the many attacks on his reputation. The attacks were justified in large by his many faults of character, but these weren't faults in his writing. The writing will survive.

I wrote twenty years ago, "American literature is vastly richer now than when Hemingway started writing, but it is not yet so rich that it can afford to disown and devalue one of its lasting treasures." I haven't changed my mind.

PETER GRIFFIN

Ernest Hemingway did not invent a style; he reminded us of one as old as the Greeks and the Gospels. It is not a simple style, but the style of simplicity where experience and expression are bound in the words. In *Green Hills of Africa* he said he aimed for a prose "With nothing that will go bad afterwards." Few writers of this century will keep as well as Hemingway.

JOHN D. MACDONALD

Any ink-stained wretch can write imitation Hemingway for laughs or plaudits. Those a trifle more skilled can imitate Faulkner. But think for a moment of the enormous problem of doing imitation Hemingway had the man never lived. One would have to invent a style, refine it, labor at it for years. And even then it might be impossible to give it the full emotional load Hemingway achieved. Forget his moments of silliness. In simple dialogue he could say more about the human condition in one page than most of us can manage in a book. He changed the way the novel is written, the way the words go together. He did it with hard work, rewriting, revising, cutting, purifying, polishing. It will live because it is good and true.

NORMAN MAILER

I would guess that with the possible exception of Mark Twain, no American author, not Faulkner nor Fitzgerald, not Melville nor Emerson, Thoreau or Whitman, has had a greater influence on other writers than Ernest Hemingway.

JEFFREY MEYERS

Hemingway described with unusual knowledge and authority physical pleasure, the natural world, violent experience and sudden death. He portrayed the heroic possibilities and tragic consequences of war, the psychic dislocation in battle and the stoicism of survival. He created unsurpassed images of Italy, France, Spain and Africa. As a man, he had intense idealism, curiosity, energy, strength and courage. He attractively combined hedonism and hard work, was a great teacher of ritual and technique, carried an aura of glamour and power. As an artist, he wrote as naturally as a hawk flies and as clearly as a lake reflects.

GEORGE MONTEIRO

As if his books were not enough to keep alive the most famous literary name in America, his very lineaments, in the faces of actress and model granddaughters, continue to appear on the world's movie and television screens. Their father, his first son, has made public-service appearances on television. Two of his sisters, his one brother and his youngest son have written memoirs. His widow has published a Hemingway-centered autobiography. And his first wife, entirely on the basis of having been married to him, has been the subject of a biography. No other American literary life has ever been as well known as that of Ernest Hemingway.

John O'Hara once proclaimed that Hemingway was the most important writer in the English language since 1616, the year Shakespeare died. The hostile reaction to O'Hara's seemingly rash statement caused him to explain just what he meant. Ten years later, in a 1960 letter, he elaborated:

> The various circumstances that have made him the most important are not all of a purely literary nature. Some are anything but. We start with a first-rate, original, conscientious artist, who caught on because of his excellence. The literary and then the general public very quickly realized that a great artist was functioning in our midst. Publicity grew and grew, and Hemingway helped it to grow, not always deliberately but sometimes deliber-

ately. He had an unusual, almost comical name; he was a big, strong, highly personable man. He associated himself, through his work, with big things: Africa, Italy, Spain, war, hunting, fishing, bullfighting, The Novel, Style, death, violence, castration, and a teasing remoteness from his homeland and from the lit'ry life. All these things make you think of Hemingway, and each and all of them add to his importance, that carries over from one writing job to another. I have a theory that there has not been a single issue of the Sunday Times book section in the past twenty years that has failed to mention Hemingway; his name is a synonym for writer with millions of people who have never read any work of fiction. (*Selected Letters of John O'Hara*, ed. Matthew J. Bruccoli [New York: Random House, 1978], p. 348)

John Ciardi once said that in the Great War soldiers did not die the way Hemingway later said they did, but that a generation later, in World War II, they did, having learned their morality and their soldierly ethics from his books. Yet Hemingway had said that the writer's great task was to tell his readers "how it was." And for more than a generation he was credited with doing just that, honestly and reliably. At first Ciardi's observation and Hemingway's writer's ethic may seem to be incompatible. They are not. It is intriguing, and perhaps not irrelevant, that in the late 1970s a majority of the Americans polled considered the most honest and trustworthy person in the country to be an anchorman on the CBS Television Network who ended his every evening newscast solemnly with a sentence beginning: "And that's the way it is."

GERALD PETIEVICH

Hemingway is a guiding light for writers because of the depth of his work. His themes—love, war, loss—are life itself. He never allowed his words, like the white cane writing that is so evident these days, to tap lightly across the issues of life. Rather than simply observing his time, he revealed truth, glimpses of what human beings do as they sail their sad little boats across life's pond.

Rather than dealing with the topical, Hemingway dealt with trackers and skinners, bullfighters and boxers, fishermen and soldiers. I think he believed that the simple endurance required to catch a big fish or win a championship fight is as close as any of us will ever get to verity. This is not a bad idea for writers to ponder.

HAROLD J. SALEMSON

The only change in my estimation of the work of Ernest Hemingway after this quarter of a century is an increased admiration for the profound effect it apparently continues to have upon new young writers. The impact of his barebones style has gone deeper and lasted longer than I imagined fifty-five years ago that it would.

Beyond that, he remains unexcelled for the manner in which *The Sun Also Rises* captured the essence and spirit of an epoch. He towers above all but one or two of his contemporaries in *A Farewell to Arms* and a number of the early short stories. He is still the master of his period in *For Whom the Bell Tolls*. But by the time this last work appeared, the predictable problem had set in.

As in the case of so many other serious American writers, with celebrity and adulation came the onset of his persona taking over in place of his talent. Where it is customary to refer to movie stars "beginning to believe their own publicity," it is less often recognized how our successful writers can be overwhelmed by their public images. To this, I attribute the fact that the balance of his output was all downhill. There were still sparks in the earlier *To Have and Have Not*, but they had been totally snuffed out by the time of the barely readable *Across the River and Through the Trees* and the slick-magazine hackwork of *The Old Man and the Sea*.

However, having created a new literary style and written two or three great novels and half a dozen of the outstanding short stories of his time is an accomplishment I feel means that his stature as of now has not diminished at all.

ROBERT O. STEPHENS

People are still discovering the power of Hemingway's writing. Each new generation of readers—students, critics, and general audience alike—finds the voices and visions of Jake Barnes and Frederic Henry, Harry of Kilimanjaro, and Robert Wilson fresh, compelling, and authoritative. Like few other figures of modern literature, they clarify the terms of our own experience and make Hemingway's writing the prism through which we see life in the twentieth century.

ARTHUR WALDHORN

Twenty years ago, Malcolm Cowley imaged Hemingway as a dead lion and warned that critical jackals and hyenas were about to violate his carcass. For nearly a decade, his prophecy held. Critics scorned Hemingway's world view as simplistic; assailed his range as narrow; and maligned his style as monochromatic. Indeed, for several years, even the number of doctoral dissertations and critical articles cited in the *MLA Bibliography* sharply diminished.

But today the lion roams once more, and a new generation of critics and biographers tracks, not a carcass, but a vital, invigorating literary spirit whose best fiction embodies a wholly American (and midwestern) reverence for the heroic, the ideal, and the traditional along with a hearty contempt for expressing that reverence abstractly.

Strands of Hemingway's sensibility still entwine our consciousness. His tender and terrible images of love and death, his superbly textured landscapes—all are ineradicably ingrained in the fibers of the American literary tradition. And as we read today his heroes' silent and courageous efforts to live in their precariously ordered worlds, we are reminded of what we have lately been and what we may wish yet again to be.

PAUL WEST

Hemingway's having been appropriated as the patron saint of prose minimalism blinds us to his passion for something seamless; more than any other American writer except maybe Faulkner (the two are mutually complementary tropics of the same concern), Hemingway saw prose as something sculpted, made with the *hands,* something pliable and plastic to be rotated and surveyed while it was being made. He reminds me of a potter too. His problem, I think, was that he tried to achieve this laudable effect with too few devices: no commas and all those *ands,* whereas Faulkner's approach is complex and many-voiced. For this reader, however, the yearning in Hemingway feels almost as good as the final effect: you can see how much he wants to deal with prose as if it were clay or bronze, and you have to respect it even if he didn't manage to pull it off. There is a manual infatuation in Hemingway that goes beyond the pared, would-be pregnant simplisms adored by his minimalist fans. I detect the presence of a complex literary artist whose bent, uncurbed, was not to simplify at all, or at least only as Giacometti does. I just wonder why he held back so much when clearly he was on the right lines and knew so tenderly what he wanted the prose medium to yield. Maybe someone knows. Too much King James Bible, I wonder? Not a *Southern* writer? He teaches writing students to be craftly, but he doesn't give them enough of the complex wherewithal.

The Pitt Poetry Series: Poetry Publishing Today

Ed Ochester

University of Pittsburgh

In the *Wall Street Journal*'s lead article of 26 September 1984, the president of the trade division of Simon and Schuster is quoted as saying, "There is no level [of quality] below which we will not go." That's not news to anybody who cares about books and has visited a bookshop in the past twenty years. "Bad money drives out good," and there seems to be an inexorable law by which books follow the same pattern. As more and more publishers become units of conglomerate corporations—Simon and Schuster is owned by Gulf and Western—the blockbuster mentality is fostered; it isn't enough for a promising title by a young author to break even or make a small profit, because an editor or division manager is judged by the bucks on the bottom line. And the chain bookstores which distribute the blockbusters really don't want to be bothered ordering a few copies of a serious novel which are probably going to have to be returned unsold or, for that matter, a book of poems by some Greek or Czech who may win the Nobel Prize next year. And the serious reader, if there are serious readers anymore, who visits the local chain bookstore isn't going to discover that young fiction writer or next year's Nobel laureate if the books aren't on the shelves.

It's a vicious circle, but its existence explains why university presses and small independent publishers increasingly have been the ones to introduce young authors and, in poetry especially, to publish established but noncommercial writers ignored by the big boys. As commercial houses such as Scribners, Simon and Schuster, and Doubleday have cut back or eliminated their poetry lists, university presses such as Pittsburgh, Wesleyan, Louisiana State, Princeton, Carnegie-Mellon, and Illinois have filled the void, as have such small presses as Graywolf, Ecco, Copper Canyon, and Black Sparrow. A look through any anthology of major American poets writing at the present time, such as A. Poulin, Jr.'s *Contemporary American Poetry*, will reveal that the large majority of writers represented were first, and often subsequently, published by university and small presses: John Ashbery, Galway Kinnell, Louis Simpson, W. S. Merwin, James Wright,

Frank O'Hara, Etheridge Knight, Denise Levertov, James Dickey, Robert Bly, Adrienne Rich, and many others. Among writers in their forties and below who have recently established their reputations or are in the process of doing so, the percentage is even higher and more striking. Though a few commercial publishers—the best among them Houghton Mifflin, Random House, Knopf, and Norton—still represent the art, American poetry, which is alive and well, is not thriving in midtown Manhattan.

At the beginning of this century Yale began the university press involvement with contemporary poetry when it established the Yale Younger Poets Series, which publishes the first book of one poet a year. Most of the early volumes have been forgotten—books such as *The White God and Other Poems* by Thomas Caldecot Chubb, *Where Lilith Dances* by Darl Macleod Boyle, *The Last Lutanist* by Dean B. Lyman, Jr., and *Up and Down* by Elizabeth Jessup Blake. Pound, Williams, and Eliot were safe from discovery. But things changed by mid-century, when Dudley Fitts became editor, and subsequently Stanley Kunitz. Yale began to take risks, and practically every year produced a book by a poet who was to make his or her mark on American letters. The list includes Rich, Merwin, Ashbery, Wright, and Alan Dugan. Fitts and Kunitz, through the 1970s, scored more palpable hits in their choices of young poets who mattered than any other editors in the history of the United States, with the possible exception of James Laughlin at New Directions in the earlier days of that press. The Yale Series continues to enjoy great prestige, and practically every poet trying to place a first book sends a copy of the manuscript to the Yale competition. Three years ago the late Richard Hugo, who was editor then, received some 1,500 poetry manuscripts.

The Wesleyan University Press poetry series began publishing during the 1950s and, particularly during the 1960s, published many of the poets who have come to be viewed as the best of their generation: Simpson, Dickey, Bly, and Wright, whose books *The Branch Will Not Break* and *Shall*

Liz Rosenberg, 1985 winner of the Agnes Lynch Starrett Poetry Prize for The Fire Music

We Gather at the River have changed the course of American poetry. During the same period Frank O'Hara and Ginsberg were being published by City Lights in San Francisco. Though during the 1960s the trade houses were still publishing poetry, much or most of what was vital and young and would dominate the rest of the century was being published by "alternative" presses.

The University of Pittsburgh Press Poetry Series—The Pitt Poetry Series—was on the drawing board in 1967, when Paul Zimmer, its first editor, was hired as associate director of the Press. The original idea was to publish one book a year, chosen through a national prize competition for younger poets. Even though Yale and Wesleyan were actively publishing poetry at this time, the opportunities for book publication by new poets were few. Frederick Hetzel, the director of the Press, and Samuel Hazo, head of Pittsburgh's International Poetry Forum, which partially funded the new competition, named it the United States Award of the International Poetry Forum. Zimmer and Hazo

served as screening judges and, for the first year, asked James Dickey, Abbie Houston Evans, and William Meredith to serve as final judges. The Series was launched, and the first volume was published in 1968.

Zimmer was particularly excited and enthusiastic about the possibilities of the Series; he suggested to Hetzel that, since the judging mechanism for the United States Award was already in place, it would make sense to publish not only the winning manuscript but also several other of the finalists. Hetzel, who has always been a strong supporter of the Series, liked the idea and agreed that Pittsburgh would publish a total of four books a year initially, two each in the fall and spring seasons.

As a young poet, Zimmer was not only enthusiastic but also nervous about the responsibility of editing poetry manuscripts. Even the mechanical details of the contest were difficult. He recalls wrapping copies of finalist manuscripts, ten or twelve in all, with light string, and offering the bundle to the tender mercies of the local post office for delivery to the final judges. Naturally, the string broke and the poems were scattered everywhere. The post office evidently did its best to collect the papers; but, Zimmer says, "I remember I got a call from James Dickey expressing some puzzlement at receiving a package that contained, in its entirety, an old green sweater and a man's belt. I was *really* inexperienced, but I was learning real fast."

During the ten years of the United States Award competition Pittsburgh published splendid work. The prizewinners include such books as Richard Shelton's *The Tattooed Desert,* Larry Levis's *Wrecking Crew,* and Gary Soto's *The Elements of San Joaquin.* What is particularly interesting, though, is that it was the additional books published, the runners-up in the competition and not the prizewinners, which received the most attention and introduced to readers the larger number of poets who have since "established themselves" in terms of subsequent publication and critical and scholarly attention. This group includes Jon Anderson, John Engels, David Young, Gary Gildner, Michael Harper, Norman Dubie, Herb Scott, John Balaban, Brendan Galvin, Carol Muske, and others.

Poets on the list developed a strong affection for Zimmer because of the amount of energy he spent not only in his editorial capacity but to promote and distribute the new books and because of his evident concern for the writers on his list. Jon Anderson used to refer to Zimmer affectionately as "Uncle Paul," but he could be a fierce uncle. The care and passion he brought to the selection and occasional defense of manuscripts was matched by his attention to even the smallest details. When I became editor in 1978 I discovered copies of letters, for example, that Zimmer had written to bookstore owners in our poets' hometowns, urging them to carry copies of the books. He knew and I've learned that selling poetry is a game of inches; the real battle only begins when the manuscript is in print.

In 1978 Zimmer decided to accept the job as director of the University of Georgia Press, and I was asked to succeed him as editor of the Poetry Series. Before his move I stopped by his office several times for nuts-and-bolts information and to get advice about matters large and small, including a few words on the proper way to ship manuscripts. One day he gave me some of the best advice I've ever gotten: "Nobody's ever going to thank you for this job," he said. He was talking, of course, not about any lack of support at the Press; nor was he denying the fact that authors are grateful when you accept their books, or that there are occasional small moments of private pleasure. Zimmer was

talking about the fact that the best editor is invisible; he works with the author to strengthen a manuscript in ways which reveal the poet's, not the editor's, genius. He was talking also, I suppose, about the endless and tedious work of writing grant proposals, about the unhappy and lonely moment when one must reject a weak manuscript by a poet whose work he generally admires.

As editor, I wanted to make some changes; Zimmer would have made them too, probably. It didn't make sense to me to continue publishing only first books and subsequent ones by Press poets. In the ten years since we'd begun, various additional first-book prizes for poetry had been established, and there had been a large growth of small independent presses which published first collections. During the same period, though, the decrease in the number of poetry books published by the major commercial houses had continued, and it was perhaps more difficult for an established poet to publish than a newcomer.

Consequently, we decided to reduce our first

Cover for the book Pittsburgh Press found "distinguished by clarity and depth of emotion"

books to one or two a year, and to publish four or five by "veteran" poets, including at least one or two who had not published previously with us. Among the latter, we've since published James Reiss, Constance Urdang, Leonard Nathan, Michael Benedikt, Ted Kooser, Carolyn Forché, Ronald Wallace, and Siv Cedering. Manuscripts from previously published poets are received during September and October of each year, and selections are currently made by February. In 1984 we received more than eighty manuscripts in this category.

External funding for our first-book prize, the United States Award, had ended before I became Series editor, but I wanted to continue some sort of cash prize to attract good young writers, to afford them added recognition as well as a bit of extra money, and to generate publicity for the books chosen. It seemed to me that this was the time to institute a handling fee for first-book manuscripts in order to fund a modest prize of $1000 and to help offset the heavy costs of processing the enormous number of manuscripts we receive; at the high-water mark of the United States Award we received 1,500 manuscripts, a staggering number for our small office to handle. I figured that among its other benefits, the handling fee would reduce the number of manuscripts from hobbyist writers, particularly if we took care to publicize the competition only in what are essentially trade journals in the field, magazines such as *CODA: Poets and Writers Newsletter*, The Associated Writing Programs' *Newsletter*, and The Academy of American Poets' *Poetry Pilot*. The strategy worked; we currently receive between 500 and 900 first-book manuscripts each year, and the percentage of quality manuscripts is higher than before.

We named the new prize the Agnes L. Starrett Poetry Prize after the first director of the Press and from the beginning have collected manuscripts for the Starrett during March and April of each year and arrived at decisions by the end of the summer. The competition is open to any poet who has not published a full-length book, but we ask that before sending a book, prospective contestants request a copy of the current rules by mailing a stamped, self-addressed envelope to Starrett Prize, University of Pittsburgh Press, 127 North Bellefield Avenue, Pittsburgh, PA 15260. The first five books chosen as Starrett winners are: Kathy Callaway's *Heart of the Garfish*, Lawrence Joseph's *Shouting at No One*, Kate Daniels's *The White Wave*, Arthur Smith's *Elegy on Independence Day*, and Liz Rosenberg's *The Fire Music* (published in 1986). The first

Starrett book was actually published in 1982, too recently for any of the young poets to have become household names, but each one of the three books published so far has received excellent reviews. Those of Kate Daniels's book, published in 1984, are typical. *Kliatt*, one of the major library reviews, said: "The language, details, and association reveal a stunning maturity of perception and insight. . . . Her language is precise and explosive at the same time. An exciting poetry experience." I mention Daniels's book not only because the response so far has been typically enthusiastic, but also because it's an example of one kind of book I'm particularly interested in, the collection of poetry that is not necessarily in anybody's camp or school, and that might not fit the mold of other publishers less creatively eclectic than Pittsburgh. A positive review in the *Village Voice* of Daniels's book emphasizes the fact that it doesn't fit neatly into one category:

> Most young, university-trained poets are in it for either the language or the feelings. Language types are usually aloof, mad for John Ashbery, and unoffended when the creation of verse is considered an emotional puzzle solvable with words. The feelings crowd is friendlier, fond of almost any recent American poets who sternly invoke words like "earth" or "blood" and who are, dammit, offended. Kate Daniels' first collection, *The White Wave*, makes it clear that she fits snugly into neither camp.
>
> Daniels' newly wise, thoughtful, occasionally fey voices tense and release, describe and direct. For all her ease of style, there's spunk to these poems.

Perhaps because there are so many poetry manuscripts in the mails today that the paperwork is causing editorial overload and burnout, or perhaps because of regional or academic alliances, my impression is that many of the books of poetry published are predictable. We have tried to avoid predictability and to maintain editorial sympathies as broad as possible.

The danger of having an eclectic editorial policy is that not everybody is going to love you all the time. Such easily accessible but powerful poets as David Huddle (*Paper Boy*) and Peter Meinke (*Trying to Surprise God*) have sold well, even going to multiple printings, and have received a fair amount of attention in newspaper reviews and articles; but they have not always sat well with some academic critics, who distrust what one called in print several years ago the "thin verbal texture" of one of these books. Conversely, Michael Burkard (*Ruby for Grief*), an "experimental" poet difficult for many readers, has received very positive attention in *American Poetry Review* and avant-garde little magazines, but relatively little from more general media.

And, of course, there are regional difficulties sometimes. New York editors and poets, like other New Yorkers, often appear to believe that life begins only east of the Hudson; California poets and editors often appear to believe that death begins east of the Rockies, perhaps east of Bolinas. Good writers can get lost in between. One of the poets I wanted to recruit during my first years as editor was Ted Kooser, a Nebraskan who'd published with good midwestern small presses. Readers of poetry in the middle of the country knew his work, but somehow his books and reputation had not permeated to the coasts. For that reason, it was a pleasure to read the beginning of Dana Gioia's review of Kooser's Pitt book, *Sure Signs*, in the Winter 1980-1981 issue of the *Hudson Review:*

> I have been suspicious of Mid-Western cultural boosterism. Therefore over the past few years when three Nebraskans I met independently recommended the work of Ted Kooser, a poet who works as an insurance underwriter in Lincoln, I smugly made the resolution to remain in blissful ignorance. Now confronted with a review copy of Kooser's new and selected poems, I abhor my snobbism and repent in dust and ashes. As penance I promise to skip the cartoons in the next five issues of *The New Yorker* and talk for five minutes to the next insurance man who calls up during dinner.

Virtue triumphs in this case because of Gioia's intelligence and good humor, but the fact is that there are regional and academic biases that are very difficult to overcome. We help mediate those, or at least attempt to. It surprises some people, for example, to learn that though we are a university press, about half the poets we have published during my editorship do not have a permanent academic affiliation, even though this is a period when colleges and universities are the major patrons of writers. Many "independent" small presses have a higher percentage of academic authors than do we.

In the early years, books in the Poetry Series were chosen largely by outside judges. That was done partly to indicate to the world our impartiality, and partly to use large poetic reputations as envois for the brave new titles we were sending out

to the world under a new and unknown imprint; we wanted imprimaturs, and under the circumstances the desire was not unreasonable. But the use of external judges generally doesn't make sense to me. As I've said, I admire the work chosen by such outstanding editors as Kunitz and Fitts at Yale, and more recently Jonathan Galassi at Houghton Mifflin and Random House. Those are editors who chose *books,* put their reputations on the line with each choice, and were willing to take chances; poetry series without one strong and intelligent editor behind them usually don't fare so well.

Examine a series where books are chosen by large editorial committees or by a succession of screening readers, and you begin to discover that a large percentage of the books look and sound alike. They seem to be what Dylan Thomas called "verbal ectoplasm served up to order." The people involved in the committees or the various screenings are undoubtedly intelligent and sensitive readers, but committees by definition tend to produce average choices; the stranger, more original or outrageous manuscripts are sure to offend someone along the way. Similarly, the time-honored system

Cover for the book chosen for the 1983 prize from 880 first-book manuscripts

in poetry publishing of choosing a very prominent poet as prize judge on a one-shot basis is rarely successful. Every poet and editor in the country, if he or she has been around long enough, has heard the delicious stories about the great Grimsby choosing a book by his/her current lover, or former student, or comrade-in-struggle because the great name naturally wanted to help a person dear to her/him and had no sense of responsibility to the poetry series itself. Perhaps also the famous poet lacks editorial experience or has stopped reading and simply doesn't know what's out there, and hence chooses a weak or very derivative work. And the visiting editor is unlikely to give much help to prospective authors, encouraging them or making editorial suggestions in the attempt to develop manuscripts.

Though for several years I've used a screening reader for the Starrett Prize, a poet whose work and judgment I very much admire and trust, I read each of the 80 to 100 "finalists," which is to say, those manuscripts with any merit at all. From the outset I wanted to make my own choices, and I was grateful to get that freedom from Hetzel when I came to the Press. Our understanding is that once every five years my work is to be reviewed by the committee of faculty and administrators which oversees Press operations. The basic criterion is the reception accorded our books by reviews. That seemed fair to me at the time and does now, since in the anarchy of contemporary criticism what more objective standard exists than the consensus of reviews? And certainly by that standard we have done well. We have been reviewed in every publication that matters which publishes poetry reviews. In terms of average number of reviews per book, at least as much attention is paid the Pitt Series as any other poetry publisher, and the large majority of reviews has always been favorable.

Why, more specifically, do we choose the books we do? When asked what jazz is, Louis Armstrong once said, "Man, if you have to ask that, you'll never know what jazz is." Though I'm willing to settle as editor for the most excellent manifestation of a mode familiar to me, I'm really looking for what I haven't seen before—not a new *style* necessarily (I agree with Ignazio Silone that mere stylistic innovation is often barren) but a new combination of elements that speaks in fresh and compelling ways for areas of the heart and intellect hitherto underrepresented in the republic of letters. Though the editor does not ignore writers' reputations, it is necessary to forget them while reading new manuscripts.

Several years before Zimmer left the Press he applied for and received one of the first grants given by the National Endowment for the Arts to a university press for poetry publishing. I've continued seeking those grants and additional support from the Pennsylvania Council on the Arts. Grants are important to us—they currently account for approximately fifteen percent of Poetry Series revenues—but it also has always seemed important to me not just to sit on grants, but actively to promote sales. One of the reasons that poetry publishing is difficult financially is that the audience for poetry, though real, is scattered; the potential volume of poetry sales is small compared to that for books with titles like *Make Millions Over Lunch* and *The Intelligent Person's Guide to Instant Gratification*. Because bad books drive out good, even bookstore owners who care about literature are afraid to risk carrying much or any poetry.

I don't have the final answer to poetry's distribution problems, but there are a few things that help. Like Zimmer, I write letters to individual bookstores and make calls when I can. I have a form letter urging our poets to be as aggressive as possible when approaching local bookstores to carry their books. After I arrived at the Press we established a larger discount for bookstores willing to sign up for standing orders. We send poetry brochures to 8,000 poetry buyers. Our publicity manager, Margie Bachman, is particularly good at calling college stores to encourage orders when one of our poets is on tour or doing a reading. Rather than take very expensive ads in such magazines as the *New Yorker* and the *New York Review of Books*, which please authors but which are not productive for sales of poetry, we place a large number of ads in smaller and less expensive media read by people particularly interested in poetry. For every book we publish we send out approximately seventy-five review copies to literary magazines and newspapers. I urge friends in academe to adopt for classes individual volumes of poetry and am convinced that, if one out of four teachers of contemporary literature and writing classes would order two or three titles by individual authors rather than using anthologies exclusively, half the publishers of poetry in the United States would immediately reach the break-even point.

It is financial small potatoes compared to megabuck publishing. But our sales have been moving up, slowly, year by year. In *Mavericks: Nine Independent Publishers* (Paycock Press, 1983), George Braziller is quoted as saying that he plans an 800-copy printing for fiction by a new, quality author. We certainly do better than that, with a minimum initial printing of 1,500 for our poets and usually higher. During the past few years we have also had to reprint many of our books. In fact, we are not too far away from the break-even point. I think that right now we could operate on a break-even basis if we refused to publish books by unknown or unfashionable writers, but we are not in the game to choose that option.

As the Series has grown in sales and reputation, poets published by the trade houses send manuscripts to us. In many cases they have grown disillusioned by the practices of those firms still concerned enough to offer poetry on their lists. They do not want to see their books go out of print in a year or two, a time period that is now the norm. They are tired of working with junior editors who know very little about poetry. They are appalled, often, by the lack of advertising and general promotion for books that are allowed to fall dead from the press. Conversely, since I have been editor only two of our poets have violated the "rights of first refusal clause" in our contract in order to move to a large trade publisher, though many could easily do so.

I want to end this account by emphasizing something I am proud of, which in several ways seems appropriate as conclusion. I like to boast that in my term here we have published only one poet who was a friend of the editor before the book was accepted for publication. And in that case the book previously had been accepted by another major university press, but had been withdrawn after an editorial disagreement. When I learned of that fact I recruited it, because I thought the book was important and that it would have good sales and good reviews. It has. It even had a title that was exactly right: *Family Reunion: New and Selected Poems*, by Paul Zimmer.

Pitt Poetry Series

Title	Author	Year	Award
Learning the Way*	James Den Boer	1968	1967 U.S. Award
Looking for Jonathan	Jon Anderson	1968	
Blood Rights*	Samuel Hazo	1968	
Homer Mitchell Place*	John Engels	1968	
Sweating Out the Winter*	David P. Young	1969	1968 U.S. Award
Body Compass*	David Steingass	1969	
First Practice	Gary Gildner	1969	
The Invention of New Jersey*	Jack Anderson	1969	
Selected Poems of Fazil Hüsnü Dağlarca*	Talât Sait Halman (translator)	1969	

The Floor Keeps Turning	Shirley Kaufman	1969	1969 U.S. Award
*Dear John, Dear Coltrane**	Michael S. Harper	1970	
*When Thy King is a Boy**	Ed Roberson	1970	
Death & Friends	Jon Anderson	1970	
*Collected Poems**	Abbie Huston Evans	1970	
*Another Kind of Rain**	Gerald W. Barrax	1970	
*The Tattooed Desert**	Richard Shelton	1970	1970 U.S. Award
The Blood of Adonis: Selected Poems of Adonis (Ali Ahmed Said)*	Samuel Hazo (translator)	1971	
*Trying to Come Apart**	James Den Boer	1971	
Alehouse Sonnets	Norman Dubie	1971	
Digging for Indians	Gary Gildner	1971	
Windows and Stones	Tomas Tranströmer May Swenson (translator)	1971	
Wrecking Crew	Larry Levis	1972	1971 U.S. Award
*Once for the Last Bandit**	Samuel Hazo	1972	
Of All the Dirty Words	Richard Shelton	1972	
Song: I Want a Witness	Michael S. Harper	1973	
*48 Small Poems**	Marc Weber	1973	1972 U.S. Award
*A Canopy in the Desert: Selected Poems**	Abba Kovner Shirley Kaufman (translator)	1973	
*101 Different Ways of Playing Solitaire and Other Poems**	Belle Randall	1973	
Gold Country	Shirley Kaufman	1973	
*American Handbook**	David Steingass	1973	

Uncle Time	Dennis Scott	1973	1974 Commonwealth Award of the Common- wealth Institute of Great Britain
Eskimo Poems from Canada and Greenland	Tom Lowenstein (translator)	1974	
*Lake Songs and Other Fears**	Judith Minty	1974	1973 U.S. Award
*In Sepia**	Jon Anderson	1974	
After Our War	John Balaban	1974	1974 Lamont Award of the Academy of American Poets
*Disguises**	Herbert Scott	1974	
*Learning to Count**	Alberta T. Turner	1974	
No Time for Good Reasons	Brendan Galvin	1974	
*The Lost Heroes**	Michael Culross	1974	
The Axion Esti	Odysseus Elytis Edmund Keeley & George Savidis (translators)	1974	1979 Nobel Prize for Literature
*Quartered**	Samuel Hazo	1974	
*Signals from the Safety Coffin**	John Engels	1975	
Exile	Thomas Rabbit	1975	1974 U.S. Award
Nails	Gary Gildner	1975	
Special Effects	Gwen Head	1975	
Camouflage	Carol Muske	1975	
The Great American Fourth of July Parade	Archibald MacLeish	1975	
*The New Body**	James Moore	1975	
*In the Dead of the Night**	Norman Dubie	1975	
You Can't Have Everything	Richard Shelton	1975	
Etai-Eken	Ed Roberson	1976	
Backroads	Mark Halperin	1976	1975 U.S. Award

*In Lieu of Mecca**	Jim Lindsey	1976	
First Selected Poems	Leo Connellan	1976	
Groceries	Herbert Scott	1976	
*The Terror of the Snows**	Paul-Marie Lapointe D. G. Jones (translator)	1976	
The Elements of San Joaquin	Gary Soto	1977	1976 U.S. Award
Blood Mountain	John Engels	1977	
The Lifeguard in the Snow	Eugene Ruggles	1977	
Reading the Ashes: An Anthology of the Poetry of Modern Macedonia	Milne Holton & Graham W. Reid	1977	
Collected Poems	Dannie Abse	1977	
*The Night Train and the Golden Bird**	Peter Meinke	1977	
*Lid and Spoon**	Alberta T. Turner	1977	
The Minutes No One Owns	Brendan Galvin	1977	
*Toward the Liberation of the Left Hand**	Jack Anderson	1977	
The Runner	Gary Gildner	1978	
The New Polish Poetry: A Bilingual Collection	Milne Holton & Paul Vangelisti	1978	
A Festering Sweetness: Poems of American People	Robert Coles	1978	
Border Crossings	Greg Pape	1978	
The Tale of Sunlight	Gary Soto	1978	
The Climbers	John Hart	1978	
*Woman Before an Aquarium**	Patricia Hampl	1978	
*The Bus to Veracruz**	Richard Shelton	1978	
From One Life to Another	Shirley Kaufman	1979	
The Ten Thousandth Night	Gwen Head	1979	

Paper Boy	David Huddle	1979	
Brass Knuckles	Stuart Dybek	1979	
A Romance	Bruce Weigl	1979	
The Names of a Hare in English	David Young	1979	
Dear Blood	Leonard Nathan	1980	1980 Commonwealth Club of California Silver Medal
Sure Signs	Ted Kooser	1980	1981 Society of Midland Authors Book Award
Satan Says	Sharon Olds	1980	1981 San Francisco Poetry Center Book Award
The Salamander Migration	Cary Waterman	1980	
The Lone Woman and Others	Constance Urdang	1980	Delmore Schwartz Memorial Poetry Award
The Badminton at Great Barrington; Or, Gustave Mahler & the Chattanooga Choo-Choo	Michael Benedikt	1980	
In the Presence of Mothers	Judith Minty	1980	
Trying to Surprise God	Peter Meinke	1981	
Northern Spy	Chase Twichell	1981	
Emplumada	Lorna Dee Cervantes	1981	1982 American Book Award of the Before Columbus Foundation
Where Sparrows Work Hard	Gary Soto	1981	
Ruby for Grief	Michael Burkard	1981	
The Middle of the World	Kathleen Norris	1981	
Holding Patterns	Leonard Nathan	1982	
Heart of the Garfish	Kathy Callaway	1982	1981 Starrett Prize
January Thaw	Bruce Guernsey	1982	
Selected Poems, 1969-1981	Richard Shelton	1982	

Flowers from the Volcano	Claribel Alegría Carolyn Forché (translator)	1982	
Express	James Reiss	1983	
Shouting at No One	Lawrence Joseph	1983	1982 Starrett Prize
Only the World	Constance Urdang	1983	
Tunes for Bears to Dance To	Ronald Wallace	1983	1983 Council for Wisconsin Writers Prize
Family Reunion	Paul Zimmer	1983	
Living in Code	Robert Louthan	1983	
Black Branches	Greg Pape	1984	
Blue Like the Heavens	Gary Gildner	1984	
The White Wave	Kate Daniels	1984	1983 Starrett Prize
Black Hair	Gary Soto	1984	
Letters from the Floating World	Siv Cedering	1984	
One World at a Time	Ted Kooser	1985	
Wyndemere	Carol Muske	1985	
Winter Stars	Larry Levis	1985	
Elegy on Independence Day	Arthur Smith	1985	1984 Starrett Prize
The Essential Etheridge Knight	Etheridge Knight	1985	

* Out of print

Literary Research Archives IV:
The John Carter Brown Library

Everett C. Wilkie, Jr.

Ever since the John Carter Brown Library, an independently managed institution for advanced research in the humanities at Brown University, opened its doors in 1904, it has collected Americana. So strong has been the library's connection with this field that one often encounters the phrase "not in JCB" as an indication of the rarity or desirability of a book. The library collection, which is now nearly 150 years old, has been built up with such single-mindedness of purpose by successive generations of owners and librarians that its name is nearly synonymous with the word *Americana*.

Although it is well known that the library was formed by successive generations of the Brown family of Providence, Rhode Island, its actual beginnings in the family are obscure. The family owned books long before the Americana library took shape, and several of these are still in the collection. Thus, there are any number of books that might be called "first," depending on the criteria one applies. The earliest family provenance now in the library is James Brown's (1698-1739) signature from about 1730 on a copy of the fourth edition of William Bradford's *The Secretary's Guide, Or, Young Man's Companion* (New York and Philadelphia, 1728). James's son, Nicholas, acquired the book in 1740 and inserted his own signature in it. This book eventually came to the library in 1904 but does not appear to have been the nucleus of the family's library of Americana. The earliest family provenance for a European book relating to America, the great strength of the library today and the area for which it is best known, is Nicholas Brown's signature from 1748 on a copy of Fayre Hall's *The Importance of the British Plantations in America to this Kingdom* (London, 1731). This book also came when the library was given to Brown University, but neither does it appear to be the earliest book in the Americana library bought with a design to create such a library.

Despite the interest of these early beginnings, there does not appear to have been an organized or deliberate attempt by the Brown family to collect Americana until John Carter Brown began to build a systematic library. The earliest provenance of a book he owned dates from 1808, when he was eleven years old, in a copy of Thomas Hobbe's *Behemoth* (London, 1679). It was not, however, until he grew older that he began to evince genuine bibliographical and collecting interests in the subject that would make him and his library famous. Although as a young man he collected books in the best Dibdinian bibliomania fashion, it was not until the 1840s that he settled upon the idea of creating an Americana library. His reasons for settling on this subject to the virtual exclusion of others are also poorly understood. By this time, Brown was in possession of a considerable fortune and had no political or other ambitions. As he once remarked, "Only let me have a cool million and others may have the offices." He continued adding to his library until his death in 1874.

It was during this time in the library's history that Brown acquired some of the books that no other library has ever been able to purchase on the market. In 1871 he ordered from Frederik Muller of Amsterdam the only known copy of Vespucci's *Van der nieuwe werelt*, his cable arriving four hours before rival collector James Lenox's order. In 1846 he acquired the unique *Copie d'une lettre venant de la Floride envoyée à Rouen* (Paris, 1565), describing an attempt to establish a Huguenot colony in America and containing the earliest printed representation of a European settlement in the present-day United States. He also acquired the library's first engraved print in 1868, Peter Gordon's *A View of Savannah* (1734?), and the library's first separate map, a manuscript version of Braddock's route in 1775 done by Christopher Gist, an engineer on the expedition itself. (This map was, however, acquired by accident, having been found folded up in a book to which it was bibliographically unrelated.)

Upon Brown's death, the library passed to his wife, Sophia Augusta. Although she was not as dedicated to pursuing Americana as her husband had been, her contributions to the library's growth can

Drawing by David MacCauley of the John Carter Brown Library (courtesy of the John Carter Brown Library at Brown University)

hardly be characterized as extraneous or unimportant. She did purchase such "great books" as the first four folio printings of Shakespeare and medieval illuminated manuscripts (the latter recently disposed of at auction) and also added to the Americana already in the library. Chief among her purchases was the acquisition of what is still the only known perfect copy in a contemporary binding of the *Bay Psalm Book* (Cambridge, 1640); the copy is also the only one known that has the autograph of one of the translators, in this case Richard Mather's.

Sophia Augusta passed control of the library to her son, John Nicholas, in 1883 but did not give him formal possession of it until 1898. (Thus, at the time of his death in 1900, he had actually owned the library only two years.) His acquisitions tended to reflect his father's idea of what belonged in the library. He purchased the only known complete copy of Juan de Zumarraga's *Doctrina breve* (Mex-

ico, 1544), the earliest book printed in the New World of which a complete copy survives. He also made many important acquisitions from Nicolas León, the famous collector of Latin American books and manuscripts, such as Pedro Font's manuscript diary (Mexico, 1776-1777). He purchased *The Case of the Inhabitants of East-Florida* (Saint Augustine, 1784), thereby ensuring that the library would eventually possess copies of both books that vie for the honor of being the first Florida imprint.

When Nicholas Brown came into possession of the library in 1898, he immediately had drawn up a will in which the library was left to the care of his brother, Harold, and George W. R. Matteson, who were supposed to see that it was disposed of according to the terms of the will. Harold himself had not participated in the formation of the "Bibliotheca Americana," as it was now called, but had, nevertheless, built up his own smaller collection of books about the Church of England and the Prot-

Portrait of John Carter Brown (1797-1874), founder of the library (courtesy of the John Carter Brown Library at Brown University)

estant Episcopal Church in the United States. Harold survived his brother by only a few days, however, and the disposition of the library was left to Matteson and Harold's replacement.

According to the terms of John Nicholas Brown's will, he left the books, a sum of money for erection of a library building (the plans for which he had approved shortly before his death), money to employ a librarian, and money for acquisitions. This bequest was not, as is commonly believed, left to Brown University, despite the family's long connection with the institution that bears their name. The library was to be given, within four years, "to a Board of Trustees, or to a corporation specially organized therefor, or to some college, university, or other institution in said State of Rhode Island, or in any other of the United States, competent in law to receive and hold the same." Brown University was settled on in 1902.

Construction of the building began that year, although minor modifications were made in the plan to accommodate the different building site. The building itself, executed in Teutonic Revival style, is significant, because it is the first separate special collections library to be built on any United States university campus. The structure, in keeping

with the terms of Brown's bequest, was made as nearly fireproof as possible. The roof is tile and, except for the flooring and some bookcases, there is almost no wood anywhere in the original structure. Certain deed restrictions also prevent Brown University from erecting other buildings too close to the library, a prudent precaution in the early twentieth century. The bookcases in the reading room are fabricated of metal and glass, thereby rendering them fireproof as well.

The library opened as a semipublic institution in May 1904. It was governed by its own independent Board of Trustees, and, according to the terms of the will, its collections could never be indiscriminately mingled with another.

Although the library was now out from under the direct control of the Brown family, a certain continuity was ensured by the appointment of George Parker Winship as its first librarian. Winship had been preceded by John Russell Bartlett, who had served the family in various capacities from 1853 until his death in 1886, thereby providing consistent advice to three of the library's private owners. Winship was hired as librarian in 1895 and served until 1915. He was followed by Champlain Burrage, who was librarian until 1917, but served with no particular distinction. Burrage was followed by Worthington Chauncey Ford, who served until 1922.

It was the period between 1923 and 1982 that saw the library grow considerably in international reputation, primarily because of the stature achieved by the only two librarians to have served during that sixty-year period. Laurence Counselman Wroth, who was librarian between 1923-1957, not only added immeasurably to the library's collections but also solidly established, in equal measure, the reputation of "scholar-librarian" for the library's chief officer. It was during his tenure that the library acquired Juan de Tovar's "Historia de la benida de los Yndios," the most fabulous manuscript relic of sixteenth-century Mexico; Bartolomé de Flores's *Obra* (Seville, 1571), the only known copy of the only printed Spanish account of the Spanish destruction of the Huguenot colony in Florida; Robert Cushman's *Sermon* (London, 1622), the first New England sermon to be printed; William Hubbard's *Narrative* (Boston, 1677), containing the first map published in the Western Hemisphere; and Asher Benjamin's *The Country Builder's Assistant* (Greenfield, 1797), the first original architectural book by a native American printed in America. Wroth was also a tireless author who actually practiced the research that he

*Librarian Laurence C. Wroth and Jeanette D. Black at one of
several sandbagged safes installed in the basement of the library
during World War II (courtesy of the John Carter Brown
Library at Brown University)*

preached. Many of his books, such as *The Way of
the Ship, Early Cartography of the Pacific,* and *A Colonial Bookshelf,* were based on the library's own collections. His many articles and books on
bibliography and interpretation justifiably made
him and the library acknowledged international resources for the study of the colonial Americas.

Wroth was followed by Thomas Randolph
Adams, who served as librarian until 1982. Adams
considerably strengthened the collections by acquiring copies of works that had eluded all his
predecessors, such as the London, 1635 edition of
A Relation of Maryland, complete with the map, a
copy of which, without the map, John Carter
Brown had purchased in 1846. He also acquired
Samuel Gale's *Essay II. On the Nature and Principles
of Publick Credit* (Saint Augustine, 1784), thereby
ensuring at last that the library owned copies of
both works that were rivals for the honor of being
the first book printed in Florida. Also added was a
perfect copy of Manuel de la Lobo's *Vida,* the only
known perfect copy of the first genuine book
printed in Guatemala, complete with a contemporary Guatemala provenance. It replaced an imperfect copy, which was long the only known copy,

already on the library's shelves. Adams also did
much to foster the role of "scholar-librarian." His
publications on British and American pamphlets of
the American Revolution were based largely on the
library's own collections, and his activities in the
world of rare book librarianship did much to ensure the continued preeminence of the library in
the field of special collection libraries and colonial
American scholarship.

Despite the seemingly monolithic face that the
library presents in the field of Americana, the
course of its collecting policy has not been so seamless. As Susan Danforth has pointed out, "Each
period in the library's history has been marked by
a characteristic signature, a direction of development determined not only by events, talents and
background of the leading figure but also by the
contemporary market situation and the 'state of the
art' in areas such as academic and popular research,
methodology and bibliography. Continuity enabled
the John Carter Brown librarians to expand and
refine the concepts of previous periods." Although
there have been numerous changes of direction in
collecting policy and numerous shifts of interest,
the thread of "Americana" has proven quite elastic
and has served to tie together the somewhat differing ideas of successive owners and librarians.

Despite the books in the library the acquisitions of which predate 1846, it is that date that
probably marks the foundation of the library on
its present design. Before that time, John Carter
Brown was generally collecting books that are more
properly described as monuments of printing or
"great books." His career as a book collector began
in 1816, the year he joined his older brother, Nicholas, in collecting books, although their libraries
were kept separate. Both were inspired, as were
many others, by the treasures in the Roxburghe
sale of 1812 and by the theories of T. F. Dibdin,
an English antiquarian whose writings have inspired several generations of book collectors. Together the brothers assembled sizable collections of
rare books, which came entirely into John Carter
Brown's possession in 1846, after he passed three
sleepless nights contemplating his brother's offer
to sell him his part of the library for $10,000. In
1846, when Nicholas decided to move to Rome,
John Carter purchased his brother's "American
books" and thus provided the genuine core of the
present library.

In many ways, Brown was groping in the dark
when he decided to build a library of Americana.
The field of "Americana" was not defined and
there were precious few people even interested in

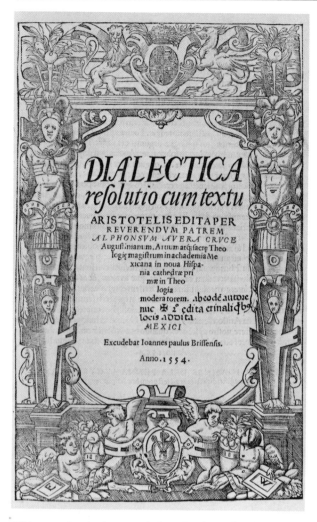

Title page for the first translation of a classical author's work published in the New World (courtesy of the John Carter Brown Library at Brown University)

it. A few bibliographical guides were available, however, particularly White Kennett's *Primordia* (London, 1713), itself not really a guide to books about America but to books once thought necessary for the education of ministers bound for America. There was also the 1837 catalogue of Henri Ternaux-Compagns's collection and Obadiah Rich's 1832 and 1845 catalogues of Spanish books. The library's copies of these works, annotated by John Carter Brown, attest to their usefulness in the early days of the library's formation. In 1846, however, the great age of Americana bibliography was still several decades away.

This lack of guidance was somewhat compensated for by the activities of Henry Stevens, who made himself one of Great Britain's most successful antiquarian book dealers by discovering and sup-

plying Americana to John Carter Brown and James Lenox, Brown's only serious American rival in the field. Stevens, whom Nathaniel Hawthorne once described as "a kindly and pleasant man," probably did more than any other individual to discover, identify, and provide Americana to John Carter Brown. The relationship between the bookseller and his client was not always smooth, however, because of Brown's financial conservatism. At one point, an aggravated Stevens even twitted Brown by remarking that books Brown considered too expensive were "selling like hotcakes" to others. In spite of these relatively minor disagreements, Stevens was Brown's most loyal book scout and a consistent source of supply for many years, much to the dismay of others, like Rich, who found Stevens's virtual monopoly hard to overcome.

Another individual who profoundly influenced the shape of Brown's library was John Russell Bartlett, who interested Brown in works concerning native American linguistics, works about the early Southwest, and early issues of Mexican and Peruvian presses. The consistent identification and purchase of such books and manuscripts were departures from Brown's own private collecting policy, which had emphasized European books about America, North American imprints, and early colonial documents. The purchases recommended by Bartlett greatly enriched the library and expanded its scope into areas it had not previously documented and in which it remains preeminent.

This early era of the library's collecting concentrated on what Brown himself jokingly used to refer to as "The Great Subject." The books and pamphlets were purchased generally with no guidance on how they fitted in with the total literature of the subject, how they related to other editions of the same work, and even without any knowledge of whether they were complete or perfect. Brown even bought manifestly imperfect copies at times, and at other times had "perfect" copies created by his book dealers or binders. Brown also does not seem to have applied any rigid chronological framework to his collecting activities, for the library possessed numerous titles that today appear almost out of place on the library's shelves but which he clearly intended to be part of his library. In many respects, what Brown collected would eventually itself define the field, an aspect of his activity which he could not then appreciate but which the publication of his first catalogue between 1865 and 1871 would make obvious to the world at large. As the volumes of the catalogue appeared, it was plain that the library's contents, collected without any real guidance other than personal taste and personal knowledge of the field, would be the touchstone of similar collections.

Ironically, Brown believed that the library was substantially complete and could be finished in his lifetime. This belief helps to explain his reluctance to pay what he deemed too dear a price for an item, because he could reasonably expect to encounter another one in the future. He could also afford to take defective copies, because it was possible, too, that he would be given the opportunity to purchase a perfect one. He even sent James Lenox a disputed copy of a Columbus letter, rather than argue with his New York rival over who should rightly possess such a rare, cornerstone item.

Sophia Augusta, Brown's widow, had somewhat different ideas about the family's collecting activities. She clearly grasped the difference between the "Bibliotheca Americana" she had inherited and the family library, which was more of a "great books" library, such as one might expect to encounter in the home of any well-heeled nineteenth-century American family. There was even some license for her concept, because her husband had himself acquired "great books," such as a collection of several hundred Aldus Manutius imprints, most of which have no Americana content whatsoever. In 1873 she had tried to get him to bid on one of the two Gutenberg Bibles in the Henry Perkins sale, although he declined to do so. Now that she was in sole possession of the library, she generously added to its treasures, purchasing such items as Caxton's printing of the "Royal Book." She was recognized by prominent dealers and librarians as a serious, qualified collector and was received as such by them.

Sophia Augusta leaned heavily on the advice of Bartlett, who was still employed as the family's librarian. In this respect, she ensured the continued existence of "The Great Subject," because Bartlett became tutor to her son John Nicholas, who would eventually acquire the library from his mother. Until his death in 1886, Bartlett tirelessly tutored the young Brown in the workings of the book trade, cataloguing, bibliography, and the contents of the library. In this manner, the father's concept was perpetuated.

John Nicholas Brown was given charge of the library in 1883 and immediately began adding to it. He did not entirely abandon the "great books" principles, however, and attempted in 1884 to purchase the Gutenberg Bible and the 1459 *Psalterium*

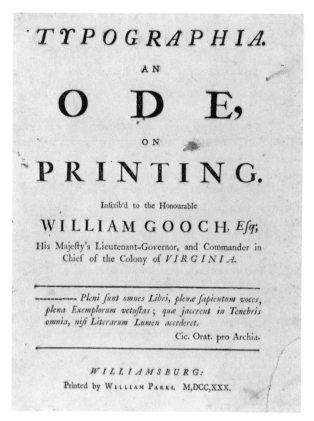

Title page of the first poem written and published in Virginia (courtesy of the John Carter Brown Library at Brown University)

at the Syston Park sale. He did succeed in purchasing a 1460 *Catholicon* and in 1881 bought a twelfth-century German gradual. Nevertheless, his great interest was in the Americana.

Brown faced a collecting situation somewhat different from what his father had faced. The subject area was now more clearly defined and the bibliographical descriptions of the pertinent books were more accurate. It was clear from such bibliographies as Joseph Sabin's *A Dictionary of Books Relating to America*, which in 1884 was well into the letter *P*, that the collection, in reality, was not so complete as his father had envisioned it to be. Some books were obviously defective; others were bibliographic "bastards," made up of leaves from any number of copies and lacking bibliographic integrity. Thus, John Nicholas Brown attempted to "trade up" to acquire perfect copies and to insist that other books he did acquire be in original condition whenever possible. Thus the sense of responsibility Brown felt to the scholarly world at large, a response impressed upon him by the large number of reference queries he received, made its presence felt in actual collecting decisions.

The library was known at this point as "la grande bibliothèque," a term that more accurately reflected its status among American libraries. In general, Brown's collecting policies followed those of his father, a retreat from the more ambitious policies his mother pursued. Nevertheless, Brown could be opportunistic and would bid at auctions when he could readily expand the library's holdings. The dispersal of several prominent libraries did permit Brown to expand the library's scope, as when he bought heavily in geographic and cartographic materials in the 1884 auction of Henry C. Murphy's library. As his father had been, Brown seemed to be reasonably hopeful that the library could be completed in his lifetime.

George Parker Winship became the first individual outside the Brown family's direct employ to be in a position to determine the library's direction. Winship had been interested in providing subject access to the collection even while he was the Brown family's private librarian and had also been interested in expanding its scope, although he was warned not to introduce too many "common books" onto its shelves. These interests continued when he assumed control of the library in 1904. Winship thus made certain crucial decisions about the library's direction, based on his knowledge of the collection. It was decided to leave the collecting of Rhode Island and other North American imprints to others and to concentrate on what were the library's unique strengths—early Spanish Americana and other European Americana. The terminus ad quem was set by Winship at 1801, a rigidity that had not been formally adhered to by the library's former owners. Winship also decided that the library would concentrate on printed material and even went so far as to transfer inappropriate material, such as early manuscript records of the City of Providence, Rhode Island, to other depositories. These libraries, in turn, did transfer some material to the John Carter Brown Library. By the time Winship departed for Harvard in 1915, he had doubled the library's original 12,000 volumes and had firmly set the library on the collecting course for which it is best known today.

The next two librarians, Burrage and Ford, did not materially alter the library's collection development, but the arrival in 1923 of Wroth marked yet another shift in the library's collecting patterns. Wroth believed in a syncretistic approach to the library's subject. Although one of his principle aims was "the perfecting of certain classes by the addition to them of important titles which for one reason or another were passed by in earlier years or which had not previously become available for purchase," his other chief goal was quite different, "the enlargement of fields partly or tentatively explored in earlier days and the establishment of new areas of interest." Thus, Wroth's most significant contribution was the expansion of the library's holdings in ancillary and background areas, such as cartographic history, geography, navigation, and mathematical sciences. (He also purchased maps in some quantity.) Wroth correctly realized that a proper understanding of these areas was necessary to the full understanding and interpretation of the voyages and travels that already filled the library's shelves. Wroth also aggressively expanded the library's collection of early Central and South American imprints. Here, again, the breakup of private libraries presented Wroth with excellent opportunities, as when he purchased fifty major Spanish Southwest titles at the 1940 sale of Herschel V. Jones's former library. Wroth also purchased the R. T. Haines Halsey collection of European engraved prints, thereby adding 258 prints depicting events or places in America. In Wroth's time, the library lost all fear of acquiring the "common book" against which Winship had been warned by the Browns.

Certain precedents for Wroth's collecting policies, particularly his expansion into ancillary areas, were already on the library's shelves, though examples of such material were hardly "common books." John Carter Brown, for example, had purchased in 1848 the Seville, 1519 edition of Enciso's *Suma de Geographia*, and John Nicholas Brown had purchased in 1893 a 1511 Maggiolo manuscript atlas of portolan charts and a 1543 Agnese manuscript portolan, the latter considered the finest example of Agnese's work. Although these items are, strictly speaking, Americana, they are more valuable for the information they contain on background areas such as geography and the history of cartography. They were, however, clearly purchased by the Browns as much for their inherent beauty and worth as "great books" as they were for their Americana content. Wroth sought to enlarge on this foundation by purchasing any book that would help interpret or complete the collections, no matter how "common" it might appear.

When Adams became librarian in 1957, he came into charge of a library that was manifestly strong but incomplete. Advances in bibliography and subject control of the field of Americana had amply demonstrated the breadth and depth of the field, which no amount of money could now hope to cover. Numerous booksellers had also become prominent in the field of Americana and offered more items than any one library could possibly hope to acquire. Adams was, therefore, faced with the problem of covering a rapidly expanding field with a limited financial base. He correctly realized that many of the "great books" were already in the library and that opportunity called elsewhere. He did, however, inherit a library that "demonstrates how the Library's collections are becoming more closely knit with each passing year," the major legacy of the Wroth era. In 1964, after the library reviewed its collecting policy, it was decided to discard the arbitrary terminus ad quem of 1801 that Winship had established and to substitute the concept that the library would collect through the colonial periods of each country in the Western Hemisphere. That decision allowed the library to expand into such areas as English and French abolition literature, where its holdings, previously all but nonexistent, now rival any such collection outside Europe and Great Britain. This policy also allowed expansion into the literature of the polar regions, the major benefit of which was the acquisition in 1966 of Bradford Swann's eminent collection of Antarctica.

Adams also continued the policy of purchasing collections when they allowed significant expansion of the library's base. For example, the library had collected architectural books for some years. Adams, however, acquired in toto an important private collection of architectural titles known to have been used in Colonial America. The library also bought heavily at the Streeter sale, realizing that this dispersal would be the end of an era and that it could no longer hope for the regular breakup of large, private Americana collections to fill its gaps.

The library during Adams's tenure also continued its policy of expanding aggressively into clearly defined, specialized collecting areas (Wroth called them "departments"), as opposed to the more diffuse policies and areas that had existed previously. Because of the expertise of Samuel Hough, the library's assistant librarian for many years, the library's collection of Italian Americana increased to major proportions. Its collection of architectural books used in British colonial North America has also grown to nearly comprehensive proportions, by building on the foundation Wroth established in this area. Finally, Adams expanded the library's collection in the sciences of shipbuilding and navigation. This concept of "cellular" acquisitions has been one of Adams's great

contributions to the library's collecting, particularly since it has been used to fill gaps, thereby better enabling researchers to approach the library's resources as a totality in the way that Wroth had envisioned.

Finally, Adams also expanded the library's collection of secondary and reference works. When he became librarian, he inherited a library that was somewhat lacking in the secondary sources necessary to interpret the materials, catalogue them, and guide acquisitions decisions. His pursuit of this previously neglected area of collection development has resulted in the formation of a reference collection that is nearly comprehensive in regard to the purposes of the library and its researchers.

Because the John Carter Brown Library has evolved through successive generations as an institution that seeks to document the American experience in only certain ways, its collecting patterns sometimes differ markedly from those found in libraries of more recent vintage. Various librarians and owners have brought to the library special interests that are revealed in the library's literature collection, such as John Carter Brown's interest in American literature, Lawrence Wroth's interest in Spanish literature, and Adams's interest in the literature of the American Revolution. The library does not own any "author collections" that seek to document an author's life or literary growth through extensive holdings of correspondence or manuscripts; has only very limited, specialized manuscript holdings; and has no archival material to speak of, except for its own archives and those of the Brown family business. The library has concentrated almost exclusively on acquiring the printed form of Americana, because that was the medium that passed America into public consciousness at large. The library has also generally limited itself to acquiring only those works that are proper Americana, thereby avoiding "inferential Americana," such as books merely read in the Americas or background books that just influenced writers about America without directly relating to the topic.

Only when it is approached in its totality may the library be properly appreciated as its collections pertain to the study of American and European literature of the Colonial period. The library does possess numerous individual works of imaginative literature, but its strength lies in its comprehensiveness, particularly in the breadth of the background sources that gave rise to the various literatures themselves. The library's strength in works printed before 1700 is especially important.

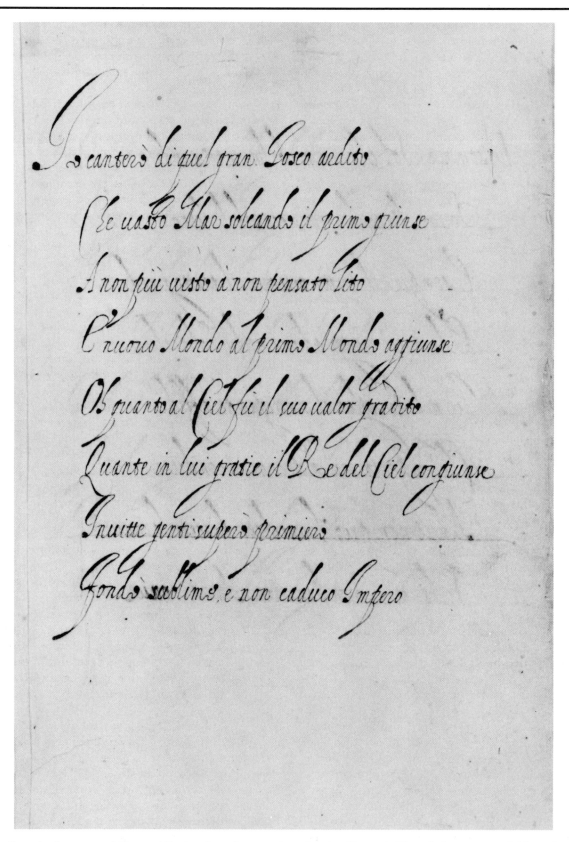

Page from the first canto of Giovanni Battista Strozzi's poem about Amerigo Vespucci. The only known copy of this work, which appeared before 1601 and is the first poem to use Vespucci as a subject, is at the John Carter Brown Library (courtesy of the John Carter Brown Library at Brown University).

The library's collection of early South and Central American authors, both native and imported, and of European authors printed there before 1700 is one of the more complete and distinguished in the United States and is set against a background of historical sources so rich that it is virtually without equal in its comprehensiveness. Numerous events in the conquest of the Spanish New World gave rise to literary reactions to those events, and the library has sought to collect especially in those areas. Particularly well represented are authors who put events of the conquest into literary form, works often read for their historical as well as their literary value. Such works as Juan de Castellano's *Primera parte de las elegias de varones ilustres de las Indias* (Madrid, 1589), Gaspar de Villagrá's *Historia de la Nueva México* (Alcala de Henares, 1610), Martín del Barco Centenera's *Argentina y conquista del Rio de la Plata* (Lisbon, 1602), and Bartolomé de Flores's *Obra nuevamente compuesta—* (Seville, 1571) are not only examples of poetry but of history versified. Other works of unquestioned literary status, such as Alonso de Ercilla y Zúñiga's *La Araucana* (Salamanca, 1574), often referred to as the *Aeneid* of Chile, are also on the library's shelves as part of the collection of early Spanish Americana.

Literature produced by the early Catholic clergy is also well represented in the library. Included in the collection are the unique copy of Julián Garce's *De Habilitate et capacitate gentium sive Indiorum Novi Mundi nucupati ad fidem Christi capessendam* (Rome, 1537), a crucial essay that argued that native American Indians were capable of being educated; and Alonso de la Veracruz's *Dialectica resolutio* (Mexico, 1554), which contains the first translation of a classical author to be published in the New World, preceding Keimer's Philadelphia, 1729 publication of Epictetus by 175 years. The library's copy is Veracruz's own, with annotations in his hand. The clergy's concern with indigenous American authors is well illustrated by the library's copy of Antonio de Saavedra Guzman's *El Peregrino Indiano* (Madrid, 1599), the first poetical work by a native Mexican to achieve publication. Among purely literary productions of the clergy are Juan Rodríguez de León's *Panegyrico augusto* (Mexico, 1639); Fernando de Valverde's *Santuario de N. Señora de Copacabana en el Perú* (Lima, 1641), an early bucolic in the style of Vergil, complete with nymphs and satyrs gamboling in the Peruvian Andes; Bernardo de Valbuena's *Grandeza Mexicana* (Mexico, 1604), a lyrical description of early Mexico City; and Francisco Corchero Carreño's *Desagravios de*

Christo en el triumpho de su cruz contra en Judaismo (Mexico, 1649), an elaborately illustrated, anti-Semitic verse history of Christ's life. The library owns a censored copy of the seventeenth-century Mexican savant Sigüenza y Góngora's *Triunpho Parthenico* (Mexico, 1683), which includes poems by various authors entered in the 1682 and 1683 competitions celebrating the Immaculate Conception, and a copy of his *Primavera Indiana* (Mexico, 1668), along with other works by this important American intellectual. Finally, the greatest American seventeenth-century Spanish female poet, Sor Juana Inés de la Cruz, Anne Bradstreet's rival for the title of "tenth muse," is well represented in both her literary works, such as *Fama, Poemas de la única poetisa Americana*, and *Villancicos*, and in her theological writings, such as *La Carta athenagórica*.

The library has also preserved a large number of occasional pieces from the earlier periods of Spanish activity in America. Numerous occasions such as the death of a prominent person, change in governmental leaders, installation of new clergy, and other significant events were memorialized by the publication of the *relación*, which described the proceedings. These proceedings, sometimes in the form of a *certamén poético* or a *máscara*, often included plays and poetry in addition to the expected speeches and sermons. Although many of the people who contributed to these processes are known only by their pieces as found in the *relaciones*, other, more prominent authors, such as Sor Juana, are often encountered in them. The library also has preserved large collections of *villancicos* and other ephemeral poetry. Included among these works are the Mexico 1657, 1659, 1660, and 1672 editions of the *Chanzonetas que se cantaron en la S. Yglesia Catedral de México*.

The eighteenth century saw the continuation of many of these themes and the introduction of others, especially those that arose from the succession of eighteenth-century wars. Religious impulses remained strong in Spanish America and were responsible for works such as Juan Carnero's *Métrica passión de el humanado Dios* (Mexico, 1729); Francisco de Castro's *La Octava maravilla* (Mexico, 1729), about the shrine at Guadelupe; the anonymous *Poético devocionario* (Mexico, 1793), religious verse about the stations of the cross; and José Agustín de Castro's *Acto de contrición* (Puebla, 1791). European literature republished in Spanish America includes Diego José Abad's *Musa Americana*, orignally published in Cadiz, 1769 in Latin but republished in Mexico, 1783 in an execrable Spanish translation; and Antonio de Escobar y Mendoza's *Nueva*

Jerusalen, published in Mexico both in 1758 and 1759.

In secular prosody, the century opened with Botello de Moraes e Vasconcelo's *El Nuevo mundo* (Barcelona, 1701), a poem that celebrated the conquests of the seventeenth century. Current events of the century are mirrored in the *Coloquio de Aristo y de Timandro* (Madrid, 1741); *Rasgo épico en que se decanta la feliz victoria* (Mexico, 1743), about the naval engagements at Guayra and Puerto Cabello in 1743; and González Maldonado's *Rasgo épico* (Mexico, 1760), occasional verse on local politics in Puebla. Purely literary activity was sustained by Bocanegra's *Canción famosa* (Mexico, 1755), which was republished several times; by Arriola's *Canción amorosa a un desengaño* (Mexico, 1755), also the first of several republications; and by Iriarte's *Música* (Mexico, 1785). The century closed as it had opened, with Escoiquez's *México conquistada* (Madrid, 1798), another poem about the conquest of Spanish America.

Literature by authors who have come to be regarded as United States authors (as opposed to British) has been collected only sporadically over the library's history. In the twentieth century, the library has largely abandoned this field to other institutions, such as the American Antiquarian Society. However, that is not to say that the John Carter Brown has no works by American authors. Because of a certain interest in this subject by various librarians and the efforts of Harold Brown, who collected works about religion in American life, the library does possess a respectable amount of American literature. The library owns several editions of Nathaniel Ward's *The Simple Cobbler of Aggawam in America,* an early satire that was quite popular. It also has a good collection of Ebenezer Cooke's poetry, including his *Sot-Weed Factor* (London, 1708), *Sotweed Redivius* (Annapolis, 1730), and *Mors omnibus communis: An Elegy on the Death of Thomas Bradley* (Annapolis, [1726?]), the last being the first poetry written and published in British North America south of Pennsylvania. It also owns the only known copy of John Markland's *Typographica* (Williamsburg, 1730), which contains the first poem written and published in Virginia. Among other unique copies of American works that the library holds is the only known copy of Rudolf Erich Raspé's *Gulliver Revived* (Brookfield, 1800). Also on the shelves is a copy of Roger Wolcott's *Poetical Meditations, Being the Improvement of Some Vacant Hours* (New London, 1725), the first volume of verse published in Connecticut and on the quality of which Tyler remarked, "For ourselves, we could

have been content, had his hours remained vacant." The library also possesses literary works composed by ministers, such as Cotton Mather's *Psalterium Americanum* (Boston, 1718), the first American translation of the Bible rendered into blank verse; Nathaniel Nile's *American Hero* (Norwich, 1775), a poem on the Battle of Bunker Hill; Mather Byle's *Poem on the Death of His Late Majesty King George* (Boston, 1727) and *Poems on Several Occasions* (Boston, 1744); and Timothy Dwight's *America* (New Haven, 1780), *Conquest of Canaan* (Hartford, 1785), *Dissertation on the History, Eloquence, and Poetry of the Bible* (New Haven, 1772), and *Greenfield Hill* (New York, 1794). Also included in these collections are such ephemera as Paul Dodge's *Poem Delivered at the Commencement of Rhode-Island College* (Providence, 1797), an occasional piece that represents the entirety of Dodge's literary career, *Muses' Address to the King* (London, 1728), *Night, a Poem* (London, 1728), *Zeuma; or, The Love of Liberty* (London, 1729), and *Sawney, An Heroic Poem* (London, 1728), an attack on Alexander Pope inspired by his *Dunciad.* Also on the library's shelves are numerous editions and translations of Joel Barlow's *Columbiad;* British editions of Jacob Ducheék's *Observations on a Variety of Subjects,* reprinted in Great Britain as *Caspapina's Letters;* an extremely rare French translation of David Humphrey's *Poem, Addressed to the Armies of the United States,* published as *Discours en vers, adressé aux officiers et aux soldats des differentes armées américaines* (Paris, 1786); and two rare British editions of *The Battle of Brooklyn, A Farce* (Cork, 1777 and Edinburgh, 1777). William Smith was the apparent author of a diatribe against Indian alcoholism originally published in New York in 1752 and twice republished in London in 1754 as *The Speech of a Creek Indian against the Immoderate Use of Spiritous Liquors* and *Some Account of the North American Indians,* both of which are on the library's shelves. Notable among the library's holdings of other Americans in Europe are editions of Helen Williams's *An Ode to Peace* (London, 1783) and *Peru* (London, 1784), which are complemented by other editions of her nonliterary works published while she traveled in Europe; of Thomas Paine's controversial works, including a copy of his *Common Sense* with manuscript corrections he dictated to his publisher during his stay in London; and of Benjamin Franklin's works, including "bagatelles" from his own press at Passy as well as more standard works, such as his autobiography.

The early imaginative literature about America by British authors is not so extensive as is its Spanish counterpart, because of the relatively late beginnings of English explorations in the New World. However, the background documents for early works are nearly comprehensive, and there are, as well, numerous distinguished examples of purely literary works written or published before 1700. In the realm of major British authors who wrote about America or lived there, the library owns the first edition of Humphrey Gilbert's *A Discourse of a Discoverie for a New Passage to Cataia* (London, 1576), which was seen through the press by George Gascoigne, who also contributed a sonnet to the work. Gilbert's work was the first publication of an English voyage by an explorer who actually tried to establish a colony in the New World. William Vaughan's *The Golden Fleece* (London, 1626), an attempt to promote his floundering Newfoundland colony, is the first English allegory set in America. Michael Drayton's *Poems* (London, 1619?) contains the first appearance of "Ode to the Virginian Voyage" as well as the immortal lines in "Idea" which begin, "Since ther's no helpe, Come let us kisse and part." Thomas Morton, in his *New English Canaan; or, New Canaan* (Amsterdam [London?], 1637), published the first extensive satire in English on the Massachusetts colony and established the "Peyton Place" genre as an American literary institution. It was followed by Nathaniel Ward's *A Trip to New England* (London, 1699), a quasi-factual satire so scurrilous that it is nearly unbelievable. The library also holds copies of the first four Shakespeare folios, wherein is contained *The Tempest,* a play set in the West Indies; numerous editions of Thomas Southerne's *Oroonoko, A Tragedy*; and several early editions of John Dryden's *The Indian Emperor; or, The Conquest of Mexico by the Spaniards.*

Minor British authors also found inspiration in the American experience, and their works reflect the impressions that the new discoveries made upon them. Richard Franck wrote *Northern Memoirs* (London, 1694), an excellent example of euphuistic literature, which has been described as "bombastic, stilted, and pedantic to a degree." Bacon's revolt in the Virginia colony provoked Aphra Behn to write *The Widdow Ranter; or, The History of Bacon in Virginia* (London, 1690), which is considered extremely valuable for the historic details of Bacon's insurrection. The developing religious events in the colonies also gave rise to poetic expression in Benjamin Antrobus's *Buds and Blossoms of Piety* (2d ed., London, 1691), which contains "A Complaint against the New-England Professors," and in Thomas Tryon's *A Dialogue between an East-Indian Brack-manny or Heathen Philosopher, and a French*

Gentleman (London, 1683), which concerns religious persecution. Francis Bugg satirized William Penn in *News from Pensilvania* (London, 1703). The perilous voyages to the New World also helped give rise to Nathaniel Boteler's influential *Six Dialogues about Sea Services* (London, 1685). The century even closed upon a literary note with the publication of the anonymous poem *Vox Britannia; or, The State of Europe* (London, 1701), which has numerous American references.

Several British authors who wrote in America but published in Britain are also represented on the library's shelves. Among them are Richard Franck, who visited America about 1690. While in the New World, he wrote *The Admirable and Indefatigable Adventures of the Nine Pious Pilgrims* (London, 1707) and *A Philosophical Treatise of the Original and Production of Things* (London, 1687). George Sandy's important translation of Ovid's *Metamorphoses* (London, 1626), the first translation of a Classical author to be done in British North America and the first poetry of any importance to be written there, is also on the library's shelves. Finally, the library also owns the first edition of Anne Bradstreet's *Tenth Muse* (London, 1650), the first volume of poetry published by a female author of arguably American extraction.

One particularly tragic event in British social experimentation was the failure of the Scots Darien colony, in present-day Panama. In addition to numerous serious political and philosophical considerations of this failed experiment, of which the library owns one of the larger collections in existence, there were, as well, several literary expressions concerning this event. Among works of this nature written early in the venture in the library are the anonymous *An Ode, made on the Welcome News of the Safe Arrival and Kind Reception of the Scottish Collony at Darien* (Edinburgh, 1699), a foolishly optimistic verse piece. When the colony's failure was obvious, satire abounded. Among such pieces are *Caledonia; or, The Pedlar Turn'd Merchant,* a tragicomedy on the settlement; *Captain Green's Last Conference with Captain Madder* (Edinburgh, 1705), a verse satire on the settlement; and Forbe's *A Pil for Pork-Eaters; or, A Scots Lancet for an English Swelling* (Edinburgh, 1705), a poem that addressed the proposed union of England and Scotland, written after the Darien settlement had clearly failed.

The progression of eighteenth-century events, riddled as they were with super-power rivalries, gave rise to numerous literary expressions, many of which are on the library's shelves. The series of wars fought over several seas and conti-

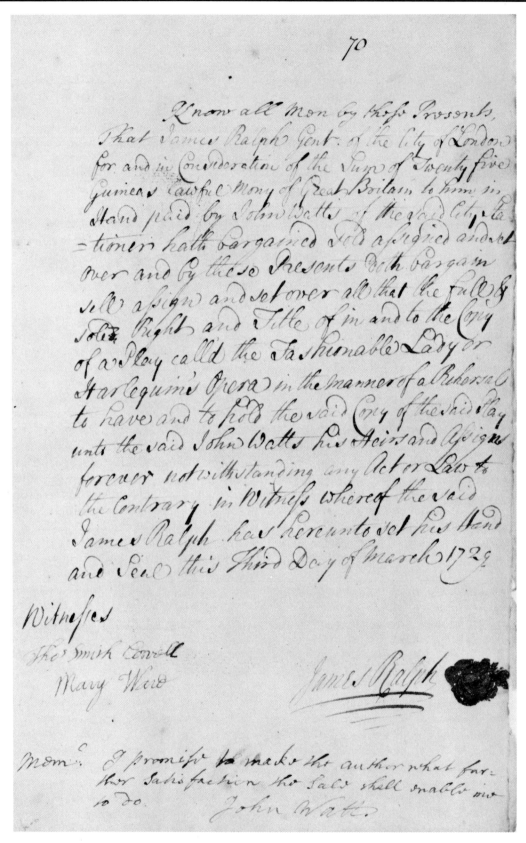

Agreement between James Ralph and publisher John Watts for publication of Ralph's play Fashionable Lady *(courtesy of the John Carter Brown Library at Brown University)*

nents, the most notable of which for American history is the so-called French and Indian War, inspired numerous authors. Among such examples in the library's collections are Thomas Martin's *A Poem on the War in the West-Indies* (London, 1742); *A Duel or No Duel; or, The Skirmish of the West-Indian Heroes* (London, 1743), a burlesque of Sir Charles Ogle's assault on Edward Trelawny, governor of Jamaica; Charles Carthy's *An Ode on the Present War with Spain* (London, 1740); Neville Valentine's *Reduction of Louisburg* (Portsmouth, 1758), a poem celebrating one of Britain's signal victories, written on the ship Orford in Louisbourg harbor; and George Cocking's *War, an Heroic Poem, from the Taking of Minorca by the French to the Reduction of the Havannah* (London, ca. 1760). The death of General Wolfe also provoked an outpouring of literary sympathy, including James Belsham's *Canadia* (London, 1760); George Cocking's *Conquest of Canada; or, The Siege of Quebec* (London, 1766), a five-act tragedy; and Elizabeth Forsyth's *Siege of Quebec; or, The Death of General Wolfe* (Strabane, 1789), a tragedy written later on the event.

No event in the British Colonies provoked such a literary outpouring, however, as the American Revolution. Even discounting such quasi-literary forms as polemics and spurious letters, the imaginative literature concerning the American Revolution is considerable, and the library owns numerous examples of it. Chief among its collections is one of the best assemblages of Richard Tickell's *Anticipation* and *The Green Box of Monsieur de Sartine*, two of the more famous satires written during this era. The library owns twenty-four separate English editions and foreign translations of these two works, published between 1778 and 1794, one of the larger such collections. These works naturally produced several spinoffs, such as *Anticipation Continued* (2d ed., London, 1779), *The Cabinet Conference* (London, 1779), *Deliberation* (London, 1779), *The English Green Box* (London, 1779), *Opposition's Mornings* (London, 1779), and *Anticipation for the Year MDCCLXXIX* (London, 1779), of which the library owns three 1779 editions.

The literary Revolutionary War was nearly as intense and as hard fought as the real one. Francis Brooke, in her famous novel *History of Emily Montague* (London, 1769), had described life in Canadian society on the eve of the Revolution; this novel was translated into French the following year and had a considerable vogue in France, because of interest there in the lost Canadian colonies. As the Revolution began in earnest, so did the literary wars. One of the opening shots was the anonymous

Civil War, A Poem ([London?], 1775), of which the John Carter Brown's copy is unique. As the war progressed, hopeful and not-so-hopeful literature was published. Among the rarer such literature in the library are Hugo Arnot's *The XLV. Chapter of the Prophecies of Thomas the Rhymer* (London, 1776), James Ogden's *The Contest* (London, 1776), Christopher Wells's *Address to the Genius of America* (London, 1776), James Murray's *The New Maid of the Oaks* (London, 1778), *Peace: A Poem* (London, 1778), Edward Burnaby Greene's *The Satires of Persius Paraphrastically Imitated* (London, 1779), and *Paul Jones; or, The Fife Coast Garland* (London, 1779). The *Congratulatory Poem on the Late Successes of the British Arms* (Dublin, 1776) celebrated the British victory in the Battle of Boston; it was soon followed by the anonymous *The Caledonian* (London, 1777), which condemned the Parliamentary minority for their support of the American rebels. Thomas Day contributed his support to the British cause with *The Devoted Legions* (London, 1776), and was seconded in his pro-British feelings by the anonymous *Reflections on the Present Combination of the American Colonies* (London, 1777), a satire on Congress that was republished in a more veracious guise as *Congress Unmasked* (London, 1781).

As the war progressed, however, and British arms did not readily prevail, causes for celebration faded in Great Britain. Robert Alves could rejoice in his *Ode to Britannia (for the Year 1780)* (Edinburgh, 1780) in the British success at Savannah and in Cornwallis's successes in the South; and British spy John André, before he lost his voice, could jest at General Wayne's problems in the Bull Ferry Affair in his *Cow Chace* (New York, 1780). Even naval disasters, such as Keppell's apparent defeat, could be celebrated, as in William Mason's *Ode to the Naval Officers of Great Britain* (London, 1779), which supported the Admiral against his detractors.

After 1779, however, not only the tenor of the actual battlefield but also that of the literary muse began to change. That year, Charles Henry Wharton published his *Poetical Epistle to His Excellency George Washington* (London, 1779), a complimentary piece. The following year John Farrar published his *America* (London, 1780); an anonymous author, writing as Harum Skarum, attacked British failures in *Account of a Debate in Coachmaker's Hall* (London, 1780). Samuel Jackson Pratt, sensing the futility of the situation, published his *Emilie Corbett; or, The Miseries of Civil War* (Dublin, 1780), the first novel on the American Revolution. Anna Seward lamented the late André in her *Monody on Major André* (Lichfield, London, Cambridge, Oxford, and Bath, 1781). Thomas Coombe's *The Peasant of Auburn; or, The Emigrant* (London, 1783), inspired by Goldsmith's *The Deserted Village*, depicted the hardships of a family that emigrated to America. Samuel Peters, a Loyalist who was tarred and feathered, published *A General History of the State of Connecticut* (London, 1781), an account so scurrilous and satiric that it is basically unbelievable. Francis Grose published his *Advice to the Officers of the British Army* (London, 1783), a satire on British efforts in North America. The anonymous *Chronicle of the Kingdom of the Cassiterides* (London, 1783) was in fact a history of the then-dismal American War disguised in the style of Jewish history. Despite such brave efforts at consolation as *The Naval Triumph* (London, 1783), which complimented Lord Rodney; the anonymous *Poems of the Several Successes in America* (1780); and John Robert's *Belloniad, An Heroic Poem, Dedicated to a Young Officer in the British Service* (London, 1785), which were pro-British, the British cause was, at that point, obviously lost. The British public no doubt agreed with the sentiments expressed by Helen Maria Williams, whose *An Ode on the Peace* (London, 1783) was once read aloud by Samuel Johnson in the author's presence.

The era closed with the anonymous *Poor Soldier, An American Tale* (London, 1789), a tale based in fact on the misfortunes of Charles Short, a Loyalist, which reflected the actual state of British fortunes at the time. One look back at former glories was provided by Henry Murphy, who published *Conquest of Quebec* (Dublin, 1790), a fond rearward glance at happier British successes in the New World. James Lowell Moore closed the century with an epic entitled *The Columbiad* (London, 1798), which recalled an era of successful conquests that the European powers would never see again in the Americas.

The wars and conflicts of the eighteenth century did not entirely eclipse normal literary activities, however, and other subjects connected with America besides war also gave rise to literary expressions. The introduction into Great Britain in 1710 of the Four Indian Kings from Canada gave rise to several poetic spinoffs, some of which persisted in various guises well into the late eighteenth century. Canada, which remained securely in British hands after the French and Indian War, also gave rise to literary endeavors. George Cartwright, who spent sixteen years in Labrador, wrote a large treatise on his experiences there which was complemented by his *Labrador, A Poetical Epistle* (Doncaster, 1785). The anonymous *An Ode, in Two Parts*

(London, 1760) also relates to Canada. B. Lacy, a mysterious figure, wrote *Miscellaneous Poems, Compos'd at Newfoundland* (London, 1729), which one critic has called "sad stuff."

The British possessions in the West Indies also provided a base for other literary endeavors, some of which were unrelated to the eighteenth-century wars. The practice of sending criminals to these islands provoked the anonymous *Elegy on the Murnful Banishment of James Campbel of Burnbank to the West-Indies* ([Edinburgh?], 1721), a poem on a celebrated banishment case. Henry Hulton, the Comptroller of Customs at Antigua and later Commissioner of Customs at Boston, was so moved by the death of one Mrs. Mitchell's husband that he wrote and published for her the consolation piece *A Poem, Addressed to a Young Lady* (Saint Johns, 1757), the circumstances of which are well documented because the library also has his holograph autobiography for the years 1751-1810. The islands occasioned Bryan Edwards's famous anthology *Poems Written Chiefly in the West-Indies* (Kingston, 1792) and Edward Rushton's *West Indian Eclogues* (London, 1788). The islands also furnished the backdrop for Richard Cumberland's famous comedy *The West Indian* (London, 1771).

British imagination was captured late in the century by the exploits of Captain Cook, whose tragic death was the occasion for several literary endeavors, and by the French Revolution, which occasioned more serious discussion than literary frivolity. In the first blush of excitement over Cook's exploits, Anna Seward published *Elegy on Captain Cook* (London, 1780). After word of Cook's death reached London, the anonymous *Death of Captain Cook* (London, 1789) put the story on the stage in a pantomine/ballet. At the end of the century, Thomas Hardy (1748-1798) took a fearful glance at the French Revolution and Thomas Paine's *Rights of Man* in his *The Patriot* (Edinburgh, 1793), in which the obvious raw nerves of the British empire are displayed.

Despite the numerous distractions the eighteenth century afforded Great Britain, the problem of slavery in the West Indies was one that persisted until 1833, when it was finally abolished by Parliament. The John Carter Brown's historical documentation of the British debate over slavery in its overseas possessions is extensive, and literary efforts to this end are also present. One of the earliest attacks on the ancien régime is the anonymous *Jamaica* (London, 1777), written in Jamaica and published at the height of the American Revolution. It was followed by Anna Letitia Barbauld's *Epistle to*

William Wilberforce (London, 1788), a conciliatory piece to the famous abolitionist consoling him on the defeat of an abolition bill then before Parliament. (Barbauld was frequently published in the United States as a children's writer.) The planters were also represented, however, by the anonymous *Abolition of the Slave Trade* (London, 1798), an attack on Wilberforce and the abolitionists.

Once the nineteenth century opened, however, the debate over abolishing the slave trade began in true earnest. Among the more famous authors in the collections are James Montgomery, who was chiefly responsible for the publication of *Poems on the Abolition of the Slave Trade* (London,

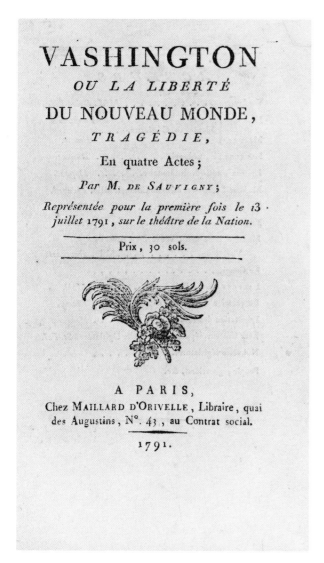

Title page of the first edition of Billiardon de Sauvigny's play about the French Revolution, in which George Washington is the protagonist (courtesy of the John Carter Brown Library at Brown University)

1809), an elegant, large-format book that was published to raise both money and sympathy for the abolition movement. Also present on the library's shelves are numerous editions of William Cowper's works, chief among which is the poem "The Task," which contains famous antislavery passages. The library also owns a copy of the abolitionist Suzanna Watts's *The Humming Bird* (London, 1825), a short-lived periodical edited and written by her; the library's copy is Watts's own with her annotations and corrections. There are also in the library numerous examples of occasional, ephemeral verse and stories that document the horrors of slavery and the slave trade. Numerous examples of these are preserved in the context of antislavery society "albums," which are made up of ephemeral literature. These literary works are found among hundreds of nonliterary pieces concerning the same subject.

The French literary response to the discovery of America was also vigorous and, at times, ingenious. The subject matter, particularly in the eighteenth century, often paralleled English themes, because of the wars fought between these two nations and their historic rivalries, often played out in part in North America. The library's collection of French literature is again set against a background of historic sources that seeks to be comprehensive.

Despite the turmoil that often occurred in North America, French literature often did not mention it. Gilles Boileau de Bouillon wrote *Les Sphères des deux mondes* (Anvers, 1555), the earliest French geography in verse that relates to America. One of these incidents is celebrated in the *Poème de six religieuses Ursulines qui se sont passées à la Martinique* (Paris, 1682), about the establishment of a convent on that island. Very early French poetry written in America is embodied in the various editions of Marc Lescarbot's *Histoire de la Nouvelle France* (Paris, 1609), which contains "Les Muses de La Nouvelle France." The library also holds several works by Gatien Courtilz de Sandras, who usually wrote under the nom de plume "Conte de Rochefort." Among his works that touch on America which are in the library are *Histoire de la guerre de Hollande* (The Hague, 1689), *Testament politique de Messire Jean Baptiste Colbert* (The Hague, [1694?]), and *Testament politique du Marquis de Louvois* (Cologne, [1695?]). Courtilz is best remembered because his quasi-truthful novels, which once landed him in the Bastille, are important precursors of the French *roman réaliste*.

Events of the eighteenth century drew forth

responses from some of the most important French literary figures of that time, who both commented directly on those events and used American themes as backdrops for other messages, particularly domestic, social, and political satire. Tales involving Indians or other exotic peoples were particularly popular. Voltaire wrote his famous satire, *L'Ingénu, histoire véritable* (Utrecht, 1767), which featured a Huron Indian and a Jansenist confined to the same cell in the Bastille, a situation that L. -S. Mercier stated to be one of the best conceived satiric juxtapositions in all of French literature until that time. Louis Le Maingre de Boucigault contributed *Les Amazons revoltées* (Rotterdam, 1737), a play that satirized historical writings. François d'Issembourg d'Happoncourt de Graffigny chose a converted Peruvian Indian princess living as a nun for the protagonist of his *Lettres d'une Peruvienne* (Paris, 1747), an epistolary novel famous for its insights into female psychology of the time. The library also owns the London, 1753, 1771, 1792 translations of this famous novel. The juxtaposition Voltaire had employed in *L'Ingénu* was taken up again in Maillet's *Telliamed* (Amsterdam, 1748), which featured an Indian philosopher and a French missionary. Jean Henri Maubert de Gouvest published two famous sets of spurious letters under the titles *Lettres Iroquoises* ([n. p.], 1752) and *Lettres Chérakéesiennes* (Rome, 1769).

As the American wars came and went, Indian themes continued to be employed. Chamfort (i. e., Nicolas-Sébastien Roch), a French moralist who eventually committed suicide rather than face the Terror, wrote his popular comedy *La Jeune Indienne* (Paris, 1764). Jean Marmontel again took up Voltaire's popular theme in *Le Huron* (Paris, 1768), which was based on Voltaire's *L'Ingénu*. Marmontel, however, looked to the experience of South American Indians as the inspiration for his popular *Les Incas* (Frankfurt & Leipsig, 1777), which satirized the Spanish for their brutal conquest of that South American Indian nation. This poem was translated into German (Frankfurt & Leipsig, 1783) and English (Dublin, 1777), both of which the library also owns. Pierre Duplessis also took up this theme in his tragedy *Pizarre; ou, La Conquête du Pérou* (Paris, 1785). Billardon de Sauvigny, another playwright, based his tragedy *Hirza* (Paris, 1767) on the Illinois Indians. The celebrated poet Saint Lambert also turned to Indian themes in his *Les Deux amix* (Paris, 1770), based on the Iroquois Indians, and in his popular short story "L'Abenaki," a pre-Romantic manifestation of the noble savage theme. Nothing is known of the anonymous author of the novel

Mémoires, vie, et aventures de Tsonnothouan, roi d'une nation indienne appellée les Têtes Rondes (Neuchâtel, 1787), which may have been mistaken in France for authentic, although it was in fact based on the English novel *Memoirs of the Life and Adventures of Tsonnonthouan* (London, 1763). The eighteenth century closed with the important *Veillées américaines* (Paris, 1795), which influenced Chateaubriand's *Atala*, and with *L'Européene sauvage* (Sables, 1797-1798), in which the circle closes in the story of Madame de Valville, who lives as an Indian for several years.

The series of wars that culminated in North America in the French and Indian War occasioned several celebrated works of literature. The English defeat at Carthagenà was responsible for the anonymous *Relation véritable et remarquable de je ne sçay quelle feste* ([Paris?], 1741), which satirized the English. Supposed English perfidy was the cause of two of the bitterest French pieces on the war. François Antoine de Chevrier satirized the English's deporting of the Acadians in *L'Acadiade; ou, Les Proüesses Angloises en Acadie* (Cassel, 1758). Antoine Léonard Thomas brought George Washington's name before the French public in his *Jumonville* (Paris, 1759), a frequently reprinted poem that bitterly criticized the future president for supposedly gunning down an unarmed French officer advancing under a flag of truce.

The period between the French and Indian War and the American Revolution saw the publication of Jacob Nicolas Moreau's *L'Observateur Hollandois* (The Hague, 1755), of which the library also owns the rare Portuguese translation (Lisbon, 1757). Marie Ann Figuet Duboccage anticipated Barlow with the publication of her *La Colombiade* (Paris, 1756), a popular poem translated into German (Glogau & Leipsig, 1762) and Italian (Milan, 1771), both of which the library also owns. The scatological Simon Nicolas Henri Linguet, taking his inspiration from Voltaire, published *La Cacomonade, ouvrage postume du Docteur Pangloss* (London & Paris, 1767), a satire with American references throughout.

The American Revolution itself gave rise to numerous works, many of them in a more celebratory vein than previous French works on the American wars. Jean Bochart Champigny commented on the war in the South in his poem *Louisiane ensanglantée* (London, 1773). The beginnings of the war were discussed in the anonymous *Entretiens de Guillaume de Nassau, Prince D'Orange, et du Général Montgommery* ([Paris?], 1776). French naval victories were celebrated in Longueville's *Ode à l'océan, sur la guerre* (2d ed., Agen 1781) and Jean Digard de Kergüette's *Le Trident* (Paris, 1781). The famous case of Asgill, a British prisoner, was the subject of J. L. Le Barbier's *Asgill* (Paris, 1785) and later of Benoît Joseph Marsollier des Vivetières's *Arnill* (Paris, 1797), the latter a comedy. (Marie Antoinette was supposed to have intervened with Washington to spare Asgill's life after he was convicted of spying.) Washington was celebrated in Billardon de Sauvigny's famous play *Vashington; ou, La Liberté du nouveau monde* (Paris, 1791), a piece that is really about the nascent French Revolution. Lafayette's amorous troubles were reviewed in Jean-Baptiste Poupart de Beaubourg's *Triomphe du beau sexe* (Boston, 1778), a supposed poetic epistle from Lafayette expressing his frustrations over his affair with Charlotte Gabrielle Elisabeth Aglae. The apparent defeat of Great Britain and the fact of the American independence brought forth a spate of celebratory verse, among them L. de Chavannes de la Giraudière's *L'Amérique délivrée* (Amsterdam, 1783) and Le Normand de Losier's *Ode sur la conquête de l'Amérique* (Le Havre, 1786).

The American Revolution produced a prodigious amount of French satire, some of which remains famous today. Among the works of this type in the library are Mathieu François Pidanzet de Mairobert's *L'Espion anglois* (London, 1779) and his *L'Observateur anglois* (London, 1777-1778). Ange Goudar, another satirist, contributed *Le Procès des trois rois* (London, 1780), which was translated into Dutch (Ostende, 1780) and German [n.p.], 1782) and followed by a supplement, *L'appel au Pape*. This mock trial features an appearance by Benjamin Franklin, who is also shown in the book's frontispiece. One Delauney wrote *L'Histoire d'un pou françois; ou, L'Espion d'une nouvelle espèce* (Paris, 1779), a satire with American references. The shadowy Baudouin de Guémadeuc assembled a satirical anthology on the American War entitled *L'Espion dvalisé* (London, 1782), which is important because it reprints the "Lettre du Comte de Chambourg," a trenchant satire on the Hessian mercenaries that was once attributed to Franklin.

Italian literature treating of the Americas has been an important part of the library's collections since the days of John Carter Brown. The library holds numerous factual, historical works by Italians or printed in Italy, beginning with the American Ur document, contemporary printings of the Columbus letter, of which the library's collection is one of the world's larger. This collection of early works is complemented by equally strong holdings of Amerigo Vespucci's *Mundus Novas* and Pietro Martire d'Anghiera's *Libretto*.

Italian literature dealing with the Americas arose in somewhat lesser quantity than that of other European nations. One of the chief figures of the early literature was Amerigo Vespucci, whose reputation was eclipsed by that of Columbus. Among the library's literary holdings concerning the man for whom America was named is the unique manuscript by Giovanni Battista Strozzi of the first poem known to use Vespucci as a subject. Raffaelo Gualterotti wrote the earliest known printed piece on Vespucci, *L'America* (Florence, 1611), but because Cosimo Medici II's patronage was not forthcoming, only the first stanza, which was the "prospectus," was ever printed. Better success was enjoyed by Girolamo Bartolomméi Smeducci, whose *L'America* (Rome, 1650) runs to over 500 pages.

Some Italian contributions to American literature are more obscure than mere writings about America. For example, a Silvio Stampiglia opera, first performed in Naples in 1699, became the first opera of any sort performed anywhere in America when it was done in Mexico City in 1711. The text and translation, Italian and Spanish on facing pages, was published as *La Partenope fiesta* (Mexico, [1760?]). Francesco Geminiani, an Italian composer and violinist living in London, contributed to British North American culture the first printed instructions for playing the violin when his *An Abstract of Geminiani's Art of Playing the Violin* (Boston, 1769) was published in Massachusetts, of which the library holds the unique copy. Other notable library holdings include a manuscript copy of Vittorio Alfieri's "La Guerra d'America" (ca. 1783), which was published as *L'America libera* (Kehl, 1787). The library also possesses numerous Italian editions of American authors, notably Benjamin Franklin, whose writings attracted a large following in Italy. Several such editions of American authors are contained in such publications as *Scelta di opuscoli interessanti* (Milan, 1776), which published Italian translations of various European and American authors.

The library's holdings of German Americana are reputed to be among the most extensive in existence and are especially strong in early historical works by German authors, such as Martin Waldseemüller's *Cosmographiae Introductio* (Saint Dié, 1507), in which was the first appearance in print of the name "America" applied to the New World. Among the library's holdings are Hartmann Schedel's *Liber Chronicarum* (Nuremberg, 1493), the first best-seller in the Western World, and Sebastien

First bill from the antiquarian book dealer Henry Stevens to John Carter Brown (courtesy of the John Carter Brown Library at Brown University)

Brant's *Stultifera Navis*, the first purely literary work to mention the discovery of America. Brant also contributed a panegyric to Carolus Verardus's *In Laudem Serenissimi Ferdinandi* (Olpe, 1494), which is also in the library. Francis Drake's first appearance in German literature is represented by the excessively rare broadside *Franciscus Draeck Nobilissimus eques Angliae* ([Germany?, ca. 1588]), which contains a German poem about the exploits of the English adventurer. Among later German authors in the collection are Johann Gottlob Benjamin Pfeil, whose novel *Der Wilde* is present in Mercier's translation as *L'Homme sauvage* (Paris, 1767), and August Friedrich Ferdinand von Kotzebue, of whose play *Der Spanier in Peru* the library holds numerous editions.

Because of the library's cross-cultural emphasis, it has accumulated significant genre collections that cut across national boundaries. One of the more important of these is its collection of imaginary voyages and utopian writings and their antecedents that concern America or are set there. Although the library does not attempt to compete with stronger collections for such obvious Americana as Daniel Defoe's *Robinson Crusoe* and Jonathan Swift's *Gulliver's Travels*, its holdings in this genre are nevertheless extensive.

Among the early antecedents of the imaginary voyage, the library numbers an extensive collection of Nuñez Cabeza de Vaca's *Relación* (2d ed., Valladolid, 1555), which may or may not be the first account of a pedestrian journey by a European across any part of the present-day western United States. Among voyages once widely believed to be true but now discounted are Nicolò and Antonio Zeno's *Dei Commentarii del viaggio in Persia* (Paris, 1558), which contains the account of their supposed 1380 journey to Labrador and Greenland; and Henry Neville's *Isle of Pines* (London, 1668), of which the library has several editions, including the recently acquired unique Swedish translation, *Een Sanfärdigh Relation* ([n. p., 1668?]). Also present are several editions of Sir Thomas More's *Utopia* and a copy of Seneca's *Tragoedia* (Venice, 1517), which contains in the play "Medea" the famous prophecy of the discovery of new, western lands, a prophecy Columbus's son later noted that his father had fulfilled.

Other voyages that may or may not combine fact with fiction are Charles de Rochefort's *Histoire naturelle et morale des iles Antilles* (Rotterdam, 1658), which contains the description of the Kingdom of Apalache, the first utopian vision set in an actual place in America and represented seriously as rest-ing on a factual basis; and Durand de Dauphiné's *Voyage d'un françois exilé pour la religion* (The Hague, 1687), a partially true account of a Huguenot's peregrinations in Europe and America in search of religious freedom. The literature of "adventure," which often involved voyages to and adventures in America, is represented, for example, by numerous editions and translations of Alexandre Olivier Exquemelin's *De americaensche zee-rovers* (Amsterdam, 1678). This book and its numerous translations, all genuine best-sellers at the time, along with John Mitchell's *A Full Account of the Proceedings in Relation to Capt. Kidd* (London, 1701) and Daniel Defoe's *A General History of the Robberies and Murders of the Most Notorious Pyrates* (London, 1724), firmly established the romance of the pirate and freebooter in the European mind and gave rise to numerous later novels, such as Robert Louis Stevenson's *Treasure Island*. The ultimate imaginary voyage is exemplified by Sor María de Jesús de Agreda's "Redondez de la tierra y de los abitadores de ella," a manuscript that gives credence to her claims that she was transported to the New World over 500 times to witness to the Indians. Equally interesting is the anonymous *Conference between a Bensalian Bishop and an English Doctor* (London, 1681), a satire in the form of a relation of a voyage to a previously unknown land near China.

The eighteenth century was the great century for this genre, however. Among the library's holdings in this century are several voyages to or descriptions of "Utopia," such as *Canary-Birds Naturaliz'd in Utopia* (London, 1709), actually a verse satire on the Act for Naturalizing Foreign Protestants, and *Relation d'un voyage de l'Isle d'Eutopie* (Delft, 1711). Among the great eighteenth-century masters of the genre, the library holds numerous editions of William Rufus Chetwood's *Voyages, Dangerous Adventures and Imminent Escapes of Captain Robert Boyle;* Antoine François Prévost's *Le Philosophe anglois*, which recounts the adventures of a supposedly bastard son of Oliver Cromwell; Alain René Le Sage's *Les Aventures de Monsieur Robert Chevalier*, who was born near Montreal and raised by Iroquois Indians; Simon Tyssot de Patot's *Voyages et aventures de Jacques Massé* and his *La Vie, les aventures, & le voyage de Groenland du Révérand Père Cordelier Pierre de Mesange* (Amsterdam, 1720), the latter being the first French imaginary voyage to the Arctic. It is complemented by the anonymous *Relation d'un voyage du Pole Arctique par le centre du monde* (Paris, 1723). Also on the shelves is James Burgh's *An Account of the First Settlement, Laws, Form of Government, and Police, of the Cessares, a People of*

South America. Lord Anson's voyage inspired Gabriel François Coyer's *A Discovery of the Island Frivola* (London, 1750), a satire on the French nation. The impending American Revolution inspired *Private Letters from an American in England to His Friends in America* (London, 1769), which shows America as the seat of government and Britain practically deserted. It was followed by Thomas Lyttleton's *Poems by a Young Nobleman* (London, 1780), which also assumes British ruin and is in the form of a letter written from a ruined Saint Paul's in 2199. Finally, the library's holdings of Louis-Sébastien Mercier's *L'An deux mille quatre cente quarante* (Amsterdam, 1771), the first modern utopian novel, are among the more extensive in existence.

The library's holdings of European and South American periodical literature printed before 1833 are also significant because a great amount of literary Americana was often published in such formats. Significant examples of such material are the library's runs of the British *Gentlemen's Magazine* (to 1827) and *The Annual Register* (to 1835), both of which have been disturbed only by being bound. Its holdings of the *Gazeta de Lima*, the *Gazetas de México*, *Mercurio Peruana*, the *Gazeta de literatura de México*, and the *Correio Braziliense* are among the most extensive in the world. The library also holds several German periodicals, among them runs of *Der Teutsche Merkur* and its continuation *Der Neue Teutsche Merkur*, the *Historische verhael*, the *Hamburgisches Magazin*, *Chronologen*, and *Wöchentliche Nachrichten*. Many of these are still in their publisher's wrappers and are pristine bibliographical examples.

The John Carter Brown Library also has a distinguished history of contribution to scholarship through its own publications. Chief among these are the library's catalogues, the first two editions of which were published while the library was still in private hands. Not only did these catalogues present to the world the expansiveness of the Brown's holdings, but they also set high standards of bibliographical description that everyone attempted to emulate. The library has continued in this tradition, established by Bartlett in the first catalogue, and now reports its holdings, still described as the highest bibliographical standards, to the Research Libraries Information Network (RLIN).

The library's catalogues are complemented by the numerous exhibition catalogues that have been put out over the years. Some of these catalogues have been so rich and extensive that they themselves set collecting standards for others in the field and have contributed much original research to the field of Americana. Among the library's catalogues that have chronicled its own growth as an institution are *In Retrospect* (1949), *A Collection's Progress* (1968), *Libros Virumque Cano: Gaudeamus* (1970), *The Italians and the Creation of America* (1980), and *The Great Subject, 'La Grande Bibliothèque', and the John Carter Brown Library* (1982). Subject catalogues that have made contributions to the field they documented include *The Colonial Scene* (1950), *Mirror of the Indian* (1958), *The French and Indian War: An Album* (1960), *The New Found Land: The English Contribution to the Discovery of America* (1965), *The British Look at America During the Age of Samuel Johnson* (1971), and *The Spanish Church and the New World in the Golden Age* (1983).

Justifiably famous among the library's publications in the rare book world are its annual reports, issued between 1901 and 1966. Especially during Wroth's tenure, these reports became more than mere dry recitations of facts and figures about acquisitions and finances. Wroth's polymathic interests and knowledge uniquely qualified him to compose annual reports that became models of their genre and made substantial contributions to the world of rare book and Americana scholarship. Toward the end of his tenure, Wroth required more than three months to write each report, and Adams, faced with the challenges of managing a library that was rapidly modernizing and expanding, had little choice but to cease writing them so that he could turn his energies to more pressing, immediate matters. Nevertheless, the annual reports, still available in reprint, were, for more than sixty years, looked forward to with great anticipation by the world of rare book scholars and librarians. They may still be read with profit.

The library has also pursued a publication program that seeks to make available to scholars reprints of its material and various scholarly articles, a goal that has been pursued since the library was in private hands. These publications include *Psalterium et Cantica* (1887), *The Influence of William Morris and the Kelmscott Press* (1912), *The First Printing in South America* (1926), *The John Carter Brown Library Conference* (1961), and *The Blathwayt Atlas* (1973-1975).

Currently under the direction of Norman Fiering, who has been director since 1983, the library is looking toward 1992 and beyond. *European Americana*, an ambitious bibliography begun by John Alden, is approaching publication of its third volume, which covers European works about America published 1701-1725, under the direction of Dennis Landis. This work is complemented by a detailed catalogue of the library's holdings of German Americana, a work in preparation under the direction of Ilse Kramer. The library also acts as a clearinghouse for information about and publicity for events and publications commemorating Columbus's discovery of the New World. Two recent grants from federal agencies have enabled the library to expand its cataloguing department and to begin work on an addition to the present building, which will also be renovated.

Contempo Caravan
Kites in a Windstorm

Tony Buttitta

Contempo was conceived during one of the darkest periods of the Depression. We have a record of the date: 28 February 1931. It's on the program of an experimental play which stirred up a theater controversy on the Chapel Hill campus. The drama was *Playthings*, Pirandello-inspired, which contrasted sharply with the fare of folk plays put on by the Carolina Playmakers. That Saturday night five of us, including the author and two backstage workers, celebrated at the Waffle Shop. Without homebrew or moonshine but, lit up by the afterglow of the event, we got just as high on waffles and pots of coffee, and the celebration blossomed into an all-night bull session instead of a campus caper or a brawl.

Much of our talk went up with cigarette smoke, but in flashes of imagination, analysis, and youthful bravado, we cursed and griped about conditions, literary, social, economic, then swapped ideas and hopes on how to set them straight. By dawn vague plans had taken on the aura of a dream reality: nothing struck us as impossible. Not even the launching of a new literary magazine—the last thing anybody might want when banks were folding, farms were foreclosed, brokers peddled apples instead of stocks on Wall Street, and little magazines vanished like kites in a windstorm.

We five had met in a philosophy class and shared a genuine admiration for our professor, Paul Green, a North Carolinian Pulitzer Prize-winner for *In Abraham's Bosom*. Green was our campus hero, a poet and playwright: a warm, outgoing,

Tony Buttitta and Langston Hughes at Chapel Hill, fall 1931 (courtesy of Tony Buttitta)

encouraging, and inspiring man from the tobacco belt with no academic or professorial pretensions. Leaning pensively against the table and running a hand through his shock of wavy dark hair, Green spoke softly about the relation of philosophy and aesthetics to the writings of Dostoyevski, Stendhal, and Joyce; he gave us the floor to sound off on relevant and timely issues rising out of his rambling remarks. We cursed the closing bell, lingered to chat with him or each other, dreading to proceed to our modern lit class where we could doze while the high-collared prof spoke from his yellowed notes that stopped with the Victorians.

The most colorful of the trio involved with *Contempo* was Shirley Carter, the assistant stage manager. He was a lyric and dramatic poet with wavy blond hair and a John Barrymore profile whose verses had been praised by Sherwood Anderson, then living in Carter's native Virginia. Vincent Garoffolo, flyman of the production, was a Newark student of the French decadents and Dada experimenters. Tony Buttitta, who wrote the play, had come up from Louisiana to do graduate work and practice playwriting with the Carolina Playmakers. The other two were Phil Liskin, a New Rochelle, New York, tennis champ whose sights were set on a Moscow match; and Milton Abernethy, of Hickory, North Carolina, who had been tossed out of the state college in Raleigh for his challenging editorial against campus military training, and who hoped to run a bookshop in a university town.

Some of our friends, there and elsewhere, scoffed at the idea of starting a literary magazine when what the country most needed in those desperate times was a good nickel cigar. Though on the fringe of farms, mills, and factories, we were not sheltered from economic problems in the serene, tree-lined campus of the University of North Carolina. Yet, with small monthly checks from home, our main concerns were the impact of Thomas Wolfe's recently published *Look Homeward, Angel*, the folksy offerings of the Playmakers, the hash at Swain Hall, and the availability of bootleg likker and girls in Durham.

The moment we settled on *Contempo* as the name—it was suggested by Buttitta, who got it from the title of a recent volume of black-and-white drawings by the illustrator John Vassos—the magazine took on a reality of its own. As we printed the word on scraps of paper, it stood out as something tangible—a charm that would help us find the answers to such questions as policy, contents, audience, financing. While speculating on them, we questioned why we were at the university and where we were heading—other than toward the dead end of the Depression.

Facing those more basic issues, we seemed to shed our dilettante liberal arts stance and slipped into an area of creative action, independence, and responsibility. *Contempo*, despite its countless pitfalls, or perhaps because of the challenge they presented, jolted our vague aims and energies into focus to create a place for ourselves. Who knows, we must have thought, the magazine might even show us a way out of the nation's debacle. Finally, as we parted Sunday morning with the feeling that *Contempo* was our answer to the times, the sun greeted us with news of an early spring.

Sunday afternoon we met—without Phil the tennis champ—in Milt Abernethy's sun-splashed room in one of the stately old ivy-draped dorms reserved for native sons. Books were everywhere. The small bookshelf yawned with them, spewing books on the floor, under the bed, and into the bathroom. They were mostly remainders of new books by established and avant-garde writers which had been dumped by their publishers, and Abernethy had gotten them from a New York outlet house for about fifty cents a copy.

We glanced at the piles and then at each other, nodding, and then suddenly we burst into laughter at the same moment. There was the answer to our problem of financing *Contempo*. It was as though Abernethy had it in the back of his mind to have a magazine as a sideline with a bookshop. Such an arrangement was not surprising; there had been previous ventures of bookshop, periodical, and publisher under one roof. In fact, early booksellers were among the first publishers who carried, in addition to their own books, those of other publishers.

When we were through laughing Abernethy said he was delighted with the prospect of turning over his collection for a bookshop to subsidize the magazine. We soon realized, however, that we would need more than a stock of remainders to attract customers to the shop. That was resolved when someone suggested that we use review copies—those that publishers would send us to be reviewed in *Contempo*—to feature on a shelf of new books and best-sellers.

Now that a bookshop was in our plans, we needed a name for it. Many were mentioned and tossed about until Buttitta came up with another winner: The Intimate Bookshop. This was no more original with him than *Contempo*; he had recently read an article about an "intimate theater" in *The-*

The Intimate Bookshop after redecorating in 1932. Milton Abernethy, seated at left; Tony Buttitta, third from right (courtesy of Tony Buttitta).

atre Arts Monthly. If that was the latest thing in theater, we decided it might be just the thing for a new literary bookshop which would appeal to the audience for our new little magazine.

We soon realized the bookshop could serve as a base of operation for both ventures and tackled them simultaneously. While the others prepared material, Abernethy would contact writers he admired such as Norman Thomas, Upton Sinclair, and Lewis Mumford for articles; Buttitta would find a site for the bookshop, canvas advertisers, and make arrangements with the printer. He had acquired some experience in these matters in connection with the programs for his play.

Before making another move, we dropped in on Paul Green, explained what we had in mind, and invited him to be one of our first contributors. He was delighted and did not try to discourage us, though he was on the editorial board of *Agora,* a magazine of the South being published in Chapel Hill, doomed to fold that spring. Also encouraging

was Phillips Russell, his brother-in-law, who taught a creative literature course at the university, and had written biographies of Franklin and Emerson; he promised us a sketch from his forthcoming book, *Harvest Men.*

When Green asked about our policy, we replied in a roundabout way that we hoped to produce an independent little review of ideas and personalities. It should be relevant to the pertinent issues of the day, without losing sight of the best new writing available to us—experimental or otherwise. Though our emphasis would be on the social and economic rather than the "arty," we aimed to carry on the pioneering spirit of Margaret Anderson's *Little Review,* which first gave us *Ulysses;* New Orleans's *Double Dealer,* which introduced William Faulkner; the American expatriates' *Broom, Secession,* and *This Quarter;* and Eugene Jolas's *transition,* the pantheon of avant-garde literature, which had published the leading international writers of the time. Now that those reviews were in limbo (except *transition,* which had temporarily suspended publication), we would solicit many of the writers for contributions—making it clear we had a policy of not paying for material—as soon as *Contempo* made its debut.

We skipped most of our classes, except Paul Green's, where we met to discuss developments. In our search for material, we learned from Green that we might get poems from Lynn Riggs and George O'Neil, who were staying at the Carolina Inn. Riggs was in town to read his *Cherokee Night* at the Playmakers; he had written *Green Grow the Lilacs,* a modest Theatre Guild success which was later turned into the musical *Oklahoma!* We knew O'Neil as a sensitive poet who appeared in various journals, and for a time was to edit Harriet Monroe's *Poetry* magazine.

We hastily made up a dummy of *Contempo*— a large sheet folded to form four pages, twelve by nineteen inches, and divided into three wide columns to the page. While Abernethy and Garoffolo called on the two writers, Buttitta collected for the ads that had financed the play's program, and went to pay his bill at the Orange Printshop and get an estimate for the printing of *Contempo.* Louis Graves, editor of the *Chapel Hill Weekly,* looked over our dummy and figured it would cost $26 for the first thousand. When Graves agreed to use good heavy stock, Caslon type, and to trust us to pay him, we shook hands on the deal.

The deal gave *Contempo* such a reality that we immediately set May first as the deadline for our first issue. Material trickled in from writers and, though some struck us as not being their best, we welcomed it all with a growing anticipation. We passed on it, edited it, and took it to the print shop. In the meantime Buttitta made the rounds of village stores and shops for ads. It was not as easy as before; merchants complained of business being slow and in some cases we agreed to take the ads out in trade. Bartering was a popular practice during the Depression, and we fell in with it.

Finally, with the corrected proofs back from the print shop, we laid out the dummy of our first issue in Ab's cluttered quarters. On the front page we pasted down the poems by Riggs and O'Neil, flanking an article by Norman Thomas on his timely new book *America's Way Out.* This was the first of a series of "authoreviews," a form we had hit upon to get name writers to use *Contempo* as a sort of open forum to answer critics and explain their latest books. The form was to attract so much attention in literary circles that a magazine soon appeared in New York featuring such reviews and calling itself the *Author Review.*

We all wrote something to fill the remaining pages—without bylines: an editorial attacking the Irish censor for condemning new American novels along with Dublin's *Ulysses,* two poems by our own poet Shirley Carter, an article on decadent literature, an advance puff on the Intimate Bookshop as a haven for the latest in international avant-garde literature, a report of the local movie guild which sponsored such films as *Ten Days That Shook the World,* and an invitation to readers to let us know what they thought of *Contempo.*

In the meantime we found the perfect location for the bookshop in the two-story Tankersly building, adjacent to the post office and across the campus. A hall ran down the middle of the second floor; offices were on both sides, all empty except the front two occupied by a dentist and a lawyer. We chose a large corner room at the rear which looked down on the garbage pails of the Cavalier Cafeteria, one of our advertisers, where we took ads out in trade. We got the rent down to fifteen dollars a month, paid in advance by Abernethy and Buttitta, and promised the landlord his asking price of twenty-five dollars when we could afford it.

We cleaned up and furnished that back room and hoped to have it ready by the time our first issue appeared. We begged, borrowed, and improvised: bookshelves, desks, a narrow couch, and a couple of chairs. We carried cartons of books from Ab's dorm and filled the shelves by authors and subjects, displaying them to advantage. Friends lent us pictures and prints to cover the bare plaster walls, and a Playmakers technician worked wonders with tricky indirect lighting for our late hours.

The Intimate Bookshop was not yet open for business when we brought up two bundles, and the oily smell of fresh print mingled with the fumes of roast beef rising from the cafeteria. We each took a copy and studied it, commenting on its contents and appearance, and speculating about how we could improve it. We didn't think too much of it but were pleased enough to mail copies to relatives and friends, hoping they would reply with $1.50 for a year's subscription; and to our favorite writers, inviting them to send anything that was close to their hearts and they could not place. We also mailed copies to the literary editors of the New York dailies and the *Saturday Review of Literature* for possible mention or review, and a bundle to Frances Steloff to sell in her Gotham Book Mart, the New York rendezvous of the avant-garde literati.

That night we spread copies around the village and stuffed mailboxes of students and professors. At classes the next morning there was no reaction, except from our friends who were kind. Two days later at the bookshop opening we were greeted by a throng of well-wishers from all over the campus who had come more out of curiosity to see what we were up to than with cash to buy books or to subscribe. We also received letters commenting on *Contempo*. While one encouraged us "to keep up the good work," another, after congratulating us "for having the nerve and verve" to start it, called us "zanies, tyros, dilettantes, and panjandrums."

With our second number the emphasis on social issues was more evident. Sinclair Lewis, in a letter praising Louis Adamic's *Dynamite*, an explosive study of the American labor movement, said that "our contemporary violence and crime was only the outcome of capitalistic greed and . . . sentimentalism on the part of labor leaders." Our lead editorial backed the "robbed, cheated, degraded" miners of Harlan, Kentucky, in their battle with sheriffs who had been ordered "to shoot to kill." There was a note on the case of the Scottsboro boys, whose death sentence in Alabama had aroused the fury of Theodore Dreiser, Lincoln Steffens, and John Dos Passos.

We balanced the controversial tone with a rambling "Travel" piece by Sherwood Anderson, reporting what he saw while driving down "the land of blossoming peach orchards and into the land of cotton"; an amusing theater bit with reference to Paul Green and the Playmakers; and a lengthy review of a biography of Jefferson Davis. There were five poems—one by our staff poet, another by Moishe Nadir, then considered the greatest living Yiddish poet. We called attention to the newly opened Intimate Bookshop and advertised specials on classics and recent fiction from 45¢ to $2.10.

Though *Contempo* was never a campus publication, our third number carried more than a page of ads to greet the opening of the university summer session. This was due to our friendship with Dr. Frank Porter Graham, who had been our history professor before becoming president of the university. In that issue we printed an official bulletin of the week's events and a message from President Graham as our lead editorial. In it he spoke "of the terrible economic conditions in the state and country" and the "radical budget proposals" of the state legislature to cut the salaries of teachers and professors as being "destructive to schools, colleges, and the public welfare."

That number veered leftward with a short story by Louis Colman, a young proletarian writer from the Northwest, and poems by Ralph Cheyney, Lucia Trent, and Norman MacLeod, who were members of Rebel Poets and edited such radical magazines as *Left* and *Unrest*. There was a review by Claude G. Bowers, political historian and keynote speaker at the National Democratic Convention in 1928; also an item on the fracas between Toscanini and the Italian fascists over his refusal to conduct "Giovinezza," their national hymn, before performances at La Scala; and another on a bill pending in the Pennsylvania legislature to penalize publishers found guilty of protecting ghost writers.

When this issue was released, a bright lad working his way through the university offered to handle a campus subscription drive during registration week for summer school. When he reported having sold about a hundred subscriptions the first day, we became suspicious and learned that the enterprising chap had placed a table at the end of the registration line and created the impression—with President Graham's editorial—that *Contempo* was an official campus publication to which they *had* to subscribe. Because of its controversial contents, this occurrence later got us and the university into hot water with the conservatives and especially with Dave Clark, who blasted the liberal policy of the university as editor of the *Southern Textile Bulletin*.

Before the opening of the summer session, President Graham, a small man with great warmth and natural dignity asked to see the *Contempo* editors. Abernethy and Buttitta, who answered his call, feared that he aimed to reprimand them for the campus subscription drive. But he only said to "please take it easy" on publishing material that might be called "radical" by conservatives until after the state had voted on the university appropriations bill.

In the meantime we had changed the *Contempo* logo to a slight variation of the style Vassos created for the title of his book of drawings, and two of our editors had gone. Liskin was on his way to the Soviet Union with a Russian dictionary under one arm and a tractor manual under the other to become a mechanic—and still play tennis. Carter left us a batch of poetry to use as fillers and wandered off with an artist friend to bum their way north doing sidewalk portraits. Late that summer the *New Republic* printed Carter's article "Wild Boys on the Road," and Hollywood had difficulty tracking him down for the film rights.

With its fifth issue *Contempo* settled down to being a biweekly. Books were coming in faster than we could review them, along with "authoreviews" by notable writers—both faster than subscriptions or the sale of books. We now had a critic who was to cover such upcoming Broadway openings as Eugene O'Neill's *Mourning Becomes Electra;* and a Paris correspondent who reported on the creative antics of the Dadaists and the avant-garde that congregated at the Dôme and the Coupole near the Boulevard Montparnasse. This number featured more unpleasant aspects of the contemporary scene: anti-Semitism—in the authoreview of *Christians Only* by George Britt, which he wrote with Heywood Broun; the United States Supreme Court—which, according to a professor, was "blessed with four narrowminded reactionaries who are sure to take the wrong side of every question"; war and peace—by a lady author who boldly declared in a letter to Secretary of War Hurley, "It would be well for us to listen to Russia which asks for complete disarmaments without any reservations such as we propose."

We front-paged "Facts About Scottsboro" by Carol Weiss King, attorney for the defense of the nine black boys languishing in the Alabama jail. Eight of them—all under twenty—were condemned to death for the alleged rape of two white women while riding in a freight car. The ninth, a lad of fourteen, was awaiting trial. The boys were to become *Contempo*'s first important "cause"—to which we were to devote two special issues. Firmly convinced of their innocence, we were determined to do what we could to break down the wall of silence and prejudice in the press for, if the facts were made known, we knew they would arouse protests that might save the boys from the electric chair.

The mid-July *Contempo* continued the defense of the Scottsboro boys with impassioned articles by Theodore Dreiser and John Dos Passos. Dreiser said they had been tried not "as human beings, they were tried as black men. . . . The case was so hastily prepared and presented" that what prevailed was the "rule of the mob over the jury. . . ." Dos Passos spoke of "our legal procedure" as "a kind of map of our ruling class mind. In the South, in a case where Negroes are involved, every white is given the luxury of being part of the ruling class. . . . A lynching is a kind of carnival."

Their remarks were illustrated by a woodcut of the nine in a dungeonlike cell with the Southern sun streaming down on them from a tiny barred window. In that same issue we ran as an editorial John Dewey's letter in defense of a Chinese student at Columbia University who was being deported for "his agitation against imperialism and his connection with the Anti-Imperialist League. I cannot believe that the United States Government will be an accomplice in sending Mr. Li to his death."

To lighten the tone of this number we chose three poems and a few odd notes. The blurb on the jacket of Nathanael West's first novel, *The Dream Life of Balso Snell,* told us that it was written "as a protest against writing books." Edwin Markham was revising his poem "The Man With the Hoe" for *Contempo.* Kahlil Gibran, author of *The Prophet,* was to be buried among the cedars of his native Lebanon. We closed with some Dadas: "If you must speak of Dada, you must speak of Dada. If you must not speak of Dada, you must still speak of Dada. Dada you are and Dada it is."

By early summer we realized the joint venture could not feed the remaining three editors. After a couple of weeks on a diet of stale bread at a nickel a loaf, a bit of cheese, and milk at a dime the quart, with an occasional meat sandwich of Swain Hall leftovers contributed by friendly students, Abernethy took a summer job chasing Japanese beetles in upstate New York for the U. S. Department of Agriculture. Buttitta gave up his room in a magnolia-scented funeral home and moved into the shop to sleep on the narrow couch, while Garoffolo survived on a small check from home.

Shortly afterward, when checks stopped coming, Garoffolo boarded a bus for Newark with the feeling that there was little future in the venture. While Buttitta was left to run the shop and put together the next few issues, Abernethy flooded him with material he was receiving from prominent writers; and he sent down Clifton Cuthbert, whose *Joy Street* had just been published, to help with the magazine. Buttitta, who was now getting his meals at the Cavalier Cafeteria for concocting gallons of lemonade *without* lemons, got Cuthbert a job there to earn his meal ticket during the two months he was on the staff.

For the rest of the summer *Contempo* had a lighter tone—poetry, authoreviews, chitchat notes, and articles with more emphasis on literature and the arts than on causes. While we ran such items as H. L. Mencken's having the best wine cellars in Baltimore, Horace Liveright was finding it hard to locate a suitable photograph for the jacket of the reprint of Maxwell Bodenheim's *Virtuous Girl,* and Frank Harris and Archibald Henderson were rushing to complete biographies of Shaw, it seems our editorial policy of controversy slowly shifted—and almost by accident—from social issues to those of the literary world.

It all started with an authoreview—Pierre Loving's, for his *Gardener of Evil,* a biography of Baudelaire. He replied to critics of the book in a piece entitled "Is Pedantry Criticism?" A young writer and poet, Edgar Johnson, answered him with a clever and sarcastic article, "Is Criticism Pedantry?" Then the New Humanism controversy brought responses from its enemies and defenders that were to continue the dispute into the fall. But the longest and most amusing controversy was over an article on the pioneering review *Secession* by Gorham B. Munson, who got into a disagreement over its early history with Malcolm Cowley, Matthew Josephson, Waldo Frank, and others, that enlivened a few issues of *Contempo.*

In the meantime we were to have a poetic authoreview by Max Eastman of his *Swamp Maple,* James Stevens's tribute to Jim Tully as "An Irish Truth Teller," an article on "The Morbidity of William Faulkner" by Cuthbert which would amuse the Mississippi writer, and "Bewildered Hollywood" by a student of films who said, "Producers think they know what the public wants. . . . It is an indictment not only against the greediness of producers but of the system that motivates 98% of American life, a system destructive to every art that depends on a hypothetical box office whether it be literature, drama, painting or music."

Erskine Caldwell wrote a piece for us entitled "Dilettantism and Propaganda" to answer critics of his *American Earth.* He said it was "a book without political affiliation," about "men and women who work and live in the fields and in the mills of America. . . . I am not an art-for-God's sake dilettante copying exquisite lines in a sky-light hall bedroom, but neither am I a propagandist writing about cracker tenant farmers . . . [who] discuss the economic causes of poverty. . . ."

That issue also carried one of the two reviews which the unknown Nathanael West was to get for *The Dream Life of Balso Snell.* Our review was written by Garoffolo, who said it was "a splendid and craftsmanlike book . . . a distinguished performance in sophisticated writing. It is with enthusiasm that we look for Mr. West's next work."

Ezra Pound and Langston Hughes, who were to join Lewis Mumford, Louis Adamic, and Paul Green as contributing editors of *Contempo,* first appeared in our September number. Hughes's short blues poem was front-paged alongside Pound's

stinging remarks, entitled "Publishers, Pamphlets, and Other Things." Among the latter, Pound said: "Years ago I spent a good deal of undergraduate energy refighting the Civil War on the southern side and on the basis of state rights. I have since come to consider the south as a morass of barbarism. . . . I behold the glorious ruins, etc. *Ma la gloria non vedo.*"

That fall, 1931, we devoted space to the founding of the Group Theatre and its first production, Paul Green's *The House of Connelly,* which garnered the unanimous praise of the Broadway critics. In the same number we featured John Middleton Murry's authoreview of *Son of Woman,* a study of D. H. Lawrence. In it Murry wrote that what struck him most in the "hostile criticisms of *Son of Woman*" was "this abysmal ignorance of Lawrence's actual writing. These so-called 'critics' have never read one single book of Lawrence's seriously. . . . It is sheer impudence on their part to write about Lawrence at all."

To offset Murry's critical blast, we let Frank Shay, the seer of Provincetown and Greenwich Village, entertain our readers with a batch of amusing items about the "factory" of Van Doren, Dreiser, Dos Passos, Mencken, Lewis, and word that Frank Harris with his "dyed hair and waxed mustache" was dead in Nice. Shay made a remark that stirred up an amusing controversy that fall: "*Contempo* can not pay for contributions and Frank Shay cannot pay for groceries. . . . Hell, men, you pay the printers and charge your subscribers and there ought to be something left over for the source of supply."

One morning in late October Abernethy showed up with a dazed William Faulkner in tow carrying a small canvas bag that bore the handwritten, unfinished manuscript of *Light in August.* Ab had picked up the Mississippi writer in New York City, rescuing him from the mad scramble of publishers who were waving contracts in his face after the sensational reception of *Sanctuary.* We put Bill up in the empty room next to the bookshop, entertained him with his favorite "jolly spot," took him to address Phillips Russell's creative writing class, but otherwise kept him incognito at his own request. Before he left, Bill promised us a chapter of *Light in August* for *Contempo,* and invited Buttitta to stop over in Oxford on his way to Louisiana that Christmas, to pick up some poetry and stories from his files of yellowing, rejected manuscripts for an All-Faulkner Number.

While Faulkner was our guest we were preparing—much to his approval—our Second Scottsboro Issue, with contributions by Lincoln Steffens,

CONTEMPO ℭA Review of Books and Personalities

Volume 1. Number 13   Dec. 1, 1931, Chapel Hill, N. C.   Ten Cents a Copy

Lynching by Law or by Lustful Mob North and South: Red and Black

By LINCOLN STEFFENS

The first time I heard of the now famous Scottsboro case, the narrator told how those colored boys under sentence saw it. And they saw what they saw of it from a rear car. There was some sort of a row—a scrap—or a fight going on in a car so far ahead that they could get glimpses of it only as the train bent around the curves till, by and by, the train stopped. Then they saw a lot of the fighters jump off that front car and run away. They went up forward to hear more about it.

It was later, when the train arrived at its destination, that those witnesses of the incident, were arrested as the scrappers and—rapists. They were so dazed that they never quite recovered from their frightful astonishment.

But you don't have to go by this casual alibi. Take the record of the trials, the speed of them, the ages of the convicted and the circumstances, and one can realize for himself that there was no justice in these cases. There was the opposite. There was righteousness in it.

In Alabama and some parts of the South the more respectable people are yielding to the Northern clamor against lynching. There is lynching in the North, too, but it is not against blacks. It is against the Reds. And it is not by mobs. It is by the police, the courts and juries; and therefore legal, regular, righteous. The righteous people of the South have been gradually waking up to the idea that they can save their face by taking justice out of the rude hands of the mob and putting it in the delicate hands of the lawyers, and judges and a few representatives of the better people in a jury. That is to say, they can lynch their blacks the way the superior North,

Christ in Alabama
By LANGSTON HUGHES

Christ is a Nigger,
Beaten and black—
O, bare your back.

Mary is His Mother—
Mammy of the South,
Silence your mouth.

God's His Father—
White Master above,
Grant us your love

Most holy bastard
Of the bleeding mouth:
Nigger Christ
On the cross of the South.

Southern Gentlemen, White Prostitutes, Mill-Owners, and Negroes

By LANGSTON HUGHES

If the 9 Scottsboro boys die, the South ought to be ashamed of itself—but the 12 million Negroes in America ought to be more ashamed than the South. Maybe it's against the law to print the transcripts of trials from a State court. I don't know. If not, every Negro paper in this country ought to immediately publish the official records of the Scottsboro cases so that both whites and blacks might see at a glance to what absurd farces an Alabama court can descend. (Or should I say an American court?) . . . The 9 boys in Kilbee Prison are Americans. 12 million Negroes are Americans, too. (And many of them far too light in color to be called Negroes, except by liars.) The judge and the jury at Scottsboro, and the governor of Alabama, are Americans. Therefore, for the sake of American justice, (if there is any) and for the honor of Southern gentlemen, (if there ever were any) let the South rise up in press and pulpit, home and school, Senate Chambers and Rotary Clubs, and petition the freedom of the dumb young blacks—so indiscreet as to travel, unwittingly, on the same freight train with two white prostitutes . . . And, incidently, let the mill-owners of Huntsville begin to pay their women decent wages so they won't need to be prostitutes. And let the sensible citizens of Alabama (if there are any) supply schools for the black populace of their state, (and for the half-black, too—the mulatto children of the Southern gentlemen. [I reckon they're gentlemen.]) so the Negroes won't be so dumb again . . . But back to the dark millions—black and half-black, brown and yellow, with a gang of white fore-parents—like me. If these 12 million Negro Americans don't raise such a howl that

Part of the front page of the Contempo *issue that aroused widespread hostility in Chapel Hill (courtesy of Thomas Cooper Library, University of South Carolina)*

Langston Hughes, Countee Cullen, and others. Hoping this time to succeed in crashing through the wall of silence and make the fate of the Scottsboro boys known to a wider public, we approached the directors of the black bank and an insurance company in Durham to subsidize an extra five thousand copies to be circulated throughout the nation. This edition of six thousand was *Contempo*'s largest during its three-year existence.

Steffens wrote of "Lynching by Law or by Lustful Mob—North and South: Red and Black." Hughes concentrated on "Southern Gentlemen, White Prostitutes, Mill-Owners, and Negroes." His

inflammatory words were on the first page: "If the 9 Scottsboro boys die, the South ought to be ashamed of itself—but the 12 million Negroes in America ought to be more ashamed than the South. . . . Dear Lord, I never knew until now that white ladies . . . travelled in freight trains. . . . And who ever heard of raping a prostitute?"

But more inflammatory—as we were soon to learn in liberal Chapel Hill—was the poem Hughes had written for *Contempo* about the Scottsboro boys. We centered his thirteen lines of "Christ in Alabama" on the front page of Vol. 1, No. 13 under the silhouette of a young Negro with holes in his

Tony Buttitta, William Faulkner, and Milton Abernethy in Chapel Hill, November 1931 (courtesy of Tony Buttitta)

hands. To quote the first and last stanzas: "Christ is a Nigger/Beaten and black—/*O, bare your back. . . .* Most holy bastard/Of the bleeding mouth:/*Nigger Christ*/On the cross of the south."

For some time our group had been tolerated by some locals and university people, not as radicals—because of how we dressed, the books in the shop, or the controversial contents of *Contempo* — but as a joke: a harmless, late-flowering of Greenwich Village bohemia in their midst. Even among the few who had some acquaintance with Marx, Engels, or Norman Thomas socialism, the moment we printed the poem by a Negro who called Christ "a nigger" there went up such a howl on the campus and in the village that "liberal" Chapel Hill overnight took on the intolerance and prejudice of a small Southern town and for a time vague threats made it unsafe for us to remain there.

In this highly charged atmosphere Langston Hughes suddenly appeared. He had been invited by some students and faculty members, including Paul Green, Guy B. Johnson, and President Graham, to read his poetry in the campus students'

hall. Such a hullabaloo arose that permission for its use that night was instantly revoked and Hughes was assigned to a smaller hall. Loudspeakers were set up so the thousand or more who had gathered on the campus could hear him read from his *The Weary Blues* and *Fine Clothes to the Jew.*

Hughes was not allowed to stay or dine at Carolina Inn, where visiting speakers were lodged. We arranged more "pleasant" quarters for him with a friendly black minister and his family; and we entertained the light-skinned poet in a main-street restaurant—passing him off as a Mexican professor. Before Hughes left, we were photographed in front of the post office—"federal territory." When Hughes wrote of this incident with some humor in his autobiography, *I Wonder As I Wander,* he closed by saying he had "walked into a lion's den, and come out, like Daniel, unscathed."

Village reaction was swift: we lost all local advertising and were unable to collect what money was due us. Leading the campaign to punish us was the Rotarian manager of the local movie house; he asked Louis Graves to stop printing *Contempo* and demanded that our landlord order us to be evicted. Fortunately, Graves was an independent publisher who liked the magazine enough to let us owe him for an issue or two; and, having signed a year's lease on our quarters, we could not be tossed out until next spring.

Soon afterward the campaign against us erupted in the Southern press as far as Montgomery, Alabama. *The Gastonia* (North Carolina) *Daily Gazette* wrote: "*Contempo* is nasty. It is common, filthy, obnoxious, putrid, rancid, nauseating, rotten, vile, and stinking. . . . If you should happen to run across a copy of it read it, by all means, and then burn it, by all means." Another North Carolina paper called on the governor of the state to censor or suspend *Contempo,* as though it was a university publication subject to such control.

Sinclair Lewis came to our rescue with a twenty-five-dollar check and a cheering note: "If nothing else would make me subscribe, the charming praise of *Contempo* from Gastonia would make me. . . . You are not on your way to 'success' until the newspapers have called you nuts, cranks and liars." In addition to praise from the New York press, we got this from Rupert Hughes, the novelist, in the Los Angeles *Examiner:* "*Contempo* is a singularly vivacious bi-monthly whose audacities are all the more amazing in a periodical issued from Chapel Hill, North Carolina."

Contempo had made its mark on the national scene, but we were unable to give away advertising space—or even barter it for necessities or an occasional trifle. From the first we had been refused book advertising—and rightly so: too many little magazines folded after the first number or two. But we made another push to get such advertising on the strength of its recognition by Horace Liveright, who "felt a personal interest when *Contempo* was mentioned in the columns all over town"; Eugene O'Neill, who wrote us that the magazine was "lively and has the stuff "; and Walter Winchell, who referred to it in his column as "that lively literary maglet."

While we struggled along on small personal loans and an occasional tie-in ad which we got with the authoreview of a prominent new book, *Contempo* continued drifting in the direction of a literary review—without losing any of its controversial spirit. The Munson-Cowley fracas went on delighting readers with reminiscences, real or imaginary, of the literary exiles in the 1920s until Ezra Pound, our leading expatriate, asked pertinent questions of Cowley and Munson, and then abruptly took up the subject of "a code of critical ethics."

Contempo soon found itself in another such imbroglio, this time spurred by Frank Shay's remark about little magazines not reimbursing "the source of the supply." Several writers promptly replied, saying they would have had no outlet for their work without them. Most prominent among them was William Carlos Williams, who had not only appeared in dozens of such publications but had been involved, like Pound, with either founding or editing several since the end of World War I.

We prompted the next controversy—not knowing that an act of providence would catapult *Contempo* into the international arena. It all started when we asked Dr. Archibald Henderson, a bookshop patron, university math professor, and "official biographer" of George Bernard Shaw since the turn of the century, to review Frank Harris's "unauthorized" biography of his hero. The professor was writing his review when death caught up with Harris and he changed his lead to read, "The late Frank Harris was, as Shaw observes, 'the most impossible of biographers.' "

In his long, detailed review, under the double-column head "Harris' Assembled Pseudo Biography of Shaw," Henderson blasted the book as a "botch—part authentic, part surmise, part innuendo, part cheap and half-baked comment. . . ." Then he went on—in an almost page-by-page rundown—to point out where, from Shaw's biographies, works, and particularly his novel *Immaturity,* Harris had deliberately "lifted," "culled," and even "falsified" some of the material for his biography.

Though Harris has been called a charlatan, a liar, and a thief, no one ever accused him of being dull—the worst crime a writer can commit. We felt sorry for the man and cabled his widow Nellie our condolences and told her we planned to honor him with a Frank Harris Memorial Issue. At the same time we mailed copies of *Contempo* to his friends and enemies in America and Europe, asking them to comment on Henderson's review and to send us a brief message of sympathy to be included in our special number.

The issue was lively enough to be read at an Irish wake. Of the dozen writers who replied, we quote briefly from three. First, his publisher Richard L. Simon of Simon and Schuster: since Shaw had edited the book and "was free to change or cut what displeased him," Henderson's "quarrel was with his subject not the biographer." Lord Alfred Douglas: "Harris' death really removed the last of my enemies. I cannot pretend to feel any regret at the old ruffian's departure. But I had mass said for him at the Catholic Church here." For our epitaph we ran the last two lines of a long poem submitted by a persistent poet: "You died in time, Frank/You died in time."

The last few issues of the twenty-two that first year contained some significant poetry and commentary. Among the poets represented were Robinson Jeffers, Witter Bynner, Alfred Kreymborg, Grace Stone Coates, Langston Hughes with a Scottsboro poem, and William Carlos Willams, whose "The Cod Head" we also issued in a limited-edition pamphlet. There was a review of Joseph Auslander's translation of the Petrarch sonnets by Frances Winwar and a two-column feature, "The Depression Has Just Begun," by Ezra Pound.

We had two other special numbers that year: one on pornography and obscenity, and the All-Faulkner Number. Leslie Baird wrote of "Censorship and the Movies"; Barrett Clark discussed forbidden words on the stage in "The Blush of Shame"; Pound did his bit with "La Merrdre"; Pierre Loving analyzed "The Meaning of Obscenity"; and Bob Brown authoreviewed his *Gems: A Censored Anthology*. Dr. Ben L. Reitman, friend of Emma Goldman, head of Chicago's literary Dill Pickle Club, and sociologist-director of the city's School of Social Pathology, contributed "Three Shades of Sex," in which he reviewed a book on prostitution, a marriage manual, and his own *Second Oldest Profession*.

With Faulkner in the spotlight because of the excitement over *Sanctuary*, our Faulkner issue was the literary scoop of early 1932 and soon became a collector's item. It marked the first publication of his poetry since 1924, when *The Marble Faun* appeared. In addition to nine poems, which were later to be included in his collection *A Green Bough*, we published his adventure story "Once Aboard the Lugger."

Contempo also paid a tribute to Faulkner in that issue as "America's most creative living writer." With the wider recognition in the 1930s of Hemingway, Dos Passos, Fitzgerald, and Wolfe, the literary world must have considered its editors brash young upstarts to take such a stand. For Faulkner had to wait more than a dozen years and several novels before Malcolm Cowley, in his introduction to *The Portable William Faulkner*, was to establish him firmly as America's outstanding writer and thus pave the way for his being awarded the Nobel Prize.

During that first year by focusing attention on Faulkner, the Scottsboro boys, Nathanael West,

William Carlos Williams, other "causes" and writers, including Ezra Pound for whose *Cantos* we helped to find a commercial publisher, *Contempo* was to establish itself—to quote John Macy—as "doing something for contemporary American literature which no other magazine attempts."

Contempo lost its broadsheet format with the beginning of Volume Two, 5 May 1932—just as George Jean Nathan, who had kept an eye on it from its inception, planned his own "literary newspaper" which made its debut that fall as the *American Spectator*. We now had the print shop fold that broadsheet once more to form eight pages; and by using a point smaller type we were able to run longer fiction, more poetry and articles, with drawings and sketches to illustrate them. Our contributing editors changed again: Faulkner, who had been one for a few months, was replaced by Kay Boyle, with Pound, Hughes, Adamic, Samuel Putnam, and Barrett Clark continuing on the board.

A week before Volume Two appeared, John Vassos and his wife Ruth, who had written the texts for his books of black and white drawings, visited us. We had been corresponding with his publishers concerning our use of his title *Contempo*—without permission from them or the artist. They had hinted at legal action, but Vassos, pleased with the quality of our magazine, told them to take no action until he had "investigated" us. The artist was so pleased with us that he drew a cartoon of Abernethy and Buttitta as "The Bad Boys of Chapel Hill," gave us a framed drawing for the shop, and wrote an article on art comes to the rescue of Big Business which we ran in our third number.

Our lead editorial reviewed *Contempo*'s policy for the benefit of new subscribers. 1: *Complete freedom from all cliques*. 2: *An asylum for aggrieved authors*—via the authoreview. 3: *Encouragement of literary controversy* which we maintained "sharpens wits and makes ideas circulate. For writers the first consideration must be . . . the finding through controversy of their convictions." 4: *Rapid reception of new ideas* in all fields. "*Contempo* lacks the space to expound these ideas but it can from time to time make known their existence."

The first issue in the smaller format featured T. Swann Harding's article "Scientific Illiteracy of Liberals," in which he described a liberal as a "strange combination of rationalist and evangelist, a curious hybrid of Rousseau and Voltaire." Also a poem by Kathleen Tankersley Young; a short story by Robert McAlmon, expatriate editor and publisher; and "Young Lonigan," a section from

Complete Issue By *WILLIAM FAULKNER*

CONTEMPO

A Review of Books and Personalities

Volume I. Number 17   February 1, 1932, Chapel Hill, N. C.   Ten Cents a Copy

I Will Not Weep for Youth

I will not weep for youth in after years
Nor will there haunt me, when I am old,
The world's face in its springtime, blurred with tears
That healed to dust harsh pageantries of gold.

Nor will dulled brain, nor ears at a sound scarce heard
Trouble old bones asleep from a sun to a sun
With a dream forgot, a scent or a senseless bird,
That now with earth and silence are brethren: one.

Poplar leaves swirl sunward, bright with rime,
To a stately minuet of wind in wheat;
And spring is blown on ruins of old time
Cruel, incurious, superbly sweet;

And swallows that arch and tighten across the heart
Will strike no hidden chord, when it is mute:
A caught breath, flash of limbs in the myrtles apart,
Dancing girls to a shrilling of lyre and lute.

Death and I'll amicably wrangle, face to face,
Mouthing dried crumbs of pains and ecstasies,
Regarding without alarm cold seas of space—
Eternity is simple where sunlight is.

Knew I Love Once

Knew I love once? Was it love or grief
This young body by where I had lain?
And my heart, this single stubborn leaf
That will not die, though root and branch be slain?
O mother Sleep, when one by one these years
Bell their bitter note, and die away
Down Time's slow evening, passionless as tears
When sorrow long has ebbed, and grief is gray;

Though warm in dark between the breasts of Death,
That other breast forgot where I did lie,
And from the stalk are stripped the leaves of breath,
There's still one stubborn leaf that will not die
But restless in the wild and bitter earth,
Gains with each dawn a death, with dusk a birth.

Twilight

Beyond the hill the sun swam downward
And he was lapped in azure seas;
The dream that hurt him, the blood that whipped him
Dustward, slowed and gave him ease.

Behind him day lay stark with labor
Of one who strives with earth for bread;
Before him sleep, tomorrow his circling
Sinister shadow round his head.

But now, with night, this was forgotten:
Phantoms of life round man spin fast;
Forgotten his father, Death, Derision
His mother, forgotten by her at last.

Nymph and faun in this dusk might riot
Beyond Time's cold greenish bar
To shrilling pipes, to cymbals' hissing
Beneath a single icy star

Where he, to his own compulsion
—A terrific figure on an urn—
Is caught between his two horizons,
Forgetting that he must return.

"Once Aboard the Lugger"

In the middle of the afternoon we made a landfall. Ever since we left the mouth of the river at dawn and felt the first lift of the sea, Pete's face had been getting yellower and yellower, until by midday and twenty four hours out of New Orleans, when we spoke to him he'd glare at us with his yellow cat's eyes, and curse Joe. Joe was his older brother. He was about thirty-five. He had some yellow diamonds big as gravel. Pete was about nineteen, in a silk shirt of gold and lavender stripes, and a stiff straw hat, and all day long he squatted in the bows, holding his hat and saying Jesus Christ to himself.

He wouldn't even drink any of the whiskey he had hooked from Joe. Joe wouldn't let us take any with us, and the Captain wouldn't have let us fetch it aboard, if he had. The Captain was a teetotaller. He had been in the outside trade before Joe hired him, where they took on cargoes of green alcohol in the West Indies and had it all flavored and aged and bottled and labeled and cased before they raised Tortugas. He said he never had heard if one would buy ever had, he'd be cured now. He was a real prohibitionist: he believed that nobody should be allowed to drink. He was a New Englander, with a face like a worn doormat.

So Pete had to hook a couple of bottles from Joe, and we brought them aboard inside our pants leg and the nigger hid them in the galley, and between wheel tricks I'd go forward where Pete was squatting, holding his hat, and have a nip. Now and then the nigger's disembodied face ducked into the port, without any expression at all, like a mask in carnival, and he passed up a cup of coffee which Pete drank and like as not threw the cup at the nigger's head just as it ducked away.

"He done busted two of them," the nigger told me. "We ain't got but four left, now. I gwine give it to him in a bakingpowder can next time."

Pete hadn't eaten any breakfast, and he flung his dinner overside and turned his back while I ate mine, his face getting yellower and yellower, and when we fetched the island—a scar of sand with surf creaming along its windward flank and tufted with gnawed purple pines on a darkling twilit sea—his face and his eyes were the same color.

The Captain held inside. We passed into the island's lee. The motion ceased and we pounded along in slack water of the clearest green. To starboard the island stretched on, bastioned and sombre, without sign of any life at all. Across the Sound a low smudge of mainland lay like a violet cloud. From beyond the island we could hear the boom and hiss of surf, but inside here the water was like a mill-pond, with sunlight slanting into it in green corridors. And then Pete got really sick, leaning overside and holding his hat on.

Twilight came swiftly. The clear green of the water, losing the sun, darkened. We beat on across a pulseless surface fading slowly to the hue of violet ink. Against the sky the tall pines stood in shabby and gaunt parade. The smudge of mainland had dissolved. Low on the water where it had been, a beacon was like a cigarette coal. Pete was still being sick.

(Continued on page four)

Visions in Spring

And at last, having followed a voice that cried within him
Through veils of changing shadow, evening fell
Upon him as he stood, aghast. Around him
Spread widening circles of a bell.

And then another bell slid star-like down the silence
Stagnant about him, and awoke
A sudden vagueness of pain. That—he said, and trembled—
Was my heart, my ancient heart that broke;

My heart that I so carefully guarded, empty
Of plant and seed, the acts of day by day
That would have made of it a garden for age to nod in,
Has broken and fallen away.

For I, who sought so much, I disregarded
The pennies one should hoard if one would buy
Peace, a corner for weary feet to stray to—
Above him, swiftly, slenderly,

The trees tossed silver arms in sleeves of green
And lustrous limbs and boughs
Moved in a hushed measure to an ancient music.
And then once more the brows

Of dancers he had dreamed before him floated,
Calm, unsaddened, in a sea of evening air;
Lips repeating the melody, sustaining the cooling sunset
In the autumned stillness of their hair.

Lightly they rose about him, quickening in magic,
And his own life, so lax within his eyes,
Stirred again: this beauty touched him, quiet, weary,
Soft hands of skies

Delicately swung the narrow moon above him
And shivered the tips of trees, until he heard
A kissing of leaves; then lo! the dream had vanished.
He raised his hand, and stirred

And would have cried aloud, but was dumb as were the branches
That tightened to a faint refrain
Clinging like gossamer about them, that softly snared him.
Then the bells again

Like falling leaves, rose mirrored up from silence;
And he, in silence, with his empty heart
Pondered: I had this thing I sought, that now has escaped me
When it was shattered apart.

For I, who toiled through corridors of harsh laughter,
Who sought for light in dark reserves of pain;—
What shall I do, who am old and weary and lonely,
Too weary to alone set forth again?

Softly above his head clear waves of darkness
Came up and filled the trees
And smoothed the rigid branches to restless coral.
He rose from stiffened knees.

Spring, blown white along the faint-starred darkness,
Arose again about him, like a wall
Beneath which he stood and watched, growing colder and colder,
A star immaculately fall.

Front page of all-Faulkner issue of Contempo, *which quickly became a collector's item (courtesy of Thomas Cooper Library, University of South Carolina)*

CONTEMPO

Volume II. Number 4   July 5, 1932, Chapel Hill, N. C.   Ten Cents a Copy

Hart Crane [1899-1932]

By WILLIAM CARLOS WILLIAMS

White Buildings (1926)

It is startling to come upon lines with such a sound of continual surf in them as these:

. . . within your breast is gathering
All bright insinuations that my years have caught
For islands where must lead inviolably
Blue latitudes and levels of your eyes,
The alternate peak and back rush of waves is clearly audible—

It begins again in the next movement:

Meticulous, past midnight in clear rime,
Infrangible and lonely, smooth as though cast
Together in one merciless white blade—
The bay estuaries fleck the hard sky limits.

This is music which an attentive and willing ear will be sure to recommend without quibble to the intelligence. And the music alone will carry all that need be said—

Then there are the words : he wrote sometimes, really, as though he were seeking to please (perhaps he was just indifferent, in view of the music) someone who had charge of a New York Sunday Book Supplement. That is to say he could be at times as bad as that—the gently bubbling putridity of the saleable—

Creation's blithe and petalled word etc, etc.

and much more of that "profound" sort in rhymed quatraines for which I can find no excuse whatever—

Worse than that, Crane wanted to be

(Continued on page four)

Miss Lonelyhearts in the Dismal Swamp

By NATHANAEL WEST

The Miss Lonelyhearts of the New York Evening Hawk (Are you in trouble? Do you need advice? Write to Miss Lonelyhearts and she will help you) sits staring through his office window into the street. Piled on his desk are letters from Broadshouldered, Broken-hearted, Disillusioned-with-tubercular-husband. Although the street is walled at both ends, he has a Bible in one hand and a philosophy book in the other. In his lap are travel, art, seed and gun catalogues.

"Ah, Tahiti . . . Like Gauguin, eh? To dream away the days on the golden sand while the sun comes up like a red pool ball across the lagoon and the rhythm of a primitive world enters your soul and you build a thatch hut and take the daughter of

(Continued on page two)

Mixcoac, Mexico
Dear CONTEMPO: March 11, 1932

You have been most generous in sending me so many issues of CONTEMPO. Please accept my sincere thanks! I've enjoyed every one of them. I think you should be congratulated both on your courage and your acumen,—the latter most of the time at least.

I haven't a thing to send you at present but the enclosed poem. *Bacardi* ought to be enough cue to explain that it represents the rather typical "colonial" attitude of two Americans in Cuba employing native labor. Anyhow, it's the sort of lingo I used to hear in the bars and cantinas when I lived in Cuba several years ago.

Cordially yours,
HART CRANE.

BACARDI SPREADS THE EAGLE'S WING

By HART CRANE

"Pablo and Pedro, and black Serafin
Bought a launch last week. It might as well
Have been made of—well, say paraffin,—
That thin and blistered . . . just a rotten shell.

"Hell! out there among the barracudas
Their engine stalled. No oars, and leaks
Oozing a-plenty. They sat like baking Buddhas.
Luckily the Cayman schooner streaks

"By just in time, and lifts 'em high and dry . . .
They're back now on that mulching job at Pepper's.
—Yes, patent-leather shoes hot enough to fry
Anyone but these native high-steppers!"

Mixcoac, Mexico
Dear CONTEMPO: April 20, 1932

Delighted to hear that you like the *Bacardi* poem and are using it.

I'm leaving for the States in a few days and can't write you a decent response at the moment. But I hope you meant what you said about sending me CONTEMPO regularly. And I should like to do reviews for you when I get settled in the north again.

Please address me from now on at Box 604, Chagrin Falls, Ohio, where I shall probably be after May 10th.

Salutations and very best wishes,

HART CRANE.

P. S. I should love to review MacLeish's *Conquistador* for you if you haven't already assigned it elsewhere.

For Hart Crane

By FORREST ANDERSON

1.
death looked at him at high-noon
her hint for exit through love's deeper solstices
where the eye expands until it fills the sea
with someone who could not fill the eye

2.
truth is in the mouths of sailors
that is why they have no certain place
in the street which is the first line to a poem
i heard what was the last line for a poet

3.
his magic angel must have met an angle
love's suppleness was unable to resolve
because the sun dipped at his arc
a ship will reach the pier at midnight

4.
others shall fall heir to these deathly pieces
shall wax to barriers less blank than noon
hell will be happy to hold this marauder
from sailor's words who found no requiem

5.
memory is a candle tonight shall burn
as through eternally beating propellors draws
this pauseless hostage to appease the long
file of the ghosts of loves — the sharks!

Confessions of a Twentieth Century Chapman

By GLENN HUGHES

A little over five years ago I had the fun of founding a series of pamphlets which I labeled *University of Washington Chapbooks.* Recently it has been found advisable to discontinue the series. The depression proved too much for the slender financial resources behind the Chapbooks.

There were several reasons for founding the Chapbooks. One was that I had been impressed by the prevalence of pamphlet publication in England and the Continent, and had wondered why more did not exist in America. Another was that I frequently encountered or heard of a manuscript which was too short for regular book publication and too important for the transience of magazine publication. A third reason was that I liked the idea of expressing my tastes and enthusiasms as an editor. Still a fourth was that I thought the University should encourage local writers by publishing their work. I was thinking particularly of certain faculty members who for one reason or another were not getting their work published.

(Continued on page three)

Front page of Contempo *issue that eulogized Hart Crane and contained an excerpt from Nathanael West's work-in-progress,* Miss Lonelyhearts *(courtesy of Thomas Cooper Library, University of South Carolina)*

Studs Lonigan which James T. Farrell was then writing in Paris.

Then came a long-overdue All-Southern Issue, with poems by Faulkner, Conrad Aiken, Evelyn Scott, and John Gould Fletcher; stories by Erskine Caldwell and William March; and an authoreview by Julia Peterkin. A Southern controversy was started when William S. Knickerbocker, editor of the *Sewanee Review,* boldly attacked his neighbors, the twelve writers at Vanderbilt University in Nashville known as the Fugitives. Knickerbocker's saying that their "agrarian" program was nothing but "O fiddlestix! O spiffledown!" brought responses pro and con that kept the spotlight on Allen Tate, Donald Davidson, and John Crowe Ransom for several weeks.

That spring we corresponded with Hart Crane while he was in Mixcoac, Mexico. He sent us the only poem he had on hand, "Bacardi," with a letter saying that it represented "the rather typical 'colonial' attitude of two Americans in Cuba employing native labor." Before we could schedule it, we read of his suicide plunge from the ship that was bringing him back to the States. We appealed to writers to send us something for a kind of memorial issue. Quick to oblige were a young poet friend who wrote a Crane-like poem which he dedicated to him, and William Carlos Williams, a longtime admirer of Crane's work, who sent us a tribute in prose and verse.

The Crane issue was to be one of our most sought-after by collectors. In addition to material relating to the poet, it had an article by Kay Boyle on "Writers Worth Reading," with a pat on the back for "Pound, our father," and a short story, "Miss Lonelyhearts in the Dismal Swamp," excerpted from Nathanael West's work-in-progress. Only two journals, *Contempo* and *Contact,* of which William Carlos Williams and West were editors at the time, were to print portions of "Miss Lonelyhearts" prior to its publication as a book the following year.

Turning our attention to European literature we asked Samuel Putnam, editor of the Paris *New Review,* to compile a special number for us. It was to feature the poetry of the German Rainer Maria Rilke, the French Ribemont-Dessaignes, and three young Russians: Vladimir Mayakovski, poet of the revolution; Serge Essenin, Isadora Duncan's slightly mad husband; and Boris Pasternak, who was to win the Nobel Prize decades later for his novel *Doctor Zhivago.*

There was a short story, "Old Man God," by Luigi Pirandello, who was the best-known of the contributors because of his *Six Characters in Search of An Author;* and an article by Putnam, "If Dada Comes to America." Putnam analyzed Surrealism as "the most fascinating aesthetic or near aesthetic manifestation in modern times. . . . Here we have a movement that is nothing if not metaphysical . . . devoted henceforth to the realization of Marxian materialism."

The Bob Brown Issue came as a complete surprise to our readers. With its publication, this playful and experimental writer of two continents had replaced Hughes as a contributing editor and Minna Abernethy was to join our editorial staff. Bob delighted all of us with his irresistible bursts of humor. His lead editorial set the tone of the issue: "I want to jeer at all polished pundits and their piddling pupils:/Hail! Hail!/ Whelps of Yale!/ To teach the young how to shoot/I wouldn't give a rooty-root!"

Containing a delightful tribute by Louis Untermeyer, who knew Brown from the old *Masses* days as a "young god of gusto," the issue was largely Brown's outbursts of linguistic madness and his dancelike freehand sketches. He happily confessed in "Optical Balloon Juice" that he was not "really interested in writing either prose or poetry. All I want is words. Words with the punch of hieroglyphics, words with the sweep and color of painters' lines, twenty-mule-team vigorous vulgar words with a hee-haw kick to them. . . ."

The next issues offered fiction, verse, and articles mostly by writers making their first appearance in our pages. There were stories by Leane Zugsmith and Julian Shapiro (John Sanford); poems by L. A. G. Strong, Charles Norman, and Charles Reznikoff; articles by Ernest Boyd, Maristan Chapman, Phyllis Bottome, Edward Dahlberg, and the modern composer George Antheil, who wrote of his years in Europe, where he had "witnessed all of the musical revolutions of the twenties"—from Schönberg to Stravinsky, Hindemith, and Alban Berg.

From *Contempo*'s earliest days we had written to Shaw, asking him to dig in his literary trunk for us. When Archibald Henderson started the controversy over the Harris biography, we made another effort to break Shaw's silence. With the forthcoming publication of Professor Henderson's new biography, we launched into our third campaign to get something from Shaw free—despite his well-publicized fee of a dollar a word.

This time Shaw replied with a long, single-spaced letter, extolling his biographer's great service in "collecting" him "into a single character . . . and thereby advanced my standing very materi-

CONTEMPO

CA BOB BROWN ISSUE

Volume II. Number 6   August 31, 1932, Chapel Hill, N. C.   Ten Cents a Copy

Party

Like rooks, the four sexes pinned down the corners of the checkered dance floor. Bottles of cognac and benedictine made sprightly knightly moves across the squares, conducted with a gliding motion by stately bishops, to people who played the part of pieces in the party.

There was hardly room on the checker board for the pawns to move. Some were too timid to advance before the flashing kings-queenly and queens-kingly; others, black and white to the soul, made fawnlike one-stepping and two-stepping leaps, their tails stiff out in the air.

"Links! Where in hell is the brandy hid?"

"Madame, your pregnant eyes! I *kuss die* hand, Madame."

The party was also a medieval tourney; a battle of flushed flowers fought to a finish on the checkered careening floor. There were favors for everybody and fat kisses, curtseys and Carmens with lip-sticky roses tempting ghoul-eyed Fausts.

Satyrs peered out behind bushy eye-brows around angular corners.

Wynn put the brandy bottle to her useful lips and put half of it inside her before somebody swan-necked it away.

"Have a heart, Wynn! Leave some for us."

"Lock the doors! Rene is going to dance!"

"*Tout le monde va nu!*"

Rene, the naughty boy, wriggled out like a white worm with lard hams.

"*Ole!* Mistinguet!"

Rene danced. Everybody laughed. Jesus wept. It was a riot.

The party was also a peasant May Day on the Village Green. All the green ran off the walls in tears of paint. Bright neck-ties gleamed out of the grass, burning their red needle way *up fancy crocheted* flannel petticoats. The girls shivered down their backs, blushed and giggled in their shawls. There was quaint kissing, cuffing and necking. A hearty rustic festival in honor of Spring, Summer, Fall and Old Man Wintah.

Ole! Ole! Ole!

Wooden shoes clicked castanets to splinters.

"I don't see sur-realism anymore. I'm trying to find something different for m y s e l f. Something more."

"George, go an' get two more bottles, that's a good doggie."

The village curate, a haughty thin-nosed man, a shrugging shoulder-perch for c o n k i n g crows, left the party in a prudish pet just because one of the

(Continued on page three)

Optical Balloon Juice

I'm not really interested in writing either prose or poetry. All I want is words. Words with the punch of hieroglyphics, words with the sweep and color of painters' lines, twenty-mule-team vigorous vulgar words with a hee-haw kick to them: Bed-fruit and death-jerks. Mud-luscious hyphenated man-seed. Hot-squat for the electric chair. Puddle-wonderful Cummingsesque living Elizabethan cackleberries crammed with chuck-streams of eye spawn. Alley apples for bricks. Human hobo slang. Alligator bait for fried liver. Inelegant but elevating. Balloon juice, heifer dust and angel food to express the mouthings of missionaries, editors and critics. Stoop-tobacco for snipes. Lillies for hands. Raspberry for heart. Thieves jargon, criminal cant. Dangler for exhibitionist. Lord's Supper for Prison food. Bone-orchard for graveyard. Splinter-belly for carpenter.

Words with optical interest wherever possible. They give me pictures. When I see heaven-reacher for preacher, I am conscious of the phonetic fun, but I see in addition William Blake's "I Want! I Want!" with his broad-minded narrow ladder reaching all the way up to some personal heaven full of soft-handed hope and houris.

I like to combine the sound and sight of letters with primitive drawings, like *Lips Looped in Lupanares* and others decorating these pages. I know the alliteration is as maddening to many as cross-word puzzles, are to me. As silly as Peter Piker picked a peck of pickled peppers, to some. Yet these things lisp in my eyes. To me they are loadsters, leering out from somewhere, loaded with leaven of life. They say what I want to say and how! whether anybody else on earth wants them winking and blinking at him or not.

With me, calligrams are as bad a habit as anagrams with Links Gillespie. Sometimes I think my lush-lips-lisp line is silly, but in twenty years I haven't tired of my eyes-on-the-half-shell calligram. From such things all my eyes squeeze juicy essences that run like bloody gravy o'er the rare roast-beef of art, (Call it half-baked, Professor) I won't argue with you or Ruskin about What is Art? If it's Art? Is there Art? Where's Art? (Why, I ain't seen him since last Toisday.)

I'm really interested only in words, and chiefly in the looks of them. I like 'em young, old, rare, blond, well-done, pregnant and brunette. Any word to

(Continued on page four)

Front page of Contempo *issue in which Bob Brown became a contributing editor (courtesy of Thomas Cooper Library, University of South Carolina)*

ally." When we showed the letter to Dr. Henderson, he had to have it for his collection; we sold it to him for the payment of our printing bill and his publisher reproduced the letter on the back cover of the book. With such a letter a Shaw Number was inevitable. We centered Shaw's communication on the front page and included, among other articles, a caricature of Shaw and the facsimile of a message Shaw wrote in long-hand to Henderson—in the form of a poem.

Contempo's last year, 1934, took on an international character without losing touch with the American scene. There were poems by D. H. Lawrence, James Joyce, Jules Romains, Wallace Stevens, and Faulkner; a translation by E. E. Cummings of Louis Aragon's controversial "The Red Front"; and thirteen hokku poems by Japanese poets from 1465 to 1775. There were stories by Kay Boyle, Paul Sifton, and Peter Neagoe, coeditor of the Paris *New Review;* articles on the drama and Eugene O'Neill by Virgil Geddes; proletarian literature and a chronicle of the leftwing magazines the *Liberator* and the old *Masses;* reviews by Aldous Huxley of Lawrence's *Etruscan Places;* Haakon Chevalier's study of Anatole France *The Ironic Temper;* and other writers on Cummings, Hemingway, Stein, West, and Joyce.

That year the international character of the political arena was reflected by literary attacks on Chancellor Hitler and Il Duce. In his "Clinical Cartoon" of Mussolini, Count Carlo Sforza analyzed the historical sources of his power and closed with a quotation from Cavour: "Any fool is able to govern with the state of siege." In his "Hitler and the Jews," Lion Feutchtwanger found it "more politic" to discuss Hitler the writer; still he had to make a last-minute change to another ship fearing he might be arrested by the Nazis as soon as it passed the three-mile limit.

Highlights of that last year were special numbers devoted to Joyce and West. The West issue marked the long-awaited publication of *Miss Lonelyhearts*. There were reviews of his work and of this novel in particular by Angel Flores, Bob Brown, Josephine Herbst, and William Carlos Williams, along with a personal portrait by S. J. Perelman. The Joyce Number was edited by Stuart Gilbert with articles by himself, Eugene Jolas, Padraic Colum, Richard Thoma; a poem by Samuel Beckett; and the publication, for the first time in America, of a selection from *Work in Progress* which later appeared as *Finnegans Wake*. In an earlier letter to us Joyce wrote, "By way of literary immortality I read *Contempo*."

Solzhenitsyn and America

Carl E. Rollyson, Jr.
Wayne State University

I have come to understand the falsehood of all revolutions in history: They destroy only *those* carriers of evil contemporary with them (and also fail, out of haste, to discriminate the carriers of good as well). And they then take to themselves as their heritage the actual evil itself, magnified still more.

This is surely the main problem of the twentieth century: is it permissible merely to carry out orders and commit one's conscience to someone else's keeping?
—From *The Gulag Archipelago*

The Soviet publication of *One Day in the Life of Ivan Denisovich* in November 1962 was electri-

fying news. Almost immediately, it brought Aleksandr I. Solzhenitsyn worldwide fame. Nikita Khrushchev publicly praised the novel, and for a brief time it was cited by his government as evidence of Stalin's criminal behavior. The "cult of personality," as Stalin's rule was deemed in the Soviet press, had resulted in labor camps that were as dehumanizing and lethal as those run by the Nazis. Solzhenitsyn's work, it was thought, would help to speed a drive toward government reforms initiated by Khrushchev in the mid-1950s as he consolidated his hold over the Communist party and the country as a whole. Very little was known about the novel's author, and because he had no

Dust jacket for the first full biography of Solzhenitsyn

by acting as the conscience of humankind. As long as he remained in the U.S.S.R., the writer would be a mystery—carefully guarding his plans among a small group of intimates, tempering and even censoring his work in the hope of getting a hearing from the Politburo. In his autobiography, *The Oak and the Calf* (Harper & Row, 1979), he explains that on the very day of his expulsion from the Soviet Union, 13 February 1974, he imagined finally encountering the highest officials of the land and debating his views; instead he was handled by security agents who were charged not to argue with him but to hasten his departure to West Germany.

Much about Solzhenitsyn has been misunderstood by both his countrymen and his foreign readers; and he often writes with the aggrieved vigor of a man who has never been given a full hearing. The Western press has often reported his opinions in piecemeal fashion and rarely has considered his politics in the context of his fiction. Solzhenitsyn has exacerbated the controversies surrounding his infrequent public appearances, occasional letter writing to American newspapers, and interviews with journalists by sounding rather intemperate and intolerant of other points of view. Similar charges were leveled at him during his last years in the Soviet Union. Even his friends acknowledge a rather austere, unforgiving side to this great novelist, but as Michael Scammell (author of *Solzhenitsyn*, 1984, the most complete biography to date) points out, the Russian writer's enormous influence is in large part due to his singularity, to his careful cultivation of independence from every person and position other than his own. His sense of destiny, of a divine providence that guided him from the camps to the world stage, inevitably results in what some regard as arrogance. He writes and speaks, however, in order to fill a void in contemporary discourse about world affairs. By standing absolutely alone (this is the myth of himself he creates in *The Oak and the Calf*) he remains uncompromised and unbeholden to any power or pressure group.

Solzhenitsyn was born on 11 December 1918, at Kislovodsk in the Northern Caucasus. His father, an army officer, died six months later. In 1924 his mother moved to Rostov-on-Don and as a typist barely managed to support herself and her son. His early schooling reflected an interest in both history and science, and he graduated from Rostov University in 1941 with a double degree in mathematics and physics. Married the previous year to Natalia Reshetovskaya, a chemist and accomplished pianist, he was inducted into the army on 18 Oc-

reputation it was presumed by those in the literary and political establishment that this neophyte could be shaped to fit the prevailing ideology. But when Khrushchev began to retreat from liberalization, he found he had unleashed an opponent with formidable moral and political resources.

Although Solzhenitsyn has compromised when his very survival was at stake, he has pursued his own program and become—as he said of great writers in *The First Circle* (Harper & Row, 1968)— a "second government." Fiercely independent, he has always maintained positions that set him apart not only from the Politburo but from fellow dissidents, Russian emigrés, and Western admirers. His last decade in the West needs to be understood in terms of that rugged individuality, a characteristic he deeply admires in his Cavendish, Vermont, neighbors.

It has only become possible in the last few years to fully investigate the phenomenon of Solzhenitsyn, a figure who has been regarded as the conscience of Russia and who has recently alienated a considerable segment of his worldwide audience

Solzhenitsyn

The GULAG Archipelago

An Experiment in Literary Investigation

For years I have with reluctant heart withheld from publication this already completed book: my obligation to those still living outweighed my obligation to the dead. But now that State Security has seized the book anyway, I have no alternative but to publish it immediately.

THE AUTHOR

Dust jacket for the book that examines Soviet repression since the October Revolution of 1917

tober 1941. By 1945 he had been twice decorated as an artillery officer. Arrested in February of 1945 for criticisms he leveled at Stalin in letters to a friend, he was sentenced on 7 July to eight years of hard labor to be followed by three years of internal exile.

Solzhenitsyn writes movingly about his arrest in *The Gulag Archipelago* (vol. 1, Harper & Row, 1974). It hit him completely by surprise, for he had believed his remarks on Stalin were permissible, and in every way he had performed as a loyal Soviet citizen. Indeed, it was already his ambition to write a series of novels on the 1917 Revolution that forever changed history—for the better, Solzhenitsyn (an orthodox Communist) believed. Even during his early, disillusioning years in the camps, he persisted in regarding his imprisonment as an aberration and the camps themselves as an error the Soviet system could correct.

Always committed to his writing, he devised ingenious ways of preserving the verse he com-

posed in the camps. With a string of beads, modeled after the rosaries religious prisoners made out of soap, he was able to remember several hundred lines of poetry. Once out of prison he worked as a physics teacher and was generally known to be deeply devoted to his students. As a disciplinarian, he was tough on both the students and himself, enforcing a strict schedule that had become second nature to him because of the rigors of army and camp life. In internal exile, he diligently but discreetly pursued the writing of poetry, plays, and—above all—fiction.

Solzhenitsyn's habits in his American home have not changed much. He still rises at dawn, begins writing at 8:00 A.M., and usually continues until 5:00 P.M., with interruptions of his work in order to attend to family matters, to the education of his three children by his second wife, or to other domestic duties. Evenings are reserved for correspondence and other business connected with his books (which have sold more than thirty million copies) and to visitors or friends. The Vermont landscape reminds him of Russia, and he is attracted to the local, town-meeting type of democracy he also admired during his year's stay in Switzerland after leaving the Soviet Union. Although he prefers rural, small-town village life, he is not hostile to modern technology. His fiction reveals admiration for engineers and other technicians, but he would like to see science used to preserve the local, regional, and national characteristics of people. To some extent, his views resemble the "small is beautiful" concept championed several years ago by Governor Jerry Brown of California.

The First Circle, completed in 1958 but revised several times afterwards, is still his finest novel because of its encyclopedic and dramatic revelation of how Soviet citizens, inside and outside of the camps, tried to cope with and rationalize the revolutionary state that repressed the very people it had been created to liberate. Throughout the years from 1962 to 1974, the author circulated various versions of the novel, sometimes excising critical chapters in the hope that authorities would approve its publication. In camp terminology, the first circle of hell is the *sharashka*, a technical institute staffed by prisoners working on spying devices. Usually work on important projects prevents the technicians from being transferred to the hard-labor camps. Given some privileges, it is ironic that in their incarceration they have a certain limited freedom to argue about politics that the so-called free people outside the *sharashka* cannot exercise.

Engineers debate the culpability of Stalin and his accomplices and argue for and against the Marxist interpretation of history—much as Solzhenitsyn did himself with friends who took both positive and negative stances toward communism. Quite aside from ideological opponents are characters like the peasant Spiridon—also modeled after a Solzhenitsyn friend. Spiridon's homespun truths, his directness and simplicity, appeal to an author who believes Soviet culture has perverted and debased a rich proverbial language expressive of a thousand years of Russian history.

In addition to the *sharashka* inmates, there are numerous prison officers and political officials whose psychology receives penetrating analyses and shrewd treatment in dialogue. For example, the apostate Innokenty Volodin, State Counselor in the Ministry of Foreign Affairs, is arrested after attempting to warn a university professor that he is in danger of being apprehended by the security police. Volodin, in turn, is one of five suspects identified in voice prints made with a crude machine developed by Rubin, a *sharashka* engineer. When Rubin protests that Volodin may not be guilty, the head of the Special Equipment Section of the Ministry of State Security, Oskolupov, replies: "Not guilty of anything at all? The security organizations will find something; they'll sort it all out." As Michael Scammell puts it: "What Soviet citizen can place his hand on his heart and declare that he is guilty of nothing? In the Soviet security service there is a saying: 'Give us the man we'll find the crime.'" *The First Circle*, Scammell observes, is "a geological cross section of Soviet society from top to bottom," and as such it is the novelist's richest exploration of every shade of opinion, of every human soul that strains to express itself for or against the State.

In both *One Day in the Life of Ivan Denisovich* (Praeger, 1963) and *The First Circle*, Solzhenitsyn commands the world's attention because he is striving to define what it means to be human in degrading conditions. Even Khrushchev could be moved by *Ivan Denisovich* because it places so much intense concentration on the value an individual put into his forced labor. A confirmed realist and traditionalist, Solzhenitsyn believes there are universals and the eternal verities of the human heart that William Faulkner spoke of in his Nobel Prize address. Categorical statements about the human soul, about good and evil, have left modern, secular readers uneasy. *Ivan Denisovich* disarms rational objections to what is ultimately a religious conviction on Solzhenitsyn's part by simply and sparely dram-

atizing the worker's day, by getting inside of Ivan's mind. Of course, there are political ramifications to the way Ivan is presented, but like so many others Khrushchev was slow to appreciate that in Ivan, Solzhenitsyn was positing an ineradicable individuality that was subversive of the Soviet regimentation of society.

The First Circle, on the contrary, is overtly political—although most of the editorializing comes through the dialogue of its characters, so that Solzhenitsyn's overall view is not easy to define, although his persistent belief in the power of individual conscience (akin to Thoreau's) is unmistakable. An artist in *The First Circle* argues for the right to envision a "*spiritual* reality" that the particular individual in his portrait may not as yet have "displayed in his life." Indeed, for all his accurate concern with the material world, Solzhenitsyn is fascinated with characters who can transcend materialism. In a criticism that presages some of the author's remarks in the last decade, one of his characters in *The First Circle* comments:

> have you ever noticed what makes Russian literary heroes different from the heroes of Western novels? The heroes of Western literature are always after careers, money, fame. The Russians can get along without food and drink—it's justice and good they're after. Right?

Although this is a crude, chauvinistic reduction of Solzhenitsyn's attitudes, the speech reflects his profound belief that the deprivation of the camps—there was precious little food or drink—actually strengthened his soul and made it possible for him to withstand the later years of intimidation in his battles with the State. Gleb Nerzhin, based in many ways on Solzhenitsyn himself, becomes the focus of attention when the narrator in *The First Circle* suggests that "in every human being's life there is one period when he manifests himself most fully, feels most profoundly himself, and acts with the deepest effect on himself and others. . . . For Nerzhin, prison was such a time." Similarly, the legacy of the camps became the basis on which Solzhenitsyn acted in the years that brought him fame, enormous power, and intense criticism.

Even to Solzhenitsyn's surprise, the publication of *Ivan Denisovich* brought forth letters from men still in the camps. Although *The Gulag Archipelago* covers the years 1918-1956, it was clear to its author that the camps remained—if no longer on the scale Stalin created (tens of millions died in the Gulag). Soviet society was hardly less repressive, given that the complete details of camp life, of an archipelago stretching across the country, were not admitted to public scrutiny and Soviet writers were under increasing pressure to avoid altogether subjects that might demoralize the people. Indeed, what troubled Solzhenitsyn was that not only politics but other grim realities such as the disease he detailed in *The Cancer Ward* (Dial, 1968) could not be published.

From 1963 until 1969 he continued rather ambiguously as an established figure—certainly a loner who was seldom published but nevertheless in good standing until his expulsion from the Russian Writers' Union on 4 November 1969. In those years he was extremely careful about releasing his work to *samizdat* (underground publication) and to the West. At the same time, however, he relentlessly went about researching and writing his Gulag books, establishing contacts with agents and writers in the West, and slowly and strategically involving himself in the dissident movement without ever joining any organizations. The failure of *Novy Mir*, the journal which published *Ivan Denisovich*, to maintain any sort of independence, the persecution of Andrei Sakharov and other dissidents, the increasing power of the KGB and the State's whole security apparatus, and the general tightening of censorship during and after Khrushchev's regime steadily pushed Solzhenitsyn into outright defiance of the government.

He made use of his prison experience in that he took advantage of every rule, cited every precedent in Soviet law and literature, for his speaking out while never explicitly attacking the authority of the State. Even his deeply critical *Letter to the Leaders of the Soviet Union* (sent on 5 September 1973, published by Harper & Row in 1975), did not challenge their right to rule but only the Marxist basis on which the government should continue. But the Nobel Prize and the publication of *The First Circle, The Cancer Ward*, and *The Gulag Archipelago* in the West lent such weight to his views that the Politburo decided to deport a writer who had, indeed, formed a "second government," one that was incredibly adept at provoking public opinion in the West to question the détente of the 1970s developed under Nixon, Kissinger, and Brezhnev.

As pressure intensified on both Solzhenitsyn and Sakharov in the year before the former was banished for treason, Western sympathy and admiration of the novelist deepened, and Sakharov and other prominent Soviet intellectuals stoutly defended their greatest living writer. Yet he contin-

ued to function as an aloof figure—even among the dissident community because of his conservatism and reservations about the West. With the appearance of *August 1914* in 1972 (Farrar, Straus & Giroux), unqualified admiration of Solzhenitsyn ended. The Western reaction to the author's first volume in a series of novels on the First World War, the Revolution, and the creation of the Soviet state, is aptly summarized by Scammell:

> Like Russian readers, the reviewers noted Solzhenitsyn's abandonment of personal testament for historical inquiry and generally regretted the loss of intensity that this entailed. Like the Russians, too, they generally preferred the battle scenes to the rest, though some found even those too encumbered with their documentary sources.

The novel lacked "aesthetic cohesiveness." Its formal devices—Dos Passos-like camera eye sections, excerpts from newspapers and heavy use of proverbial language—seemed to reviewers unnecessary diversions from the main narrative. Debates in Russia over the content of the novel, especially Solzhenitsyn's growing sympathy for pre-revolutionary Russian government, dismayed his contemporaries who looked not to the past but to the present Western models of social democracy. This book was the beginning of a revaluation of both his style and his convictions that is still the subject of vigorous debate. Both his literary and political views have been subject to steadily antagonistic reactions.

As Scammell and many others sympathetic to Solzhenitsyn have pointed out, the Russian author has not helped himself by his tendency to go to extremes. In *Solzhenitsyn in Exile* (Hoover Institution Press, 1985), John Dunlop demonstrates that it is in the nature of his subject to attack sharply, to engage in polemics, when his purpose is to shift public opinion. In point of fact, many of Solzhenitsyn's approving comments on the West and on America could be cited to show that he is not hostile to democracy as such, but his major concern is not to congratulate Americans for their generous help to other countries and their previous steadfastness in the face of Soviet aggression. He fears, rather, for the erosion in opposition to communism fostered by détente in the 1970s and for the future unwillingness of Americans to fight for freedom. His comments, however, have caused much confusion because he veers between suggesting that a decline in American resolve has already taken place and warning that he is alerting the U.S. to alarming trends that could result in weakness. Perhaps the clearest way of explaining his position is to say he is frightened by America's unwillingness to contend with growing Soviet strength, especially since Western Europe, in his view, has already signified its eagerness to collaborate with the U.S.S.R.

In *Warning to the West* (Farrar, Straus & Giroux, 1976) Solzhenitsyn writes that "only firmness makes it possible to withstand the assaults of communist totalitarianism" and goes on to cite approvingly the examples of the Berlin airlift in 1948, the Korean conflict in 1950, and the Cuban Missile Crisis in 1962. Yet Americans now flinch from John F. Kennedy's ringing declaration that the country would pay any price to preserve freedom. Sounding, in fact, like a latter-day JFK, Solzhenitsyn also affirms in *Warning to the West* that "you cannot love freedom for yourselves alone. . . ." Vietnam, in his view, "was the least of a long chain of similar trials which awaits you in the near future."

As of August 1976 an official resident of Cavendish, Vermont, Solzhenitsyn began to set his sights directly on the infirmity of popular culture, largely dominated by American influences. At Harvard University on 8 June 1978 he scored the West for its loss of "civic courage," its dependence on legality rather than on morality, its "TV stupor . . . intolerable music." Behaving to his auditors like a fundamentalist preacher bemoaning a Godless society, Solzhenitsyn succeeded in arousing the press's ire—evidently to his surprise, even though he had singled it out for its superficiality and miseducation of the people. In a series of editorials and columns attacking his speech, the easygoing, tolerant, and even decadent qualities of the West were defended as the price of freedom. Because Solzhenitsyn was not willing to recognize democracy as a form of government that was everywhere realizable, he was excoriated as an authoritarian Russian mystic, a throwback to the nineteenth-century slavophiles who zealously tried to protect their country from contamination with Western liberal and radical ideas.

Solzhenitsyn does indeed have grave objections to Western democracy, and he doubts that it could be applied to Russia. In this respect, he differs not only from many Western observers but also from Russian dissidents who look to the West for help. Yet he admires the power of public opinion in the West and knows, from his own experience, of its power to do good, and he was shocked to find that his harsh criticism would be dismissed so quickly. His most cherished belief in the West is

that it can be self-critical—this is its strongest attribute and is what sets it apart from the U.S.S.R.

Solzhenitsyn has attributed his negative press to the unwillingness of Westerners to accept warnings that put in jeopardy a rather complacent and comfortable view of coexistence with the Soviet Union. Before the House Committee on Foreign Affairs, he asked how can the United States trust the Soviet Union in formal written agreements when its rulers "have never observed their own constitution?" As he knows, were Western governments and their citizens actually to accede to his admonitions and attempt to remedy their fatal tolerance toward the U.S.S.R., an enormous sacrifice would be called for. In effect, the West would have to proceed on the belief that the Soviet Union is indeed the "evil empire" to which President Reagan referred in his much-criticized press conference. Solzhenitsyn counsels the American government to strike harder bargains with its Soviet counterpart; he insists on what he calls genuine détente, not "pseudo-détente."

Solzhenitsyn has disturbed Americans and their allies because his vocabulary hearkens back to the simplistic caricatures of communism so prevalent in the early postwar and pre-détente period. Like Reagan, in fact, the Russian author has been accused of ignorance. He is on solid ground, of course, when he details the abhorrent universe of the Gulag, but what does he really know about foreign policy and about the designs of Soviet policymakers?

Breaking with Moscow (1985), Arkady Shevchenko's recent memoir of his career as a Soviet diplomat, confirms many of Solzhenitsyn's recent statements about the unremitting tyranny and expansionist goals of the Soviet Union. As a matter of fact, Shevchenko decided to defect after years of waiting to detect signs that the U.S.S.R. might be able to reform and to liberalize aspects of its brutally repressive system. Shevchenko is particularly convincing because of his long devotion to a career within the ranks of privileged government officials and because of the position he held at the United Nations as an advisor to Andrei Gromyko. Shevchenko shows that the varying personalities of officials and the extent to which they might have reservations about their government's policies hardly matter in the light of an overwhelming requirement that all servants of the State conform to a single objective: the systematic pursuit of world conquest—not, Shevchenko hastens to add, by world war but by subversion of various kinds. In the long run, in the total picture of things, differences of opinion among Soviet officials do not matter. Dominating as much of the world as possible is the perennial principle of the U.S.S.R.'s foreign and domestic policy, and this has been the case, Solzhenitsyn insists, from the very beginning of the Bolshevik revolution. Communism, inside and outside his native land, is basically the same, he adds to the dismay of those who count on the redeemable features of Marxism in other countries. Reform, he insists, is impossible; communism must be rooted out everywhere if humankind and the precious conscience of individuals are to survive anywhere. It is the universal threat of communism, and not its putative Russian roots, that Western and particularly American "experts" on the Soviet Union should recognize, he notes in "Misconceptions About Russia Are a Threat to America," in the Spring 1980 issue of *Foreign Affairs*.

This is not a new position for Solzhenitsyn; rather it is an understanding he has come to express with some urgency now that he has seen first-hand the illusions that prevent the West from saving itself. Although he has been accused of simplifying the historiography of American scholarship on the Soviet Union, he writes not as a scholar but as a product and participant of Soviet culture. His reading of American political scientists and his research at Stanford's Hoover Institution and at other American universities has confirmed his belief that the West knows very little about a country three quarters of which is closed to foreign visitors.

Unlike many Soviet intellectuals, Solzhenitsyn has lived in various remote parts of the U.S.S.R. and taken a deep interest in its various ethnic and religious groups, its peasants and workers. As John Dunlop suggests, Solzhenitsyn's traditionalism is probably more popular in his native land than the Westernized views of Sakharov and other dissidents. The novelist's vision is nothing less than apocalyptic and, yes, religious in the sense that he rejects the contemporary secularization of human behavior, a secularization that shrinks from absolute categories of good and evil. Having little patience with the sophisticated relativism of Westerners, he naturally struggles for a breakthrough in consciousness that would convince the anticommunist world that what is at stake are the very values that constitute a free human being.

The centerpiece of Solzhenitsyn's vision is *The Gulag Archipelago*, an astonishing feat of the historical and literary imagination. His three massive volumes on the unremitting cruelty of the camps require extraordinary dedication on the reader's part. While the author's energy never flags—he confronts himself and his readers with case after case of the heroism and corruption of the Gulag—it is a fact that the audience remaining for the final pages of his trilogy has been greatly diminished. Professor Edward E. Ericson's recent abridgment of the Gulag books (Harper & Row, 1985) attempts to remedy this dissipation of interest by reducing 1,800 pages to fewer than 500 while keeping the seven-part structure of the work intact and making room for additional comments by Solzhenitsyn which do not appear in previous editions. As a result, Solzhenitsyn's professed goal of affirming, in Ericson's words, an "innate human dignity" by writing a work that provides both a moral uplift and a "catharsis" is now readily accessible for those who were daunted by the scope of his epic. Judging by the morality of *The Gulag Archipelago*, the West must learn, as did some of the survivors of the camps, to acknowledge the worst in humankind before it can hope to reach the best. If his recent condemnation of Western weakness seems harsh, it reflects the same hard evaluation he conducts in regard to himself and his native land:

> When people express vexation, in my presence, over the West's tendency to crumble, its political short-sightedness, divisiveness, its confusions—I recall too: "Were we, before passing through the Archipelago, more steadfast? Firmer in our thoughts?"

This is, of course, Solzhenitsyn's point: the West has not passed through the Gulag.

The very first chapter of his account of the camps shifts quickly into the second person as he tries to put the reader in his place: "If *you* are arrested, can anything else remain unshattered by this cataclysm?" Before his arrest, Solzhenitsyn was no more a believer in the pervasiveness of the camps than his readers may be. Thus he makes of his own innocence an example that would surely be replicated in the lives of his readers. "Me? What for?" were his first words after the arrest. The camps, he proceeds to demonstrate in descriptions of the Gulag's millions of victims, were not there just to punish or liquidate political opponents. On the contrary, people of various persuasions—many of whom were loyal to the Soviet state—suddenly found themselves worked to death by a regimen of forced labor that leveled all human beings to the same degraded mass. Thousands of people, for example, were worked to death in a single construction project, and Solzhenitsyn's conclusion is that this lowering and elimination of human life was the necessary outcome of the revolution. His life's work, a series of historical novels entitled *August 1914* (Farrar, Straus & Giroux, 1972), "October 1916," and "11 March 1917," has been dedicated to proving that the triumph of Bolshevism was a fatal turning point in human history that calls into question the future of humankind itself. Lenin, once the projected hero of the author's fiction, has become the founding villain of totalitarianism.

Can the camps, begun during Lenin's rule, serve as a metaphor for the nature not only of Soviet life but of twentieth-century history? Every imaginable category of human being was included in the camps. Peasants, intellectuals, clergy, various ethnic groups and nationalities, high party officials, common thieves, children—the Archipelago contained a composite of the whole Soviet world and, by extension, the West, since many of its inhabitants were incarcerated for no other reason except that as soldiers they had been prisoners of war in Germany or had other contacts with Westerners. And the West, particularly Great Britain, Solzhenitsyn has pointed out in an electrifying appearance on British television, abetted Stalin by forcibly returning Russian émigrés after the Second World War to certain imprisonment and often death in the camps.

Solzhenitsyn had an extraordinary opportunity to learn about entire classes of people and elements of society that those outside the camps could not hope to understand. His prison experience, moreover, differs from what one would find in the West because of the opportunity he had to witness the lives of fellow writers, ideological opponents, and thinkers of every stripe. There is no twentieth-century author whose range of experience has been so all-encompassing. As a result, his remarkable individuality is matched by an equally noteworthy respect for the collective efforts of mankind. As Michael Scammell observes, *The Gulag Archipelago* is like one of those "vast and vaunted construction projects of the early Soviet years," except that Solzhenitsyn has restored the very humanity those projects destroyed.

After the appearance of *Ivan Denisovich*, Solzhenitsyn was besieged with letters and inquiries from camp inmates eager to ratify his experience with their own. It was then that he set out to write a monumental history of the camps that includes but transcends the novelist's fate. As Scammell concludes, from at least the time of *Ivan Denisovich*, the author realized he was living not only for himself but for the countless numbers of correspondents and interviewees who began to supply him with

testimony and documentation concerning the Gulag.

In America, John Dunlop demonstrates, Solzhenitsyn has not been as isolated as the press has supposed. In fact, he has made a point of traveling and of meeting all types of Americans. Naturally, there are aspects of American life and of Western values he does not fully appreciate, but on fundamental issues he seems reasonably well briefed. Not since de Tocqueville has a foreign writer exerted so much influence on American life. Far from being an intruder into American politics, Solzhenitsyn has been invited to speak on numerous occasions in this country and has evidently secured a fond place in the hearts of his Cavendish neighbors who have honored his obsession with privacy, especially after he attended a town meeting to explain that both the seclusion of the community and the climate reminiscent of his Russian days made him choose Cavendish for a home.

As in his fiction, so in his life Solzhenitsyn has proven to be close to the land and its people. He has been critical of American media and politicians for not reflecting the genuine values of the American heartland through which he has traveled and commented favorably upon. Never really a city intellectual, his conservatism has much in common with the American agrarian tradition and with the attitudes, if not the style, of writers like William Faulkner, who have fiercely maintained that the right of privacy and of self-determination are one and the same. Like the Faulkner of the 1950s, who wrote essays on the corruption of American values, Solzhenitsyn has been appalled by the superficiality of popular culture. It is not necessary to accept his evaluation of contemporary affairs, of course, but it is a facile notion indeed to suppose that his serious reservations are merely the result of lack of information or insensitivity. Solzhenitsyn has always been an inquisitive traveler and an impulsive deliverer of his opinions. His aloofness, however, is largely the result of his working life; people have often been inspired by his good humor, his energetic behavior, and his magnetic presence. On almost all public occasions he has spoken Russian, but he is fluent in German, and his English is adequate.

Solzhenitsyn is vitally concerned with the health and integrity of American culture not only because it represents the best means of checking Soviet aggressiveness but because he dreads the forces of mass culture that undermine a national identity from within. The mass media and press, in particular, seem artificial to him, for they frag-

Dust jacket for a 1974 English translation of the photographic and documentary account originally published by The Nobel Foundation

ment what should be the continuity of American life. There is so much abrupt switching from one topic to another that nothing can be followed in its entirety. His trilogy, most of which still has not been translated into English, reflects an old-fashioned emphasis on narrative, on a careful detailing of the causes and consequences of history because Soviet authorities have permitted only the official party view of the past. A government official in *The First Circle,* for example, speaks only of the "Party con-

science," of what the government chooses for its subjects to remember and to feel responsible for.

If *The First Circle* leaves the impression that Stalin alone is responsible for this tyranny, *Lenin in Zurich* (Farrar, Straus & Giroux, 1976), made up of selected chapters from Solzhenitsyn's series of historical novels, focuses on the founder of the Soviet state as an alien figure hostile to his own people:

How could you knead sad Russian dough

into any sort of shape! Why was he born in that uncouth country? Just because a quarter of his blood was Russian, fate had hitched him to the ramshackle Russian rattletrap. A quarter of his blood, but nothing in his character, his will, his inclinations made him kin to that slovenly, slapdash, eternally drunken country.

Lenin stands for the diminution of Russian character, and his ideology is directed toward wrecking the country's religious heritage, its language, its very rootedness in its thousand-year history.

The destruction of the Russian peasantry— begun under Lenin's leadership—as they were herded into collective farms reflects the systematic destruction of a whole people's identity. Solzhenitsyn's reliance on proverbs and on folk history constitutes his determined effort to recover the color, the variety, the texture of a land that has been denuded and depleted—its environment wrecked by a rapacious regime that cares for nothing but its own supremacy. And the West, he believes, is heading for a similar political, religious, literary, and ecological disaster if it does not recognize in time its own tendencies toward a deadening uniformity.

Not all has been lost, Solzhenitsyn shows toward the end of *The Gulag Archipelago*. In the late 1940s and early 1950s prisoners in the Gulag were gradually able to recreate a sense of public opinion among themselves that is reminiscent of the Solidarity movement in Poland. They were able to resist Stalinism and to establish an ever-widening area of freedom for themselves. Eventually that public opinion led to overt acts of resistance against the State, and while the State itself was not overthrown, conditions in the camps improved.

The Gulag is much more than just a history of the camps; it is a metaphor of the times. Its author staunchly defends the documentary, philosophical, and historical quality of his books, but he is a novelist first—which he emphasizes by titling *The Gulag Archipelago* "an experiment in literary investigation." The novelist has to do more than summarize, study, analyze his subject; he must make it live. History in his work has to flow, and the novel must provide an intricate environment that is complete in itself, an environment which is destroyed when one critiques it and breaks it down into its constituent parts. As Solzhenitsyn said to one of the critics of *Lenin in Zurich*, "your criticism is tantamount to draining an aquarium in order to study the life of the fish in it." The big fish, in this

case, is Lenin. Solzhenitsyn attempts to penetrate the great Bolshevik's psychology, one that is brutal, almost entirely self-centered and exculpatory. Lenin ruthlessly refuses to associate consistently and truthfully with any human being. The only possible exception is his love for Inessa, a fellow revolutionary whom he indulges in extraordinary ways. She represents the humanity he otherwise repels. For her, he will be tactful, conciliatory, sensitive to her moods. Every other individual is useful only in terms of the historical moment as Lenin interprets it. Terribly isolated in Zurich on the eve of the 1917 Revolution in Russia, he is also cut off from his fellow human beings.

Nowhere in the novel is such an explicit condemnation of Lenin expressed; on the contrary, the fiction is sympathetic to him in the sense that he speaks and thinks for himself, and a bond is formed between the revolutionary and the reader, since the vigor of Solzhenitsyn's prose admirably captures the energy of Lenin's mind. Inescapably an identification is made with this towering figure who doubts until the very moment of his arrival in Russia the efficacy of his life's work.

Something in Solzhenitsyn's own character perhaps accounts for the strength of his portrayal of the Soviet state's first ruler. If the author condemns the character, he cannot deny the force of that character's actions. In other words, Solzhenitsyn succeeds in revivifying history. It would have been easy for him to use only Lenin's words and to have him convict himself. That kind of irony is practiced in *Lenin in Zurich*, but a Jamesian narrator—close to but not synonymous with Lenin— provides an incisive commentary on the nature of Lenin's mind. In no sense, however, is the commentary omniscient; rather it is a shrewd voice that arises out of the historical conditions.

The year Solzhenitsyn spent in Zurich after his expulsion from the Soviet Union was an extremely difficult time, in which he had to re-establish his working habits, reconsider the impact of his fiction and public statements on the U.S.S.R. and on the rest of the world, and decide where it was he would live. At the same time, he was gathering additional material for *Lenin in Zurich* which was not available to him in the Soviet Union. Like Lenin, Solzhenitsyn was at a crossroads, gearing himself up to renew his commitment to a lifetime's work. Did Solzhenitsyn see himself in his reverse image, in the fiction he could not wait to publish until his series of historical novels was complete? While not conceding these parallels between himself and Lenin, he remarked that "I am writing him only out of his own characteristics . . . [but] I cannot describe him without myself having reached a certain level of psychology and experience. . . ." For Lenin, it was a matter of reaching the stage where he could return to Russia, having overcome his sense of being cut off from his homeland. For Solzhenitsyn, as Scammell suggests, exile meant coming to terms with the creator of the Soviet state: "Long after his disillusionment with Stalin, Lenin had remained his idol, the shining knight of the revolution, and it had taken him a long time before he plucked up the courage to tear him from his pedestal." With the abandonment of his last illusions, Solzhenitsyn set out to awaken the West, to become its exemplar and call its attention to values that were in danger of disappearing.

To his Vermont neighbors at a town meeting, Solzhenitsyn emphasized his rootedness in the Russian soil. Appealing to their own sense of identity, he noted, "I shall soon be sixty, but in all my life before, I have never had a permanent home." It was a "bitter fate to think and look back at his country," and on the day the Russian people "can be liberated from the Soviet system" he would thank them "very much for being good friends and neighbours" and go home. It is fascinating to see how hospitable he could be in the place he had chosen temporarily to call home, and his warm words, which were greeted with loud applause, were in striking contrast to the strident tones of his political speeches—perhaps because those speeches attack a world he cannot call home, a world that is, in his view, inhospitable to humanity.

Imagine the last twenty years without Solzhenitsyn. The last pages of Scammell's biography describe three of Solzhenitsyn's appearances on American, French, and English television; in each case, whatever reservations about his opinions were expressed by the public and the press, the overwhelming impression conveyed was of a prophet, of a human being who deserved a privileged status as modern minister to the fundamental ailments of society.

References:

Ronald Berman, et al., *Solzhenitsyn at Harvard: The Address, Twelve Early Responses, and Six Later Reflections* (Washington, D.C.: Ethics & Public Policy Center, 1980);

John B. Dunlop, Richard Haugh, and Alexis Klimoff, eds., *Aleksandr Solzhenitsyn: Critical Essays and Documentary Materials* (Belmont, Mass.: Nordland, 1973);

Dunlop, Haugh, and Michael Nicholson, eds., *Solzhenitsyn in Exile: Critical Essays and Documentary Materials* (Stanford, Cal.: Hoover Institution Press, 1985);

Kathryn Feuer, *Solzhenitsyn: A Collection of Critical Essays* (Englewood Cliffs, N.J.: Prentice-Hall, 1976);

Zhores Medvedev, *Ten Years after Ivan Denisovich* (New York: Knopf, 1973);

Michael Scammell, *Solzhenitsyn: A Biography* (London: Hutchinson, 1984).

Fifty Penguin Years

Philippa Toomey

In 1985 Penguin Books celebrated "Fifty Penguin Years" with a program of events to mark an anniversary which would have seemed impossible in the days of the firm's founding in 1935. An exhibition at London's Royal Festival Hall showed in extraordinary detail the progression of editorial trends and graphic design, as well as the march of Penguin's progress (usually in the vanguard of publishing). On sale in the Exhibition's bookshop was the billionth Penguin.

The founder and inspirer of this publishing company with its international reputation was Allen Lane. Born in 1902, Lane was at home in the publishing world. His uncle, John Lane, founded The Bodley Head, a publishing house which had had its scandalous moments (Oscar Wilde was one of the Bodley Head authors, and they had also published *The Yellow Book)*; but by the time Allen Lane joined the firm in a relatively junior capacity, it had become reputable, reliable, and rather dull—with a board of directors devoted to caution and respectability.

Allen Lane, as a possible heir to the business, was looked on with some disquiet. He had involved the firm in an embarrassing scandal in 1925 over the publication of *The Whispering Gallery,* allegedly the sensational memoirs of a well-known diplomat, but in fact written by Hesketh Pearson. When challenged, Hesketh Pearson had named Sir Rennell Rodd, the British Ambassador in Rome, as the author. This was untrue (Pearson later said it was "a joke") and the case ended up in the courts. Three weeks later, John Lane was dead, and Allen Lane had inherited the support of the major shareholder, Lane's widow; but he had a board of directors which was conservative and now distrusted his judgment.

All his life Allen Lane mixed business with pleasure, enjoying parties and social contacts with his authors. It brought him many books and friendships. The legendary beginning of Penguin Books occurred when he had a long rail journey back from Devon, where he had been visiting Agatha Christie. An hour spent on the platform at Exeter waiting for a connection revealed nothing to read,

Sir Allen Lane, founder of Penguin Books (courtesy of Penguin Books)

and as J. E. Morpurgo, Allen Lane's biographer, wrote, "The long bookless journey back to London would have been unbearable had it not set him to mulling over notions that had been present, if vague, in his mind for several years."

Paperback editions were by no means new. Victor Gollancz, an inspired and inspiring English publisher, had begun to publish in paperback; but the first books had not been successful, and the project was abandoned. There were the Tauchnitz editions and Albatross books on the Continent, but in 1935 Allen Lane was thinking of reprints of quality fiction and nonfiction to be sold at sixpence—

even then a very low price, comparable to the cost of ten cigarettes.

Allen Lane had two allies at the beginning of this venture—his brothers Dick and John. All three were bachelors and lived together in a flat in Talbot Square. All were involved, more or less indirectly, with publishing and The Bodley Head. The bathroom at Talbot Square was the "think tank" for discussion, argument, laughter, and preparations for a business decision which was to change publishing. The first reactions were not favorable. Where would the authors come from, allowing that The Bodley Head could not supply them all? What would be the reactions of rival publishers? Sixpence was an absurd price—where would any profit come from? And how would booksellers react? All this and more had to be faced before any action could be taken.

The board of directors at The Bodley Head were appalled: recipe for bankruptcy; one of Allen's mad schemes. Allen Lane, encouraged by Dick and John, would not be put down. He managed to persuade the board that he could go ahead with preparations for cheap paperback reprints, that he had authority to negotiate with Bodley Head authors and their agents as well as other publishers, and that they could use the Bodley Head staff and facilities—provided that there was no interruption of *normal* Bodley Head business. It looked like certain disaster. Moreover, when Allen Lane and his brothers began the approach to other publishers, they received almost as cold a reception as they had had from their own board. A bright young man with new ideas is not always welcome: he may fail, or he may be a successful rival. Why, they asked, would readers buy their books for 7s 6d if by waiting for the paperback they could pay a mere sixpence?

Allen Lane had to argue his case to any audience he could find. The three Lanes believed in their project, and some of the younger members of the staff at The Bodley Head were equally enthusiastic. They had to go out and sell the idea. At the booksellers' annual conference Allen Lane was greeted with open hostility, even heckled. It was a new idea, and booksellers are highly conservative in their outlook. Why, they asked, should they give valuable shelf space to books which (at 6d) would give them a very small profit? Would paperback books not fall apart? Would the small, easily pocketable books not be an easy prey for the pilferer? If successful, they pondered, it might ruin them all.

Opposition not only sharpened Allen Lane's

thoughts but opened new avenues for the book trade. The Lanes had the view that the books should not only be cheap but also well designed, well printed, produced in large numbers, and sold in equally large numbers—not necessarily in bookshops, but in places like Woolworth's. But, first of all, they had to have some titles to sell. Before they had any contracts to sign, the Lanes decided that they would have ten books to launch the venture, and then a series of successors. The first publisher to agree to have his titles reprinted was Jonathan Cape, a successful and innovative publisher, who said in later years that as he reckoned Allen Lane would go bankrupt in any case, he might just as well make as much profit as he could while the getting was good.

No author or publisher would become rich from the contracts the Lanes were offering. It is strange to look back from the present time, when paperback advances are very high, to a contract which offered a £25 advance against royalties, or £1 for every thousand copies sold. As the Lanes planned to publish at most 20,000 copies of each title, it would be very unlikely that an author could earn more than the advance. Favored authors offered £50 would only earn more if their books sold 48,000 copies—unthinkable at the time.

Of the ten books for the launch, only two came from The Bodley Head. As part of the fiftieth anniversary, Penguin published a facsimile set of the first group of titles, and it was a curious collection. It was the best that Allen Lane could get in the circumstances, bearing in mind that there was no editor and there was no editorial policy apart from providing a good, readable book for 6d. The Bodley Head pair were Agatha Christie's *The Mysterious Affair at Styles* and *Ariel*, André Maurois's biography of Shelley. Compton Mackenzie's *Carnival* came from Martin Secker (it had been published some twenty years earlier). From Jonathan Cape came six titles: Ernest Hemingway's *A Farewell to Arms*, Eric Linklater's *Poet's Pub*, Susan Ertz's *Madame Claire*, Beverley Nichols's *Twenty-five*, E. H. Young's *William*, and Mary Webb's *Gone to Earth*. Dorothy L. Sayers's *The Unpleasantness at the Bellona Club* came from Ernest Benn. It is said that the last title gave Allen Lane particular pleasure in that Dorothy L. Sayers was a Gollancz author, and Victor Gollancz had been particularly dismissive of Allen Lane's approaches. (The novel in question had been written when Sayers was a Benn author.) The result was that Gollancz retained his hatred of Penguin and all paperbacks for the next twenty years, and it is only now in the 1980s that Gollancz

The first ten Penguins, which appeared in July 1935 and established the form of the Penguin cover (courtesy of Penguin Books)

has opened its own paperback house. Victor Gollancz became a Penguin author in 1955—a feud resolved at last.

For the last fifty years we might well have been reading Dolphin Books, the first choice of name, but Dolphin belonged elsewhere, and Porpoise (the next choice) was being used by Faber and Faber. No one has ever claimed the original inspiration for Penguin, but a junior member of the staff who was an amateur artist was sent off to the London Zoo to draw some penguins. His original drawing, with some alterations, has remained the colophon. The artist's name was Edward Young, and in later years he was to write the Penguin numbered 1000, *One of our Submarines,* having become a medal-winning submarine commander.

Allen, John, and Dick Lane went on selling trips around the country, and John wrote to his overseas contacts. From abroad the welcome was favorable but resulted in few orders. The orders that Allen Lane had received did not even cover the expenses of his trip, and Dick had few orders to report. Two bookshops had shown enthusiasm—Bumpus and Selfridges, which had offered an Oxford Street window for a Penguin display. The totals, however, were dismal; an average of 7,000 a title was not even the halfway point.

Then there happened one of the strokes of luck which can turn a publishing house from disaster to triumph (or the other way round). Allen Lane revived his notion of selling through Woolworth's, whose policy at that time was to sell nothing that cost more than 6d. There is a nice story, revealed as a myth, that the chief buyer at Woolworth's turned down Penguins, but his wife, seeing them, said that they looked very good ar.d at 6d a time she would buy the lot. The truth is that Woolworth's put in a small consignment order, which meant sending stock to every Woolworth store, and confirmed the order a fortnight before publication at 63,500 copies. This improved the whole climate of opinion, and other booksellers became convinced that there might be something in a crazy idea after all.

Meanwhile the Lanes, with uncharacteristic prudence, had printed 20,000 of each title, but bound only half of them. Frenzied exertions on the part of staff and printers ensured that by 30 July 1935, 20,000 copies of each title had been printed, packed, delivered, and invoiced. One of the survivors of those exciting days remembers writing out invoices for every single Woolworth store by hand. At this moment, also, very large

A scene from Penguin's first offices, in the crypt of Holy Trinity Church, London, 1936 (courtesy of Penguin Books)

sums of The Bodley Head's money had been spent with no return in sight for the anxious directors who viewed the activities of the Lanes with much mistrust. But too much was at stake to withdraw.

The result was a publishing triumph. From the very first moment, Penguins were a success. It is difficult to analyze just why this should be so: the idea matched the moment. There was no coherent editorial or marketing strategy, and while there were plans for the future, these were vague. At no time did anyone guess that the word *Penguin* would become synonymous with "a paperback book." As J. E. Morpurgo points out, in the first hundred Penguins, there were not more than a dozen worth reprinting forty years on. In fact, Norman Douglas's novel *South Wind,* first published by Penguin as No. 11 in October 1935, is the book that has been longest in print, where it remains to this day. Financial success came more slowly. It was three years before Dick Lane could cease the regular visits to a friendly bank manager in order to keep their credit extended.

Hasty arrangements were made for Penguin Books to operate out of the crypt of Holy Trinity Church in the Marylebone Road. It had its disadvantages. There was no room for offices, and female staff could not be employed because there were no lavatories. It became part of the Penguin legend—of eighteen-hour days, with the Lanes themselves packing and invoicing. Stories abound of collapsing walls revealing coffins and skeletons, of six pennies a week being given to each man to use the men's lavatory at the nearby Great Portland Street underground station—and the curious smell (attributed to mice) of some of the books.

By January 1936 it was clear that the relationship between Penguin Books and The Bodley Head would have to be regularized. With a capital of £100 the three brothers set up the company Penguin Books Limited with themselves as directors. Allen then resigned from The Bodley Head. In January it was announced that the millionth Penguin had been sold. Overhead was low: the staff was small and poorly paid. John and Dick Lane took no salary for the first two years, and Allen Lane himself was paid only £1,000 a year. A combination of circumstances—the overcrowding in the crypt, the lack of office space, and a visit from a health inspector—made it essential to find new premises just at a time when costs, including the cost of paper and printing, were beginning to rise. Once again, a decision of Allen Lane's proved a master stroke.

Property in the traditional publishing area in central London was extremely expensive. Why not look for a site outside London? Dick Lane was put in charge of the search and finally settled on a three-and-a-half-acre site in Middlesex, a place called Harmondsworth, fifteen miles from central London. It was what is now called a green field site; the Underground system was only two miles away; it was within easy reach of the main-line railway; it was well sited for roads. The only snag appeared to be that in addition to the price of £2,000, the owner wanted an additional £200 for a crop of cabbages. Even so, it was a bargain, financed once again by the amiable Martin's Bank. The Lanes did not know that Heathrow Airport would be built on the open fields across the road.

In 1937, by chance (as so much seemed to be) Penguin issued six Shakespeare plays edited by G. B. Harrison, launched with a glamorous party at which, as Morpurgo says, "there were crammed into the Talbot Square flat almost every leading actor and actress who could be persuaded to come, but not one representative of the universities or the schools except the series editor." It heralded the turn toward the educational, the classic, and the foundation of Pelican Books.

George Bernard Shaw was the next to fall victim to Allen Lane. Though notoriously difficult over publishing matters (he employed no agent and bargained ably for himself), he accepted the standard, niggardly Penguin terms and updated his book *The Intelligent Woman's Guide to Socialism, Capitalism, Sovietism and Fascism* to two volumes. It then struck Allen Lane that this could be the start of a new series, the Pelicans. To the Shaw title was rapidly added *Last and First Men* by Olaf Stapledon, *Digging*

Cover for one of the first nine books published under the Pelican imprint, May 1937

Up the Past by Leonard Woolley, *A Short History of the World* by H. G. Wells, G. D. H. Cole's *Practical Economics, Essays in Popular Science* by Julian Huxley, *The Floating Republic* by Bonamy Dobrée and G. E. Manwaring, *A History of the English People in 1815* by Elie Halévy, and *The Mysterious Universe* by Sir James Jeans. A signpost to the future was *Practical Economics*, which was not a reprint, but the first of the Penguin originals. Obviously a list like Pelican could not be assembled in such a haphazard fashion for long, and Krishna Menon was invited to become editorial director, with an advisory panel of three other editors. Fifty Pelicans were published between 1937 and the outbreak of the war in 1939.

In 1937 the first Penguin Special was published. Penguin Specials have always been a kind of journalism, and *Germany Puts the Clock Back* by Edgar Mowrer, the Pulitzer Prize-winning American journalist, set the pattern. Mowrer had been thrown out of Germany by the Nazis for his forthright reporting of their rise to power. An initial print run of 50,000 copies had to be reprinted within a week. While the fortunes of the Specials have varied over the years, in 1985 Penguin declared their support for the series by announcing eight new titles to be published from September 1985 onward. This list included Lord Lever and Christopher Huhne's *Debt and Danger: the World Economic Crisis,* Tom Hadden and Kevin Boyle's *Ireland: A Positive Proposal,* William Keegan's *Britain Without Oil,* and Geoffrey Cannon's *The National Diet.*

From 1939, Penguin, in common with all other publishers, faced paper rationing and the departure for war service of many of the staff. In spite of the war, 1939 had seen the first titles of the King Penguin series of illustrated books, beginning with *British Birds on Lake, River and Stream* by John Gould, and Redouté's *A Book of Roses.* Penguin was in a comparatively good position over paper stocks. The quota was determined on prewar output, and Penguin's output had been prodigious for a staff of under forty people. The demand for reading matter during the war years was equally prodigious. Light, pocketable Penguins were ideal for sending to the forces overseas. Much traditional entertainment was closed down; Penguin flourished, bringing out Puffin Picture Books in 1940, and in the same year the first *Penguin New Writing,* edited by John Lehmann. It was a publishing legend in itself. At its peak, it sold more than 100,000 an issue, using five tons of paper each time—an amount equal to the entire paper ration allocated to some publishing houses. Puffin Story Books be-

gan in 1941 with Barbara Euphan Todd's *Worzel Gummidge*—a tale of a scarecrow, apparently immortal in that the books are still selling. The Penguin Forces Book Club was set up to satisfy demand for reading matter, and given the virtual monopoly that Penguin achieved, it was also very profitable for the company. By 1945 four out of every five titles published were originals, not reprints.

With the peace came new challenges. The close relationship between the three brothers, so vital to the enterprise and so rewarding in human terms, had been broken in 1942 by the death of John. Allen, a long-time happy bachelor, much interested in many women, married in 1941. His brothers had resented the marriage, and the relationship was never quite the same again. Allen and Lettice Lane had two daughters, but he was not a domestic man, and there were difficulties in the marriage, leading later in life to a virtual separation. He was always too much involved in his work (closely linked with his active social life) to make a great success as a husband and father.

As an employer, Lane also had his limitations. He took fancies to people and then dropped them. Old established staff who had worked for him for years were wounded by his lack of concern. On occasion, he behaved very badly to people to whom he owed a lot. Salaries continued to be very low and conditions far from ideal. But he had the great gift of inspiring people to follow him, the ability to make work fun, and an instinct for publishing for which people forgave him a great deal. He also picked some extremely talented people to work for him. His secretary, Eunice Frost, became one of the best editors in the publishing world. Nikolaus Pevsner was employed to edit the Buildings of England series, which was launched in 1951 and grew into forty-six magisterial volumes by the time of its completion in 1974. Pevsner also edited the Pelican History of Art, projected at forty-eight volumes, forty-four of which have appeared; the eventual sixty will be completed in 1995.

In the grey days after the war came the 1946 announcement of the first Penguin Classic, E. V. Rieu's translation of Homer's *Odyssey.* Not a good idea, said some. There were already eight translations, none of which had sold more than 3,000 copies. Allen Lane persisted. Today it is in Penguin's top six sellers—equal with Chaucer's *Canterbury Tales*—with more than three million copies sold. It was the beginning of a series which now has 750 titles. There were less successful ventures. Ptarmigans, a series on parlor games, lasted only a

Cover for one of the Puffin Picture Books, a series of children's books illustrated by autolithography to keep their cost low

couple of years. Penguin Modern Painters and Penguin Music Scores proved too expensive to produce and were closed down. The real troubles were to come later.

In 1946 Penguin brought out ten Bernard Shaw titles to mark his ninetieth birthday—the Shaw Million, it was called, with a hundred thousand of each title. It was a moment for gathering publicity, a grand gesture of the kind that Allen Lane loved and at which he excelled. An unprecedented demand, with runs on bookshops and Penguin's switchboard jammed on the first day, led to the selling out of the edition in six weeks. In 1960 Penguin had a more unexpected million. With the change in the climate of public opinion and the passing of the 1959 Obscene Publications Act, Penguin felt able to publish the first unabridged edition of D. H. Lawrence's *Lady Chatterley's Lover*. The

Crown decided to prosecute Penguin, and the case of *Regina* v. *Penguin Books Ltd.* provided some excellent, vintage entertainment for the five days of the trial. A selection of the great and famous in the literary world stepped into the witness box to give testimonials to Lawrence, and the prosecution's case was not improved when the Crown's lawyer suggested it was not a book that any man would wish his wife or maidservant to read. It was a test case, and Allen Lane might have been in trouble had he lost it. However, he had gambled on winning, had doubled the print run, and two million copies were sold in the six weeks following the trial. *Lady Chatterley* is also one of Penguin's top six, at four million copies to date.

As the 1960s progressed, the scene became less rosy for Penguin. For the first time they faced serious competition in their own field. Other publishers joined together to form Pan Books, a serious rival. (Later, in the 1970s, a trio of publishers who had hitherto had a friendly relationship with Penguin joined to form Triad, to publish their paperbacks under this new imprint.) Penguin's Canadian company had been formed in 1940, and the Australian company in 1946. Penguin Books Limited was beginning to be too large and complex for one man to direct. Allen Lane had no successor, no son to pass the business on to; and while he was adept at finding new and younger people to join the staff, he either would not or could not bring himself to name a successor or establish the future of Penguin Books when he retired. It was clear that something had to be done.

In 1960 Tony Godwin joined Penguin Books. He was a man much in the Allen Lane mold. In Morpurgo's description, "Godwin's assertiveness, energy, briskness and that strain in him which is best described as chirpiness reminded Allen of himself when he was Godwin's age." However, there were differences. Godwin was extremely talented but lived on his nerves, with periods of depression or aggression. Moreover, he saw the need for changes, many of which did not appeal to Allen Lane. He also, like Lane, had the ability to attract followers and admirers, particularly among the younger members of staff. Godwin updated the image of Penguin by bringing in the pictorial covers—a change much opposed by Allen Lane, but essential. He brought new blood and new authors to the list. During his six years at Penguin as editorial director he gave much and planted the seeds for the next decade. It was more than unfortunate that Allen Lane grew to dislike him and that the relationship which could possibly have been so fruitful was broken up in 1967. He had aspired to taking over from Allen Lane, but he was dismissed. For all that, the 1960s were a period of expansion. The Puffin lists flourished under the incomparable children's editor Kaye Webb, producing magazines and a club to add to the list. Today the Puffin list accounts for nearly forty percent of all children's paperbacks sold in the United Kingdom.

In 1969 Allen Lane celebrated fifty years in the publishing trade with the three thousandth Penguin title, James Joyce's *Ulysses*. He had been honored by a knighthood; now he was made a Companion of Honour, but he was suffering from the cancer which was to kill him in 1970. The day after his death the newspapers carried a statement from acting chairman Sir Edward Boyle, managing editor Christopher Dolley, and the directors of Penguin Books Limited announcing a merger with Pearson Longman. For the next few years, though there were successes—the formation of the Federation of Puffin School Book Clubs (in 1985 accounting for over two million Puffins sold a year), the beginning of Penguin Books in New Zealand, and the reforming of Penguin Books, Canada—Penguin Education closed after only six years of life. A considerable group of Penguin authors' rights, including those of Virginia Woolf and Somerset Maugham, reverted to their hardback publishers and were not renewed. There was increasing competition from other paperback houses, but a step toward broadening Penguin's coverage was taken with the acquisition of the American publishing house The Viking Press in 1975. It increased Penguin's American publishing opportunities and added some excellent authors, such as Saul Bellow, John Steinbeck, Arthur Miller, and Nadine Gordimer, to Penguin's list. But it was widely felt that the central direction of the firm had been lost, and that, increasingly, the employees were no longer willing to put up with the pay and conditions.

In 1978 the decision was made to appoint a chief executive, and the choice fell on Peter Mayer. Mayer, an American with an excellent record in paperback publishing in the United States, found himself faced with a large company, regarded in Britain with pride as an institution, which was rapidly sinking under increasing losses. His arrival also coincided with the beginning of a recession which was to shake the book trade during the 1970s. Mayer had a difficult task. First he had to reduce the number of staff by one hundred. For the first time there was industrial action taken by the staff, attracting bitter criticism of Mayer, and a great deal of unfavorable publicity. Everything that Mayer did or said was scrutinized in no very friendly spirit. In the years since the early bitter struggles, his policies have turned the losses into profits of £8M in 1985. His success seems to be attributable partly to the old traditional virtues of attention to detail, including careful estimation of print runs and the redesigning of covers, and partly to the newer disciplines of aggressive selling and marketing. Large sums were being offered for paperback rights in the 1970s, and Mayer dragged Penguin into the popular market, much to the horror of the traditionalists. It was, however, a question of sheer survival.

One of his "popular" novels was *The Far Pavilions* (1979) by a then-unknown author, M. M.

Colophons for Penguin, Pelican, and Puffin books

Kaye. At a slightly higher price, and in a large format, with an aggressive marketing campaign, it sold 400,000 copies in eight months. He also capitalized on the famous backlist. Before his arrival, no novel by Graham Greene had sold more than 70,000 copies in a year. With a newly designed cover, *The Human Factor* sold 300,000 in three months. In 1980, within forty-eight hours Penguin secured the paperback rights to five of the seven shortlisted titles for the Booker Prize, the largest literary prize in Britain, and delivered finished copies to the bookshops a week later.

In the 1980s began the rise of the Penguin Bookshops—the first was opened in 1980 in Covent Garden, then newly refurbished as an attractive area for shopping, leisure, and the arts. By 1985 there were nine Penguin Bookshops and a Puffin Bookshop, specializing in children's books. The Penguin shop-within-a-shop has grown at the same time—in bookshops and in other kinds of retail outlets. Today, Penguin claims, a Penguin is sold every 1.5 seconds somewhere in the world.

Additions to the series continue. King Penguins were launched in 1981, or rather, reinvented. No longer picture books, they became a series of literary works in a slightly larger format: Puffin Classics, Fighting Fantasy, The Penguin Travel Library, Penguin Passnotes (review aids for students), and a Lives and Letters series, to be followed by Lives of Modern Women.

During Peter Mayer's reign (as King Penguin, some would call him) there have been acquisitions which have changed the character of the company. In 1983 Penguin bought the old publishing house of Frederick Warne, best known as publishers of Beatrix Potter. In 1984 a small American trade publisher, Stephen Greene Press, was bought. In 1985, the anniversary year, it was announced that Penguin Books Limited had bought five of the companies forming the main part of the publishing empire of Thomson International. These firms included two hardback publishers, Hamish Hamilton and Michael Joseph; Rainbird, an international book packaging company; the paperback house Sphere Books; and TBL Book Services, a warehousing and distribution firm. Penguin Books is a very large and influential hardback and paperback publishing house with international connections. Best-sellers like Dick Francis, James Herriot, and Danielle Steel now appear on Penguin's list.

Today, with companies in five countries, Penguin adds 1,200 titles to the list every year—at least one third of which are commissioned by the firm. In the United Kingdom alone 700 new Penguin titles are published, as well as 2,500 reissues. When the imprint was launched in 1935, there were jokes about a series named for a bird that could not fly. That bird has hopped and waddled a great distance during the last half century.

Sinclair Lewis Centennial Conference

Martin Bucco
Colorado State University

In 1945 Sinclair Lewis, at sixty, admitted that he wondered unendingly "whether I might not have been a much better writer had I spent all my life, except for a year or two in the East, for contrast, in my native Minnesota." Less prone than Lewis to such wondering, the Minnesota House of Representatives passed a resolution commemorating the 100th birthday—7 February 1985—of the state's only, and America's first, Nobel laureate in literature.

To celebrate the man and to reassess his work, St. Cloud State University, situated on the west bluff of the Mississippi, hosted a Sinclair Lewis Conference on 7-9 February. Directed by Michael Connaughton of the English Department and supported by faculty, students, townspeople, and the Minnesota Humanities Commission, the gathering drew scholars and writers from throughout the region and the nation. Between continental breakfasts, buffet luncheons, coffee breaks, and nightly banquets, celebrants picked among the more than fifty items on the program—appreciations, films, recollections, interpretations, exhibits, history, pedagogy, tours, and even a new play about Lewis.

Most of the events took place in the university's Atwood Memorial Center. Writer John Koblas presented "Home at Last," a slide show of Sinclair Lewis's Minnesota residences. At the first banquet, Virginia Lewis of San Francisco, reminiscing about "My Uncle Hal," read samples of letters he had written to her when she was a schoolgirl in St. Cloud. Afterward, novelist and raconteur Frederick Manfred related in his talk, "Memories of Sinclair Lewis," how the famous author had befriended him as a struggling young writer. The next afternoon Ida Kay Compton declaimed in "Dear Red . . . Love Ida" on how she persuaded her friend not to publish an early version of his last novel, *World So Wide*.

Scholarly papers ranged widely, treating connections between Sinclair Lewis and satire (T. J. Matheson), social criticism (W. Gordon Milne), literary journalism (Martin Bucco), the short story (Clara Lee Moodie), the small town (James Marshall, Lydia Blanchard), the Midwest (James Lundquist), the South (Edward J. Piacentino), Europe (Salley E. Parry), Hungary (Anna B. Katona), blacks (Robert Fleming), Jews (Barry M. Gross), humanism (Stephen L. Tanner), religion (Elmer Suderman), technology (Glen Love), the screen (Wheeler Dixon), marriage (Bea Knodel), alcohol (Roger Forseth), Jack London (Robert Coard), Grant Wood (David Crowe), J. F. Powers (Walter H. Clark), and Garrison Keillor (Wayne Meyer, Garvin Davenport).

One session tackled problems in teaching *Main Street, Babbitt,* and *It Can't Happen Here.* An-

Cover of playbill for drama by Lance S. Belville commissioned by St. Cloud State University for their national conference on Sinclair Lewis, February 1985

145

other presented dramatic readings of *Cass Timber-lane*. The film festival showed adaptations of four Sinclair Lewis novels: Guy Kibbee and Aline MacMahon in *Babbitt* (First National, 1934); Walter Huston and Ruth Chatterton in *Dodsworth* (United Artists, 1936); Spencer Tracy and Lana Turner in *Cass Timberlane* (M-G-M, 1947); and Burt Lancaster and Jean Simmons in *Elmer Gantry* (United Artists, 1960). The Atwood Center, Alumni House, and Learning Resource Center displayed books and other Lewis material.

After William Morgan's lecture on community values in Main Street architecture, buses toured nearby Sauk Centre, the town that raged against her native son yesterday but raves about him today. The calendar of the Sauk Centre Centennial Committee ran from January to October—with everything from unveilings of a bronze bust, a postage stamp, and a medallion to the raw stuff of another *Main Street*— readings, discussions, and recitations; writing, photography, and cake-decorating contests; window displays, musicals, and snow sculptures; carnivals, races, and treasure hunts; antique, auto, and air shows.

Braving the cold, attendees stopped at the Interpretive Center, crossed Original Main Street and Sinclair Lewis Avenue, and looked in on Lewis's boyhood home "restored to turn-of-the-century apple-pie order." They glimpsed Bryant Library,

the *Sauk Centre Herald,* Main Street Drug, Sauk Lake, and Greenwood Cemetery.

At the town's Little Theatre in Sauk Centre High School, first-nighters saw Lance S. Belville's commissioned play, *Exile from Main Street: A Portrait of Sinclair Lewis.* Directed by John Orlock of the Great North American History Theatre, the monologic tour de force starred Jay Nickerson, who had previously portrayed F. Scott Fitzgerald in Belville's *Scott and Zelda: The Beautiful Fools.* Playing Sinclair Lewis, an irrepressible parlor mimic, Nickerson mimed seventeen parts, among them Billy Sunday, H. L. Mencken, Alfred Harcourt, Grace Hegger Lewis, Dorothy Thompson, and Marcella Powers.

Finally, David D. Anderson of Michigan State University gave the capstone address, "Sinclair Lewis and the Midwest Tradition." Mentioned almost as much as the name "Sinclair Lewis" was the name "Mark Schorer." More than a few at the conference argued that Schorer's jumbo biography, though brilliant, displays insufficient sympathy for Lewis. Among other outcomes, the centennial stimulated the republication of James Lundquist's 1973 short study, *Sinclair Lewis* (Ungar, 1984); the sale of a three-volume set of letters and diaries edited by John Koblas and David Page—*Selected Letters of Sinclair Lewis* and brother Claude B. Lewis's diaries, *Sinclair Lewis and Mantrap: The Saskatchewan Trip,* and *Sinclair Lewis: Final Voyage* (Main Street Press,

View from Lewis's boyhood home down Sinclair Lewis Avenue toward the intersection with Main Street (AP Laserphoto)

Dave Jacobson, president of the Sinclair Lewis Foundation, in front of Lewis's boyhood home (AP Laserphoto)

1985); the printing of *Sinclair Lewis at 100* (St. Cloud State University, 1985); the conference proceedings edited by Michael Connaughton; the publication of Martin Bucco's volume, *Critical Essays on Sinclair Lewis* (G. K. Hall, forthcoming in 1986); and the production of a PBS television documen-

tary by Gene Dent. On 7 February a feature in the *Minneapolis Star And Tribune* proclaimed: "All Is Forgiven, Sinclair—Happy Birthday!" Ten days later the book page announced: "Lewis Reputation Gets Big Boost At Saint Cloud Conference."

Lardner 100: Ring Lardner Centennial Symposium

Hal Wyss
Albion College

A national celebration and symposium in recognition of the one hundredth anniversary of the birth of Ring W. Lardner was held on the campus of Albion College, Albion, Michigan, 5-8 March 1985. Lardner was born in Niles, Michigan, 6 March 1885.

The intent of the four planners of "Lardner 100," Albion professors Russell Aiuto, Charles Crupi, James Diedrick, and Hal Wyss, was that the event should include both festivities honoring Lardner and a working conference interpreting and evaluating Lardner's contribution to American letters. Two days of panel discussions, addresses, and responses were bracketed by the premiere performance of *Ring Lardner's America* (an original play by Aiuto and Crupi written for the symposium), a birthday banquet, a production of Lardner and Kaufman's 1929 Broadway play *June Moon,* and several exhibitions. Invited to participate were editors of Lardner's stories and letters, biographers, novelists, scholars of sports literature, literary historians, and members of the Lardner family. Six Lardners were in attendance including Ring Lardner's son Ring, Jr. and his wife Frances, granddaughters Susan and Katy, and grandson James and his wife Natalie. Susan, James, and Ring Lardner, Jr. took part in conference panel discussions.

The birthday banquet on the evening of 6 March, which was attended by 160 participants and visitors, was both a ceremonial gathering and the beginning of a serious investigation of Lardner as a writer. Following the reading of proclamations by the Michigan State Legislature and Governor Blanchard and a lighthearted reminiscence by Ring Lardner, Jr. was the keynote address of Jonathan Yardley, book critic for the *Washington Post* and author of the most recent biography of Lardner (*Ring,* 1977). To the surprise of most of the audience, Yardley both refused to claim great stature for Lardner as a writer and warned other participants not to overestimate him. "I should like to begin with a cautionary note. It is in the nature of gatherings such as this one to sing loud the praises of the person in whose honor they assemble. This is not merely natural but appropriate. There is al-

ways the temptation though, and it is often succumbed to, to heap upon the remains of the honoree more praise than he or she can bear. . . . So I begin with both a plea and a judgment. The plea is that, in the interests of common sense and scholarly standards, we keep our heads about us. The judgment, which is directly related to the plea, is that the most that can be said of the writer whom we are celebrating is that he was a distinctly minor figure in American literature and, so far as I can tell, a figure of no moment at all in international literature." Yardley continued in this vein for a substantial portion of his address. "A large audience read him for about two decades in the teens and twenties, but almost nobody reads him now. . . . Most of his work now seems irretrievably dated. . . . He did not do the work he could and should have done, and the work he did do is not sufficient to permit him the substantial place in American writing that I among others most devoutly wish were his."

Eventually, and to those in attendance it seemed much later in the address than it actually was, Yardley reached a transition. "But this is really quite enough of facing up to the hard truths with which I believe Ring Lardner presents us. Let us now turn to those aspects of his life and work which we still have cause to celebrate." First among these aspects is baseball writing: "In the small landscape of baseball writing he is now, as he always has been, a dominant figure." Having said this, however, Yardley found more "hard truths" to face up to, particularly that Lardner never wrote a novel and, although the short story had some prominence in Lardner's day, "the short story, to put it as mildly as possible, no longer occupies any such role in American culture today." And yet, said Yardley, "Lardner lives." He lives, not directly through his stories, but indirectly through the influence the language of those stories has had on the styles of his contemporaries and many American authors since. "Ring tried to capture the way people really sound and to an extraordinary degree he succeeded. What he did seems commonplace to us now for the simple reason that it is indeed so common, but in

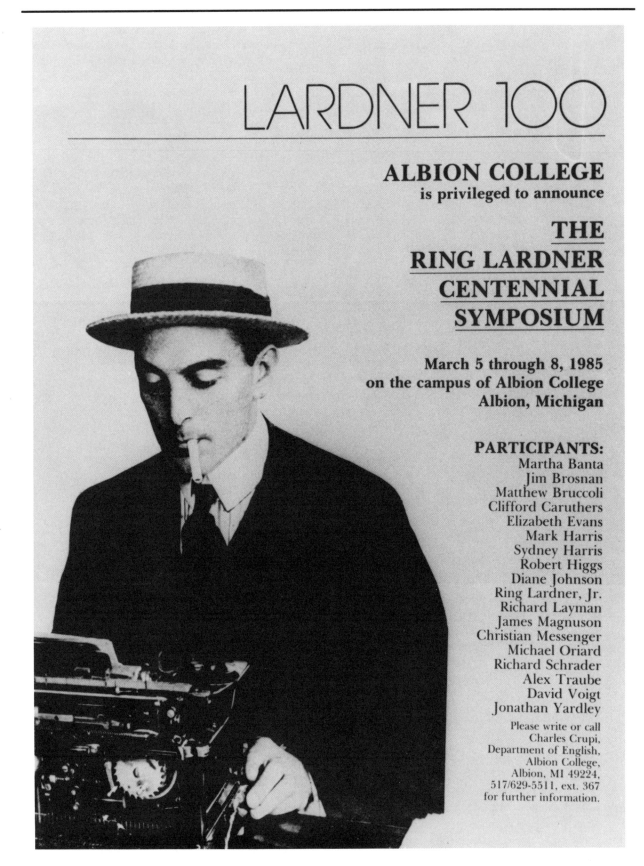

Announcement for the Lardner celebration

Ring's day it was revolutionary. In fact, it just about knocked H. L. Mencken's socks off, and it opened the way for everyone else." Finally, according to Yardley, "Ring lives in the way Americans see and define themselves," in the "detached and skeptical view of the reality behind the American dream," which is "near universal now" but was "a far piece from near universal seven decades ago when Ring started to articulate it."

Jonathan Yardley's address was balanced and thoughtful, but his "hard truths" came first and tended to echo in the ears of other participants louder and longer than the accolades he accorded Lardner in the second half of his address. During the ensuing two days, those speakers not delivering prepared papers (that is, members of panels and respondents to addresses) devoted at least part of their time to disagreeing with one or more of Yardley's judgments, and a dialogue developed on the related questions of Lardner's place in American literature and whether such rankings mean anything in the long run. Yardley himself, participating with Ring Lardner, Jr. and Clifford Caruthers in a panel on "Lardner's Life and Times" the following morning, said that it had not been his intention to rank Ring Lardner; "If I presented that impression, I'm certainly sorry." He went on to explain: "It is my judgment and I can only present it as such . . . that there is not much of enduring quality to Ring's fiction, and I am not measuring that against Scott Fitzgerald or Theodore Dreiser or anybody else; I am measuring it for its own weight, and I find relatively little weight there."

The other two panel members found more weight in Lardner's stories. Clifford Caruthers, editor of *Letters from Ring* and *Ring Around the Max*, recalled that in *Letters from Ring* he had said Ring Lardner created more vivid and more accurate characterizations than any of his contemporaries including Fitzgerald and Hemingway. "As I reread my words yesterday, I still believe them. . . . Jack Keefe, Alibi Ike, the barber in 'Haircut,' the 'Golden Honeymooners,' all stick in my mind even more vividly than Jay Gatsby or Frederic Henry or Robert Jordan." Ring Lardner, Jr. disagreed with the contention that his father excelled only as a baseball writer. "I think that some of the best stories are the non-baseball stories, and I think he was working on his craft all the time." He cited three non-baseball stories—"Some Like Them Cold," "I Can't Breathe," and "Who Dealt?"—as examples of memorable works containing "some of the most revealing writing about people."

Various later speakers took issue with some

of Yardley's ideas, but it was Richard Layman, coeditor (with Matthew J. Bruccoli) of *Some Champions* and *Ring Lardner: A Descriptive Bibliography*, who, speaking the afternoon of 8 March and having had two days to think about it, provided the most complete response to Yardley's contention that Lardner is a "distinctly minor figure in American literature." Layman began by answering in the affirmative the question of whether literary critics should establish rankings of writers. "There is clearly a compelling need to study literature and understand literary traditions. It follows that we must make value judgments about what we read, and we must rank writers in order to order the chaos of literature that is thrown at us." The problem is that students of literature may not agree on the criteria upon which such rankings are based or on the proper ways of applying those criteria. "Universality is certainly a criterion that we can use to judge Lardner's works. We are told that while his characters tell us something about the way people were during the twenties and thirties, they tell us almost nothing about the way we are now. I disagree. I think most of us, perhaps, disagree with that statement. . . . I feel that Lardner's strength as a writer is his ability to draw strikingly accurate characters as recognizable now as ever."

Layman acknowledged that Lardner should be ranked behind some novelists. "Great short story writers take their place behind great novelists because they attempted less." Given that, Lardner's achievement should not depend on what he never attempted to do, write a novel, but on what he did do. "It seems to me that when we look at Lardner as literary historians, it is necessary to see him in the proper context as a journalist, as a humorist, and as a short story writer." Discussing these three separately, Layman said first that "as a journalist Lardner seems to me to have very little importance today." However, "Lardner ranks very highly among American humorists. He was the best of the lot during what has been called the golden age of American humor." Finally, according to Layman, "It is as a short story writer that Lardner truly distinguishes himself. . . . The status-conscious suburbia of Lardner's 1920s stories with his pretentious, self-deluded, pitiful little people struggling for recognition is still profoundly useful for its insight into what makes us the way we are and into what makes our world the way it is." "It's a mistake," concluded Layman, "to underestimate and to undervalue works like Lardner's. If we're not careful, we're going to wake up one morning and find that all good writers are gone, that we've buried them, that they're relegated to the status of being minor figures and buried in the stacks of unused libraries."

Whatever Lardner's rightful place in a literary hierarchy may be, much of the centennial symposium focused on other subjects such as his influence on later writers, the context in which his career developed, the literary genres his works do or do not fit into, the nature and influence of his vernacular, and his attitude toward 1920s American cultural values. There were three addresses (in addition to Yardley's) with respondents and four panel sessions.

The first panel the morning of 7 March was the one on "Lardner's Life and Times" mentioned above which included Clifford Caruthers, Ring Lardner, Jr., and Jonathan Yardley and was moderated by Arthur Kinney of the University of Massachusetts. That afternoon Mark Harris, author of a dozen novels including *The Southpaw* and *Bang the Drum Slowly*, gave an address on Lardner's baseball fiction. More accurately, Harris discussed Lardner's influence on his own baseball fiction, particularly the development of the personality and speaking style of his best-known narrator, Henry Wiggin. Harris said that he wasn't conscious of any influence when he began his series of baseball novels and only later remembered having read Lardner stories in the *Saturday Evening Post* when he was a boy. Respondent Robert J. Higgs of East Tennessee State University (author of *Laurel and Thorn: The Athlete in American Literature*) made reference to Northrup Frye's system for classifying literary types and argued that Harris's and Lardner's works belonged to separate classes. However similar their main characters may be, their purposes and methods differ. Harris's Henry Wiggin is a fictional narrator; Lardner's narrators are, for the most part, satiric personae. Christian Messenger (author of *Sport and the Spirit of Play in American Fiction*), from the University of Illinois at Chicago, began by reminding the audience that the topic of the session was supposed to be "Lardner's Baseball Fiction." Messenger demonstrated that Lardner did not suddenly and miraculously invent a whole new kind of literature in his baseball stories but rather made original use of a number of sports journalism traditions already well established when he came upon the scene in 1908.

This was followed by a panel on "Lardner and American Sports." Richard J. Schrader, Boston College, moderated; participants were James Magnuson, playwright and novelist (*Open Season*), Michael Oriard, Oregon State University (*Dreaming of Heroes* and *The End of Autumn*), and David Q. Voigt, Albright College (*America Through Baseball* and *American Baseball*). Oriard provided a summary of America's historical attitude toward sport, ambivalent in that sport has been seen both as a contradiction of the Puritan work ethic and a necessary part of the development of the ideal young man, especially during the era immediately preceding Lardner. In Lardner's work this ambivalence appears as the theme of innocence and corruption; in responses to his work, he is both praised for being the country's best writer about sport and criticized for only writing about sport. Like Oriard, baseball historian Voigt examined historical trends present at the beginning of Lardner's career. In particular, Voigt concentrated on baseball journalism and expanded on an idea raised earlier by Messenger, that Lardner built on traditions begun at least a half a century earlier by writers like Henry Chadwick. Magnuson gave examples of modern athletes behaving like Lardnerian characters and of modern authors portraying sports figures in this way and wondered how one should respond to these characters. "At the moment," he concluded, "nothing seems more important and more relevant than what Dorothy Parker called 'Ring Lardner's strange, bitter pity.'"

That evening *Chicago Sun Times* syndicated columnist Sydney Harris, who claimed neither a great deal of knowledge about Lardner nor any resemblance to him, gave an address on the rewards and pitfalls of being a syndicated daily columnist with total freedom of subject choice. Respondents were Caruthers, Layman, and Elizabeth Evans of the Georgia Institute of Technology (author of *Ring Lardner*). Evans expressed interest in the relationship between Lardner's columns and stories. "[The] 'In the Wake of the News' articles and columns are perfectly fascinating because here one sees all sorts of seeds that came to life in some of the very best short stories."

The final day of the symposium, 8 March, began with a panel on "Lardner and American Literature" moderated by Kinney; participants included Higgs, Evans, Schrader, and Susan Lardner, Ring Lardner's granddaughter and a staff writer for the *New Yorker*. Lardner spoke first and gave a brief, witty account of the legacy she has from her grandfather, namely traits of shyness, cigarette smoking, two-fingered typing, and, in writing, "the light touch." Schrader and Evans discussed the influence of Lardner's vernacular on other writers using Anita Loos and Flannery O'Connor as illustrations, as Higgs expanded on

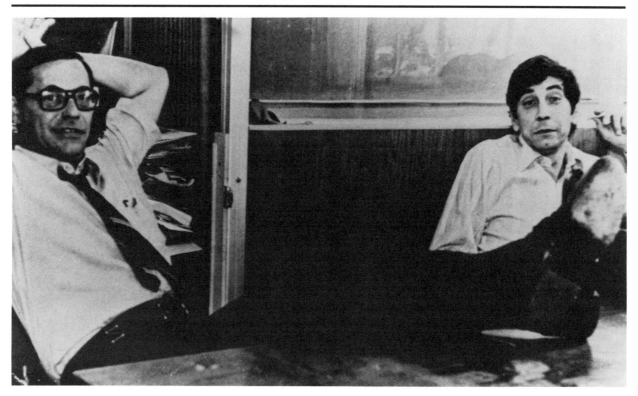

Russell Aiuto and Charles Crupi, authors of Ring Lardner's America, *a play written for the Ring Lardner Centennial Symposium*

his contention that Lardner should be evaluated only in comparison with other authors who wrote in the same literary genres as he did.

That afternoon Martha Banta of U.C.L.A. (*Failure and Success in America*) delivered an address entitled "Ring Lardner and the Failure of Success." Banta carefully documented a developing American cultural schism which culminated in the first quarter of this century, "the essential split between two mentalities, that of the will to succeed and that of the intellect that fails, that of the masculine type that prevails and that of the feminine type who faints by the wayside." The first she referred to as highbrow or genteel, the second as lowbrow or the tradition represented by Teddy Roosevelt. Authors of the time, including Lardner, were fascinated by the lure of financial success (lowbrow) but in all other respects were more at home in the contemplative highbrow tradition. The division provided them the subjects for their fiction but created personal disorder and impelled them toward disillusionment, perhaps best represented for Lardner by the Black Sox Scandal.

Respondents were Voigt, Layman, and Lardner's grandson James Lardner, staff writer for the *New Yorker.* Lardner acknowledged the cultural division described by Banta but added, "I don't feel

that my grandfather suffered from this as much as some others." His background was not especially genteel; "he had what may have been the good fortune of his parents' losing their money early." In his highbrow and lowbrow characters, theater people and baseball players, there is "an essentially common element; they don't seem fundamentally different." Voigt argued that once an author decides his subject is baseball, the way the sport itself defines success may prevail over broader cultural definitions, and baseball is not divided; success means pecuniary success. Layman gave the response to Yardley discussed earlier.

The final panel, "Lardner's Achievement," was moderated by Oriard and included Banta, Mark Harris, and Messenger. Banta offered a kind of shopping list of subjects the symposium hadn't gotten around to discussing, such things as Lardner's depiction of women, his handling of verbal social conventions, and his creative use of qualifiers and conjunctions. Harris discussed the difficulty of defining success and the fallacy of applying an "imposed definition" condemning a writer for not doing what he never had intended to do in the first place. And Messenger, like Layman, identified several major strengths in Lardner's works. "He created American speech again in the mold of its frontier comedy and platform humor, but he overlaid that with the wisecracking cynicism of the city desk and of urban and suburban America." "He possessed a sure ability in the short story form to accomplish a great deal."

The Ring Lardner Centennial Symposium was sponsored by Albion College and the Michigan Council for the Humanities with additional support from the Chicago Tribune Foundation and the Gannett Foundation. The Newberry Library, the

Beinecke Library, the Bentley Library, and the Kent State Library generously contributed Lardner papers, letters, and editions which, in company with a number of unpublished photographs brought by Ring Lardner, Jr., made up a comprehensive exhibit open to visitors for the duration or the celebration. And there was an exhibition of baseball photographs by Alex Traube. The proceedings of the symposium are being prepared for publication under the title *Lardner 100*.

The New Variorum Shakespeare

Robert Kean Turner
University of Wisconsin-Milwaukee

Guilty of fornication, a capital crime in Vienna, Claudio waits in prison to learn whether his sister has persuaded Angelo, the deputy ruler, to grant him clemency. Under the eye of the Provost, Claudio is visited by the city's Duke, who, disguised as a friar, seizes this opportunity to strengthen Claudio's spiritual integrity by convincing him to reject his natural hope to live in order to become better prepared to die. So begins act 3 scene 1 of Shakespeare's *Measure for Measure*, quite an exciting part of the action because we soon learn that Claudio can be pardoned if his sister Isabel, about to enter a convent, will give herself to Angelo (who then would commit the very crime he has condemned in Claudio), and we hear Claudio, forgetting all about spiritual integrity, beg her to do it.

The two pages of the scene reproduced here are from Mark Eccles's 1980 edition of the play, one of a series called the New Variorum Shakespeare. More than a page and a half of notes and commentary, full of abbreviations and special symbols adopted for compactness, hang from only nine lines of text. The edition is not primarily designed for reading through (although people do sometimes read their Shakespeare in Variorums) but for reference and research. The notes are extensive because they, along with information elsewhere in the book, bring together every significant critical action ever performed upon the nine Shakespearean lines, and since Shakespeare has been the most

edited and the most explained writer in English, the record is lengthy. Beneath the notes lie the energies of generations of interpreters who may disagree sharply with each other but who are united in their devotion to Shakespeare's work. For almost four hundred years they have striven to give the public the very words Shakespeare wrote and whatever information they could to aid the understanding or appreciation of those words. The New Variorums are the most comprehensive record of that effort.

Each page has three sections. At the top are the text and its appurtenances—an act and scene heading, a stage-direction, prefixes identifying the speaker of each speech, and line numbers, aids to reference. The text is not just any version; it is a careful reprint of the earliest form of *Measure for Measure* to survive, the copy published in 1623, one play among the first collected dramatic works of Shakespeare. Since this version is as close as we can get to Shakespeare's own lost manuscript, the Variorum preserves its features with considerable fidelity—for instance, the old *u* for *v* in *haue, liue,* and *Seruile;* such old spellings as *onely* and *loose;* the unusual contraction *I'haue;* and the unexpected hyphen in *skyie-influences.* It is with this text in this form that all criticism of *Measure for Measure* begins.

Directly beneath the text are textual notes, a record of every meaningful change ("emendation") made in the text by fifty-nine editions of the play ranging in date from 1623 to 1974, the last im-

---

Actus Tertius. Scena Prima.   3.1

Enter Duke, Claudio, and Prouost.

Du. So then you hope of pardon from Lord *Angelo?*
Cla. The miserable haue no other medicine   1205
But onely hope: I'haue hope to liue, and am prepar'd to
die.
Duke. Be absolute for death: either death or life

1202 *The Prison.* ROWE1-SIS, ARD2
1204 you] you've JOHN   of] for HAN1
1205–11 *Lines ending* medicine . . . am . . . die. . . . life . . . thus . . . lose . . . breath HAN1; medicine, . . . hope: . . . dye. (*then as* F1) CAP-KNT2, HAL-WH1, STAU-GLO, DYCE2-DYCE3, HUD2+; have . . . hope. . . . die. (*then as* F1) COL; medicine, . . . am . . . death; . . . sweeter. . . . Life: . . . thing . . . art, mTBY1 *conj.,* KTLY
    1206 I'haue] I've ROWE1-JOHN2, WH, CAM1, GLO, DYCE2, DYCE3, HUD2, CAM2, ARD1, NLSN   hope to] hop'd to BLAIR
    1208 either] or COT (p. 173), POPE1-JOHN2

    1204 hope of] Hope for (*OED, v.* 1), as in *Ant.* 1.1.61–2 (75–6).
    1205–7 THEOBALD (1909, p. 283): Cf. Palingenius, *Zodiacus Vitae* (ed. 1832, 7:353–4): "Ignorance and hope are the two medicines which have been bestowed on us." [So in *The Zodiake of Life* (1576, pp. 114–15): "Man of all creatures most miserable. . . . *Hope* and *Follie* medicines be."] Cf. TILLEY (H602).
    1206 I'haue] WILSON (ed. 1922): "N.E.D. quotes no examples of mod. contracted form 'I've' before eighteenth century." But FRANZ §52 cites *I'ue* in *Ham.* (F) 5.2.237 (3678) and KÖKERITZ (1953, p. 277) adds *Ham.* (F) 4.7.84 (3080). HOWARD-HILL (1972, pp. 44, 48–50, 89) notes that Crane wrote *I'haue* in two transcripts of Middleton's *Game at Chesse* and that the only two Jonsonian apostrophes in ten Folio comedies are this and *I'am* in *Tmp.* 1.1.58 (64).
    1208–44 ROBERTSON (1897, p. 52): "The whole speech may be said to be a synthesis of favourite propositions of Montaigne." HOOKER (1902, p. 326): It "seems to collect many of Montaigne's remarks" (citing parallels on pp. 326–47, 358–62). HARRISON (1934, pp. 2–3) compares Lucretius, *De Rerum Natura,* 3:

Pages from the New Variorum Shakespeare edition of Measure for Measure, *edited by Mark Eccles (New York: Modern Language Association of America, 1980)*

Shall thereby be the sweeter. Reason thus with life:
If I do loose thee, I do loose a thing   1210
That none but fooles would keepe: a breath thou art,
Seruile to all the skyie-influences,

1211 keepe] reck THEO, WARB   thou art,] *Om.* HAN1
1212 *In parentheses* PORSON *conj. in* MALONE (1780, 1:98), RANN-v1821, SING,
KNT1, KNT2, HAL, HENL

830–1094. HARMON (1942, pp. 1000–1): "The Duke's speech is, as Robertson says,
made up of Stoic comments on life and death. Most of these were universally familiar
as commonplaces of consolation against the fear of death." Sh. could have read some
of them in Cicero, Seneca, Lucretius, Pliny, or Marcus Aurelius, and many were
gathered in Erasmus's *Adagia* and in English books. "No one passage which I cite can
be pointed out definitely as Shakespeare's source—indeed in this speech he has
adapted, fused, and compressed his material more perhaps than in any of the passages
from his plays quoted above. . . . Seneca's commonplaces are probably a main source."
MARTIN (1945, pp. 177–9): "The arguments may be chiefly of Stoical origin, but
. . . some of the notions recommended by the Duke to Claudio are at least as near
to Lucretius the heretic, as they are to Seneca." BALDWIN (1944, 2:84–6): Sh.'s
argumentatio or reasoning "is in clear-cut conformity with the type" described in *Ad
Herennium: propositio* (1208–9), *ratio* (1210–11), *rationis confirmatio* (1211–44), *con-
clusio* (1245–7). "The Duke has emphasized his confirmations." DUNCAN-JONES
(1977, p. 442): Sh. "might also have cast his eye over" *A Discourse of Life and Death*,
written in French by Philippe du Plessis-Mornay and tr. by Mary Sidney, Countess
of Pembroke (1592), "which could have served him as a quarry for the Duke's
arguments." HARMON (1942, p. 1006) notes that Mornay's *Discourse* "itself depends
to a great extent upon Seneca."
     1208 Be . . . death] JOHNSON (ed. 1765): "Be determined to die, without any
hope of life." *OED* (Absolute *a.* 11): "Positive, perfectly certain, decided," first
quotation in this sense.
     either] Monosyllabic. See nn. 851, 1082.
     1211 keepe] WARBURTON (in THEOBALD, ed. 1733): "But this Reading is not
only contrary to all Sense and Reason; but to the Drift of this moral Discourse.
. . . The Sense of the Lines, in this Reading, is a direct Perswasive to *Suicide!* I make
no Doubt, but the Poet wrote, *That none but Fools would* reck. i.e. care for, be anxious
about, regret the Loss of." JOHNSON (ed. 1765): "The meaning seems plainly this,
that *none but fools would* wish *to keep life;* or, *none but fools would keep* it, if choice were
allowed. A sense, which, whether true or not, is certainly innocent." STEEVENS (Var.
1778): *"Keep . . .* may not signify *preserve,* but *care for."* MALONE (1780, 1:97): Cf.
Webster, *Dutchesse of Malfy,* 4.2.188: "Of what is't fools make such vain keeping?",
"apparently used for *account, estimation."* HALLIWELL (ed. 1854): "The word is here
used in its ordinary sense, in contrast with *lose.*" Cf. Daniel, *Cleopatra* (1601, 5.2.1):
"What doe I lose, that haue but life to lose?" HANKINS (1953, pp. 136–7): Cf. *The
Zodiake of Life* (1576, p. 107): "who fears to dye Is but a foole."
     1212 Seruile] SCHMIDT (1875): "Meanly subject." *OED* (*a.* 5): "Subject *to* the
control of something else; not free."
     skyie] JOHNSON (1755): *"Adj.* <from *sky.* Not very elegantly formed.>
Ethereal." SCHMIDT (1875): "Pertaining to the sky (as the cause of the weather)."

portant one published before this Variorum. These fifty-nine editions were compared ("collated") with the Variorum's text word for word and punctuation mark for punctuation mark in order to determine just what alterations editors have thought necessary. In addition, readings from other sources, such as manuscript annotations or editions of secondary importance, are occasionally represented. The abbreviations ("sigla") stand for these sources, and a complete list of the sigla and their meanings on the endpapers of the book enables us to make sense of such a formula as ROWE-SIS, ARD2 ("all editions collated from Rowe's first edition of 1709 through Sisson's edition of 1954, plus the second Arden edition, published 1965"). As for what the notes record, some of the information is routine or of merely passing interest. Note 1202 says that all but a few modern editors specify a prison as the scene; those who do not probably omit this detail because Shakespeare did or because an attentive reader can easily deduce it. Note 1204 shows two eighteenth-century editors modernizing the language, emendations adopted by no others. Note 1205-11 is more significant. It indicates that many editions have found the lineation of the text not to accord with Shakespeare's wishes, but they do not entirely agree on what his wishes were. Because the lineation should reflect Shakespeare's principles of dramatic versification, the disagreement arose in part because these principles were somewhat flexible, his basic iambic pentameter line sometimes containing other feet than iambs and more or fewer syllables than ten as well as elisions that cause some syllables, in effect, not to count. Of the remaining notes, the most striking shows the replacement of *keepe* by *reck* in THEO and WARB, early-eighteenth-century editions, implying that *reck* is the word Shakespeare wrote, or should have written, or would have written if only the unfortunate implications of *keepe* had been pointed out to him. And in another part of the book where conjectural emendations never adopted in any edition are recorded, we discover that a later critic thought the word should be *weep*.

We thus see that Shakespeare's text is in flux; even today the words printed as his in different editions of the same play rarely accord throughout. The textual notes of the Variorum present editorial history concisely and, for these lines of *Measure for Measure* at least, show that apart from the lineation of 1205-11 no significant change to the early text has won permanent approval. Elsewhere the case is different. Later in the scene, for example, the Duke, wishing to hear Isabel's report to Claudio,

orders the Provost, "Bring them to heare me speake, where I may be concealed." The line is garbled, and no one believes Shakespeare intended it to be that way. Before a remedy was agreed upon, however, editors essayed a number of emendations:

> Bring them to speake, where I may be conceal'd, yet heare them
> Bring me where I conceal'd may hear them speak
> Bring me to stand where I may be conceal'd yet hear them speak
> Bring me to hear them speak, where I may be conceal'd, yet hear them
> Bring me to hear them speak, where I may be conceal'd

The last is the current favorite; it allows the early reading to be accounted for simply as a transposition error, perhaps made by the compositor who set the line for the 1623 edition. But if this emendation seems fairly certain, another does not. Still later in the scene Claudio, brave for the moment, will not have his life bought at the price of his sister's virtue, and Isabel vehemently condemns the depravity of her would-be rapist, "this outward sainted Deputie" who is, she says, a devil within, a pond deep as hell, full of filth. Claudio replies, "The prinzie, *Angelo?*" *Prinzie* is the problem, and it is the more problematical because a few lines later Isabel speaks of the livery (probably *disguise* here) of hell covering the damnedest body in *prenzie gardes* (*trimming* or *dress*). Neither Shakespeare nor anyone before or since, as far as we know, has ever used *prinzie* again, so its meaning, if it means anything, is a mystery. If it is a word, as its recurrence might suggest, is it a noun or an adjective? If it is a repeated error, what is it an error for? Emendations and conjectures have been numerous: princely, priestly, precise (*puritanical*), primzie (*demure*, Scottish), prenze (*prince*, Italian), and pensive, among many others. Nothing proposed so far, however, has been generally convincing. The Variorum reviews all the efforts, its editor for good reasons favoring *precise*, but he makes it clear that since 1831, when *precise* was proposed, quite a few people have found it unsatisfactory. What the Variorum's notes show in this instance is that Shakespeare's intended word may be gone forever. The urge to repair is probably not exhausted, however, and it is surprising how often a reader of today inspired to think *prinzie* (or some other reading) should be another word will discover in the

Variorum that his bright idea was tried and rejected long ago.

If it makes acceptable sense and the versification of the lines seems regular enough, few critics would care to change the early text, yet it contains obsolete words and antiquated usages and constructions that require definition or explanation. The third range of notes on the Variorum page serves these purposes, and the notes deal with other matters as well—for example, where Shakespeare found the ideas the characters are expressing, whether he used the same words or turns of phrase elsewhere (which helps to authenticate and define them), or how the stage action may have gone if the dialogue does not make this clear. So note 1204 tells us that *hope of*, somewhat old-fashioned today, was acceptable in Shakespeare's time (the authority being the *Oxford English Dictionary*) and that Shakespeare used the idiom again in *Antony and Cleopatra*. Note 1205-7 indicates that the ideas the lines express were commonplace; they were, in fact, embodied in a proverb (the authority being M. P. Tilley's collection of early English proverbs). Note 1206 raises a different kind of issue, an important one in understanding why the early text takes the form it does. Part of the note establishes that the contraction *I've* was used by Shakespeare and so *I'have* is likely to signify that (one syllable) rather than *I have* (two), but the rest points out that *I'have*, rather than Shakespeare's form, was an occasional characteristic of an early-seventeenth-century scribe, Ralph Crane. Only one of Crane's traits to manifest itself in *Measure for Measure* (the hyphen in *skyie-influences* is likely to be another), the *I'have* testifies that two people, a scribe and a compositor, each capable of making his own kind of deliberate changes as well as mistakes, shared in transmitting each word of the text. Note 1208-44 deals with the sources of the Duke's address to Claudio, which contains many familiar reasons why one should hold his own life in low esteem. Perhaps the remark most striking to those acquainted with Shakespeare's way of handling derivative ideas is that in the speech "he has adopted, fused, and compressed his material" extraordinarily, through the power of distinctive thought and expression making it his own. And, to consider but one more, note 1211 shows us why *reck* briefly stood for *keepe*. William Warburton, a clergyman later to be a bishop of the English church, thought the lines with *keepe* to be irreligious, "contrary to all Sense and Reason," and therefore wrong. This detail may seem merely antiquarian, yet editors today emend the old texts because they too find readings contrary to sense

and reason and so un-Shakespearean. It is sobering to think that years hence the reasons given for these alterations may seem as quaintly beside the point as Warburton's do now.

About half the Variorum *Measure for Measure* is made up of pages like the ones just examined; the rest of the edition contains information about the play that does not lend itself to line-by-line arrangement and is not so explicitly directed toward the words. An essay on the text assesses how the accuracy of the 1623 version may have been affected by Crane's transcript of Shakespeare's papers and by the typesetter's transformation of Crane's manuscript to print. Another examines the external and internal evidence for the play's date. Another quite long section reprints Shakespeare's main source (a two-part play of 1578, *Promos and Cassandra*, by George Whetstone) and two subsidiary sources; it also remarks briefly on other stories similar in plot to *Measure for Measure* and on more general influences, such as that of the Bible. Yet another long section is an anthology of criticism—general comments on the nature of the play as a whole, its strengths, its weaknesses, and its place in Shakespeare's development as a writer; then more specific remarks on its genre (comedy, tragedy, tragicomedy, or problem play), its characters, literary style, dramatic technique, and themes. A calendar of past performances is provided, with references to additional information about them. The earliest known music for the play's one song is given, as well as a list of where many other settings may be found. All the essays quote heavily from the comments of critics, the quotations carefully arranged by the Variorum editor, who when necessary expresses his own opinion too, in order to give the clearest, fullest, and most objective account possible of what has been learned and thought about *Measure for Measure* from its first appearance to the present.

The term *variorum* is borrowed from classical scholarship; an edition of a Latin author *cum notis variorum* is one with notes by various commentators. The first edition of Shakespeare recognizable as a variorum was published in 1773, ten volumes of the plays and commentary, the first volume half occupied by prefatory matter. The editors were Samuel Johnson, the great lexicographer and critic, and George Steevens. During the next fifty years a half-dozen more such editions appeared, each bulkier than its predecessor. These culminated in the famous *Plays and Poems* of 1821, twenty-one volumes, including three of prefatory matter, edited by James Boswell, the son of Johnson's biographer. The 1821 variorum was the standard work of reference until the 1860s, when there began to appear in England the Cambridge Shakespeare, an edition with textual notes but little commentary, and in the United States the New Variorum, initiated by Horace Howard Furness. Furness had come to love Shakespeare through the readings of Fanny Kemble, a famous actress, and in 1860 he joined the Shakspere Society of Philadelphia, a group which attempted serious critical studies. Too often, however, the Shakspere Apostles, as they called themselves, were handicapped by using the 1821 variorum; so much commentary had collected in forty years that it was outdated, and the society, as Furness wrote, "were constantly threshing old straw." So Furness "made a mighty variorum *Hamlet* cutting out the notes of five or six editions besides the Variorum of 1821 and pasting them on a page with a little rivulet of text." The experiment was well received, yet the difficulty of collecting, studying, condensing, and synthesizing the deluge of modern work on Shakespeare may be gauged by the fact that although the first New Variorum to be published, *Romeo and Juliet,* appeared in 1871, the series is not yet complete and, because the old variorums' problem of instant obsolescence cannot really be solved, may never be. Necessarily the work goes slowly; the 555 pages of *Measure for Measure* took thirty years to finish. At present twenty-six volumes have been published. New editions of eleven of these are in progress besides editions of five plays not yet represented in the series. Twenty-eight editors and their assistants are involved, some in England and Germany but most in the United States.

Is the effort worth it? Opinions differ. Some think the Variorum's compilation so ponderous that the play, the literary creation that really mat-

ters, vanishes beneath it. Some think the task so massive that the editors cannot in every detail be as rigorous and as accurate as they should be. Some directors and actors find their spontaneity stifled by what seems the dead weight of the past; knowing the meaning of *prenzie* or finding that Shakespeare drew the Duke's speech from stoic sources does not block the play, design the costumes, or show how the complexity of Isabel's nature is to be revealed in stage action. Yet other directors and actors are avid to know everything possible about the work in which their energies and reputations will be invested. If *prenzie* is *precise*, one more detail indicates that Angelo should in speech, motion, and dress be puritanically cold, his blood a very snow-broth until Isabel sets it afire. If the Duke voices stoic ideas, he is marked by their import a philosophical man who can give powerful statement to his age's best secular reasons for the love of easeful death ("Thou hast nor youth, nor age But as it were an after-dinner sleepe Dreaming on both . . ."). From such details as these the actor's interpretation and the director's sense of how the play should move are built up. The preservation of such long-discarded readings as Warburton's *reck* may occasionally make the edition seem a game preserve for March hares, but that is the price of comprehensiveness and a reminder that the canons of criticism change. To the student, the theatrical professional, and the general reader the Variorum gives answers and some sense of the intellectual struggle involved in achieving them. For the scholar and critic it clears the ground by laying out what has been accomplished, and if the prospect is dim he is challenged to clarify it. If a vast work cannot be perfectly done, it can nevertheless be well done. So is it worth it? Of course.

John Steinbeck Research Center
San Jose State University

John R. Douglas
San Jose State University

The Steinbeck Research Center was the outgrowth of a conference and film festival held on the San Jose State University campus in 1971. The three-day celebration of Steinbeck and his work attracted more than 800 participants from around the world. It was at that time that the Library acquired the nucleus of its Steinbeck collection, 180 items, including copies of all Steinbeck's important published works.

The Steinbeck Center was formally dedicated in March 1974 with a weekend conference focusing on the author's *Of Mice and Men*. Participants did not just study the novel; they also saw the 1939 film version of the work, the prize-winning drama, and

John Steinbeck at Pacific Grove, November 1960 (courtesy of the Steinbeck Research Center)

Carlisle Floyd's operatic version staged by San Francisco's Spring Opera.

The collection, housed in the Steinbeck Room of the Wahlquist Library, now consists of more than 5,000 items, including books, correspondence, galleys, manuscripts, periodicals, copies of literary criticism, portraits, and memorabilia. The book collection includes first editions of all Steinbeck's works, and many signed presentation copies.

The rapid growth of the Center's collection and activities has necessitated a move this year to greatly expanded quarters adjacent to the Library's Special Collections Department. The new facility allows for greater opportunities to display the many graphic materials, posters, and lobby cards from films of the author's works, Steinbeck portraits, illustrations of "Steinbeck country," and selections from one of the world's largest Steinbeck photograph collections. The many Steinbeck related materials in audiovisual format, including slide-tape presentations, phonorecords, videotapes, and films, require additional equipment which can be readily accommodated in the new quarters.

The development of the Center as a vital research institution is due largely to the efforts of Dr. Martha Heasley Cox, professor of English and Steinbeck scholar at San Jose State University, who served as the founding director (1974-1980). Under the stewardship of the Steinbeck Center's new director, Robert DeMott, an internationally recognized Steinbeck scholar whose most recent book, *Steinbeck's Reading* (1984), has added a new dimension to Steinbeck research, there has been a vital resurgence of activity at the Center.

The Steinbeck collection is more than just a rare book collection. Because of its comprehensive collection of critical, historical, and biographical material, the Center has increased our knowledge and understanding of Steinbeck, his writings, and the time in which he lived. As a resource for a regular English Department course on Steinbeck taught by Professor DeMott, it allows the University's students an opportunity to understand the character and creative habits of one of the country's leading writers.

The Center also sponsors conferences, lectures, Steinbeck film festivals, tours of Steinbeck country, and other activities. In a recent program to celebrate the eleventh anniversary of the Center's founding and the author's eighty-third birthday, Steinbeck scholar Warren French presented a lecture entitled "John Steinbeck and American Literature."

This was also an occasion to introduce two important new publications under the Steinbeck Center's imprint: Robert Woodward's *The Steinbeck Research Center at San Jose State University: A Descriptive Catalogue,* and *Your Only Weapon is Your Work: A Letter by John Steinbeck to Dennis Murphy.* The latter is a limited edition booklet which includes supporting material by editor DeMott. It marks the first appearance in print of this original letter by Steinbeck.

Through all of its programs, the Center has become an important force in Steinbeck research, serving serious scholars from around the world, as well as students and faculty of the University and the region in which Steinbeck lived for much of his life.

The Center is a repository of all the author's published works in various editions including autographed presentation copies and foreign language editions. The Center has original editions of many anthologies containing Steinbeck's contributions, as well as periodicals containing his stories, essays, articles, and serialized or condensed books.

The Center has a copy of the manuscript of *The Grapes of Wrath,* supplied by the University of Virginia as well as copies of the corrected galley proofs and typescripts of both *The Grapes of Wrath* and *The Sea of Cortez.* The major autograph manuscript held by the Center is the author's copybook containing commentary on his life and work, as well as fragments from his novels, unpublished stories, and early versions of short stories which were to appear in *The Long Valley.* Shorter manuscripts include an original of the author's obituary of his friend Ernie Pyle, a typescript for the screenplay *The Pearl,* and the original manuscript of *The Wizard,* an early attempt at playwriting.

A growing number of original letters and postcards are among the Center's holdings. The most recent additions are several letters from Steinbeck to the young novelist Dennis Murphy, written from 1956 to 1959, and a series of thirty-one letters to Steinbeck's confidante Wanda Van Brunt, written from 1948 to 1949. The Van Brunt letters,

purchased by the Center in the summer of 1985, are of exceptional biographical value for the years following Steinbeck's divorce from his second wife, Gwyndolyn.

The Center also houses copies of virtually every book published on Steinbeck and his work, an extensive file of scholarly articles, and copies of newspaper articles, reviews, and commentaries. Several scrapbooks contain clippings relating to Steinbeck's works, including announcements and reviews of his plays, as well as background information about his friends, homes, and haunts. The Center maintains a file of all doctoral dissertations and selected masters theses relating to Steinbeck.

Taped interviews by Dr. Martha Cox with relatives, friends, and associates of the author are available at the Center.

A particularly rich collection of photographs of the writer and his family, especially for the period of Steinbeck's second marriage, are part of the Center's holdings. In addition, there is a series of photos of Steinbeck country by Peter Stackpole. Photographical stills of productions of the author's plays and films are also part of the Center's photo files. Many of these photos appeared for the first time in the authorized biography of Steinbeck, *The True Adventures of John Steinbeck, Writer* (Viking, 1984), by Jackson Benson.

Colored photographs of Steinbeck country by Ron Burda, a portrait of the author by Barnaby Conrad, and an oil caricature of Steinbeck by his friend Pepe Romero decorate the walls. The Center's most recent acquisition, donated by Steinbeck's son Thom, is the portable typewriter used by the author on the trip across American which he wrote about in *Travels with Charley.* The Center also houses a collection of books from Steinbeck's personal library.

Also located at the Center are items relating to Edward F. Ricketts and his Pacific Biological Laboratory, including the Laboratory's catalogue, and some preserved specimens. Ricketts, who was the author's friend and mentor, was the model for the character "Doc" in Steinbeck's *Cannery Row* and *Sweet Thursday.* Of particular note is a copy of a forty-nine-page verbatim transcription of Ricketts's notes on the Gulf of California trip, on which he and Steinbeck coauthored the book *The Sea of Cortez,* as well as photographs of Ricketts and his laboratory.

The Center is indebted to the author's widow, Elaine Steinbeck, his friends and relatives, his publisher, his literary estate, the University of Virginia,

Robert DeMott, John R. Douglas, and Bernadine Beutler examining recently acquired Steinbeck-Van Brunt correspondence

and the John Steinbeck Library of Salinas for their continued support.

John Steinbeck stands out among American authors who have written about the land and the people who work upon it. His novels and stories focus on enduring values which are relevant to each succeeding generation. Not always supported by the critical establishment, his writings have continued to be read by people of all nationalities who find a form of spiritual renewal in Steinbeck's stories. The continual flow of theatrical and cinematic adaptations of his work is further evidence that he has touched upon something elemental in the American psyche.

The John Steinbeck Research Center, with its varied resources, is dedicated to increasing the world's understanding of the author's life and writings. We hope that those who seek information and those who have knowledge and resources to share will find our facilities fruitful environment for their endeavors.

James Joyce Conference
Philadelphia, Pennsylvania: 12-16 June 1985

Michael Groden
University of Western Ontario

Joyce specialists and enthusiasts enjoy meeting to talk about Joyce and his works. Since 1967, the year of the First International James Joyce Symposium in Dublin, nine biannual conferences have taken place in Europe, and in the early 1970s smaller gatherings in North America began to fill the gaps between the international meetings. One day of these conferences is always Bloomsday, or June 16, the day on which *Ulysses* takes place. In 1985, a non-European year (in 1982, Joyce's centenary, the international symposia were switched to even-numbered years), a five-day conference took place in Philadelphia. This conference was the biggest, longest, and most elaborate of the non-European meetings, and the organizers secured a memorable setting for the occasion. Sessions met at the Curtis Institute of Music (which had never before opened its facilities to an outside conference), the Art Alliance of Philadelphia, and the Dolan-Maxwell Gallery, all in Center City on or close to historic Rittenhouse Square, and a Bloomsday Banquet (a Joyce conference tradition) was held on June 16 at the Horticultural Center in Fairmount Park.

Joyce conferences always reflect the participants' range of interests. Unlike many academic conferences, which consist of a few hour-long papers delivered exclusively by major figures in the field, the Joyce meetings are organized on democratic principles. Most sessions consist of panels, workshops, and short papers, and anyone who wants to can sit on a panel or deliver a short paper. (In Philadelphia there were no formal, full-length papers at all.) Some people come to hear and talk about Joyce's early works, *Dubliners* and *A Portrait of the Artist as a Young Man;* some are most interested in *Ulysses;* while others attend primarily for *Finnegans Wake.* Some are interested in precise interpretive problems, others in broad theoretical issues. The diversity of interest was reflected in the range of panels and workshops at the conference. For example, a workshop that met to analyze two

Cover for James Joyce Conference booklet

pages of *Finnegans Wake* followed a theoretical panel called "Character as a Palimpsest: A Continuing Theme in Joyce's Work," while a four-session panel/workshop that discussed problems in one episode of *Ulysses* was surrounded by panels on such topics as "Joyce and Issues of Authority," "Feminist Approaches," "Joyce after Deconstruction," and "Representations and Patterns of Reading in Joyce."

Panels and workshops devoted to the state of the texts themselves have occurred regularly at these conferences ever since a group of people met at the first symposium in Dublin to consider the possibility of producing a definitive edition of *Ulysses*. By the late 1970s the preparation of a new edition was underway, and *Ulysses: A Critical and Synoptic Edition*, edited by Hans Walter Gabler with Wolfhard Steppe, Claus Melchior, and others, was officially published on Bloomsday (naturally) 1984 by Garland Publishing. The Philadelphia conference thus took place after the new edition of *Ulysses* had been available for exactly a year, and reactions to and assessments of the edition formed a major part of the gathering, both formally in a couple of the panels and in many informal discussions between and after the official sessions. (The new edition was also an important topic of discussion at a textual studies conference held in New York in April 1985, a Joyce seminar in Monaco in May, and a Vico and Joyce conference in Venice that took place just after the Philadelphia meeting in June, and it was the subject of a panel at the annual Modern Language Association convention in Chicago in December.) The title of one Philadelphia panel, "The New Edition of *Ulysses*: An Assessment of Its Usefulness One Year Later," suggests the process of adjustment that is taking place as readers, teachers, and scholars respond and adapt to a major change in the set of texts that they have been working with for many years.

Ulysses: A Critical and Synoptic Edition represents far more than simply a new appearance of a familiar text. Hans Gabler and his editorial team attempted to reconstruct Joyce's writing of *Ulysses* and to produce a text that represents as closely as possible the first edition of 1922 as it would have appeared had thousands of errors not slipped in during the eight-year process of composition and publication. Since Joyce revised each part of *Ulysses* over and over again, sometimes as many as eight or nine times, and since these revisions usually involved additions to the text, often communicated directly on the book's proofs to the French-speaking printers, the chances for error were great indeed. The new edition represents, in Gabler's words, "the author's own text as established from the documents of composition"—it is thus a "critical" edition—and it considers all errors, misprints, and variants in the ten previously published editions, from the 1922 first edition to the three commercial editions now available (1960 Bodley Head, 1961 Random House, and 1968 Penguin), as departures from the author's text that has now been critically established. (The surviving evidence is not quite complete, and it is sometimes contradictory, so the critical edition has no illusions about being

"definitive." It is unlikely that such a text of *Ulysses* can ever be produced.) The new edition thus does not "correct" any of the existing texts in the sense of looking for errors and fixing them; rather, it sets out independently of all existing versions to recreate the text Joyce wrote and wanted to see in print and only incidentally and indirectly corrects the existing versions. The first edition, the 1961 Random House edition, and every other version that was collated for the new edition each reveals about five thousand departures from the critically established text; the different editions do not always reveal the same departures, but the number remains fairly constant. This staggering number of variants, about seven per page, means that anyone at all familiar with *Ulysses* will constantly encounter words and phrases he or she has never seen before in the book, as well as familiar passages that now appear reworded or repunctuated. (For more detailed information elaborating on this short summation, see Hans Walter Gabler's "Afterword" in volume three of his edition; Michael Groden's article, "Foostering Over Those Changes: The New *Ulysses*," in the *James Joyce Quarterly*, volume 22, [Winter 1985]; or Ira B. Nadel's "The New *Ulysses*" in the *Dictionary of Literary Biography Yearbook 1984*.)

The edition is both "critical" and "synoptic." It not only builds its text of *Ulysses* from the ground up as Joyce originally wrote it but also, using a set of diacritical marks, offers a synoptic presentation of the text's genesis on the left-hand pages, with the corresponding clear text on the right. The synoptic text indicates the first appearance of any word or phrase as well as any text that Joyce rejected through either deletion or replacement; using the left-hand pages, a reader can trace the development of the text that Joyce created and that Gabler and his associates have recreated. The clear text on the right-hand pages offers a reading text based on the synoptic text; when the commercial publishers of *Ulysses* present new one-volume editions sometime after June 1986, they will reproduce a version of the critical edition's clear text. (The interested reader can find one pair of synoptic- and clear-text pages reproduced in both the *James Joyce Quarterly* and *Dictionary of Literary Biography* articles cited above; the edition itself contains a full explanation of the symbols used in the synoptic presentation.)

The panels in Philadelphia featured two approaches to *Ulysses: A Critical and Synoptic Edition*. A session on "Joyce Manuscripts" included papers that focused on the documents that were used to recreate Joyce's writing of *Ulysses* and described

Hans Gabler's methods of producing the edition. James Card discussed the "Penelope" episode (Molly Bloom's soliloquy) and showed how, because of the new edition's synoptic presentation, scholars no longer need to perform the laborious task of retrieving all the prepublication documents. Card argued that words lost in the original transmission of the text from manuscript to print should be restored, unless Joyce explicitly asked for their deletion. Michael Groden talked about the only beginning-to-end manuscript of *Ulysses*, a document that now belongs to the Rosenbach Museum and Library in Philadelphia and so is known as the Rosenbach Manuscript. Earlier research on this manuscript had questioned its assumed status as the starting-point for Joyce's subsequent work on some parts of *Ulysses*, but the new edition, because it accepts evidence in Joyce's hand over transcriptions from other sources (typescripts, proofs, printed versions), gives a great deal of prominence to the Rosenbach Manuscript.

Another panel, "The New Edition of *Ulysses*: An Assessment of Its Usefulness One Year Later," focused not on the production of the edition but, as Jane Ford, who chaired the session, put it, on the "practical aspects of dealing with Joyce's work in its new format." Bonnie Kime Scott, in a paper on using the new *Ulysses* in the classroom called "Teaching with Synoptic Authority," considered the practical but usually unnoted problems involved in switching from a familiar copy of a text to a reset, repaginated, and sometimes reworded one. For example, how do you adjust from the familiar method of referring to passages in the text by page number to the recommended new but seemingly unnatural system of episode and line numbers? (This odd system is recommended because the commercial paperback editions will not duplicate the three-volume edition's pagination, but they will follow its lineation; using episode and line numbers will ensure compatibility among all the printings based on the new text.) How do you teach from the new edition when all the students are reading old versions? Scott went on to talk about the real values of the new edition in the classroom. Attention to Joyce's writing of *Ulysses* and to errors in the existing texts caused her class to focus on "essential qualities of the chapters" and led to considerations of the different kinds of interpretations that are possible. For instance, a misprint might have suggested a highly symbolic reading of a passage, whereas Joyce's actual words were more realistic. (A restoration in the opposite direction is equally possible.) Scott concluded with a few remarks about current readers' likely "problems of adjustment" to a text of *Ulysses* that offers about five thousand unfamiliar readings and a new format: "It has occurred to me very quickly that many of my efforts to present the new edition are transitional ones, soon to be obsolete.... In a year or two, the revised word will be in all students' hands.... The problem of adjustment will be something that dates us. New readers will be dealing with what to them is, quite simply, *Ulysses*."

A second paper at the session focused on scholarship and the new edition. Jane Ford, interested in possible correspondences between *Ulysses* and Joseph Conrad's *The Secret Agent*, demonstrated how a reader can use the synoptic text on the left-hand pages as well as the textual apparatus at the end of the edition to learn quickly and easily when Joyce introduced particular words and passages into the text. (Until the new edition appeared a scholar could have discovered this information only by visits to the libraries owning the manuscripts or by consulting reproductions of the manuscripts in *The James Joyce Archive*.) The new text also invalidates some existing readings. For example, critics have suggested that a sailor who appears near the end of *Ulysses* is a caricature of the Irish poet W. B. Yeats; the sailor's name, W. B. Murphy, sparked the association. But the new edition negates any possible Yeatsian connection, since it prints the sailor's name as D. B. Murphy.

A third paper considered the most frequently discussed passage in the new edition. In the third episode of all editions of *Ulysses*, Stephen Dedalus asks himself, "What is that word known to all men?," and in a passage from the fifteenth episode where he imagines a conversation with his recently deceased mother, he asks her "eagerly" to "tell me the word, mother, if you know now. The word known to all men." A passage restored to the ninth episode of the new edition suggests that Stephen knows the answer to his question; he thinks there, "Do you know what you are talking about? Love, yes. Word known to all men. *Amor vero aliquid alicui bonum vult unde et ea quae concupiscimus....*" Some critics and reviewers have been quite excited by this recovered passage; a few have even called it a key to *Ulysses*. In a paper discussing the passage Jean Kimball analyzed the Latin words from St. Thomas Aquinas's *Summa Contra Gentiles* that enter Stephen's mind after he thinks about love (she cited as a translation, "But love wills something good to someone: hence, those things which we want ..."), and she showed that Stephen quotes parts of two separate sentences from Aquinas and in doing so reveals two definitions of "love." In the primary definition, "love-of-friendship, love has as its object the *someone*—and this may be oneself as well as another," and "in the secondary sense ['love-of-desire'] the object of love is the *something* willed to or for someone." Kimball argued that Stephen leaves the quotation unfinished and that by doing this "he undercuts the assurance of his identification of the word known to all men as 'Love, yes' with his reminder that love has more than one meaning. And we are back in the familiar ambivalent *Ulysses* territory" and therefore far from any newly provided "key" to the meaning of the book.

Finally, Fritz Senn, responding to the three papers, expressed some skepticism about the text of *Ulysses* ever being established with certainty and about readers ever fully accepting that it has been established. He claimed that nonbibliographers' responses are tinged by subjective preferences: "we want *Ulysses* to be the way we have come to like it." And he argued that no editorial principle, no matter how sound, can determine for him exactly what Joyce wanted. "So we are thrown back on our sense of judgment precisely when it may matter most."

Besides descriptions of how *Ulysses: A Critical and Synoptic Edition* was produced and accounts of attempts to adjust to and work with it, a third kind of response has developed, one that in Philadelphia was addressed only unofficially. A new edition of a book like *Ulysses* will inevitably arouse controversy, and this one will do so for at least two reasons. For one thing, readers who feel reluctant to let go of a text that they know, however corrupt it may be, will understandably greet an edition that introduces five thousand unfamiliar readings with some skepticism. Second, Hans Walter Gabler's method of editing the book, that of recreating Joyce's original composition, goes in a few basic ways against some commonly held ideas about editing. For example, if a word or passage in Joyce's hand differs from the subsequent typed or printed versions but Joyce gave no instruction that survives or can be posited for the change, then Gabler accepts the handwritten reading unless there is clear evidence that Joyce accepted the transcribed version. In doing this, Gabler rejects an idea called "passive authorization" with its argument that, since Joyce probably saw the printed text several times without restoring his original formulation, he therefore accepted the printed version. Gabler insists on concrete evidence (such as further authorial revision of the printed passage) before he will accept a reprinted variant over Joyce's handwritten

inscription. Given Joyce's intense desire for control over the appearance of his text, Gabler's theory and methods are certainly justifiable, but it would be possible to produce an edition of *Ulysses* based on different theories and procedures, such as, for example, one that reverses Gabler's principles and follows the 1922 first edition unless there is a compelling reason to depart from it. (In a review of the new edition published in *Criticism*, volume 27 [Summer 1985], Jerome J. McGann outlines the different theories of editing that could lie behind an edition of *Ulysses*, and he describes the kind of text that would result from an application of each theory.)

The most sustained attack on Gabler's procedures has come from John Kidd, who, after telling a *Washington Post* reporter that "I think what I have to say is going to blow the whole Joyce establishment wide open" and that "4,000 of Gabler's [five thousand] changes are unnecessary," delivered a paper on "errors of execution" in the new edition at an April textual studies conference in New York. Kidd's paper included some potentially useful suggestions for specific corrections to the edition. (One of the reasons for a two-year gap between the publication of the scholarly Garland edition and the commercial Random House, Bodley Head, and Penguin printings is to give time for any errors in the edition to be noticed and corrected.) But, the claims Kidd made in the newspaper notwithstanding, his argument in the paper rested on a refusal to acknowledge the difference between the kind of edition he wanted to see (one based on the first edition) and the kind Gabler actually produced (one based on Joyce's manuscripts). Gabler's procedures and choices are bound to seem suspect or thoroughly erroneous to someone who believes that the first edition and later printed versions of the text should take precedence over the manuscript materials, but it will take some time for a useful debate to develop among editors and textual specialists who are aware of and acknowledge the various options and possibilities for an edition of *Ulysses*.

Critics, scholars, and general readers have only begun to voice their responses to *Ulysses: A Critical and Synoptic Edition*. As Bonnie Scott noted in Philadelphia, we are now halfway through a unique transitional period that will end in June 1986 when the new text becomes the only one available for purchase throughout the world, and from then on the "new" *Ulysses* will be "quite simply, *Ulysses*." Nothing regarding *Ulysses*, however, is ever

—Marinà, Stephen said, a child of storm, Miranda, a wonder, Perdita, that which was lost. What was lost is given back to him: his daughter's child. *My dearest wife*, Pericles says, *was like this maid*. Will any man love the daughter if he has not loved the mother?

5   —The art of being a grandfather, Mr Best ⌐(B)⌐[murmured.] gan murmur. *L'art^c d'être grandp .....^⌐(B)⌐*

—Will^c he not see reborn in her, with the memory of his own youth added, another image?

Do you know what you are talking about? Love, yes. Word known to
10 all men. *Amor vero aliquid alicui bonum vult unde et ea quae concupiscimus ...*

—His own image to a man with that queer thing genius is the standard of
˙ all experience, material and moral. Such an appeal will touch him. The images of other males of his ⌐(B)⌐[brood] blood°^⌐(B)⌐ will repel him. He will see
15 in them grotesque attempts of nature to foretell or to° repeat himself.

The benign forehead of the quaker librarian enkindled rosily with hope.

—I hope Mr Dedalus will work out his theory for the enlightenment of the public. And we ought to mention another Irish commentator,° ⌐⁶Mr^c George
20 Bernard Shaw. Nor should we forget⌐⁶⌐ Mr Frank Harris. His articles on Shakespeare in the *Saturday Review* ⟨are⟩ were surely brilliant. Oddly enough he too draws for us an unhappy relation with the dark lady of the sonnets. The favoured rival is William Herbert, earl of Pembroke. I own that if the poet ⌐(B)⌐[is to] must^(B)⌐ be rejected such a rejection would seem
25 more in harmony with — what shall I say? — our notions of what ought not to have been.

Felicitously he ceased and held° a meek head among them, auk's egg, prize of their fray.

He thous ⌐(B)⌐and thees^(B)⌐ her with grave husbandwords. Dost love,
30 Miriam? Dost love thy man?

—That may be too, Stephen said. There's° a saying of Goethe's which Mr Magee likes to quote. Beware of what you wish for in youth because you ^will^ get it in middle life. Why does he send to one who is a *buonaroba*,° a bay where all men ride, a maid of honour with a scandalous girlhood, a
35 lordling to woo for him?° He was himself a lord of language and had made himself a coistrel gentleman and he° had written *Romeo and Juliet*. Why?

---

6 *L'art--grandp .....*] aC; NU tC   7-11 —*Will--concupiscimus ...*] STET aR; ABSENT tC (EYE-SKIP); →TN   14 blood] →TN   15 to] aR; ABSENT tC (MARGIN)   19 commentator,] (aW):tC; commentator aR   19-20 Mr--forget] CF 'ARCHIVE', 23.303   27 held] CF held out LR

Pages in the Garland Ulysses *most frequently discussed by scholars*

—Marina, Stephen said, a child of storm, Miranda, a wonder, Perdita, that
which was lost. What was lost is given back to him: his daughter's child.
My dearest wife, Pericles says, *was like this maid*. Will any man love the
daughter if he has not loved the mother?

—The art of being a grandfather, Mr Best gan murmur. *L'art d'être*   425
grandp .....

—Will he not see reborn in her, with the memory of his own youth added,
another image?

Do you know what you are talking about? Love, yes. Word known to
all men. *Amor vero aliquid alicui bonum vult unde et ea quae*   430
concupiscimus ...

—His own image to a man with that queer thing genius is the standard of
all experience, material and moral. Such an appeal will touch him. The
images of other males of his blood will repel him. He will see in them
grotesque attempts of nature to foretell or to repeat himself.   435

The benign forehead of the quaker librarian enkindled rosily with
hope.

—I hope Mr Dedalus will work out his theory for the enlightenment of the
public. And we ought to mention another Irish commentator, Mr George
Bernard Shaw. Nor should we forget Mr Frank Harris. His articles on   440
Shakespeare in the *Saturday Review* were surely brilliant. Oddly enough
he too draws for us an unhappy relation with the dark lady of the sonnets.
The favoured rival is William Herbert, earl of Pembroke. I own that if the
poet must be rejected such a rejection would seem more in harmony with —
what shall I say? — our notions of what ought not to have been.   445

Felicitously he ceased and held a meek head among them, auk's egg,
prize of their fray.

He thous and thees her with grave husbandwords. Dost love,
Miriam? Dost love thy man?

—That may be too, Stephen said. There's a saying of Goethe's which Mr   450
Magee likes to quote. Beware of what you wish for in youth because you
will get it in middle life. Why does he send to one who is a *buonaroba*, a bay
where all men ride, a maid of honour with a scandalous girlhood, a lordling
to woo for him? He was himself a lord of language and had made himself a
coistrel gentleman and he had written *Romeo and Juliet*. Why? Belief in   455

---

31 There's] e; There is (aW):tC; There's|is aR   33 *buonaroba*,] aC; ʌɛ aR,tC   35 him?]
(aW):tC; him. aR   36 he] aR; *ABSENT* tC

very simple, and the newly edited text will certainly be a prominent topic of interest and debate as Joy-

ceans gather together to discuss *Ulysses* and Joyce's other works on many future Bloomsdays.

Conference on Modern Biography

Philippa Levine
Flinders University of South Australia

The Conference on Modern Biography hosted by the School of English and American Studies at the University of East Anglia (Norwich, United Kingdom) from 12-14 April 1985 was something of a departure from the normal routine of academic conferences, not merely in its subject matter but in its structure. Deviating from the standard practice of formal papers delivered by academics, organizers John Charmley and Philippa Levine (both English historians) and Eric Homberger (an American literature specialist) chose to highlight the problems of particular areas of biographical writing by inviting working biographers to participate in panel-based discussions. In addition to the private panel sessions, there were three major and well-attended public lectures over the course of the weekend, delivered by Robert Skidelsky, Professor of International Relations at Warwick University and biographer of both Oswald Mosley and John Maynard Keynes; Victoria Glendinning, whose recent biography of Vita Sackville-West has been well received and who has worked previously on novelists Elizabeth Bowen and Edith Sitwell; and Lord Blake, Provost of The Queen's College, Oxford, historian of the Conservative party, and biographer of Benjamin Disraeli.

A further distinguishing feature of this Conference was the large amount of nonacademic interest which it attracted. Biography as a literary medium has often been the butt of academic criticism and has in consequence frequently found itself denied a place within the historical or literary canon, a theme taken up by many of those invited to speak. One of the recurrent questions thus posited throughout the three days of this Conference was what status biography could claim within the world of letters, and whether its popular reception connoted a consequent loss of academic dignity, and indeed rigor. At the end of three days' discussion of these controversial issues, few of the

Conference participants could have doubted the sound intellectual pedigree of modern biography.

The proceedings were opened by Robert Skidelsky, whose lecture "Modern Biography: A Case of Indecent Exposure?" was a blend of the psychological and philosophical considerations addressed by the biographer. He began with a historiographical survey of the development of the art, focusing on Freud as a watershed after whose work critical considerations of individual motivation came to be demanded of the biographer. Classifying the great biographies of the Victorian age as examples of the old adage "Let us now praise famous men," Skidelsky identified their most characteristic hallmark as incuriosity. Biography as hagiography was the common currency of the nineteenth-century phenomenon of "Lives and Letters," models of virtue and achievement intended for emulation. Skidelsky's assertion that the biography of the post-Freudian world had turned its attention to subject matter well beyond the arena of public achievement is an important one. His point raised the question of what features of an individual's life make the construction of a biography intrinsically interesting. Skidelsky maintained that, in the aftermath of Freudian influence, public achievement continued to dominate justifications for the writing of biography, but that the author now automatically sought to analyze the motivations and specific history which inspired the individual in the context of Freud's psychoanalytic model. In particular, the idea that the will to achieve is in essence a diverted and sublimated form of sexual drive became a commonplace of the biographer's commentary, and a somewhat reductionist notion of achievement as displacement replaced the laudatory paeans favored by earlier writers.

Inevitably, Skidelsky's remarks led to the thorny issue of concealment as a conscious and de-

Left to right: Richard Shannon, Kenneth Morgan, and Ruth Dudley Edwards

liberate act. Modern conceptions of biography necessarily raise questions about what responsibilities the modern biographer has in laying bare areas hitherto regarded as beyond the limits of public concern and consumption, about the relationship pertaining between the public and the private sphere. In short, could the subject of a biography still retain a private life?

Much of the discussion which followed Professor Skidelsky's provocative lecture centered upon this theme. How, asked Michael Holroyd, did he evaluate and indeed define "gossip"? Where were the boundaries to be drawn between personally explicit information employed to illustrate aspects of an individual's life that are material to the biographer's concern, and information, principally sexual in nature, offered for its own sake or perhaps with malicious intent? This was to be a theme constantly and problematically invoked throughout the Conference, and one which made clear the decision of the organizers to concentrate attention upon modern biography. The discreet silences maintained by earlier biographers marked quite

clearly those areas which have become emblematic of the preoccupations of their latter-day successors.

Skidelsky's lecture also raised the question of the status of the individual within the genre of biography, represented by Malcolm Bradbury as the divide between those theories which promote individual inspiration and creativity and those emphasizing the significance of external cultural factors. The social existence of heroes and heroines would, Professor Bradbury implied, undercut the essentially individualist nature of the biographic enterprise. The necessity to suggest modes of exploring a dialectic between an individual and his or her cultural determinants became a further issue with which the conference participants found themselves grappling.

The following morning the first of the panels brought together Hugh Brogan, biographer of Arthur Ransome; Susan Crosland, whose life of her late politician-husband Tony Crosland continues to excite considerable interest; and historian Alistair Horne, currently engaged on the life of former British Prime Minister Harold Macmillan. Susan

Crosland spoke first, amplifying her thoughts on biography as a mode of psychological drama. She was followed by Hugh Brogan, who returned us to the historiographical approach proffered by Robert Skidelsky the previous evening. Praising Boswell and Lytton Strachey as the "presiding geniuses" of English biography and dismissing the Victorian devotion to the discipline as "the dark ages," Brogan identified the overwhelming tendency of modern proponents of the art to choose literary subjects. Biography has become, he said, little more than the lives of writers, a phenomenon which has served to open up the divide between the literary world and "the rest." Turning from literary to historical considerations, Alistair Horne speculated on ways of marking out the separate territories of the biographer and the historian, a more acute problem in cases where the subject is still alive. He saw the biographer as an excavator, his or her subject as the "living fossil." He gave the audience some entertaining examples of table-talk delivered by his own subject, Harold Macmillan.

The questions which followed centered largely on the ethical issue of whether a potential subject had the right to request that no biography be written; how far could the biographer supersede the wishes of the dead subject or of surviving relatives who sought to prohibit access to material or publication of information? There was some attempt among the panelists to distinguish between the rights of the living and the rights of the dead, with some concern for the feelings and reputation of those who might survive the subject.

In the afternoon, Victoria Glendinning delivered the second of the three public lectures. Her talk, "Modern Biography: Lies and Silences," touched on many of the themes already treated during the two previous sessions of the Conference, but she introduced fresh considerations. Much of her lecture dwelt on the element of chance which dogs the biographer: the writer's limitation to those materials which have survived the passage of time. The necessarily intuitive and imaginative features of biographic writing and the concomitant problem of writing about another as an oblique means of investigating one's own life were matters, she felt, to which commentators perhaps paid too much attention. Glendinning counseled that the avoidance of hero worship was perhaps a more pressing consideration of which one should remain constantly and sharply aware. By way of example, she cited the tendency to use biography as a means of what she called "author theology," whereby the exemplary subject of the biography served the same purpose as the adulatory epics so favored a century earlier. Returning to a problem she had aired in the introduction to her book *Vita,* she spoke of the distorting vision offered by the spotlight nature of biography. That is, characters other than the principal subject acquire an inevitably peripheral status within the narrative, creating a "double vision" effect which filters the reader's experience of the subject through both the biographer's and the subject's eyes. The reader is thus at third remove. In attaching significance to the chosen individual in this way, biography thus could not but lend itself to falsification in its reading of events and personalities allied to but separate from that central character.

By the time the panel on literary biography met, those attending the Conference were in little doubt as to the range of intellectual and ethical problems confronting the potential biographer, both literary and historical. Michael Holroyd, Andrew Sinclair, and Hilary Spurling further fueled this sense of the complexities of the medium. Holroyd, the biographer of Lytton Strachey and Augustus John, now engaged on a life of George Bernard Shaw, spoke first, offering a snippet of autobiography in explanation of his own intellectual predilections and dubbing himself an amateur for his lack of a general theory of biography. Both he and Hilary Spurling, who followed him, spoke of the cross-fertilization of fiction and nonfiction which mapped out the biographer's territory. Spurling dwelt at length on the responsibilities the writer faces in drawing together an objective record of events in an individual's life with the unavoidable fictions caused not simply by gaps in the writer's factual knowledge but by the very process of annotation and subsequent interpretation inherent in the commentary. Drawing startling and effective analogies with both the rules of legal evidence and portrait painting, the biographer of Ivy Compton-Burnett spoke of her chosen profession as a mode of construction and performance.

Andrew Sinclair introduced a new note into the discussion with his declaration that modern biography was often overwhelmed by too great a wealth of information, which he feels can be detrimental to the imaginative power of reconstruction necessary to this form of writing. The biographer of Dylan Thomas, and more recently of Sir Walter Raleigh, Sinclair was of the opinion that the lack of evidence lamented by previous panelists could be a positive source of inspiration for the archive-weary biographer. In the light of this opinion, his comments regarding the challenge

Left to right: Matthew Evans, Hilary Rubinstein, Christopher Sinclair-Stevenson, and Bob Woodings

posed by subjects who *never* tell the truth both amused and taxed his audience.

In the third and final lecture of the weekend, Robert, Baron Blake, returned to the historiographical approach first brought up by Professor Skidelsky. He concurred with all those who had preceded him on this theme in deeming Victorian biography little more than moral fable. He was most explicit, however, in his contention that the biographer's concern was with those of outstanding achievement and ability and not with what he termed "the common man." His own work as historian and biographer of Bonar Law and Disraeli certainly implies that the biographer's subjects are those whose interest for the reader derives precisely from their separateness and their publicly acknowledged achievement. In keeping with his own meticulous attention to detail, he devoted considerable time to the problems of presentation, exhorting his listeners to careful, thoughtful accuracy; his was one of the rare voices at the Conference which thus took up the question of form in the strictest sense of the word.

On Sunday morning, Richard Shannon, Kenneth Morgan, and Ruth Dudley Edwards formed the panel whose theme was political biography.

This panel differed markedly from those of the previous day in its almost exclusive attention to the tradition of historical biography. Shannon, a former lecturer at the University of East Anglia and now professor of history at University College, Swansea, and author of a biography of William Gladstone, emphasized the crucial distinction between historical and political biography pertinent to the concerns of a panel charged with considering the latter. The political biography is, he maintained, a more specifically selective work excluding matters which do not impinge upon the political life of the subject. A working academic as well as a biographer, he staunchly argued that academic historians are fundamentally antipathetic to the aims of biography.

This more concrete and specific approach whereby Professor Shannon spoke of his own reassessment of Gladstone and that of Lord Blake on Disraeli was rehearsed too by Kenneth Morgan, known best for his work on Edwardian Liberalism. His biographies of politicians Lloyd George and Keir Hardie, and that of Viscount Addison, which he coauthored with his wife, Jane Morgan, formed the basis for his comments. He departed from the view of biography offered by Lord Blake: biography, said Dr. Morgan, was "not only about Titans." The main thrust of his argument was to suggest a reading of biography as symbolic, taking his own subject Addison as his example. Addison was an important subject not simply in and for himself but in representing the political evolution of the British Left. His career thus transcended the particular details of his life as an individual. This point went back, in a sense, to the problem voiced at the opening session of the Conference: the status and importance of the individual—simultaneously the raison d'etre of the art of biography and yet perhaps no more than the symbol of more powerful and far-reaching cultural forces shaping the life of the individual.

In keeping with her fellow panelists, Ruth Dudley Edwards concentrated her talk on her work on Irish nationalist and martyr Patrick Pearse. She quietly catalogued the extraordinary reception which her book has received, ranging from vilification to extravagant praise. She used this contrast to draw out her theme of the troubled relations between myth and history, between fiction and fact in the world of biography. She concluded her controversial argument with this phrase: "Where myth sits comfortably, truth becomes treachery." Edwards's concept of biography is far removed from the *Pilgrim's Progress* which Shannon had exemplified by reference to Morley's life of Gladstone, and indeed from the slightly indulgent writing about writers which Hugh Brogan had brought up the previous morning. Under discussion here was biography as a powerful weapon of politics, cutting through generations of myth and crude idealization to expose the dangers of sentiment.

On Sunday afternoon, the final panel was convened. Once again, the Conference was to offer a new and unusual practice. Matthew Evans of Faber and Faber, Christopher Sinclair-Stevenson of Hamish Hamilton (both publishers with large biography lists), and Hilary Rubinstein of the London literary agency A. P. Watt took the floor and spoke of the more practical considerations of biography as a trade. Their agreement that biography is an important element in the list of a general publisher, offering competitive rates of return, was heartening for hopeful writers in the audience. The fact that it is creative, though nonfictional, lends it high regard in the more commercial areas of the literary world. However, it is an area hedged with political, legal, and diplomatic problems often requiring delicate negotiation. At the end of the last day, in a more practical context, the final panel returned to questions raised early on in the proceedings. Among them were considerations of a moral nature which had been posed the previous morning with regard to the rights of the subject and of the subject's kin. Equally the status of biography within the catalogue categories laid down by publishing houses rekindled the frequent point about biographical writings defying the orthodox boundaries of fact and fiction, of literature and history. In the context of this Conference, it served not only to bring together these sometimes disparate disciplines and their proponents, but also to effect considerable harmony between the academics and the motivated amateurs who attended this highly successful Conference on Modern Biography.

Writers' Forum

Alexander Blackburn
(Editor, *Writers' Forum*)

Back in the old days, the 1940s, when imaginative literature was welcomed by publishing houses and when editors and writers could still regard the printed word as almost holy, Robert Frost cheerfully told a group of student writers at Duke, "Your teacher is paid to love you, and your editor is paid to hate you." In other words, the teacher of writers would encourage talent, and the editor would put it to the test. Hate it properly, so to say. The teaching and editing of literary composition represented two necessary sides of the same cultural coin minted from language and tradition. New writers surfacing from discoveries in the buried self had to find understanding somewhere, especially in America, a puritanical country where art is a concupiscence with the devil only to be forgiven by a blessed issue of dollars; new writers needed nurturing and fortifying of the spirit against the day of editorial hating, the chastening

Cover for a recent issue

of style, the ordeal of learning how hard it is to write but also that good writing earns a place and, once in a while, an audience, even a living. Well, those were the days. Whereas teachers of writers are everywhere now, a hard editor is good to find. Now, like as not, your editor is not paid to hate you but to ignore you; that is, if you write fiction or poetry and have some dreamy notion of a national literature which endures, not easily disposed of, not Kleenex. Perhaps what such writers now must fear most is not a failure of nerve and talent before the criteria of lucidity, force, and exactitude but exclusion from access to readers. And that is a condition of intolerable silence, silence of the voices of truth and beauty, silence that is insidiously enervating to a nation's soul—its literature. Faced with the prospect of such silence, then, many thousands of gifted writers, not only the new but also the experienced, have turned for the love and hate, the encouragement and chastening, the renewal of pride in their work, to what used to be called the "little" magazines, the literary magazines that rarely pay, rarely have a circulation over 1,000 but can play a caretaker role with respect to literature. One need only look at *The International Directory of Little Magazines & Small Presses* to realize what a glorious number of magazines exists to bring voices out of the silence.

In 1974, I became editor of *Writers' Forum* in order to become one of the caretakers. I confess at once to evangelical zeal in the proceedings, perhaps by inheritance of folly: my grandparents tried to convert the Persians (of all people!) to a weird form of Christianity, and my father's cousin wrote 2,000 hymns such as "Throw Out the Lifeline, Someone is Drifting Away." Righteousness, however, is of no use to teachers, who are paid to love, or to editors, who, even if unpaid, must hate you properly. The missionary drive is there without, I hope, the objections. Still, where money is concerned, few literary editors whom I know ever seem to have much for their magazines. It must be faith that fuels us. Every so often I recall Grandpa Blackburn's assertion, "The Lord will provide," and think, He better. And lo! we go to press with another thick volume of *Writers' Forum*, and, blow me down, miracles happen. For instance, a few years ago, when I didn't have $1,900 to pay a typesetter, he completed his job, suffered a nervous breakdown, blew town, and obligingly never submitted a bill. Similarly, when I noted the discrepancy between the $2,000 in my account and the $7,000 required to produce our tenth volume, a local literate, clearly prescient tentacle of a huge international publishing house offered to compose and print the book for $3,000, as a charitable contribution; and a remarkable increase in book sales more than made up the difference. Like Wilkins Micawber, I've become doggedly optimistic.

From the beginning I conceived of the magazine as a congregation of and forum for writers, editors, teachers of writers, and critics. Once in the early 1950s, myself an inchoate and floundering writer, I had joined an audience of hundreds at the University of North Carolina at Greensboro to hear William Blackburn (my father) and Robert Penn Warren deliver public critique of student stories printed for the occasion in a campus magazine. The idea was simple: a love feast where everyone present had read the stories and could participate in what my father, with characteristically heavy sigh, liked to describe as "a civilized dialogue that has been going on since Aristotle." The results of that forum were superb: quite a few new writers were encouraged, the most famous of them being Mac Hyman, who a few years later would write *No Time for Sergeants*. Thus *Writers' Forum* came about, though the Rocky Mountains did not seem the right place for Aristotle's *Poetics* (later, I knew I was dead wrong about this: when Pike's Peak looms over your psyche, catharsis of excessive pity and fear just comes with the territory). I would send out a call for stories and poems throughout the Rockies, publish the best of them, distribute the magazine to writers and others, and, on a day in March 1974, assemble them to hear a discussion led by John Williams, John Wideman, and James Yaffe, who would then award cash prizes. So it came to pass, with 150 excited people coming to Colorado Springs from as far away as Albuquerque, New Mexico, and Laramie, Wyoming. The First Prizes went to Yusef Komunyakaa for poetry and to Russell Martin for fiction, both writers who have gone on to establish for themselves national reputations.

The conference was held annually for four consecutive years. Each time, a volume of *Writers' Forum* was readied in advance. Among distinguished writers to speak at a conference were Richard Hugo, John Nichols, Max Steele, Rudolfo Anaya, Ron Sukenick, Bill Tremblay, and one Pulitzer Prize-winning poet whose name I won't mention because he came drunk, stayed drunk, and cursed all writers. After spending an evening trying to restrain a hundred aspiring writers from lynching that gentleman, I vowed to devote myself to editing and to open the pages of *Writers' Forum* to writers everywhere, unrestricted by region. Conferences ended, the magazine was reborn, which since 1978 has but figuratively brought writers together, new writers (often post-M.F.A.) with contemporary masters, among them Fred Chappell, Reynolds Price, Paul Engle, William Stafford, John Hermann, James B. Hall, William Peden, Gladys Swan, David Ray, Reg Saner, Joyce Thompson, and Charles Baxter. We continue to find "firsts," sometimes stories by minority persons such as Hispanics and Native Americans whose problems with the Great Silence are far greater than those of graduates from creative writing programs. After we published Craig Lesley's first story in 1978, it became the basis of his novel, *Winterkill* (Houghton Mifflin, 1984), which has just won first prize in fiction from the Pacific Northwest Booksellers Association. After we published Julian Silva's second story in 1979, he—having been ignored by publishers for two decades while he wrote novels as richly textured as those of Henry James—placed one of them, *The Gunnysack Castle*, with Ohio University Press. All in all, over eleven years, out of tens of thousands of manuscript submissions, we have published more than 1,000 poems by more than 225 poets and 150 stories or novel-excerpts by more than 100 fiction writers. One story has won a Pushcart Prize. *Writer's Digest* has ranked *Writers' Forum* first among university-sponsored literary magazines in their list of the top thirty nonpaying fiction markets.

Having learned from experience not to restrict the magazine's pages to those writers available to attend a conference, I have nevertheless continued to emphasize the role of *Writers' Forum* as publisher of new American literature about or from the West. There is good reason for this emphasis: one, serious Western writing (opposite of the "western" of international fantasy) has often fared badly in the Eastern publishing "establishment," and, two, the West is the most vital literary region in the United States today. In its recent past are Robinson Jeffers, Willa Cather, John Steinbeck, and Walter Van Tilburg Clark; in its vigorous present are Frank Waters, Wallace Stegner, Edward Abbey, and many more, with Waters a literary giant who stands in relation to the West as William Faulkner stood to the South. Rich in writing but poor in publishing, the West cannot long remain misrepresented or unknown. A region as vast as Western Europe, the West is the ancient heartland of the continent, has a deep and tragic history, and, in spite of suffering many of the ills that afflict the nation elsewhere, offers through its towering mountains and fragile deserts a spiritual wonder that ignites passions and lifts the heart. So the stories of this magnificent land are being told—some have been told for thousands of years—and *Writers' Forum* is specifically dedicated to listening to and publishing them.

When I joined the English faculty of the University of Colorado at Colorado Springs in 1973, it was a small campus accommodating 1,200 students of all ages in a few scattered buildings, the most imposing of which had once been the world's greatest tuberculosis sanatorium. One of the Pulitzers had died in this building, an event that was the closest I had come to a literary tradition when, during spring break in 1974, *Writers' Forum One* went to press, if that's the word. Most of my budget of $300 had been expended on the typing, on stencils, of 192 8 1/2 by 11 inch pages and on reams of mimeograph paper sufficient to produce 300 copies; the remainder of the money would go to a bindery. The university—which, by the way, now has 6,000 students and capacious new buildings—had no Xerox copying and collating machines, nor could it provide secretarial or "work-study" assistance. One simply ran projects on empty. So there I was, going to press in the basement of a building haunted by the ghosts of departed lungers, on a deserted campus, and with three days to go to meet the bindery's deadline. I did the mimeographing myself, for thirty consecutive hours cranking up

and feeding a ga-thunking A.B. Dick machine until pages grew into stacks, stacks into columns reaching to the ceiling like the legendary manuscripts of Thomas Wolfe. Late Saturday night the job was done, or so I foolishly believed, and I went home with my clothes soaked in ink and my head ringing in a sort of rapture. Collating the pages next day by hand *did*, somewhere in the recesses of my spaced-out brain, seem a bit formidable, so I called one of my students, Dan "Duck" Pond, a retired Marine colonel who had hit the beaches in three wars, and he volunteered to help me next morning. I poured myself a double Jack Daniels, saluted Parnassus and the gods of little magazines, and fell into fitful sleep with visions of millions of sheets of paper blowing in the wind like bleached autumnal leaves.

Sunday morning was gray with the threat of snow. Duck showed up at ten, and together we lugged 57,600 sheets of paper from the basement to a large room that had once been the sanatorium's morgue. On tables that might once have been slabs for stiffs, we assembled 192 stacks, each 300 sheets thick. Then Duck made the first-ever *Forum* book, bending over 192 times in a sort of automatized agony; I made the second book. When we were done, twenty minutes had passed, and a metaphorical lightbulb had become incandescent behind my wrinkled millimetric brow.

"Duck," I said in a half audible croak, "it's impossible."

Duck laughed. He probably laughed at Iwo Jima and Porkchop Hill. "Yup," he nodded after a pause.

"What are we going to do?"

"Call more grunts," Duck said.

We did that. After dialing a dozen numbers

Craig Lesley and Bret Lott, fiction editors for Writers' Forum

without result, I got through to Michelle's Restaurant ("World Famous Ice Cream Creations as Featured in *Life* Magazine") where the girlfriend of another one of my students worked as a waitress on Sunday. Sure, she'd come after work. And call Mark. And Mark would call his friends and they would call theirs and. . . . No problem.

An hour later, several platoons of volunteer book collators might have been observed in the morgue going happily round and round, bobbing and straightening. Big pregnant hippies down from the communes. Mountain men with shovel beards. Poets, cowboys, high school dropouts who began every utterance with "man," waitresses still in uniforms splotched with hot fudge sundae, Snow White and the Seven Dwarfs and all the Lost Tribes of Israel. Someone brought coffee and sandwiches. Someone else brought six-packs of Coors. At the stroke of midnight the last copy of *Writers' Forum One* had been assembled and stowed in the trunk of my '64 Dodge, and these wonderful princes and princesses had departed on their motorcycles and pumpkins as a quiet snow drifted across them, like a benediction.

As I write this, *Writers' Forum Eleven* has gone to press, a real press, and soon there will be 1,000 copies of a 200-page book, 8 1/2 by 5 1/2 inches, printed on 60 pound Nekoosa white, with a three-color cover, fourteen stories, twice that number of poems, and an entire section devoted to the writings of Frank Waters. At $8.95 a copy, the book-size magazine will cost less than two movie tickets. Library subscriptions are coming in from the Bodleian to Buffalo, from Cornell to California, though we're going to need more if this little literary magazine is to survive and its editors allowed to love and hate properly. Soon, 20,000 flyers will be mailed to high school and college English teachers, with some suggestions for including Western American literature in their curricula, not excluding *Writers' Forum*. An endowment fund drive has been launched, the income from which will enable *Writers' Forum* to establish a large national literary prize.

Beyond that, who knows? Perhaps one day we'll hire an editor. I hope he doesn't wear a pin-stripe suit, drink three dry martinis for lunch, send out printed rejection slips, or think that fiction in the *New Yorker* is ever more than "charming"—the kiss of death by the standards of us "littles." But if he has a copy of *The Poetics* tucked in blue jeans, we might put him on the waiting list.

The National Jewish Book Awards

Rena Leibovitch

Established in 1949, the National Jewish Book Awards are the oldest and most prestigious awards for North American Judaic literature. The Jewish Welfare Board Jewish Book Council presents these prizes annually to authors and translators of meritorious books of Jewish interest. Past winners have included Isaac Bashevis Singer, Chaim Grade, Rabbi Joseph B. Soloveitchik, Cynthia Ozick, and Dr. Emil L. Fackenheim. The purpose of the awards is to stimulate the writing, publishing, and reading of worthy books of Jewish content.

Currently the awards are given in eleven categories: biography, children's literature, fiction, Jewish history, Jewish thought, Holocaust, illustrated children's books, Israel, scholarship, visual arts, and Yiddish literature. Books are submitted by publishers, but judges also seek other eligible books. This procedure has been developed to encompass as broad a range of publications as possible. There is no nominating fee.

To be eligible, books must be written by either American or Canadian citizens. They also must have been published during the preceding year. Thus, books published in 1985 may be submitted for a 1986 award. In addition to awards in specific categories, there are also awards to recognize lifetime achievement. In 1959 Sadie Rose Weilerstein received the Children's Literature Award for a series of books about *K'tonton*, the Jewish Tom Thumb. And, in 1979, Salo W. Baron, author of

Blu Greenberg, left, President of the JWB Jewish Book Council, with award-winning authors David Wyman and Joan Peters at the 1985 National Jewish Book Awards ceremony

the multivolume *A Social and Religious History of the Jews* and many other historical works, won the Jewish History Award for his cumulative contribution to Jewish history.

Books are examined by a three-member panel of judges in each category. The judges first decide on three nominees from which the winning selection is chosen. The author or translator receives a citation and a cash prize of $750. The publisher of the award-winning entry also receives a citation at the Awards ceremony held each spring in New York City.

Many literary personalities, scholars, and leaders of the Jewish community have volunteered to serve as judges for the awards. In 1986 Harvey Shapiro of the *New York Times* and Robert Kotlowitz of PBS are among the judges.

Awards are part of the Council's continuing effort to promote American Jewish literature. In 1940 representatives from major Jewish organizations formed a committee to sponsor Jewish Book Week. By 1943 the committee emerged as the Jewish Book Council with the National Jewish Welfare Board joining as the sponsor and coordinator in 1944. This national organization, now known as

JWB, provides financial and professional support for the Council. The Council has an Executive Board comprising authors, educators, and representatives of publishers and Jewish organizations.

The National Jewish Book Awards incorporated two literary prizes previously offered·by the Jewish Community Councils of Philadelphia and Washington for books of Jewish interest. In 1949 there were only two categories: fiction and nonfiction. The nonfiction award was given to Dr. Harry Wolfson for *Philo,* and the fiction award went to Howard Fast for *My Glorious Brothers.*

In 1950 a poetry category was added and private sponsorship of awards was begun. Funding for the poetry award was provided by the family of the late Harry Kovner. And the award was presented for the best books of poetry written in English, Yiddish, and Hebrew. Lack of funds has forced the elimination of this category for the past five years.

The 1950 nonfiction award was sponsored by a group of friends of the late Isadore Hershfield, who was actively involved with Jewish Communal affairs in Washington, D.C. Gradually, this category has been subdivided into several awards, including awards for works on the Holocaust and Israel.

The newest awards are presented for biography and illustrated children's books. Ruth S. Frank, past Director of the Book Council, explained that the various categories have been established with the hope that all genres of Jewish books will be recognized. They are also intended to encourage writing and publishing in areas where there is now a scarcity of good material, such as visual arts and illustrated children's books.

The National Jewish Book Awards were first presented to authors at the annual meeting of the Council held in New York City. With increased recognition the awards soon merited a ceremony of their own. In recent years this ceremony has been held in the Trustees' Room of the New York Public Library.

The awards have a history of recognizing rising talent. Isaac Bashevis Singer won the Fiction Award in 1963 for *The Slave*—twenty-five years before he received the Nobel Prize for literature.

The choice of an award-winning book is based solely on its scholarship or literary merit. The topic of Jewish interest need not be a conventional one nor must the author be popular or even Jewish. For example, in 1950 the Fiction Award was conferred upon Pulitzer Prize winner John Hersey for *The Wall*, his best-seller which deals with the destruction of the Warsaw Ghetto.

Another example of merit outweighing controversy is Howard Fast, who, as was mentioned before, received the first Fiction Award for *My Glorious Brothers*. The author was criticized at the time for his political affiliation. The judges saw beyond this controversy, though, and selected this outstanding novel for the prize. Howard Fast later commented that "the granting of this award represents an act of real independence and courage in the best tradition of Judaism."

In the late 1940s the Fiction Award was refused by one winner. Laura Z. Hobson, author of *Gentleman's Agreement*, declined the prize because she felt that her acceptance would label her novel as a "Jewish" book. Since her novel had been written to condemn sectarianism, she felt the award would negate the message of the book.

In 1985 David Wyman, a devout Christian, received the Holocaust Award for *The Abandonment of the Jews*. At the awards ceremony Professor Wyman explained that he wrote this book in order to avoid another Holocaust. He expressed regret that recognition for the book had come overwhelmingly from Jews and that it has not stirred the response he had hoped from non-Jews.

The importance of the National Jewish Book Awards is acknowledged by authors and publishers alike. They realize the award increases a book's visibility and often mention it in their advertisements and publicity. In wide use are the "National Jewish Book Award" seals which are available from the Book Council to be placed on the winning books. Frequently, when a book is reissued or published in paperback, the award will be prominently mentioned on the book itself.

In the future, the Book Council hopes to continue to expand the awards program and to fund the awards through endowments, rather than annual contributions. This method would allow larger cash prizes and the revival of the translation and poetry awards, which have lapsed.

"There has been an explosion of Jewish publishing in the last decade," states Blu Greenberg, President of the Book Council. "In fact, there are now over six hundred books of Jewish interest in English published each year. This situation makes the judges' task more difficult as both the number and the quality of books increase, but this is one problem we are pleased to have."

According to Greenberg, the readership for Jewish books continues to be mostly Jewish. This situation is beginning to change, though, as more publishers print books of Jewish interest which appeal to the general public. Another encouraging sign is that more books on Jewish subjects are now being written by non-Jews, David Wyman being just one notable example. The Council is pleased by these developments and hopes an increased awareness of Jewish literature and scholarship will help create better understanding between the Jewish and non-Jewish communities in America today.

Audio Art in America: A Personal Memoir

Richard Kostelanetz

> In communications we tend to become aware of the
> basic characteristics of a medium only after a new
> one has replaced or coexists with it.
> —Tony Schwartz, *Media: The Second God* (1981)

My recollection is that my first appearance on radio as an adult had something to do with meeting, in early 1964, a staff producer for WBAI-FM, the listener-supported Pacifica station in New York City. He invited me to record some long essays that I had just written about recent theater and recent fiction. I remember being terribly displeased with my declamation. It went on much too long; I got bored talking to a microphone. I cannot recall whether these talks were broadcast; I hope they were not.

In London the following year, I was advised to call Phillip French, who was then working as a

Richard Kostelanetz at work in the multifaceted production of his audio art (J. Nebraska Gifford)

BBC radio "talks" producer. French asked me to submit an essay on the American Absurd Novel. This I did; and when he accepted my typed-out text, I was invited to transcribe it. I remember being disappointed again with my reading; I did not know how to sustain a lively pitch while talking to a microphone. After correcting my Americanisms ("Sart," he said, not "Sart-re"; and "Ee-o-nes-co," not "Ion-esco"; and V. "spelled with the letter V and a full stop"), French judged that my delivery sounded "too lecturish." Instead, he wanted me to sound as though I were speaking in a British living room. I asked him to demonstrate the difference; but this he was unable to do. Once home I asked my resident landlord, Wallas Eaton, himself a veteran radio comedian, what to do. Eaton recommended that I speak as though I were talking over the telephone to a *girl* friend. Back in the BBC studios for a second trip, I did this. French accepted it. Around Easter, 1965, I heard a terribly breathy American voice begin, "In the American novel today, . . ." Though the fantasies have changed since then, the mental trick remains viable.

In the following decade, I did occasional radio interviews, usually about books of mine that had recently been published. I taped at least one more lecture on recent literature for WBAI. (I remember emerging from the shower one Saturday afternoon and thinking that the voice on the blaring radio sounded awfully familiar. It took me a few seconds to realize that the voice was mine!) Since I was, in general, disinclined to give lectures, even to live audiences, because I disliked speaking what was written to appear in print, I was no more enthusiastic about radio "talks."

I had not thought of working creatively in radio until the Ithaca poet Tom Hanna called, early in 1975, to invite me to participate in a festival of radio creation at Rochester's new FM station, WXXI. At first I turned him down, remembering that I had neither a taste for speaking my words aloud nor ideas for working creatively with tape; but fortunately, he insisted. I brought along a few experimental texts, vaguely thinking that I would perhaps find ways for reading them more interesting and viable than a straight live declamation.

At first I did short pieces that depended upon putting different voices of myself on two sides of a stereo track. I used a synthesizer as background for one piece and electronic reverberation for another. Once I saw the eight-track machine at WXXI-FM, I realized that it could enhance my *Recyclings,* a book-length collection of single-page texts of nonsyntactic prose. Now I could read these pages in progressively augmented nonsynchronous choruses of myself. (The reason why there are only seven voices in the concluding section of *Recyclings* is that one of the eight WXXI tracks was dead. Since I was the first person ever to use this new machine, the fault was not discovered before. "I'm the visiting artist," I could joke. "I'm here to test your new machinery.")

I returned to WXXI-FM the following year to make *Openings & Closings,* which was then my longest single piece; *Declaration of Independence,* in which I used all eight tracks for an almost unison chorus of myself; and then *Foreshortenings,* in which my solo voice alternates with a unison quartet of my voice. The radio show that WXXI put together from its visiting artists was called "The Intergalactic Poetry Energy Circus." Broadcast initially in Rochester in 1976, it won from the Corporation for Public Broadcasting a national prize for innovative local programming and was later rebroadcast over the National Public Radio network. By the end of 1976, I wrote my first manifesto on "Audio Art" in which I defined my central aim as doing on tape a language art that would be impossible in live performance.

For the next few years my most ambitious audio efforts were stymied. Because my pieces required sophisticated technology (that was, and still is, well beyond my personal means), I became necessarily dependent upon invitations to work in tape studios (and, after that, upon the generosity and enthusiasm of sophisticated engineers). However, between 1976 and 1981, it was almost impossible for me to get access to another professional situation. I made proposals; proposals were made on my behalf. All the recognition notwithstanding, none succeeded, some for scandalous reasons. I continued doing interviews about my new books and even coordinated for Voice of America a series of fifty programs on *American Writing Today.* On one program devoted to my own work, I played some of these aging creative tapes. National Public Radio distributed some of them over its Modular Arts Service (which went out weekly to member stations, to use whenever, and if, they wished). In 1978, Australian Broadcasting produced a 45-minute retrospective of my early Audio Art. The previous year, WBAI-FM's Morning Music program devoted two hours to my audio work, and then rebroadcast this program in the evening. Beth Anderson included me in her 1981 "Poetry Is Music" series which was distributed over the successor to the NPR Modular Arts Service, the Satellite Program Development Fund. Examples of my early work, as well as an interview with me, were featured on a 1981 Westdeutscher Rundfunk program on "Text-Sound-Sound Poetry USA." In addition, I gave scores of concerts of these early tapes at universities and art museums across the land. From time to time there were fan letters. However, aside from an invitation to work for two hours at Davis & Elkins College and a short evening in a rather limited private studio, it was impossible for me to do new work; these were the years in the audio wilderness.

The second breakthrough came in the wake of an invitation to be a 1981 guest of the DAAD Künstlerprogramm in Berlin. The year before, to my New York home came an enthusiast named Klaus Schoning, who was (and still is) Westdeutscher Rundfunk's legendary producer and advocate of *Neue Horspiel* (or new radio plays). He put into my head the vision that, once I got to Germany, I would be able to do the kinds of adventurous audio art that was impossible here. And he was right. My first week in Berlin, the local radio station commissioned field recordings toward a sixty-minute piece. These tapes were sent to the Electronic Music Studio of Stockholm, whose director, Lars Gunnar Bodin, offered me a hundred hours of studio time gratis. (To comprehend the magnitude of this gift, remember that all previous works of mine were made within a dozen hours of studio time!) Later that year, Schoning himself invited me to do for WDR a pair of major pieces, one in German, the other in English.

Looking back, I think I can identify my encompassing ambition as using audio technologies to create unusual, innovative verbal-acoustic experiences. My works generally start with texts (that could, no doubt, also be read in mundane ways). Although these texts invariably precede my involvement with tape, I use audio technologies precisely to realize speech structures that cannot be done live: a single voice subjected to steadily increasing reverberation; my own voice talking sprightly to a chorus of itself; different versions of my voice emerging from separate speakers in series of discrete fictions, a self-interview and even a self-seduction; an interwoven collection of stories in which my voice is transformed into sixteen audibly different versions of itself. I also put into the same acoustic space the prayers of over sixty ministers, speaking roughly two dozen different languages—people who would never be "live" in the same place together, let alone pray in the same space together. Thanks to audio multitracking I was also able to have four English-speaking ministers recite the Gospels simultaneously and then do another piece in which four German ministers did likewise.

One way that my work has always differed from that of other poets and "sound poets," as well as composers, is that I rarely do pieces for live performance; my medium is not the traditional concert hall (or coffee house) but the new venue of audiotape. Until recently, I have been reluctant to use sounds other than speech, whether music or sound effects. (That reluctance might have something to do with literary purism, also evident in my visual poetry, or a desire to echew what I find compromised, if not vulgar, in others.) My pieces are not based upon expressions of sensibility, as is much monologue radio, but with premeditation, originality, experimental procedures and, at times, painstaking execution. Rarely have I tried to imitate the illusion of live theater (or, beyond it, of "the real world"), because one of my esthetic ideals is mediumistic integrity, which here means doing in sound what can only be done with sound. Another ideal has been to create pieces so strong, and distinctive, that each would implant in every listener's head a series of *after-sounds*, or particular aural-verbal impressions.

As for critical categories, I once preferred "text-sound" to "sound poetry," in part because most of my pieces draw upon texts that are ultimately closer to prose, as traditionally defined, than poetry, as traditionally defined. My preference for recognizable words also separates me from those "sound poets" who work primarily with verbal sounds, or "vocables" that may be words or parts of words. On the other hand, once subjected to audio techniques, most of my pieces eventually become not text-sound but something else that I prefer to call Audio Art, in that they exploit audio technologies to enhance language and can exist only on audiotape. Needless to say perhaps, Audio Art could not exist before the second half of the twentieth century; it could come only from some-

one born after the first quarter of this century.

One strategy distinguishing my own creative adventure has been bringing to the creation and performance of language certain intelligence gained from a long appreciation of contemporary music. A dozen or so years ago, it became clear to me that the richest, most advanced ideas about artistic creation were not in literature, my initial field, or in visual art, where I have done some work, but in music. Even though my initial material has always been language, my audio work reflects in certain structures the musics of Terry Riley and Philip Glass and, in certain attitudes, both John Cage and Milton Babbitt. From Cage, for instance, comes my sense that anything and everything can be incorporated into the vocabulary of one's art, as well as my taste for compositional procedures so definite and distinctive that many details of their execution could be left to chance. From Babbitt comes my taste for rigorous structures and empirical explanations of an artist's esthetics. Perhaps my sense of a literature that necessarily exists only on audiotape owes something to his notion of musical ideas so complex that only on tape can they be accurately represented, which is to say that tape is neither a documentation of a live performance nor a substitute for it, but a presentational medium with its own integrity. One general way in which my works are closer to music than traditional radio programs is that they eschew explanatory frames or interruptions; they contain nothing other than themselves. It could be said, with this background in mind, that my radio work represents my attempt to compose primarily, if not exclusively, with words.

Another characteristic of my creative method, in audio as well as other arts, is generating a wealth of possibilities within certain particular purposes and ideals. Once I put my visions on paper or, better, test them in a recording studio, I can get a surer sense of not only which possibilities are best but which imply the most fertile suggestions for future work. Since radio is less costly than film or video or theater—less expensive to produce and less expensive to disseminate—it is more conducive to radical experiments that, alas, have no immediate commercial future. Given these purposes and biases, I sense that I have hardly exhausted the capabilities of the current technologies or imagined the usefulness of audio technologies to come. All this is another way of saying that I have scarcely reached the end of my adventure with musical ideas in taping language sound.

One theme I should like to explore further is

the possibilities of artificial voices, not only for sacred texts (that electronic techniques can make more mysterious) but for comedy. It seems to me that electronic artists have been slow to realize how audio machinery can generate humor for many of the same reasons that film animation does. When semblances of human beings are portrayed as performing in super-human ways—say faster, or in self-echo—the artifice is invariably funny. This plan will get me beyond tape manipulation into computer-assisted voice synthesis and other new techniques.

It was Marshall McLuhan who suggested that the emergence of a new medium reveals the particular nature, previously hidden, of the earlier dominant medium. Now that television has securely superceded radio, we have the precondition and freedom to discover the intrinsic possibilities of the older medium. A further McLuhan notion was that such essentially esthetic discoveries would be made not by media professionals, so concerned with mastering conventions and meeting day-to-day obligations, but by outside artists, whose creative roots were planted elsewhere, whose professional careers were not dependent upon income from radio. With that last thought in mind, we can understand why the major recent innovations in German *horspiel* (literally, ear-plays) have come from artists known initially as poets and composers. While American radio professionals mostly play records, conduct interviews, answer telephones and read either advertisements or the news, artists from someplace else can discover something else.

Nothing has curbed the development of my audio art more than circumstances beyond my control. The first is the fact that in America, unlike Europe, there is no tradition of support for experimental radio. (Remember that electronic music in Europe matured largely in studios attached to radio stations. There was no analogue here for such institutional concern about any aspect of radio art.) There are no Guggenheims for radio work; the Rockefeller Foundation has not explicitly supported it since 1940 (the year I was born). At the

Media Program at the National Endowment for the Arts, documentaries are allowed to pass for Art and receive a preponderance of the awards. Indicatively, we have television reviewers, but no radio critics (which are common in Europe). We have national awards for film, records, and television, but none of consequence for radio (again unlike Europe).

American radio art today resembles American poetry in 1915 in this respect—advanced artists must go abroad to produce and distribute their more important work. There are scarce means for making it here and, once it is made, scarcely any means for disseminating it. National Public Radio hasn't been much good; its newer competitor, American Public Radio, has yet to prove itself better. The same long pieces of mine that have gone out over European stations are sometimes played in America, if I get to work the station myself, sometimes taking it home as well, my wallet no heavier than before. Until American broadcasters become more receptive to experimental endeavors, ideas like mine are likely to appear here first in print, long before they are embodied on tape. That is a secondary reason for my writing about my Audio Art.

Bibliography:

Charles Amirkhanian, *10 + 2 American Text-Sound Artists* [record] (Berkeley, Cal.: 1750 Arch Street, 1976);

Richard Kostelanetz, *Experimental Prose* [audiocassette, with "Excelsior," "Plateaux," "Recyclings," "Declaration of Independence"] (New York: Assembling Press, 1976);

Kostelanetz, *Openings & Closings* [audiocassette] (New York: RK Editions, 1977);

Kostelanetz, *Foreshortenings & Other Stories* [audiocassette] (New York: RK Editions, 1977);

Tony Schwartz, *Media: The Second God* (New York: Random House, 1981);

Kostelanetz, *Invocations* (New York: Folkways Records, 1983).

The Fugitives and the Agrarians: The First Exhibition

David Havird
University of Virginia

From 28 April to 3 September 1985, the paneled and book-lined McGregor Room in the University of Virginia's Alderman Library provided an elegant setting for the first major exhibition ever mounted of works by the Fugitives and the Agrarians. Since titles by John Crowe Ransom, Donald Davidson, Allen Tate, and Robert Penn Warren dominated the exhibition, Ben C. Toledano (whose private collection comprised most of the items) wisely cautioned viewers against regarding the Fugitives and the Agrarians "as one group with interchangeable designations." As Toledano explained in the introduction to the commemora-

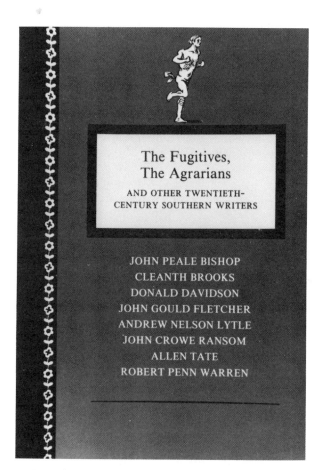

Cover for commemorative booklet (courtesy of Warren Chappell, designer)

tive booklet, "The Fugitives, not to be confused with the Agrarians, were poets from Tennessee and Kentucky, with the exception of Laura Riding, who became a member of the group in 1925." Centered in Nashville, these poets published, from April 1922 to December 1925, nineteen separate issues of *The Fugitive,* a poetry journal. Of the sixteen Fugitive poets, only Ransom, Davidson, Tate, and Warren were also Agrarians, in that they, along with eight other Southerners, contributed essays to *I'll Take My Stand* (1930), "an anthology," as Louise Cowan has described it in *The Fugitive Group: A Literary History,* "attacking industrialism and its basic dogma, the belief in the perfectability of man through secular progress."

It was Toledano's purchase, in 1950, of a secondhand copy of *I'll Take My Stand* that started his book collecting. During his student days at the University of North Carolina, Toledano (now a Charlottesville resident) happened upon the anthology, whose provocative title compelled him to purchase it. As he explained in an interview, "The anti-materialistic, spiritual nature of the essays, which I read as a declaration of war on the dehumanizing forces in society"—the very society he was just then poised to enter—"struck a chord in me." Back home in his native New Orleans, whose public libraries lacked the titles he now felt inspired to try to find, Toledano, a lawyer, began accumulating a library of his own. Autographed by Warren, Davidson, Andrew Lytle, Tate, and Ransom, Toledano's copy of *I'll Take My Stand* and his similarly inscribed copy of its "surprisingly neglected sequel," *Who Owns America?* (1936)—together with a rare complete run of the *Fugitive*—composed the thematic centerpiece of the exhibition.

Cleanth Brooks, who contributed an article ("A Plea to the Protestant Churches") to Herbert Agar and Allen Tate's *Who Owns America?*, opened the exhibition with an informal talk, which emphasized the influence of Ransom, Tate, and Warren on a host of younger Southern writers. George Garrett, who introduced Brooks to an audience of several hundred, reiterated this theme in his mem-

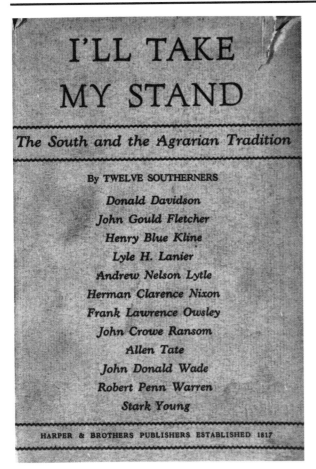

I'LL TAKE MY STAND

The South and the Agrarian Tradition

By TWELVE SOUTHERNERS

Donald Davidson

John Gould Fletcher

Henry Blue Kline

Lyle H. Lanier

Andrew Nelson Lytle

Herman Clarence Nixon

Frank Lawrence Owsley

John Crowe Ransom

Allen Tate

John Donald Wade

Robert Penn Warren

Stark Young

HARPER & BROTHERS PUBLISHERS ESTABLISHED 1817

Cover for a 1930 symposium that Ben Toledano describes as a "counterattack against the forces which threatened a depletion of the whole person in civil society ..." (courtesy of Ben Toledano)

oir in the commemorative booklet: "There is not," he declared, "a Southern writer alive who doesn't owe a great deal ... to the example and enormous success of the Fugitives (and their authorized disciples) in bringing Southern literature out of the shadows, the imposed obscurity of defeat and poverty, and into the front rank of modern writing." An anecdote illustrated this younger Southern writer's ambivalent relationship with the group: In 1958 Garrett won a *Sewanee Review* Fellowship in Poetry. "Together with the award," as he explained, "came a message from Andrew Lytle [an editor of the journal] that the award was *not* by any means to be misconstrued by me as offering any approval whatsoever for my prose fiction which was, in those days, sassy and irreverent and indifferent to (though not at all ignorant of) certain standard rules and regulations of acceptable Fugitive fiction."

No wonder Garrett "was never," as he put it, "a member in good standing of the club"—as was Peter Taylor, an "authorized disciple" whose first book, *The Long Fourth* (1948), contained an introduction by Warren, who had been—along with Brooks—one of Taylor's mentors at Louisiana State University in 1940. (A first edition of this volume of Taylor's stories, together with a later collection, *The Widows of Thornton* [1954], dedicated to Tate and Caroline Gordon, was included in the exhibition.) Unable himself to attend the opening, Taylor (whom Garrett recently succeeded as Henry Hoyns Professor of Creative Writing at the University) also reminisced, in the keepsake, about the Fugitives who were his teachers: Tate at Southwestern at Memphis, Ransom at Vanderbilt and Kenyon, Warren and Brooks at Louisiana State University. Tate, as Taylor remembered—speaking for himself and other writers of his generation—"inspired us with ideas concerning the importance of becoming a writer.... One never again doubted what one's calling was." To Taylor and to Robert Lowell (housemates at Kenyon), Ransom "was the father we had not quarrelled with, the father who was not a lawyer or a businessman, and was the man we wished to become...." These two memoirs, Taylor's and Garrett's books, brought to life the displays of periodicals and manuscripts.

As Louise Cowan has maintained, "In a critical evaluation of the Fugitive movement ..., it is to the work of the four poets who were also Agrarians that one turns, since Ransom, Davidson, and Tate were, in Tate's words, the 'final causes' of the movement and Warren was in many senses its product." Even so, the displays began with titles by John Gould Fletcher (an Agrarian who, as a prominent Imagist in London, contributed verse to the *Fugitive*) and by John Peale Bishop (neither a Fugitive nor an Agrarian, but an intimate friend of Tate). The publication of Fletcher's first book, *Fire and Wine* (1913), preceded by a month the publication of *The Book of Nature 1910-1912*. In the displayed copy of this, his second volume of verse, the author had noted at the end of each poem the date and place of composition. One of two copies of the poet's *The Tree of Life* (1918) bore Fletcher's inscription to Vachel Lindsay, while the other revealed the ownership signature of Allen Ginsberg's father, Louis Ginsberg of Woodbine, New Jersey. As for Bishop, a first edition of *Green Fruit* (1917), his first collection of poems, lay beside Fletcher's early volumes. Elsewhere in the exhibition was

Bishop's book of stories, *Many Thousands Gone* (1931), which he had inscribed to his Princeton schoolmate Scott Fitzgerald, "with affection, admiration/—and gratitude/John/May 19, 1931." Copies of Bishop's *Minute Particulars* (1935), a book of poems published in a limited edition by the Alcestis Press, and of *Act of Darkness* (1935), his only novel, were also on display.

Poet Laura Riding (the only female Fugitive, a native New Yorker, wife of an instructor at the University of Louisville, and one of only three Fugitives who enjoyed an international reputation) and the unjustly neglected novelist Andrew Lytle (whose poems saw publication in the *Fugitive* when he, like Warren, was still an undergraduate at Vanderbilt and whose provocatively titled essay, "The Hind Tit," on "farming as a way of life" appeared in *I'll Take My Stand*) both had volumes on display. Their titles were easy to miss amid the crush of titles by the Big Four. Riding was represented by an autographed copy of her *Love as Love, Death as Death* (1928). In addition to first editions of Lytle's novels—such as an autographed *The Velvet Horn* (1957), his most ambitious novel, which the University of the South has recently reprinted—Lytle's *Bedford Forrest and His Critter Company* (1931), inscribed to Toledano, appeared alongside other biographies of men who fought or otherwise figured in the Civil War: Tate's *Stonewall Jackson: The Good Soldier* (1928), his *Jefferson Davis: His Rise and Fall* (1929), and Warren's *John Brown, The Making of a Martyr* (1929).

At about the same time as verse by the Fugitives was coming to light in their own journal, other journals were featuring their work—not only such legendary little magazines as the *Double Dealer*, the *American Review*, *Poetry*, and *transition*, but even littler magazines such as *S4N*, the *Wave*, *Alcestis*, *Voices*, the *Measure*, and the *Reviewer*. In the *Hound and Horn*, which had once been a Harvard literary magazine and for which, after its move to New York, Tate became a regional editor in 1933, the names of the Vanderbilt poets mingled with those of Wallace Stevens, William Carlos Williams, E. E. Cummings, John Dos Passos, Kay Boyle, T. S. Eliot, and Basil Bunting. The Curator of American Literature Collections at Alderman Library, Joan Crane, expressed (in an afterword in the keepsake) particular satisfaction that the display included copies of these periodicals, whose covers gave the exhibition its period look.

When Ransom returned to Vanderbilt after World War I, he had in hand a volume of verse, *Poems about God* (1919), commercially published while he was still "1st Lieut. Field Artillery, A.E.F.," as he was identified on the title page. An even rarer item than Ransom's first book (a first edition of which was on display) was a fragile pamphlet, published in 1923 by the Poetry Society of South Carolina, which contained his poem "Armageddon," winner that year of the Society's Southern Prize, and a poem ("A Fragment") by William Alexander Percy and another ("Avalon") by Davidson. "It is fair to say," observed Toledano, "that that small pamphlet containing only three poems is of more than minor interest to serious book collectors, not to mention serious booksellers," whose catalogues have listed the item for as much as $2000.

In 1924 Robert Graves, whose poem "The Corner Knot" appeared in the last issue of the *Fugitive*, published in England a selection of Ransom's poems, *Grace After Meat*, which included verse from *Poems About God* and later, uncollected work. In the foreword, Graves compared Ransom's "manner" and "matter" with that of the New Englander Robert Frost: "Neither Frost nor Ransom had any local poetic tradition on which to build and had each to evolve his own." Graves went on to assert that Ransom was doing for Tennessee "what Frost has done for New England, Vachel Lindsay for his Middle-West, and Carl Sandburg for Chicago." Allen Tate found this assertion absurd. In his review, which the *Nation* printed in 1927, of Ransom's *Two Gentlemen in Bonds*, Tate declared that Graves's "remarks . . . constitute one of the most astonishing criticisms of American poetry . . . that we have yet heard. Mr. Graves, in effect, announced to the British public that here was a poet giving utterance to the illiterates and poor white of Tennessee. . . ." Ransom was for Tate "the last pure manifestation of the culture of the eighteenth-century South." In addition to a first edition of *Grace After Meat*, which never saw publication in the United States, first editions of *Chills and Fever* (1924) and *Two Gentlemen in Bonds* (1927) testified to Ransom's productivity during his one decade of writing poems.

The appearance of his essay in *I'll Take My Stand* and the publication a year afterwards of *God without Thunder* (1931) confirmed the poet's shift of interest from verse to prose. If Ransom took the lead among the Southern group in turning to social and literary criticism, Tate and Davidson and Brooks followed, and the next ten years witnessed the publication not only of Ransom's *The World's Body* (1938) and *The New Criticism* (1941) but also of Tate's *Reactionary Essays on Poetry and Ideas* (1936) and his *Reason in Madness* (1941), Davidson's *The*

AN OUTLAND PIPER

I followed till the pipes trilled sweet
At the winding end of an unknown street,
And none of all the mob was nigh,
Nor door nor window cracked an eye,
And — "Follow me no more," he said,
"Though I be of thy father bred,
And though I speak from thine own blood,
Yet I am not of mortal brood;
And follow not my piping sweet
To find the walking world a cheat;
And cherish not my outland grace,
Nor pride in likeness to my face,
For children of an earthly mother
Cry out upon their demon brother."
His smile flashed out a sudden dawn,
In the dark street, — then he was gone;
And through the town where he had sung
The futile ravelled silence hung.

I heard, but I could not forget,
And through the world I follow yet,
And many a time I pause and sigh,

[4]

Pages from Donald Davidson's first book of lyrics, annotated by the poet (courtesy of the Alderman Library, University of Virginia)

AN OUTLAND PIPER

Thinking I hear his melody;
And peer at all men's charactery
To find that image so like me;
And wonder that his piping sweet
Left me to know a world's deceit,
Left me to seek an unknown kin
Through all the streets I travel in.

Revised from "A Demon Brother" (Fugitive: April '22. the first issue). One of the first poems I wrote after the group began to meet regularly. The main writing of the poem took just about an hour (or less) of fiery mood one Saturday afternoon before Fugitive meeting. The strange piper is, of course, my _Alter Ego_ – _mon semblable_, _mon frère_ – the ideal self, glimpsed once or twice, rarely seen again though always sought.

Attack on Leviathan: Regionalism and Nationalism in the United States (1938), and Brooks's *Modern Poetry and the Tradition* (1939)—first editions of which were on display.

While Davidson's rather old-fashioned poetry never enjoyed the high critical esteem of Ransom's or Tate's or Warren's, Davidson was himself (as William Pratt has observed in his anthology *The Fugitive Poets*) "the main cementing force of the Fugitives." In some ways, the copy of Davidson's rare first volume of lyrics, *An Outland Piper* (1924), annotated throughout by the poet himself, was the most interesting item there. George Marion O'Donnell, who purchased the volume secondhand at a Fourth Avenue book stall, seems to have been so incensed that the original owner had sold it that he scissored off the page that bore an inscription from the author. Davidson's annotations reflected his mature assessment of his Fugitive verse. Take for instance his comment on "The Tiger-Woman," a ballad published in the second issue of the *Fugitive:* "I believe this is the first *real* poem I ever wrote (if it *is* a real one). It belongs to the spring of 1921." Davidson regarded "Redivivus" (published in the fourth issue of the *Fugitive*) as "one of [his] personal favorites." "The last stanza," he contended, "might receive a subtitle: 'Credo for Modern American Poet' ":

> let my skeleton soul
> > Writhe upward from the loam,
> Drink red morning again
> > And look gently home.

A piece of realism in blank verse, reminiscent of lines by E. A. Robinson, "The Man Who Would Not Die" (which appeared in the sixth issue of the *Fugitive*) anticipated later verse—"Aunt Maria and the Gourds," for example. But among the poems in *An Outland Piper* it may be unique in that it "draws from the local scene. The landscape and persons," Davidson explains, "are reconstructed from the country around Mulberry, near Fayetteville, Tennessee."

Other commentary on his own poetry came in a handwritten letter of 28 May 1934, on letterhead of Vanderbilt's Department of English, to Miss Belle O'D. Battey, treasurer of the Poetry Society of Georgia in Savannah, which had awarded a twenty-five-dollar prize to Davidson's "Old Black Joe Comes Home." In his gracious acknowledgement the poet confidently declared that this poem, written during his stay (in the fall, winter, and spring of 1932-1933) in Marshallville, Georgia, was

to be "one of a series of pastorals." First published in the *Poetry Society of Georgia X* (1933-1934), "Old Black Joe Comes Home" appeared later as one of "Two Georgia Pastorals" alongside the superior "Randall, My Son" in *Lee in the Mountains and Other Poems* (1938). Toledano's inscribed copy of this book of poems also contained the poet's correction of a typographical error in "On a Replica of the Parthenon" that had transformed "motion"—the "blind motion" that went into the vain construction of the Nashville Parthenon—into "notion": "The word should be *motion*, not *notion*," wrote Davidson, "for the modern multitude knows only *motion*."

Meanwhile, he was advancing the regional cause in prose. Of all the Fugitives, according to William Pratt (who alludes to two of Davidson's best-known poems), Davidson "remains the most convinced Southerner, the least ironic in his loyalty to the 'Sanctuary' of the Southern wilderness and the 'Hermitage' built by his forefathers." This statement applies equally well to the essayist as to the poet. In fact, it was Davidson who "objected strongly," as Louis Rubin remarks in his introduction to a 1977 edition of *I'll Take My Stand,* to Rubin's depiction, in an earlier edition, of agrarianism as "an extended metaphor, of which the image of the agrarian community is the figure, standing for and embodying ... modern society. Of this society the South is a part, and, for the purposes of the metaphor, the correlative."

An open letter (of 20 September 1930) from Davidson, Tate, and Ransom to Stringfellow Barr betrayed nothing but a literal-minded conviction as to the practicality of agrarianism. Barr had marked his accession (on 1 October 1930) to the editorship of the *Virginia Quarterly Review* with an article advocating the South's "sympathetic cooperation" with and "control" of industry. Granting that inequity and exploitation characterized industrial societies (which he found to be as pernicious in some ways as the slave society of the Old South), Barr nevertheless maintained that industrialization did not have to produce an evil social system—and would not in the South if the "traditionalist" (who "by pouting in the corner ... will not keep the factory out") would only recognize "that it lies in his own power, not to eject industry indeed but to regulate its application." The "horror" of industrialism and laissez-faire economics, Barr declared, "has derived not from the intelligent use of more powerful tools but from their gross misuse." In a separate letter to Barr, which accompanied the open letter, Davidson charged, "You stand squarely with the Chambers of Commerce. I should not be

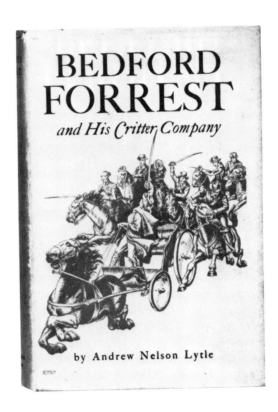

Dust jackets for Civil War biographies displayed together at the first Fugitives and Agrarians exhibition (courtesy of Ben Toledano)

surprised to see them quote copiously from your article in their future advertisements." Together Davidson, Tate, and Ransom asserted,

> The task of confronting the South today is to discourage industrialism on the whole, and make it go slow. Unmitigated industrialism is an evil even when it employs neither child labor nor cheap labor. Its consequences are to be seen in the perfect industrial communities of the East. Looking at these, the South may not be so anxious to duplicate their charming features as to preserve its own traditional way of life.

This significant correspondence preceded by a month or more the publication in November of *I'll Take My Stand.*

If Ransom's reputation as a poet grew out of a modest number of poems written during a single decade, Tate won the esteem of critics and poets alike with an equally meager output that spanned three decades. Perhaps it was because his meager output contained an extraordinarily high percentage of major poems that limited, collector's editions figured so prominently among his book publications. In fact, Tate began his association with private presses while he was still an undergraduate at Vanderbilt in 1923 when he and Ridley Wills (a fellow Fugitive) composed in one evening their spoof of conventional and experimental verse, *The Golden Mean and Other Poems,* which they dedicated to "The Fugitive." (The title satirized the literary course advocated by one of their professors, Edwin Mims—to whom, incidentally, Tate later attributed a "desire to break up the Nashville group." In a letter, on display, of 4 June 1937, the year of Ransom's departure from Vanderbilt to Kenyon, Tate confided to Lambert Davis, then editor of the *Virginia Quarterly Review,* "When [Mims] addresses Rotary Clubs he 'points with pride' to the group, but for years he has carried on a campaign of detraction in devious ways against the men who have made the prestige of his department.—He let Warren go to Louisiana, after vile treatment of him. . . . Now it is Ransom. When he gets Davidson alone, he will persecute him.") *The Golden Mean* contained, in addition to parodies by Tate and Wills, an introduction and three verse tributes to the two authors by Merrill Moore (another Fugitive), whose "tongue," Tate later remarked, "was not [then] where it should have been"—it was in his cheek. Published in a limited edition of 200 copies and signed on the dedication page by Tate and Wills,

this fragile pamphlet—consisting of 32 stapled pages—can sell for as much as $3000.

An even more fragile pamphlet, published by Minton, Balch in 1930 in an edition of 125 copies (of which 25 were numbered and signed by the author), contained only three poems: the newly "revised and final version" of "Ode to the Confederate Dead," "Message from Abroad," and "The Cross." Other works appeared in fine limited editions. *The Mediterranean and Other Poems* (of which J. Ronald Lane Latimer's Alcestis Press published, in 1936, 165 numbered and signed copies) stood out as Tate's first volume of new verse since 1928. That year had seen the commercial publication of *Mr. Pope and Other Poems*—an autographed first edition of which was also on view. In 1943 Tate began an association with the Cummington Press in Massachusetts, which that year printed 430 copies of his translation of the *Pervigilium Veneris, The Vigil of Venus.* On exhibit was Tate's personal copy. The next year, 1944, saw the publication, also by Cummington Press, of *A Winter Sea.* This important volume contained, among other poems, such major ones as "Seasons of the Soul," "Winter Mask," and "Ode to Our Young Pro-consuls of the Air." A "Reviewer's Advance Proof" revealed the ownership signature of poet Weldon Kees. Finally, in 1950, Cummington Press printed on handmade paper 300 copies of *Two Conceits,* Tate's metaphysical nursery rhymes.

Warren's popularity, if not his critical esteem, arose from his fiction. He had yet to write his highly acclaimed first novel, *Night Rider* (1939), when he edited *A Southern Harvest* (1937), an anthology of short stories by contemporary Southern writers. Warren's astute selection included William Faulkner's "That Evening Sun," Katherine Anne Porter's "He," Caroline Gordon's "Old Red," Lytle's "Jericho, Jericho, Jericho," and other stories by Jesse Stuart, Erskine Caldwell, Elizabeth Madox Roberts, John Peale Bishop, Thomas Wolfe, Stark Young, and Marjorie Kinnan Rawlings—proof that Southern literature was hardly in an early stage of efflorescence but was indeed ripe for harvest.

The display of Warren's fiction included a limited edition, from Cummington Press, of his most famous short story, "Blackberry Winter" (1946), a signed first edition of *All the King's Men* (1946), and three distinct editions of *World Enough and Time* (1950): a "special Kentucky Edition" of one thousand signed copies, a copy for presentation to the booksellers of America, and a paperback reprint with the pictorial, descriptive wrapper panel over heavy paper covers.

Even though Warren received a Pulitzer Prize for *Promises: Poems 1954-1956* and the Bollingen Prize for his *Selected Poems: New and Old, 1923-1966,* only since the publication of his widely reviewed *Selected Poems: 1923-1975* has the reputation of the poet begun to overtake that of the novelist. The exhibition had the salutary effect of reminding viewers that Warren began as a poet—as one whose promise was unmistakable to the older Fugitives. In 1924, when Warren was nineteen, Davidson voiced their opinion of him in a letter on exhibit to Louis Gilmore, editor of the *Double Dealer,* which was preparing to publish the same poems by Warren as the *Fugitive* was bringing out: "I am sure he can send you others," Davidson assured Gilmore, "and he told me he would do so. . . . He is, by the way, a brilliant youngster who is going to do fine things,—or so we feel." The exhibition included a copy of Warren's first volume of verse, *Thirty-Six Poems* (1935), and the corrected galley proofs of *Thirty-Six Poems*—both originally owned by George Marion O'Donnell. The galleys have numerous corrections by the publisher (J. R. L. Latimer of the Alcestis Press) as well as by the poet. The book, which contained only one of Warren's Fugitive poems, "To a Face in a Crowd," had appeared in an edition of 165 signed copies.

As the exhibition moved from the McGregor Room into an adjoining gallery, it acquired a distinctively local color. To enter this gallery was in effect to start the exhibition over, for Tate and Warren appeared again at the outset of their careers in letters. Only here they were mostly playing the role of wishful contributors rather than editors. For example, in a letter of 24 November 1931 to Stringfellow Barr (whose lax editorial standards they were no more willing to let pass than they were his "liberal" politics), Tate came to the defense of Warren, whose poems Barr had just rejected. Tate pointed out that Barr had taken the same attitude toward Tate's work:

> In my own case you have steadily rejected my best poems—The Idiot is the sole exception—only to print immediately afterwards very second rate work by Untermeyer or Aline Kilmer or Henry Bellaman. . . . Do you happen to know that the Virginia Quarterly is famous for its rotten poetry? Well, it is, and if you haven't heard it before this, it is because I am the first person rude enough to tell you. . . . I have heard some of your New York contributors speak lightly of placing articles with you that they couldn't place

elsewhere. In general the opinion of the Quarterly is this: it is a place to sell facile stuff.

A letter to Barr from the twenty-six-year-old Warren followed within three days, in which he wrote, "I can say without laying myself open to the charge of vanity that at least two of the pieces recently offered you would satisfactorily meet the standard of poetic excellence in the *Quarterly*"—following which assertion Warren proceeded to expose as "a tissue of *cliche*" a recently published poem by Frances M. Frost. "This poem is not an isolated example," Warren insisted. "If you aren't inclined to agree, ask somebody who reads poetry seriously."

Barr may or may not have responded to Warren; he certainly responded, apparently rather defensively, to Tate, who found Barr's excuses evasive. Tate lambasted the editor for his "confession" that public taste influenced his judgment: "I had always supposed that a quarterly's duty is to form the public taste by publishing the best according to its lights. I must conclude," Tate continued bitterly, ". . . that what I had taken to be an effect is an intention—your lack of seriousness. I think you may be Governor of Virginia some day, and I wish you well."

As the youthful editors of a little magazine, which had achieved international recognition, and now as mature poets, Tate and Warren (along with the other Fugitives) had set a standard of excellence for regional writing. It was in the interest of the region, as well as in their own self-interest, for "the outstanding literary review of the South" (as John Gould Fletcher called the *Virginia Quarterly Review*) to uphold that standard—"to air the Southern tradition," as Tate proposed, ". . . specifically by printing Southern writers, whether they've been to New York or not, and equally by printing good writers elsewhere. . . ."

An exemplary letter of 20 February 1932 from Tate to Leigh Hanes, who had submitted verse for possible publication in a special Southern issue of *Poetry,* which Tate was editing, showed him exercising his own stern editorial judgment. Tate prescribed the study of Ezra Pound, "the finest craftsman in English," as an antidote for Hanes's "poeticism":

> If you are ever to do anything with a fine talent you will have to alter your whole sense of form. Take some of your lyrics: out of material just as slight and casual, Pound

makes something overwhelming, while your lyrics, in spite of beautiful imagery, are dead as herrings. . . . Why not study a couple of poets who are great craftsmen but fundamentally different from you, and who for that reason offer an objective study of form?—Marianne Moore and John Crowe Ransom? *All poets must begin with their slightly older contemporaries*; we go to the remoter past through them, and *only* in that way.

Tate was still fighting the war the Fugitives

had declared against "conventionalism, whether old or new," as Davidson put it earlier to a news-woman in a letter (quoted by Cowan) of 10 March 1923. Of the Fugitives Davidson had written, "They hope to keep in touch with and to utilize in their work the best qualities of modern poetry, without at the same time casting aside as unworthy all that is established as good in the past." In their defense of this seemingly modest cause, these social conservatives fought as revolutionaries.

Small Presses II: The Spirit That Moves Us Press

Morty Sklar

Sitting down to write a prose piece brings to mind something basic about being in noncommercial literary publishing: although my publishing has at its roots my being a writer (of poetry and fiction), it has in a way cut me off from my own writing. That is something I hope to remedy soon (I've been saying for years). Some people are capable of writing, editing, publishing, raising a family, and working at structured jobs on an ongoing basis, but I'm not one of them. I can, so far, involve myself fully in only one thing at a time, and since 1975 that thing has been publishing. Not that you would think so, judging by The Spirit That Moves Us Press's output—only twenty-two publications—but during that time I have carried each publication from the announcement/solicitation stage through reading, decision-making, editing, typesetting, proofreading, layout, design, distribution, promotion, and fundraising, with all the clerical work related to those activities, except for small periods of time when someone helps me.

Something I can't do by myself is finance the press. Until October 1984, my best-selling book was *Editor's Choice: Literature & Graphics from the U.S. Small Press, 1965-1977*, and that has sold only 2,000 copies—even though it is indexed in *Granger's Index to Poetry* and has received fine reviews. Distributors get up to fifty-eight percent of the proceeds; bookstores and library jobbers get up to forty percent. My best shot so far—and ironically enough the publication I promoted the least—was a book of poetry by Jaroslav Seifert, titled *The Casting of Bells*,

which I published in 1983. A year later Seifert won the Nobel Prize for literature. The media coverage couldn't have been much better (*The Casting of Bells* was Seifert's only collection in English in the U.S., his only one in *Books in Print*). On 11 October 1984 I received phone calls from, and was interviewed by, the *New York Times*, the *Wall Street Journal*, the *Washington Post, U.S.A. Today, Publishers Weekly, Small Press*, Radio Free Europe, the *Des Moines Register*, "Good Morning America," and other television and radio programs. The translators of *The Casting of Bells*, Tom O'Grady and Paul Jagasich, were interviewed by *Time, People*, and others. On 12 October all the daily papers had pieces based on the interviews, and the weeklies and air media followed.

The National Book Award for poetry results in the sale of around 1,200 copies. A Nobel poet's only collection in English in the U.S.A.?—4,000 copies to date. (Faber and Faber has recently bought United Kingdom rights and *The Casting of Bells* from The Spirit That Moves Us Press.) The National Endowment for the Arts and the state arts councils (and previously the now long-defunct magazine grants from the Coordinating Council of Literary Magazines) are why The Spirit That Moves Us and many other small presses and "little" magazines are still operating. The history of The Spirit That Moves Us's funding from outside sources includes, first, money received personally by the editor when he was relocated in 1973 as a result of urban renewal in Iowa City. That took care of Vol-

Morty Sklar, 1979 (Shelley Sterling)

ume 1, no. 1 of *The Spirit That Moves Us.* Volume 1, no. 2, and Volume 1, no. 3 were both financed through money from State Vocational Rehabilitation in Iowa. Having published three issues of the magazine by 1976, The Spirit That Moves Us was eligible to apply to the Coordinating Council of Literary Magazines for a grant, which it did, and was awarded. The National Endowment for the Arts was awarding grants to magazines for special issues. The Spirit That Moves Us applied for and received one for *The Actualist Anthology* (Volume 2, nos. 2 & 3). It also applied to the Iowa Arts Council for a grant for that special issue and was rejected. Because that issue would contain fourteen poets who lived and interacted in Iowa City, the editor felt that literature wasn't getting a fair shake in Iowa, and so he, Allan Kornblum of Toothpaste Press, and Jim Mulac asked the Iowa Arts Council if they could talk to the Board of Directors about the place and importance of the small press, and the small press's need of funding through grants. Permission was granted, and, assisted by letters

from William Meredith, Consultant in Poetry to the Library of Congress, and other people, we made our presentation. The Council was understanding, and from that time on has awarded grants to small presses.

Nongovernment funding for literature is another story. In attempting to get matching funds for *Editor's Choice,* The Spirit That Moves Us asked forty-two foundations and corporations for grant application guidelines. Of the thirty or so which responded, only four seemed possible, and only one of these awarded us a grant—the Gannett Foundation, because of their connection to (and a recommendation by) the *Iowa City Press-Citizen.* The amount was $500. We fared better going door-to-door to businesses in Iowa City, getting an average donation of around $20. That netted $1,500. Recently we got another shot in the arm in the form of an Editor's Grant by the Coordinating Council of Literary Magazines, as one of the ten best editors of the year. (Consideration was given also to past performance, future plans, and vision.)

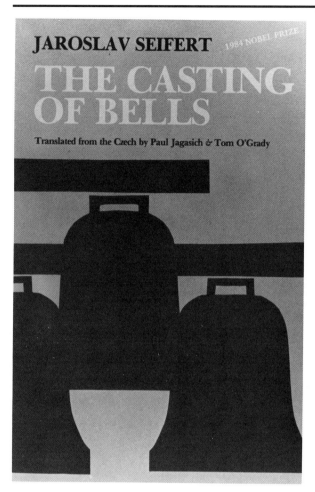

JAROSLAV SEIFERT 1984 NOBEL PRIZE

THE CASTING OF BELLS

Translated from the Czech by Paul Jagasich & Tom O'Grady

Cover for a collection of poems by 1984 Czech Nobel laureate

Why be a publisher if you're a writer? My own reasons were several, among them the enjoyment of collecting some works among many into a volume. Writing requires more of an original creative effort than publishing, but good publishing, like teaching, is a creative process. Another reason for my publishing is that it's a way to help me define and reinforce my own aesthetics. The defining process includes, along with showing what one already knows, discovering what one didn't know he would like—or didn't even know existed. Still another reason is wanting to influence the way literature is being written, and what is being read. I favor writing which is expressive of feeling. The imagination and experiment I like are those which are related to, and come out of, living. I want writing to affect people on an emotional level as well as intellectually. And although I'm open to many different styles of writing, I'm not a magnanimous editor—I won't publish something just because I think it is well written. I have to be fond of it.

I have given some reasons for my publishing *The Spirit That Moves Us,* but those reasons were seeds. The fertile ground in which they began to take root was the community of writers and "little" magazine publishers which thrived in Iowa City most heartily from the early to mid-1970s—outside the university and the renowned Writers Workshop. I began to know some of them soon after I moved here in 1971 from New York City, where I was born and raised. Among them was Allan Kornblum, who then published the mimeo magazine *Toothpaste,* and went on to establish Toothpaste Press, a fine letterpress house. Allan asked me for poems for *Toothpaste,* and later wanted a manuscript, which he published from his letterpress in 1977, titled *The Night We Stood Up for Our Rights: Poems 1969-1975.*

My Iowa City experience was most important for me both as a writer and as a publisher. In New York, where I had been writing a lot of poetry for three years prior to my leaving, I didn't associate much with other poets or go to open readings, because I was afraid (at the beginning of my poetry writing) to be influenced before I could get a real feel for how I wanted to write. When I became somewhat confident of my writing, I wanted to be with other poets, but I was shy and found it difficult to walk into a tavern where they might be hanging out, or go to an open reading. So I submitted a manuscript to and was accepted for a poetry workshop to be presided over by Isabella Gardner. According to the rules of the 92nd Street YM-YWHA, which sponsored the workshop, we were to meet at the Y. We did the first time, but then Isabella invited us to have our workshop at her Hotel Chelsea apartment at 23rd Street and Seventh Avenue. When we were about two-thirds through our sessions, Isabella would bring out some wine and snacks; after the sessions some of us would meet at the corner Horn & Hardardt's cafeteria for coffee and talk.

Isabella's workshops were, as I think of them now, the first of the one-two punch which set me straight in the literary world. I had the great good fortune to be one of twelve individual poets in the group—that is, if you read a collection of poems of theirs, you *wouldn't* be able to switch their names and fool anyone. I didn't realize then that the gathering of twelve individual poets into one workshop was something Isabella must have aimed for, and it wasn't until years later that I realized she had hardly ever told me what I should or should not do. It was her presence, part of which was her openness and her nurturing attitude, which influ-

enced me. When I now read some of the poems—
or versions of them—I had brought to workshop,
I see how raw or artless they were, either in part
or entirely. But Isabella was never critical, though
in her own way she made me think about those
poems and my writing of them. And the other
workshop members were helpful—especially since
they were coming from varied sensibilities.

With Isabella and her workshop, I was reinforced in my beliefs about how writing should be,
how one should write. But it wasn't until I came to
Iowa City that I realized how publishing should
be—both the sending out of one's writing to be
published, and publishing as a publisher. Until
then I felt that success was achieved by having one's
work accepted by established, well-known publications and presses. I had a list of magazines, and
would send three to five poems to each; when they
were returned, I'd circulate them among the others. Only one poem of the forty or so I'd been
sending out was published during that period—by
the *New York Quarterly*. So I am understanding and
tolerant of some people's (both readers' and writers') attitude that "little" magazines and small
presses are somehow second-best, that one starts
there, perhaps, but must climb the ladder of success
to the large commercial publishers. When Allan
Kornblum first asked me for poems for *Toothpaste*,
and later a manuscript for his press, I thought, who
will read *Toothpaste*? Some local people, some people on his small subscription list, some with whom
Allan exchanged issues, some who might pick up
the magazine in a literary bookstore? And if I publish a book of poems with him, how many bookstores will carry it, and how much promotion could
he do, and what reviewers will pay attention?

In the early to mid-1970s in Iowa City, we
wrote a lot, got together at the places of two or
three people who had apartments (rather than
rooms) to talk, read, help collate and staple the
latest issues of *Toothpaste, Search for Tomorrow*
(George Mattingly, who later ran Blue Wind Press),
Gum (Dave Morice, who later published *Poetry Com-
ics*), *Suction* (Darrell Gray, who later coedited with
me *The Actualist Anthology*, and was the "father" of
Actualism), *Me Too* (Mary Stroh and Patty Mar-
kert). And we had poetry readings around town,
one of the most organized of which was a weekly
series at the Sanctuary Tavern which lasted more
than a year. That was organized by Jim Mulac (who
later edited *Editor's Choice* with me) and served as
a forum not only for us, but for anyone who might
want to read, including people from New York,
Indianapolis, Madison, and Chicago. We also went

to read in their cities from time to time. We made
our own posters: Dave Morice would do a series in
his inimitable style, then Jim Mulac in his, then I
and then others. Jim later purchased what he re-
named Jim's Used Books & Records, and other
reading series ensued, broadened in scope by the
inclusion of writers who had come to Iowa City
from all around the world for the International
Writing Program.

In 1974 Jim Mulac asked me why I didn't do
a magazine. The question seemed strange then; I
wasn't sure why he asked it. A year later he asked
me again, and the idea seemed right, exciting. At
that point I had read enough magazines and books
to come to feel I could pack in a lot more good
stuff than most I'd seen—and I wanted to do that,
not only for egotistical reasons, but to give something to people: to readers, good literature; to writers, an opportunity to be read. The magazine was
and still is open—over ninety-five percent of what
I publish is unsolicited. The first issue was all poetry, and produced by myself with a mimeograph
machine, with a photo-offset cover added. Volume
7, no. 2 (Spring 1985) was all fiction—seventeen
pieces by seventeen writers, from award-winning
W. P. Kinsella, Sallie Bingham, Pat Carr, and Lester
Goldberg, to two previously unpublished writers.
It's titled *Here's The Story: Fiction with Heart*. All issues have contained artwork, and all have had covers by artists—except the first, which had a family
photo of my grandmother Rose and one-year-old
me on the cover. Most issues contain both poetry
and fiction, by many authors.

In 1977 I published *The Actualist Anthology*.
It consists of a generous selection of poetry by fourteen people, with photos of each and of readings
and events, plus autobiographical notes and bibliographies. This was the first book-format issue of
The Spirit That Moves Us, with ISBNs, CIP data, and
in a smythe-sewn cloth edition as well as a trade
paperback edition. It is Volume 2, nos. 2 and 3,
and was indexed in *Granger's Index to Poetry. Editor's
Choice: Literature & Graphics from the U.S. Small Press,
1965-1977* (1980), a 501-page collection of poetry,
fiction, essays, and artwork, consists of work nominated by editors of other "littles" and small presses.
I desired to do that book (and Editor's Choice II,
now in production and coedited by Mary Biggs, the
first woman editor of *Library Quarterly*, and a writer
and little-mag editor herself) because I saw so much
excellent work scattered around the small-press
world, most of which is seen by very few people. I
also wanted to see what was going on in the far

Cover for a 1980 anthology of poetry, fiction, essays, and artwork

recesses of the world of literary writing and publishing.

By 1981 I was very dissatisfied with the distribution of *The Spirit That Moves Us*. I felt that not only wasn't the magazine paying for itself (even with an occasional grant and some excellent reviews), but it wasn't seen enough. So I published in 1982 *The Spirit That Moves Us Reader: Seventh Anniversary Anthology*. This contains poetry, fiction, and art, culled from all issues of the magazine; reproductions of all previous covers; and two indexes—one according to issue-appearance, and the other in alphabetical order. This was the third book-format issue (the second was *Cross-Fertilization: The Human Spirit as Peace*, published in 1980). It was taken on by some small-press distributors and by Baker & Taylor's Approval Program. Copies of this, and other book-issues, were sent to book-reviewers also, and have received some excellent reviews.

Although *The Actualist Anthology* was the first book-format issue, I didn't know enough about book publishing and distribution to gain the best advantage for exposure. I did not know at the time, for instance, that reviews in *Publishers Weekly, Library Journal* and some other places were pre-publication reviews, and required either galleys or bound copies sent as far in advance of publication date as twelve to fifteen weeks. When *The Spirit That Moves Us Reader* was ready for publication, I was much wiser about such things.

In 1982 I was approached by Tom O'Grady, a little-magger, poet, and translator, about the possibility of my publishing the Seifert book, which he and Paul Jagasich had translated into English. As I read *The Casting of Bells*, the poet grew on me, but I told O'Grady, "What's the use? A book of poetry by an unknown (practically everywhere but in Czechoslovakia) would sell even less than my other publications." Then I said, "Okay, but in two years. That way I can apply for a grant with which to do it, and can catch up with my publishing schedule." O'Grady said that the author was dying, and that Jagasich was going to Prague that summer to visit him. He said that he wasn't sure if Seifert would get the books if we mailed them to him, as his books had been suppressed by the Czech government since the 1968 "Prague Spring," during which he had spoken out for free speech. In 1983 the book was out, with the assistance of O'Grady's college, which guaranteed the purchase of enough copies to pay for the printing. In October 1984 Seifert won the Nobel Prize for literature. The discouraging lack of financial success of a book I'd published earlier that year, *Nuke, Rebuke: Writers & Artists Against Nuclear Energy & Weapons* (poetry, fiction, essays, artwork), had put me at the lowest point in my publishing career. Now, in one day, I was at the literary, if not financial, zenith. In 1985 I published two chapbooks by Seifert: *Mozart in Prague: Thirteen Rondels* (bilingual; translated by O'Grady & Jagasich), and *Eight Days: An Elegy for Thomas Garrigue Masaryk* (bilingual; translated by O'Grady & Jagasich, and including Seifert's acceptance speech for the honorary doctorate given him by Hampden-Sydney College in Virginia, where the translators teach).

I have published two other single-author poetry chapbooks. One was *The Poem You Asked For* (1977), by Marianne Wolfe, who sent so much good work to the magazine that I had to give her her own publication. It was our first nonmagazine issue, single-author book. The other was *The Farm in Calabria & Other Poems* (1980) by David Ray, with photographs by Judy Ray (published back-to-back with a regular issue of *The Spirit That Moves Us*—Volume 5, nos. 1 & 2). Some of the other poets I've published are Robert Bly, Marge Piercy, Charles Bukowski, Gary Snyder, Margaret Randall, William Stafford, and Robert Creeley. In 1978 I published a set of 16 x 11-inch *Poetry with Drawings in the Buses,* with an accompanying edition of the same in postcard format. It contains the work of eight poets, with drawings commissioned from eight visual artists and a "cover" illustration. Forthcoming after *Editor's Choice II* are two special issues: "Men & Women: Together & Apart" (coedited with Mary Biggs, and consisting of poetry and artwork), and an as-yet untitled book of poems by Chuck Miller, one of our finest little-known poets.

Distribution of The Spirit That Moves Us publications is now done mainly through small-press distributors and "mainstream" library jobbers. We sell direct also, with around twenty-five percent of our distribution being done that way. Distributors who sell our publications (on consignment, with discounts varying from fifty to fifty-eight percent) are Bookpeople, Bookslinger, Inland Book Company, Small Press Distribution, Publishers Group West, The Distributors, and

Book Dynamics. Our major library jobbers are Baker & Taylor, Blackwell North America, Midwest Library Service, and Book House. Eight to ten other jobbers periodically order from us as well. Orders are generated through two main sources: direct-mail promotion and reviews. Other sources are advertisements and listings in our distributors' catalogues, our use of CIP data, listings in *Books In Print,* occasional display ads in review journals, bookfair and convention displays, and word-of-mouth. Recently we mailed out 12,000 copies of a 16-page catalogue of backlist/new/forthcoming publications.

Publications are sold either as monographs or by subscription. Because of the varying sizes and prices, subscriptions are based on twenty percent off the cover price, to simplify things. For non-subscription publications, a fifteen percent discount is given for two or more pieces (titles and bindings may be combined). Complete sets of *The Spirit That Moves Us* are still available, as are cumulative indexes. A complete list of *The Spirit That Moves Us* publications may be had in a 1985/1986 descriptive catalogue from The Spirit That Moves Us Press, P.O. Box 1585, Iowa City, IA 52244.

The Practice of Biography IV

AN INTERVIEW ————————————

with WILLIAM MANCHESTER

Before he began writing books, William Manchester was a newsman for seven years, serving the *Baltimore Sun* as reporter, Washington correspondent, and foreign correspondent in the Middle East, India, and Southeast Asia. His first book was *Disturber of the Peace: The Life of H. L. Mencken* (1951). Probably best known for his 1967 account of the John Fitzgerald Kennedy assassination, *The Death of a President,* Manchester is a historian, essayist, and novelist as well as a biographer. His additional nonfiction includes *A Rockefeller Family Portrait* (1959); *Portrait of a President* (1962); *The Arms of Krupp* (1968); *The Glory and the Dream: A Narrative History of America, 1932-1972* (1974); *Con-*

troversy and Other Essays in Journalism (1976); *American Caesar: Douglas MacArthur, 1880-1964* (1978); *Goodbye, Darkness* (1980); *One Brief, Shining Moment* (1983); and *The Last Lion: Winston Spencer Churchill, Visions of Glory* (1983). His novels are *The City of Anger* (1953), *Shadow of the Monsoon* (1956), *Beard the Lion* (1958), and *The Long Gainer* (1961). Since 1955, Manchester has been a writer-in-residence at Wesleyan University. He is currently at work on the second volume of his Churchill biography.

DLB: You were reading seriously and writing when you were quite young. Was biography something you thought you'd like to do specifically, or did it just evolve through your Master's thesis on H. L. Mencken?

MANCHESTER: Actually I don't think of myself

Dust jacket for the book that William L. Shirer said "brought home the misery and horror of combat . . ."

as a biographer at all. In this country we tend to pigeonhole professionals. If people know that you write, they ask what sort of author you are. That is not true elsewhere. In France, for example, you are a writer, period. You may write a novel one month, a play the next, then a book of poems, a letter to the editor, a philosophical work, or a volume of nonfiction. It seems that half the time I'm called a historian and the other half a biographer. In fact I've published fifteen books. Three of them are serious novels; the reviews were marvelous, but they have found few buyers. One is a collection of essays, and another a book of diversion—an entertainment, to use Graham Greene's word. The rest are nonfiction. But *The Death of a President*, which is perhaps my best-known work, is not a biography at all; it's a history.

DLB: What techniques of fiction do you think are useful and fair to bring to the writing of biography?

MANCHESTER: Although it has not yet been recognized, over the last twenty-five years a wholly new literary form has evolved. If you pick up a book of nonfiction published before World War II, it's likely to be pedestrian in style, with no scholarly apparatus at the end—in fact, you're lucky to find an index.

Since the war, such writers as Barbara Tuchman, William L. Shirer, John Brooks, and Walter Lord have developed a new genre, writing popular history and biography as literature, with a scholarly apparatus in the back providing annotation—what the French call *les justifications*. Shirer, like most of us, started as a novelist. The writer of fiction is familiar with such techniques as characterization, scene setting, and plotting without contrivance. It's like counterpoint in music. Events are happening simultaneously, and so you switch from one theme to another and back. This is elementary plotting. You know the story of the two men in a rooming house: the man in the upstairs bedroom drops a shoe with a thud, and, regretting this, he lowers the other shoe softly. After fifteen minutes the man downstairs says, "For God's sake, drop the other shoe!" You write a passage and you leave a situation unresolved. The reader wants it settled the way he wants to scratch an itch. But at that point you introduce another scene, and again you drop a shoe. You return to the first situation and resolve it, and so on. You're not limited to two, of course. You may have five subplots running simultaneously, leaving the reader dangling from various cliffs, confident that you will rescue him.

These are fictive techniques. They were used by Dickens and Trollope more often than by our modern novelists, but they are a way of attracting and holding readers. As I often remind my colleagues at Wesleyan, a professor has a captive audience. A writer does not; the reader can throw the book aside at any time. Using the fictive devices I taught myself as a novelist (and believe me, that's the way you learn any writing—not in a workshop), I have attempted to write nonfiction as literature. I'm not alone in this. We have academic historians and popular historians. Barbara Tuchman is depressed because she gets bad reviews from academic historians. Well, the academic historians are writing for one another. Writers like Barbara and Bill Shirer are reaching out for the large audience. I think the fact that my four novels were succes d'estime does not mean that time was wasted. I learned skills I use in all my work.

DLB: Some critics felt that you showed too much

partiality to John F. Kennedy in *The Death of a President*. Later, researching *American Caesar,* you said that you felt General Douglas MacArthur resisted being understood. Is a certain balance of feeling for the subject you're writing about necessary to good writing?

MANCHESTER: If I am partial, I declare my partiality at the outset, and there it is. My God, if you look through history, this is done again and again. Boswell is certainly Johnson's advocate, and Macaulay is Marlborough's prosecutor. In *The Death of a President,* it is clear from the outset that I was close to Jack Kennedy and mourned him, but so did most Americans. I didn't find Johnson sympathetic, but I did not attack him. My partiality is more evident in the other two books I wrote about Jack, *Portrait of a President* and *One Brief, Shining Moment.*

 In *American Caesar* and *The Arms of Krupp* and *The Glory and the Dream,* and with Winston Churchill, I have pointed out flaws as well as the attractive aspects of my subject. There's room for both. The difficulty lies in the confusion of biography and history; they are frequently misunderstood by historians, who hardly admit the existence of biography as an independent discipline. But the difference is quite clear. History is a chronological account of events. Biography centers on one man, and the events are context.

DLB: But biography and history are hard to separate because they are often so intertwined.

MANCHESTER: In my biography of Churchill, which is going into two volumes, you cannot ignore history; he was a statesman. The history is accurate, and so is the personal material. But in analyzing Churchill personally, I'm not tied down by chronology. I can range back and forth throughout his life to demonstrate aspects of his personality.

DLB: Disturber of the Peace would seem to have been done under the best conditions for biography because of your personal relationship with Mencken.

MANCHESTER: I worked for the *Baltimore Sun* for seven years as a reporter, a Washington correspondent, and a foreign correspondent in the Middle East, India, and Southeast Asia. In the last year of Mencken's life I took a leave of absence to be with him. For seven years he had been a surrogate father to me. That was my first book, and I knew very little about publishing. It appeared on the

third day of January 1951. In those days hardly anyone ever brought out a book in January, so I was misled by the great attention it received. Also, that generation of book reviewers and book review editors had been enchanted by Mencken. I got a marvelous press, and they were too kind to me. I had the cover of the *Saturday Review* and the lead review in the *New Yorker* and *Time.* As I look back, I see that book was written under the influence of Mencken. Most first books are under some writer's influence. My second book, my first novel, *City of Anger*—which is my favorite—is entirely my style.

DLB: You've noted that all subjects present their own unique difficulties. Is there one of yours that's been most difficult, either emotionally or in other ways?

MANCHESTER: The hardest, emotionally, was *The Death of a President.* The most difficult book to research and write was *The Arms of Krupp.* I was working in German, and I'm not a linguist; and I was also dealing with hostile subjects who didn't want me to write anything at all. I might say that the present work on Churchill is extremely difficult. I should have begun the second Churchill volume as soon as I finished the first. Instead, I wrote *One Brief, Shining Moment* as sort of a farewell to Jack, and the return to Churchill has been a struggle. Also, I'd never done more than one volume before. I find that you're writing volume two and you realize that in volume one there's an anecdote that would be absolutely perfect, but you can't use it.

DLB: Working with a subject for so long, do you ever get tired of being in his company day after day?

MANCHESTER: No, I don't. I have a one-track mind; I concentrate entirely on one topic. Arthur Schlesinger can write books, teach, be a social celebrity, write movie criticism, and do all of these things well. I cannot. I have my work and my family and the Wesleyan community and I avoid going to New York whenever possible—and it's usually possible.

DLB: I'm sure it can be very distracting.

MANCHESTER: It's the *caput mundi* of literary politics. I went down a year and a half ago for the New York Public Library's Literary Lions Award. I was surrounded by people I knew or knew of— Herman Wouk, Arthur Miller, Bill Styron, Philip

Roth, Susan Sontag—and there was a lot of politicking going on. I'm uncomfortable with that. I have friends who are writers, but we don't talk about writing; we talk about ideas. When my first book was published, Harold Ross offered me a job at the *New Yorker* working on "The Talk of the Town." I asked him if I would have to live in Manhattan, and he said yes. I said, "Well, I'm sorry. I can't do that." Greenwich Village bars are full of young men and women talking about the books they say they're going to write and never will, because they get rid of them by talking. I think that books are important and writers are not. If a writer reaches a point at which he finds his own life more interesting and more exciting than his work, he's in trouble. Writers are very vulnerable to that, particularly in New York. It's not good for them and it's not good for literature.

DLB: You're known for your prodigious research. Do you try to do all of it before you actually get down to the writing, or do the two processes overlap?

MANCHESTER: They overlap. I do all of the research that I can think of doing before I begin writing, but inevitably as I'm working along I come to a subject that requires more investigation.

DLB: Are there certain sources that you always rely heavily on, such as newspapers and unpublished documents?

MANCHESTER: There are primary and secondary sources. In dealing with the past you work with letters and diaries, with documents. Actually, the present is more difficult to research because of the telephone. I know more about the assassination of President Kennedy and the transfer of power to the new administration than anybody else on earth, but I know still more about the Gallipoli Campaign of 1915, because back then everybody put everything in writing. Interviews are important when people are still alive. I don't like to use secondary sources, but sometimes it's unavoidable.

DLB: In doing interviews for a book, do you ever find that other people's recollections of the subject conflict with your own to the extent that it becomes a problem?

MANCHESTER: Yes, and it's important to check. Interviewing is an art all its own. You're born with talent; you learn research; and you teach yourself interviewing. I build an interview so that, if I ask a question and I get an unexpected answer, about ten or fifteen minutes later I'll ask the same question differently phrased to see if I get the same answer. I may even do it a third time. In Dallas, for example, when there were six people in the car in the motorcade, I interviewed all six. If one saw something that five didn't, I concluded that it didn't happen. If five saw it and one didn't, I concluded that it did. And I did interview everyone in the motorcade and in the hospital—doctors, nurses, orderlies, elevator operators, switchboard operators. Then you have to take it all and spread it out on the living room floor; you see how it matches up and try to recreate what happened.

DLB: Current subjects must be especially hard because there isn't the perspective of time to approach them from.

MANCHESTER: And because there are so many living witnesses. When I wrote *The Arms of Krupp*, a history of four centuries of the Krupp dynasty, in certain periods the documentation was rather thin. In dealing with the mid-nineteenth century, I was working with a couple of diaries, a sheaf of letters, company records, and diaries and letters written by friends. It was not very substantial. When I was researching *The Death of a President*, I interviewed over a thousand people, and I had Xeroxes of the diaries and notes of all the members of the government. Nevertheless, there were people who popped up and said, "It didn't happen this way, and I was there"—which seems irrefutable, except that other people were there and they saw it differently.

DLB: What writers have particularly influenced your own work?

MANCHESTER: As a young writer, I was influenced by Mencken and by E. M. Forster, whom I never met, though we had an extensive correspondence when I was living in India. Mostly I was influenced by the nineteenth-century writers I read in my father's library when I was a child: Macaulay, Huxley, Ruskin, Matthew Arnold. Then, when I was twelve, I discovered Shakespeare. It was the pit of the Depression, and there was a forty-volume Shakespeare for sale in a second-hand bookstore. It cost four dollars. Only *Macbeth* was missing, and I knew where I could get a *Macbeth* for a dime. I put a dollar down, and it took me three months to get the other three dollars. I still have those volumes. I read all of Shakespeare and fell in love with his work.

DLB: Are you ever able to get away from the writing and do any sort of reading for relaxation?

MANCHESTER: Yes, and I try to read something as far as possible from what I'm working on. For example, right now I'm writing about Churchill, and I tend to read light fiction. When I was writing fiction, I read nonfiction. I think it's dangerous to read something for diversion in your own field. You're tempted to imitate style, and even borrow phrases and similes unconsciously.

DLB: Working on any subject that many other people have written about, such as Churchill, what do you hope to bring to it that will be new?

MANCHESTER: I have frequently been told when I've embarked on a project that it's been done. Early in 1964 Bobby Kennedy announced at a press conference that I was going to write *The Death of a President.* At that time the Associated Press had published a book called *The Torch Is Passed,* and UPI had put out another, *Four Days.* The UPI and AP reporters came to me afterward and said, "Why do you bother? It's already been done." When I started MacArthur, people said the same thing, and they said it again with Churchill. But I take the arrogant view that it hasn't been done until I do it. And in each case I have managed to find that there is a wealth of material that has not been covered. I've never gone into a subject and not found extraordinary material.

One of the traits necessary in research is a capacity for drudgery. Recently I went through 40,000 pages of British foreign policy documents from 1919 to 1939. That was very hard work, but I did come up with some extraordinary discoveries. Similarly, when I was working on MacArthur I read many World War II divisional histories, and nothing could be deadlier. Sometimes I would pick up an anecdote or two at most, and sometimes I'd pick up nothing. I can be a speed reader, depending on whether I'm reading for entertainment or for work. When necessary, I can push myself up to 3000 words per minute.

DLB: Would you undertake another authorized biography if the opportunity arose?

MANCHESTER: Given again the circumstances under which I undertook *The Death of a President,* no, I would not. I drew up all of the conditions of that work. I drew up the Memorandum of Understanding. I stipulated that my profits would go to the Kennedy Library, because I did not want to make money from the death of a friend; that there would be no television or motion picture use of the material; that the Kennedys would have the right of manuscript review and approval. I did everything I could to guard against misunderstanding, but misunderstanding arose because although it was Jackie who had asked me to write the book, she had told me, "Work through Bobby." Bobby, after a four-month review of the manuscript by five men who had been special assistants to President Kennedy, approved the publication in writing—in a special delivery letter to Harper's and a telegram to me. He then participated in the auction of magazine rights, which went to *Look.* Then, to his horror and mine, Jackie changed her mind. She hadn't read the book but didn't want it published. The prospect of publicity alarmed her. What she didn't understand was that contracts had been signed all over the world. Bobby and I could have been sued for everything we had. Bobby's position was much worse than mine. At that time he was very much a presidential possibility. He could afford a rift with Lyndon Johnson, but not with his sister-in-law.

DLB: It must have been a very difficult time for you.

MANCHESTER: It was ghastly. There are writers who enjoy celebrity, but I don't; I hate it. I cherish anonymity.

DLB: In *Goodbye, Darkness* you wove your memoir into the story of World War II. I'm sure it can be hard emotionally to retrace the war sites and recall the events. Is it in some ways hardest to write about one's self, do you think?

MANCHESTER: It was a hard book. I've just finished reading galleys for an introduction to a new edition of *The Death of a President.* In that book, and in *Goodbye, Darkness,* both the writer and, if the writing's true, the reader experience catharsis. Such books are moving when you read them, but afterward you may feel purged and at peace.

DLB: Your writing and your work at Wesleyan seem to have been mutually enriching. How much time do you spend in the classroom?

MANCHESTER: I don't spend any time any more.

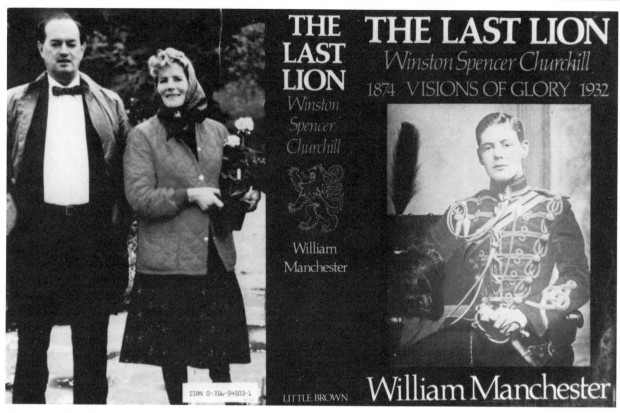

Dust jacket for the first volume of Manchester's projected two-volume Churchill biography. At left, the author with Churchill's daughter, Lady Soames.

I have a few tutorials for seniors who are candidates for honors, but I no longer teach classes.

DLB: The Churchill biography, you said, may take another three years. Is it too early for you to have thought beyond that to another subject?

MANCHESTER: I can tell you that this is the last 1000-page annotated book I'm going to do. I have 800 categories of Churchill material; ten years ago I could carry all this around in my head easily, but now it's become a strain. Russ Baker and I were on the *Baltimore Sun* together. We went to work at the same time; we went abroad as foreign correspondents together, he to London and I to India, and we left at the same time. Long ago we said we were going to write our reminiscences. Russ is writing his now, and I'll write mine when I finish Churchill. And then I have some other books I want to do.

DLB: There was talk about another novel a few years back. Will you do one?

MANCHESTER: There was and is talk, and I've been offered very large advances. But *The Death of a President* was the only book I've written that was not my idea; that was Jackie's. I work best with my own ideas. I'm just not comfortable with the suggestions of others.

—*Jean W. Ross*

The Year in Literary Biography

Jeffrey Meyers
University of Colorado

Biography
Is better than Geography,
Geography's about maps,
Biography's about chaps.

—Auden & MacNeice,
Letters from Iceland

Winfield Scott remarked, in his review of Mark Schorer's *Sinclair Lewis* (*New Republic*, 20 November 1961): "Our saddest stories are biographies of 20th Century American writers, Thomas Wolfe, Hart Crane, Vachel Lindsay, Scott Fitzgerald, Edna Millay, Eugene O'Neill, probably Hemingway when we know it. . . . It would require . . . a combination of psychologist, sociologist, literary historian and critic, as well as an expert in alcoholism, to try to explain why." And Richard Blackmur, after reading this review, "asked himself why so many 'eager young talents' had turned 'abortive and sterile,' or why, if they 'succeeded in keeping their talent alive into middle age, [they] either reduced their standards, fell silent, became eccentric, or went abroad.' Perhaps the writer carried with him the seeds of his own destruction" (Russell Fraser, *A Mingled Yarn*).

The 1985 harvest of letters, diaries, memoirs, and biographies, on American if not on the more sane and stable English writers, tends to substantiate these observations. Apart from John Crowe Ransom and Thornton Wilder, the two cautious exceptions, we are confronted in these books with Pound's treason and madness, Jarrell's breakdown and suicide, Jane Bowles's disease and mania, Louise Bogan's sad loves and sterility, Hemingway's shock treatment and shotgun blast, James Jones's pathetic failures, Norman Mailer's violence, Tennessee Williams's alcoholism and drug addiction.

Most of the twenty-seven books considered in this essay, inflating their subject and straining to be definitive, are too long. The abundance of trivial detail reverses Mies van der Rohe's aphorism and shows that "more is less." It is also a great pity that full cloth bindings have virtually disappeared and that clear footnotes have usually been replaced by confusing cue words at the end of the text. Many of these works are competent, but only a few—Robert Martin's *FitzGerald* and Tim Hilton's *Ruskin*—have the qualities that characterize great modern biographies: exhaustive research, sceptical evaluation of evidence, scrupulous honesty, clarity and coherence, discriminating selectivity, and sympathetic attraction to the subject.

If Victorian biographies were mainly eulogistic, modern lives (though sympathetic) are more honest and more critical. The biographer must not merely discover new facts that bring the subject to life, but also master the material and interpret what these facts mean. He must select the essential and convincing details, find the appropriate length, effect a strategy of presentation, and create a dramatic form that clarifies the pattern of the life. He must possess a lively narrative style, find striking openings, whether chronological or dramatic, and persuasive summations for his chapters. He must often struggle against the subject's rage for privacy and—while dealing with the sexual and medical aspects as well as the end and extinction of the life—combine lucidity with subtlety to achieve the vivid realism of a Flemish painting. He must reveal how the seeds of genius developed, how experience was transformed into art, and how the writer imposed his vision on the world. He must show the changes that occur during the passage of time and the multiple lives contained within a single subject. He must balance external events with crucial moments of the inner life, do justice to the minor characters and to the cultural milieu. Finally, he

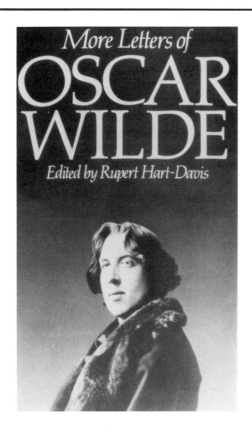

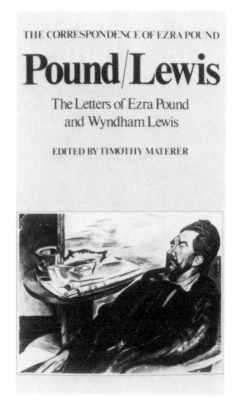

Dust jackets for four new collections of literary correspondence

must define the subject's achievement, influence, and place in the literary tradition, and illuminate human nature through individual character.

The greatest letters in English—by Byron, Keats, and Lawrence—are marked by intuitive sympathy, vital energy, intellectual audacity, and imaginative intensity. The liveliest correspondents in these volumes are Oscar Wilde, Katherine Mansfield, and Wyndham Lewis; the dullest are Ransom and Shaw.

Both Flaubert and Turgenev—similar in age, profession, and stature—thought writing was a solitary and lonely art, and felt an intense need to communicate with a kindred spirit. From 1863, when they met and were instantly attracted at one of the famous literary dinners at Magny's restaurant, until Flaubert's death in 1880, they exchanged about 230 letters—competently translated, introduced, and edited by Barbara Beaumont—and moved from flattery to friendship. Since many of the letters in *Flaubert & Turgenev: A Friendship in Letters* contain trivial details and requisite formalities, and tend to skirt serious literary and political issues, they are not nearly as interesting as the Freud-Jung or Thomas Mann-Erich Kahler correspondence.

Flaubert believed that Turgenev was "the only man in existence really devoted to literature," and poured out a lava of anger in letters to his sympathetic friend. Flaubert insists that Théophile Gautier "died poisoned by the filth of modern life." He is "overwhelmed by public Stupidity," feels "a wave of relentless Barbarism rising up from below the ground" and hopes "to be dead before all [he values] is swept away." Yet he wants to live long enough, at least, to empty "a few more buckets of sh-- on the heads of my fellow men." A slight ray of hope appears when a distinguished French nobleman is arrested for sodomy and "judges' robes hang over the latrines"—"Such stories cheer one up and help to make life bearable."

When the decay of their bodies matched the disintegration of their world, both writers expressed profound pessimism about fate, suffering, and death. Turgenev—impotent, old, gouty, and crippled—lamented that "illness, slow disgust, painful stirrings of useless memories are all that await us once we're past the age of fifty." The genius of George Sand, he said, was reduced by death to a "horrible relentless hole in the ground, silent and stupid, that doesn't even know what it's devouring."

More Letters of Oscar Wilde (Vanguard), excel-

lently annotated by Rupert Hart-Davis, contains 164 epistles that have been discovered since the original edition of 1962. Both a supplement and a self-contained volume, it also reprints as a lagniappe two interviews with Wilde. The letters are characteristically stylish, lively and witty, with hints of sincerity beneath the artifice. They concern Wilde's lectures and journalism, the publication of his books and staging of his plays, his response to imprisonment and late destitution.

A college friend called Wilde "aesthetic to the last degree, passionately fond of secondary colours, low tones and Morris papers." Wilde contests an "extortionate and exorbitant" bill, complains of "the coarse impertinence of having a work officially rejected which has been no less officially sought for" and, his voice extinguished by illness, offers to offer his homage, "even though it be in dumb-show." The chill London winter, "so pitiless, so precise—gives one form where one wants colour, definiteness where one needs mystery"; the burning Parisian summer produces "streets of brass in which the passers—few in number—crawl like black flies." He praises "the sinless master whom mortals call Flaubert" and visits Whitman in Camden. He lectures to 2,500 people in Chicago and in Sioux City finds himself confused "among cañons and coyotes: one is a sort of fox, the other a deep ravine: I don't know which is which." He is lionized, adored, assailed, mocked, and worshipped in America, "but of course as usual quite triumphant."

In the only surviving letter from Algiers, where Wilde and Lord Alfred Douglas ran into André Gide and smoked hashish, he notes that the brown shepherd boys are quite lovely: "The beggars here have profiles, so the problem of poverty is easily solved." After the fatal, idiotic step of action at law against the Marquess of Queensberry, Wilde is incarcerated in Reading Gaol, an admirable address "from the ethical point of view," and is forced to spend eighteen relaxing months in the Thames Valley. He agrees that his children should change their surname but hopes, when they are older, that they may be proud to acknowledge him as their father. After losing his position and power, he observes that the English have denied him "even the barren recognition one gives to the dead." Desperate for money and cadging on his friends, he is still capable of a glittering *mot:* "Bankruptcy is always in store for those who pay their debts." This book shows Wilde as a brave and brilliant man.

The 989 pages of *Collected Letters, 1911-1925* (Viking) reveal Bernard Shaw—the antithesis of

Wilde—as the great bore of modern literature. They expose his labored humor, his exaggerated posturing, his perverse response to emotional experience, his non-starter love affairs, his cocky omniscience, his prejudicial opinions, his half-truth arguments, his tedious causes, and his dated, stupefying plays.

The headnotes by the editor, Dan Laurence, are informative and a few of the letters are intermittently interesting: the condemnation of Archibald Henderson's biography, the twenty-nine-page autobiographical letter, the reaction to the 1916 Easter Rising in Dublin, the defense of Roger Casement, the condolences to Stella Campbell and Lady Gregory after the death of their sons in the war, the negative response to *Ulysses,* the analysis of the character of T. E. Lawrence, and the attempt to get Lawrence a government pension. And there is the curt rejection of the extortionate demands of his Polish translator, Floryan Sobieniowski, the lover and blackmailer of Katherine Mansfield: "You must at once set about making a new set of friends with the requisite money; for I cannot go on financing you. . . . I will never see you again if I can possibly help it: it costs me too much."

Katherine Mansfield's *Collected Letters: Volume 1, 1903-1917* (Oxford), edited by Vincent O'Sullivan and Margaret Scott, are, like her stories, among the best written in this century. They are passionate, witty, dramatic, receptive, and sensitive, evocative of mood, place, and people. Mansfield was highly critical of New Zealand while she lived there. But in adult life she idealized the atmosphere and landscape in nostalgic evocations of childhood. Her selfish parents—the father absorbed in business, the mother in herself—failed to recognize their daughter's genius and did not give her the money and love that she so desperately needed. Her life became a depressing series of domestic, financial, emotional, and medical crises. Despite her numerous friends, she suffered terribly from isolation and loneliness. So letters were for her a great occasion, a treat, and a solace. At once guarded and open, she was, as Lytton Strachey observed, "an odd satirical woman behind a regular mask of a face."

Mansfield, a talented actress, cautiously warned, "don't lower your mask until you have another mask prepared beneath. As terrible as you like—but a *mask.*" But she loved to expose herself to experience, had a self-destructive streak, and was drawn to men who treated her badly. One lover gave her gonorrhea; Garnet Trowell abandoned her when she was pregnant; Francis Carco crassly

Dust jacket for a biography based largely on Edward FitzGerald's letters

used her; Middleton Murry treated her like a dilatory housemaid, neglected her illness, and exploited her work after her death.

Living in a constant state of transition, Mansfield often found herself "alone all day, ill, in a house whose every sound seems foreign." She would despair in the atmosphere of that dreadful world, having no hiding place and no cover. She was attractive, talented, and brave. It was tragic that she became mortally ill just as she had mastered her art and begun to write her finest works. She rushed out her mature stories during the last five years of her life and died in 1923—after a disastrous entanglement with the charlatan Gurdjieff—at the age of thirty-four. Mansfield was as fastidious as if she had written with acid. When she managed to sweep away the last veil between herself and the heart of things, she brought all that she saw and felt into harmony with a rare vision of life. Her best letters and stories have the vivid clarity and precise detail of a fine engraving.

The second volume of E. M. Forster's *Selected Letters* (Harvard), excellently if over-abundantly edited by Mary Lago and P. N. Furbank (whose annotations are sometimes longer than the letters), covers the last fifty years of his life and portrays him in the role of inconspicuous public figure, unstrident propagandist of good causes. A witty though rather dreary fellow, Forster lived almost entirely in a homosexual milieu, and his main correspondents were secret sharers of his sexual taste: G. L. Dickinson, Housman, J. R. Ackerley, Cavafy, Sassoon, T. E. Lawrence, William Plomer, Isherwood, Spender, John Lehmann, Britten, and Forster's great love, the married policeman Bob Buckingham. He jealously described the constable's unusually tolerant wife as "domineering, sly and *knowing* and at present she seems to have got him down." Forster had his first sexual experience in Egypt at the age of thirty-eight, and his fictional impulse dried up soon after his sex life began.

Forster's best letters concern his last novel, his friends, and his attitude toward love, sex, pain, and death. He told Virginia Woolf that he disliked the documentary aspects of the novel but recognized "that when cut away these detach with them something that ought to remain." He found it difficult, when completing *A Passage to India*, "to strike a balance between self-expression and personal loyalty." While writing the novel he thought it a failure, but was encouraged to finish it by Leonard Woolf. He mistakenly "tried to show that India is an unexplainable muddle by introducing an unexplained muddle—Miss Quested's experience in the cave." When asked what happened there, he replied: "I don't know." He was always opposed to film versions of his novels and in 1947 refused $25,000 for rights to *A Room With a View*: "Nothing would have survived of the original except my name, and if I had tried to control the production I should have broken my heart at Hollywood."

Forster made some acute observations about his friends. He "turned his backside" to Bloomsbury: "they will never have the grace to penetrate it, their inquisitiveness never had any spunk, that is why one loathes it so." And he was "bored by Virginia's superciliousness and maliciousness, which she has often wounded me with in the past." He found the dreaded Wyndham Lewis, the great enemy of Bloomsbury, surprisingly sympathetic: "He is a curious mixture of insolence and nervousness, and has been quite agreeable to me." The odd

and alarming T. E. Lawrence had a sure sign of genius: "The power of making one feel one could do all he has done." He planned to edit Lawrence's letters and could have produced a "gem" of a book, but fell out with the executors over the question of indemnity for libel. The best letter, by far, in the book is Frieda Lawrence's brilliant reply to Forster's condolence note after the death of D. H. Lawrence.

Forster wondered whether " 'fondness' and 'love' lead to intimacies that are different in quality" and believed "we communicate dimly—except for the special occasions when we go to bed with one another." Pain is good, he thought, only when "it's incidental to love." Forster strained mildly against his loss of independence while living with his mother, and when she finally died, aged 90, he noted: "the famous death-rattle wasn't too bad." When shocked by death, he longed "to think or look at warm obscenities—this has happened to me when upset all my life." Ackerley wanted to discuss nature, but the octogenarian Forster preferred to talk about "cockstands." As Buckingham's son was dying of cancer, Forster was helped by his "disbelief in the existence of god. . . . As soon as one realises that the universe is neither for us or against us one feels steadier."

In his 1951 review of Ezra Pound's *Letters*, Wyndham Lewis described the tone as "authoritative, not to say pontificatory" but also said that "his rock-drill action is impressive: he blasts away tirelessly, prodding and coaxing." So *Pound/Lewis: The Letters of Ezra Pound and Wyndham Lewis* (New Directions), the correspondence of two of the most lively, energetic, and original minds of the twentieth century, was bound to be interesting. Since both men had notoriously rebarbative personalities, only profound mutual respect could have enabled their friendship to survive the vicissitudes of poverty and prison, blindness and madness.

Timothy Materer has done a superb job of transcribing and annotating these learned and allusive letters, and has provided an illuminating commentary on each phase of the friendship. Yet Pound's exasperating style and repulsive content after about 1930—when he became obsessed with economics, Fascism, and anti-Semitism and lapsed into a private language—are torture to read. Lewis found Pound's last letters impenetrable.

The main emphasis of the early letters is on how the loyal Pound can get Lewis money, publishers, exhibitions as well as—through the influence of powerful patrons—promotion to officer and then transfer out of the Royal Artillery. Lewis was temperamentally unfit to do any good for himself; Pound was a master at handling patrons, sceptical dealers, and lonesome tycoons. So there was no question of Lewis doing anything for Pound, who was also (if not equally) hard up.

Lewis's Great War letters are the best in this volume. He was characteristically vituperative, showed real courage in combat and continued to write at the front. He was eager for violent experience that he could use in his art, thought firing Howitzers was appropriate for the editor of BLAST, endured heavy fire every day, and fought at Passchendaele.

Lewis named Pound his literary executor, instructed him to look after his two illegitimate children, and asked him to write a memoir (as he had done for Gaudier) if Lewis were killed. But all Pound's extraordinary efforts, Lewis menacingly exclaimed in 1925, did "not give you a mandate to interfere when you think fit . . . with my career." To which Pound bluntly replied: "There are some matters in which you really do behave like, and really do write like, a God damn fool."

In 1925 Lewis had jokingly asked: "Could you get me the Nobel Prize next year? or do you want it yourself?" In 1948, when their close friend Eliot creamed off all the honors, Lewis was still impoverished and obscure, Pound confined to an asylum for the criminally insane. Struck by the irony of their situation, Lewis observed: "You might almost have contrived this climax to your respective careers: yours so Villonesque and Eliot's super-Tennysonian."

The first generation of modern American poets—Frost, Stevens, Williams, Eliot—led relatively respectable and orderly lives (Pound was the great exception) compared to their drunken and deranged successors: Roethke, Berryman, Jarrell, and Lowell. John Crowe Ransom, a strong contrast to Allen Tate, who had twins with his third wife at the age of 68, follows this conservative pattern. He was decent, homely, and cheerful but—even as a young man—pompous, formal, and humorless. He studiously avoided controversy and, after narrowly missing a First as a Rhodes Scholar at Christ Church, Oxford ("I consider it a moral defeat rather than intellectual"), had a peaceful war as an artillery instructor in Saumur.

His *Selected Letters* (Louisiana State), edited by Thomas Daniel Young and George Cope, often little lectures to literary luminaries like Graves, Stevens, Tate, Warren, Trilling, and Empson, are rather dull: "Art is our refusal to yield to the blandishments of 'constructive' philosophy and permit the poignant & actual Dichotomy to be dissipated

in a Trichotomy." But Ransom was a powerful figure in modern literature; and the letters occasionally throw off sparks of interest about his move from Vanderbilt to Kenyon, the founding of the *Kenyon Review* and the School of English (which later moved to Indiana), the attempt to merge with the folding *Southern Review*, and the choice of successors to his throne (Jarrell refused, Robie Macauley accepted).

There is a revealing contrast between his assertion in 1913 that "country conditions operate to produce in country people the qualities of stolidity, conformity, mental and spiritual inertia, callousness, monotony" and the principles of his reactionary Agrarian manifesto, *I'll Take My Stand,* in 1930. He makes some perceptive remarks about the mischievous, paranoid poet Laura Riding: "she is a little politician that plays dirty tricks," but is unaware of her affair with Robert Graves: they "are up in London, where they find they can work better without the distractions of [his] family."

The editors tend to overrate Ransom's poetry and criticism, though not his literary influence, and absurdly claim that he "made Gambier the literary capital of the United States." But there are some notable lapses in Ransom's extremely prim and prudish critical outlook. He missed the depth in Frost and disliked Warren's fiction, was terrified of covert homosexuality in Robert Duncan's poems, was blind to the originality of Edmund Wilson's *Memoirs of Hecate County,* and dismissed *Lolita* as a "pretty pointless . . . naughty novel." The introduction to this small-print volume is mechanical and the editing good but not perfect.

Born in Nashville, Randall Jarrell was educated at Vanderbilt and Kenyon, began his poetic career under Ransom, Tate, and Warren, and remained faithful to the principles of his mentors. He spent the war years at army bases in Texas, Illinois, and Arizona. Washed out of pilot training after going into a spin on a test flight, he became a ground instructor in a model airplane that simulated flying conditions.

Jarrell, known for his scrupulous and merciless criticism, increased his power and prestige when he became literary editor of the *Nation* during 1946-1947. He wanted to be more constructive and less entertaining in his reviews, but could not restrain himself when confronted with inferior verse. Though he lectured at the Salzburg Seminars in 1948, was Poetry Consultant at the Library of Congress during 1956-1958, and won the National Book Award for *The Woman at the Washington Zoo* in 1961, he justly felt he had not won his share of the major prizes, honors, and awards.

Jarrell was an extremely intelligent writer, a brilliant novelist, and the best poetry critic of his time. He wrote pioneering essays on Whitman, Frost, Williams, Auden, and Lowell; after forty years, his judgments still seem unerringly accurate. Yet he had less poetic talent than his peers and lacked Lowell's rhetoric, Berryman's originality, and Roethke's lyricism. Jarrell's letters are curiously guarded and impersonal. They are not especially witty and contain some tedious rhapsodizing about his cats. But they have acute analyses of poems by Lowell and Adrienne Rich as well as interesting explanations of the genesis of his academic satire, *Pictures from an Institution.*

Jarrell's *Letters* (Houghton Mifflin) are too important to be entrusted to the amateurish and subjective editing of his widow. Mary Jarrell provides

JOHN RUSKIN

THE EARLY YEARS

TIM HILTON

Dust jacket for a biography concerned with the development of Ruskin's ideas and the significance of his work

a display of egoism and self-praise by including seventy love letters, written during his year at Princeton and shortly before their marriage, which repetitively celebrate her virtues. The text of the letters is inaccurately transcribed; words are carelessly omitted and the punctuation is changed.

Mrs. Jarrell's exculpatory edition tries to preempt a biography without answering the essential questions about his life: his background, parents, and unhappy childhood; his love for Amy Breyer, Elizabeth Eisler, and other women; his lack of children, divorce from his first wife, behavior as a stepfather; the problems of his second marriage; his physical illness, mania, breakdown, and suicide.

The life of Jane Bowles (1917-1973) was even more nomadic and bizarre than that of her friend Tennessee Williams. (With Capote, Beaton, Burroughs, and Ginsberg, Williams was part of her homosexual set in Tangier.) Bowles disastrously combined the illness of Carson McCullers with the marriage of Vita Sackville-West. Her husband—a writer and composer—was apparently homosexual and she was lesbian. Her lovers included Iris Barry, who had been the mistress of Wyndham Lewis and mother of his children. Bowles completed all her work, a novel, a play, and seven stories, in her early thirties; then struggled with a writer's block that coincided with her passion for an extortionate Arab woman: "My experience is probably of no interest to anyone. . . . I must hate the written word no matter how I use it." On a visit to Ceylon her hair fell out; she alternated between depression and hysteria, and consumed great quantities of gin. She suffered a brain lesion after a severe stroke at the age of forty, had a series of nervous breakdowns, endured shock treatments, and died in a psychiatric clinic in Málaga.

Bowles's 133 letters, *Out in the World* (Black Sparrow), written between 1935 and 1970, have a mannered style, gossipy content (there are no ideas) and campy humor: "Poor Michael Duff's son was born dead. I don't hear from them. Just a funny postcard now and then." Many of them—which she called "agonizers"—are nagging letters to her husband and friends about travel details and lack of money: "There seems too much really to write about—I mean . . . Africa altogether and my failure to like in it what you do and to like what you do at all anywhere. . . . I can get chicken heads and giblets for a penny a pile but have no eating companion." The later letters, pathetic and depressing, are mainly about her illness: "My life is one of great pain and torment. . . . Please come and see me and if possible to get me." The editing of the letters by Bowles's biographer, Millicent Dillon, is poor. The notes are inadequate (though the same information about Bowles's stroke is repeated on four different pages), many figures are not identified, and the relations between the various people (including Paul and Jane Bowles) remain obscure.

Siegfried Sassoon touched all the bases. He was a homosexual, a husband, and a father; a Protestant, a Catholic, and a Jew. His paternal ancestor, born in Bombay in 1791, spoke only Arabic, Hindi, and Hebrew. Sassoon had experienced the major events of his life and written his best book of poems—*Counter-Attack* (1918), "a spark sailing up from the bonfire of 1914-1918"—by the early 1920s. The entry for 27 March 1923 accurately predicts his tranquil future life: "Some day, when I have 'settled down' and come into a fortune, I will buy a little manor house in good hunting country."

Diaries, 1923-1925 (Faber), the third volume in this sequence, records Sassoon's activities during his late thirties and his struggles to become an accomplished writer. (His royalties in 1923 were £3 for 98 copies sold.) He excised all reference to "affairs of the heart," yet retained a keen eye for homosexuality: spanked choirboys, overenthusiastic scoutmasters, and T. E. Lawrence's soldier-friends. He also failed to preserve a conversation between T. E. and Thomas Hardy, and his own response to D. H. Lawrence's "The Fox." But the diaries—which concern steeplechase racing, soothing music, posh holidays, and a new car—are unusually lively and perceptive. Though Rupert Hart-Davis's introduction could have been more substantial, his editing is excellent and his notes often contain fascinating bits of information.

The best parts of the *Diaries* are Sassoon's comments on artists and writers. The painter Stanley Spencer is a "nice little chap, and a genius, but very exhausting as he talks incessantly." Edmund Gosse is "an artist in [all the] amenities." Hardy insists: "I'm not interested in my novels. I haven't written one for more than thirty years." Osbert Sitwell's works always leave the impression "of spiteful gossip and 'pretty' writing." H. G. Wells remarks: "It's a great advantage, when dealing with pompous people, to be a cad!" T. E. Lawrence, a queer figure with a grimy face and fur-lined cap, "hacks his way down to reality, never sparing himself." Virginia Woolf observes that the only way to treat Old Tom Eliot is to pull his leg: "otherwise he behaves with such absurd formality and primness." The "famous fiction-fabricator," E. M. Fors-

ter, is wistful and attenuated; disheartened by the nearly completed *A Passage to India* and then "pleased but unexultant" when his novel sells 10,000 copies in the first five weeks.

Angelica Garnett's memoir, *Deceived with Kindness* (Harcourt Brace Jovanovich)—another "sensitive," trivial, and entirely familiar book about privileged life in Bloomsbury—provides an adolescent view of Vanessa and Virginia, like Richard Kennedy's *A Boy at the Hogarth Press:* "My doll Judy was also there, her stockinette limbs splashed with red ink, which, as I carefully explained, resulted from numerous operations." Angelica, the illegitimate daughter of Vanessa Bell and Duncan Grant, did not discover her true father until just after her brother Julian had been killed in Spain and just before she was bullied into a semi-incestuous marriage to the overpowering David Garnett. (Her parents, like Virginia and Leonard, had virtually no sex life—though Vanessa took Roger Fry as her lover.)

Garnett was twenty-six years older than Angelica, had been in love with her mother and been seduced by her father. Though she had two fathers, neither seemed fully her own: "by denying me my real father, [Vanessa] was treating me even before my birth as an object." The philistine and puritanical Leonard Woolf seemed to be the paternal figure who was missing in her life. This self-indulgent and self-pitying exorcism expresses Angelica's disaffection with the past: her resentment against her dominant mother and withdrawn father as well as the emotional failure of the complacent Clive Bell. Meanwhile, they all got on with the buttered scones and "life at Charleston continued, bathed it seemed in the glow of a perpetual summer."

Thornton Wilder was clearly a cultivated and intelligent man, but a middle-brow, second-rate writer. His *Journals, 1939-1961*, edited by Donald Gallup (Yale)—accompanied by an automatic puff from Malcolm Cowley—lacks the insight, style, and wit to bridge the gaps between the disparate entries on his polyglot reading and his abortive literary schemes: a massive tome on Lope de Vega, lectures on classic American writers (a feeble echo of Lawrence), and "The Emporium," a disastrously misconceived play "influenced by both Kierkegaard and Gertrude Stein, combining the atmosphere of Kafka's *The Castle* with a Horatio Alger theme."

As Official Man-of-Letters and Roving Ambassador of Kulchur, Wilder meets Camus ("The whole visit has faded from my memory, probably because I did not like anything about him, nor he about me"), and exchanges banalities with Adenauer ("any contact between us would come to the barest civilities, or nothing"). He absorbs the absurdities of Gurdjieff ("In the world, everybody idiot. Twenty-one kinds of idiot") and the fatuous claims of his disciples ("the Master can speak all the languages of the world without having learned them"). But he fails to see through that supreme charlatan and concludes that "he was very clever." Wilder's best *mot* comes after a Waldorf dinner to celebrate the birthday of Robert Frost, who was "too big for friendship, too small for apotheosis." Though Wilder had the supreme distinction of graduating from Yale, it is difficult to see why the Press wished to publish his flatulent *Nachlass*.

Jean-Paul Sartre wrote his *War Diaries: November 1939-March 1940* (Pantheon) while serving as a private in the Meteorological Service near Strasbourg during the long calm of the Phoney War: "The Germans are 250 metres away, we can see them quite clearly. They used to play in the grass and had accordions and harmonicas." During the 1930s he had taught philosophy in several *Lycées* and won a certain renown for *Nausea* and *The Wall*. Since nothing much happens to him, he records more about the books he has read—by Flaubert, Gide, Malraux, Saint-Exupéry, Koestler—than the events he has experienced. He describes the reaction to his naked mates during a medical examination, the looting of evacuated houses in Alsace, an introspective moment of mental strain: "My eyes suddenly flicker and half fail and I have a quarter of an hour of empty, nervous anguish—which in 1935 I used to take for madness." His philosophical ideas seem more like Woody Allen than Martin Heidegger: "This impalpable gratuitousness is there, stretched out across the whole of consciousness. . . . *Life* is the transcendent, psychic object constructed by human reality in search of its own foundation."

The editor and translator, Quintin Hoare, lists Sartre's literary virtues as pungency, directness, freedom, spirit of inquiry, humor, self-knowledge, and a confidence in human reason; and claims the disappearance of nine of the fourteen diaries is "surely one of the great intellectual losses in our century." In fact, Sartre's journals, "a calling into question of myself," are dull and disappointing. Ill at ease in war, as he was in peace, he realistically admits that his diary contains "a series of pages that I know and feel to be definitely mediocre." These narcissistic notations end when Sartre is captured by the Germans during the spring offensive of 1940 that started the real war in the west.

The life of Edward FitzGerald (1809-1883) had no dramatic events. Robert Bernard Martin, author of earlier biographies of Kingsley and Tennyson, has mastered the Victorian period and produced a subtle and elegant life—*With Friends Possessed* (Atheneum)——based largely on FitzGerald's lively and learned letters. He concentrates on the sexually ambiguous aspects of his personality and on his lifelong kindness to friends.

FitzGerald's family had a streak of eccentricity, even madness. But his mother inherited one of the great English fortunes (which did not prevent his father from going bankrupt in coal mining), and there was no need for their son to work after studies at Trinity College, Cambridge. He was a close friend of Tennyson and Thackeray at the university and later became an intimate of Carlyle. Crabbe's son described the young FitzGerald as "proud and very punctilious . . . always like a grave middle-aged man"; and in middle age he combined excessive vulnerability with apprehensive hauteur. He desperately tried to cling to those he loved, was painfully open about the innocent homoerotic emotions he attempted to avoid, and was extremely generous with money. His profound loneliness was leavened by his talent for male friendship, his literary labors were mixed with laziness and self-indulgence, and his commentary on life in this voluminous correspondence eventually "became the surrogate for living it." At age forty-nine he had a brief, absurd marriage to an unattractive older woman who accepted his proposal without his having made it. His ideal, his Billy Budd, was a bluff Suffolk sailor, "Posh" Fletcher. It is doubtful that FitzGerald ever had physical relations with either sex.

FitzGerald had no originality as a poet; but he did competent translations of Aeschylus, Sophocles, and Calderón, and recreated a magnificent version of *The Rubaiyat of Omar Khayyam*. "It was fidelity to the spirit of Omar he sought, not to the text." Martin convincingly explains the basis of FitzGerald's attraction to the poem by the "old Mohammedan blackguard," the special significance it had for him and the reasons for its belated but astonishing success—which led to 310 editions, mostly pirated, by 1929.

Tim Hilton's learned and lively *John Ruskin: The Early Years* (Yale) concentrates on the development of his ideas and the significance of his work, and surpasses the previous biographies by John Rosenberg (1961), Joan Abse (1980), and John Dixon Hunt (1982). Hilton's provocative foreword challenges previous assumptions about his subject: he criticizes the limitations of the massive Cook-Wedderburn edition, questions the discretions and distortions of *Praeterita,* and emphasizes the latter part of Ruskin's life.

This volume is dominated by Ruskin's relations with his parents, his disastrous marriage to Euphemia Gray, and his creation of the monumental *Modern Painters.* Ruskin's father founded the prosperous sherry and brandy firm of Pedro Domecq, and young John fell hopelessly in love with Domecq's sophisticated daughter, Adèle. An only child, he was intensely attached to his parents, who accompanied him when he was a student at Oxford. Hilton shows how Ruskin was emotionally incapacitated by their sacrificial, devouring love. He was selfish and solitary, preferred mountains to matrimony, and confessed he had "no heart nor eyes for anything but stone."

Like Franz Kafka, Ruskin warned his fiancée, with pathetic honesty, that he was nervous, weak, dreamy, ill, and broken down. There were many reasons why their marriage had to remain unconsummated: his hatred of putty-like children, religious beliefs, desire to preserve Effie's beauty. He had imagined women were quite different and was disgusted by her body on their wedding night. He even told her father that Effie's desire for conjugal relations was "an illness bordering on incipient insanity." Hilton cautiously speculates on Ruskin's mysterious disgust and suggests the possibility of his impotence or her menstruation. But he does not employ the insights of psychoanalysis nor mention the theory that Ruskin might have been shocked by her pubic hair. After an intense triangular relationship with John Millais, the Ruskins finally had their marriage annulled. Effie then married the painter and bore him eight children.

Ruskin's lifelong endeavor was to celebrate Turner above all other artists. Ruskin's love of detail, marked visual sense, extravagant prose, ability to grasp both natural and architectural subjects by rendering them in drawings, and taste for early Italian painting made him seem, in contrast to conventional critics, "like a Luther of the arts." After the publication of *Modern Painters* he was venerated by George Eliot, and many others, as "one of the great teachers of the day." After Turner's death, Ruskin helped to restore 19,000 drawings bequeathed to the nation, burned a number of "grossly obscene" works, and claimed that Turner was, at the end, insane.

Hilton's first volume ends halfway through this industrious life. At forty, the great pedophile

Dust jacket for a biography of the Swedish playwright and novelist

encountered the child Rose La Touche (his great love) and made the final drive to complete the fifth volume of *Modern Painters.* The threat of madness, not manifest till 1878, darkened his future.

Strindberg (Random House) by Michael Meyer, the biographer of Ibsen, is a massive compendium of dull facts (with a line missing on 438: 3-4) in which the major patterns of the life are obscured and lost in the rigid and relentless chronological scheme. Though better than the recent life of Strindberg by Olaf Lagerkrantz (1984), Meyer's book fails to evoke sympathy for his loathsome subject: anti-Semitic, misogynistic, mendacious; "repulsive, self-worshipping, perfidious and cowardly."

Strindberg needed misery to spark his writing. He had serious problems on his wedding nights. He throttled his second wife (later the mistress of Frank Wedekind and Augustus John) while dreaming of his first and claimed that his third wife (who later bore his fifth child) had a prolapsed uterus, an "inverted" vagina, and no clitoris. Three disastrous marriages—to a Finn, an Austrian, and a Norwegian (the latter looks astonishingly like his mother)—exile ("France is absinthe and self-abuse; Switzerland matriarchal sentimentality"), several trials for blasphemy and obscenity, extreme poverty, quarrels with all his friends, bleeding eczema, absinthe poisoning, and near madness enabled him to turn out an enormous quantity of second-rate painting and writing. He produced novels, autobiographies, history, art and literary criticism, travel books, Swedenborgian mysticism and pseudo-science (he tried to make gold and did not believe sulphur was an element), as well as a few great plays about men and women in extreme emotional states. (He completed *The Father* and *Miss Julie* in only two weeks.) Strindberg corresponded with Nietzsche, knew Zola, Gauguin, Munch, Shaw, and Yeats. But he seemed to have learned very little from them. He was a genius who behaved like a lunatic.

The theme of Mary Lou Kohfeldt's *Lady Gregory* (Atheneum) is the emergence of a woman from a privileged but rather repressive childhood and the mild restraints of a comfortable marriage; the achievement, in widowhood, through energy and ambition, of a significant managerial and dramatic career in the Abbey Theatre: "a good cause in which to put herself centerstage." Yeats wrote of her circle of authors: "They came like swallows and like swallows went,/ And yet a woman's powerful character/ Could keep a swallow to its first intent."

Augusta Gregory (1852-1932) was born into the wealthy Protestant landowning class in Ireland: "we looked upon our tenants as animals, they looked on us as kings." At the age of twenty-seven, she married the sixty-three-year-old Sir William Gregory, a cultivated gentleman, Master of Coole Park and former Governor of Ceylon. She had a love affair with the poet and nationalist Wilfrid Scawen Blunt (tolerated by her elderly husband), platonic affairs with Yeats and the patron John Quinn, and friendships with Synge and O'Casey. Blunt's legacy was a critical "attitude about the British Empire that set her apart from her own class without really damaging her position in it." Her friendship with Yeats was like Sylvia Beach's with Joyce: both women provided care, comfort, order, and stability. Yeats was inspired by the aristocratic traditions of Coole Park and elegized her pilot son (accidentally shot down by his allies over Italy in 1918). He was grateful for her attentions and observed: "I cannot realize the world without her—

she brought to my wavering thoughts steadfast nobility."

Lady Gregory, through her connections more than her creations, is an important subject. But this biography, though competent, suffers from a graceless style, simplistic portrayal of the political background, longueurs in the narrative, and tiresome discussions of Gregory's folklore collections and her nineteen Irish plays.

The life of Radclyffe Hall, one of the famous literary lesbians in the early twentieth century, was an unholy combination of animal worship, spiritualism, pseudo-science, and inversion. She emerges from Michael Baker's sympathetic but extremely prolix biography, *Our Three Selves* (Morrow), as a revolting poseur who led a trivial and self-indulgent life, wrote third-rate novels and insincere verse: "Ah! Faith, I'd barter all I own to know/ But one brief moment of your magic charm." Hall had a miserable childhood, but her compensatory leading lovers were married women with children and accommodating husbands. Baker does not discuss the details of her sexual life, though it seems clear she was the "male" partner. But he does confusingly mention her correspondence in the 1920s with an otherwise unidentified "Gerard Manley Hopkins." Since the Jesuit priest died without issue in 1889, this chap may be the unmanly French translator Gerard Hopkins.

Hall saw herself as a woman trapped in a man's body. She is best known for *The Well of Loneliness*, whose message was that "inverts have a raw deal out of all proportion to their 'crime.'" Leonard Woolf thought the book was a failure; Cyril Connolly found it "long, tedious, and absolutely humourless"; and even lesbian writers like Violet Trefusis, Vita Sackville-West, and Romaine Brooks felt it was loathsome, ridiculous, and trite. In 1928—though lesbianism itself was not a criminal offense—the novel was attacked in the press, withdrawn by the publisher Jonathan Cape, tried in court (where Forster and Virginia Woolf appeared for the defense), and condemned as obscene. Though rather tame, it became notorious and at the time of Hall's death in 1934 was selling a remarkable 100,000 copies a year.

Louise Bogan (in contrast to Lady Gregory and Radclyffe Hall) came from a poor Irish Catholic background and moved from the mill towns and boardinghouses of New England to the little magazines and literary salons of New York. She had two failed marriages, one daughter, and a number of lovers—including, in 1934, Theodore Roethke: "physically overwhelming and emotionally gargantuan, a floating continent of exquisite sensitivity, towering despair, insatiable appetite, and howling self-ignorance." Edmund Wilson and Rolfe Humphries, who portrayed her in their work, were her close platonic friends; and she also inspired the lesbian love of May Sarton. Bogan (like Jane Bowles) was pathologically jealous, had several nervous breakdowns, and endured shock therapy in 1965. There were at least two Louise Bogans: "one a tender, passionate, intensely sexual being, and the other a violent, cruel, and deeply suspicious fiend." As her own creative work diminished and the invitations and honors came in at the end of her life, she became increasingly resentful about her lack of recognition.

Elizabeth Frank's 460-page *Louise Bogan* (Knopf), which follows Ruth Limmer's editions of Bogan's letters and autobiography, is intelligent and well written. But it is far too long for its distinctly minor subject and contains extensive analyses of trivial poems and tedious stories: "she could feel the poignant mystery of time and things, but failed to get what she believed to be the whole truth from herself." Bogan is now better known for the reviews she wrote for the *New Yorker* from 1931 to 1969 than for her own poetry, which, in Frank's inflated judgment, "belongs securely within the great tradition of the English lyric, along with that of Herbert and Hopkins."

Amy Lowell was the Gertrude Stein of Imagism. Both women were obese, unattractive, wealthy, well-connected, ambitious, domineering, egocentric, and emotionally deprived. Lowell combined execrable poetry with patronizing pomposity. Most of *The Letters of D. H. Lawrence & Amy Lowell, 1914-1925* (Black Sparrow) have been previously published, and all of Lawrence's letters up to June 1921 have appeared in the Cambridge edition. But this handsome volume of ninety-three letters (including five from Frieda Lawrence), competently edited by Claire Healey and Keith Cushman, is the first to print the complete—though rather disappointing—correspondence.

Lawrence and Amy Lowell met thrice in England in the summer of 1914 and corresponded until her death in May 1925. Their friendship was based on mutual exploitation: the extreme individualist benefited from the money and influence of his only personal contact in America while the crude careerist captured his poetic genius for her Amygist anthologies. She tried to collect money owed to Lawrence by his slippery American publisher, Mitchell Kennerley; and at Frieda Lawrence's request sent the sick and penniless "charity-boy of literature" £60 in October 1916 and $100 in January 1920. Despite her generosity, Lowell sometimes exasperated Lawrence, who in March 1921 described the sinking lady as "trying to keep afloat on the gas of her own importance: hard work, considering her bulk." Their uneasy de haut en bas relations surfaced when Lawrence wrote, "Not having a secretary to [type and] sign my letter I sign it myself" and when he gave his Sicilian landlord, en route to Boston, a letter of introduction. Lowell, who could not conceive of a connection with a cook, replied: "I will look up your Sicilian, although I cannot see what good it will do as I am not by way of being able to employ him."

Lawrence's letters concern the misery of the war, his sudden expulsion from Cornwall, and his antagonism to Lloyd George, "a clever little Welsh *rat,* absolutely dead at the core, sterile, barren, mechanical"; his new red beard, Frieda Lawrence's futile attempt to see her young children and awkward encounter with her former husband, Ernest Weekley (which foreshadows *The Virgin and the Gipsy);* Lawrence's impressions of Ceylon and New Mexico, his descriptions of the furious waves on the Cornish coast and of fallen apples "like green lights in the grass." Lawrence impertinently criticizes her verse and exhorts her to abandon affectation, yet Lowell expresses her fervent admiration for his work. She also makes a nice distinction between Lawrence's suppressed books and the "pure obscenities perpetrated by James Joyce." She defends her literary territory, discourages Lawrence's journey to America and especially to Boston. Then she relents and invites him for only three days. But Frieda Lawrence has an urgent dental appointment in New York and they neglect to come.

Though Anthony Burgess's deepest affinity is with Joyce rather than with Lawrence, he visited (while making a television documentary) all the places Lawrence wrote about and has produced a personal, perceptive, enthusiastic, and stimulating centennial tribute. *Flame Into Being: The Life and Work of D. H. Lawrence* (Arbor House)—a discussion of the works in the context of the life rather than a comprehensive biography—reveals unusual points of interest in *Mr. Noon* and *Kangaroo,* makes Lawrence come alive, and is an excellent introduction to his art.

Burgess's imaginative disregard for facts has allowed some errors to seep into the text. Katherine Mansfield *was* reconciled to Lawrence after receiving his postcard from New Zealand and wrote affectionately about him to Murry in October and November 1922. Mabel Luhan did not "donate" the ranch to the Lawrences, but exchanged it for the manuscript of *Sons and Lovers*. Lawrence did not become impotent in 1922, but toward the end of 1926. His ashes, not his body, were taken to Taos for reburial. Surely Nabokov and Koestler, as well as Huxley, assimilated enough science to bring a new intellectual rigor to the novel. And was not Mellors's unwillingness to kiss Connie related to Lawrence's contagious disease?

Burgess (an expatriate writer) believes that by living abroad Lawrence was trying "to get out of the narrow cage that inhibits the British novel, to acquire a continental point of view." He admires Lawrence's "outstanding talent for always saying the uncomfortable thing" and credits him with the Protestant virtues of cleanliness and hard work, with courage and with charm "when he wished to have it." Lawrence has a "cheeky reliance on intuition." His orthodox stylistic faults become idiosyncratic virtues, and his "intensity of image and rhythm . . . suggests poetry while remaining prose." His outstanding quality is physical particularity, an "almost hallucinatory exactness of notation."

According to Burgess, Lawrence always strives for the "sinking beneath identity to the 'elemental,'" to pure being untortured by thought and feeling. In the act of physical love, "he was able to shed the obsessions of a powerful ego that could not be subdued by the exercise of the will." His homoerotic impulse was "an innate power hunger, cognate with the creative urge, [that] had to be exercised over some chosen man, since it did not work with the chosen woman." His political ideas are antidemocratic, but not fascistic: "he was merely honest enough to state openly that we all need living models of superior energy and genius, that there is a canaille around, and that politicians are, for the most part, inferior animals."

Fernanda Pivano, a distinguished Italian critic, journalist, and translator of modern American literature, has written an introduction to Hemingway's life for Italian readers. Her interpretation is based on her meetings with Hemingway in 1948-1949, 1954, and 1956. The narrative of *Hemingway* (Rusconi), divided into highly condensed chapters, is not chronological. She relies heavily on printed sources and thus repeats some myths and makes a few errors. The Hemingway she knew had film-star status in Italy. Pivano notes the quantity of his luggage; the lavishness of his hospitality in grand hotels, where he loved to preside over large tables of friends and hangers-on; the scale and pace of his travels on ocean liners and trains, and in the

big black Buick that appears in one of the excellent photographs by Pivano's husband, Ettore Sottsass.

They met for the first time in October 1948, when Hemingway invited Pivano to visit him in Cortina, during his first trip to Italy since 1923. He heard that she had been arrested in a Nazi raid on the Einaudi publishers in Torino, after a contract for her translation of *A Farewell to Arms* was found. (The book was banned by Mussolini because of its depiction of the Italian retreat from Caporetto.) Hemingway greeted her warmly; he valued her work, wrote to her often about her translations, and took an interest in her career. She translated *A Farewell to Arms*, to replace the pirated versions, as well as *Across the River and into the Trees* and *The Old Man and the Sea*. Young, warm-hearted, and intellectual, Pivano esteemed him as a writer and found him sympathetic as a man. She conveys a lively sense of his physical presence: his shyness and vulnerability under the confident mask; his

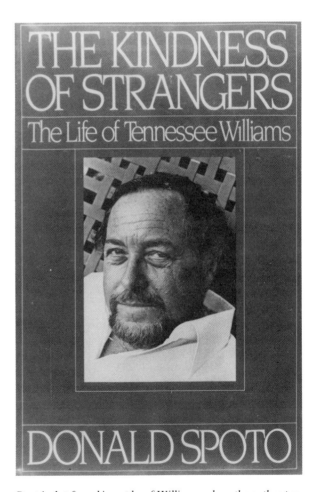

Dust jacket for a biography of Williams, whom the author portrays as "a man more disturbing, more dramatic, richer and more wonderful than any character he ever created"

tendency to talk almost in a whisper, as if communicating secret information; his capacity to invest ordinary activity with a sense of wonder.

The publisher claims that *Along with Youth* (Oxford), the first installment of a projected three-volume life, "promises to become the definitive Hemingway biography." Peter Griffin's two important discoveries are Hemingway's letters to his Red Cross friend Bill Horne and new information about their commanding officer, Captain Jim Gamble. In the late 1970s, Mary Hemingway allowed Griffin to remove five early stories, not good enough to publish in his lifetime, from the Hemingway Collection at the Kennedy Library and to print them in this book.

Hemingway's apprentice fiction, mixed in with rather than separate from Griffin's own text, brings his limping narrative to a halt. Though Griffin does not actually discuss these stories, he unconvincingly claims that Hemingway's style and vision were formed in Oak Park before he went to Paris. Just as birth anticipates death, so, for Griffin, everything written in youth "anticipates the mature Hemingway voice." Hemingway's style was not modeled on literary masters, but on the "unaffected in tone, sonorous, rhythmical" letters of his first wife, Hadley, which "set a standard for Ernest." Since dozens of Hadley's repetitious letters are quoted, we can judge for ourselves how profoundly her characteristic sentences—"I wanted to run down and holler my undying affection in your too distant ear" and "I love you so highly and lowly and like a boy and girl warmly"—influenced her husband's work. Griffin first quotes a letter in which Hadley admits having "all this low sex feeling" for a woman friend, then says she has no lesbian tendencies. And Griffin falsely attributes to Hemingway—"the style is unmistakable"—a flat and commonplace unsigned story in the *Kansas City Star*.

Both the method and accuracy of this biography are radically flawed. There are more than forty typographical and spelling errors; the discussion of sources repeats material in the text; the footnotes are neither numbered nor keyed to pages; and the index is inadequate. The style is often awkward, at times ungrammatical; and some sentences make no sense: "At *three*, Ernest's favorite doll was [one] that Clarence had given him for his *fifth* birthday . . . [italics added]."

Griffin describes in excruciating detail the buds and lawn in Oak Park and the kinds of apples at Walloon Lake, a sister's dress and a walk to a dance, his uncle's handkerchief and the temperature in Kansas City, what Hadley made for breakfast and wore on her honeymoon. But he does not fully discuss the influence of the Civil War, the church and high school in Oak Park, the marriage of Grace and Clarence Hemingway, Hemingway's conflict with his parents, his writing for papers in Kansas City, Toronto, and Chicago, the psychological effects of his wound and, most importantly, how the dominant traits of his character emerged from his early life. Griffin's laundered Hemingway is a conventional chap who shows no indication of future greatness. This portrait is likely to please the immediate family (Jack Hemingway writes a laudatory preface), but few others. If Griffin plans to continue this ambitious project, he will have to raise his standards.

Hemingway's reputation has survived his decline, his death, and his detractors, and he is now recognized as the most important and influential novelist of the twentieth century. Jeffrey Meyers's *Hemingway: A Biography* (Harper & Row), the first complete life to appear in sixteen years, presents new material from archives and interviews. It covers Hemingway's wound in the Great War, the background of the Greco-Turkish War, his friendship with Chink Dorman-Smith, his Catholicism, his periods of impotence, his quarrel with his sister Carol, his affair with Jane Mason, Dr. Lawrence Kubie's suppressed psychoanalytic essay on Hemingway, the latter's friendship with Gustavo Durán, the lesbianism of Jinny and Pauline Pfeiffer, Hemingway's Cuban friends, his sexual problems with Martha Gellhorn, Gellhorn's supposed liaison with the jai alai player Felix Areitio, Hemingway's political ideas, the FBI file on him, his relations with Adriana Ivancich, his bitter fight with his son Gregory, his infatuation with Slim Hayward and Jigee Viertel, his second African safari, his relations with the bullfighters Dominguín and Ordoñez, his affair with Valerie Danby-Smith, his medical problems and treatment at the Mayo Clinic, the reasons for his suicide, and the aftermath of his death. This book also shows the literary influence of writers outside the American tradition: Tolstoy, Kipling, Crane, Conrad, Joyce, D. H. Lawrence, and T. E. Lawrence; and provides new interpretations of several major works: "The Short Happy Life of Francis Macomber," "The Snows of Kilimanjaro," *To Have and Have Not, Across the River and into the Trees,* and *A Moveable Feast.*

Meyers portrays the evolution of several different and distinct Hemingways, for he changed greatly from the confident genius of the 1920s and swaggering hero of the 1930s to the braggart of the 1940s and sad wreck of the late 1950s. But certain significant patterns, which recurred throughout his life, showed a consistency of character. He fell in love during wartime, became involved with his future wives while still married to his present ones, revised reality to fit his personal mythology, sought a scapegoat and blamed others for his own faults, quarreled with those who helped him, befriended a series of military heroes, and adopted a number of substitute sons. At the end of his life he tried to repeat earlier triumphs by returning to Africa, Paris, and Spain, and by falling in love with two nineteen-year-old girls. Hemingway was not always an attractive man, but his faults were an essential part of his character; without them, he would be a far less interesting and exciting writer. Though most books published after his death described him as a boorish bully, Hemingway emerges from this biography as a surprisingly sensitive, serious, and intellectual artist.

Frank MacShane's *Into Eternity: The Life of James Jones* (Houghton Mifflin) is a lively, interesting, and sympathetic narrative that captures the essence of the man and offers a fair appraisal of his work. Jones was a Midwest country bumpkin, a child of the Depression and World War II. He grew up in Robinson, Illinois, the son of a diabetic harpy and of a drunken dentist who had lost everything in the Wall Street crash and shot himself in 1942. Rejected by his contemporaries at school, Jones enlisted in the army in 1939, was sent to Schofield Barracks in Honolulu, and served ingloriously as a clerk. He was slightly wounded in the head by a random mortar shell soon after he arrived in Guadalcanal and discharged in 1944 after injuring his ankle playing football. He finished *From Here to Eternity* in a trailer park in North Hollywood and achieved immediate critical and popular success.

Irwin Shaw noted that Jones "grappled with the ghost of Hemingway all his life, excoriating him, mocking him, worried about what Hemingway meant to him." MacShane quotes Hemingway's vituperative and pathological attack on *Eternity* in a letter to Charles Scribner, but does not explain that it was inspired by profound insecurity about Hemingway's own literary stature. After the failure of *Across the River,* he had a deep-rooted fear of younger literary rivals who challenged him by writing about the war.

Mailer thought *Eternity* was better than *The Naked and the Dead.* Styron, throwing his arms around Jones and Mailer, exclaimed: "Here we are, the three best writers of our generation, and we're

all together!" But their intense rivalry and sense of art as a lethal game led to Mailer's attack on his contemporaries in *Advertisements for Myself.* As Mailer and Styron matured as artists, Jones remained static and feared he had lost his "drive to write because of being successful."

Jones compared *Some Came Running* to *War and Peace,* but its commonplace plot and boring characters were condemned by the critics. In 1958, after his marriage to the sexy Gloria Mosolino, a bit-part actress from "an underground background" in Pottsville, Pennsylvania, Jones escaped to Paris. He wrote lucrative scripts for films that were never made, consorted with wealthy expatriates and courtiers. After sixteen years in Europe, he remained an ignorant, apolitical tourist, with scant knowledge of French language and culture. Jones died of heart disease after dictating the end of *Whistle* from his hospital bed.

Jones had unpromising origins, no education, limited intelligence, and a crude style. Driven by a powerful urge to write, he had nothing much to say, produced closely autobiographical novels, and was essentially a one-book author. Wilfrid Sheed (using Orwell's phrase) called him the "king of the good-bad writers." Mailer convincingly stated that Jones was "the worst writer of prose ever to give intimations of greatness."

Norman Mailer, a brilliant subject, has had bad luck with biographers. Hilary Mills's book (1982) was superficial and obtuse; Peter Manso's *Mailer: His Life and Times* (Simon & Schuster) portrays the writer as celebrity and vulgarian, and epitomizes the corruption it describes. This undeveloped embryo is not a biography, but a crude compilation of extracts from 200 interviews. There is no introduction to or transition between the entries, no coherent structure or narrative, no evaluation or interpretation of these egoistic and anecdotal fragments. This is not valuable oral history but a monstrous gossip column in which no detail is too trivial or disgusting to record.

The "little Jewish guy with a lot of hair and big ears," smothered in mother's love, emerges as the boy genius, mad about writing. The letters to his Arkansas army friend are surprisingly dull, but he is the most perceptive analyst of his own character. Though merely a cook in the army, he transformed that involuntary experience into *The Naked and the Dead,* which made him famous at twenty-five and thrust him into Hollywood. Fame also "lobotomized" his past and forced him to invent his public persona.

The failures of *Barbary Shore* and *The Deer*

Park temporarily helped to return him to reality. But he was determined to bring mind and discipline to bear on the eruption of instinct, to do things that frightened him. He indulged in bourbon and Seconal, marijuana, peyote and mescal; tried Orgone boxes and became host to succubi; broke with friends. He entered the condition of panic, became unbalanced and dangerous, had several breakdowns. He lost his idealism and his artistic integrity and was charged with plagiarism for his book on Marilyn Monroe. Finally, he stabbed his second wife when she attacked his virility and (freed from criminal charges) complained how awful it was that people "gently move knives away so they're out of my reach."

Mailer, who has none of Hemingway's redeeming features and lacks the protective isolation of Cuba, imitates and exaggerates all the debased aspects of Hemingway's life. The sportsman participates in head bashing and ear biting; the fighter (told that his dog is queer) is beaten up; the competitor attacks all his fictional friends and rivals in print; the celebrity makes a public fool of himself; the lover is inexperienced and insecure. Like Hemingway, Mailer feels obliged to hide, even extinguish, the bookish and introspective side of his character.

Donald Spoto's *The Kindness of Strangers* (Little, Brown) is particularly interesting on Tennessee Williams's early life in Mississippi and St. Louis, and on the bizarre family that provided the raw material for his art. His father was a lecherous drunkard; his mother, a faded Southern belle who survived the brutality of the world by illusory memories of the Old South; his sister, an invalid cast into unreality by a savage lobotomy. There was no hint of greatness in the shy, withdrawn young man who had a patchy education at Missouri, Washington University, and Iowa, and a long struggle before achieving fame with *The Glass Menagerie* in 1945. He wrote half a dozen great plays by 1960 and in the following decade sold ten of his works to Hollywood for nine million dollars.

This lively but loathsome playwright epitomizes the catastrophe of success. His life was dominated by frenetic travels and an obsession with work and sex. He hated being homosexual, sacrificed humanity to carnality, and treated people as items on a menu. His soap-operatic affairs led to rages and hysterics. He surrounded himself with parasites who resembled rejects from a road company of *Streetcar*; broke with his closest friends: his brother Dakin, his longtime lover Frank Merlo, his

agent Audrey Wood; became addicted to a deadly combination of drink and drugs; and lapsed into a comatose condition "unable to complete a coherent sentence, unable to negotiate five steps without stumbling."

Williams's sharp decline during the last twenty years of his life, his self-projected image of a burnt-out case on television and in his *Memoirs*, his tendency to revise pointlessly and even to sabotage his work, his lapse into the Gothic mode and use of sensational themes, his sentimentality and lack of coherence all tend to obscure the considerable achievement in his finest works. Spoto has mastered his material and tells a fascinating story. But his book is limited by an undistinguished style, a moralistic tone, and a lack of critical insight and of psychological depth. Williams's deep-rooted self-hatred ("I'm just a pathetic faggot") seems a more convincing explanation of his personal tragedy than Spoto's belief that his life was poisoned by fame.

This torrent of literary biography, nearly one book a week (if all were considered) for an entire year, would seem by now to have exhausted the subject. Yet we can still look forward to the appearance of a great many major works in progress: Max Novak's *Defoe*, Donald Greene's *Johnson*, Marvin Mudrick's *Boswell*, Aileen Ward's *Blake*, Richard Holmes's *Coleridge*, Kenneth Silverman's *Poe*, Peter Ackroyd's *Dickens*, John Hall's *Trollope*, Geoffrey Wolff's *Melville*, Millicent Bell's *Henry James*, Robert Bernard Martin's *Hopkins*, Norman White's *Hopkins*, Richard Ellmann's *Wilde*, Michael Holroyd's *Shaw*, Thomas Pinney's *Kipling*, Roy Foster's *Yeats*, James Gindin's *Galsworthy*, John Worthen, Mark Kinkead-Weekes and David Ellis's three-volume *Lawrence*, Humphrey Carpenter's *Pound*, Charles Molesworth's *Marianne Moore*, Jon Stallworthy's *Sassoon*, Victoria Glendinning's *Rebecca West*, Charles Doyle's *Aldington*, Nancy Milford's *Millay*, H. R. Winnick's *MacLeish*, Lewis Dabney's *Edmund Wilson*, Stephen Oates's *Faulkner*, Hans Bak's *Malcolm Cowley*, Kenneth Lynn's *Hemingway*, James Mellow's *Hemingway*, Frances Spalding's *Stevie Smith*, Norman Sherry's *Greene*, Ronald Hayman's *Sartre*, John Haffenden's *Empson*, Deirdre Bair's *de Beauvoir*, Anthony Curtis's *Rattigan*, Scott Donaldson's *Cheever*, Ian MacNiven's *Durrell*, Carol Gelderman's *Mary McCarthy*, William Pritchard's *Jarrell*, Paul Mariani's *Berryman*, David Roberts's *Jean Stafford*, Charlotte Goodman's *Jean Stafford*, and Jeffrey Meyers's group biography of *Lowell*,

Berryman, Roethke, and *Jarrell.* Despite these ambitious projects, a few good biographical subjects miraculously remain: Burns, Wordsworth, Norris, Stevens, Jeffers, Waley, Tate, Trilling, Betjeman, Spender, Bishop, and Larkin.

The Year in Drama

Howard Kissel

A brief list of some of the premises of plays that opened in New York in 1985 might suggest it was a stimulating year in the theater. After all, there were plays about the private lives of T. S. Eliot and Virginia Woolf, a play about the thought of V. S. Naipaul, a play in which one of the characters makes an intellectual case for the politics of Henry Kissinger, and one in which the crises of liberalism over the last few decades were reflected in the professional and personal problems of an architect trying to win approval for a housing development in the impoverished East End of London.

Interestingly, all of the above plays were imported from London. What they shared with their less intellectually ambitious American cousins was an inability to develop a premise beyond provocations into genuine drama.

The one exception is Michael Frayn's *Benefactors,* a play in which the changing moods of the times are skillfully depicted in the disintegrating friendship of two couples. Three of the four friends are university graduates, definitely activists. The fourth is a nurse, who seems entirely passive. David is an architect. In the late 1960s, when the play begins, he is planning a huge public housing development on an East End street called Basuto Road, which, he points out, evokes the years of Empire, when streets were named for the lands and people the British had conquered.

David is supported enthusiastically by his wife and opposed by his friend Colin, the nurse's husband, a journalist filled with the negativism and cynicism that seem endemic to the profession. While battles of ideas rage around her, the nurse, Sheila, seems unable to cope. She seems absolutely dependent on the solicitousness of David and Jane merely to survive, but as the play proceeds we see an unsuspected strength beneath this seeming helplessness. Eventually David and Jane become dependent on her need for their help.

"What should we do without them?" Colin asks Sheila. "What would they do without us? We make them feel good. It's our one contribution to the world. . . . We keep that marriage together." In certain ways Colin and Sheila resemble the East Enders whose housing problems David is trying to solve. David acknowledges this when he speaks of "the redevelopment of Colin and Sheila . . . a twilight area—that's what Colin and Sheila were when we started working on them." He then compares them to Basuto Road. They too are "full of hidden sewers."

It seems clear that one of the things Frayn's rich play is about is intellectual imperialism, the attempt men make to subdue human nature, which invariably eludes them. But Frayn never uses his characters simply as chess pieces in some carefully schematized arrangement. The changes they undergo all seem natural, even inevitable. The ideas lurking behind the shifting relationships make this theater rather than soap opera, which it could easily become were it not for Frayn's adroit wit.

Most of the British plays that now come to New York originate at the Royal Court Theater in London and are brought here, often with most of their original casts, by the New York Shakespeare Festival. Among these were several about British literary figures, of which the most arresting was probably Edna O'Brien's *Virginia,* which used the writing of both Virginia and Leonard Woolf to convey some sense of this enormously sensitive, vulnerable, and ultimately disturbed woman. We follow her from a childhood trauma to her marriage to Woolf to an affair with Vita Sackville-West to her suicide by drowning in the early years of World War II.

"I love cruelty," Virginia says early in the play.

"I would eat it on a spoon, like malt and oil." Later she says, "There's a queer, disreputable pleasure in being abused." Leonard tells us his wife says of herself that "her soft crevices are lined with hooks." The suggestion of a certain masochism in her character helps one understand why O'Brien may have considered her a prime subject for dramatic development. Unfortunately Woolf's desire for cruelty did not lead her to seek it in others; she seems to have been bent on inflicting it on herself. Her husband is a gentle soul and her lover a thoughtful one. (Apart from a brief look at her father, these are the only characters we see other than Woolf herself.)

The text is full of eloquence—so much so that one constantly wonders which volume of the letters, which novel, which diary each line may have come from. There is a sharpness and pungency we have grown unaccustomed to in the theater. Nevertheless the brooding of so introspective a woman never really lends itself to engrossing action. Virginia analyzes what has happened to her. She almost never does anything directly. Moreover the knowledge that the text has been drawn from her writings adds another veil—however spontaneous the actors make lines sound, however artfully O'Brien has woven them together, it is hard to shake the feeling that we are hearing a distillation of experience rather than the thing itself, raw, not yet filtered through the intelligence.

A similar feeling prevailed in Michael Hastings's *Tom and Viv*, which concerns T. S. Eliot and his first wife, Vivian, from their first meeting in 1915 to her death in 1947. Hastings portrays Eliot as cold and cheerless, but ultimately the character is not so much forbidding as merely tepid. Because she is dotty, Vivian is obviously more interesting and sympathetic. We now know that she had hormonal imbalances that caused her endless sexual and mental grief. This was especially painful in a period when medical knowledge and social understanding of sexual problems were extremely limited. Hastings deals with this material in a style that is not prurient, but not very interesting either. He piques our curiosity about the Eliots but never develops much of what he knows about them into dramatically cogent material.

As he did in *Plenty*, David Hare places a cynic at the center of his new play, *A Map of the World*. In this play the cynic, a man with a rich and mournful sense of man's capacity for idiocy and self-destruction, seems closely modeled after novelist V. S. Naipaul, who comes from the Third World but refuses to share the West's romanticization of it.

The novelist is called Victor Mehta, and for much of the play the action simply consists of a British journalist of conventional leftist sentiments arguing with and fuming at him. Toward the end of the play the journalist tells Mehta he must renounce his own fiction because of its "hopelessness," charging that it reflects "the jealousy of a man who does not take part." This is a standard leftist literary ploy to downgrade writers who are clearheaded and refuse to offset their vision with a rosy view of the future.

Unfortunately *A Map of the World* never really puts Mehta's (or Naipaul's) ideas into focus. It offers instead a play within a play that raises a lot of interesting side issues that detract from the real ones. Nor does Hare ever present a convincing opposition to Mehta. Toward the end the journalist tells Mehta to read a statement disavowing his ideas to a Third World audience he is to address. "If you wish to be human," the journalist says, "parrot whatever rubbish you're handed . . . at least you'll experience an emotion that's not disdain." Can Hare really expect us to think this sort of apparatchik thinking counterbalances Mehta's eloquent "not to speak is not to be a writer, not to be a man."

As the play proceeds Hare finds Mehta increasingly sympathetic. He seems to have started *Map* as an attack on the Naipaul point of view but ends by accepting it. Again, since a similarly aloof character was the focal point of his *Plenty*, one suspects *Map* is really a failed effort at self-criticism. Hare cannot effectively combat his own cynicism.

One of the Royal Court imports was Ron Hutchinson's *Rat in the Skull*, a play about the troubles in Northern Ireland. Its parochialism was apparent as soon as one entered the theater and was handed, along with the program, a glossary of names, places, and jargon. The play takes the form of an interrogation of a suspected IRA activist, but for the most part it seems like a pretext for some provocative spoken essays on this difficult subject.

A more fetching entry was Louise Page's *Salonika*, set on the beach that was an important battlefield in World War I. In its exploration of five characters, it is a capsule history of Britain from the beginning of the century. The youngest of the characters is a dead man, the ghost of one of the hundreds of thousands of young Englishmen who died in World War I. He is a man of ideals and innocence, but, as we come to see, there is no natural strength or nobility in this combination. We see him more and more as selfish and bewildered and ultimately self-destructive.

His counterpart, a young man of today, is

Playbills for a selection of 1985 productions

several years older than the tommy was when he died. He seems lazy and self-indulgent, but the more we get to know him the more we are touched by the gentleness of which he is capable. He too is self-destructive and more knowledgeable about it. The two images of British youth balance one another poignantly and disturbingly. The other male character is a seventy-five-year-old survivor of both wars, decent, sensible, lacking the sensitivity and poetry of the other men. If anything he seems an overgrown Boy Scout, a comic specter perhaps of what the tommy might have become had he less tragic potential.

The two women in the play are the eighty-four-year-old widow of the tommy and her sixty-five-year-old daughter, who was conceived just before her father went off to war. The two, like many who have lived together so long, seem in a state of uneasy truce. They have left their home in northern England to visit the beach where their husband/father died and is buried. The Mediterranean has little effect on them, since they bring the cramped, suspicious mood of the North Country with them to the beach. It acts as a natural shield, allowing them to retain the little bitternesses that seem to animate their lives together.

The play, a remarkable one for a twenty-six-year-old writer, is full of humor, wit, and an overriding sadness. In its touching portrait of these wasted lives, it seems a chilling indictment of the English character in the twentieth century.

One of the plays in the Royal Court exchange was commissioned by the Shakespeare Festival from an American playwright. But Wallace Shawn's *Aunt Dan and Lemon* was first produced in England and brought here in that production. The play seems an exercise in liberal-baiting, a harmless pastime to be sure, but not one to be confused with playwriting.

Aunt Dan and Lemon has very little in the way of dialogue. For the most part the characters lecture one another and us. The intention of these speeches seems less to inform than to taunt. Aunt Dan, for example, is a passionate admirer of Henry Kissinger. Much of the play is set during the Vietnam War, and Aunt Dan defends his policies as if they stemmed from a profound philosophical point of view, as if their execution caused him great emotional anguish. A defense of Kissinger as a shrewd strategist might be stimulating, but the excess and grandiosity of the presentation here seem designed mainly to annoy. To make matters worse none of the characters onstage presents any counterweight to her arguments.

Aunt Dan has a formidable influence on the young girl whose nickname is Lemon, who comes to espouse views that suggest she has bettered Aunt Dan's instruction. At the end of the play she declares that none of us really is capable of compassion. The reason, she maintains, that we are fascinated to read about the Nazis is that their actions are easier for us to identify with than their well-meaning opponents'. And after all, every society has been guilty of persecuting and murdering some minority in order to create its own civilizations. So can we sneer at the Germans, who wanted to return to the purity of their primitive past, before all these foreigners came in and mucked them up?

These are Lemon's final remarks, so of course no other character can argue with her. There is too little evidence of wit or humor in the play to suspect Shawn is being ironic. The whole thrust of the character is to shock and disturb the audience, which is an exercise on a different level than dramaturgy. In a play we would see such arguments as a reflection of some carefully developed character. We would also see other characters with conflicting viewpoints of equal force and we would be forced to see where we stand between the two positions. Here the characters exist only as mouthpieces for irritating rhetoric.

The other American plays produced by the New York Shakespeare Festival this year were Christopher Durang's *The Marriage of Bette and Boo,* an idiosyncratically collegiate look at an unhappy marriage, and Gerard Brown's *Jonin',* an unconvincing play about contemporary black fraternity life. The NYSF also produced one of two plays about the AIDS epidemic. Larry Kramer's *The Normal Heart* is an unmistakably autobiographical play about Kramer's political experiences while trying to organize New York's homosexual community to recognize the gravity of its situation and to force the city to do something about a health crisis of epidemic proportions.

The tone is clearly one of *j'accuse.* Very often the writing is didactic. We are given a huge amount of information to absorb. If the facts were not so outrageous, so troubling, they might seem more suited to a lecture or an editorial. But their presence in the play—there were even statistics in the sets—is like a series of exposed wires filling the stage—live, dangerous, combustible.

Parallel to the political plot is an equally self-revealing love story between the abrasive activist and a younger man, who is handsome, bright, and determined enough to break through the wall of hostility and self-hatred with which the "enragee" surrounds himself. The older man's growing capacity to experience—and accept—love becomes more poignant when his lover contracts AIDS. The tragedy the older man is trying to combat in the community defeats him at home.

The Normal Heart is very much a play of the moment, one that may lose its force when AIDS comes under medical control. Unlike a "play of the moment" of fifty years ago, Clifford Odets's *Waiting for Lefty,* it never reduces its characters or the society around them to simple stereotypes.

The other AIDS play, *As Is,* by William Hoffman, was coproduced by Circle Repertory Company and The Glines, an organization dedicated to fostering art by and about homosexuals. After a successful run at Circle Rep, it was transferred to a Broadway theater. Hoffman's play is important because it focuses on basic things—the reconciliation of brothers, for example—that under normal circumstances we tend to regard as banal or sentimental. In the shadow of death these things regain their actual importance.

As Is is a more carefully structured play than *The Normal Heart.* It concerns two former lovers who finally come to terms with each other when one gets AIDS. The touching scenes (often enlivened by bitchy humor) are balanced by witty vignettes of the gay world around them. The comedy never descends to vulgarity, even when depicting the darker sides of contemporary homosexual life.

Both these plays brought a foreign and sometimes alienating world within the ken and sympathy of the general audience. Deliberately gay plays have been part of the New York theater scene for many years, but often they were geared toward exclusively gay audiences, "in" material for "in" groups. These new plays are really not so much about gay life as about death, which gives them universal significance.

What seems remarkable about 1985 is how many major American theater voices were heard— Neil Simon, Sam Shepard, Lanford Wilson, Herb Gardner, and David Mamet all had new work performed.

Biloxi Blues, the Neil Simon play, begins with five young recruits on a dismal train carrying them from Fort Dix, New Jersey, to Mississippi during World War II. The first scene is full of jokes about flatulence and body smells, suggesting a typical Simon yock-filled evening. But the mood changes very quickly when the boys arrive in training camp. It is a play about coming of age in America during a difficult time. More important it is a play about a New York Jew coming to terms with his identity in the rough atmosphere of an army barracks. It is really the first time Simon has come to terms with his own identity, the source of his humor. In several recent plays Simon has deliberately cosmeticized the Jewish roots of his comedy, with unsatisfying results. Here he is willing to risk scenes of great discomfort and chilling humor to be honest about his own experience. It seems a very courageous play for Simon, an assertion that there are things that matter more to him than the reassuring sound of the audience's laughter, certainly an admirable leap forward.

Sam Shepard's *A Lie of the Mind* draws on some of the same images as his last play, *Fool for Love.* Again, love is violent, possibly even a kind of insanity—it is depicted as an ungoing battle that stems from and then results in madness. As in *Fool for Love* there is a suggestion that love puts one in some state beyond ordinary reckoning. Here all the characters seem convinced that the ones they love, from whom they are separated, are dead. A violent young man fears he has killed his mistress and longs for her. He has in fact beaten her so badly that she has suffered brain damage. She too imagines he has died and longs for him. The young man's mother, still in love with her husband, is convinced he is alive—he is in fact dead. In all these cases Shepard creates a feeling of romantic yearning quite worthy of the nineteenth century though he does so in his own style, one that evokes the grandeur of the American West and the sometimes poignant, sometimes comic aloneness of men against it.

Though Shepard is skillful at interweaving themes of guilt and love, violence and death, the play is not always convincing when it dwells on these heavy themes. It is more successful in the earthy comedy that serves as counterpoint to these highflown images.

Lanford Wilson's *Talley and Son* is a revised, strengthened version of his 1981 play *A Tale Told.* It is set during World War II, when the Talleys are at the apex of their power, ruling their little Missouri town as firmly, as imperiously as any feudal lords. When one of the Talleys expresses his objections to the family business being absorbed into a conglomerate, when he talks about such things as pride in craftsmanship, we know the clan is not ready for the new spirit of corporate America being strengthened by the war.

The play takes place on 4 July 1944, the same evening Sally Talley is being courted by Matt Friedman in the boathouse (the action of Wilson's 1979

Talley's Folly). In the earlier play WASP America, in the person of Sally, comes to terms with a Jew full of subversive ideas and love. In the house on the hill that night, we see people for whom WASP and America are synonymous, who do not realize the postwar world will not treat them with the same deference.

Though Wilson views the Talleys with a certain wryness he also sees their tragedy. On this same night they learn their young son has been killed in the Pacific. The dead character floats in and out of the action, bringing a disarming and very American innocence with him that serves as a delicate foil to the cynicism of much of what the Talleys do. The more one dwells on the last of the three Talley plays, the more one admires the skill, the poetry with which Wilson has captured the spirit of America from World War II to Vietnam.

Herb Gardner's *I'm Not Rappaport* is about two men in their early eighties: Nat, a Jew who has battled all of society's lost causes and several of his own, and Midge, a black about to be dismissed from the Central Park West building where he has been the superintendent for many years. For much of the play the two sit on a bench in Central Park. Like a writer and an editor, Nat spins stories and Midge pokes holes through them until the reality breaks through. The rhythms of their speech have a jazzlike quality, Nat's riffs buttressed by Midge's ironic and plangent chords. Their idyllic life is interrupted by the New York of today—a mugger, a former junkie, and her pusher. The intrusion of plot generally is an annoyance—Gardner's play is at its strongest when his two men simply speak to one another.

Two David Mamet one-acts, *Prairie du Chien* and *Shawl*, both subtitled "ghost stories," were presented at Lincoln Center as yet another management tried to bring theater to the Vivian Beaumont. Mamet's efforts were slight, though *Shawl* is a skillfully written piece of storytelling concerning a medium, an anxious upper-class client, and the medium's manipulative black lover. An element of the supernatural gives the play its charm and strength.

A possible new voice presented itself in *Orphans*, a new play by Lyle Kessler given a brilliant production by the Steppenwolf Company of Chi-

cago. The play is set in the shabby, garbage-strewn living room of a house in North Philadelphia, which suggests a primitive, forgotten island where the natives have not evolved beyond a simian existence. Two brothers live here rather like Lost Boys in some contemporary Never-Never Land.

Where J. M. Barrie's boys longed for a mother, Kessler's get a father, a man who, like the boys, is an orphan. He is brought home by the older brother who hopes to hold him for ransom. But the man quickly outwits the boys and takes charge of their house. He transforms the living room from a garbage heap to a room of restrained elegance and changes their diet from one of exclusively tuna and mayonnaise to such rarified dishes as bouillabaisse. The boys lose their animality and their rough edges. Their introduction to civilization is surprisingly lacking in discontents.

The play has echoes of Sam Shepard and Harold Pinter, especially the latter in its atmosphere of inarticulate menace. The style of Kessler's writing is allusive and assertive. We don't see human behavior unfolding naturally but rather are shown a series of gripping and comic episodes, like tableaux in some surreal theater. Exactly how these actions hang together, exactly how true they are to human nature one does not question until after leaving the theater because the production is so persuasive. Whatever the ultimate value of the play, Kessler's writing is lean and solid, full of theatrical vitality.

Much of Lily Tomlin's one-woman show, *The Search for Signs of Intelligent Life in the Universe,* written by Jane Wagner, is conventional stand-up comedy, though all of the material comes from the voices of a group of out-of-kilter women, never simply that of a comedienne. In the second act, however, there is an extended sequence about a Los Angeles woman and her friends that perfectly captures the comedy, the foibles, and the sharp sadness of the women's movement, of liberal trendiness over the last decade and a half. It is an astonishing piece of theater, which might be just as funny if all the roles were played by different actresses, but is especially so performed by a virtuoso soloist. Among other things this piece called attention to how ripe contemporary America is for dramatization and how rarely our theater deals with it at all.

The Year in Poetry

Lewis Turco

In *Dictionary of Literary Biography: 1983,* we noted in the Year in Poetry essay that there were uncertain signs that formal poetry might be returning to favor in the United States after an absence of twenty or twenty-five years from American publishing and the academic writing workshops. This year the signs are stronger; in fact, 1985 ends with the publication, by Harper and Row, of *Strong Measures,* an anthology edited by Philip Dacey and David Jauss, subtitled "Contemporary American Poetry in Traditional Forms." This is the first such book to be published by a major company since *The New Poets of England and America: Second Selection,* edited by Donald Hall *et alia* in 1962 (although the very catholic and still available *New Yorker Book of Poems,* 1969, contains many fine formal poems). The *New Poets* "First Selection," which appeared in 1957, launched the so-called "War of the Anthologies" that pitted the "Academic Poets" of the 1950s against "The Beats" and "The Black Mountaineers." Amazingly enough, both Beat and Black Mountain poets, including Allen Ginsberg and Robert Creeley, are represented in the 1985 anthology.

This war was won in the 1960s by the hosts of the latter armies who managed to convince a generation of poets that to write in verse meant to learn craft, and craft was a product of the military-industrial complex no less than napalm. One of those academic poets, Robert Bly—who had, in fact, appeared in both the *New Poets* anthologies— spent the next decade or two explaining to Hall, James Wright, James Dickey, and others that in order to write quintessentially "American" poetry one had quixotically to study the work of the Chilean Pablo Neruda and the Scandinavians including Gunnar Ekelof and Thomas Tranströmer. If one did this, it led to the so-called "deep-image" that welled up out of the unconscious, which in turn was the basis of a wonderfully "sincere" surrealism that addressed the world by plumbing the depths of the brute in us all. The academics abandoned their posts, stopped teaching anything basic or substantial in the way of craft to their students, and for at least fifteen years the graduate writing programs were smothered in the "pink fog," to use a term of the Upstate New York poet Dugan Gilman, of Deep Imagist bathos and confessional sentimentality.

Unlike every other art taught in the academy, poetry became the bastard child of "intuition." If anyone wanted to find out what he or she was actually doing with pen, muse, and paper, it had to be learned privately, on one's own in the lonely hours. And now it turns out that numbers of young poets have been doing just that. If publishing reports are correct, the Dacey-Jauss anthology will soon be joined by at least one other, and perhaps yet a third. Where there was nothing, there will shortly at least be something, if not an abundance.

Last year we noted that Blymagism, if one may coin a term, was at last dead and that the newest fad among the graduate workshoppers and others is the school of abstract or "musical syntax" poetry led by John Ashbery. The so-called "New York School" of poetry was going national, through the so-called "LANGUAGE" poets, after many years of confinement to Manhattan, though its originator, Wallace Stevens, was perhaps one of the great Modernists.

In some ways 1985 might be considered "The Year of the Anthology," for several interesting and unusual ones were published. *The Harvard Book of Contemporary Poetry,* edited by the critic Helen Vendler (Harvard University Press), is so unusual it is peculiar. It does not begin to live up to its title before page 113, where Howard Nemerov puts in an appearance as the first poet included who is still living. The anthology begins with Stevens, who died in 1955, and it proceeds through Langston Hughes (d. 1967), Theodore Roethke (1963), Elizabeth Bishop (1979), Robert Hayden (1980), Randall Jarrell (1965), John Berryman (1972), and Robert Lowell (1977). Later, we have poems by Frank O'Hara (d. 1966), James Wright (1980), Anne Sexton (1974), and Sylvia Plath (1963). Beyond those, there are poets who are truly contemporary, but the editor's inclusions become extremely subjective, almost as though they were those people whose books Vendler has willy-nilly

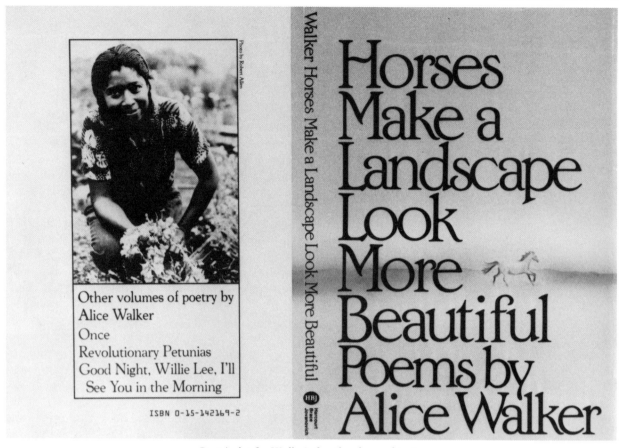

Dust jacket for Walker's fourth volume of poetry

been asked to review over the years. This book is a monument to personal preference masquerading as a standard anthology. One noticed large stacks of the volumes piled on the floor in the Harvard Bookstore in the fall, but no one seemed to be buying them. It is a hard thing to imagine the course for which this might be the text.

A much more representative selection of contemporary American poetry is *The Bread Loaf Anthology of Contemporary American Poetry* edited by Robert Pack, Sydney Lea, and Jay Parini (University Press of New England). All the contributors are still living and writing. This book is projected as the first in a series of pentennial collections. Pack, it will be noted, was one of the original triumvirate of editors who launched The War of the Anthologies nearly a quarter-century ago.

Two important anthologies of ethnic poetry were published during the year. The first, edited by Ferdinando Alfonsi of Fordham University, is titled *Poeti Italo-Americani/Italo-American Poets*. A bilingual compilation published by Antonio Carello Editore of Catanzaro, Italy, this book is the most

comprehensive collection of its kind ever assembled, and it is sure to be the standard for decades. It ranges from immigrant poets who wrote primarily in Italian to contemporaries who do not even know the language of their forebears; it is thus a literary chronicle of the assimilation by one culture of another.

The Dream Book: An Anthology of Writings by Italian-American Women, edited by Helen Barolini (Schocken Books), contains fiction, drama, and nonfiction by American poets of Italian extraction as well as poetry. There is very little overlapping between this book and *Poeti Italo-Americani*—only three of the women appear in both collections. Another interesting book in the general category of women's studies is *Woman Poet: The Midwest*. This is volume three in a series under the general editorship of Elaine Dallman, published by Women-in-Literature, of Reno, Nevada.

Finally, a couple of annual anthologies might be mentioned. Robert Wallace's third collection of light verse and humorous poetry, *Light Year '86* (Bits Press), is fatter and funnier than ever. The

Anthology of Magazine Verse and Yearbook of American Poetry edited by Alan F. Pater (Monitor Book Company) is as fat as ever, but it is not funny. This collection is a yearly indiscriminate compilation of what are purportedly the "best" poems to appear in the periodicals during a given year. In fact, however, it is a vanity press book that makes a living for its publishers from the desperation of scores of poets who want to see their work between hard covers. Not only does the book not pay its contributors; it doesn't even give them a free copy. Contributors must purchase it if they want one.

The winner this year of the Yale Series of Younger Poets is Pamela Alexander for her first book, *Navigable Waterways* (Yale University Press), chosen by James Merrill. Last year in this article we discussed the revival of narrative in poetry, and Alexander writes short narratives in this collection; however, poetry is that genre in which the writer focuses upon the language itself, not on story lines and characters, and one wonders why these nearly styleless pieces weren't written out in straight prose sentences rather than broken arbitrarily, as they are, into something resembling verse lines that do not operate on any of the levels of verse, not even the rhythms inherent in parallel structures repeated, as in Whitman and Ginsberg, Jeffers and William Everson. Speaking, in his introduction, of "Talking to Myself at Thirty," Merrill says that "the poem all but shudders into prose"—but that is exactly what it began with, so it does not "shudder" into anything. Here are a few lines from the first poem, "Flight":

> The rumble of the red and gold
> Electra wakes the air, shakes stars
> down their strings until
> they hang outside the cockpit, close enough
> to touch. Squares, like quickened days, take turns
> showing her senses
>
> what to do. The fragrance of blooming
> orange orchards carries to considerable
> altitudes.

Why do some lines end with unimportant, medial words like *until, enough?* Why is there a break after *senses?* Why are there stops two or three syllables into a line, as after *to touch, what to do,* and *altitudes?* What is lost by writing these *lines* out as sentences, thus?

> The rumble of the red and gold Electra
> wakes the air, shakes stars down their strings

until they hang outside the cockpit, close enough to touch. Squares, like quickened days, take turns showing her senses what to do. The fragrance of blooming orange orchards carries to considerable altitudes.

In fact, it appears that there is a great deal to be gained in the way of grace, rhythm, sense, and sensation by being straight about the prose. Alexander writes well, but she disguises the fact.

Maxine Kumin chose the winner this year of the Eileen W. Barnes Award "for a first book by a woman poet over the age of forty," Anne Nicodemus Carpenter, author of *Ma's Ram* (Saturday Press). Born in 1914, Carpenter is well over forty, but her performance here shows considerably more youth, in fact more life, than many another collection that has come across this desk during the past three years. Though she is a prose poet in most of her work, she breaks her lines where the

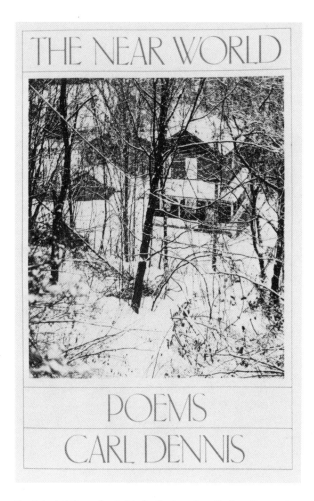

Dust jacket for a book Linda Pastan described as "engaging, human, and wise"

phrases and clauses end, so that her work *does* have a sense of the line.

Jim Daniels has won the inaugural Brittingham Prize for his book *Places/Everyone* (University of Wisconsin Press). C. K. Williams was the judge who, in a foreword, describes this book as "proletariat poetry." Daniels tells stories about blue-collar people in short-line prose poems, for the most part. The characters and situations are concrete, and the poet keeps his eye on the particular at all times. Though these scenes from the lives of working folk are clear and believable, the sentimentality of the poet as he tells his tales can be cloying; it undercuts the empathy a reader might have felt had a more objective approach been employed rather than this partisan voice, this condescending manner. The best part of the book is section two, a series about a character named Digger. Here the poet often achieves the distance he needs in order to let the reader live the life of the worker without the author getting in the way, as in "Digger Laid Off":

> Tonight you beat up four little kids
> to get a baseball at Tiger Stadium.
> After the game you sit in a bar
> watching fat naked women
> rub mud over their bodies.
> You throw your ball in the mud pit
> and a dancer picks it up
> rubs it over her muddy crotch
> and throws it back to you.
> In the parking lot
> you throw the ball against a windshield
> but it will not crack.

Daniel Halpern selected a winner this year in the Open Competition of the National Poetry Series: Kathy Fagan for her first book, *The Raft* (Dutton). Fagan has evidently escaped all the fads of the graduate programs and hued to her goal: to become a writer, which she has achieved. Although her poems are not traditionally formal, she has learned a range of technique that enables her to use the prose line as lyrically as others might use the verse line. Her subject is the past, how it arises constantly in the present, shapes it, ties us down to an inevitable future. Her evocations are of something more than nostalgia—something as palpable as her father, in "Fire," long before she was born, roasting potatoes at a burning trash can at Lenox and 116th Street while her future mother forgets the daughter she has never had and goes to sleep on the other side of the city. The past, present, and

"future" become one thing, solid as the dream you cannot forget. Here is a young poet to watch; she is certain to become something fine, for she is already something extraordinary.

Carolyn Forché was not so astute in her choice of Robert L. Jones's *Wild Onion* as a winner in the same competition. Perhaps she was seduced by the combination of machismo and "sensitivity" in these disingenuous mass-productions of the West Coast graduate workshops. If these poems rhymed and metered, perhaps Glen Campbell or John Denver could sing them.

The winner in the Pacific Poetry Series Competition for 1984 was Marina Makarova for her book *For Yesterday;* W. S. Merwin was the judge. Makarova's collection has things in common with several of the other books reviewed in this section: it is proletariat poetry; it is nostalgic and often particular (though at times it is egopoetic and vague); there is a certain toughness in its viewpoints and stances; it is prose poetry. But, finally, it fails to hold the attention, perhaps because there does not appear to be a center to it, or maybe a unifying vision on the part of its creator.

Eric Pankey's *For the New Year* (Atheneum) is the 1984 winner of the Walt Whitman Award of the Academy of American Poets. The judge was Mark Strand, and the prize is funded by a grant from the National Endowment for the Arts. Although the *I* narrator here is sometimes a persona other than the author, it is not frequently so; usually it is the egopoetic *I* which, eventually, despite good writing, becomes numbing. The reader would now and again like to become the Other, not the Author.

The Academy's other book prize, The Lamont Award, was won by Philip Schultz for his collection *Deep Within the Ravine* (Viking); the judges were Louise Glück, Charles Simic, and David Wagoner. This volume is reminiscent of W. D. Snodgrass's *Heart's Needle* (1959), the story of separation and adjustment to being single again, even to the central title-poem sequence. But the lyricism of Snodgrass has been dropped and the breast-beating of Robert Lowell's *Life Studies* (also 1959) as well. What has been substituted is an urbane, city-dwelling sensibility, a talent for telling a story well, and an ability to turn a summary phrase, as in this quotation from "The Rounds Continue; Christmas 1980": "a bullish apocalypse/where hope is bought on credit & death/is just another sad cliché wrapped in tinsel."

The Agnes Lynch Starrett Poetry Prize was won by Arthur Smith for his *Elegy on Independence*

Day (University of Pittsburgh Press). The first poem, "Tarantulas," is as hard, clear, concrete, and dark a poem as anyone could ask for. It should have set the tone for a book that walks steadily forward into existential loss and acceptance of loss—in this case the loss of a beloved wife. The book could have been a survival manual for the human animal; instead, it turns too far inward and softens. The writing is always good, but its impact never again achieves the level of impression made by the initial poem.

Silver and Information by Bruce Smith (University of Georgia Press) was selected by Hayden Carruth and published in the National Poetry Series. The first section of this three-part book is simultaneously a narrative of the relationship between a son and his father, and an elegy to that father. The viewpoint is third-person rather than first-person, and for that reason the reader is allowed in to empathize with the mourning son. The second section begins to turn away—the narrative becomes second- and sometimes first-person. By the third section, the turning has gone wholly inward and confessional. As a result, this book's impact is anticlimactic—it is strongest in the beginning and weakest at the end. Its final effect is maudlin, despite some tough-sounding diction.

Here we are again with Robert Bly, in *Loving a Woman in Two Worlds* (Dial), mucking about in supersentimental "deep image" surrealism. His voice-of-choice is always the egopoetic *I* which goes jumping about from one non sequitur to another, and we are in the topography of the poet's mind, without landmarks or guideposts. Here is "Such Different Wants":

> The board floats on the river.
> The board wants nothing
> but is pulled from beneath
> on into deeper waters.
>
> And the elephant dwelling
> on the mountains wants
> a trumpet so its dying cry
> can be heard by the stars.
>
> The wakeful heron striding
> through reeds at dawn wants
> the god of sun and moon
> to see his long skinny neck.
>
> You must say what you want.
> I want to be the man
> and I am who will love you
> when your hair is white.

The only lines that make sense are the last two, and they are the least interesting, the most trite.

What a relief to turn to Amy Clampitt's *What the Light Was Like* (Knopf). Instead of getting bogged down among the miasmas of the self, Clampitt jumps into the world, embraces it, and embodies it in a language strong enough to show us ourselves in a strangely familiar landscape, as in these lines from "Cloudberry Summer":

> 　　　　　　　Rancor
> is rarely simple, least so in the dank
> sector of organic
>
> chemistry. Likewise
> its lack, as in these strangely sallow-
> tinged, blandly baked-apple-
> flavored thimble nubbins, singly borne, no
> more than inches from the bog's
> sour surface.

It's wonderful to run into a poet who loves the language, its heft and swing and color.

Charles Edward Eaton is a poet whose level of competence has always been, and continues to be, extraordinarily high. His new book, *The Work of the Wrench* (Cornwall Books), is full of good formal poems which, if they do not often rise to the level of inspiration, nevertheless compel the attention and quicken admiration. The words that come readiest to mind in considering this work are pleasurable and interesting, neither to be taken in any pejorative sense. Eaton has held his ground and his standards over the past two decades and more. His work deserves the recognition of an intelligent audience.

Hayden Carruth is said, on the jacket of his *Asphalt Georgics* (New Directions), to have written this long poem about ordinary people "in the common speech of Upstate New York." In order "to capture the rhythms of their very colloquial language, Hayden Carruth has invented a new verse form, his Georgics—quatrains in strict syllables and rhyme, though with no accentual pattern—which achieve by their special artifice a classic and earthy elegance."

The syllable counts of the quatrains are 8-6-8-6. There is nothing new about quantitative syllabics (if that is what these are). The rhyme scheme is *abcb, defe,* and so on—nothing new there, either. Carruth breaks words wherever he likes between syllables, and makes these lines rhyme—unusual, but not new; the technical term is "apocopated rhyme." Georgics is a rhymed handbook in the arts and crafts; Carruth is redefining the term here—by it he seems to mean something like "bucolics" or, more accurately, "suburbics." The declaration that these quatrains have "no accentual pattern" is dead wrong. The long lines have four stresses, the short ones three, almost invariably. If one scans out a whole stanza as though it were one line, one will find verse feet, primarily iambs and anapests.The book is moderate fun to read, like listening to conversations in a bar.

Last year, reviewing John Ciardi's *Selected Poems* here, we discussed his wonderful way with narratives. Now, fresh from that collection, Ciardi gives us a book mainly of lyrics. This poet does not need to invent a "new" prosody or form in order to speak colloquially—the old kinds do very well in *The Birds of Pompeii* (University of Arkansas Press), just as they did for Ciardi's Bread Loaf colleague of many years, Robert Frost. When Ciardi wants to be subjective he knows he must sing to us to keep our attention, and there are few poets currently writing who can sing as well. Ciardi simply does everything well, and has been doing so for years. Here's how and why, "At Least with Good Whiskey":

> She gave me a drink and told me she had tried
> to read my book but had had to put it down
> because it depressed her. Why, she wanted to know,
> couldn't I turn my talent (I raised my glass)
> to happier things? Did I suppose it was smart
> to be forever dying? Not forever,
> I told her, sipping; by actuarial tables
> ten years should about do it. See what I mean?
> she hurried to say—always that terrible sadness.
> Well, maybe, I said. (This is good whiskey, I said.)
> But ten years, plus or minus, is not much time
> for getting it said—do you see what I mean?—which
>   leaves me
> too busy to make a hobby of being sad.

Another New England bard is Louis Coxe, whose *The North Well* (Godine) contains less formally traditional lyrics than most of his books have done. His vision has changed little, though; it is still dark and darkly stoical. These are the finely wrought poems of a survivor, whose survival has perhaps been made possible by the writing of such laments as "Aphasia":

> It never came on time
> to reach me, the late news:
> my dates were wrong, the beam

swept out but didn't scan.

> Out there blip and beep
> came on ticking the time
> to others. Caught in the sweep
> I turned them out of tune

> into shapes of plot and pattern
> that leapt on the scope and died
> telling me "No matter."
> Whatever I did, they lied

> to me alone. This sickness
> fingered and fed with dark
> stands as sole witness
> to a long night's work.

This is what Louis Ginsberg, Allen Ginsberg's father, was writing in *The Grub Street Book of Verse*, edited by its publisher, Henry Harrison, in 1927—it is from a poem titled "To My Two Sons":

> My little sons, because I know
> That Love perpetuates only woe,
> I write these lines so you may read
> Some night upon your hour of need.

According to Allen Ginsberg's *Collected Poems 1947-1980* (Harper and Row), this is what the son was writing in his 1948 pre-Beat days—from a poem titled "A Very Dove":

> A very Dove will have her love
>   ere the dove has died;
> the spirit, vanity approve,
>   will even love in pride.

And this is Allen Ginsberg returning to his roots in verses titled "Love Forgiven," written in 1979:

> Straight and slender
> Youthful tender
> Love shows the way
>   and never says nay

There is even a 1980 poem with a Greek title written in Sapphic stanzas! In between are all the prose "poems" for which Ginsberg became notorious if not famous. Perhaps the current return to formalism now underway around the nation is not an unmixed blessing.

When John Ciardi was poetry editor of the *Saturday Review*, he was asked how he managed to read all the hundreds of "poems" that came across his desk each month. He replied that he didn't read

Dust jacket for a new collection by Kunitz

them all; he simply read the first line of a poem, and if he liked that line he read the second, and so on until he hit a line he didn't like, at which point he went on to the next poem. If he was pulled by liking clear through a poem, he put it on the "To Be Reconsidered" pile.

One must have some sort of approach like that if one is to review annually dozens of books. One has to *select,* for space and health so dictate. This year I decided to screen these books by looking through each to find how often the first-person, singular "I" prevailed. If it appeared often, I looked to see if it were the egopoetic, the narrative, or the dramatic "I." If it were egopoetic I looked to see if the poet made palatable this spreading of ego upon the page with craft or art, wit or intelligence, or *something* that could keep the reader's interest or draw him into the poet's sensibility. If none of these prevailed, I put the book aside.

Except—for there are always exceptions— when the book in question is one a reviewer feels obliged, for one reason or another, to consider. Such a volume is *The Triumph of Achilles* by Louise Glück (Ecco Press), for whom extravagant claims are made on the dust jacket by Helen Vendler, who writes, "A very peculiar power, and a new style, commanding in its indifference to current modes"; and by Dave Smith, who says, "She has the chance as few ever do to become a major poet." Let the reader judge. Here is a typical piece, "Seated Figure":

It was as though you were a man in a wheelchair,
your legs cut off at the knee.
But I wanted you to walk.
I wanted us to walk like lovers,
arm in arm in the summer evening,
and believed so powerfully in that projection
that I had to speak, I had to press you to stand.
Why did you let me speak?
I took your silence as I took the anguish in your face,
as part of the effort to move—
It seemed I stood forever, holding out my hand.
And all that time, you could no more heal yourself
than I could accept what I saw.

Patricia Goedicke, in *The Wind of Our Going* (Copper Canyon Press), combines a driving rhetoric often, but not always, harnessed to a couplet stanza set up in grammatic parallel constructions, with a minutely discerning eye that twists reality surrealistically. Here is a portion of "The Husband and Wife Team" seen as a piano duo:

Dominating the concert hall
The giant portraits of our parents

Insist we go on playing for them

For each of us has a piano on his back
And sits in front of one forever.

With eyes like the polished depths
Of mahogany

The man looks at his wife over the black
Glistening humpback of a whale,

The woman sights along the lifted ridge
Of an open flying fish to see her husband

Full of overtones, the gold strings
Tangled like candy, like smooth satin

Valentines under the raised lids. . . .

What catches and keeps the attention is this combination of the sensory and the sonic.

In *Assumptions* (Knopf), her fourth collection, Marilyn Hacker shows us once again that she is the complete poet. She is one of the new generation of formalists now making their presence felt after years of absence from the American literary scene. Hacker's range of formal approaches is wide; she writes in unrhymed syllabics as well as in strict sestinas, heroic couplets, and sonnets. Her voice is meditative and quiet, and her mind is clear; her diction follows it faithfully and easily, despite—or perhaps because of—the discipline she imposes upon herself. This is a poet whose artistry is solidly grounded in craft.

Michael Harper in his most recent book, *Healing Song for the Inner Ear* (University of Illinois Press), continues to write out of his black heritage using the referents and rhythms of jazz and blues. His language, however, is never used as a bar for excluding the reader of another race or minority; rather, Harper writes to include, to initiate and welcome. Nothing is overdone, nor is it rarefied. What we have here is good writing about the human condition in a style that is both personal and ethnic.

Shore Guide to Flocking Names (Fanferon Press) is a bird chapbook in a limited edition by Robert Huff, one of the older formalists. These sometimes rueful, usually descriptive, always light-verse pieces are enjoyable to read, but perhaps the audience for which they appear to be intended—older children—will have little chance to see them in this package.

Cross Ties (University of Georgia Press) is an important book, for it is X. J. Kennedy's selected poems. It "contains every poem that the poet cares to save" from all his books and chapbooks, ranging from his first collection, *Nude Descending a Staircase* (1961), to *Hangover Mass*, reviewed here last year. Kennedy is a traditional formalist who was trained in the 1950s to believe that one can do whatever one wishes with the English language, provided

only that one has the talent and the intelligence to do it. His voice is naturally bent to the humorous, but it is a humor with depth that probes the issues of living and dying. There are far too many fine pieces here to quote with representative examples, but here are two cautionary epigrams:

THE DEVIL'S ADVICE TO POETS

Molt that skin! lift that face! you'll go far.
Grow like Proteus yet more bizarre.
    In perpetual throes
    Majors metamorphose—
Only minors remain who they are.

TO THE ONE-EYED POETS

Creeley, Penn Warren, and James Seay,
Did sight hold sway, and mind,
The likes of you might well be kings
In this country of the blind.

Maxine Kumin is one of those formerly formalist poets who, in the 1960s, became "confessional" poets. Her transformation occurred under the influence, in particular, of her close friend Anne Sexton. *The Long Approach* (Viking) is, then, another of those egopoetic exceptions mentioned above. Or is it? One of the things Kumin never forgot how to do is to tell a story. These poems, though they log the subjective voyages of the heart, never exclude through excessive privacy, for the reader is always shown the compass, the latitude and the longitude of those voyages, and we are immersed in the particular. Those poems in this book that make the strongest impression are those that are longer-lined, that approach, and sometimes achieve, the condition of verse; the weaker poems are line-phrased prose. Nevertheless, this is a strong collection, one that gives sustained pleasure to the reader.

Next-to-Last Things by Stanley Kunitz (Atlantic Monthly Press) is a collection of verse and prose poems, essays, an interview, and a concluding section of aphorisms and observations—distinctly a mixed bag. It is sometimes difficult to tell where the boundaries lie between the kinds of writing. In the essays Kunitz writes of poets as diverse as Keats, whom he admires for his particularity, and Whitman, Keats's vast and nebulous polar opposite, whom Kunitz nevertheless manages to admire also. But it is the poems that are wonderful. Here are a few quotes that delight the senses and stimulate the mind:

"Now that the nights are chill
and the annuals spent,
I should have thought them gone,
in a torpor of blood
slipped to the nether world
before the sickle frost."
                    (from "The Snakes of September")

"Our lives are spinning out
from world to world;
the shapes of things
are shifting in the wind.
What do we know
beyond the rapture and the dread?"
                    (from "The Abduction")

"The way I look
at it, I'm passing through a phase;
gradually I'm changing to a word.
Whatever you choose to claim
of me is always yours;
nothing is truly mine
except my name. I only
borrowed this dust."
                    (from "Passing Through—on my
                             seventy-ninth birthday.")

Those Who Trespass by Dan Masterson (University of Arkansas Press) is, inexplicably, only the second book by this widely known and well-published poet. The heart of his work is the narrative—perhaps that is the reason for his neglect, for the last quarter-century has been the Age of the Naked Ego. Masterson does not neglect the self—by the time we have read these poems we know more about the poet-narrator than we do of the ego-centrists from Whitman to the Feminists. But our knowledge is gained in passing, by reflection from the stories of multifarious people in their human situations. Masterson makes us part of his world and therefore a part of him. By the time we reach the last, long title poem and help him close the door on his parents' house, left empty and filling up with stagnant time, we are ourselves members of his family.

Jerome Mazzaro's *The Caves of Love* (Jazz Press) contains poems of phrased prose, syllabics, and accentual-syllabics manifested especially in an astonishing English ode several pages in length, "Kansas Interior," which, thematically, is much like Masterson's "Those Who Trespass." The range of approaches here is lyrical to narrative, confessional to epigrammatic. By far the most usual approach, however, is the formally lyrical. The book is refreshing and readable, intelligent and affecting.

Carrying On: New and Selected Poems by Leon-ard Nathan (University of Pittsburgh Press) publishes better than a score of the poet's new poems and gathers work from six collections ranging back to his second book, *The Glad and Sorry Seasons* (1963). Over the years Nathan has steadily developed a personal "middle" style. His lines never pop off the page, but the level of their discourse is high, seldom if ever slipping beneath intelligence and wit. It is the ideational level that interests Nathan and his reader, but the sonic supports his thought unobtrusively. These poems are a pleasure to read.

Joel Oppenheimer, in his *New Spaces: Poems 1975-1983* (Black Sparrow Press) is the democratic poet, speaking to the American Everyman from the perspective of the guy next to him at the bar. His subjects are what happened today at work, or in the park, or sitting in the kitchen waiting for the coffee to be done. The poems are readable and objectifying: we see ourselves from a little distance, as though we were the stars in a drama of the ordinary, and we even laugh a little at ourselves now and again.

Forever Wider, Poems New and Selected: 1954-1984 by Charles Plymell (Scarecrow Press), has an "Appreciation" by Rod McKuen as a foreword. Plymell doesn't *quite* deserve it.

Vern Rutsala's books are nearly all the same. Each is dedicated to his wife Joan, like *Backtracking* (Story Line Press) and a chapbook, *The Mystery of Lost Shoes* (Lynx House Press); each is filled with poems that are unmistakably Rutsala, even those truly flat prose poems of *The Harmful State* (1971) and *Paragraphs* (1978). In them things lie in wait to trip us out of our ordinary walks of life, to take us down where surfaces close over our heads and we breathe dread and fascination. We know who writes "X's Poems":

These are the poems which steal,
which siphon gas, which
break in at night. These poems
are cat burglars, cold-eyed
prowlers. These poems shoplift
your cart empty at the store.
When you've read these poems
you're picked clean, you're naked
and alone, you're bankrupt
without hope or gender. It's then
these poems bring
a freezing wind, foul and piercing,
from the arctic dump.
These poems take everything
but ice and bone. Each one writes
each reader's elegy in cold blood.

There are two kinds of poems in David St. John's *No Heaven* (Houghton Mifflin). The most prominent are in the new abstract syntax style of John Ashbery and the LANGUAGE poets (Ashbery has provided a blurb for the jacket). The other kind are prose narratives of a meditative nature containing low-voltage epiphanies of the upper-middle classes. Some of the poems are written in long lines like James Dickey's with eye-breaks instead of punctuation.

A great change has taken place in Grace Schulman's work since her previous book, *Burn Down the Icons* (1977). In *Hemispheres* (Sheep Meadow Press) there is a much wider range of subjects treated—the poet literarily moves from country to country. Her style, likewise, changes from poem to poem: at one point it is biblical, at another, neo-Anglo-Saxon; and there is greater aesthetic distance in the new work, less of the purely personal. As a result, this book is constantly surprising and always interesting—a fine showcase of the poet's abilities.

There is nothing fancy about Dave Smith's poems in *The Roundhouse Voices: Selected and New Poems* (Harper and Row). The quiet narratives are here, the fine writing, the compassionate sensibility. The only thing operating to keep this work from being totally enjoyable is a willful obscurity that runs parallel to the story line in some of the poems. It's as though the poet felt that to be perfectly clear is unpoetic; that a little fuzziness is good for the reader and mandatory for the poet. Not so, of course. Otherwise, this is uncommonly good work, singular, not fashionable.

Remains: A Sequence of Poems by W. D. Snodgrass (BOA Editions) is a new edition of the 1970 volume which was a very limited issue of those poems the poet published under the anagram pseudonym "S. S. Gardons." The chapbook is made of those pieces Snodgrass felt at the time were too personal and familial even for the original "confessional" poet to publish.

Song of the Sky: Versions of Native American Songs & Poems by Brian Swann is the latest publication of one of the most prolific poets in America. The book is a scholarly collection of American Indian songs but, despite the full introduction and the notes, even several pages of musical notation, the emphasis here is on *versions,* not translations, and there is a heavy emphasis also in many of the poems upon the typographical level, something that could not have been a part of the oral originals. Those originals are not included, so the scholarship of the book is incomplete, but the versions themselves are

very good. Swann, despite his fecundity, maintains a high standard of writing always.

It was a distinct pleasure to discover, after turning to it with trepidation, that *Facing Nature* by John Updike (Knopf) contained some poems that had substance, even an intellectual wit substituted for the clever surfaces and mechanical rhymes and meters one expects to find in Updike verses. The light section of this book, unfortunately the last section, is still like that; otherwise, this is the popular novelist's best collection of versework.

The simplicity of the prose poems in Alice Walker's *Horses Make a Landscape Look More Beautiful* (Harcourt Brace Jovanovich), the driving, repetitive rhythms of the biblical parallels, are disarming. These are songs of joy and grievance. They are poems that have points to make about social injustice, historical evils perpetrated by Europeans upon native Americans and blacks, about love and affirmation despite it all; but the poems are not strident. Walker can make us listen and enjoy the pain.

Blues & Roots/Rue & Bluets by Jonathan Williams (Duke University Press) is an enlarged edition of the 1971 collection. In a forenote the author writes, "Twelve texts have been pared; and thirty-three have been added—eight of which are printed for the first time." The book is, according to Herbert Leibowitz's introduction, "an unofficial oral history in verse of the Southern Appalachian folk often vilified and dismissed as hillbillies." It is certainly *not* in "verse," and it is difficult to see how some of these texts could have been "pared." Here is one of the many entries that are shorter than their titles, "A Pileated Woodpecker's Response to Four Dogwood Berries":

kuk

kuk kuk

kuk●kuk

kukkuk

A new edition of William Carlos Williams's *Selected Poems* (New Directions), edited by Charles Tomlinson, contains many of the finest poems of one of the finest and most humane poets of the twentieth century. New Directions has brought out as well a companion volume, *Something to Say: William Carlos Williams on Younger Poets,* edited by James E. B. Breslin. According to the jacket (and, in similar words, the preface by Breslin), this volume "collects all of Williams' known writings—reviews, essays, introductions, and letters to the editor—on the two generations of poets that fol-

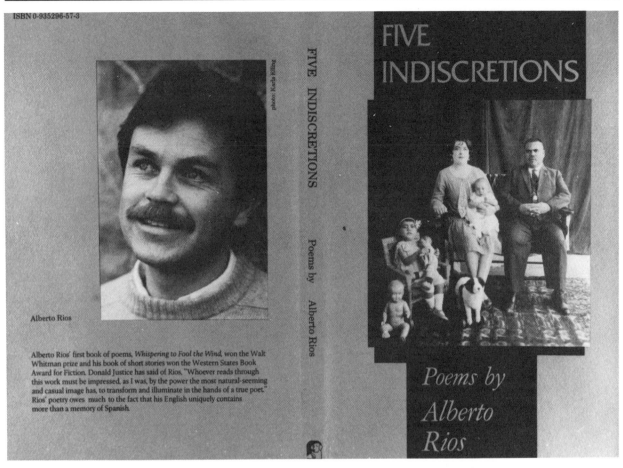

ISBN 0-935296-57-3

FIVE INDISCRETIONS

Poems by Alberto Rios

Alberto Rios

Alberto Rios' first book of poems, *Whispering to Fool the Wind*, won the Walt Whitman prize and his book of short stories won the Western States Book Award for Fiction. Donald Justice has said of Rios, "Whoever reads through this work must be impressed, as I was, by the power the most natural-seeming and casual image has, to transform and illuminate in the hands of a true poet." Rios' poetry owes much to the fact that his English uniquely contains more than a memory of Spanish.

FIVE INDISCRETIONS

Poems by Alberto Rios

Dust jacket for a book of poems that explore the Spanish-American experience

lowed him, from Kenneth Rexroth and Louis Zukofsky to Robert Lowell and Allen Ginsberg." None of the great Modernists, not even Ezra Pound, was more generous and welcoming to new talent, more encouraging of the development of new voices. This is a truly remarkable and important book of criticism, offering us insights into the American personality and culture by a great poet who never forgot where he came from.

The Salt Stone: Selected Poems by John Woods (Dragon Gate) is another important event in poetry publication during 1985. Reviewing another of Woods's books here two years ago, we called the poet "an old master formalist." Here is the proof. This volume selects poems from the six collections Woods published between 1955 and 1976, the first five of which are out of print. It is a completely engaging collection, a showcase of talent and intelligence, sensibility and insight, broadened and deepened by craft and a sense of tradition.

A Season of Loss by Jim Barnes (Purdue University Press) is another book inspired by the Amer-ican Indian culture, but the forms in which this heritage is distilled range from straight prose poems in paragraphs to complicated medieval Welsh forms—Barnes moves easily in and out of the traces.

Sydney Lea says in his foreword to Leo Connellan's *The Clear Blue Lobster-Water Country* (Harcourt Brace Jovanovich), "By holding to an achingly candid poetry—devoid of posture, composed in isolation, and without external reward, yet founded on human love—Connellan has certified the importance of his own voice.... It is a voice like no other in current poetry." And Richard Eberhart says that the poet "has achieved a masterwork in narrative verse...." One sincerely hopes that this is a narrative, not a confessional work. The story begins, "Father, we'll/meet again./ /You can tell me you love me then." On page 11 the narrator says to his dead father, "We'll meet again./You can tell me you love me then." And on page 15 the same. On page 18, "My only brother and I/never had a chance/to ever like each other," and shortly thereafter, "We were robbed of/our mother and/cheated of each other.//We are the children/of violation." On page 37, "We'll meet again and you/can tell me you love me then. . . ." But at the beginning of the second section there is a quantum shift: "Mother, we'll meet again./I will tell you I love you then." On page 126, it is back to an older theme: "Father we'll/meet again.//You can tell me you love me then." The effect of all this, despite the entrance of various voices and attempts at colloquial rhythms in some of the speeches, is of incessant whining and puling. As for Connellan's not being rewarded for his poetry with an academic sinecure of which Lea makes much in his introduction, Connellan at least won the Shelley Memorial Award of the Academy of American Poets in 1982 and a grant from the Connecticut Commission on the Arts for this "Whitmanesque" production.

A truly narrative poem is Bruce Cutler's *Dark Fire* (BkMk Press), which has to do with the disappearance in a midwestern town of Holly Shay, a teacher, after the death of her father. It is as good a read as a good short novel, and in some ways it reminds one of the narratives of Conrad Aiken.

One keeps forgetting, going through these books, what it is like to read *writing*, work by someone who enjoys putting the language to work on real human themes having to do with recognizably human beings, but now and again one runs across a book like Carl Dennis's *The Near World* (William Morrow) and simply becomes immersed in it, forgetting one is reading at all. Here is the beginning of "The Connoisseur," chosen because of its subject, to be compared with Connellan's work above:

> If my father had praised me a little when I
> climbed the tree,
> If when I swam the stream he hadn't looked
> away,
> Maybe I wouldn't need your praise now
> When I tell you what the still lives of Cezanne
> Say about pears and pitchers, tables and
> tablecloths.
> You could believe or disbelieve. I'd be happy
> enough
> Making my point with a graceful gesture
> under the gray eyes
> Of eternity, eyes like my own but colder and
> more removed.

The Luftwaffe in Chaos by Nicholas Rinaldi (Negative Capability Press) is another in the swatch of books of poetry about World War II that include William Heyen's *The Swastika Poems* (1977), *Erika:*

Poems of the Holocaust (1984), and W. D. Snodgrass's *The Fuhrer Bunker* (1977). Rinaldi's narrative and dramatic representations of Nazi characters and situations, and his embodiment of them in language, are as good as anyone's and as interesting. The only question is, How many of those who lived through that war and those times can put aside their feelings long enough to be objective and "enjoy" such productions? It is a painful kind of pleasure, to say the least.

In Alberto Rios's *Five Indiscretions* (Sheep Meadow Press), a wonderful ethnicity envelops the reader, who is welcomed into the families and situations of real people doing recognizable things, having feelings we understand and facing problems we must all face.

Robert Ronnow was praised here on another occasion. Now, in *White Waits* (Barnwood Press), we are offered a more traditional collection of poems,

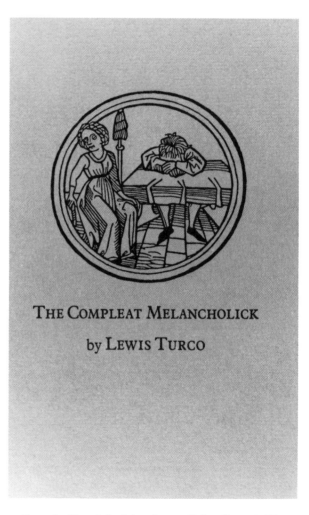

Cover for Turco's book based upon Robert Burton's The Anatomy of Melancholy *(1621)*

but there is no slackening of the talent, and there is an opening up of range and style. It appears that Ronnow is so much the craftsman that he can do anything he wants with the English language in any form from prose poem to iambic blank verse. This is an excellent book, well printed and designed.

Stan Sanvel Rubin's *Midnight* (State Street Press) is a book of contemplations and elegies, each poem written in a quiet voice that has depth as well as surface, sense beside sound. Each celebrates a moment, like "First Waxwing":

I need to understand the cry
of the one bird who hangs upside down
straddling berries with his thin claws.
He is like a parenthesis
carved out of morning, his gray monk's head
encompasses everything. His darting beak,
quick as a dagger, drives sunlight home.

A third collection this year that derives its substance from the North American Indian culture is *Little Dog of Iron* by Philip St. Clair (Ahsahta Press). This is a series of poems about Coyote, the trickster of Native American myth. As Howard McCord says in his introduction, this book might well be subtitled " 'The True History of Coyote in Our Times,' for St. Clair reveals Coyote in his historically American manifestations, from folk hero-demon to law student, from relisher of field-mice canapes to lecher-philosopher. From hunter to hunted, in a fundamentally slapstick universe." And managed very well at that. My favorite poem is the "Coyote Villanelle," in which the quintessential West merges and blends with a medieval Provençal verse form to produce a unique experience.

A fine formal poet is Gjertrud Schnackenberg in *The Lamplit Answer* (Farrar, Straus & Giroux). She is one of that apparently sizable group of younger writers who, over the past decade or so, appear to have been quietly honing technical skills and developing the ability to understand human natures other than their own in intelligent idioms and personal styles that manifest themselves in traditional forms. Ms. Schnackenberg is represented in the Dacey-Jauss *Strong Measures* anthology, with three poems, one of which, "Darwin in 1881," is to

be found in this, her second collection.

Again we will end this overview of the year with a look at some chapbooks, most of them published by Robert L. Barth. Turner Cassity has entered the lists with *The Book of Alna: A Narrative of the Mormon Wars* written in narrative blank verse. Cassity is one of our fine writers, with sure grasp of character, scene, and event. Raymond Oliver in *Other Times* is classically epigrammatic, handling the language surely and lyrically in traditional and simple forms that lend themselves well to the twists of the poet's thought. A bit looser and less traditional in her approaches is Nancy Winters in *A Sad and Solemn Ground* but, oddly enough, the effect of the poems is more commonplace. Timothy Dekin's *Carnival* in quiet quatrains takes on subjects like murder, violence, the savagery of the classroom and makes them real enough to touch, at least with our feelings and our minds. Charles Gullans whispers us away with his *Local Winds*, the sounds of the lines chiming against the syntax to make almost perfect artifacts with which to stave off the inroads of time.

Finally, we ought to notice H. R. Coursen's *War Stories* (Cider Mill Press), a chapbook full of quantitative syllabic poems whose subject, for the most part, is nostalgia, but not the kind that cloys, the kind that illuminates the present by casting a sharp glow over the past. The poems begin in the 1950s when Coursen was a fighter pilot, and they work forward to 1984. In effect, then, this is a biography, but it is first of all the story of days spent in intense living, both physically and intellectually. Coursen, too, is a formalist—there is even a sestina here, but the forms do not hinder his telling any more than they hindered his colleague and fellow Maine poet Louis Coxe. These are readable and interesting, and Coursen is long overdue for a book of selected poems from a major publisher.

Editor's Note. In 1985 Lewis Turco published a collection of poems, *The Compleat Melancholick,* "Being a Sequence of Found, Composite, and Composed Poems, based largely upon Robert Burton's *The Anatomy of Melancholy*" (Bieler Press).

The Year in Fiction

George Garrett
University of Virginia

One major development in 1985 which is peripheral to but seriously impinges upon the world of newly published hardcover works of fiction, the chief concern of this annual essay, was the sudden expansion of the trade paperback business, so that trade paperbacks, including a great deal of recent fiction, were much in evidence in bookstores throughout the country. Both Vintage (Random House) and Penguin (Viking) came on the scene with extensive lines of serious contemporary fiction, including books from 1984 and some rediscoveries; and there were others, William Morrow's Quill Books, for example. Simultaneous with this rapid growth in the reprint market, there were new books which were successfully published in both hardcover and trade paperback editions, the most prominent example being Carolyn Chute's *The Beans of Egypt, Maine* which had only a modest sale in hardcover (Ticknor and Fields), but a large and successful sale in trade paperback (Houghton Mifflin). And, of course, many university presses, Louisiana State University for instance, have long brought out fiction simultaneously in both forms.

The flowering of the trade paperback is a significant change in the American literary scene with many implications for our fiction. Ironically, it is good news rising from the ashes of bad news. The bad news was that over the past decade the familiar mass-market paperback, routinely available in newsstands, in airports and bus and railroad stations, in drugstores and supermarkets, had all but turned away from fiction except the genres—suspense, Western, fantasy, romance—and the blockbusters of popular fiction. The mass market offered fewer books with the aim of selling more copies of fewer titles. Gradually, then, the goal of subsidiary paperback rights for publishers (and thus authors) of serious fiction had begun to seem unobtainable. Since almost all first novels and, indeed, most serious novels at any stage of a writer's career have depended on subsidiary rights to break even, things looked bad, in general, for serious fiction. Two things happened to change this precarious situation. First, the surge in the trade paperback business, with some apparent success—based, as it is,

on much smaller initial advances against royalties than the mass-market books, but, by the same token, offering writers and publishers at least *some* subsidiary income. Second, according to agents and others closely involved in the commerce of American publishing, in the world of popular fiction, the market for all but the extraordinary blockbuster, widely advertised and massively promoted, has dried up. Near misses have proved to be expensive disasters. The lesser luminaries of popular fiction now, in fact, sell no better than serious fiction. With what result? "Nowadays I regularly get calls from publishers asking me if I have any good *literary* novels available," a bemused agent told me. Some of these calls, she added, come from the new, emerging crowd of very young editors in American publishing, "the baby editors," as they are called. At least for the time being these new editors appear to be more committed to serious fiction than their predecessors. With all these changes in progress, both in fact and attitude, it is no wonder that 1985 proved to be an exciting and adventurous year in fiction.

It needs to be noted, however, that the separation, now really a divorce, between the best-sellers and the best books has never seemed quite so final. Of the ten best-selling works of fiction in hardcover in 1985, according to the list published in the *New York Times*, 6 January 1986, only two—John Irving's *The Cider House Rules* (Morrow) and James Michener's *Texas* (Random House)—had any overtly serious literary pretensions. Most of the rest, composed of works by the likes of Carl Sagan (*Contact,* Simon and Schuster), Sidney Sheldon (*If Tomorrow Comes,* Morrow), Jean M. Auel (*The Mammoth Hunters,* Crown), Stephen King (*Skeleton Crew,* Putnam), Danielle Steel (*Secrets* and *Family Album,* both published by Delacorte) are without more intention than solid commercial entertainment. There are two wonderful exceptions to all the rules (and an exception rate of twenty percent is likely to signal more than mere accident), books which are without pretensions and without most of the usual ingredients of major blockbuster fiction and are, therefore, surprising arrivals on a list of this

"Indeed there is no living American writer whose work I admire so much as Taylor's."
—**Jonathan Yardley**

"No one writing in English can do more with a short story...he is a master."
—**Geoffrey Wolff**, *Newsweek*

"His *Collected Stories* is one of the major works of our literature."
—**Joyce Carol Oates**

"One of the finest short story writers of our time."
—**Albert Griffith**, *Commonweal*

"I am tempted to say that Peter Taylor is the greatest living short story writer, but I shall be prudent and suggest he is the greatest one writing in English today."
—**Linda Kuehl**, *Saturday Review*

ISBN: 0-385-27983-3

PETER TAYLOR

The Old Forest
—*and Other Stories*

The Old Forest
and Other Stories
PETER TAYLOR

THE DIAL PRESS

Dust jacket for a book collecting stories of Southern domestic life during the 1930s and 1940s

kind. *The Hunt For Red October,* by Tom Clancy, a first novel and the first work of fiction ever published by the otherwise special-interest Naval Institute Press, was number six nationally and the number-one best-seller for the year in Washington, D.C. It was simply and accurately described by the *Washington Post* as "a technically accurate and finely developed thriller about a Soviet submarine commander who tries to defect." Experience has shown that only "thrillers" by established names, massively advertised and promoted (while *Red October* certainly was not) can make the best-sellers lists. In 1985 experience proved dead wrong in this case. Perhaps most astonishing of all, when one pauses to think about it, was the number-one best-seller in hardcover fiction for 1985, a book which has almost none of the conventional elements of the blockbuster—Garrison Keillor's *Lake Woebegon Days* (Viking). Based firmly on his radio show, "The Prairie Home Companion" on National Public Radio, it is a work of humor and nostalgia without

sentimentality or bias. The perhaps more cynical and sophisticated *New York Times Book Review* offers no real explanation for this extraordinary success, but the *Washington Post* touches on the subject: "Lake Woebegon may not be Everytown, but the events of its people are for everyone." It is too early to guess, but it may be that the whole publishing industry has been out of touch for years with the real interests and concerns of the potential American public for popular fiction.

1985 was a fine year, vintage really, for book publication of short fiction. The familiar annual anthologies—*The Best American Short Stories,* edited by Shannon Ravenel and (this year only) Gail Godwin, and *Prize Stories 1985: The O. Henry Awards,* as usual edited by William Abrahams, were both adventurous and excellent in their selections and, for once, just about equally divided between tried and true, safe choices and newer names and voices.

Both have (finally!) begun to try to represent what is truly happening in our short fiction by ranging far and wide among the multitude of small literary magazines searching for excellence and finding it often in a variety of places, from the *Missouri Review* to *Tendril*, from *Ploughshares* to the *Texas Review*. Clearly Abrahams and Ravenel/Godwin are still firmly committed to the care and preservation of the literary status quo (which, after all, includes themselves), but the evidence suggests that they are increasingly aware of other reputable points of view and, therefore, increasingly defensive—a generally healthy condition. Abrahams is more openly so, as he feels it necessary to protest that "excellence—transcending genre, theme, subject, and place of publication is decisive." Meanwhile Gail Godwin has included "a small confession of antipathies to give you a back room glimpse of the selection process, which, I believe, is as individual as the vagaries and the passions and the prejudices of each judge." A similar, somewhat defensive stance to justify the editorial process is taken by DeWitt Henry in his first-rate gathering of stories from *Ploughshares*—*The Ploughshares Reader: New Fiction for the Eighties,* when he insists: "The selection is my own; among possible bests, I have chosen, finally, according to my own vision, stories worthy of each other, stories that enlarge and strengthen the whole, stories that have withstood, compelled and grown with my re-reading and remain permanently new, and that suggest the mix of subjects, sensibilities, and the approaches characteristic of the magazine." The magazine has always been, by and large, conservative in a literary sense, though always trendy also, a situation which might seem paradoxical were it not for the fact that conservation is more a trend of these times than exploration and discovery. Nevertheless this gathering of thirty-three stories at the least proves that *Ploughshares* has attracted the best efforts of some of our very best and best-known story writers and has encouraged a few fine beginners. This was a year, also, for the reappearance of established masters of the short story. Among others, Alice Adams (*Return Trips,* Knopf), Hortense Calisher (*Saratoga Hot,* Doubleday), Italo Calvino (*Mr. Palomar,* Harcourt Brace Jovanovich/ Helen and Kurt Wolff), Penelope Gilliatt (*They Sleep Without Dreaming,* Dodd, Mead), Irvin Faust (*The Year of the Hot Jock and Other Stories,* Dutton), Mavis Gallant (*Home Truths,* Random House), Jack Matthews (*Crazy Women,* Johns Hopkins University Press), R. K. Narayan (*Under the Banyan Tree,* Viking), Grace Paley (*Later the Same Day,* Farrar, Straus and Giroux), Isaac Bashevis Singer (*The Im-*

age, Farrar, Straus and Giroux), and Marguerite Yourcenar (*Oriental Tales,* Farrar, Straus and Giroux) brought out impressive and well-received new collections. Meanwhile larger gatherings of new and selected stories came from Tennessee Williams (*Collected Stories,* New Directions) and Peter Taylor (*The Old Forest,* Doubleday); and additional books included *The Stories of Muriel Spark* (Dutton), *The Collected Stories of John O'Hara* (Random House), *The Collected Stories of William Humphrey* (Delacorte), George Garrett's *An Evening Performance* (Doubleday), and William Goyen's *Had I A Hundred Mouths* (Clarkson N. Potter). Most of these collections received excellent, widespread, and thorough review coverage; though, as is usual in the contemporary American scene, there were, even here, flagrant examples of whimsical injustice and consensual if not actually collusive negligence. For example, it was a great pleasure to his admirers, myself among them, to see Peter Taylor's *The Old Forest* receive well-deserved attention (though the reviewers' obsessive assertion that Taylor is almost "unknown" and thus to be "discovered" was, at the least, unfactual). But it was a bitter disappointment to his equally ardent admirers (myself, again, to be counted) that William Goyen's posthumous gathering did not gain much critical attention: lyrical, elegiac, humorous, and exalted, Goyen's stories are powerfully original, among the few and finest of our times. Yet not even an introduction by Joyce Carol Oates, a final interview by his literary executor, Reginald Gibbons, or the knowledge that with this volume all the known stories of Goyen have now been published (there is at least one unpublished novel in manuscript) could bring the books the sort of attention well earned by Goyen.

Second chances are as rare as unicorns in the story of modern and contemporary American letters. And yet there was in 1985 an unusual and unusually interesting exception to this fact—the reprinting, by Atlanta's Peachtree Press, of three out-of-print short story collections under one cover—*3 By 3: Masterworks of the Southern Gothic.* This volume offers *Beasts of The Southern Wild,* by Doris Betts (1973); *McAfee County,* by Mark Steadman (1971); and the much-honored first book by Shirley Ann Grau, *The Black Prince and Other Stories* (1955). (Grau's latest book, *Nine Women,* has just appeared as a 1986 offering from Knopf.) Although the emphasis on the "Gothic" is more gimmick than fact here, the book is of great interest and value; and from it Doris Betts emerges as one of the finest artists of the Southern story.

Among the masters it is worth calling attention to an oddity of the season, the discovery and publication of five short stories by Ernest Hemingway as a part of Peter Griffin's biography of the early Hemingway years—*Along With Youth* (Oxford University Press). There were impressive collections of stories from authors who, though not beginners by any means, are still in the early years of their careers. Among the very best of these is Charles Baxter's *Through The Safety Net* (Viking), eleven elegantly crafted and deeply moving stories whose greatest strength and interest is in Baxter's sympathetic depth of characterization. Baxter's first collection, published in 1984 by the University of Missouri Press, was winner of the Associated Writing Program's annual competition. Tobias Wolff, whose *The Barracks Thief* won a PEN/Faulkner Award for himself and Ecco Press, has moved to Houghton Mifflin for *Back In The World,* ten stories of post-Vietnam America which originally appeared in magazines ranging from *Ploughshares* to *Vanity Fair.* Wolff received considerable, if mixed, critical attention for this gathering, some reviewers detecting a falling off since his first collection, *In The Garden of the North American Martyrs* (Ecco). Barry Hannah, who has become a kind of literary cult figure, at least since the publication by Knopf of his first collection of stories, *Airships* (described by his publishers as "now-legendary"), was represented by the highly original *Captain Maximus* (Knopf), a gathering of seven openly autobiographical stories, highly literary, sophisticated, and eccentric, and the short novel *Power and Light,* previously published (1983) in book form by Palaemon Press and identified as "An Idea For Film." Hannah is like nobody else, baffling, sometimes simply amazing, afflicted with cuteness, and yet alive with, yes, power and light. Mary Morris, in *The Bus of Dreams* (Houghton Mifflin), tells her stories straightforwardly and clearly, yet with an unusually strongly evoked sense of place; *places,* rather, for the variety of realized settings—Greece, the Caribbean, Central America, and Europe, as well as Lake Michigan and Manhattan—is her most original characteristic. Variety in almost everything—form, setting, situation, tone of voice—dominates the second collection of short fiction by T. Coraghessan Boyle, *Greasy Lake and Other Stories* (Viking), a writer of great gifts and energy, accurately described by his publisher as "a master storyteller and a pyrotechnic stylist, able to switch gears from funky to Augustan with practiced ease and flair." Many of these stories are extremely funny, and at least one is a little masterpiece, "The Hector Quesadilla

Story," a tale which is a strong contender for the best baseball story of our time.

The year was also an excellent one for first collections. These appeared, as they have over the past few years, with a clear-cut demarcation between the kinds of writers and stories being introduced by the commercial publishers and those who have been brought out by university presses and small presses, both inside and outside the specific context of contests. My personal impression is that the university presses and small publishers offer a more representative sense of what interests both American writers and readers at this time, and that certainly these publishers offer a greater range and variety of form and content, vision and voice. Some of the best collections come from the university presses. From Pittsburgh University Press came (early and late in the year) two winners of the Drue Heinz Literature Prize—Randal Silvis and his *The Luckiest Man In The World,* and *The Man Who Loved Levittown* by W. D. Wetherell. Illinois University Press marked the tenth anniversary of its short story series with four good collections: *The Christmas Wife,* by Helen Norris; *Getting To Know The Weather,* by Pamela Painter; *Tentacles of Unreason,* by Joan Givner; and *Honeymoon,* by Merrill Joan Gerber. Missouri's Breakthrough Series produced three outstanding collections—Gerald Flaherty's *Filthy The Man,* Rod Kessler's *Off In Zimbabwe,* and the marvelously realized, precisely crafted stories of Mary Peterson in *Mercy Flights.* From Louisiana State University, which busily publishes both novels and stories, there was Lou A. Crabtree's *Sweet Hollow.* And under the guidance of story writer Charles East and the judgeship of George Garrett, the University of Georgia Press came forward with four winners of the Flannery O'Conner Award for Short Fiction. These were *Why Men Are Afraid of Women,* by François Camoin; *Living With Snakes,* by Daniel Curley (neither of these *first* collections); *Rough Translations,* by Molly Giles; and best of all the batch, in the opinion of the final judge, Mary Hood's *How Far She Went,* stories mostly concerned with country people in the contemporary South (and mostly previously published in the *Georgia Review*), with one of them, "Lonesome Road Blues," perhaps the finest American story dealing with the country music scene. Mary Hood has been "discovered" by Ticknor and Fields, who will publish her next collection late in 1986. From the small presses there was a multitude of story collections of every kind and form and of various quality. Among the best of those that I have seen are *Pictures Moving,* by James Thomas (Dragon Gate); *All*

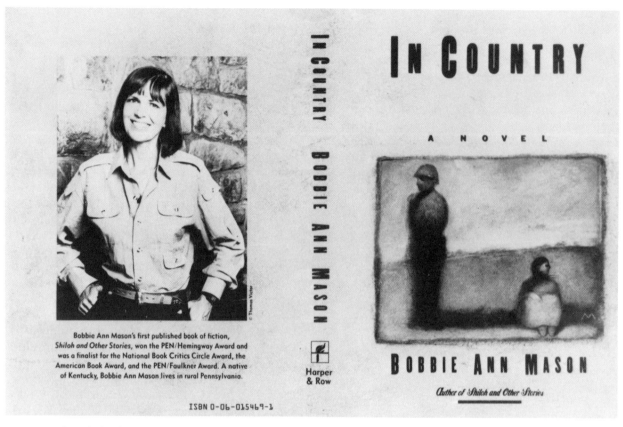

Dust jacket for the first novel by a Kentucky author whose short stories have appeared in the New Yorker

Set About With Fever Trees, by Pam Durban (Godine); and Jascha Kessler's cockamamy retailing of our irrepressible consciousness of classical myths in *Classical Illusions* (McPherson).

Better known by far, because more often and more widely reviewed and rewarded with prizes and recognition, more often extravagantly blurbed, and more likely to be picked up for reprinting in trade paperback editions, are the first collections from the commercial publishers. By and large these stories are apt to be a little more fashionable and trendy (the basic trend remains a slick, enigmatic kind of minimalism), often de-emphasize variety in favor of some sort of apparent unity or uniformity; and more often than not (though somewhat less than earlier) the stories have appeared, individually, more in commercial than literary magazines. Still, some excellent collections emerged from this limited area. *Mr. and Mrs. Baby* (Knopf), by Mark Strand, is basically silly fun and games at the expense of silly-putty characters. But Strand is a poet of considerable reputation, and the language and imagination are uniformly lively. Lorrie Moore's *Self-Help* (Knopf) offers oddly mov-

ing stories of women of the times in language and forms at once clever and cool; though this book seems more injured than aided by the insistence on improvising throughout in the idea of self-help manuals with titles like "How To Be An Other Woman," "How to Talk to Your Mother (Notes)," and "How to Become a Writer." The excellent stories in *Easy In The Islands* (Crown), by Bob Shacochis, which has already won him the American Book Award for the best first book of 1985, are neatly and successfully united by their exclusive concern with the wild life and times (". . . nothing made sense, unless you were a mystic or a politician, or studied both with ambition") of the Caribbean islands, a crazy clash of cultures and assumptions, of old virtues. Frank Conroy's slender volume (eight stories, 149 pages) *Midair* has the unity of an autobiographical mode, which is not surprising since his other book, a minor American classic, *Stop-Time,* was de facto autobiography. His stories are marked by clarity and depth of characterization, by an unsentimental compassion for others and himself. They are neither minimal nor fantastic. The publisher's (Dutton/Seymour Lawrence) note

Elizabeth Tallent in Kensington Gardens, London, May 1985 (©Allan Titmuss)

on "a common thread"—"a man's growing aware-ness of the world around himself and his increasing engagement with the world"—is unjustly vague. And the rich plethora of heartfelt blurbs by Jayne Anne Phillips, Robert Stone, Thomas McGuane, Tobias Wolff, Doris Grumbach, Joan Williams, and Geoffrey Wolff, though it may win the Blurb Prize for 1985, is entirely unnecessary, though perhaps not entirely surprising since Conroy is director of the literature program of the National Endowment for the Arts. In any case, his stories are distin-guished enough to stand on their own.

The three best first collections coming from the commercial publishers in 1985 are, in my judg-ment, Sharon Sheehe Stark's *The Dealer's Yard* (Morrow), James Robison's *Rumor* (Summit), and Amy Hempel's *Reasons To Live* (Knopf). Stark's and Robison's books, came, like *Midair*, heavily bur-dened with their almost irrelevant camouflage of big-time blurbs. Is this blatant, hardsell hustling a sign that the big-city publishing houses are some-what on the defensive, feeling vaguely threatened by all that uncontrolled literary activity going on out there in the provinces, with or without their imprimatur? Or does it, more likely, indicate that in the clamor and constant struggle for attention

on all sides, even (perhaps especially) the best new work may be lost to us without benefit of some extraordinary sorts of promotion and support? James Robison is frankly described by his publisher as "one of the brilliant young *New Yorker* writers"; and, indeed, only one of the stories in his collection previously appeared in any other magazine. Lean rather than minimal, evocative rather than smart, yet polished to a high gloss, precisely fashionable and nevertheless often deeply moving, Robison's stories present the very best that that famous mag-azine has to offer these days. Like all *New Yorker* writers, past and present, he is a superbly gifted and strictly limited artist. Somewhat less intense, but at once more various and original, is *The Dealer's Yard*. Stark has style, depth of perception and char-acterization, and a brilliantly authoritative bravado in these stories of modern-day rural Pennsylva-nia—all of which, by the way, appeared first in literary magazines. But it is her credible voice which is the source of her striking originality, what her publisher correctly describes as "her ability to dash and dance among these phenomena in an entirely unique way." Equally original in style, form, and content are the sad/funny, brief stories in Amy Hempel's *Reasons To Live*. Though deliberately flat, almost casual in tone, these are the creations of a stylist of the first order, and her stories have the mysterious impact of poems without looking or sounding like poems at all. Fashionably nihilistic in context, each of these stories overcomes its own presuppositions, not cheating with "happy endings," but gracefully arriving at resonance and meaning. Hempel catches the eye and could well develop into a major talent.

Even in a good year for serious short fiction it is, finally, the novel that is the infantry for the art of fiction. Fiction wins or loses, rises or falls in concordance with the health and welfare of the novel. It was a busy year for the serious novelists. The *New York Times Book Review* lists 50 novels in its "Christmas '85" annotated list of 200 notable books of all kinds for the year. These include new novels by writers like Anne Tyler, Ursula K. Le Guin, John Hersey, William Gaddis, John Irving, Russell Banks, Elie Wiesel, Gail Godwin, Kurt Vonnegut, Elmore Leonard, Doris Lessing, Lore Segal, Louis Auchincloss, Anita Brookner, Bobbie Ann Mason, Larry McMurtry, Ann Beattie, Marguerite Duras, John Fowles, Benedict Kiely, Carlos Fuentes, Joyce Carol Oates, Stanley Elkin, Don DeLillo, E. L. Doctorow, and Philip Roth. An impressive list of established talent, and all the more so when one notes that there were many more serious novels by known writers which, for one reason and another, did not manage to make this list. None of the books on the list can be called exactly surprising, since each was, to a greater or lesser degree, heralded, promoted, and predestined as potentially "notable" if not necessarily a best-seller. In the rough and tumble of the marketplace—judging, as one must, by the guesswork of public sales figures and by the extent and nature of the review coverage nationwide—some of these have done very well, others less well than might be expected. Yet even though all the preliminaries of advance attention must be executed, the fate of a given book, at the hands of reviewers at least, is not fully controllable. Serious fiction frankly depends upon reviews to have its day in the marketplace.

The list itself (and never mind, for a moment, significant works which did not earn a place on the list), offers classic examples of the eccentricities of fate. Three books given major promotion and attention, evidently in about equal measure, were Don DeLillo's *White Noise* (Viking), William Gaddis's *Carpenter's Gothic* (Viking) and John Hawkes's

Adventures In The Alaskan Skin Trade (Simon and Schuster). All these writers are mature and recognized serious novelists whose time, it was felt generally, had arrived. *White Noise* received skillful promotion and widespread, favorable reviews. Apparently its sales were modest, but the book hung on for a time and has received the American Book Award For Fiction given in 1986 for books published in 1985. Since it was already available only in paperback edition, it was Penguin which advertised the book's award in the *New York Times Book Review* (12 January 1986). Gaddis's book, his third novel in a thirty-year period, and, as well, the author himself, received a very heavy dose of deferential attention on a national level. Interviews and reviews stressed the gritty integrity of the author and praised *Carpenter's Gothic* as his most "accessible" work to date. And it may yet win some of the prizes; certainly Gaddis is eligible and due. But, once again, there proved to be a very small audience for this writer, touted in the *Times* as "mazily and mercilessly adroit." Maybe "adroit" is not quite enough. Certainly John Hawkes came on the scene this year with a reputation as one of the most brilliantly adroit novelists of his generation. Published by a major commercial house, with full fanfare and full-scale promotional activity (this for the first time in Hawkes's distinguished career), the book received mixed reviews, had modest sales, did not (as alert readers will have noticed) find Hawkes's usual place on the *Times* list of notable books. It is beginning to seem, after all this time, ten novels, and extensive critical attention at all levels, that the fiction of John Hawkes is a hard case. Year after year readers are told of its merits and virtues. Year after year readers look elsewhere for delight and instruction. All three of the novels just mentioned speak for the disaffected Left, are politically based on the solid-rock intellectual assumptions of the 1960s; but DeLillo's book, though a satirical attack on the outward and visible and inward and spiritual pollution of the 1980s, is grotesquely funny and summons up (safely) the Nazis as the real heavies. It may be that Gaddis and Hawkes are more out of touch with and contemptuous of an America that has twice elected Ronald Reagan its president. Equally a strong supporter of the Left and a more active public campaigner against the sins of America is E. L. Doctorow, who, in *World's Fair*, has turned back to the great New York World's Fair of 1939-1940 and to a memoir of his own boyhood. It is a book which is rich with nostalgia and, without question, "accessible" (except, perhaps, for his usual hybrid mixture of fact and fiction). *World's*

Fair (Random House) has held a place on the *Times* best-seller list for some months.

Among the excellent novels by women on the list are three which were given the full treatment with slightly different results. This was to be Anne Tyler's year, and in a sense it was that, as *The Accidental Tourist* (Knopf), her gracefully crafted, funny, and devastatingly accurate study of love and social class in contemporary Baltimore, won a wide reading audience and received uniformly excellent and thorough reviews. Her characters, no matter how determinedly eccentric, are always worth knowing, and she treats them honorably. And very few writers have created a really fine dog like the utterly unmanageable Welsh Corgi Edward. Ann Beattie's *Love Always* (Random House), which seemed to me her finest work to date, is a comedy with plenty of laughter of all kinds, at all levels of being, and plenty of satirical bite also. (" 'The enlightenment of women can allow for a new radiance in our society. Pectoral power, not penis envy,' the woman said, hitting the counter. 'I would suggest that in place of those Debbie Harry and Annie Lennox stills, you hang pictures of women such as Margaret Bourke-White and Dr. Helen Caldicott.' ") *Love Always* earned mixed reviews; some reviewers missed the humor of it, something which is increasingly a problem for American writers in comic modes. Readers may not have any trouble knowing when to laugh and when to cry, but reviewers are often unsure and, typically, anxious not to be caught doing the wrong thing. Few books in 1985, or in any year, have received the kind of respectful public attention which greeted the arrival of Bobbie Ann Mason's first novel, *In Country* (Harper and Row), a *very* contemporary American story of a teenage girl named Sam Hughes, of Hopewell, Kentucky, whose father was killed in Vietnam before she was born. All the virtues of Mason's much-praised collection of stories, *Shiloh* (Harper and Row), are present, as is her established scholarly expertise in the finer points of popular culture—the brand names, pop tunes and TV allusions are always right on the money, if sometimes a little mechanical. But this novel, in the end, evoked a very mixed reaction. Something about the subject, the search now for the meaning of the Vietnam experience, perhaps. Certainly some intellectuals among the reviewers found it somewhat *obvious*, maybe lacking experience, themselves, in any place like Hopewell, Kentucky. By the same token, many American readers might find both the assumptions and conclusions of the book to be, still, debatable. Certainly, all intellectual and media protestation to

the contrary, we have not yet arrived at any consensus concerning the 1960s and the Vietnam years. It may be that the subject is still too close and too politicized to be successfully captured in fiction. Another problem faced by Mason was the reaction of some reviewers that she is too condescending and superior to her characters. That, like humor, is a difficult and almost wholly subjective judgment; but, true or false, it is a risk that Bobbie Ann Mason runs with her particular kind of rhetorical stance—all knowing and yet somehow, herself, aloof from all these people and their problems.

A notable book which, it seems to me, was doomed by an odd combination of honorable respect and condescension on the part of the literary journalists was John Hersey's huge accounting of the life of an American missionary in China, *The Call* (Knopf). Somehow they made it sound dull and even pedantic. I found it one of Hersey's most adventurous works, boldly mixing fact and fiction to get at truth and even mixing letters and journals with straight narrative. I also found its picture of life in China during the 1930s and World War II to be compelling and fascinating. I can only conclude that its size went against it—reviewers have busy schedules and limited time for reading fat books—and that the subject of the life of a *missionary* was less interesting to intellectuals than to the general reading public.

Three best-selling novels on the notable list, each by a serious writer of real reputation, seem instructive in a different way. Kurt Vonnegut's *Galápagos* (Seymour Lawrence/Delacorte) seems a fairly thin experience, certainly not one of his most successful novels, though at least much of its method and manner are typical. It is, of course, entirely honorable; but it is hard to imagine how and why it is a best-seller except that Vonnegut has at last become a kind of public figure and, to an extent, a household name. John Irving has likewise become a kind of public figure, known beyond the boundaries of literature, ever since *Garp* with its T-shirts and bumper stickers. Reviews for his latest novel, *The Cider House Rules* (Morrow), were overwhelmingly favorable; yet it seems at best archly contrived, historically anachronistic, trendy and "relevant" in the worst sense of both words, and crudely overwritten. Larry McMurtry's large novel *Lonesome Dove* (Simon and Schuster), which has sold very well though to a mixed reception, seems to be a masterpiece and surely the finest work yet created by the gifted McMurtry, a splendidly written, wonderfully vital recreation of the Old West which is at once authentic enough and original enough so

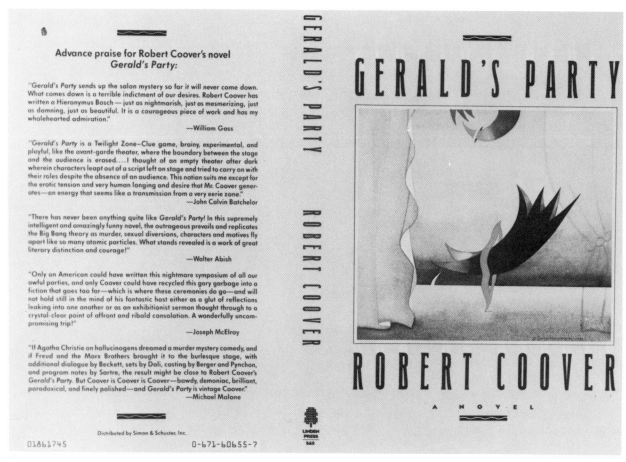

Dust jacket for Coover's new novel, which, according to his publisher, is "part murder mystery, part British parlor drama, part meditation on the nature of Time, Theater . . . and Love . . ."

that you can feel and perceive how the myths of the West came to be and what are the truths behind them. In its own way, and at the other end of the time scale, it is as important a book to the literature of the West as was Owen Wister's *The Virginian* many years ago. It is hard to believe that there was a better novel of any kind published in 1985.

Of the relative newcomers on the list two seem worthy first novels—T. R. Pearson's beautiful *A Short History of a Small Place* (Linden) and Elizabeth Benedict's *Slow Dancing* (Knopf). Two—Denis Johnson's *Fiskadoro* (Knopf) and Brad Leithauser's *Equal Distance* (Knopf)—seem at once derivative and greatly overrated. Johnson's book, though full of admirable assumptions and right ideas, is a latecomer to the after-the-nuclear-war literature. Leithauser's story is described on the dust jacket as "an update of Hemingway's 'Sun Also Rises,'" set in modern Japan. Trying to imitate Hemingway, poet Leithauser is out of his league. Carolyn Chute's *The Beans of Egypt, Maine* (Ticknor and

Fields) is like no other novel past or present, unless it shares a little bit with the early Erskine Caldwell who also wrote about poverty-ridden and unvanquished rural people. Chute's book was deservedly a huge success for a first novel, though as much for sociological reasons as for literary ones. Two other novels by newcomers are quite marvelous, delightful surprises in any year, for any list. Elizabeth Tallent's first novel, *Museum Pieces* (she had already published a fine collection of stories, *In Constant Flight,* and a critical study of John Updike), has many obvious virtues. Her publisher, Knopf, celebrates her "unfailing generosity toward her characters, a precise depiction of complicated emotions, a sensual evocation of the American Southwest." All true. Add to these a luminous, graceful, unself-consciously beautiful sense of style in which each sentence sings and dances without effort and with natural grace, and you have a writer who will surely give us much more. Madison Smartt Bell's *Waiting For The End Of The World* (Ticknor and

246

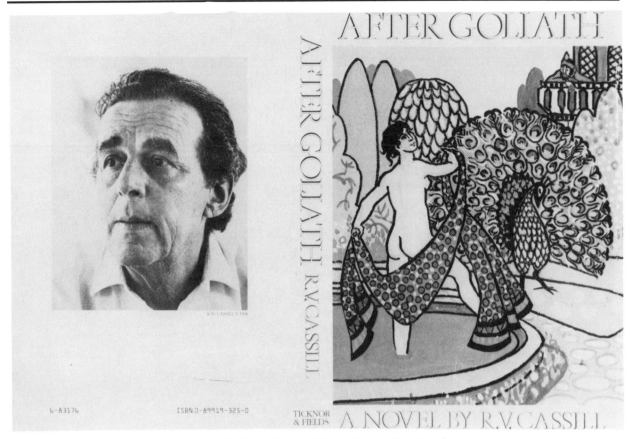

Dust jacket for R. V. Cassill's novel about King David

Fields), followed hard on the heels of his successful *The Washington Square Ensemble* (1984). The new novel is a story of five terrorists with an apocalyptic scheme for New York City which seems altogether reasonable and possible. A taut plot line, memorable characters, and an energetic, admirable prose style serve to make this an outstanding novel and, taken together with his first book, the sign of a major novelistic talent.

On the vague borderline where popular and serious literature meet and sometimes merge, 1985 could well be remembered as the year of Elmore Leonard. Leonard has been around for years, mainly writing Westerns and, more recently, thrillers set in and around his hometown, Detroit, and sometimes Florida. These books have been, and continue to be, very successful as mass-market paperbacks, and some have been made into movies. This year Arbor House bought out Leonard's latest, *Glitz*, to the tune of a massive and somewhat unusual advertising campaign (for example, full-page ads in the regular news section of the daily *New York Times*) and an adroitly orchestrated campaign of publicity, interviews, and profiles, which in turn resulted in high-visibility reviews. (None of this campaign was or is furtive; for, as if part of a second wave, there was a series of articles in a variety of business publications and in the business sections of newspapers, describing the ways and means of selling *Glitz* and Leonard to the public.) *Glitz* found a firm niche on the best-seller lists for several months. Perhaps not Leonard's best thriller, it is nevertheless a fine, polished, altogether professional job, with plenty of action and lively, memorable dialogue, and the introduction of a new and interesting detective to his gallery of good and bad cops—Lieutenant Vincent Mora of Miami. Less successful than *Glitz* at the marketplace, though both writers have been there before, were John D. MacDonald's latest Travis McGee novel, *The Lonely Silver Rain* (Knopf) and George V. Higgins's *Penance for Jerry Kennedy* (Knopf). The latter is much less a thriller than a gritty, often witty novel of Jerry Kennedy, a Boston criminal lawyer who hustles hard for the almighty dollar in a very different world than the high-priced, high-toned attorneys-at-law in 1985's other major novel of the legal world—Louis Auchincloss's highly regarded *Hon-*

orable Men (Houghton Mifflin), which in its own way is more a social history of the Vietnam War and its impact on the moral fabric of American society. Finely wrought, elegant and ironic, it has all the virtues of serious fiction except perhaps the pure entertainment factor. This may be more a matter of the choice of protagonist than anything else. Chip Benedict—"the perfect corporate executive": forward looking, ambitious, lauded in *Fortune* and *Forbes*—just does not have the juice that Jerry Kennedy does.

Arriving so late in the year that the book was not physically available in provincial bookstores until well into January 1986, Robert Coover's new novel, *Gerald's Party,* his first full-size fiction since *The Public Burning* (1977), has already received major national review attention and serious critical consideration. Not surprisingly, the book is a kind of grotesque literary send-up of the salon mystery, perhaps best described by Michael Malone, with as much accuracy as wit: "If Agatha Christie on hallucinogens dreamed a murder mystery comedy, and if Freud and the Marx Brothers brought it to the burlesque stage, with additional dialogue by Beckett, sets by Dali, casting by Berger and Pynchon, and program notes by Sartre, the result might be close to Robert Coover's *Gerald's Party*." Coover's fans (not a few) ought to be delighted. And the disadvantages of a very late 1985 publication are offset, as was the case with Don DeLillo's *White Noise* last year, by the fact that the book thus becomes eligible for prizes in *both* years, at least doubling the odds of prizes and awards. This is a truth Coover, who has served as a judge himself for national awards, would have to be fully aware of.

Beyond the limits of official lists and the quick-claim precincts of end-of-the-year summings-up (including, alas and inevitably, this one) there are a great number of novels which, moderately successful or mildly unsuccessful, the work of well-known or little-known writers, new or old, stand up strongly in the personal experience of the critic-reviewer. Some of these are as good in quality as anything on any list of notables. Some are better. And because the life of a book perhaps in reprint and certainly in the more or less timeless quiet of libraries is more than a season, it is not only worthwhile but also a kind of bounden duty for me to end with some sort of listing and acknowledgement of other novels of 1985 which (for a wild variety of reasons and impulses) have demanded and kept my attention. Here then is an alphabetical listing of these:

John Calvin Batchelor, *American Falls* (Norton). A highly imaginative Civil War spy novel, plotted on a large scale and told in an authoritative, quasi-documentary manner.

Anita Brookner, *Family And Friends* (Pantheon). Her *Hotel Du Lac,* published earlier in the year, received much attention and found a place on the honor lists. This one, coming late, is slightly different from her other work by dint of its autobiographical parallels and implications, though it, too, is high style in its cool abstraction.

Anthony Burgess, *The Kingdom Of The Wicked* (Arbor House). Burgess, always energetic and entertaining, here turns his eccentric attention to the coming of Christianity to decadent Rome, telling a tale which his principal narrator, Sadoc, advertises to be composed of (among other things): "pork-eating, lechery, adultery, bigamy, sodomy, bestiality, the most ingenious variety of cruelty, assassination, the worship of false gods and the sin of being uncircumcised."

Janet Burroway, *Opening Nights* (Atheneum). A complex, yet brilliantly accessible story of two interesting women who have been married to the same man, a theater director. Intelligent and up-to-date in its depiction of the high and low worlds of show biz and academe.

Fred Chappell, *I Am One of You Forever* (Louisiana State University Press). Another outstanding novel coming from a university press, this one the fifth novel by a poet (he won the Bollingen Prize for 1985) and story writer of great distinction. Linked chapters, almost as separate and independent as stories, tell eloquently and simply of a young boy growing up in the Carolina mountains in the years around World War II.

R. V. Cassill, *After Goliath* (Ticknor and Fields). The daring truth about this one is that it comes out only a few months after Joseph Heller's very similar *God Knows* (Knopf, 1984). The sad truth is that it is a much better novel than Heller's, a superior and satirically anachronistic version of the life of King David and the lives of his kith and kin. Perhaps the finest character is Joab, every bit as modern as Moshe Dayan or Menachem Begin and cut from some of the same cloth. Brilliant satire by one of our most gifted professionals.

Bret Easton Ellis, *Less Than Zero* (Simon and Schuster). The other end of the scale—bright tour de force by a talented beginner. In the form of a "what I did over Christmas vacation" memoir he tells the story of a too-rich, too-bored generation of teenagers in Los Angeles. Grownups were apparently shocked by all the "sex, drugs, and disaffection." They were supposed to be. It is, as his former teacher, novelist Nicholas Delbranco, has written, "a memorable debut."

Garrett Epps, *The Floating Island* (Houghton Mifflin). A very funny and, at times, savagely accurate satire of contemporary life in Washington, D. C., written by a former *Washington Post* reporter. His first novel, *The Shad Treatment,* is considered the definitive treatment of modern Virginia politics.

Francine du Plessix Gray, *October Blood* (Simon and Schuster). Gray's fifth book is high comedy dealing with the odd little world of high fashion. It took a beating from the major reviewers who didn't seem to get the joke. Too bad. Much fun and games.

William Holinger, *The Fence Walker* (State University of New York Press). Winner of the Associated Writing Program's novel contest, *The Fence Walker* is a story of uneasy Korea during the Vietnam War. National Public Radio critic Alan Cheuse has hailed this as worthy of comparison with William Styron's *The Long March* and James Jones's *The Pistol.*

Edmund Keeley, *A Wilderness Called Peace* (Simon and Schuster). A wonderfully realized story which somehow got lost to the larger audience. This novel, by a man who knows it inside out, is perhaps the definitive piece of American writing about the history and honor of contemporary Cambodia.

Brian Moore, *Black Robe* (Dutton). A powerful and moving story of a Jesuit priest in the wilderness of seventeenth century Canada, told with consummate skill by one of the finest of living novelists in the language. This one was, I think, misread and misunderstood by many reviewers who began by being unsympathetic to the subject. Certainly Moore's finest work to date.

Richard Powers, *Three Farmers On Their Way To A Dance* (Morrow). Virtuoso first novel, an almost wholly original concept and construct, effectively bringing together three distinct stories, two from our times and one from early 1914, to tell the century's sad story in human terms.

Kit Reed, *Fort Privilege* (Doubleday). This is novel number ten by an extravagantly gifted writer who is inexcusably too little known. Here the story is the decline and fall of the Big Apple on the occasion of a festive celebration by "the last of New York's rich and famous."

Nicholas Rinaldi, *Bridge Fall Down* (St. Martin's). Wildly imaginative caper novel by a young poet. The caper is a covert action in a nameless and

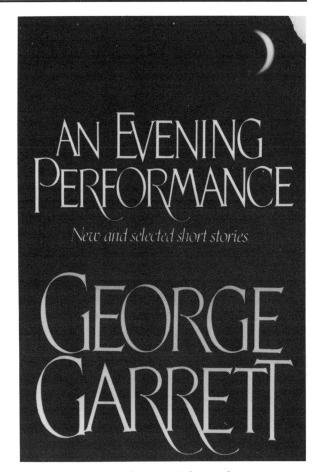

Dust jacket for Garrett's latest volume

hostile Third World country. A regular zoo of eccentric characters and unusual, provocative events.

May Sarton, *The Magnificent Spinster* (Norton). A strong, gracefully executed traditional novel, with autobiographical shadows, dealing with the fifty-year friendship of two women who are so realized as characters that we feel they have really lived and we have known them. The eighteenth novel of one of our major writers, for whom full honors are still due.

Lee Smith, *Family Linen* (Putnam's). Best and richest work so far by the greatly gifted and productive Smith. She has already proved herself in five good novels and an outstanding story collection *(Cakewalk).* Here she combines murder story with rowdy Southern comedy to explore some of the mysteries of family. It all works like a charm.

Robert Taylor, Jr., *Fiddle and Bow* (Algonquin). Another top-flight novel from a new small press which has already earned a good name for its quality fiction. Story-writer Taylor's account of the history of a large Southern family, his own in fact, is doubly interesting since he is the nephew of the distinguished writer Peter Taylor, who has made much memorable fiction from the same family, seen from a slightly different angle.

To arrive at an ending I should like to call attention to a book of the year which many readers, perhaps most, may not have heard of: *William Styron's Lie Down in Darkness: A Screenplay By Richard Yates* (Ploughshares). Both Styron and Yates are leading American novelists, and to have them together in this form is of great interest, especially since Yates's screenplay, often wondered about by those in the know, is available for the first time. Here is yet another example of the special kind of contribution which has been made by the small press at this time.

OBITUARIES

Heinrich Böll

(21 December 1917-16 July 1985)

Robert C. Conard
University of Dayton

If not for aesthetic reasons, then at least for ethical ones, many people thought on 16 July 1985 that Germany had lost its most important living writer. The press in Germany and around the world mourned the death of "the conscience of the nation." More obituaries spoke of Böll the moralist than of Böll the writer, the man who just thirteen years before had received the Nobel Prize for literature. Whereas the quality of Böll's life may have been easy to assess, the quality of his work has been more difficult to judge. He was a short story writer, novelist, poet, essayist, public speaker, dramatist, film author, and the man who refined the simple interview and journalistic dialogue to an art form; but he was foremost a satirist. In his writing, whatever the genre, his satiric talent dominated.

Since the satirist is always a moralist, it comes as no surprise that Böll's work was associated with the religious-humanist positions he took as a conscientious citizen of a democratic society. That he managed to be a popular writer and an intellectual with a message at the same time, that through his work he spoke to readers in the West and the East, in the first world as well as the third, made Böll a literary phenomenon like no other writer of this century. While he experimented from work to work with time, narrative perspective, and form, even creating the dramatic novel (a novel in play form) with his last work—published shortly after his death—his works were never written for a literate elite, but for the average reader. He directed his writing to the conscience of the ordinary person of goodwill. These readers recognized that in Böll they had an author concerned with their problems.

Since in his personal life he took the same moral positions as in his work, it is difficult to say whether his person or his writing was more influential. Perhaps it is accurate to say that while he lived the two were one, his life and work a single achievement.

Böll's place in German letters and in world literature will surely change with time, but in the future his place is likely to be more, rather than less, secure. Some of his novels were poorly re-

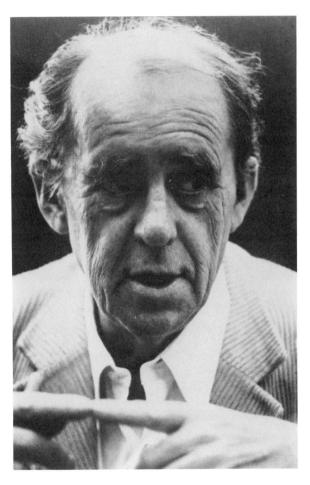

Heinrich Böll

ceived by critics, but his short stories were almost universally acclaimed, and some of his satires, because of their Swiftian brilliance and ethical relevance, have already acquired the status of masterpieces.

Because it is generally known that Böll's work took a clear position for humanity and against injustice, it is important to explain how this general statement expressed itself in particulars. He was against war, militarism, and all hypocrisy in politics, religion, and human relations. He excoriated the opportunism of Nazis who became overnight democrats after 1945, and he refused to let Germans forget their recent past. He railed against the Catholic church, of which he was a member, for its cooperation in German rearmament and its role in the restoration of German capitalism. He pointed out repeatedly in the 1950s and 1960s the dangers of the cold war. In the 1960s and 1970s he supported Willy Brandt's *Ostpolitik* and campaigned for him in the 1972 election. In the 1980s his practical idealism led him to support the newly formed Green party. He was consistently active in the peace movement throughout the postwar era and in the 1980s demonstrated against the deployment of Pershing II and cruise missiles on German soil.

Equally clear was what he stood for: democratic socialism with its inherent respect for people, especially the "little people" of the world who are often without a spokesman or advocate. Böll's work, however, never failed to criticize the politics of the Left when practicing socialism showed disregard for the rights of ordinary people, dissidents, and writers, as in the Soviet Union, Poland, or Czechoslovakia. Still, he never disguised his social ideal: a utopian Christian-Marxism. Although he was no Communist, he dreamed, as he once said to Heinz Ludwig Arnold, of a "profitless, classless society," and he argued persuasively through his characters for a gentle, natural, undogmatic socialism based on enduring religious-humanistic principles.

As with few other artists, the discussion of his life and work went together. The ideals Böll advocated in public, on radio or TV, he put into his novels, stories, plays, and poetry, as well as practiced in his private life. Because he said he preferred to write for his own age instead of for posterity, and because he always insisted, as he stated most clearly in his 1983 speech in acceptance of honorary citizenship of the city of Cologne, that "articles, reviews, and speeches are literature too," it is not surprising that essays represent about half of his oeuvre. Böll lived what he wrote and wrote what he lived. He intended with his work, as he stated in his lectures on aesthetics at the University of Frankfurt, to construct with his writing "an inhabitable language in an inhabitable land." Thus, to comprehend his importance as a writer, his life and his work must be taken as a whole.

Christian Linder argues correctly in the article "Seine Kindheit war seine Heimat" ("His Childhood Was His Home" —*Bösenblatt*, 23 July 1985) that to understand Böll it is necessary to understand his youth. Böll was born during World War I and claimed his earliest memory was of being held in his mother's arms while he looked out their apartment window to see Hindenburg's defeated army march through Cologne. That would have been in 1919. By 1923 the inflation caused by Germany's defeat ravaged the German population worse than the war had done. Böll remembered his father, a master furniture maker, going to the bank to get money in a cart to pay the employees in the family workshop. The money had to be spent immediately because it would be without purchasing power the next day. Böll never forgot the misery brought to his family, friends, and neighbors by the inflation of the 1920s. The stock market crash of 1929 brought the Depression and the unemployment of the 1930s which caused even more economic suffering than the inflation of the 1920s. The economic uncertainty of that period also helped fire the flames of hatred in the recently formed National Socialist party, and Böll witnessed the first Nazi marches through the streets of Cologne and saw how the Nazi terror made the once peaceful streets unsafe for ordinary citizens.

His family, like everyone else he knew, lost what financial security they had and with it their faith in an economic-political system that had failed twice in a decade. The fear of social turmoil became part of the traumatized psyche of every German. Economic insecurity, the concern for the next meal and a place to stay became the daily worry of a generation. To survive these times when hard work and the skill of Böll's father, a master craftsman, were not enough, the Bölls had to rely on family solidarity, mutual help, and religious faith for survival.

Although the setting for Böll's stories became Germany after World War II, in essence, it is the experience of these earlier times and variations of these formative experiences that determined his oeuvre. The simple security of love, the values of food and drink, the luxury of a cigarette (things often taken for granted in an affluent world, especially in Germany of the economic miracle) pervade his work. These existential values stand in stark contrast to the commercial virtues of the modern world of industrial plenty and provide a stable standard of humanity in times of surfeit consumption determined by the advertising media. Never far from the surface of Böll's stories is his distrust of prosperity because he knew that wealth could disappear overnight and that it was often the enemy of familial cohesiveness and of social unity when it began to divide people into haves and have-nots.

The Bölls themselves survived the 1920s, 1930s, and the war of the 1940s by never loosening the bonds that held them together. This familial model—this strategy for survival, one might call it—forms the essence of Böll's work. Whether his characters are the working poor not knowing where money for rent and food will come from, or whether his characters are the rich without financial worry facing the troubles of affluence, the solution for their problems lies in the maintenance of family ties.

This solution may seem simplistic, naive, or sentimental, and all these objections have been raised against Böll's work, but the power of his prose, the realism of his situations, the moral imperative in his writing triumph over these voiced shortcomings. Because Böll's work tries to preserve traditional human values within the person, family, neighborhood, and society, because he was suspicious of progress, technology, and prosperity, fearful of all power over others that resulted from wealth and position, Böll the leftist can be called a conservative writer.

Böll acknowledged this tendency in his work to maintain lost values. Speaking of his hope for Germany after 1945, he revealed in a different context what has been said above: "If I am conservative, and I tend to accept that judgement, not just as author, but also as a contemporary, then it is because I wish to conserve, if possible, that which held more or less all Germans together in 1945, the feeling of liberation, the hope for a new state with a new communality after the common suffering of the fascist period which was a terror system, an absolute 12 years of permanent terror—which, however, we don't like to admit. And 1945 was the liberation from this terror. And I conserve permanently within myself, if I can use this expression, the moment of this liberation. I live from it; my whole life, my family life, my work, all live from it. In this sense I am a conservative." This kind of conservatism confers on Böll's work a utopian dimension which manifests itself in his use of multiple variations of simple symbols and elemental themes, and his treatment of contemporary political and moral problems.

In 1937, when Böll completed his secondary education, he went to Bonn to begin an apprenticeship to a book dealer. But his training was interrupted during the winter of 1938-1939 by induction into the labor service. After completion of this semi-military obligation, he enrolled briefly as a student at the University of Cologne where he intended to study philology. But even before he could really call himself a student, three months before the Second World War started, he was

drafted into the *Wehrmacht*. In the course of the next six years he served as an infantryman on the Western front in France and on the Eastern front in Russia and in other Eastern European countries as the *Wehrmacht* retreated before the Red Army. In these six years Böll was wounded four times and reached the rank of corporal. Although it was customary for soldiers with his education to be officers, his hatred of war and army life prevented him from cooperation with the military. At the risk of court-martial and summary execution, he frequently forged papers to see his family or, after his marriage to Annemarie Cech in 1942, to visit his wife in the Rhineland. In April of 1945 Böll was taken prisoner by American troops and interned in allied POW camps until September of 1945. After his release, he immediately returned to Cologne, a city which lay eighty percent in ruins, to begin his life as a writer. Böll knew from the age of seventeen that writing was all he wanted to do. As a young man before the war he wrote novels and poems, but all of these early writings were destroyed in the bombing of Cologne.

The existential conditions for Böll, as for many Germans, when he returned home were reminiscent of the struggle for food and shelter after World War I; only now it was not just the problem of earning money for rent but finding an apartment still standing, not just buying food but finding food at all, not just paying for heat but finding fuel of any kind. In these first years after the war, Böll's wife earned most of the family income as a teacher of English while he took only random employment in order to dedicate most of his time to writing. Even his reenrollment in the university was merely a strategy to obtain a legal ration card without employment to be able to spend more time writing.

In these early years, Böll, like other postwar German writers, had to struggle with finding a new German literary language. Under the Nazis the German language had become polluted by fascist ideology. The German literary tradition which had served Böll's older contemporaries belonging to the generation of Thomas Mann no longer seemed valid in a post-Auschwitz age. Böll was fortunate in that he found his own style early, one appropriate for his ideas and suitable to the content of his stories. The style he found can be described as a kind of Hemingway-like minimalism—simple words in simple sentences—a laconic plainness commensurate with the Germany of 1945, a time when the expression of truth, to be believable again, had to possess the certainty and simplicity of a mathematical statement like $2+2=4$. The

Robert C. Conard; Heinrich Böll; Böll's wife Annemarie; Viktor Böll, Böll's nephew and Director of the Böll Archive. Taken at Böll's home in Langenbroich, 29 May 1985 (courtesy of Robert C. Conard).

opening lines of any of the stories written before 1950 illustrate the style. "Damals in Odessa" ("That Time We Were in Odessa") starts with the seven words: "In Odessa it was very cold then." It concludes: "It was cold in Odessa, the weather was beautifully clear, and we boarded the plane; and as it rose, we knew suddenly that we would never return, never. . . . " Between the terse opening sentence and the final lines, the story tells of soldiers eating and drinking to forget their fear before going to die. In the history of German literature Böll's sober language has the place accorded a Shaker chair in the history of American furniture.

In 1947 these first stories began to appear in various periodicals. They were collected in 1951 in *Wanderer, kommst du nach Spa. . . .* In 1983 twenty-two more of these early stories were discovered in the Böll Archive in Cologne and published in the collection *Die Verwundung.* Of these early stories only a small part is available in English in the collection *Children Are Civilians Too.* The subject matter

of these earliest works was Böll's and Germany's most recent experience: the war and the return of soldiers to a homeland morally impoverished and physically destroyed. Böll's war stories contained none of the heroism and gallantry of popular war literature written during the Weimar Republic. In Böll's narratives men died without honor for an inhuman cause. But despite the stark realism of war Böll did not dwell on battle scenes; he more often depicted the boredom of military life and fear of death. In these tales the only haven from despair was found in transcendental love, discovered in momentary encounters between soldiers and women on the periphery of the war.

The two novellas *Der Zug war pünktlich (The Train Was on Time),* 1949; *Das Vermächtnis (The Legacy),* written in 1948, published in 1982; and the episodic novel *Wo warst du, Adam? (And Where Were You, Adam?)* represent Böll's longer treatment of the war. While they differ from one another in structure, they, like the shorter works, share the same earthly fatalism that death is bigger than life and proclaim the same Christian optimism that heavenly consolation is greater than suffering. Thus, all the war narratives acknowledge that God is still in his heaven, although all is not right with the world.

Böll's motto for the novel *Adam* (which he took from Antoine de Saint-Exupéry's *Flight to Arras)* can stand as a motto for all his war stories from this period: "When I was younger, I took part in real adventures: establishing postal air routes across the Sahara and South America. But war is no true adventure; it is only a substitute for adventure. War is a disease just like typhus." Alan Bance claims that this apolitical perspective on the war was typical of German literature in the 1940s and 1950s. He even sees a kind of "realism" in this political vagueness because, as he says, "war is not conducive to clear thinking." In Böll's case this unanalytical response to the war (seeing international conflict as a natural illness) was compounded by his feeling of being a lucky survivor, for only one in four German men in Böll's age group returned from battle. This sense of destiny forced Böll to deal subjectively rather than objectively with the suffering of the Hitler years. This narrow perspective manifests itself in Böll's simplistic division of characters into two groups: victims and executioners, with the victims often being the Germans themselves. This dichotomous view of World War II is understandable and even accurate for someone who was himself an antifascist and a sufferer of twelve prolonged years of oppression. Still, the result of this dichotomy is that the war stories cannot reveal what the war was about because the limited categories of suffering innocents and brutal henchmen are too unrefined to do the job. This kind of dualism, as Walter Soket calls it, which is characteristic of Böll's work in this period, disappears from the later stories as they become more sophisticated in their characterizations. Günter Wirth's indictment of Böll's war stories as "timeless irrationalism" is to the point because certainly war is not like typhus or any other sickness which has biological causes. War is not nature's making; it is made by people who have political and economic interests.

But the novel *Adam* also has a second motto taken from the war-time diaries of the Catholic writer Theodor Haecker: "A world catastrophe can serve many ends, one of which is to find an alibi before God. Where were you, Adam? 'I was in the World War.' " Of these two mottos the one from Haecker is clearly the more important, for Böll takes the title of his novel from it. Clear also is

Haecker's irony which informs Böll's novel: war is no excuse before God. Ultimately people are responsible for what they do. This message goes far to undercut the metaphor that war is like typhus, especially since the main chapter of the novel is the one in which a Nazi commandant of a concentration camp murders all his Jewish prisoners. This episode established Böll as one of the first German writers to acknowledge the Holocaust in literature. Clear also in the way the novel recounts the circumstances surrounding this episode is that all who cooperated with the Nazi system of extermination, from those who transported the victims to those who ordered and did the killing, are guilty. The excuse—"we did not intend what happened"—finds no support within the economy of the novel.

This bold, honest attitude casts an undiminished moral light throughout Böll's writing. Though he may have viewed the world unhistorically in the 1940s and early 1950s under the influence of Christian existentialism, he learned quickly in the 1950s that without recognizing the forces of history he could not understand what was going on in Europe around him. Böll's literary development from ahistoricity to historicity, from presenting only men and women suffering to presenting and analyzing the causes of their suffering by giving the historical background of events, is a fundamental change in Böll's work.

Written contemporaneously with these war stories were those that recounted conditions in Germany immediately after the war. The narrators of these stories are often weary veterans who refuse to work on Germany's restoration because they suffer physical and emotional debilitation from too much war and too many years of having been ordered about. Now that tyrannical authority has disappeared from their lives they cannot on their own conjure up the energy to struggle with existence. Through these passive characters Böll began his criticism of postwar German society. His lethargic heroes stand in opposition to the robust, dynamic Germans eager to readjust, rebuild, and make money. These opportunists, men without a sense of guilt, who have already forgotten Hitler's six years of war and twelve years of oppression and murder, dominate the political, social, and economic scene. These new democrats rush headlong into the economic race, leaving behind the slow starters burdened with a memory and a conscience. Satire became Böll's main weapon in his chastisement of Germany. Stories like "Nicht nur zur Weihnachtszeit" ("Christmas Everyday"), 1951; "Dr. Murkes gesammeltes Schweigen" ("Dr. Murke's

Collected Silences"), 1955; and "Der Wegwerfer" ("The Thrower Away"), 1957, have become classics of postwar German literature. A humorous, bizarre fantasy characterizes these satires of developing West German society. In "Nicht nur zur Weihnachtszeit" a tyranical old aunt demands Christmas everyday to avoid confronting the guilt of the Hitler years. In "Dr. Murkes gesammeltes Schweigen" a Ph.D. in psychology, working for a radio station, tries to preserve his sanity by collecting on tape snips of dead air cut from cultural programs. In "Der Wegwerfer" a fanatic time-study expert makes a place for himself in the business world by systematically destroying junk mail, the surplus production of the ad industry. It is Böll's success in this genre, the satirical short story, that led critics like Erhard Friedrichsmeyer, James Henderson Reid, and Walter Jens to conclude that Böll's acutest artistic sense is his eye for satire. These stories have garnered such high critical acclaim because they take to task the shortcomings of all Western democracies although they are grounded in West German economic and political reality. When one reads the criticism of the Eastern bloc, one recognizes between the lines that Böll's satire hits the mark there also where culture too is an industry, where production, though not for profit, often leads to waste and people avoid just as tenaciously confronting the unpleasant past.

Böll's sense of satire, however, is also the high point of many of his novels and raises them in some cases to great literature and in others saves them from the doldrums. For example in *Ansichten eines Clowns* (*The Clown*), 1963, the scene of the penniless clown pantomiming his blindness during the visit of his millionaire industrialist father contains the essence of the novel's political content, and in *Entfernung von der Truppe* (*Absent without Leave*), 1964, the narrator's account of his latrine duty in World War II is more than just humorous satire of the army; it reveals the narrator's total alienation from society. In *Ende einer Dienstfahrt* (*End of a Mission*), 1966, Böll's choice of a pedantic, objective tone fraught with understatement confers on the novel the main feature of its readability. The dry reporting of the events of a trial of father and son accused of burning an army jeep discloses how the courts and the press keep political protest under control. And Böll's last novel, *Frauen vor Flußlandschaft* (*Women before a River Landscape*), 1985, published just after his death, reaches its high point in a long interior monologue by a disenchanted intellectual whose job for his party requires him to write speeches for a corrupt and stupid Christian Democratic minister. Here the monologue summarizes the novel's political intent by revealing the politician's incompetence and moral emptiness as well as the intellectual's sellout of his ideals. This chapter confirms that Böll's satiric talent remained intact right up to his death.

Beginning with his very first short story of 1947 about a veteran returning from the war, Böll began choosing themes, drawing characters, and selecting events tied directly to current developments in Germany. For this reason, one of the best histories of the Federal Republic is Böll's collected work. Fritz Raddatz even calls Böll "the Balzac of the Second Republic." Read chronologically, Böll's work goes through every significant phase in West German history from its establishment in 1949 to the mid-1980s, forming a running chronicle of the first thirty-five years of the Second Republic. While Böll's work deals with contemporary West Germany, it does not do so as if the present were separated from the past or as if a new German history began in 1945. It treats the postwar era in light of the Hitler years and of German history since the turn of the century. In its totality Böll's oeuvre accomplishes two things. It helps establish West German literature after the war, and it contributes to a political and social understanding of Germany in this century. The young man in his late twenties and early thirties who began by publishing pathetic, realistic accounts of the misery of war developed into an astute chronicler of his nation's history.

Moreover, a guiding philosophical position informs this running chronicle of the Second Republic. Böll's oeuvre shows the little people of history to be the objects of social forces, often victims of the decisions of others. This Weltanschauung which lies at the heart of Böll's work surprises no one who is aware of the events which Böll has stated are important in his own formation as an individual: two world wars, inflation, depression, and economic restoration. His novel *Die verlorene Ehre der Katharine Blum* (*The Lost Honor of Katharina Blum*), 1974, because it demonstrates how an unpolitical, law-abiding young woman can be turned into a vengeful murderer by society's toleration of social injustice, may be the best illustration of this social philosophy.

Böll's assumption that a person is a product of social forces could be called Marxist, and may be just that, except that it is thoroughly religious, lacks the happy dimension of Marxist optimism, and never suggests social change through political organization. Social solutions are not found in Böll's work. Implied, however, is the truism that if people in power acted with more concern for those subject to their power, practiced more compassion in the execution of their offices, society, especially West German society, would be a more just place in which to live. In general, a certain sadness prevails in Böll's work about the human condition even though a mild optimism flourishes within narrow limits. His heroes and heroines always make important decisions regarding their own lives. They are not completely passive; they do not yield to or reluctantly accept injustice. Their decisions affirm their individual human dignity and assert a militant humanism. Although their actions may be vain in effecting significant social change and merely permit themselves to live with their consciences, their decisiveness functions as symbolic opposition to an unjust world and, as such, suggests that social awareness and conscious opposition are the way to a better future. The story of Katharina Blum's vengeance neither recommends nor condones murder, but merely illustrates the simple truth that injustice tolerated is often the cause of social violence.

This tendency to decisiveness and action on the part of individuals is a prevailing pattern in Böll's work. At the conclusion of *Und sagte kein einziges Wort* (*And He Never Said a Word*), 1951; *Haus ohne Hüter* (*The Unguarded House*), 1954; *Billard um halbzehn* (*Billiards at Half-past Nine*), 1959; *Fürsorgliche Belagerung* (*The Safety Net*), 1979; and *Frauen vor Flußlandschaft*, 1985, the main characters make decisions that alter their lives. They assert that individuals can be courageous and virtuous even if as individuals they cannot change society. Moreover, the decisions made at the end of Böll's novels frequently involve more than one person. They are often group decisions made by members of a family or by a circle of friends. These small groups who decide to put their own moral lives in order represent Böll's model for a more humane society.

When the Swedish Academy awarded Böll the Nobel Prize in 1972, it singled out the novel *Gruppenbild mit Dame* (*Group Portrait with Lady*), 1971, for special praise, calling that work the summation of Böll's oeuvre. Although Böll continued to publish novels, stories, poems, plays, and essays regularly after 1971, *Gruppenbild mit Dame* still maintained that unique place in his writings as the single work which came closest to representing the whole of Heinrich Böll. The book was both summary and summation in that it recapitulated his major themes and culminated their formulation.

Politically the novel condemned practicing communism as strongly as it did capitalist society. Because the work criticized specific actions of the Communist party in the period between the Russo-German nonaggression pact of 1939 and the Warsaw Pact invasion of Czechoslovakia in 1968, the novel has appeared in the Soviet Union only in abridged form, lacking all criticism of the party and even omitting some sensitive sexual passages. Despite a political evenhandedness in the novel, Böll's criticism of the Western and Eastern systems differed. He showed a society based on production for profit instead of human needs to lack compassion and want for justice. The practice of capitalism as presented in the novel assumed the status of a philosophy of greed run amok. His criticism of communism, in contrast, is not of its ideals but of its failure to live up to its precepts. From this point of view the novel's criticism of established socialism paralleled its criticism of the institutional church. Through the main character, Leni, and especially her son Lev, Böll demonstrated that socialist and religious principles go hand in hand as partners of a shared humanism. The novel is, indeed, the summation of Böll's writing, for it crystallizes the radical message that runs through all of his work: Christianity and capitalism are incompatible; their long-standing marriage survives only because organized religion continually surrenders its humanistic values to the demands of economics and politics.

On 11 June, one month before his death, Böll made the following statement in an interview on North German Radio. Speaking of the end of the war, he said: "It was not a pleasant condition to be German in 1945. German was probably the most despised label one could have. When I compare that condition with the resonating self-confidence of German politicians today—politicians who are about my age—it all seems strange indeed."

One reading these words may remember a similar sentiment expressed in 1945 by Robert Jackson, U.S. Chief Consul at the Nuremberg trials. The German nation, he said, had sunk to a new low of human depravity, and it could expect "no early deliverance." But today in the Soviet Union, Poland, Czechoslovakia, in France, England, Holland, Belgium, the U.S., and in all countries around the world, Germany has been readmitted to the Human community, and Böll has often stood as a model for this renewed Germany. Germans now justifiably speak in tones of "resonating self-confidence." This change in world public opinion in such a short time, this "early deliverance," was made possible by a host of "good" Germans, but most notably by Heinrich Böll. Because he did not forget what it was to be German in 1945, because his work is built upon this memory, his artistic oeuvre has aided immeasurably the cause of Germany's moral restoration. For this reason, because reconciliation is always preferable to hatred, not only Germans, but all people, owe a debt to Heinrich Böll that in full measure can never be repaid.

References:
Robert Conard, wnd ed. (Berlin: Rütten & Loening, 1973);

Hans Joachim Bernhard, *Die Romane Heinrich Bölls: Gesellschaftskritik und Gemeinschaftsutopie*, 2nd ed. (Berlin: Rütten & Loening, 1973);

Robert Conrad, *Heinrich Böll* (Boston: G. K. Hall, 1981);

Enid MacPherson, *A Student's Guide to Böll* (London: Heinemann, 1972);

Rainer Nägele, *Böll: Einführung in das Werk und in die Forschung* (Frankfurt am Main: Fischer Taschenbuch, 1976);

James Henderson Reid, *Heinrich Böll: Withdrawal and Re-emergence* (London: Oswald, 1973).

A TRIBUTE

from ERHARD FRIEDRICHSMEYER

The humanity and persuasive artistry of Heinrich Böll will continue to attract readers in both the East and the West. His vision of postwar Germany, at once or in turn mournful, acerbic, humorous, may have been the most astute and compelling of his generation.

A TRIBUTE

from HENRY AND SHIRLEY GLADE

Heinrich Böll was a unique friend whose concern for others and gift of words live on through all who knew him and his writings.

A TRIBUTE

from RALPH LEY

On occasion Böll remarked that a writer should not be praised or damned for his convictions and dispositions—they are after all, gratis. He should be judged on the basis of his talent. However, in Böll's case, the two elements were inseparable. Böll was a writer of stature because his spiritual outlook went into the fashioning of the characters, mood, atmosphere, and setting of his fictional world. If one can say that Böll afforded his readers the pleasure of gaining a deeper insight into the meaning of human dignity and decency through his talent and his ethos, and I think one can, then one has indeed said a great deal. An early work, *Und sagte kein einziges Wort (And He Never Said a Word*, 1951), is probably the finest Christian novel of postwar Germany. His masterpiece, *Gruppenbild mit Dame (Group Portrait with Lady*, 1971), is a humanitarian document of our times which can stand comparison with the best efforts of a Silone, a Camus, or a Brecht. This novel may well be the most forceful plea in German literature on behalf of human solidarity and equality since Lessing's *Nathan der Weise (Nathan the Wise*, 1779).

Robert Graves
(24 July 1895-7 December 1985)

Patrick J. Keane
LeMoyne College

A full biblical seventy years after he was pronounced dead of war wounds, Robert Graves passed away on the Mediterranean island that had been his home for more than half a century. His posthumous life had been rich and strange, with Graves himself emerging as a figure larger than life: soldier, scholar, craftsman. He was, undeniably, an odd mix: a man who retreated to an island, from which he courted, and attained, world fame; an immensely learned and perceptive scholar given to idiosyncratic, sometimes crackpot theories; a poet, classicist, and "uncommercial man" who earned a considerable living by writing prose, some of it "best-selling" popular fiction. Above all, he was prolific.

Starting in 1916, the year he had been prematurely declared dead, Graves published some 120 volumes—poetry, criticism, autobiography, short stories, historical novels, mythography, biblical "reconstructions," translations. Graves always insisted that his prose works were his "show dogs," bred to support his cherished "cat," poetry. But despite his insistence that it was as a poet that he wanted to be judged by history, and despite the staggering quantity and variety of his work, Graves's world fame rests on just a few volumes, all prose works: *Good-bye to All That* (1929, 1957), *I, Claudius* and *Claudius the God and His Wife Messalina* (both 1934), *The White Goddess* (1948, later revised), and the widely read two-volume work, *The Greek Myths* (1955).

Written a decade after the horrors of the trench fighting it recounts, *Good-bye to All That,* perhaps the most moving yet ironically funny account of men in modern war, is at once brutally direct and bemusedly distanced: a money-making theatrical performance by a master farceur which is both a personal exorcism and a dismissal of the very audience that paid to have Graves thumb his nose at it. The critically and commercially successful Claudius novels, awarded the Hawthornden and James Tait Black Memorial prizes in 1935, reached a far wider international audience forty years later through the superb BBC television adaptations.

Robert Graves (Gale International Portrait Gallery)

The White Goddess, Graves's erudite and eccentric "Historical Grammar of Poetic Myth," brought him to world attention as the champion of a matriarchal as opposed to patriarchal vision, with Graves himself revealed as the scholar-vassal of a Muse-Goddess who inspires, comforts, and ultimately destroys her chosen acolyte. The same blend of classical and anthropological erudition and intuitive audacity, a mixture that understandably infuriates conventional scholars, is displayed in *The Greek Myths,* a retelling of the old stories buttressed by Gravesian glosses that are intriguing even when they are most dubious.

The sixty-odd years of Graves's career as a writer spanned two world wars and man's landing on the very moon associated with his Goddess—indeed the whole technological revolution, including the abiding terror of nuclear stalemate. Robert Graves had first-hand experience of the horrors of our century, of what he deplored as the replacement of instinct and love by a rationality gone mad, with war as the final product of modern, male technology. Given that vision, he insisted that, far from retreating into an atavistic aberration, he was affirming the persistent survival of something timeless when he chose as his unifying theme the "antique story" celebrated in "all true poetry". He described the story as the battle between the rival gods of the waxing and waning year for the love of the capricious and all-powerful Triple Goddess, who functions on the personal and literary level as the poet's femme fatale and Muse.

In his devotion to this fatal Muse and, after 1959, to her kindlier but related black sister, Graves struck an often precarious balance. Though he was attracted to the mysteries and primitivistic rites surrounding his Goddess, Graves's British common sense, intellectual sophistication, and passionately skeptical Anglo-Irish temperament combined to keep his shamanistic tendencies in balance. As Patrick Keane wrote in *A Wild Civility* (1980), "Even after Graves's attraction to the irrational and mystical was solemnized in his official bewitchment by the White Goddess, that ecstatic allegiance did not preclude experimentation with sophisticated techniques of alliteration and assonance, meter and rhyme; nor did it overwhelm intelligible communication: the lucidity and almost-Horation impassioned plainness that mark Graves's work in both poetry and prose."

Having survived his own "death" on the Somme in 1916, Robert Graves, it began to seem, would outlive us all. He had emerged from that "brief demise," he wrote in his poem "The Second Fated," having learned to "scorn your factitious universe/Ruled by the death which we had flouted." We had come to cherish that imperial audacity; even, with time, to understand if not agree with his arrogant and cranky dismissals of the idols in the modernist pantheon: Pound, Eliot, Auden, Dylan Thomas, and—most persistently and unrelentingly—W. B. Yeats.

What Graves called "the old-clothesmen of literature," the critics, have not been kind to the poetry of his last years, which Graves overvalued at the expense of some of his finest earlier work. Nevertheless, most of the old-clothesmen have been in accord with W. H. Auden, who described Graves a quarter century ago as "a poet of honor," a craftsman who had respect for his tools, a man

who often succeeded in transforming his experience of love into art.

Art is long, and, in Graves's case, so was life. In the popular imagination, Robert Graves, there on his island, had come to resemble a modern Prospero, an archaic talisman against death itself. He had, apparently, written nothing in his final decade; but his survival, even in silence, had begun to assume a kind of mythological status. It was comforting to think of the old man, all that honorable and arduous toil behind him, poking about the house in Deyá, cared for by his wife Beryl—revealed in Martin Seymour-Smith's recent biography as a loving, patient, and understanding woman. So it was still with something of a shock that we learned that Robert Graves had, in fact, died, on Majorca, in his ninetieth year.

There persists a sign of spring beyond that winter death. In *The Golden Fleece*, the novel Graves was working on when he was overwhelmed by the figure of the White Goddess, Orpheus sings of the dead Eurydice:

> She tells her love while half asleep,
>   In the dark hours,
>   With half-words whispered low;
> As Earth stirs in her winter sleep
>   And puts out grass and flowers
>   Despite the snow,
>   Despite the falling snow.

It is Graves's unimprovable final work on his recurrent theme of midwinter spring, here captured in an exquisite short lyric that combines eternally springing hope and plangent elegy.

That fusion is characteristic of Graves's finest poems, in which, despite awareness of the irreplaceability of individuals, he wistfully longed to circumscribe suffering within a fuller glory—what Nietzsche called a "higher, overmastering joy" and order so transforming terror that "lamentation itself becomes a song of praise." Lamentation becomes a song of praise in Graves's central mythological poems, "Darien," "To Juan at the Winter Solstice," and "The White Goddess."

In "Darien," the middle-aged poet, a representative of the departing year, must willingly yield up his old self in order to create the vital new poetry inherent in his visionary marriage with the Muse—a promise embodied in the living form of their son, "The new green of my hope." Graves's best-known poem, "To Juan at the Winter Solstice," synopsizes the antique story of the solar hero's relationship with the Triple Goddess, his union with her, and his inevitable death at her hands or by her command. "But nothing promised that is not performed": the negative construction of that final affirmation confirms her dual role, fecund yet fatal. As her devotee, Graves accepts his fate with *sprezzatura*, aristocratic nonchalance. Even in mid-winter, we are "gifted," in the quest poem "The White Goddess," with so great a sense of her magnificence that "We forget cruelty and past betrayal,/Heedless of where the next bright bolt may fall."

Graves clung to the Goddess, for all her cruelty, as the guarantor of his poetic immortality. The time, he knew, was not propitious for his kind of poetry. As an inconoclastic critic, bombarding the fashionable figures and modes, he repeatedly referred to the "foul tidal basin" of Franco-American "modernism" as a stagnant deviation from the "mainstream." Scorning the modernist mode in the confidence that his commitment was to the true Muse of poetic tradition, he gradually "ceased to feel the frantic strain of swimming against the stream of time." While Graves may not have been a major figure in the modernist "swim," his accomplishment makes him too good an artist to be politely dismissed, and "considerably more than an archaic torso washed up at Majorca and out of the swing of the sea."

Robert Graves remains a man and a poet "of honor," author of many fascinating books and of a handful of magical poems that will indeed guarantee his immortality. During the First World War, Graves had found himself "among men whom detestable trench conditions and persistent danger either destroyed or ennobled." He saw the parallel with the writing of poetry:

> Holding a trench to the last round of ammunition and the last man, taking a one-in-three chance of life when rescuing a badly wounded comrade from no-man's-land, keeping up a defiant pride in our soldierly appearance: these were poetic virtues. Our reward lay in their practice, with possible survival as a small bright light seen at the end of a long tunnel.

After the war, Graves swore "a poetic oath never again to be anyone's servant but my own," and the defiant pride that had characterized the Royal Welch Fusilier governed throughout his life the poet's service to his craft and his Muse. His reward lay both in his ennobling practice of that craft and, at the end of the long tunnel, in the more than "possible survival" of a number of poems certain to live.

A TRIBUTE   *from DANIEL HOFFMAN*

Robert Graves is the most accomplished metaphysical love poet in English in our century. His poems are impassioned and elegant, yet ecstasy is everywhere straitened by guilt and terror. Although his own aesthetic theories (elaborated in *The White Goddess*) demand the poet be true to "one story and one story only," the poet's subjection to the Muse, much of Graves's best poetry embodies a different theme—the destruction by the First World War of a rational world. Graves's poems of the 1920s and 1930s (such as "Rocky Acres," "Warning to Children," "Alice," "The Pier Glass"), though brief, are comparable to Eliot's *The Waste Land* in their powerful representation of a world whose social and spiritual underpinnings have been blown away.

A compulsive seeker of unity, Graves everywhere reveals his doubleness: both a romantic and a classicist; a writer committed to conventional language and versification, he uses traditions in unexampled ways; compelled by the unassuageable urgency of his intuitive life, he is a rationalist explainer and solver of riddles. Graves not only avoided but denounced the shattering of forms by which the modernist poets embodied the breaking apart of social institutions and released the energies of the id, yet those institutions are ignored, those energies rippled, in Graves's poems. Graves is a prime instance of Eliot's diagnosis of the dilemma of contemporary sensibility, its dissociation. With reason and feeling ever at odds, in Graves's best work the oppositions of his own nature are intertwined. His unmistakably wry lyricism results from the tension between them.

His prose alone attests his significance. It is no small thing to have written the most memorable account of trench warfare (*Good-bye to All That*), or the most vivid re-creation of the Roman Empire (*I, Claudius*). His *White Goddess*, "a historical grammar of poetic myth," ransacks the history of language, myth, and poetry with determinist clarity so overwhelming that it will continue to convince and inspire readers and poets. In prose as well as poetry, Graves was an original.

Shiva Naipaul

(25 February 1945-13 August 1985)

Joseph Caldwell

BOOKS: *Fireflies* (London: Deutsch, 1970; New York: Knopf, 1971);

The Chip-Chip Gatherers (London: Deutsch, 1973; New York: Knopf, 1973);

North of South: An African Journey (London: Deutsch, 1978; New York: Simon & Schuster, 1979);

Black and White (London: Hamish Hamilton, 1980); republished as *Journey to Nowhere: A New World Tragedy* (New York: Simon & Schuster, 1981);

A Hot Country (London: Hamish Hamilton, 1983); republished as *Love and Death in a Hot Country* (New York: Viking, 1984);

Beyond the Dragon's Mouth: Stories and Pieces (London: Hamish Hamilton, 1984; New York: Viking, 1985).

PERIODICAL PUBLICATIONS: "Notebook," *Spectator,* 240 (25 February 1978): 5;

"Notebook," *Spectator,* 241 (29 July 1978): 5;

"I cannot disown Trinidad and it cannot disown me," *Listener,* 107 (10 June 1982): 13-14;

"Discussing Uganda," *Spectator,* 252 (24 March 1984): 13-14;

"Aborigines," *New Republic,* 192 (22 April 1985): 25-30;

"A Thousand Million Invisible Men," *Spectator,* 254 (18 May 1985): 9-11;

"Family Affair," *New Republic,* 192 (27 May 1985): 26-30.

Shiva Naipaul (photo ©Jerry Bauer)

Shiva Naipaul claimed, in his essay "My Brother and I," published in the British periodical *Time and Tide,* that he "never made a decision to become a 'writer.' It happened." He explained that he wrote a sentence—"The Lutchmans lived in a part of the city where the houses, tall and narrow...."—and "started to follow it. At that moment I was propelled by inquisitiveness, not by literary anticipation. I wanted to see where—how far—that sentence would take me. It took me a long way." The sentence led to his first novel, *Fireflies* (1970), and helped to establish him in the ca-

reer that won him much acclaim. He produced three novels, a travel book, an account of the People's Temple massacre in Jonestown, Guyana, and a collection of stories and shorter journalism. He had begun work on a book about Australia when he died of a heart attack at the age of forty.

Born 25 February 1945 in Port of Spain, Trinidad, Shivadar Srinivasa Naipaul was the second son of Seepersad and Bropatie Capildeo Naipaul. His education began at Queen's Royal College and continued at St. Mary's College, where he won one of the four Island Scholarships the Trinidad government offered for study abroad. In late 1963 Naipaul departed for Great Britain. He attended University College, Oxford, on an open scholarship and, at first, read philosophy, psychology, and physiology. After he lost interest in these subjects, he shifted his study to classical Chinese and took his degree in 1968. In 1967 Naipaul married Virginia Margaret Stuart, an Englishwoman, and they settled in London; their son Tarun was born in 1974.

The novel Naipaul had begun near the end of his academic study, the novel that had "happened," won the John Llewelyn Rhys Memorial Prize and the Royal Society of Literature's Winifred Holtby Memorial Prize in 1970, and in 1971 the Jock Campbell New Statesman Award.

Set in a Port of Spain neighborhood of indeterminate status—it is bounded on the north by a botanical garden and the homes of the rich, on the south by gas stations, cinemas, and nightclubs—*Fireflies* traces the decline of two families: the Khojas, a powerful landowning clan, and the Lutchmans, poor relations on the fringes of Khoja influence. Baby Lutchman, great-niece of the Khoja matriarch, and Govind Khoja, head of the clan after his mother becomes blind, are the protagonists. Naipaul amusingly caricatures Govind, who greatly admires his own wisdom and writes long, tractlike letters to the local newspapers extolling the values of hard labor and education, neither of which he has experienced. Vain, conservative, and shallow, Govind is the product of his sisters' adulation. His confidence in his authority and self-worth arises from his childhood grooming as future ruler of the family. Having never been contradicted, having always been praised for the genius of his mediocre thought, Govind cannot deal with rebellion or accept criticism. When, after his mother's death, his family breaks into loyal and disloyal factions warring over the distribution of wealth, Govind retreats into a walled house where he continues to write letters and dispense justice to those willing to accept his authority.

Among those loyal to Govind is Baby, whose loyalty goes unappreciated. In his characterization of Baby, Naipaul demonstrates great tenderness, for, despite her lack of education and the unremitting drudgery of her life as wife and mother, Baby never retreats from hardship and never withholds her love from those who do not acknowledge her gift, though they benefit from it. Only at the end of the novel, which chronicles more than twenty years of death, desertion, and defeat, does Baby lose her optimism and begin to long for nothingness.

Reviewers noted the fullness of Naipaul's de-

tail in describing his characters' lives and complained at the length to which he went to realize it. "Neither Mrs. Lutchman, her family, nor the stuffy and beautifully realized Mr. Khoja, who provides the novel with its desperately needed comic relief," wrote Sara Blackburn in her review for *Book World*, "serve to justify its great length. It is because of this, in combination with the very authenticity of its airless, constrained atmosphere, that I found myself wavering constantly between admiration and exasperation." Blackburn concluded that Naipaul "has written a novel that is highly accomplished; my real disappointment is that its length makes it highly pretentious as well." Though Linda Hess found the novel to be an admirable first effort, she was bothered by "a quality of style that . . . is stable, thorough, emotionally limited. Not that it's boring: the details of dialogue and description are consistently sharp and well selected. But for a panoramic human comedy it seems to lack lightness."

The novel's length befits the period of time reviewed. Naipaul recalled incidents from the lives of his family and his own experience. His "stable, thorough, emotionally limited" style helped to insulate him from material he could not, because of its painful familiarity, treat with objectivity.

Naipaul's second novel, *The Chip-Chip Gatherers* (1973), is similar to *Fireflies* but lacks the compassion and humor of its predecessor. Here Naipaul traced forty years of life in the Settlement, a squalid rural community on the fringes of nowhere, and the nearby town of Victoria, where the only family of importance, the Ramsarans, live. No joy eases the burdens of frustration and deprivation that grind the lives of Egbert and Wilbert Ramsaran, Sushila and Sita, Vishnu Bholai, and Basdai to nothing. Their small and malicious dreams thwarted by the dearth of resources needed to fulfill them, these people dissipate their energies in petty schemes of vengeance, querulous protest at injustice, and unshakable despair at the futility of action. None acts for any other reason than to escape, in some way, the barrenness of the Settlement. None succeeds.

Egbert Ramsaran, though born in the Settlement, possesses the single-minded drive to accumulate the fortune needed to escape it. But he returns to Victoria with his transport company so that he can exercise his wealth as power. An unforgiving man, he enjoys abusing his neighbors in the Settlement for their earlier contempt for his desire to better himself. Soon Egbert becomes corrupt, derelict, and unaware that he is either. When his wife Rani dies, he becomes the prey of beautiful and vivaciously cunning Sushila, whose own sense of the outrages done her by her neighbors makes her as formidable an ally as a foe. Seeking to control Egbert and his fortune, Sushila moves into his house, and a contest of wills begins that exhausts them both. Sushila, driven nearly mad by her defeat, flees the house; Egbert collapses into decrepitude and death.

Wilbert Ramsaran, strangely placid in comparison with his father, is the book's most pathetic character. From his birth, the direction of his life is set. His father's power and place will pass to him, he is told; and he waits impatiently for fulfillment of this destiny. Sadly, Wilbert lacks imagination and cannot conceive that he has the right to choose his own direction. Browbeaten into passivity, he endures a nameless dissatisfaction and learns, at his father's death, that he has neither the mettle nor the desire to rule. He allows himself to be guided into a loveless marriage and, while honeymooning at his beach house, has an epiphany of his life's futility. Sitting beside the ocean, he watches women and children from a nearby village harvest chip-chip, "filling the baskets and basins with the pink and yellow shells which were the size and shape of a long fingernail. Inside each was the sought-after prize: a miniscule kernel of insipid flesh. A full bucket of shells would provide them with a mouthful. But they were not deterred by the disproportion between their labours and their gains. Rather, the very meagreness of their reward seemed to spur them on . . . Wilbert would marvel at the dogged application that was displayed and the passions fruitlessly squandered."

Though Naipaul's language was sometimes clichéd, critics praised *The Chip-Chip Gatherers*—it was given the Whitbread Literary Award in 1973—as further proof of the promise of his talent. In a review for the *Christian Science Monitor*, A. L. Hendricks said that Naipaul "is a skillful storyteller. He wastes no words on elaborate descriptions or philosophizing, but lets his characters make his point. He draws them sympathetically and yet never loses his artistic detachment." Writing for *New Statesman*, Martin Amis noted that "a primitive society offers a Hobson's choice of styles to its authors: tantrumese, noble-savagery, or a combination of irony and pathos. But like all limitations this brings special liberties. Irony and pathos are essentially downward-looking viewpoints, so a society of grotesques, fools, snobs, show-offs, martinets and ingenues who think and talk in illiterate clichés has obvious perks for a writer with as delicate a touch" as Naipaul's. Amis added that "if the book isn't quite as

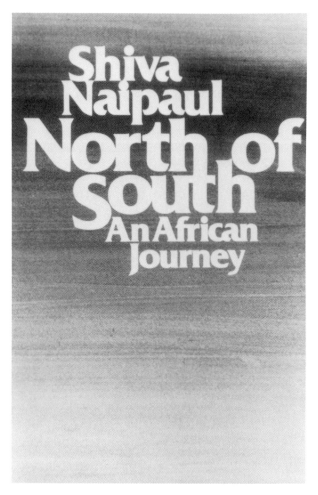

Dust jacket for Naipaul's record of a trip through Kenya, Tanzania, and Zambia

successful as the startlingly mature *Fireflies*, it is because Mr. Naipaul has started to deal with the problem of focus. He is concentrating on nuance rather than ambiance, shaving down his sentences, and holding his vast—perhaps Dickensian—comic talents carefully in check."

Widely admired, Naipaul was inevitably compared with his elder brother, V. S. Naipaul, whose work offered similar commentary on the emotional, intellectual, and physical distresses of the small, poverty-constrained community. Ronald Bryden, in reviewing *The Chip-Chip Gatherers* for *Listener*, began by saying that "it would be polite but ridiculous to talk about Shiva Naipaul as if he had leapt, full-armed and *sui generis*, into a world miraculously swept of all footprints of his famous brother V. S." Early reviews, indeed, had skirted the issue of comparison on grounds that it would be impolite or impolitic; but, as Naipaul noted later, comparisons were inevitable between "two men, both of denuded Indian ancestry, both born on the same island, both of roughly similar concerns, both exercising the complementary arts of fiction and journalism. . . . Our being brothers is interesting. But it is not intrinsically so. In the end it is the work that matters, not the relationship." Those who found the relationship more interesting were usually of the opinion that Shiva Naipaul's work suffered in comparison to that of V. S. Naipaul.

Bryden displayed deeper consideration in his comparison. "The relationship between the two is fraternal in much the same sense as that between Chekhov and Gorky. Like Chekhov, the elder Naipaul works from a fastidious, ironic private sensibility to humane public conclusions: because people behave badly, the world needs changing. The younger, more sweeping and less fastidious, starts where his brother ends: because the world needs changing, people behave badly. Bred within the old imperial culture, V. S. Naipaul sees its failure as one of individual wills, brains, imaginations. For his brother, born in 1945, it is the culture that blights the brains and wills. Like Gorky, he's fascinated by the perverse energies of primitive capitalism, the ferocious battling for a better life which, re-channeled, could transform society. In its raw appetite, depressing to his brother, he finds backhanded hope. For its casualties, pitiful and exasperating to the elder Naipaul in their self-delusion, he has only pity."

Following publication of *The Chip-Chip Gatherers*, Naipaul was named a fellow in the Royal Society of Literature. That same year he departed on a trip to India, the first in a series of wanderings that, in 1976, took him to Africa. At the request of his English publisher, he toured Kenya, Tanzania, and Zambia for six months to gather material for his next book, *North of South* (1978).

Subtitled "An African Journey," *North of South* records Naipaul's impressions of revolution in new African states, of the romanticizing of early European penetration into Africa, of the precarious position in Africa of the East Indian, whose exclusivities of caste, clan, and religion have prevented his assimilation into African society and made him universally despised by blacks and whites. This last consideration made it difficult for Naipaul to maintain an objective outlook on his subject, for his Hindu West Indian ancestry earned him the ire and suspicion of many African officials who relished persecuting him subtly and overtly. Nor did Naipaul reserve any sympathy for the threatened East Indians, whose property had been confiscated

and who awaited expulsion from the countries where they had made their livelihoods and raised their families. He felt these people had made no attempt to establish an African character for themselves, nor had they fought to retain what was theirs, relying pathetically on their status as British citizens to gain them safe exit. Throughout this work, Naipaul's tone shifts between despair, annoyance, and frustration, yet his style in relating the incidents that elicit these responses remains sharp, economical, and bitterly ironic.

Reviewers' annoyance with Naipaul was as sharply expressed as Naipaul's with Africa. Jack Beatty, in his *New Republic* review, called *North of South* "a remarkably bad-tempered book." What troubled Beatty was Naipaul's tone. "There is much pain in what he describes, but he shows little sympathy for it; his forte is describing the illusion. . . . Africa is unproblematic to Naipaul. He needn't have gone there at all; he could have written his book straight from his prejudices. Those prejudices light up the plight of the marginal men, the Asian population in the new black nations, but they stand between the reader and Africa. This would not be a problem in a novel but in a work which claims to be transparent on reality it causes a loss of belief, it induces an indiscriminate skepticism, finally it makes the reader as churlish and ungenerous as Mr. Naipaul." In contrast, Beatty noted that "testy as it is, *North of South* is a first-rate book—spirited, funny, written with economy and care. . . ."

In the *New York Times Book Review*, John Darnton wrote that "Naipaul's central thesis is that black-white relations in independent Africa are rotten to the core. . . . There is, of course, some truth to the construct. From the point of view of social integration, Kenya's multiracial society is a myth. Whites do enjoy inordinate privilege, many blacks do aspire to European possessions if not lifestyles, and the Indians remain a group apart. . . . But to see in these remnants of the past the whole future, and in these individual truths the single overriding truth, is to ignore some contradictory evidence. . . ."

Naipaul attempted to live in the United States in 1979, settling briefly in San Francisco and then New York. He found that he was happier in London and returned there in 1980. While in the United States, Naipaul had begun an investigation of the People's Temple massacre in Jonestown, Guyana. His research took him to Guyana briefly, but he finished it in San Francisco. In 1980 his conclusions were published as *Black and White* (in the United States as *Journey to Nowhere: A New World Tragedy* in 1981).

Naipaul researched the massacre well; he interviewed survivors, people who had escaped the Jones cult, corrupt officials of Guyana; but he went deeper than the massacre. He traced Jim Jones's origins as a charismatic and self-proclaimed prophet. He addressed the rootlessness and fear of Jones's nearly all-black congregation and found implications that poverty and a sense of alienation had created a Third World of America's ghettos. Jones had tapped his congregation's fear, had preyed upon and reinforced it, had been corrupted by it, and had used it to destroy them utterly.

Naipaul traced the sense of rootlessness that motivated many to join Jones's church to the corruption of 1960s ideals of nonconformism, instant intimacy, and the rejection of rigorously disciplined thought. The generation of brotherhood and free love had become the "me" generation, interested in acquisition and personal gratification but at the same time vaguely disturbed by a sense of spiritual nullity. This generation was ripe for the likes of Werner Erhard, Sun Myung Moon, and Jim Jones, who offered easy assurance that the world could be made a better place if people would but care and believe that their caring was effective. Followers were discouraged from thinking deeply about difficult moral questions; their leaders would do that for them. In this intellectual climate, epitomized by the countless subcultures of California, Naipaul notes that it is no wonder so many people could be led to the jungles of a foreign country to commit, said Jones, "an act of revolutionary suicide protesting the conditions of an inhuman world."

Diane Johnson, writing for the *New York Review of Books*, said that Naipaul was "right about many of our native forms of foolishness, but wrong to connect these to Jonestown." Too, she questioned his objectivity and his qualifications as a commentator on the American scene. Naipaul, she said, "writes from the perspective of Oxford, where, he says, the Sixties were barely noticed and there is something corrective in his mistrust, which makes one examine and on balance wish to defend our no doubt goofy American hopefulness. It's almost enough to put one crazily on Jim Jones's side."

In the *New York Times Book Review*, Peter L. Berger offered a more objective consideration of the book when he noted that Naipaul's "is a harsh perspective; it is also a very persuasive one. To be sure, a less idiosyncratic writer would have softened his interpretation, introduced more nuances, perhaps shown more compassion. One strength of the book is that Mr. Naipaul does none of these things, letting the reader make his own modifications. . . ." Berger also noted the major omission in Naipaul's investigation that weakened his presentation: the motivations of Jones's mostly black congregation. "By no stretch of the imagination," said Berger, "can they be seen as products of the 'California Syndrome.' . . . It would have been important to enter into their story too, along with the stories of all those assorted gangsters, revolutionaries and deranged intellectuals. What is more, an examination of their story might have introduced the note of compassion that one misses in this book."

Naipaul returned to England from his trip to Guyana with enough material for his first novel-length fiction in ten years. Set in Cuyama, "a tract of land perched uneasily on the sloping shoulder of South America. . . . a tract of land on the fringe of an Empire whose interests had always lain elsewhere," *A Hot Country* (1983) is a work of foreboding and despair on the eve of a dictator's ascension to power and the descent of a young couple's marriage into loveless frustration. Dina and Aubrey St. Pierre, Naipaul's protagonists, make an unlikely pair, Dina withdrawn and vaguely malcontent, passively seeking an unnameable excitement, Aubrey a pompous pedagogue and ineffectual pamphleteer vainly attempting to make his life meaningful. One of his angry letters protesting the forthcoming "revision" of Cuyama's constitution attracts the interest of an English schoolmate, Alex, who visits the island to renew his acquaintance and to gather material for an article. Alex spends a week of desultory notetaking on the island, the whole time regretting his visit, at the end concluding that "maybe one day, if he felt in the mood, he might write a paragraph or two about it." He destroys his notes and returns to England untouched by the despair of his friends.

At one point, on the day before his departure from Cuyama, Alex hears an affecting confession from Dina: "I grew up, you know, without allegiance to anything. I'm nothing but a mongrelised ghost of a human being living in a mongrelised ghost of a country. There's nothing holding me together. Every day I have to reinvent myself." Alex, who comes from a complete culture, does not understand Dina's anguish. The impossibility of the individual's escaping the constraints of his environment, the ambiguities of race relations, the volatility of the political situation, and the absurdity of intellectual pretension in a community interested only in consumption and mimicry escape Alex's notice. But they do not escape Naipaul's notice.

SHIVA NAIPAUL·
MEMORIAL FUND

Shiva Naipaul was one of the most gifted and accomplished writers of our time. When he died in August 1985 at the age of 40, the Spectator announced that it was setting up a fund in his memory. We are now able to announce the purposes of the fund in more detail.

On the first page of a recent notebook, Shiva Naipaul wrote: 'All journeys begin the same way. All travel is a form of self-extinction.' As a man outside every tribe, Shiva Naipaul saw himself as a traveller in the world, observing curiously the loyalties of men which he could not share. It was from this observation that he derived his greatest insights. He also wrote:

> A journey, one hopes, will become its own justification, will assume patterns, reveal its possibilities — reveal, even, its layers of meaning — as one goes along, trusting to chance, to instinct, to hunch. Journeys undertaken in this spirit — acknowledging, that is, the obscurity of the impulses that have provoked them — resemble a work of the imagination: a piece of fiction, say. Sometimes when we set out to write a novel all we have to begin with are stray, enigmatic images, evanescent scraps of feeling and intuition, which unite to create an intimation of possibility. Our literary labours delve after that possibility and seek to bring it to the surface and give it form. When you start off you do not necessarily know where you are going or why.

The Memorial Fund will be used to establish an annual prize to be awarded to the writer best able to describe a visit to a foreign place or people. The award will not be for travel writing in the conventional sense, but for the most acute and profound observation of cultures and/or scenes evidently alien to the writer. Such scenes and/or cultures might be found as easily within the writer's native country as outside it. The award will be open to English language writers of any nationality under the age of 35. Submissions should not previously have been published and should be about 4,000 words (a length at which Shiva Naipaul particularly excelled). The winning entry will be published in the Spectator.

To reflect its importance the prize will also carry a substantial financial reward. The fund has already received a good number of contributions, but more money will be needed to secure the future of the award. We shall be most grateful for all contributions of whatever size. These should be sent to the Spectator Shiva Naipaul Memorial Fund (Account No. 261529), Drummonds Bank, 49 Charing Cross, London SW1A 2DX.

The precise rules will be announced when the first competition is launched in the spring.

Announcement of a prize honoring Naipaul's literary achievement (Spectator, *4 January 1986*)

Dust jacket for Naipaul's last novel, set in South America

Through the pained and searching perceptions of Dina, he filters his own bitter indictment of the mediocre masquerading as the grand, his plea of compassion for the person who must reinvent himself everyday.

Critics received the book both cautiously and enthusiastically. In her *New Statesman* review, Harriett Gilbert summed up the consensus with her statement that "whatever one's opinion of Naipaul's perception, there is skill to be admired in his recreation of a tropical city sustained by nothing but the habits of hatred and corruption." Though Gene Lyons, in his *Newsweek* essay, noted that "few will be comforted by its deeply pessimistic vision," he concluded that "this novel establishes Shiva Naipaul as a novelist of rare gifts and great authority." Nicholas Rankin called *A Hot Country* "a sad book

about waste, but a work of art that delights with its craft as it dismays with its vision."

At the time he was writing *A Hot Country*, Naipaul was scrutinizing his own identity and his place in the world. He had returned to Trinidad at the invitation of BBC2 to do a talk for their "Writers and Places" series. Naipaul recalled the early years of his education, "a barely controlled frenzy" to determine whether he would escape the island by winning a scholarship or fail and go "mad or bad with despair." His talk, published in *Listener*, became the basis of the title essay in his latest book, *Beyond the Dragon's Mouth* (1984).

Beyond the Dragon's Mouth, along with Naipaul's meditation on the special nature of his identity, was comprised of short stories, journalism, and travel essays that enlarged his themes of alienation, disillusion, and mimicry in the Third World. Naipaul began his title essay with a recollection of the death of his friend Steve, a Presbyterian convert destined for success, a scholarship winner enrolled with Naipaul at University College. Steve had died accidentally in his sleep after vomiting aspirin taken for a cold. The suddenness and, to Naipaul's mind, capriciousness of death had destroyed Naipaul's fragile conception of his place in the world: "The only emotion I felt was terror. Terror for myself. If someone like Steve could be snatched away like that, could be so swiftly and incomprehensibly annihilated, what about me?. . . Wasn't I too in imminent danger of being swallowed up and annihilated? My last vestiges of certainty and optimism melted away."

Naipaul reports that several days after his friend's burial he suffered a debilitating attack of anxiety that caused him to reconsider the expectations he had brought to London from Trinidad. After recreating the background he had struggled from, a western district of Port of Spain called St. James, he states, "I grew up in a no-man's land. . . . Such definition as I do now possess has its roots in nothing other than personal exigency. Every day, I have to redefine myself."

Naipaul sought definition through his writing. The story "Beyond the Dragon's Mouth" ends with Naipaul's academic career and a new beginning: "On a sunny afternoon I turned my back on Oxford. The future was not merely indistinct but murky. . . . In my meagre baggage was the beginning of a novel, the outlines of which had occurred to me one bilious and despairing afternoon as, sick in mind and body, I gazed at the mossy apple tree that grew in the unkempt garden of the flat I had been renting. It wasn't much to be taking away after four years, but it was better than nothing: it gave me, however unreliably, a reason to go on living."

Reviews of the book were few but appreciative. In his notice for *Spectator*, Peter Levi called Naipaul "the kind of writer one used to imagine in the future 30 years ago; intellectual in the sense of Camus or Malraux, widely travelled, perfectly serious, not tied to any kind of establishment, with Orwell's incision, with rich material and a tough flexible prose style. . . . He is like a late Roman historian of stern provincial culture but mixed tradition, Lucian, as it were, if Lucian had not composed in Greek, writing in crisp and sparkling Latin about the Burgundians." Ryszard Kapusćiński, writing for *New Republic*, noted that "Naipaul's man is a feeble creature, reconciled to fate, at best busy figuring out a strategy for survival, but always within the frame-work of the existing order. Everything takes place in a heavy, numbing climate. And that is why, although there is much disarming, warm humor and scathing, merciless irony . . . in the end this book is like the world in which we live: there are few reasons for joy in it."

Naipaul had traveled to Australia, via South-east Asia, in 1984 to gather material for a book about the island. An essay about the politicization of Aboriginal blackness was published but the work was not finished. Naipaul died of a heart attack 13 August 1985. His death attracted little notice in the United States, but in Great Britain critics and friends expressed regret that his career had ended with its promise unfulfilled. His crisis of identity to some degree resolved, his work earning consideration for its own value independent of its relation to his elder brother's work, Naipaul seemed ready to produce his masterpiece. His three novels had shown a progress toward a work that would gather his experience of the mixed cultures of Trinidad and London and the material he accumulated in his travels into a final definition of himself. In a talk he gave for the British television program "Opinions," Naipaul stated that "one of the greatest honours we can confer on other people is to see them as they are; to recognize not only that they exist but that they exist in specific ways and have specific realities." Though his career ended just as it was beginning, the quality of his work has earned him the honor of a specific response.

Theodore Sturgeon

(26 February 1918- 8 May 1985)

Reginald Bretnor

See also the Sturgeon entry in *DLB 8, Twentieth-Century American Science Fiction Writers*, Part 2: M-Z.

All working artists, and writers are no exception, can survive beyond their lifetimes in two ways: because of the persisting vitality and human relevance of their works and because shadows of their personalities endure in biographies and the reminiscences of their contemporaries. Theodore Sturgeon was a vital, virile, complex man, intensely interested in life and people and the world. Much has been—and probably more will be—written about this personal aspect, about the trials and triumphs of his life and how they may have affected his work and less directly, perhaps, the work of

other writers influenced by him. But he will live on as surely, and possibly more truly, in his short stories and novels and critical writings.

In his essay "Science Fiction, Morals, and Religion," written for my symposium, *Science Fiction, Today and Tomorrow* (Harper & Row, 1974), Sturgeon defended his genre:

> There is a force operating upon that body of literature called, or miscalled, science fiction, which, quite aside from the substantive content of the field, is moral and religious in nature. . . .
> This force shows itself in critical snobbery, in the "ghettoization" of science fiction, in the wide and erroneous conviction among the general reading (and viewing) public that

"Oh, I never read science fiction." What they really mean is that they consciously avoid that which is *called* science fiction, while attending in droves performances of *The Andromeda Strain* or *Lord of the Flies* or any of scores of other science fiction films, [and reading] novels, and short stories written by "mainstream" writers for the most part—those who have cut their creative teeth elsewhere than in the pages of the science fiction magazines. The assumption is that the magazines themselves, and therefore all of their authors' products, are trash and junk, poorly conceived and poorly written, and concern bolts, nuts, nuclei, zap-guns, and bug-eyed monsters; and anyway, ninety percent of it in concept and execution is trash.

Conceded, but then (and this has come to be known as Sturgeon's Law) ninety percent of *everything* is trash. The best of science fiction is as good as the best of any modern literature—articulate, poetic, philosophical, provocative, searching, courageous, insightful, and virtually anything else you expect of the best. Science fiction alone among the labels is consistently tarred with its own bad examples; the very same reader who knows the difference between *Hopalong Cassidy* and *Shane*, or between Mickey Spillane and Graham Greene, utterly fails to discriminate between the good and the bad in science fiction; utterly fails even to try, and says (in the words of Kingsley Amis), "This is science fiction—it can't be good," or, "This is good—it can't be science fiction"! And with this, we reach the point—the isolation of this genuinely religious force which has created such an injustice to the practitioners of science fiction—and which has committed such arrant robbery upon the reading public. For it has missed many delights, many excitements, and many beneficial explosions of mind.

This defense of science fiction was made necessary by an intellectual set of mind which, especially between the two World Wars, exiled science fiction from the mainstream of literature. Ted Sturgeon, like all of us in those years, entered this environment without choice, and it did not satisfy him. At its core was a fraudulent realism—fraudulent because of the constricting terms in which it defined human motivations, actions, aspirations. It was rooted in the decay and destruction of traditional values, and it consistently trumpeted the false dichotomy of "the warm human emotions" on the one hand and "cold, inhuman science" on the other, as though the two were not functions of the same human minds and bodies. Unhappily, it still survives today, not only in the mainstream, but in the science fiction field itself.

Here is the difference between this restricted literature and what Ted Sturgeon wrote: the pseudo-realistic writer has been content to hail the decay of values, or to rant against its effects on men and women, or to face it with a masochistic acquiescence. In each case, his attitude is one of acceptance. Ted Sturgeon was not content with such an attitude. Fully aware that values were decaying, he still perceived that a society cannot survive with no values whatsoever, and that decay, a symptom of change, warns us of the processes producing it, processes which require analysis—and which, once understood, can perhaps be adjusted to, directed, and controlled. He recognized that this, like any other problem of survival, is what the problem-solving mind of man exists to do, and the awareness permeates much of his work, science fiction, science fantasy, even pure fantasy. It is probably best illustrated in his novel *More Than Human* (1953), where he explicitly sets forth a beautifully conceived basis for a new ethics and, derived from that, a functional definition of morality.

In this connection, Ted Sturgeon did not shy away from controversial subjects such as aberrant

Theodore Sturgeon (Jay Kay Klein)

sexuality; indeed, some of his stories pioneered in the area. The difference between him and many another writer was that he never, *never* wallowed in it. If it was necessary to a story, he used it, but always with empathy and compassion. His stories were, in the best sense of the word, moral tales.

Fantasy and science fiction can be more than entertainment. They are literary tools for examining, questioning, and displaying the human condition; and at their best—as in so much of Sturgeon's work—they can do this with a precision, a keenness of insight, and a foreseeing almost-clairvoyance far more truthful than the so often duller and cruder tools of purblind realism. They are, in that sense, infinitely more realistic.

I have emphasized Ted's concern with the values and the rules of human life simply because I believe that, to handle these subjects adequately while simultaneously riveting the attention of the reader and "entertaining" him, and to do this well in our unsane, perilous world, requires much more than a facile talent: it demands high intelligence, more than a touch of genius, and—perhaps above all—intellectual courage.

All this leads to another area where Ted excelled in the writing of science fiction concerned with such "soft sciences" as psychology, psychiatry, and parapsychology. The writers who have dared in this area and *really* succeeded are few in number, and I can think of none who succeed quite as well so consistently, for in order to achieve that willing suspension of disbelief essential to the success of the imaginative in literature, not only must the writer be flawless in his logic, no matter how far out his premises, but he must entice his readers into following it, and involve them wholly in the passions and desires, the joys and fears, of his characters—something difficult enough, in all conscience, even when one is writing within the narrow boundaries of everyday experience. *More Than Human* involves psychology, parapsychology, and the possible destiny of man; and certain of Sturgeon's short stories come immediately to mind—"Maturity" is one, "The Other Man" another, "The Graveside Reader" a third. The first two deal directly with psychology and psychiatry; the last does not—it invents a basically intuitive soft science, which can be taught and learned, and which explores the human psyche more thoroughly than any system yet imagined. There are, of course, many, many more.

I think the secret of their success is the fact that Ted's characters are always more than puppets manipulated by the author to make the plot come

out. He *feels* with them; he *desires* with them; he *fears* with them—and, because of his mastery of his medium, he conveys their emotions to the readers who encounter them. Here a writer must share the qualities that make a good psychologist, a good parish priest, or—on a different level—a really good first sergeant. He must have a high order of empathy. He must understand that all men have their complexities. He must have his own clearly defined concepts of human cause and effect, of right and wrong, and he must be well enough balanced so that these concepts never become rigidly two-valued, allowing no more subtle, no more accurate, interpretations. Above all, he must possess the quality of mercy, so that he can pity his characters and weep with them and, when necessary, forgive them for their sins.

I certainly do not mean that everything Ted Sturgeon wrote was perfect, that every one of his characters was fully realized, that each of his plot schemes was without a flaw. That would be asking too much of any man, and especially of any man who only too often has been paid at a disgracefully low rate. But my object here is not the sort of analysis that searches for defects, even for the perhaps worthwhile purpose of instruction. It is simply to point out how very successful Ted was in the difficult tasks he set himself, and the degree to which he outshone the great majority of his compeers, and why he was able to accomplish this.

First, there was the man himself. *I have never heard anyone—fellow writer or editor or fan—say a bad word about him.* I found him to be warm and open, tremendously interested in people and what they did and what made them tick. I felt immediately that he genuinely *liked* people. Obviously, he was widely and deeply read, and in his conversation, as in his writing, taking delight in the language and his command of it.

Damon Knight has called Ted "the most accomplished technician the field has ever produced, bar none," and with this I would agree, though I might be tempted to substitute the word *artist* for technician. His mastery of using the right word at the right time in the right place was almost uncanny and invariably delightful, something that implies not only a rich vocabulary but also a tremendous sensitivity to words, phrases, sentences, their meanings and nuances. He was incredibly generous with this descriptive and narrative talent; his keen eye and excellent memory for the so-often-significant phenomena of nature, for those details which evoke our own memories and associations and so enable us to feel what his characters are feeling,

Dust jacket for Sturgeon's 1984 story collection about which Ray Bradbury declared, "the most complimentary thing I can think to say of Sturgeon is that I hated his damned, efficient, witty guts"

say that whatever effort and persistence it required certainly were worth it to those who have enjoyed his work, to those who will continue to enjoy it, and to all those writers who have learned and profited by reading it—and who will continue to do so in the future.

A TRIBUTE

from ARTHUR C. CLARKE

Ted Sturgeon was the best of us all, and he earned his place the hard way. He once told me how his step-father discovered his hidden cache of science-fiction magazines—and spent hours tearing them into shreds. Yet there was no anger in his voice: only a wistful regret. I do not think that Ted was capable of hatred.

Perhaps my best tribute to him is to admit something that I realized only recently. My own favorite story, "Transit of Earth," was undoubtedly inspired by his masterpiece, "The Man Who Lost the Sea."

I'm only sorry, Ted, that the day I spent with you, Marion, and Robin in 1952 had to serve for a lifetime.

A TRIBUTE

from JUDITH MERRIL

The best that may be here is yours, for you
Have given me a world of narrative
And verse. The colors of the dreams I knew
Now may be limned in words as sensitive.
Know that the finest phrase I can construe
Stems from a radiance inchoative

That you took pleasant pains to bring to bright
Edged focus. Luster in the words I write
Derives directly from your gift of light.

A TRIBUTE

from FREDERIK POHL

When Ted Sturgeon first burst on the science-fiction scene in the late 1930s it was my considered opinion that the only reason any of the rest of us ever got published at all was because it was simply physically impossible for him to write enough sto-

enabled him to enrich innumerable scenes and sentences, *especially where the drama and emotion of the story demanded it.* What can a writer do but stimulate his readers to create, in their own minds, that which he himself has experienced through the creation of his characters and their stories? At this, Ted was truly great. That is why his work is so believable, so enjoyable, and so worth experiencing.

This is true of his science fiction, of stories such as his memorable "Killdozer," and possibly even more true of his fantasy and soft-science fiction, where the preliminary evocations in the reader's mind are of even more critical importance. He once told me that he did not write easily, and had I not been a writer I might have found this difficult to believe in the light of the unimpeded flow of his words and sentences and paragraphs. Now we can

ries to fill all the blank pages. In grace of writing, in invention and in a dozen other ways he was, quite simply, the best there was. I wish we had that bright, kind presence back.

A TRIBUTE

from JOHN BRUNNER

If memory serves, the first time I took notice of the name Theodore Sturgeon was when I read, in the British edition of *Unknown,* that terrifying story "He Shuttles." It gave me nightmares; I was in my early teens.

But I already knew enough to recognize an exceptional talent. I was delighted to find "There is No Defense" in *Astounding*—and then, of course, there followed "The Dreaming Jewels," and eventually the stunning "More than Human."

I finally made his acquaintance in California in 1964, and took to him at once, as people generally did. But I had no chance to get to know him properly until he made his first trip to Europe. (Funny, that! Aware that he had held a seaman's ticket, I'd assumed he was a much-traveled man.)

My wife and I, and Ted, were at the Metz Science Fiction Festival, and planned to continue to the Ferrara Convention in Italy. We suggested he might like to come. He countered doubtfully, "Do you think they'd want me?"

I said approximately, "You *must* be kidding!" and proceeded to send a cable to Ferrara. (Ever try dictating a telegram in English for an Italian des-tination to a French telephone operator? It's not something you can handle in a hurry.) The reply was YES in capital letters with neon lights, so we piled him and his bags into the back seat of our open sports car and took him along. I remember how struck he was by the sight of Fiat's fourteen-wheel truck-and-trailer rigs on the *autostrade;* he said to him *Fiat* had always meant a compact car and nothing more. His fascination with heavy machinery no doubt went back to his days of driving bulldozers.

Not having planned to extend his trip this way, he had to borrow some Italian money from us. Within an hour or two of our arrival in Ferrara, he rushed up to pay it back, exclaiming, "An Italian publisher just said, 'You're Sturgeon? I owe you three thousand dollars and I didn't know where to send it! Here you are!' "

Well, he did have one bad habit. He never—but *never*—answered his mail. . . .

After the convention, he used some of this windfall to visit his brother in Austria whom he hadn't seen in twelve years. For a first-time visitor to Europe, he was certainly getting around.

We could not have wished for better company on that memorable trip. That's how I want to re-member Ted: all his senses alert to this strange new environment, picking out details that a thousand other travelers might miss, entertaining us constantly with anecdotes and reminiscences.

I count myself immensely fortunate to have known him, as it were, off duty, when he wasn't obliged to play the writer, or the guru, but could simply be his own impressive self.

UPDATED ENTRIES

Graham Greene
(2 October 1904-   )

Richard Hauer Costa
Texas A & M University

See also the Greene entry in *DLB 15, British Novelists, 1930-1959, Part I (A-L)*.

NEW BOOKS: *Dr. Fischer of Geneva; or the Bomb Party* (New York: Simon & Schuster, 1980; London: Bodley Head, 1980);

Monsignor Quixote (Toronto: Lester & Orpen Denys, 1982; New York: Simon & Schuster, 1982; London: Bodley Head, 1982);

J'Accuse: The Dark Side of Nice (London: Bodley Head, 1982);

Getting to Know the General (New York: Simon & Schuster, 1984; London: Bodley Head, 1984);

The Tenth Man (New York: Simon & Schuster, 1985; London: Bodley Head, 1985).

How many novelists can be said to be writing at or near the top of their form in their sixties, let alone their seventies? Lawrence Durrell and Angus Wilson are producing good books in their seventies; Anthony Burgess, Doris Lessing, Iris Murdoch, and Muriel Spark are almost book-a-year people in their sixties. But none has produced two novels as a septuagenarian that received reviews as distinguished as those accorded Graham Greene's *The Honorary Consul* and *The Human Factor*, published when he was seventy and seventy-four, respectively. Then, as Greene closed in on his eightieth year, he published to almost as much acclaim his twenty-first and twenty-second novels, *Doctor Fischer of Geneva; or the Bomb Party* (1980) and *Monsignor Quixote* (1982), plus a revealing memoir, *Getting to Know the General* (1984), issued a few weeks before his eightieth birthday.

"There is a point . . . in the careers of important and prolific novelists," writes Thomas F. Staley in *Commonweal*, "when each new work becomes a piece in the larger picture of their total work, and the entire picture becomes far more important than the latest piece." Staley is writing about *Monsignor Quixote*, but his sense of a canon just as surely applies to that book's immediate predecessor. Both short novels—156 and 221 pages, respectively—

return to landscape features of "Greeneland"—that is, to the terrain of man's fall. In *Doctor Fischer*, these are failure, betrayal, boredom fictionally implemented by such Greene staples as Russian roulette—*de facto*—and suicide—botched. In *Monsignor Quixote*, there is Greene's deployment of "opposite forces"—announced thirty years ago in the classic short story "The Destructors"—and here made dialectically vibrant in a running dialogue, frequently softened by wine, between a Quixote figure and a Sancho figure contrasting and comparing Communism and Catholicism.

The narrator of *Doctor Fischer* is Alfred Jones, a middle-aged Englishman with a minor secretarial job in a Swiss chocolate firm, who meets, falls in love with, and marries Anna-Luise Fischer, the very young daughter of the famous man of the title. Fischer, inventor-tycoon of "Dentophil Bouquet," the best-selling toothpaste in Europe, has in the manner of the Duke in Browning's "My Last Duchess" murdered his wife, Anna-Luise's mother, for "betraying" him by indulging her taste for music with a minor clerk. His revenge only exacerbating his despair, Fischer makes a hobby of dinner parties that are spiritually of a Grand Guignol character: laboratory experiments in the depths of human greed and self-degradation. Rightly perceiving that the rich are not less but more pathetically greedy than the poor, Fischer invites to his repasts a gallery of affluent grotesques whom Anna-Luise dubs the "Toads." He humiliates them in various ways, which they gladly tolerate for the sake of the expensive "presents" they know he will give them at the end of the ordeal. As Frank McConnell notes in *Commonweal*, they are "like the tests of a vengeful Jehovah eager to see, not who might be saved, but whom he can damn." Greene's sense of man's depravity has intensified since *A Burnt-Out Case* (1961). He leaves nothing ambiguous in his misanthropism. Anna-Luise dies—absurdly—and Jones, after a bungled suicide attempt, agrees reluctantly to attend Doctor Fischer's last supper. The party, McConnell wisely observes, "is a kind of communal Russian roulette." Looking at

Dust jacket for the Canadian first edition of Greene's most recent novel

the dead body of Fischer, Jones thinks: "This . . . was the bit of rubbish I had once compared in my mind with Jehovah and Satan."

For McConnell, with *The Honorary Consul* and *The Human Factor*, this book forms a trilogy that suggests Kafka's major unfinished books, *The Trial* and *The Castle*. He writes, "Just as Kafka banishes all virtues but Hope from his characters' moral repertoire, so Greene banishes all but Love. And in both cases, the odd and fascinating allegories that result are in fact acts of a distinctively modern, existential Faith in the very center of the abyss."

One would hesitate to excoriate Greene comically, as hack novelist-academic Garnet Bowen in Kingsley Amis's *I Like It Here* does for forcing him annually to add another title to his lecture notes. Also, one would not readily take it for granted that Greene has finally terminated what Frank Tuohy has praised as "the last complete literary career, moving from strength to strength." Nevertheless, it would appear that *Monsignor Quixote* constitutes the subsuming statement—part comedy, part allegory, all compelling—that culminates for Greene,

at seventy-eight, a career which began almost sixty years ago.

Robert Towers (*New York Times Book Review*) finds that the book presents the mixture as before. "In this seriocomic offshoot of Cervantes's romantic fable, we encounter once more that compound of Catholic faith and Communist sympathy that has contributed its peculiar tensions to so much of Greene's fiction. . . . The rejection of dogmatic authority—whether of the church, the party or the state—is the presiding theme of the book. . . . [Greene's] sympathies lie with human weakness rather than rectitude."

Maria Coute (in the *New Statesman*) reverses any verdict that Greene has "mellowed" by turning to fable, believing that *Monsignor Quixote* "creates a devastating blend of humour and sharp insight." She points to a tongue-in-cheek juxtaposition of the Gospels, the breviary, and the Communist Manifesto; the Roman Curia and the Politburo; the Protestant and the Euro-Communist; Torquemada and Stalin; the Cross and the Hammer and Sickle. "The bond between the fellow travellers is strengthened by a shared doubt and the implicit awareness that their respective faiths have not done away with either nationalism or imperialism . . . [the forces] that cause war."

Recently elevated to the rank of Monsignor, Father Quixote teams up with a Communist ex-mayor whom he dubs Sancho Panza, and together they set off across Spain for Madrid to buy the purple socks and bib that are the insignia of the new Monsignor's rank. They encounter as many windmills as their literary ancestors. Their mutual ineptitude scandalizes the bishop and nearly lands them in jail. A night in a brothel, a confession of an undertaker, an X-rated movie, and other adventures never disturb the pair's innocence. Through all of these adventures, which have their obvious parallels with Cervantes's novel, there is a running dialogue comparing Communism and Catholicism, but in the most human and personal terms, free from the intense emotional charges that longtime Greene watchers will remember from his earlier years.

Professor Staley concludes that Greene's concern, dramatized first in his early masterpiece *The Power and the Glory*, remains steadfast in *Monsignor Quixote:* the transforming power of illusion and the transforming power of love. "For Greene, love lies deeper than faith. Both Quixote and Sancho realize this at the end. After the priest dies, Sancho, the avowed Communist and dear friend, says, 'I wish I could come upon St. Paul now by accident and for the first time.'"

As he approached his eightieth year, the rarely interviewed Greene made no effort to deny that writing, which he always viewed as a means to fend off boredom, no longer sustains him. He told John Vinocur, Paris Bureau chief of the *New York Times*, that he still *wants* to feel like writing but doesn't feel like it. "I'm afraid of living too long away from writing." Since he has described writing as something like squeezing a boil, he awaits the irritation to develop. As he waits, Greene makes entries into the journal he keeps of his dreams. "There are more than 800 pages and they are indexed by letter, like the phone book, so that he can find a dream about the sea or a hotel or Khrushchev or Haiti," Vinocur reports.

He is managing throughout the 1980s to maintain his book-a-year pace, but what curious books they are. *J'Accuse* (1982), which is hardly a book at all, does no honor to its distinguished namesake. It is an exposé of links among the police, the courts, and the underworld in Nice, the French Riviera city ten miles from Antibes where Greene lives as a semirecluse in a modest two-room apartment overlooking the harbor. The background for *J'Accuse* dates from 1960 when Greene was in Africa doing research for *A Burnt-Out Case*. He became friendly with a French-Swiss family living there. Six years later, when he moved to Antibes, he discovered the family was living not far away in Juan-Les-Pins. They renewed their friendship; the wife became Greene's secretary, and the daughter, Martine, a surrogate niece.

Martine worked as a TV announcer in Monte Carlo and in 1972 married a suave real estate salesman named Daniel Guy. They divorced in 1979. The settlement, says Greene, was "monstrous." Martine got custody of the two children, but she had to live within 500 yards of her ex-husband and could never leave work later than 8:30 P.M.. According to Martine, Daniel snatched their older child after the settlement, roughing up his father-in-law, while Martine sprayed Daniel with tear gas. Afterward, the French courts gave Daniel custody of the child. To the rescue of his friend's daughter came Greene. First he caused a small sensation by returning his Legion of Honor to the French government (it was returned to him with the word that it could be forfeited only in death or disgrace). Then Greene appealed to Alain Peyrefitte, a fellow writer and minister of justice under former President Valery Giscard d'Estaing. His own investigation, Greene charged, had revealed that Daniel had served three prison terms for crimes of theft and violence in the 1960s. Although a special investigator agreed with Greene that the situation was "horrifying," nothing substantive was done; Greene decided to write and publish his polemic, a pale sound-alike of Emile Zola's courageous stand on the Dreyfus case nearly a century ago. Legal battles followed but with no redress for Greene's side.

The year 1984 saw the publication of still another slim book—*Getting to Know the General*—which may have provided the only clues Greene is likely to give to the guarded side of the traveling man in his seventies. It is a memoir of Omar Torrijos Herrera, the Panamanian strong man through whose skillful diplomatic maneuvering the Panama Canal was returned to Panama in 1978. Torrijos was also a romantic figure who could have stepped out of a novel by Graham Greene. In fact, he did step out of it. The novel Greene wanted to write was to have been called *On the Way Back;* it was to be about a woman who is invited to interview Panama's leader and who nearly becomes the lover of the leader's closest friend. The novel was aborted,

Front cover for Greene's bilingual exposé of the Nice criminal world

a victim of the tyranny truth can impose on fiction when it is not only stranger but stronger. In its place, built from the same blocks of remembrance, is this memoir of a six-year involvement between the most international of living authors and a revolutionary with a touch of the poet. It was in August 1981, while packing for his fifth trip to Panama, that Greene received word that Torrijos had died in a plane crash. He was moved to declare that "I have never lost as good a friend as Omar Torrijos." Although Greene had said substantially the same thing when Evelyn Waugh died, there is no book to prove it. *Getting to Know the General* is Greene's eulogy for General Torrijos, but it is a lot more besides.

There is something compelling about authors who travel to exotic places for their materials, make wars or revolutions parts of the action, and install

heroes who somehow perform honorably despite a paralysis of spirit. The Graham Greene hero records his daily grappling with the demons of a "despairing romanticism" that is always associated with boredom. Boredom, predictably, is a major ingredient here too in a book that might better have been titled *Getting to Wait for the General*. It is based on Greene's four trips to Panama, expenses paid, as the guest of an admirer—Torrijos—before, during, and after the book's centerpiece: the Washington signing by Torrijos and President Carter of a pair of treaties under which the U.S. agreed to relinquish control of the Canal by the year 2000. With Greene joining another "temporary Panamanian," Colombian novelist Gabriel García Márquez, in the Torrijos entourage, the twelve pages devoted to the signing produce the memoir's first real interest (after 130 pages). Up to then, Greene has relied on his diary for those matters even a great storyteller would otherwise have forgotten: the waiting around, the missed or canceled flights, the excursions to places where the measure of interest more often than not was the quality of the rum punches and pisco sours.

But in Washington, Greene's portrait of the Panama leader deepens.

"I am nervous," Torrijos tells Greene, "but Carter is more nervous and that comforts me a little." Torrijos expresses dismay that Carter had invited the South American military dictators—Videla of Argentina, Pinochet of Chile, Banzer of Bolivia, Stroessner of Paraguay. He would have preferred only those moderates who had supported him in his long negotiations—from Colombia, Venezuela, Peru.

Someone has said, perhaps only partly in jest, that if another general—Eisenhower—had appointed Hemingway ambassador to Cuba in the 1950s, the Bay of Pigs disaster might never have occurred under President Kennedy in the early 1960s. Whether, with dictators, the pen can ever be mightier than the sword is doubtful. Nevertheless, it is a virtue of this book to bring Latin American strong men and their politics down to something more human than media-vantage stereotype. Thus, on his final journey as Torrijos's posthumous emissary (January 1983) Greene returns to Nicaragua as a signal to the Sandinista leaders that the Torrijos spirit was still alive in Panama. He visits Cuba, where, at their first meeting since 1966, Greene finds a Castro who says he is reading *Monsignor Quixote*. Greene goes, finally, to a jungle village, built by refugees from El Salvador, who had been rescued from their perilous exile in Honduras by Torrijos.

The book promised to be as controversial among American readers as his anti-U.S. novel *The Quiet American* of thirty years ago. But Greene is not an idealogue; he has lived his life under a torment of faith of which his political views are the merest suggestion. Anyone interested in knowing about the enormous commitment in sweat and sacrifice that went into building the Panama Canal and the extraordinary dramas behind its disposition should not look into this brief memoir. What the reader gets are sidebars of the master storyteller's craft; and his pictures are not only of General Torrijos but of his associates, the byproducts, in this case, of the abandoned novelist.

Although the reviews of this, Greene's most recent significant book, were largely favorable, its creator's own view was that *Getting to Know the General* is "very unsatisfactory," too dispersed, not clearly enough a memoir or an autobiography or a travel book.

If *The Tenth Man* (1985) should prove the last work by Greene published in his lifetime, it would be, in the worst sense, ironic. This 30,000-word melodrama, described by its publisher as Greene's "newly discovered novella," dates from the midst of World War II—1944—when the 40-year-old author was doing some screenwriting for M-G-M. Greene, who declares in his straight-faced introduction that he remembered the manuscript only as a filmscript outline of a few pages, purports now to welcome the "discovery" and even hints that he finds it superior in craft to his rightly celebrated scenario for *The Third Man*. The opening, in fact, is vintage Graham Greene. Thirty imprisoned Frenchmen draw lots to determine which three of them will be executed in retaliation for three slayings by the resistance. The wealthiest of the pris-

oners, Jean-Louis Chavel, an attorney, draws one of the unlucky lots, but cheats death by signing away his fortune and ancestral home to the family of a young clerk—the tenth man—who takes his place before the firing squad. This opening section provides a model of economy, the sort of taut writing and plotting that were trademarks of the "entertainments" of Greene's earliest period. However, once Greene allows the war to end and the lawyer to return to the estate that is no longer his, the novella turns wholly implausible. *The Tenth Man* has sold briskly in England and the U.S.

Talk of failure punctuated Greene's recent conversation with John Vinocur. He would rather use the word *doubt,* which, he says, was the theme of *Monsignor Quixote,* the finest of his recent fiction. He would also like to set the record straight on a number of sore matters. It had been made out that he didn't like the United States, which he last visited in the 1960s, and that he once said he preferred to live in the Soviet Union than in California. He placed President Reagan on the same level as Pope John Paul II, men he didn't care for a bit. The comment on Russia and California, he told Vinocur, "was meant to be ironic. I would end my days much quicker in Russia than in California, because the Russians take writing seriously, so I would soon find myself in a gulag, which is in a way a compliment to a writer. Whereas one might drag out one's years in California in some backwater."

Greene is invariably wry when the subject turns to mortality. Asked point-blank by Anthony Burgess when he was going to get the Nobel Prize, Greene replied that when he was asked the same question by a Swedish journalist he had said he was looking forward to getting a bigger prize than the Nobel. "Which one?" asked Burgess. "Death," Greene answered, followed immediately by a request that they end the interview and have lunch.

Doris Lessing

(2 October 1919-   )

Mary Doll

See also the Lessing entry in *DLB 15, British Novelists, 1930-1959, Part I (A-L)*.

NEW BOOKS: *Documents Relating to the Sentimental Agents in the Volyen Empire* (New York: Knopf, 1983; London: Cape, 1983);
The Diary of a Good Neighbor, as Jane Somers (London: Michael Joseph, 1983; New York: Knopf, 1983);
If the Old Could . . . , as Jane Somers (London: Michael Joseph, 1984; New York: Knopf, 1984);
The Diaries of Jane Somers (New York: Knopf, 1984);
The Good Terrorist (London: Cape, 1985; New York: Knopf, 1985).

Doris Lessing's career continues to be marked by surprises. Her venture into space fiction, with the five-novel sequence entitled Canopus in Argos: Archives, was a departure from the emphasis in the Children of Violence sequence (1964-1969) on feminism and psychic wholeness. Her writing under the pseudonym Jane Somers caused a literary storm. *The Diary of a Good Neighbor* (1983) and *If the Old Could . . .* (1984), later published together as *The Diaries of Jane Somers* (1984), were written pseudonymously to prove a point about the plight of new writers on the publishing scene. In tone, style, and theme *The Diaries of Jane Somers* are entirely different from the Canopus series, for in *The Diaries,* Lessing returned to romantic storytelling. Her latest novel, *The Good Terrorist* (1985), is realistic and doubly unromantic in its depiction of the day-to-day existence of a band of terrorists in London.

Stylistically, Lessing is a chronicler of daily events, preferring the mode of documents, reports, journal entries, and diaries over traditional narration. Her novels tend to run in series. For her, a story is ongoing, evolutionary, or cyclical rather than linear or closed. Her forms allow her to demonstrate the creative potential that lies within flux. Her emphasis on ordinary objects and impressions gives further testimony to her belief that it is not the grand design or the "great man that" moves

historical events; it is, rather, the small personal voice.

Thematically, the Canopus series gives Lessing a vantage point from which to criticize the place of ideology in the rise and fall of empires. Major galactic empires, Canopus, Sirius, and Puttiora, engage in rivalries that emerge out of differing social theories of man. Even in outer space, such ideas as conformity, self-indulgence, and rationality lead to decline. The fifth and last book of the Canopus series is a continuation of Lessing's expression of contempt for societies that fall prey to inner decay because they lack love, compassion, and vitality. Here she restates the theme of *The Four-Gated City* (1969), among others of her works: that rational attempts to wrest order from chaos will staunch life's flow. Her political and visionary satires remain consistent with her conviction, expressed early on, that social constraint destroys psychic creativity.

Another theme that has been consistent in Lessing's work is the struggle of women for selfhood in a male-dominated world. The Jane Somers diaries continue this theme. They detail the fabric and texture of life from the every day concern with food, shelter, and clothing. These basic needs acquire political and psychological dimension as we watch Jane Somers cope, first, with a lonely old woman of ninety, and then with a sudden romance in her own middle years. Although opposite in style and emphasis, the Canopus series and *The Diaries* reflect two prongs of Lessing's vision: the political and the psychological. *The Good Terrorist* deals with both.

The earlier books in the Canopus series are *Shikasta* (1979); *The Marriage Between Zones Three, Four, and Five* (1980); *The Sirian Experiments* (1981); and *The Making of the Representative for Planet 8* (1982). *Documents Relating to the Sentimental Agents in the Volyen Empire* (1983), written as a collection of documents including reports in dialogue form, relates the impressions of a mature agent, Klorathy, as he comments on the collapsing empire, Volyen, and guides a younger agent, Incent, in the Path of

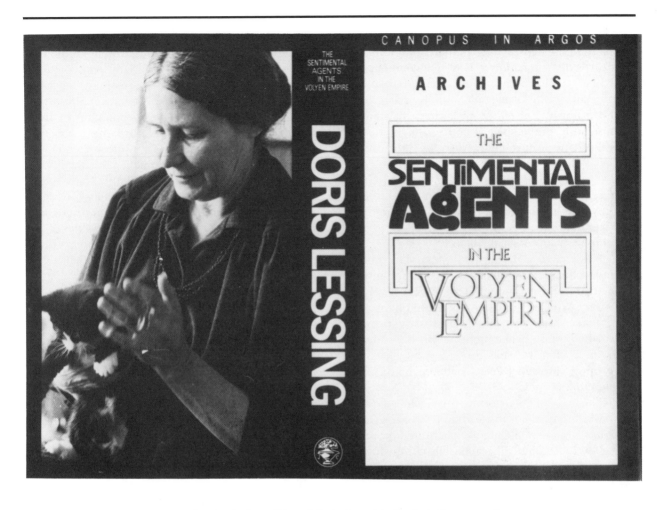

Dust jacket for the first edition of the last novel in Lessing's Canopus series

the Purpose. For the Canopean empire, the Purpose is not to be a victim of words. Incent is a "sentimental" agent because, no matter how many times he is sent to the Hospital for Rhetorical Diseases, he remains ill of free will and cannot develop an immunity to the meaning of language. Klorathy must train agents to avoid emotional response to words so that they may become effective tyrants. Tyrants exercise language control and stimulus control, and encourage crowds of people to behave like animals. Tyrants are at home in abstraction, with the abstract goal of power. "And so a career develops that has no future in the existing order, but relates only to an idea; the aspiring one, as he or she looks about at the chaos, the ugliness, the disorder of a time of disintegration, sees beyond it some infinitely noble society ruled by himself." So writes Klorathy, approvingly, of a training process that could as well be describing a social experiment such as fascism, nazism, or communism.

The agents' conditioning involves learning to develop clever talk about comradeship, social responsibility, peace, and friendship while at the same time learning to organize a machinery of brutality. To this end, Incent is surrounded by an artificial environment: he is isolated in a stimulus-free white room that is intended to prepare his mind for "passionless stuff": "It was as silent as in a cave deep under the earth, as silent as if we floated in the black spaces between galaxies. . . . At first you are allowed only glimpses of circles, triangles, squares, all a luminous white on flat white. . . . soon, however, the mind begins to protest against changelessness, longs for relief, and . . . you understand that this is your thought—hunger transmuted from a sharp need into the passionless stuff of the mind. . . ." Far from being cured of emotion, Incent acquires a reborn love of shape and design, seeing the revolving mathematicals not as abstractions but as dancing rhombohedrons.

The novel's interest focuses in part on Incent's periodic lapses into human emotion and Klorathy's determination to lead the agent back to the Path of the Purpose. Lessing's main satire, however, occurs in the scenes of a public trial, where the governor of Volyen, Grice, accuses the state of manipulating the people. "I accuse Volyen of not providing me—representing for the purpose of this trial all Volyen's citizens—with real information as to our basic nature. . . ." Governor Grice operates under the delusion that he can criticize tyranny. He assumes that his logical training can now be put to a different revolutionary aim: to save the empire from internal collapse.

The trial is a drama of tyrants. The public defender, Spascock, obstructs the issues and mocks judicial procedure. The publicity expert, Krolgul, has a face "full of the vitality of triumphant cruelty." Later, this cruel inner nature is expressed outwardly by his apelike motions. He walks on all fours and, when he talks, presses a knuckle into the ground. The chief Peer, Arithamea, knits and simpers in a corner.

The trial takes a serious turn when Grice's chief witness is called to the stand. Stil, educated from hardship in a satellite of the empire, presents himself as an example of responsible citizenship by his story of diligence and work, putting to shame the population of Volyen, "allowed to go to flesh." Lessing's portrayal of the masses' herd instinct demonstrates her belief that tyranny cultivates the animal brain in man. When rhetorical manipulation succeeds, people swallow a set of ideas that soften them and arrest the life force. Once energetic, self-disciplined, and questioning, a people become bored, uninspired, self-indulgent.

The novel ends in Volyen's defeat by the planet Maken. In her vision of galactic empires, Lessing introduces conquerers who are successively lower on the evolutionary scale. It is not survival of the fittest, but the reverse of Darwinism: from human to monkey to reptile. The Makens are maggot-headed birdmen who ride on the backs of lizards and wear animal bodysuits. Their undeveloped nature is revealed by their external appearance: glittering eyes, thick black fur, thunderous wings, claws, beaks. And while outwardly they are primitive and frightening, inwardly they are even worse. They are "all alike. All, all absolutely alike."

Variety, the interplay of opposites, color: these are the "sentiments" Lessing sees as essential for political and psychological well-being. A range of shape, size, and texture becomes the external manifestation of inner health and rootedness. More than words or speeches, a display of the texture of clothing and routine of daily living patterns will illustrate, conclusively in Lessing's view, the state of the psyche. And so it becomes an important point for the novel that, at the moment of their defeat by a lower order of creature, the degenerate Volyens look at themselves for the first time. In contrast to the all-alike birdmen, the Volyens appear suddenly, sadly, in a new light: "hair yellow and brown and red and silver and black, in skins that were white and cream and grey and pink and yellow and brown and black; they could not get enough of gazing at one another, and marvelling at . . . the surprises and amazingness of what they were."

Rosemary Herbert, reviewing *Documents* in the *Christian Science Monitor*, wrote, "Incent's earnest rhetoric makes good material for satire and humor, two elements that make this novel the most approachable of Lessing's Canopean fare." But other critics treated it as harshly as they did the previous books in the series. Edward Rothstein, writing for the *New York Times Book Review*, said: "Whatever promise it offers of satire and enlightened vision dissipates into cliché and platitude. The humor falls flat, the rhetorical jests become tiresome and the political insights seem derivative. The tone wavers uncertainly, mixing farce, cynicism and banal religiosity." And writing for the *Times Literary Supplement*, F. L. Wallis commented: "Formerly Lessing offered keen appraisals of the insidious seductions of orthodoxy; now she has relaxed and is merely orthodox. To be orthodox is to be incapable of irony, it seems. . . . Unfortunately, [the book's] imperial theme . . . attracts authors who have ceased to examine myths and are looking for somewhere to establish and enforce them." The critics generally felt that the book was, in the words of Susan Lardner in the *New Yorker*, inept and flimsy.

Part of the difficulty of *Documents* lies in the reader's total lack of personal identity with the narrator, Klorathy. Klorathy first made an appearance in *The Sirian Experiments* (1981), volume three of the series, as a Canopean administrator; but even familiarity with him does not reveal who he is. He is only administrator: without personality, capable of objective description only. He does his duty, makes his reports, and with a single-mindedness that precludes the slightest doubt, is humorless and unperceptive. Such a nonhuman ideologist becomes the vehicle for Lessing's irony: commitment to an idea turns an individual into a pawn. *Docu-*

ments is dull reading because its narrator's mind is dulled by the zeal of the empire.

Although she is still working with a basic dialectic between ideology and sentiment, politics and psychology, Lessing's theme here lacks the tension of its earlier expression in *The Golden Notebook* (1962). There public and private, political and personal, historical and fictional, male and female become oppositions that play off against each other in exciting, creative ways among five notebooks. The five notebooks—black, red, yellow, blue, and golden—express the varying parts of a whole, no one part or color offering total truth. The Canopean series is also in five parts, each part its own novel. But here the fifth book does not offer the golden vision of the fifth notebook, which fused the other four viewpoints into one complex whole. Rather, the fifth novel of the Canopean series ends in disintegration and fragmentation, suggesting a reversal of the author's earlier theme that out of chaos could come a creative, integrative order. Lessing's outlook in the 1980s is more apocalyptic and pessimistic than her golden view of the 1960s.

The style and tone of *The Diary of a Good Neighbor* and *If the Old Could . . .* are clearly more concerned with the ordinary and are less moralistic, but the insistence on political and psychological variety marks them as Lessing works. The question of why a famous author would wish to write under a pseudonym is fascinating. Traditionally, women used male pen names to protect their female identity, as was the case with George Eliot and George Sand. Or male writers selected other names to suggest a sense of the exotic, as with Stendhal and Saki. But Doris Lessing had other reasons. She explained her motives fully, after the true identity of Jane Somers was made public, in the preface to the 1984 Vintage edition of *The Diaries of Jane Somers.* "I wanted to be reviewed on merit, as a new writer, without the benefit of a 'name,'" she wrote. With a degree of relish obviously aimed at the reviewers and publicists, she outlined three other reasons for her experiment into pseudonymous writing. First, she wanted to shake off the labels that had been customarily attached to her work, seeing herself as not just a political writer and more than an author of space fiction. Second, she wanted to encourage new writers by illustrating with her case that certain publishing procedures are unrelated to an author's talent. And third, she offered this "faintly malicious" motive: "some reviewers complained they hated my Canopus series, why didn't I write realistically, the way I used to before?" In presenting her work under the Jane Somers pseudonym, Less-

ing proved that her writing style completely eluded the reviewers.

The publishing story of Jane Somers's diaries, referred to by *Time* reviewer Richard Zoglin as "the golden hoax book," is as follows. With her agent Jonathan Clowes, Lessing decided to submit *The Diary of a Good Neighbor* to her main British publishers, Jonathan Cape and Granada. Both turned the manuscript down as "too depressing," although her editor at Cape, Tom Maschler, never read it. "I saw the readers' reports," Lessing said, "and was reminded how patronized and put-down new writers are." A third British publisher, Michael Joseph Limited, accepted the work—reportedly when the editorial director there, Phillippa Harrison, commented that the manuscript reminded her of Doris Lessing. *Diary* was published by Michael Joseph in April of 1983, and also by publishers in France, Germany, Holland, and America. The following June, *If the Old Could . . .* was published as a sequel. The only reference to Lessing was a veiled statement by the publishers, who had been brought in on the secret, that Jane Somers was the pseudonym of "an English journalist."

The reaction to Jane Somers by Lessing's American publisher, Alfred Knopf, was very different. Her editor there, Robert Gottlieb, saw the manuscript and had an immediate response. "As soon as I read it," he said, "I burst into laughter because it was a voice that is so well known to me." For two and a half years, from the time of his first reading until Knopf republished it under Lessing's name in 1984, Gottlieb was "afraid to make any signal" lest his colleagues in the field expose the pseudonym scheme. Recalling the events in a *Time* interview the week of the Vintage publication, Gottlieb said, "It seemed to me a true Doris notion, and I was enjoying watching her at her most playfully perverse. . . . she is not only a famous writer but a great woman, and it was my job to help her."

Ironically, helping her initially meant doing little to promote Jane Somers. *The Diary of a Good Neighbor* sold only 2800 copies in America and 1500 in England, even though it was reviewed favorably. *Publishers Weekly*, for example, carried a review which should have spurred interest in Jane Somers: "From the unlikely subject of geriatrics, this spirited and entertaining novel emerges. Janna is a modish Londoner, a smugly successful magazine editor. . . . Maudie, an ancient bundle of smelly rags, whom Janna casually befriends, is the catalyst for a new way of living. . . . Although overlong, this novel is original, brimming with vitality and, like Maudie, funny and sad." But when *If the Old Could*

. . . came out a year later, Somers had not gained a following, despite reviews in three American book review supplements, including the *New York Times,* which called Jane Somers "a courageous writer."

Gottlieb confirmed Lessing's contention that, without publicity and promotion, a new writer has difficulty. For proof, Gottlieb cited the sales differences between the two Knopf printings: while Jane Somers had a sales record of about 3000 copies each for the first printing, the second printing, entitled *The Diaries of Jane Somers* by Doris Lessing, sold six times that number: between 17,500 and 20,000 copies. According to Gottlieb, the reissued *Diaries* was not only more than the standard paperback sales, it was more than Lessing's normal sales of between 15,000 and 30,000 copies for fiction. Lessing's point was that were it not for her unmasking, "poor old Jane Somers could have faded away forever."

The critics, however, tended to regard Lessing's experiment with skepticism. Some were downright hostile. Jonathan Yardley argued in the *Washington Post* that the Lessing scam was evidence of the fairness of literary marketing: not only could new writers get published, they could get reviewed. Others felt Lessing had engaged in a cheap publicity stunt, beneath the dignity of her reputation as an established author. But there were those, like Ellen Goodman, who praised Lessing's act as "an extraordinary, vulnerable piece of risk-taking." Writing also for the *Washington Post,* Goodman was sympathetic to the notion of pseudonymous writing in general, suggesting that famous writers may be particularly susceptible to fraudulent promotion tactics.

Clearly, Doris Lessing's reputation has been anchored by the academic community. Her status as a major literary figure of the twentieth century has been confirmed not only by the formation of a Doris Lessing Society but also by the Modern Language Association, which in December 1984 devoted two sessions to her work. At one session, on the theme of Lessing's politics and ideology, scholars presented papers on her African stories, her languages of feminism, and her futurist fiction. The other session, on the politics of Lessing's fiction, presented a range of ideas from her subversion of the "ideology of coherence" to the importance "of women's things." Scholars from the University of Reading, Columbia University, and the University of East Anglia were among those making presentations. Despite this academic acclaim, however, Lessing has nothing but scorn for those makers or breakers of literary reputation, the book pundits and promoters who failed to recognize in the works of Jane Somers the identifying traits of Doris Lessing's writings.

Among these traits is Lessing's interest in the way the things of daily life, such as food and clothing, both disguise and reveal identity. In *The Summer Before the Dark* (1973) this motif becomes itself the point of an experiment conducted by Kate Brown. She assumes two guises, first as a disheveled woman dressed in unbecoming clothes. Passing in front of a group of construction workers, Kate makes no impression on them. She is invisible in that space. But crossing that same space again, this time in the guise of a stylish woman, Kate becomes visibly an object of desire. Clothing is like a tag, or a famous label, to which others will respond.

Clothing and food are used in the Jane Somers books as indicators of economic and social class; more, they breach political gaps to become a shared concern of female relationships. That which stitches women together—throughout time, throughout class distinction—is the "stuff" of life. *The Diary of a Good Neighbor* makes this theme explicit. It is the story of a four-year relationship between Janna Somers, a successful editor of a fashion magazine, and Mrs. Maudie Fowler, a widow in her nineties. The phrase "good neighbor" refers to a type of social worker who provides needed comforts to shut-ins. But Janna's relationship does not arise out of social concern; it arises out of love. She is, she insists, Maudie's companion: there to defend her against the laws of the state and to befriend her as she approaches death. Their times together are filled with the ups and downs of daily emotion. Oddly, it is Maudie, dying of cancer, who gives the life sense to Janna: "She was chilly, she was sick, she was weak—but I could feel the vitality beating there: life. How strong it is, life. I had . . . never felt life in that way, as I did then, washing Maudie Fowler, a fierce angry old woman. Oh how angry: it occurred to me that all vitality is in her anger. I must not, must *not,* resent it or want to hit it back."

Maudie and Janna share a mutual attraction like that between nail and magnet. Maudie is sharp and hard: an ancient crone, with a little wedge of a face; she is a little fury, her body a cage of bones; she is a crooked witch, her nose and chin meeting. These sharp features make her both like and unlike Janna. Janna works for a magazine called *Lilith.* In mythology, Lilith was a witch who roamed desolate places. Lessing implies that both women connect with their mutual at-homeness in the extremities of the heart; they share a sharp loneliness. But they are also attracting opposites. Janna, a public person, does all the right things: she wears fine clothes, has excellent taste, and conveys in her life a magical unity. Publicly, she is a magnet of energy and dynamism. But privately, Janna's brilliance has cracks. Her husband's death from cancer left a gap in her life; she wonders if she ever really loved him. Her sister has values that are not hers. Somehow, Maudie expresses the rage that Janna is not able to express. A dynamism of negative emotion pulls their opposite poles together; Maudie's "horror-shivering masochism" sets Janna's magnetism alive.

Janna acquires her sense of self as she becomes emotionally attached to another generation of woman. Partly, it is a historical appreciation (she is a writer of historical novels). But also it is a confirmation, abstractly appreciated in literature and concretely realized with Maudie, that small daily doings can plug the cracks of her own private fears. "When I read diaries from the past, what fascinates me is what they wore, what they ate, all the details . . . how did a woman make up her bed, or lay her table, or wash her underclothes; what did she have for breakfast, in 1780, in a middle-class household. . . ." Maudie thus becomes representative of a bygone era, when the objects of life were valued not for their commercial but for their aesthetic qualities. When Maudie fondles Janna's hat, there is a knowingness to her touch: "She looks at the satin that lines the hat, the way the lining is stitched in—blown in, rather; oh yes, the one who did this hat knew her work all right! And the little white quills. . . ."

The question *The Diary of a Good Neighbor* raises comes out of such small moments and goes to the heart of Lessing's concerns as a writer. How do we value ourselves? And by what? Janna's work is satisfying, but it does not give her the value of human relationship. Only when she gives of herself to geriatrics like Maudie Fowler or Eliza Bates or Annie Reeves does Jane Somers find dimension in her life. She shares with these ancients a moment, as when a hat is fingered or a cream cake eaten, and time becomes charming and utterly real.

If the Old Could . . . is the second part of Jane Somers's diary and takes up where *Good Neighbor* leaves off, after Maudie's death. The title is taken from a French proverb—"If the young knew . . . If the old could . . ."—to suggest an incapability of human will to alter the course of events. Here the unalterable event is a love story between Jane—as she now calls herself—and Richard. But is is also the story of the way in which a very ordered career

person allows her life to become filled with complications. More than her relationship with Richard, the diary charts an impossible situation when Jane allows her niece Kate to come live with her. A totally different female partnership evolves in this book of the diaries; yet, as the second mirrors the first, it reflects the infinitely complex, infinitely open possibilities of human potential.

Jane meets Richard by chance one morning on the way to work. Fate throws them together, but also keeps them apart; for no matter how strong the attraction, they are prevented from forming an alliance. Richard's marriage to Silvia has produced three children. One of them has Down's syndrome; one of them spies on Richard and Jane; and the third son, Matthew, of college age, falls in love with Jane. Richard and Jane share a public romance, meeting in elegant restaurants and pubs, taking long walks on Hampstead Heath, talking on the phone at work. They do not go to bed together. Their attraction arises from a need each feels for release from their other life. Despite the lack of physical consummation, the relationship—like that between Jane and Maudie—is one of two souls who find delight and magic in each other's company.

The other focal point of *If the Old Could . . .* , Kate and Jane's relationship, is really the more interesting because of its sadomasochistic undertones. Kate, the youngest of Jane's sister's daughters, with a history of mental instability, comes unannounced to live with Jane. Jane would never have willed such a flatmate; to Jane, her living space is sacred, containing such cherished objects as "two elegant little armchairs, yellow and bright, with candy-striped cushions." Kate makes the light color of the living room gray and slowly spreads her gray distress throughout the flat. But Jane's resilience reminds the reader of Maudie's fierceness; she is able somehow to give back, blow for blow, what comes her way.

Lessing suggests that this resilience is sensual in a nonsexual way. Sensuality is implied by the way Jane delights in her body and in the fabrics she wears: "When the rooms were all tidy, I had a bath, not one of 'my' baths lasting hours which are so rare now, but a bath for effect. I stood in front of the mirror in my Janet Reger knickers and let the silk of the petticoat slide over my head, ivory with coffee lace. . . ." The other side of this frank determination to luxuriate is a need to tidy. When Kate's friends from the squat, or commune, come into Jane's living room, she achieves peace of mind by insisting on her style of hostessing. She waits on her grubby guests, offering them her best cups and

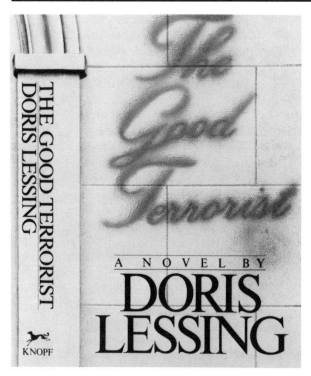

Dust jacket for the American edition of Lessing's most recent novel

saucers, delicious coffee, and a large fruitcake. It is as if, by the erection of social barriers, she can protect herself from falling apart.

Eating habits also reveal psychological dimensions about Lessing's characters. Maudie shows her style and also her fragility, in the *Good Neighbor* diary, by eating off of big old cracked plates and drinking from a flowered Worchester teapot, also cracked. Tommy in the *Golden Notebook* establishes bullying behavior when he eats slowly, sullenly. Kate's choice of poor food and her animal-like eating mannerisms illustrate the degree to which she is alienated not only from others but from herself: "Kate sat eating shortbread biscuits with a total avid concentration, both hands at work, one lining up the next biscuit to be consumed, while the other actually fed her mouth." After a suicide attempt, Kate evidences her disassociation by plunging pickled onions into her mouth.

Being able to respond to color in food, clothing, and living space is another indicator of one's sensual being. Jane is fully conscious of beauty in even the most mundane arrangements. "I make supper.... But probably she [Kate] doesn't connect the red mush on her plate which sets off the slim brown frankfurters with the silken magenta marvel she brought in from that wonderhouse,

London." Indeed, Jane occupies a fully sensuous world and is a textured, complicated person. This is what makes Jane Somers, in Lessing's view, whole. She is open, as well, to the different colorations of her inner emotions and is unafraid of her sometimes wild contradictions: "I hate Matthew ... I am in love with him. I am sick with concern over Kate ... I admire and rely on Hannah. I love Richard. I dream of Freddie."

Lessing's portraits of the three ages of women in these diaries are richly affirming of the middle and older years. In their second half of life, women are seen as vital and sensual, even in physical frailty. They are what the psychologist Carl Jung would call fully individuated, having made contact with their dark side without breaking down. Indeed, Jane knows her boundaries. She is like a window that looks out on the night sky. The colors of the London nights—orange, purple, pink, and pearl—give texture to the darkness without disturbing the calm. Lessing's women are deeply textured, or complicated, with dimensions of feeling; but they manage their lives from a still point.

In *The Good Terrorist* (1985), Lessing returns to political ideas in a drably realistic mode. Alice Mellings, the thirty-six-year-old central character described in the book's title, tries to impose order and even beauty on her setting, but she lacks the vision or intelligence to be a romantic—or even a strong central character. One of Lessing's caretaking women, she manages to turn a disheveled London house that is slated for destruction into a comfortable squat for a loosely bonded group of fellow radicals, mostly members of the Communist Centre Union. Alice's considerable energy is misplaced—on her companions, on the house, and on her cause. Jasper, with whom she has lived for fifteen years, is a homosexual. Alice has not allowed herself sexual feelings, though she would rather not have other people know her relationship with Jasper is asexual. Although he treats her coldly and contributes nothing to their maintenance, Alice regards Jasper with "admiration and wistful love."

To keep the house and its occupants (most of whom, like Alice, do not have or want jobs), she steals from her father and mother. That the thefts can have serious economic effects on her parents does not occur to Alice, nor does she think of herself as a thief: "she had always been honest," she believes, "had never stolen anything, not even as a child."

Alice and the other terrorists have a very unclear idea of their aims and targets. Jasper and Bert Barnes, a housemate, go to Ireland to offer the group's services to the Irish Republican Army but are rejected. Alice reasons that "if the IRA wouldn't have Bert and Jasper (and, by extension, the rest of them, Alice included), then something else of the kind would certainly make its appearance. They all wanted to be of use, to serve!" When their house becomes the site for the CCU Congress, reading material displayed on a hall table includes *"The Case for the IRA,* all the Greenpeace pamphlets, several books about Lenin, a long poem in free verse about Greenham Common, a large variety of pamphlets for the Women's Movement, and on antivivisection, vegetarianism, the use of chemicals in foodstuffs, Cruise, Trident, the dumping of radioactive waste in the sea, the ill-treatment of calves and chickens, and the conditions inside Britain's prisons."

Alice is a good terrorist partly because she cares for the others, but also in the sense that she is still the "good girl" self she remembers being as a child, outwardly serene and smiling but "shaky and trembling inside, where her anger lived." Lessing may also be saying that Alice is a good terrorist because she is a *bad* terrorist, in practical terms. She dislikes the idea of hurting innocent people, though she becomes involved in doing so.

In the *New York Times Book Review,* Denis Donoghue calls Lessing's characters "types rather than individuals, exemplars of aging youth, inhabitors of an experience that asserted its international character, fifteen years ago, in clothes, language, attitude, music, and gesture." He commented that *The Good Terrorist* "is bound to give comfort to the middle classes, if only because their enemies, Alice and her friends, are so ludicrously inept." Even amateur terrorists, however, can make bombs that kill and maim at random, and Lessing is clearly making this point.

Alison Lurie, in the *New York Review of Books,* noted that the characters seem "makeshift, sharp-edged, and unfinished,"—the way their homemade bombs look—but called the book "one of the best novels in English I have read about the terrorist mentality and the inner life of a revolutionary group since Conrad's *The Secret Agent.*"

The Good Terrorist has connections with much of Lessing's earlier work not only in its political interest (though it makes no specific political statement), but also in its conflict between generations and its detailed depiction of a woman who spends her energies "cooking and nannying for other people," as Alice's mother describes both Alice and herself. Though Alice never sees herself clearly and therefore never grows as a character in any way, she is successful at least by the author's aims for

her: Lessing told Caryn James (in a brief interview that accompanies Donoghue's review) that the novel was about "a kind of self-styled revolutionary that can only be produced by affluent societies," and that the contradiction between the nurturing and terroristic sides of Alice's personality is "a pretty common characteristic in this type of person."

In a 1983 interview conducted by William Phillips of the *Partisan Review,* Lessing gave the impression of being a modest person. But when asked what her ambition was, she gave an altogether different kind of impression. "I had in mind the kind of book she saw as her ideal work," Phillips said, explaining his question. "Her answer shocked me so, I hardly knew what to say. She said she wanted to conquer England, and she had already accomplished that. I thought of all the conquerers who had preceded her, and could scarcely find a basis of comparison with this small, gentle, soft-spoken woman."

Lessing's reply to Phillips's question would seem to be but another of her surprises. She is a woman of enormous ambition and strange humor. Her use of inventive fantasy in Canopus in Argos: Archives as a vehicle for her social imagination and her fun with the critics as Jane Somers indicate the turns of her humor. But in *The Good Terrorist* she is completely serious. In Lurie's opinion, *The Diaries of Jane Somers* and the Canopus in Argos series "considered in combination . . . were disturbing. They suggested that the creative high-tension in Doris Lessing between wild, imaginative energy and practical realism had finally snapped, splitting her into manic and depressive selves who produced, respectively, cloudy, optimistic fantasy and pessimistic tales of modern life." But in *The Good Terrorist,* Lurie concluded, "the two Doris Lessings are happily reunited." Clearly Lessing is capable of many more surprises. But whatever the theme or style of her writing, she is certain to outrage her critics and please her fans.

References:

Walter Clemons, with Donna Foote and Ray Saw-hill, "What's in a Literary Name?," *Newsweek,* 104 (1 October 1984): 89;

Denis Donoghue, "Alice, the Radical *Homemaker,*" *New York Times Book Review,* 22 September 1985, VII: 3, 29;

Howard Fields, "Doris Lessing Reveals Hoax of Two Novels," *Publishers Weekly,* 226 (5 October 1984): 22;

Ellen Goodman, "The Doris Lessing Hoax," *Wash-*

ington Post, 29 September 1984, p. 19A;
Susan Lardner, "Angle on the Ordinary," *New Yorker,* 59 (19 September 1983): 140-144;
Alison Lurie, "Bad Housekeeping," *New York Review of Books,* 19 December 1985, pp. 8-10;
William Phillips, "Four Portraits," *Partisan Review,* 50 (Spring 1983): 536-547;

Jonathan Yardley, "An 'Unknown' Author and the Success Syndrome," *Washington Post,* 1 October 1984, p. 81;
Richard Zoglin, "The Golden Hoax Book," *Time,* 124 (1 October 1984): 83.

James Merrill
(3 March 1926-)

Stephen Sandy
Bennington College

See also the Merrill entry in *DLB 5: American Poets Since World War II, Part 2: L-Z.*

NEW BOOKS: *Scripts for the Pageant* (New York: Atheneum, 1980);
The Changing Light at Sandover (New York: Atheneum, 1982);
Santorini: Stopping the Leak (Worcester, Mass: Metacom, 1982);
Marbled Paper (Portland, Ore.: Seluzicki, 1982);
From the First Nine: Poems 1946-1976 (New York: Atheneum, 1983);
Late Settings (New York: Atheneum, 1985).

PERIODICAL PUBLICATION: "Divine Poem," *New Republic,* 183 (29 November 1980): 29-34.

James Merrill has completed the occult epic *The Changing Light at Sandover,* a 15,000-line elegiac trilogy of such variety and force that the reader may have difficulty at first in seeing it steadily or whole. Its structure and intention are unprecedented in American letters. It is an inspired poem, and it undoubtedly merits consideration in the context of the Western epic tradition. It brims with the knowledge which great poetry makes and makes available. Further, the style of the trilogy is new; as the critic Rachel Jacoff has said, "there are, I believe, no precedents for a funny philosophical poem."

The 560-page poem is built around an armature of dialogue among spirits and the poet's friends, whom some will think of as masked selves of the poet, his constellated personae. The work

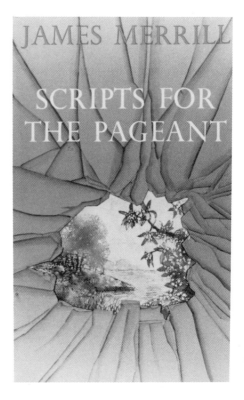

Dust jacket for the third part of Merrill's philosophical verse trilogy

was written during a quarter of a century and published between 1976 and 1982 in three installments. These correspond to the poem's three movements, or canticles, divided according to the design of the Ouija board. "The Book of Ephraim" is the initial movement and comprised ninety pages of *Divine Comedies* (1976) before it appeared as the first part of the trilogy. It consists of twenty-six parts, one for each letter of the alphabet. *Mirabell: Books of Number* (1978), the second part of the trilogy, is made up of one hundred parts, ten for each of the Arabic numerals on the board, zero through nine. *Scripts for the Pageant* (1980) has three parts in accord with the board's only complete words, "Yes," "And," and "No," with eighteen subdivisions each to "Yes" and "No" and fourteen to the central "And" or ampersand. The final canticle contains twenty-five "lessons," ten in the first and last parts, five in the middle section. In 1982, the whole poem was published under the title *The Changing Light at Sandover* with a coda, "The Higher Keys" (and minor revisions through the text). Merrill closes the epilogue by beginning to read his poem to an audience made largely of those who have influenced him as a writer, a turn of tranquil confidence and a witty acknowledgement of debts without anxieties. (*Late Settings,* Merrill's 1985 collection, contains a sheaf of discards from the dictations, "From the Cutting-Room Floor.")

The poet (JM) and his companion David Jackson (DJ) pass time at their homes in Stonington, Connecticut, and in Athens, in a parlor game (Merrill has been "trying to make sense" of Yeats's *A Vision*): they manipulate a dimestore china tea cup on a Ouija board, encounter spirits, and take dictation from them. The mortal protagonists in "The Book of Ephraim" meet departed friends, family, various dead persons both famous and unknown, in a vaguely Dantesque frame; they communicate with, and usually through, a jocular but inadequate guide, a first-century Greek Jew at the court of Tiberius (how limited and yet integral he is the sequel shows). There is much that is novelistic in this first section; indeed, the poem claims to have sprung from the scattered remains of a lost novel. Foundations are laid for the main body of the work; the reader grows acquainted with the principal characters and their situations, while the protagonists, through their contact with the other world, achieve preliminary insights and are tested for further revelations.

In "The Book of Ephraim," images of twilight and sunset abound; mere notations or extravagant descriptions, which provide a leitmotiv for the canticle:

> Sunset; mild azure; sable bulks awince
> With fire—and all these visible at once
> While Heaven, quartered like a billionaire's
> Coat of arms, put on stupendous airs.

There are more images of sunset than sunrise; the poet verges on middle age and looks upon youth and its marches through the lenses of time.

Merrill's financier father, the father of "the broken home" of earlier poems, dies while the poet is visiting Japan, the "land of the rising sun." (Charles Merrill's death seems to be alluded to in the lines likening a sun-fired sky to a rich man's pretensions, which recall, as well, Emily Dickinson's "before the door of God," and her epithet "Burglar! Banker—Father!") The poet has traveled to Mount Koya, a bastion of esoteric Buddhism for a sect devoted to magical exercises and mystical pictures; a monastery now, mostly, a treasury of art:

> word comes of my father's
> Peaceful death, his funeral tomorrow.
> There will be no way to fly back in time.

From Japan there is "no way" for the poet to reach America in time for the funeral. He has lost his father; the last opportunity for communication—this side the grave—canceled. The past is not to be recaptured. It cannot be extended longer to dovetail with the present.

Such verbal play in presenting the death of the father is matched, almost in the same breath, by glimpses of erotic revelry, couched in equally witty language:

> half-stoned couples
> Doing the Chicken-and-the-Egg till dawn.
> Which came first? And would two never come
> Together . . .?

Such delight in the doublings language makes possible; joy in the world's baubles! So much levity, called up by the puns, the spoonerisms ("the heart before the course"; "swirls before pine"), and the brilliant use of difficult verse forms: the high jinks and joviality might allow for the charge of frivolity were the poem not weighted—balanced—by the compound advent of death: the poet's father; his friend Hans; Maya Deren, the first living person, after the protagonists, to enter the drama; a guest who dines, dances, sits with JM and DJ at the board midway through *Ephraim*, dies before its close, and becomes one of the spirits in frequent communication with the operatives at the Ouija board. Yet the presence of Jackson's aged parents, visiting Stonington or whiling away the time in their "senior/Citizen desert ghetto," is the most trenchant emblem of dissolution in the early part of the trilogy.

> They are senile and violent at once,
>
> > the poor old
> > Helpless woman and the rich old skinflint
> > Who now, if no one's there to stop him, beats
> > Intelligence back into her, or tries.

The surroundings of their "sunset years" in the Southwest—

> their "lawn" (gravel dyed green) and view:
> Other pastel, gadget-run bungalows

—are symbols of the artificial meanness and superficiality of their "senior" existences. David Jackson's parents, Matt and Mary, live and die through the course of the trilogy, a small contingent in the multiple elegy. More saliently, they are an example of a fresh theme and circumstance in American life and letters, the burden of the adult child. This figure, altogether a recent arrival, is the American Aeneas who must, through the wonder of medicine, for years bear up under his parents' prolonged decline and scientifically postponed death; he experiences death not only qualitatively but also quantitatively. Merrill and Jackson exhibit the Aeneas syndrome and exemplify, in their affections, adult children.

The inclusion of the American West in a poem set largely in "the mysterious East" and in Europe affords the occasion for a final example of oblivion, of dissolving sunset. The poet touches on nuclear destruction; however light the touch, the point is surely made. Finding himself near Los Alamos, he turns to "nearby nuclear research/Our instinct first is to deplore." But then he turns from thoughts of "closing time in the gardens of the West"—Cyril Connolly's phrase—to another time, to the Golden age of China, and the poet Witter Bynner reciting

> Renderings of T'ang poetry he made
> As a young man. Firelight on spinach jade
> Or white jade buckles . . . .

It is as if even the idea of extinction loses force and meaning unless it is seen in the warm light of poetry and art, retrospective lamps of civilization.

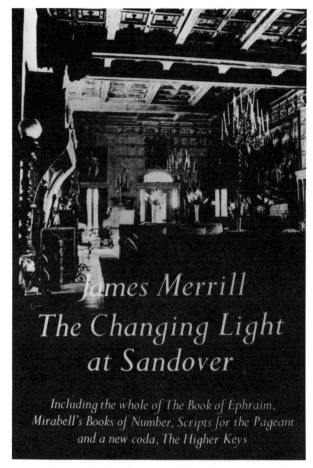

Dust jacket for the collection of Merrill's trilogy into one volume, with selections from The Black Swan *(1946),* The Yellow Pages *(1974), and* First Poems *(1951)*

In *Mirabell: Books of Number* the form Merrill invents is clearly established; the poet no longer relies on novelistic props; and the poem is no longer buttressed as the first canticle had been by appearing in a book called *Divine Comedies*. Here we find the poet confident of his own devices—if he is not as at home with them as he grows to be in *Scripts for the Pageant*. The scene becomes (more or less) a classroom, and the poem's argument takes on the "modern" world, where science is the dominant faith. Here are some slow stretches: the red tape which made heaven a bureaucracy, a sort of celestial Pentagon, in "The Book of Ephraim" was amusing. In *Mirabell* there is an exponential increase in detail, and the numerological discourse may give pause to even the most avid reader. The guide Ephraim is replaced by another spirit, the "bad angel" Mirabell. Otherworldly speakers employ scientific terms (now simplistically, now technically) to explain, in a domesticating pastiche of science's way of looking at the world, the nature of the cosmos and the divine intention. Presences, who are fallen angels and must be imagined as bats (though spirits, of course, in fact have no form), speak through the Ouija board and tell Merrill to write "POEMS OF SCIENCE." (Ouija boards have only Roman capitals. Angels and other immortals of high rank speak in syllabics—verse measured by number of syllables—and humans in an approximate pentameter. We may disapprove the angelic syllabics and find them, as Johnson found the writing of metaphysical poets, "very often such verses as stand the trial of the finger better than of the ear.") The critic Phoebe Pettingell has summarized the central matter of *Mirabell:*

> Mysterious powers who "SPEAK FROM WITHIN THE ATOM" ... have come to tell of the dangers of atomic energy. "Maria and Wystan," who also communicate through the board, describe them as enormous black bats with gargoyle faces and red eyes. The voices identify themselves as "bad angels," the negative charge of energy, creators of the black holes in space, and pure reason without matter. Their fall was a nuclear explosion brought about when they tried to wrest power from the positive forces. They founded, then destroyed Arcadia on Atlantis.... Since 1938, when Enrico Fermi first split the atom, mankind has teetered on the brink of a similar cataclysm, but God Biology does not want his supreme creation destroyed. Therefore these messengers, repentant of their former mischief, have arrived to warn against the evil of energy that does not come from the sun.

All is not hortatory and didactic in this jaunty drama, however. Whether it is *Mirabell* or *Scripts,* gossip mixes with metaphysics, banter with theology, interludes of intense song with the immortals' simmering lectures of admonishment and explication.

The lyrical interludes function like arias in an opera; their graceful interruptions give needed pause and tensile strength to the exposition of cosmic system. At the same time, their singing reminds the reader of the controlling role of the lyric poet Merrill, and his familiar technical mastery of forms, such as this passage, from "The Book of Ephraim," in sonnet form:

> Powers of lightness, darkness, powers that be
> Come, go, in mists of calculus and rumor

Heavens above us. Does it still appear
We'll get our senses somehow purified

Back? Will figures of authority
Who lived, like Mallarmé and Montezuma,
So far above their subjects as to fear
Them not at all, still welcome us inside

Their thoughts? The one we picture garlanded
With afterimages, fire-sheer
Solar plume on plume;

The other, with having said
The world was made to end ("pour aboutir")
In a slim volume.

Or, these closing lines of a passage in terza rima from *Mirabell* (one such passage appears near the close of each canticle, each pointing its allusion to the *Divine Comedy* by concluding with the image of stars). Here, JM's and DJ's wise and good friend Robert Morse leaves their home, as it turns out for the last time; Morse speaks of Merrill's poem.

> "Everything in Dante knew its place.
> In this guidebook of yours, how do you tell
> Up from down? Is Heaven's interface
>
> What your new friends tactfully don't call Hell?
> Splendid as metaphor. The real no-no
> Is jargon, falling back on terms that smell
>
> Just a touch fishy when the tide is low:
> 'Molecular structures'—cup and hand—obey
> 'Electric waves'? Don't *dream* of saying so!
>
> —So says this dinosaur whom Chem 1A
> Thrilled, sort of. Even then I put the heart
> Before the course ..." And at the door: "Today
>
> We celebrate Maria's Himmelfahrt
> And yours. You're climbing, do you know how high?
> While tiny me, unable to take part,
>
> Waves you onward. *Don't look down.* Goodbye."
> —Answered with two blithe au reservoirs,
> He's gone. Our good friend. As it strikes me, my
>
> Head is in my hands. I'm seeing stars.

The most notable interlude in the trilogy is "Samos," the canzone (a complex verse form of Italian origin), which opens the middle section, "&," of *Scripts.* It begins

> And still, at sea all night, we had a sense
> Of sunrise, golden oil poured upon water,

Soothing its heave, letting the sleeper sense
What inborn, amniotic homing sense
Was ferrying him—now through the dream-fire
In which (it has been felt) each human sense
Burns, now through ship's radar's cool sixth sense,
Or mere unerring starlight—to an island.
Here we were. The twins of Sea and Land,
Up and about for hours—hues, cries, scents—
Had placed at eye level a single light
Croissant: the harbor glazed with warm pink light.

It is important to understand, first, the authority such lyrics lend to this difficult, sometimes eccentric text, the focus they give to the sublime theme, and the aid they offer to the reader's belief in both voice and theme. Then, they work formally simply as structural devices, as a mortar not only to comment on but also to clasp one section to another. One of countless examples is this little silver buckle of a transition from *Scripts*, written in a stanza that recalls Donne or Herbert—or Herrick:

(Beneath my incredulity
All at once is flowing

Joy, the flash of the unbaited hook—
Yes, yes, it fits, it's right, it had to be!
Intuition weightless and ongoing

Like stanzas in a book
Or golden scales in the melodic brook—)

The third canticle, *Scripts for the Pageant*, continues in the vein of *Mirabell* and enlarges on its themes. *Scripts* offers a further glimpse of other worlds (Arcadia; a place beneath the Earth's crust; the garden at the rosebrick manor called Sandover), more creation myth, exuberant celestial soireés (in part celebrating the twenty-fifth anniversary of JM and DJ, and DJ's fifty-fifth birthday). The archangel Michael takes over from Mirabell as guide and is now master of ceremonies. His voice and manner are alternately likable or sublime; if he seems familiar, like a friend remembered, it is because he shows some of the poet's courtly authority and witty condescension; and because Ephraim, at the close of the trilogy, is disclosed to have been an incarnation of Michael. God B,

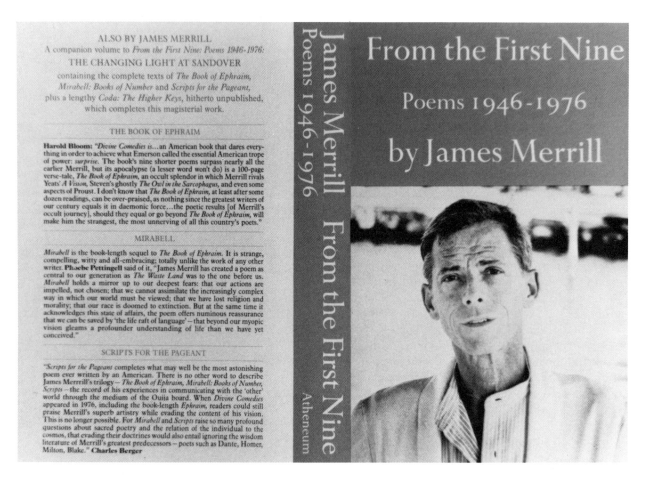

Dust jacket for Merrill's selection of poems from nine of his books

though offstage, plays a part and seems familiar, in this case because he bears some resemblance to the Judeo-Christian deity; a Miltonic father who loves his creation and shows compassion for it; he would arrange matters so that humankind does not destroy itself through having tapped destructive and unnatural energies (the atom). *Scripts* affirms, in highly serious language and without inflated rhetoric, the stability of man's bond with Nature but emphasizes man's disobedience to God B in consuming fruits of forbidden or destructive scientific knowledge. If Michael, God B's favorite, possesses the "CALM ELATE INTELLIGENCE" of Apollo and is the Vishnu of this pantheon, then Gabriel the bringer of death is its Shiva, ever ready to dance the destruction of the universe. Merrill admits evil, conceived of as death, a presence which the poem's affability only momentarily veils. The power of dissolution is everywhere, as friends and family of Merrill and Jackson continually succumb to it; in *Scripts* the agency of Gabriel emerges as a force at least as powerful as God's will to preserve His Creation.

Much of the interest in *The Changing Light at Sandover*, this side of its metaphysical speculations, lies in the fates of the poet's four friends, W. H. Auden (the poet), Maria Mitsotáki (a woman of Athens), George Cotzias (a Greek biochemist), and Robert Morse (a Connecticut pianist). The ongoing fortunes of this quartet provide what the critic Stephen Yenser calls the plot of the poem.

In *Mirabell* and *Scripts*, for example, Robert Morse, the friend who dies during the composition of the poem, stands more and more revealed as an ideal of human behavior and insight. Unlike another friend, Hans Lodeizen, who remains a shadowy cipher, a distant silhouette, and unlike Auden, who though admirably rendered is perhaps too "altogether otherworldly now," Morse achieves definition and presence as a full personality in this world—and the next. The reader meets him alive once in *Mirabell*, is entertained, and feels the poet's anguish at his passing; in *Scripts* the reader experiences Morse's death from *his* viewpoint, listens to his posthumous, endearing discourse, and witnesses him in his reincarnation as the composer "Tom." With Wystan Auden and Maria Mitsotáki, the figure of Morse, if more lightly drawn than these two major presences, is central in the trilogy. As "elegy" the poem focuses on him more than on many others in the train of the departed, and his is a crowning example of the consolation the poem may provide in an immediate, personal sense for the reader who is apt to accept the generative premise of the poem. (To be reborn, like Auden's friend Chester Kallman, as an African dictator or like Maria as a tree—though this fate is rescinded in favor of a more heroic future role for her—is not much help.) Yet Morse is a leaf upon the stream and shows slight freedom of will. His childlike, delighting, and resigned relation to his existence offers an example of Buddhist acceptance, an equilibrium born of an achieved desirelessness; he is a willing boater adrift on the Heraclitean flux.

The Changing Light at Sandover recommends the performance of "V work," the conserving and creative labors of the mind and heart. To Auden's question "Why the four of us?" (Maria, Merrill, Jackson, himself), Mirabell replies

KEEP IN MIND THE CHILDLESSNESS WE
SHARE THIS   TURNS US
OUTWARD TO THE LESSONS
& THE MYSTERIES.

Helen Vendler articulates one view of the cluster of Merrill's themes. " 'Mirabell' is a poem about the dead," she notes, "in part because it is a poem of the single life and childlessness; since there is no question of posterity, life is composed of oneself and one's friends, the dead as much as the living . . . [V work] is encouraged, according to Mirabell, by loves that do not envision the production of bodies." The myth of childlessness as a means to intellectual vision, artistic creativity, and inspiration is jestingly challenged by JM and DJ: "Come now, admit that certain very great/Poets and musicians have been straight." The claim, Vendler concludes, "however whimsical, has been made, and the whole of Merrill's trilogy can be seen as a substitution of the virtues of mind and heart . . . for the civic and familial and martial virtues usually espoused by the epic." The idea of fatherhood as a bar to other kinds of creativity looks to be at odds with facts (consider Dante and Bach) and seems almost a mask veiling more fundamental issues. The theme of the benefits of childlessness outlined by Vendler (doing her own V work), is adumbrated by Richard Saez, who relates a childless dedication to art to the oedipal triangle; and he rightly turns to the question of the role of evil in Merrill's cosmos to shed light on the connections among these themes. Initially, some critics spent much fire power on irrelevant bastions—for example, the numbing Roman caps, the plenum of puns, homosexuality, the questionable reliability of Ouija boards—

whereas the poem's center, where its strengths are massed, is its explanation of and response to the facts of pain, loss, suffering, death; and the question of "evil."

The poet seldom mentions evil. He speaks of "THE OTHER," "THE UNDOER," and of "NOTHING" and "THE VOIDS" and "THE BLACK." His "God Biology" opposes "IT." There is a negative force at the earth's core called "the monitor." It is as if Merrill had hoped that the universe was all to the good, but that he learned, as he so often affirms, that creation requires resistance, and that some negative force must be posited in order to explain anything, from higher physics to table manners; and that he, a poet with "shyness/Vis-à-vis 'ideas,'" only slowly and with effort approaches the concept of a negating force, of evil or of darkness, a process of defining akin to that of approaching a limit.

To view death and evil as coequal, as Merrill does, is to say that death is only the result of an organic process, that the end of withering is alone evil, and immortality only freedom from entropy. But many would affirm that while death is evil, evil is not death; mortality means more than a husk in an autumn field. It is as if Merrill would rewrite Yeats, "Bodily decrepitude is evil; young we loved each other and were good." Reductive as this conclusion may be, the stand, apparently, has been taken, and we can only contribute our troubled assent.

Richard Saez sees a tension between a vision of theodicy, in which suffering is educative and enlightening, and a Manichean view, in which the soul is possessed by the dark body of the physical and must free itself from matter, flesh, thingness. "There is a relationship between the trilogy's concern with childlessness and its apparent surrender to Manicheism," he says. "The surrender of free will in a universe created by the cloning of supernatural agents or the control of a mechanistic Monitor . . . is also the surrender of any personal responsibility for the sacrifice of life—childlessness and all—to an aesthetic vocation."

If God is good, whence evil? But this God is the supreme deity, God A, not Merrill's God B. God B is locked in certain struggle with "the Black," for God Biology is a deity of local dominion, not supreme, but one of a pantheon which rules the galaxy, who is "HARD PREST" by "Gods as powerful" from beyond this universe, gods who indeed have infected God B's creation with a small but cancerous dollop of the black and negating Other. So pain is not merely educative, and there are more

transcendent devastations to come. "Evil" is not just a passive fact (men experience pain) but also a passional agency (men give pain). The poem tends to give the negating power more attention, scope, and force as it goes along. Initially this concern seems to be a motif included for the sake of symmetry, pro forma, but finally it becomes an organic part of the scheme—and of Merrill's creed, hard as this is to distinguish in the welter of surmise and suggestive image. Yet Merrill's way of looking at the world is sunnily benevolent, amoral when it comes to cases, and this neutrality thrives in the mechanistic view of creation which Merrill adopts. Inevitability in the workings of the cosmic machine allows the poet to minimize holocaust by comparing a subterranean atomic explosion to a toothache; enables him to find passivity a strength and childlessness an opportunity. "The washing of the hands represented by a cloned, mechanistically controlled universe," Saez notes, ". . . is, in fact, a vigorous assertion of the free will in the disguise of passivity." In a view in which the universe is the proverbial mechanism of a timepiece, passivity and its consequences (among them, childlessness) is not what it is in a black-and-white universe charged with moral contest where each soul must take a stand in the cosmic struggle.

Merrill has been on a psychic roll of the most prolific kind in *Mirabell* and *Scripts*. It is as if the basket of his thought, learning, and experience had tilted and the whole contents had poured into the text. Merrill includes everything; he has it both ways ("Yes" and "No"); he has anticipated (like a great theologian) every objection and has covered each plot of ground before the reader touches it. Thus, apparently, the poem is "about" salvation, if not explicitly. But the quest for transcendence, of which salvation is the result, implies a feeling of guilt, an efficient motion of guilt, and this does not seem to be a part of the poem. So it is not, implicitly, a poem about salvation, though certain persons, such as Morse when he becomes the composer "Tom" and Maria when she becomes the Mughal inventor (without, apparently, losing all "Morseness" or "Marianess"), do achieve a kind of salvation, if only in the non-Christian valences of reincarnation.

The work of art survives in the valley of its happening, where those downtown would never want to tamper. All the same, the work presents questions. Even though the system the poet propounds to explain cosmos and suffering and fate turns out to be a partial, limited one, nevertheless in liberating ourselves across the threshold of this great verse edifice we are sorely tempted to read Merrill's structure as overarching.

And so it is difficult to understand, and at once necessary to ask, what Merrill's religious belief is. Perhaps he lacks one. This system was *received*. "And maddening—it's all by someone else!" says Merrill in *Mirabell*. It was arbitrarily dictated (in an extreme instance of Hebraism as opposed to Hellenism). All this restitutive doctrine comes to the poet across the threshold of the Ouija board from the Beyond. "This scribe, my hand," says Merrill, quoting Keats. The reincarnations are equally poetic artifice and embraced belief. Love? Salvation? Evil? This, our present? These—as the poet Chard deNiord notes—are hard to account for in such a closed, synergistic system as the trilogy.

"God has put eternity into man's mind but so that he will not find out what God has done from beginning to end" (*Ecclesiastes* 7:14). Perhaps too God has put the notions of God B's cosmos into JM's head to a similar end. And the common reader, coming to this text from his Bible or his *Comedia*, may ask, what of God A?

There is another important issue. To the extremes of its formalism and artifice, to Merrill's sweet, made melodies—the poetry that is there for its own sake—one must oppose the quest for divine knowledge, absolute awareness; as well, His approbation and conferring of commission ("POET FROM THIS MAKE A V WORK") and the consequent involvement of a quest for salvation (of which this text must be the record). Dante had revealed three levels of transcendence: the physical, the aesthetic, and the spiritual. Perhaps Merrill's work considers only two of these. For the reflexive convolutions of artifice—the baroque accomplishment that the poem is—and the quest for personal salvation are enterprises which are mutually exclusive from just about every point of view. The opposed concerns of this inspired poem raise a crucial question as to its success, for someone who is writing with such artifice and ornate obscurity has created a mode at odds with a focused spiritual quest for transcendence.

There has never been a poem of philosophy and metaphysics with such sustained levity. The sense of tradition, the mastery of craft, the music, the "sentence" make much writing look, in contrast, wanting. Even if the trilogy is not a complete success and not always sustained (some day there will be an annotated edition; one day an abridgement,

a "Shorter *Changing Light at Sandover*"), the poem deserves the reader's soberest attention, the benefits of his doubts, disbelief suspended. The absence of conventional plot and contributive quest by the hero on what the *Bhagavadgita* calls "the field of decision"—Samuel Johnson's "one great action achieved by a hero"—gives measure to the degree to which *The Changing Light at Sandover* challenges the epic tradition and rings changes on it. Its protagonists lack the civic involvement of conventional epic heros; they do not perform the actions tradition requires ("NOTHING is exactly what we do"). This quest is internalized; and just as there is closet drama, why not parlor epic? The central figure of the poet does indeed perform a quest, one quintessentially Promethean.

Yeats and Blake, Proust and Pound, Byron and Cowper, Cowley and Pope, Milton and Dante: a host of precursors and influences stand behind the poem. The mass of its inspired length, its foursquare rhetoric alternating with exquisite interludes of song, ode, and narrative leave a music in the mind's ear that enchants and lingers long after one has put down the book.

If we can compare Merrill's unusual stenography with automatic writing, we may remember what the French poet Bonnefoy said: that automatic writing is not dissolution for the writer but deliverance. So the chance encounter by Merrill with a Ouija board opened to him a grand and original scheme for poetry and occasioned the great turn in his career, offering him by far the greatest employment of his extraordinary poetic gift, and from a parlor game stemmed a great trope of the literary imagination. However untuned the ear, *The Changing Light at Sandover* communicates its matter and its music to the reader willing to immerse himself in it. As Wallace Stevens wrote, "Anyone who has read a long poem day after day . . . knows how the poem comes to possess the reader and how it naturalizes him in its own imagination and liberates him there." The dialogue with presences, the spirits who may well be the personae of a vastly cultivated sensibility, is an imagined one, therefore affirmative, liberating. The high-spirited philosophical comedy revealing a surprisingly involved angelic order, combined with Merrill's customary lyric finish and allusive density makes this poem an unprecedented achievement. For now many would turn what Conrad Aiken said of John Berryman's "Homage to Mistress Bradstreet" to Merrill's account: "He bided his time and wrote the poem of his generation." The trilogy is long and new; we are strangers to its densities and must get to know them better. The poem must bide its time.

In 1983, following the publication of the one-volume edition of *The Changing Light at Sandover*, *From the First Nine: Poems 1946-1976* was published. The title refers to the selection made from Merrill's nine collections of shorter poems before the trilogy, and alludes as well to the nine stages of enlightenment he is told of by the instructors at Sandover. The suggestion is one of ascent to greater lyric proficiency and poetic vision; the inference is a valid one. The collection (in spite of the poet's having grandly "touched up," as he puts it, early work) shows a clear rise to greater craft, scope, and self-knowledge and strongly illustrates his ability to find fresh occasions for his subjects, to explore his themes with increasing thoroughness, understanding, ease, and a more inclusive diction. The poems about dwellings, for example, are seen together here from a half dozen books, from "The House" (*First Poems*, 1951) to "An Urban Convalescence" (*Water Street*, 1962) through many other examples of the development of this theme to the apocalyptic "18 West 11th Street" (*Braving the Elements*, 1972) and beyond. The thinning throws into relief recurrent images, such as clothes or majestic birds; growing preoccupations, as when "Willow" (1951) appears near "Willowware Cup" (1972), and the willowware tea cup JM and DJ use as a "pointer" in the trilogy crops up in the first Ouija board poem, "Voices from Another World" (1959). By bringing together his twenty-odd most important lyrics in this selection of 139 poems, from "The Charioteer of Delphi" to "Lost in Translation," Merrill illustrates the coherence and consistency of the themes which have engaged him: love, loss, nostalgia, metamorphosis, art in the vise of time. The gathering focuses sharply the accomplishment of thirty years.

At the end of *From the First Nine*, Merrill prints "Clearing the Title" as a "Postscript (1980)"; this narrative poem also appears at the opening of his most recent collection, *Late Settings* (1985), and presents the setting and the theme of the new book. The poet has abandoned Greece ("Athens was no longer a livable place" said Merrill in a *Paris Review* interview); now David Jackson has bought a home in Key West; the axis shifts from Stonington/Athens to Connecticut/Florida. "Clearing the Title" is both the proving of ownership for Jackson of the new house, and a seal of liberation from the trilogy, now after many years finished, titled, given to the press and public. (Scraps and bits of contact with the board swirl in the epic's wake, as probably they

will always for two men who have spent years at one game.) "Clearing the Title" closes with a Key West sundown. The poet joins a motley platoon that gathers on a pier to witness the sun sink below the horizon; here is the ever widening index of Merrill's poetic diction (" 'Give or Ah'll clobber yew!' and *grunt* go the trombones." " 'Let's hear it for the sun.' ") As the sun sinks, a clown releases balloons. With distance, "the balloons, mere hueless dots now, stars/Or periods" are conflated: the man-made gewgaw; the star of a galaxy beyond time; the period, the mark of an ending. A period points the close of a thought; the completion of a series of events; the chronological division of a life. So Merrill inserts a fresh disc and offers a collection with broader diction and a chattier ease of manner; and at once controlled, more somber, grittier than ever: at least in the three texts central to this volume, "Clearing the Title" at the outset, "Bronze" in the middle, and "Santorini: Stopping the Leak" at the close. "Santorini" is a delightful and menacing looping back, as if for one last glimpse, to Greece, the spirits of the trilogy; and a confrontation with a plantar wart, a growth treated by "God willing lethal x/Rays," lethal to warts but also (as one has learned from the trilogy) lethally desiccating to souls. In this meditation Merrill addresses the problem of "psychic incontinence" and approaches the "confessional" mode. Yet this masterful poem is not, finally, so revealing, so dramatically charged, or so abruptly presumptive as "Bronze."

A curious, brooding, proleptic run of eight sections, the narrative "Bronze" explores a dark harmony of doublings. Since "Bronze" is a matrix of pairings, it has no center; the paradoxical nature of twinning hints that all is not only "both/and" but also "either/or," yes *and* no at once. The occasion of the poem is an (initially canceled) visit to Florence to see the great bronze statues of Riace; the epigraph makes the theme of doubling clear in alluding to the two Greek warriors found in 1972. No one knows if these sculptures were intended to "go together" since it is uncertain whom they represent; but they have been together, a pair in the Ionian Sea off the Calabrian town of Riace, for 2500 years. One is older, helmeted; each is larger than life and, whether god or man, is fiercely warlike; but the salient point is that these naked figures are frightening; their inlaid eyes glance brutally; they are blatantly sensual, forbidding. Speaking of the "unabashed physicality" of these soldiers, the art historian James Beck finds them "cruel, muscle-bound supermen who represent an ancient race that has yet to be Christianized, who can eat their own children as easily as commit incest with them." Merrill and Jackson are to visit these works of art where they are on exhibit in Florence, (a few hundred yards from Michelangelo's David). Visiting a friend near Florence, Merrill watches his host and "David the Fair" study train schedules. The aged Umberto (secretly the son of the old Italian king Umberto) holds "the timetable/Dense as himself with station and connection." David refuses to go: " 'Close connections . . . /Harm the soul.' " Merrill and Jackson differ. At dinner Umberto tells a tale of his own wartime heroism; one sees Umberto young and Umberto old. The sculptures from the sea become figures of the father, repellant yet magnetic; of enduring companionship; of isolation and a life dedicated to art ("Here at my desk, but fathoms deep"). The statues sing of their dislike of being art objects, in a dactyllic measure that sounds less classically Greek than contemporarily American, like the poet Ben Belitt. These figures are threatening:

> Not tea-gowned ephebes like the driver
> At Delphi, but men in their prime
> With the endocrine clout so rebarbative
> To the eternally boyish
> Of whichever sex.

The splendid men "dealt death" and "divide the spoils."

The poet's response to these works in the Archeological Museum is omitted; but the ellipsis gives breath to his response. Time has wrenched the poet from his lair. His companion goes off by himself. "Our separate routes. A month. A year." Things fall apart. Or together. Umberto dies, and his estate, intended as a "retreat for scholars," he leaves instead to the butler, Mario. Back home in Stonington, a young stranger embraces not Merrill but a bust of him at six, a child now unrecognizable in the older man. The poet remembers that the sculptor of the bronze bust was murdered by his sons. "QUEENS/MAN AXED BY SONS" the headline had read; the American violence calls up both Aeschylus and the murderous athletes of Riace. A strange fable with manifold circuitry, this narrative acknowledges the inevitability and cost of loss in the inexorable progression of pairings (David and David, Umberto old and Umberto young, Umberto's true and his false father, Jackson and Merrill the "two halves" of this poem, the child Merrill and Merrill the man, the paired warrior brothers of antiquity). The "life created" has been a secure

> castle built
> To nurture intellect, art, love
> Together with, let's face it, guilt,
> Deception, strife.

In "Bronze" Merrill faces "it" in a sturdy and intricate study of dispersion, dissolution, survival; of random pairings and willed ones. The poet hews to a hard line of separation as attachment and, leaving the city of high art and culture, sings soberly of "the entropy of Florence."

Interviews:

Helen Vendler, "James Merrill's Myth: An Interview," *New York Review of Books,* 26 (3 May 1979): 12-13;

Ross Labrie, "James Merrill at Home: An Interview," *Arizona Quarterly,* 38 (Spring 1982): 19-36;

J. D. McClatchy, "The Art of Poetry XXXI: James Merrill," *Paris Review,* 84 (Summer 1982): 184-219.

References:

William Harmon, "The Metaphors and Metamorphoses of M," *Parnassus: Poetry in Review,* 8 (1980): 29-41;

Michael Harrington, "Paradise or Disintegration," *Commonweal,* 110 (November 1983): 585-589;

John Hollander, "A Poetry of Restitution," *Yale Review,* 70 (Winter 1981): 161-186;

Richard Howard, "James Merrill," in *Alone with America* (New York: Atheneum, 1980): 386-411;

David Kalstone, "Transparent Things," in *Five Temperaments* (New York: Oxford University Press, 1977): 77-128;

David Lehman and Charles Berger, eds., *James Merrill: Essays in Criticism* (Ithaca: Cornell University Press, 1983);

J. D. McClatchy, "Lost Paradises: The Poetry of James Merrill," *Parnassus: Poetry in Review,* 5 (Fall/Winter 1976): 305-320;

Judith Moffett, *James Merrill, An Introduction to the Poetry* (New York: Columbia University Press, 1984);

Jay Parini, "A Poet's Life," *Horizon,* 26 (September 1983): 16-20;

Joseph Parisi, "Ghostwriting," *Poetry,* 135 (December 1979): 161-173;

Phoebe Pettingell, "God and JM," *New Leader* (6 October 1980): 14-15;

Pettingell, "Merrill's Ascent," *New Leader* (21 February 1983): 14-15;

Pettingell, "Voices from the Atom," *New Leader* (4 December 1978): 14-15;

Richard Saez, "James Merrill's Oedipal Fire," *Parnassus: Poetry in Review*, 3 (Fall/Winter 1974): 159-184;

Henry Sloss, "James Merrill's *The Book of Ephraim*," *Shenandoah*, 27 (Summer 1976): 63-91; and *Shenandoah*, 28 (Fall 1976): 83-110;

Helen Vendler, "James Merrill," in *Part of Nature,*

Part of Us (Cambridge: Harvard University Press, 1980): 205-232;

Robert von Hallberg, "James Merrill: 'Revealing by Obscuring,' " in *American Poetry and Culture 1945-1980* (Cambridge: Harvard University Press, 1985): 93-116;

Edmund White, "On James Merrill," *American Poetry Review* (September/October 1979): 9-11;

Stephen Yenser, "The Fullness of Time: James Merrill's *Book of Ephraim*," *Canto*, 3 (Spring 1980): 130-159.

Tom Stoppard

(3 July 1937-   )

Carl E. Rollyson, Jr.
Wayne State University

See also the Stoppard entry in *DLB 13, British Dramatists Since World War II, Part 2 (M-Z).*

NEW PRODUCTIONS: *The Real Thing*, Strand Theatre, London, 16 November 1982; Plymouth Theater, New York, 5 January 1984;
The Dog It Was That Died, BBC Radio 3, 9 December 1982;
Squaring the Circle, TVS (Britain), May 1984.

NEW BOOKS: *The Real Thing* (London: Faber & Faber, 1982);
The Dog It Was That Died and Other Plays (London: Faber & Faber, 1983);
Squaring the Circle (London: Faber & Faber, 1984).

RECENT AWARDS: New York Drama Critics Circle Award and a Tony for *The Real Thing*, best new play of 1983-1984.

The reception of Tom Stoppard's most recent stage play, *The Real Thing* (first produced in London, 1982), confirms the reputation he has acquired as a major playwright since his brilliant debut in 1966 with *Rosencrantz and Guildenstern Are Dead*. A big hit in London and New York, *The Real Thing* has nevertheless been criticized for its superficiality and slickness, and the playwright's great verbal gifts have once again aroused suspicion among commentators who question his sincerity in grappling with serious themes—in this case with marriage, adultery, fidelity, politics, and art. For

some reviewers, Stoppard's winning way with words comes too easily, and they seem frustrated by his unwillingness to commit himself to a position, to one side or the other of the arguments put forward by his disputatious characters. Other reviewers, and an increasing number of academic critics, are beginning to respond positively—as the playwright's audiences always have—to the remarkably funny and complex rhetoric, the inimitable style of Stoppard's figures. For that is what they usually are—figures, not fully developed characters, who are free to indulge in a witty vocabulary that is not in the possession of most realistic characters in the works of other playwrights. Stoppard has stuck to the theatricality of his writing and has not pretended that his stage is the world at large, although he certainly has contended that his plays are part of a world that values art as essential to life. In *The Real Thing*, he has confronted more directly than ever before his profoundest feelings about life and art and has, at the same time, provided a characteristically clever response to the doubters of his integrity.

A sampling of critical opinion on the play reveals both a deep distrust and admiration of Stoppard's success. Gerald Weales in *Commentary* remarks that "despite the witty lines, the play is essentially sentimental, which may be why it is so popular, and it ends on a lightly, lubriciously happy note that seems benignly fake to me." Catharine Hughes in *America* faults the playwright for his "smug cleverness" while acknowledging his "ingen-

Tom Stoppard

ious manipulation of theatrical conventions and his adroit mastery of apt literary allusion." Elliott Sirkin in the *Nation* recognizes Stoppard as a "subtle, astute, complicated writer," but he attacks the New York production of *The Real Thing* for overly emphasizing its old-fashioned aspects in a refined style reminiscent of Noel Coward and Philip Barry. On the other hand, Robert E. Lauder in *America* and Hersh Zeifman in *Modern Drama,* viewing Stoppard carefully in the context of his whole career, discover, in Lauder's words, "a significant development in the vision of one of the most stimulating and thought-provoking of our contemporary playwrights." Zeifman, who provides the most thorough analysis of the play to date, finds that Stoppard rigorously follows through with the major theme of his latest stage work: "we thus find ourselves at the end invariably questioning, among a host of other 'realities,' the precise nature of love—as Stoppard, of course, intended."

The Real Thing is divided into twelve scenes, the first of which engages in a familiar Stoppardian ploy of presenting a play within a play. The difference in this instance is that the audience is not aware that the first scene is, in effect, a fake until the second scene reveals that Max and Charlotte have been on stage performing part of her husband Henry's play, *House of Cards.* Right from the beginning, then, the playwright challenges the audience to sort out what is real and what is feigned.

Judging by the reviews and the reaction of a New York audience, it comes as something of a shock to realize that Max and Charlotte are actors, even though in retrospect the artificiality of their dialogue is apparent. Gradually their "real" lives come to resemble their stage roles, but the point is that the theatricality of human lives is as "real" as anything else about the nature of their existence. This is not to say that there is no difference between theater and everyday life, but how one tells the difference is what *The Real Thing* is all about. Henry, for example, is manipulative as both a playwright and a husband deceiving his wife Charlotte by having an affair with Max's wife, Annie. But it is only after the initial scene of *House of Cards* that Henry, and the audience, begin to learn how to discriminate between dialogue in a play and dialogue in real life. As Charlotte predicts, Henry will not be so witty or so polished as his cuckolded character in *House of Cards* when Henry learns that he has been deceived.

The following dialogue from scene 2 illustrates how Henry and Charlotte cannot talk without making their conversation into a commentary on their lives and on Henry's art:

> HENRY: How was last night, by the way?
>
> CHARLOTTE: I had to fake it again.
>
> HENRY: Very witty woman, my present wife. Actually I was talking about my play.
>
> CHARLOTTE: Actually, so was I.

Husband and wife are doing this scene for Max's benefit. Naturally these theatrical characters will be especially adept at fudging the distinctions between real and imagined life, but their dialogue is not simply characterizing them; it also reveals how people portray themselves in front of others on stage and off. Real life, in other words, is also staged and scripted; and theatrical life also has its own standards of realism and authenticity. In scene 2, neither Charlotte nor Max knows that Henry is having an affair with Annie, who makes her first entrance a short time later, an entrance that has been calculated to give her some time with Henry while seeming to be joining her husband Max on a social visit.

Annie, actually, is the character who would most like to drop the pretense of theatricality, for she urges Henry to escape from the false scene he has created and would like to prolong until, as she puts it, "you'll know it wasn't the real thing." She wants Henry to take some responsibility for his feelings instead of shaming principles like "I don't steal other men's wives." For this is exactly what he is doing, and she bluntly tells him off: *Sod* you." Her straightforwardness is in sharp contrast to Henry's histrionic and stylized manner. Even when he is joking and covering his tracks, he is also foreshadowing, like a good playwright, his lack of commitment to his "present wife."

Almost like one of Stoppard's critics, Annie tries to get Henry to commit himself. She is playful, but she is also serious, and she wants a frank demonstration of his feelings. The flat speech, the declarative style is a challenge to him:

HENRY: I love you.

ANNIE: Touch me then. They'll come in or they won't. Take a chance. Kiss me.

HENRY: For Christ's sake.

ANNIE: Quick one on the carpet then.

HENRY: You're crackers.

ANNIE: I'm not interested in your mind.

HENRY: Yes, you are.

ANNIE: No, I'm not, I lied to you.

Words will take Henry a long way, but they will not suffice for Annie. When Max discovers her infidelity in scene 3 she does not finesse her motivations as Henry would. She tells Max that she loves Henry and he loves her. "That's that, isn't it. I'm sorry it's awful. But it's better really. All that lying." Max would prefer to pretend that Annie does not love Henry and would prefer to be let down easily, but Annie will not play such a scene for him.

The Real Thing is Stoppard's most autobiographical play. He is not Henry, to be sure, but Henry is certainly representative of one of Stoppard's guises as a literary man exuberantly living off of his style who is suspected of not having "real" convictions. At the same time, however, Annie is hardly a satisfactory antidote to the equivocating stylist. She can be tactless and cruel, and she values content over style so highly that she is put in the ridiculous position of supporting Brodie, an oafish young man involved in protesting against nuclear weapons in Britain.

Brodie writes an awkward, amateurish play

that Annie badgers Henry to fix up. Henry is appalled at both Brodie's style and his opinions. He is even more revolted by Brodie's idea that politics has an objective reality like a coffee mug that can be handled straightforwardly and without the necessary ambiguity and humility of a supple style. Politics, justice, and patriotism have no reality "separate from our perceptions of them," Henry tells Annie. His argument cannot be fairly summarized because it depends so heavily on his own style, a style that implies there is no such thing as just a bald statement of the facts. The relationship between Henry and Annie, for example, is not as simple as the words Annie uses with Max: "I love him. . . . Yes, I do. And he loves me." The play progresses by breaking down her neat formula so that she will have to make exceptions to it—make room for Billie, an actor who plays Brodie in Brodie's atrocious play. Henry, in fact, is the one who wants to be loved without qualifications or exceptions, and he is the one who espouses a simple-minded view of fidelity that Annie has to reject in a style not nearly so rigid as the one she employed in the early scenes when her life seemed much tidier. Indeed she rivals Henry's facility in finding verbal equivalents of her complicated feelings about Billie: "He sort of got in under the radar. Acting daft on a train. Next thing I'm looking round for him, makes the day feel better, it's like love or something: no—love, absolutely, how can I say it wasn't? You weren't replaced, or even replaceable. But I . . . ." The involved syntax, the questioning and qualification of her feelings, and the way she now elaborately punctuates her experience in scene 11 suggest the theatrical bent of this wife and actress. Love means, in one of its manifestations, "acting daft." Love is, in fact, theatrical but also real; it is a complex emotion that cannot be encompassed in the monosyllabic style Annie favored when speaking with Max.

The accommodation Henry and Annie eventually reach at the end of *The Real Thing* is a melding of content and style, a melding that has also taken place in Stoppard's writing of the play. The husband and wife seem very much like "the real thing" in their gradual and loving recognition of each other's similarities and differences. The playwright has found a credible way of getting them to talk like each other, to adopt each other's styles. In doing so, he has also slyly supported his own reliance on language for its dialectical grasp of reality. His characters have convictions; Stoppard has convictions, but the convictions shift with time and place and are dependent on the context in which they get expressed.

Take Max as a final example of the playwright's reply to his critics. In scene 1 he is thoroughly convincing as a cool and witty Noel Cowardian husband who has been deceived by his wife; the same Max—that is the man and actor who has Annie as his wife—is movingly broken by the evidence of adultery: Henry's bloodied handkerchief in Annie's automobile:

> It looks filthy. It's dried filthy.
> You're filthy.
> You filthy cow.
> You rotten filthy—

Max starts to cry; he drops his genuine but still histrionic actor's reaction, is immobilized by deep feeling, and says to Annie in a barely audible voice: "It's not true, is it?" The audience can tell where the acting, the style, leave off and the crude content begins, but it can also respond to how closely connected theater and life are to each other in Stoppard's art.

Stoppard was a journalist before he was a playwright, and the world of facts continues to bemuse him even as he recognizes how malleable reality becomes in the prism of language. He is an artist who is also proud of his ability to entertain and to write for hire. He speaks in interviews of his "assignments," and he seems to relish the opportunity to shape his techniques and themes not only for the conventions of the stage but also for radio and television. Since the mid-1970s he has become increasingly interested in politics—in political intrigue really—and has explored what happens to the language of art in authoritarian countries, especially in Central Europe, where he was born.

It is not surprising, then, that Stoppard should write an introduction to *Squaring the Circle* (produced May 1984), his television play about Solidarity in Poland, that reviews his involvement in writing an accurate and artistically defensible script. He had the services of a professional researcher and was soon in command of "tens of thousands of facts about Poland." How to integrate them into coherent and trustworthy drama, however, was not clear since neither Stoppard nor his researcher could "*know* what happened and what was said." Instead, the playwright had to construe a plot from a reported reality, which meant he could easily reproduce the errors and mistaken speculations of sources that could not be verified.

Stoppard's search for a solution to the problem of veracity led him "to the idea of having a narrator with *acknowledged fallibility.*" Viewers, right from the beginning, would know they were seeing the expression of a "qualified reality." *Squaring the Circle* would have a "self-skeptical tone" and a "witness" would be present to correct the narrator. Thus the dialectical structure of Stoppard's plays became part of his television docudrama. As in *Travesties* (produced 1975), there is no reliable, authoritative source, but the respect for the historical record—for what historical personages actually said—is largely left intact.

The dialectical method in *Squaring the Circle*, as in *Travesties*, has limitations that become apparent when the structure and the dialogue are closely examined. The television play is divided into four parts: "The First Secretary" (centering on Edward Gierek, Poland's leader in June 1980), "Congress" (devoted to the Solidarity meeting in Gdansk that met to decide a course of action after the Government failed to honor its promises), "The General" (following the rise of a new leader, Jaruzelski, who eventually declared martial law in December of 1981 and suppressed Solidarity). While this structure admirably captures the dynamic of shifting energy and power between the union and the Communist authorities, the issue of what was really at stake for both sides is never completely engaged because officials like Gierek and Jaruzelski are much more mysterious than the Solidarity leaders like Walesa and Kuron. The dissenting unionists have personalities and private lives that have been documented in many interviews and profiles. Gierek and Jaruzelski may also have fascinating personalities, and Stoppard does his best to enliven our sense of their psychology, but in his respect for fact he has to be more conservative with them, more noncommittal about what they really felt. And where the playwright does take the liberty of personalizing Gierek's or Jaruzelski's or Brezhnev's reactions, the viewer has to wonder what his warrant is for doing so. Certainly Stoppard's speculations are plausible, but they are not as real as his portrayals of Walesa and other Solidarity officials.

As a television docudrama, however, *Squaring the Circle* has no doubt broken new ground, for Stoppard has consistently found a way of reminding viewers that the 122 interior and exterior scenes of his script are just that—scenes, flawed and fragmented approximations of what actually happened during the sixteen-month period of Solidarity's public life. For example, scene "I. EXT. SEA SHORE. SUMMER DAY" purports to give a dialogue between Brezhnev and Gierek, but the narrator, after setting the scene in a voice-over, suddenly appears in a close-up in the same location to explain "this isn't the Black Sea. Everything is true except the words and the pictures." A meeting took place, but the narrator cannot be sure of the terms or even the location and is only speculating. Similarly, he will have Brezhnev and other officials talk in a variety of styles, since he is trying to penetrate the reality behind the Government's rhetoric. He cannot be successful, but he can stimulate the viewer's thinking about the elusive personalities of these powerful figures. As the narrator puts it, however doubtful his version, "there was something going on which remains true even when the words and pictures are mostly made up."

Stoppard shrewdly has the narrator enter the

Program for the 1984 Broadway production of Stoppard's latest stage play, which won the New York Drama Critics Circle and Tony awards

frame in scene 6, for that is a way of stressing that the narrator is not an authority; he is a kind of coordinator of events and personalities. Occasionally the narrator and the witness argue about which version of events is correct, as in scene 18, when the witness calls the narrator's emphasis on the importance of intellectuals "horse manure." A rapid series of very short scenes (77-79) picture the narrator's difficulties in following events, his discarding of drafts of his narrative, and confessing he does not know "who's winning"—Solidarity or the Government.

Such scenes, where the narrator gets caught up in the flux of history, are especially convincing, since for a time it was not clear to historical participants like Walesa and Jaruzelski who was winning. On the one hand, Solidarity made enormous strides in getting access to the media and in enlisting more than ten million people in its union. On the other hand, it was never successful in getting the government to honor the agreement in August of 1980 that would have meant a true liberalization of peoples' lives, considerable freedom of expression, and some self-government. Scene 111 (a card game between Jaruzelski, Glemp, and Walesa) is Stoppard's most brilliantly imaginative touch because in it he gives three different versions of what the Church, Solidarity, and the government expected to get out of a secret meeting that is still not fully understood. By starting and stopping the scene three times, the playwright mimics the repetitive and circular nature of interpretations of history, interpretations that necessarily go over the same ground from different perspectives in the hope that an all-encompassing account can be developed.

In his introduction, Stoppard recognizes that the narrator is still a problem in the presentation of history. The playwright wanted the narrator to be identified with himself, so that a personality would emerge, as one does in *Travesties* where it becomes clear that Henry Carr is really the fallible narrator of the fragmented and distorted history dramatized in the play. In *Squaring the Circle*, the principle of fallibility is preserved, but the peculiar individuality, the quirkiness of a Stoppardian character is not present. For commercial reasons, Stoppard had to concede the narrator's role to an actor, Richard Crenna, who "*played* him much better than I could have ever *been* him," but the playwright still regrets *Squaring the Circle* did not fulfill his intention of producing "a kind of personal dramatized essay." If Stoppard offers this work on Solidarity as a compromised piece, it is nevertheless a remarkably innovative use of television that does express his aim of "distancing the film from the conventional kind of docudrama which (falsely) purports to reconstruct history."

The Dog It Was That Died, Stoppard's most recent play for radio, is a superb tragicomedy about the farcical world of spies in which "the real thing" is difficult to define. The following exchange between Rupert Purvis, a double agent working for Giles Blair, head of Britain's Q6 intelligence agency, shows the playwright at his very best, for he is under no constraint to hew to the facts or to balance his facility with words against the action or visualization needed for the stage and screen. Stoppard has always worked well in radio and has produced for it some of his most innovative probings of human psychology. Here he effectively opens up the gap that arises in Purvis's mind that causes him to question his identity, to attempt and to finally succeed at suicide after having been put into a mental institution where almost nothing is as it seems:

> PURVIS: Well, I'm pretty sure that when I told Gell that all this was going on, I was also acting on Rashnikov's instructions.
>
> *(Pause)*
>
> BLAIR: But, if that were so, no doubt you told Gell that it *was* so. No doubt you told Gell that Rashnikov has told you to tell Gell that Rashnikov had told you to tell him that you were being offered the bait.
>
> PURVIS: That's what I can't remember. I've forgotten who is my primary employer and who my secondary. For years I've been feeding stuff in both directions, following my instructions from either side, having been instructed to do so by the other, and since each side wanted the other side to believe that I was working for *it,* both sides were often giving me genuine stuff to pass on to the other side . . . so the side I was actually working for became . . . well, a matter of opinion really . . . it got lost.
>
> *(Pause)*
>
> Blair?

Purvis can be no more than "pretty sure" of his intentions. The first pause indicates just how uncertain both he and his boss are about where he stands. Blair then tries to straighten Purvis out, to

be logical about what the double agent intended, but as his syntax demonstrates, he is also confused by double talk. He begins by knowing where to put the emphasis (on *was*) and lamely ends by using the phrase "no doubt" that clearly suggests everything is in doubt. The ellipses in Purvis's next speech mimic the breakdown in memory, in logical processes, in the faith that one can reason through the confusion. He is no longer able to connect his "so" to a conclusion. His sentences are inconclusive, and inconclusiveness is all that is left "really," which means he is "lost"—waiting for some assurance from his boss Blair. Instead, there is only another pause, worse than the first, because Blair goes on to ignore the dilemma.

Only a writer who cares deeply about convictions would dare to write plays to call his own convictions and those of others to account. Lovers, politicians, and secret agents of various kinds are winning and losing their convictions all of the time in Stoppard's plays. The sense of intrigue and doubt that pervaded *Rosencrantz and Guildenstern* still informs Stoppard's work today. As his career has progressed, he has been willing to test his principles and his lack of principles more directly and personally even as he has taken on profoundly difficult historical and political subjects that many artists of his stature would shy away from. If he has seemed slippery to critics who would like to pin him down, the playwright shows no inclination to anchor himself in mid-career. As he recently told Mel Gussow for the *New York Times Magazine:*"You have to get everything in proportion. You compensate, rebalance yourself so that you maintain your angle to your world. When the world shifts, you shift."

Whether adapting the work of others, construing the plots of current events, or creating his own real things, Tom Stoppard continues to play with the balance between imagination and fact that can only be captured in the permanence of great language. As Henry, the character closest to his author states:"I don't think writers are sacred, but words are. They deserve respect. If you get the right ones in the right order, you can nudge the world a little or make a poem which children will speak for you when you're dead."

The themes of love and marriage in *The Real Thing* reflect, no doubt, some of Stoppard's own experiences, although he is reticent about discussing the connections between his plays and his private life. He continues to live near London with his second wife, Miriam, a physician and popular author on health issues, and his four sons, two of whom are from his first marriage. In recent years, he has become increasingly active in supporting the human rights movement. His primary area of concern is Czechoslovakia and Central Europe. He has written letters and cables to Moscow, participated in vigils, and worked through the British magazine *Index Against Censorship*. In the interview with Mel Gussow he lists "among his possible future projects . . . an original play dealing with the role of presidential bodyguards, and an English adaptation of 'Conspirators,' an unproduced play by the Czechoslovak dissident Vaclav Havel."

Interviews:

"Trad Tom Pops in: Tom Stoppard in interview with David Gollob and David Roper," *Gambit*, 37 (1981): 5-17;

Nancy S. Hardin, "An Interview with Tom Stoppard," *Contemporary Literature*, 22 (1981): 153-166;

Mel Gussow, "The Real Tom Stoppard," *New York Times Magazine*, 1 January 1984, pp. 18-23.

Bibliography:

David Bratt, *Tom Stoppard: A Reference Guide* (Boston: G. K. Hall, 1982).

References:

Tim Brassell, *Tom Stoppard: An Assessment* (London: Macmillan, 1985);

Richard Corballis, *Stoppard: The Mystery and the Clockwork* (New York: Methuen, 1984);

Lucina Paquet Gabbard, *The Stoppard Plays* (Troy, N.Y.: Whitson, 1982);

Jim Hunter, *Tom Stoppard's Plays* (New York: Grove, 1982);

Andrew K. Kennedy, "Tom Stoppard's Dissident Comedies," *Modern Drama*, 25 (1982): 469-476;

Robert E. Lauder, "Tom Stoppard's Mystery and Metaphysics," *America*, 11 May 1985, pp. 393-394;

Roger Scruton, "The Real Stoppard," *Encounter*, 60 (1983): 44-47;

Elliott Sirkin, "Theater," *Nation*, 238 (1984): 200-201;

Kenneth Tynan, *Show People* (London: Weidenfeld & Nicolson, 1980);

Gerald Weales, "Playwright's Dilemma," *Commonweal*, 111 (1984): 404-405;

Thomas R. Whitaker, *Tom Stoppard* (New York: Grove, 1983);

Hersh Zeifman, "Comedy of Ambush: Tom Stoppard's *The Real Thing*," *Modern Drama*, 26 (1983): 139-149;

Zeifman, "Tomfoolery: Stoppard's Theatrical Puns," *Yearbook of English Studies* (1979): 204-220.

Thomas Wolfe

(3 October 1900-15 September 1938)

Carol Johnston
Clemson University

See also the Wolfe entries in *DLB 9: American Novelists, 1910-1945*, Part 3, and *DLB Documentary Series 2*.

NEW BOOKS: *The London Tower*, edited by Aldo P. Magi (N.p.: Thomas Wolfe Society, 1980);

The Streets of Durham, edited by Richard Walser (Raleigh, N.C.: Wolf's Head Press, 1982);

K-19: Salvaged Pieces, edited by John L. Idol, Jr. (N.p.: Thomas Wolfe Society, 1983);

My Other Loneliness: Letters of Thomas Wolfe and Aline Bernstein, edited by Suzanne Stutman (Chapel Hill: University of North Carolina Press, 1983);

The Autobiography of An American Novelist, edited by Leslie Field (Cambridge, Mass.: Harvard University Press, 1983);

Beyond Love and Loyalty: The Letters of Thomas Wolfe and Elizabeth Nowell, edited by Richard S. Kennedy (Chapel Hill: University of North Carolina Press, 1983);

Welcome To Our City: A Play in Ten Scenes, edited by Kennedy (Baton Rouge: Louisiana State University Press, 1983);

The Train and the City, edited by Kennedy (N.p.: Thomas Wolfe Society, 1984);

Thomas Wolfe Interviewed: 1929-1938, edited by Magi and Walser (Baton Rouge & London: Louisiana State University Press, 1985);

Mannerhouse: A Play in Four Acts, edited by Louis Rubin and Idol (Baton Rouge: Louisiana State University Press, 1985);

Holding On For Heaven: The Cables and Postcards of Thomas Wolfe and Aline Bernstein, edited by Stutman (N.p.: Thomas Wolfe Society, 1985).

PERIODICAL PUBLICATION: "Last Poem," *Vanity Fair*, 46 (October 1983): 61.

Thomas Wolfe examining some of his manuscripts (photo by Robert Disraeli)

The six-year period spanning 1979 (the fiftieth anniversary of the publication of *Look Homeward, Angel*) and 1985 (the fiftieth anniversary of the publication of *Of Time and the River*) has been particularly rich in Wolfe scholarship. Of the eighteen volumes pertaining to Wolfe published in that time, four are either first editions of or new scholarly editions of works by Wolfe; three are limited editions of difficult-to-locate Wolfe items; eight are books or pamphlets of historical and biographical interest (three volumes of previously unpublished correspondence, a collection of interviews, and four volumes of reminiscences); and three are critical works. Six of these are products of major university presses (Louisiana State University, University of North Carolina, and Harvard); two are publications of commercial houses (Ungar and G. K. Hall); three have been printed by small private presses (Croissant and Willamette); and seven are publications, with limited distribution, of the Thomas Wolfe Society. The proportion of textual and scholarly work to critical work during this period (about four to one) is noteworthy, marking a pivotal moment in Wolfe studies: important attempts by scholars to come to grips with complex textual problems in the Wolfe canon.

Few years between 1979 and 1985 were uneventful; 1980, 1981, 1983, and 1985, however, were the most productive. The years of "Wolfegate," 1980-1981, a controversy focusing on John Halberstadt's 1980 *Yale Review* article, "The Making of Thomas Wolfe's Posthumous Novels," were the most turbulent and inglorious. The teapot tempest that found its way into the pages of the *New York Times Book Review*, the *New York Review of Books*, the *Chronicle of Higher Education*, the *Boston Globe*, and the *San Francisco Chronicle*, among others, centered on Halberstadt's misuse of Wolfe-estate material and on the decision made by the Houghton Library at Harvard (where the materials were housed) that he be barred from the library for a year. Halberstadt did not fabricate the textual problems he saw in the Wolfe canon, and he actually quoted fewer than ten words from previously unpublished Wolfe material, but his charges of literary fraud and his vociferous insistence that Wolfe had really not written his posthumous novels sensationalized and distorted material which had been made public nearly two decades earlier by Richard S. Kennedy in *The Window of Memory* (Chapel Hill: University of North Carolina Press, 1962). What Kennedy perceived to be "creative editing" on the part of Edward C. Aswell, Wolfe's editor at Harpers and later his literary executor, made necessary by Wolfe's death in 1938, Halberstadt perceived to be a conspiracy of secrecy designed to disguise the "true author" of Wolfe's posthumous novels. His scenario oversimplified and generalized the complex relationship between editor and writer, presenting sensitive Wolfe-estate material to the general reading public in the worst possible light.

In 1983 and 1985, more responsible Wolfe scholars plumbed a rich vein of archival material. In 1983 Wolfe's unpublished "Last Poem" was discovered by Charles Scribner, III, in a desk once belonging to Maxwell Perkins; and John L. Idol,

Dust jacket for a previously unpublished version of the play

Jr., convinced a private Wolfe collector to allow him to facsimile the only extant copy of the dummy of the first chapter of Wolfe's abortive second novel, *K-19*. That same year, Richard S. Kennedy included a previously unpublished Wolfe story, "No More Rivers," in his edition of Wolfe's correspondence with Elizabeth Nowell. New versions of previously published Wolfe works, *Welcome To Our City*, *The Story of A Novel*, and "Writing and Living," were published by Kennedy and Leslie Field. In addition, Kennedy, the most indefatigable of Wolfe scholars, edited the correspondence of Wolfe and Elizabeth Nowell, *Beyond Love and Loyalty*, while Suzanne Stutman, who began her work as a dissertation under Kennedy's direction at Temple University, edited the correspondence of Wolfe and Aline Bernstein under the title *My Other Loneliness*. Although 1983 was certainly the banner year in Wolfe studies, 1985 came close to rivaling its productivity. In 1985 Louis Rubin and Idol pieced together a jigsaw puzzle of documents to reconstruct Wolfe's play *Mannerhouse;* Richard Walser and Aldo P. Magi tirelessly searched for Wolfe interviews to be published as *Thomas Wolfe Interviewed;* and Suzanne Stutman added to her edition of the Wolfe-Bernstein correspondence in a pamphlet titled *Holding On For Heaven.* The year 1986 promises publication of Pulitzer Prize-winner David Herbert Donald's long-awaited Wolfe biography, the Thomas Wolfe Society's publication of the previously unpublished *The Hound of Darkness,* and the University of Pittsburgh Press's *Thomas Wolfe: A Descriptive Bibliography.*

Clearly, the most important contributions to Wolfe scholarship over the past six years are the first editions and new versions of Wolfe works; of parallel interest, because of the light it sheds on the facts of the publication of Wolfe's work and because of the autobiographical nature of his writing, is the recent biographical and historical scholarship on Wolfe.

One of the central issues facing Wolfe scholarship today is the establishment of authoritative texts of Wolfe's posthumous publications. Prior to 1980 much of the critical work published on Wolfe was tentative and defensive: tentative because so much archival material remained unpublished; defensive because charges of editorial collaboration (first leveled by Bernard DeVoto in 1936) clouded the authority of many published Wolfe texts. Of the twenty-eight volumes of Wolfe material published to date, sixteen were written for publication, and eleven of those sixteen were published posthumously. Three of these eleven, *The Web and the Rock, You Can't Go Home Again,* and *The Hills Beyond,* are central to the Wolfe canon. Had these posthumous publications been simple transferals of author-sanctioned typescripts into print, textual problems might still exist, but would be minimal. The task faced by Edward C. Aswell in preparing these volumes for publication after Wolfe's death in 1938 was complicated by the length of Wolfe's works, the proliferation of his drafts, and the complex synchronistic nature of Wolfe's writing which often defies sequential patterning. Doubtless, the volumes produced by Aswell unaided by Wolfe would differ from those same volumes had they been produced with Wolfe's assistance. The question—still awaiting an answer—is to what degree they would differ.

Over the past six years, textual, biographical, and historical scholarship have opened up the archives, and scholars have responded with enthusiasm. Denials of the existence of textual problems have been replaced by energetic efforts to create

authoritative texts of minor works in the Wolfe canon and by intriguing studies of the complex interaction between editor and writer. Among responsible Wolfe scholars, Kennedy, Field, Rubin, and Idol have taken the lead in coming to grips with these problems. Their editions of *The Story of A Novel,* "Writing and Living," *K-19, Welcome To Our City,* and *Mannerhouse* not only make authoritative texts of these works accessible to the scholarly community but also make genuine inroads into establishing policies and procedures for dealing with Wolfe's other posthumous publications.

Three additions were made to the Wolfe canon between 1979 and 1985: a poem, a chapter from an unfinished novel, and a short story. All are of greater historical than literary value, but have interesting publication histories. The last two also shed some light on Wolfe's relation to his editor, Edward Aswell, and his literary agent, Elizabeth Nowell. Wolfe's thirty-six-line "Last Poem" lay hidden in the recesses of a Scribners desk for nearly fifty years before it was unearthed. The desk used by John Hall Wheelock and Burroughs Mitchell, after Maxwell Perkins, offered up its treasure only when Scribner sought to discover why a stubborn drawer would not close. Behind the drawer, blocking its movement, were two crumpled sheets of paper and a photograph of Wolfe. The poem, apparently written in Brooklyn in 1934, is an undistinguished Faustian cry over lost creative power, of the kind that haunts many writers' notebooks and journals. It recalls a "wild first force" and an "old madness."

John Idol's edition of *K-19,* over half of which was appropriated by Aswell after Wolfe's death for use in chapter five of *You Can't Go Home Again,* is a less-heralded but ultimately more important publication. Idol facsimiles a ten-page publisher's dummy printing the first chapter of what was to have been Wolfe's second novel. Prepared sometime during the summer or fall of 1932, the dummy, complete with dust jacket, title page, an epigraph from Heine, and a prologue, was tossed into a trash basket at Scribners when the book was cancelled. Leo H. Linder retrieved it and kept it until 1959, when it was sold to a private collector. Idol postulates that Aswell edited passages of the work prior to including it in *You Can't Go Home Again* because "if left unedited, [it] would have eloquently betrayed the fact that it was a product of Wolfe the rhapsodic novelist rather than of Wolfe the less spendthrift and poetic writer in the final years of his career." The publication of *K-19* will enable students of *You Can't Go Home Again* to deal more successfully with material appearing on pages 48-51 of that novel and to understand more clearly the steps taken by Aswell to publish Wolfe's work following Wolfe's death in 1938.

"No More Rivers," a thirty-four-page typescript whittled from sixty-three pages by Wolfe with the help of Elizabeth Nowell, was accepted by the *Yale Review* just prior to Wolfe's death. Maxwell Perkins, who objected to the story because it included vignettes reflecting on Charles Scribner, Whitney Darrow, and Robert Bridges, successfully blocked its publication, and it remained unpublished until Richard S. Kennedy appended it to his edition of the Wolfe-Nowell correspondence, *Beyond Love and Loyalty*, as an example of Nowell's editing. The story, although not vintage Wolfe, contains several powerful passages about the morning traffic on the East River, the freight cars of the American railroads, and the landscape of the upper Mississippi. As Kennedy notes, it shows Wolfe experimenting with a nonautobiographical consciousness—sympathetically depicting a man totally different from himself.

Three recent products of Wolfe scholarship, Leslie Field's *The Autobiography of An American Novelist*, Richard S. Kennedy's *Welcome To Our City*, and Louis Rubin and John L. Idol's *Mannerhouse*, suggest the textual problems surrounding much Wolfe material. All have been previously published: *The Autobiography of An American Novelist* prints texts of *The Story of A Novel*, first published serially by the *Saturday Review of Literature* on 14, 21, and 28 December 1935 and then, in book form, by Scribners in 1936, and of Wolfe's Purdue Speech, "Writing and Living," edited by Field and William Braswell and published in the Purdue University Studies series in 1964; *Welcome To Our City* was first printed in *Esquire* in 1957; and *Mannerhouse* was first published in 1948 by Harper and Brothers. With the exception of "Writing and Living," which is printed much as it appeared in 1964, all are important new versions of these works based on copy-texts that differ substantively from those used in the earlier editions. (Copy-text is that version of a work, often one of a number of extant versions, that an editor decides to adhere to when preparing his edition of that work in all respects except in those instances in which there is compelling reason to change.) All contain introductions describing their editorial policies and outlining the transmission of the text; none contains textual apparatus; all are editions of essentially minor works in the Wolfe canon and are intended for general readers. One, "Writing and Living," retains the text of the earlier edition; two,

The Story of A Novel and *Welcome To Our City*, select their copy-texts on the basis of what the editors perceive to be the relative strengths of the available versions of these works; and one, *Mannerhouse*, chooses copy-text on the basis of authorial intent. In all cases, the research is excellent; the texts are readable; and the books are genuine contributions to Wolfe scholarship.

Field's ingenious juxtaposition of texts of Wolfe's two most important creative statements, *The Story of A Novel* and "Writing and Living," within a single volume, *The Autobiography of An American Novelist*, should be well received by students of Wolfe (it fills a genuine need), although Field's preface, a brief historical study of each work, is somewhat misleading. It implies that both texts are new versions of these works, when, in fact, only *The Story of A Novel* is here published, in its entirety, for the first time.

In his 1982 article "A 'True Text' Experience: Thomas Wolfe and Posthumous Publication" (the *Thomas Wolfe Review*, 6 [Fall 1982]: 27-34), Field describes the complex task of reconstructing Wolfe's Purdue Speech "Writing and Living," which he undertook with William Braswell in the early 1960s. The obstacles overcome by Field and Braswell in producing an authoritative text of Wolfe's speech are impressive; the apparatus of the 1964 edition speaks for their rigorous scholarship. In contrast, Field's "A Note on the Manuscripts and Editorial Method," prefatory to the text of *The Autobiography of An American Novelist*, is only three paragraphs and leaves far too many questions unanswered.

The text of "Writing and Living" used by Field here (Field states that it appears for the first time in its "original form") is essentially the same as the 1964 text, without apparatus, but with some forty words, the product of manuscript mutilation (originally marked in the 1964 edition by brackets containing the italicized word *hiatus*), now supplied. Assuming that scholars working on "Writing and Living" would turn to the apparatus of the 1964 edition, making its reprinting here unnecessary, it still seems strange that Field should supply forty-odd words without explanation. Have they been supplied conjecturally? Are they the result of further investigation? Surely some suitable explanation could have been given in the prefatory matter.

In the case of the 1983 publication of *The Story of A Novel*, the other text printed in Field's *Autobiography of An American Novelist*, it is, again, the brief prefatory note on editorial methods that raises questions. In choosing a copy-text for this

Dust jacket for the book that chronicles Wolfe's most important love affair

work, Field turned to an early seventy-four-page typescript, the original version that was later severely edited by Elizabeth Nowell for serial publication in the *Saturday Review of Literature* in 1935. Field's decision to use the extended version written by Wolfe, instead of the truncated version prepared by Nowell to meet the space limitations of magazine publication, is sound. It is more difficult to understand, however, why he should feel that the early typescript is more authoritative than the text of the 1936 Scribners edition, labored over by Wolfe, in which the author replaced much but not all that had earlier been cut by Nowell. Surely, prompted by Scribners to create a book out of an article, Wolfe would have been pressured to expand, not contract the text. The 1936 text is the text in which Wolfe chose to accept or reject Nowell's editorial emendations; it is his final say.

Field's decisions may emanate from his desire to present these texts in versions that approximate

the speeches originally delivered by Wolfe in 1935 at the University of Colorado Writer's Conference and in 1938 at the annual Literary Awards Banquet at Purdue University. The problems created by this volume may not reside as much in the texts printed by Field as in the truncated nature of his introduction. In a time marked by controversy over the textual problems posed by Wolfe's works, it is probably unwise for even as competent and authoritative a scholar as Field to produce editions without justifying copy-text and fully describing editorial procedures.

Richard S. Kennedy, faced with easily as complicated a copy-text decision in editing *Welcome To Our City*, elaborates at length on his choice of copy-text finally making a good case for choosing an early version of the text ("Text A"—the version prepared by Wolfe and George Pierce Baker for presentation by the 47 Workshop at the Agassiz House Theatre on 11 and 12 May 1923) over an apparently more authoritative text ("Text B"—a later, expanded version prepared by Wolfe for and then rejected by the Theatre Guild) as copy-text. "Text B," abridged by Edward Aswell, was published in 1957 in *Esquire;* "Text A" had never been published. As in the case of *The Story of A Novel,* "Text B," Wolfe's last say, initially appears to be the authoritative text. Kennedy argues convincingly, however, that the unwieldy "Text B," prepared by Wolfe under the misapprehension that he was creating a new medium for the stage, is less dramatically sound than "Text A"—which both Wolfe and Baker worked on. *Welcome To Our City* is, essentially, a minor work in the Wolfe canon, more of value for what it discloses about Wolfe than for its literary value. Kennedy's edition presents the play in an authoritative text representing the version that drew applause at the Agassiz House Theatre, rather than the version that failed to stimulate the Theatre Guild readers.

The most interesting textual study of a single work by Wolfe to date is, however, John L. Idol, Jr.'s discussion of "The Text and the Background" of *Mannerhouse,* prefatory to the edition of that play prepared by Louis Rubin and Idol for the Louisiana State University Press. Rubin and Idol found that many unacknowledged changes—some minor, others major—were made in preparing the play for publication. Although Rubin and Idol postulate in the prefatory matter to this edition that Edward Aswell made these changes, evidence has arisen since the publication of the 1985 edition suggesting that Franklin Heller, who oversaw the production of the play by the Yale Dramatic Society (not Drama

School) in 1948 may have assisted Aswell in arranging the text. The minor changes were primarily matters of consistency and house style; the major changes involved the less justifiable collapsing of two acts into one, deleting single lines and whole scenes, removal of characters, rearrangement of scenes, and addition of stage directions. The 1948 *Mannerhouse* appeared in a prologue and three acts; the Rubin/Idol edition is printed in a prologue and four acts. Rubin and Idol took as their copy-text the text of the play as prepared in early 1925, a typescript of 167 sheets with more than 130 corrections in Wolfe's hand. In addition to discussing revisions made in the 1948 edition and the editorial policies and copy-text decision used in preparing the 1985 edition, Rubin and Idol conclude by stating a policy that may well be of use to future editors of Wolfe: "Whether a cut or rearrangement made for a better play or not, Aswell took liberties with Wolfe's play and presented to American literature a work not wholly of Wolfe's creation. No such liberties are taken in this edition." It is, of course, impossible to extrapolate from the textual histories of *K-19* and *Mannerhouse* whether similar "liberties" were taken with other posthumously published works by Thomas Wolfe. Future Wolfe scholars, however, would do well to look to Rubin and Idol's edition for suggestions about the kinds of "liberties" taken with Wolfe's texts and for an intelligent discussion of the way in which these "liberties" should be handled.

Of the seven volumes of historical/biographical material published on Thomas Wolfe since 1979, four—three volumes of previously unpublished correspondence and one volume of interviews—are of major importance. Two of the volumes of correspondence, Richard S. Kennedy's *Beyond Love and Loyalty: The Letters of Thomas Wolfe and Elizabeth Nowell* and Suzanne Stutman's *My Other Loneliness: Letters of Thomas Wolfe and Aline Bernstein*, were published almost simultaneously by the University of North Carolina Press in 1983.

Kennedy's solidly edited little volume, although less dramatic than Stutman's edition of Wolfe's impassioned correspondence with his mistress, Aline Bernstein, will probably prove to be the more valuable to scholars. Wolfe published thirty-eight short stories in magazines prior to his death, some of which, like "Boom Town," "The Child by Tiger," "I Have A Thing To Tell You," "The Lost Boy," and "The Party at Jacks," although virtually ignored since then by critics, demonstrate valuable fictional skills. Nowell was largely responsible for these publications, consistently cutting Wolfe's vo-

luminous prose to meet magazine publication specifications and then successfully marketing his stories. Her correspondence with Wolfe is a spirited exchange between two intelligent professionals, one struggling to keep his work intact, the other paring and refining to strengthen character development and dramatic structure. Surprisingly, Wolfe's relationship to Nowell, who acted as unofficial editor of his short fiction only in addition to her task as literary agent, was the least adversarial of his relations to any of his editors. She justified her cuts, changes, and rearrangements to Wolfe—and, ultimately, he came to respect the discipline and objectivity with which she approached his work. By 1935 it is clear that Nowell, in addition to marketing and editing Wolfe's short stories, had begun to pore through the unused portions of Wolfe's manuscripts, salvaging publishable segments. It is with genuine surprise that Wolfe writes her in April 1935 upon learning through English agent A. S. Frere-Reeves of the publication of four of his stories. Where the hell, he asks, did she find them? Nowell had salvaged all four, "In the Park," "Arnold Pentland," "The Cottage By the Track," and "Only The Dead Know Brooklyn," from unused portions of the manuscript of *Of Time and the River*. Kennedy's well-annotated edition will be invaluable to students of Wolfe's short fiction. It prints not only the entirety of the Nowell correspondence for the first time, but a large number of Wolfe's letters to Nowell which Nowell chose not to include in her 1956 edition of *The Letters of Thomas Wolfe*. Of the thirty-eight letters and cards from Wolfe to Nowell published by Kennedy, twenty-four do not appear in *The Letters of Thomas Wolfe*.

The facts of the celebrated love affair between Thomas Wolfe and Aline Bernstein, recorded in fictionalized accounts in Wolfe's *The Web and the Rock* and *You Can't Go Home Again* and in Bernstein's *Three Blue Suits* and *The Journey Down*, are revealed in the primary documents of their correspondence, from which Suzanne Stutman selected 162 letters for publication in *Beyond Love and Loyalty*. On one level the book reads like an epistolary novel, detailing the Wolfe-Bernstein affair from its initial passion through stormy renunciation and accusation; on another level, it reads like a history text offering glimpses into the world of the 1930s. The letters are as passionate and egocentric as their gifted and tormented writers. Stutman's edition, supplemented in 1985 by her seventy-page *Holding On For Heaven* (a Thomas Wolfe Society publication printing cables and post-

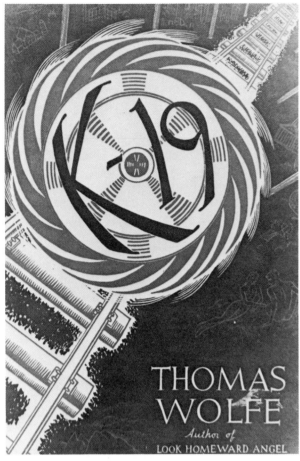

Cover for the facsimile of the dummy for Wolfe's aborted 1932 novel

creative artist as can be found in the more traditional sources of *The Story of A Novel* and "Writing and Living." One interview, published in the *Berliner Tageblatt* on 5 August 1936 (translated by Magi and Walser into English), shows Wolfe at his most adept, casually tossing out references to his bewildering productivity. He comments first on the peace of the scenery and then on his need for a vacation: "I am," he notes, "working on six books, you know."

No survey of Wolfe material published between 1979 and 1985 would be complete without mention of the three reprintings of hard-to-locate Wolfe items; the four volumes of reminiscences; the two critical collections; and the single biographical/critical work published during that time. The reprintings, all limited printings in pamphlet form of small Wolfe items prepared by the Thomas Wolfe Society for distribution to members, include *The London Tower,* a reprint of a 19 July 1925 *Asheville-Citizen* article; *The Streets of Durham,* a short play first published by Wolfe on 18 November 1919 in the *University of North Carolina Tar Baby;* and *The Train and the City,* a short story first published by Wolfe in the May 1933 issue of *Scribner's Magazine.* Of additional interest are Samuel Marx's four-page reminiscence of his encounter with Wolfe at Metro-Goldwyn-Mayer Studios, *Thomas Wolfe and Hollywood;* Madeleine Boyd's account of the significant role she played in placing Wolfe's first novel, *Look Homeward, Angel,* with Scribners, *Thomas Wolfe: The Discovery of A Genius;* a series of papers and reminiscences delivered at the second annual meeting of the Thomas Wolfe Society, *Thomas Wolfe of North Carolina;* and texts of Edward M. Miller's recollections of and Brian F. Berger's reconstruction of Wolfe's last journey through the midwest in 1938, *Thomas Wolfe: The Final Journey.* Only three full-length critical studies, two collections and a biographical/critical book, were published between 1979 and 1985: Richard S. Kennedy's *Thomas Wolfe: A Harvard Perspective* (a collection of eight papers presented at the Third Annual Meeting of the Thomas Wolfe Society); John Phillipson's *Critical Essays on Thomas Wolfe* (a collection of previously published essays); and Elizabeth Evans's *Thomas Wolfe* (a well-documented introduction to Wolfe containing sound, if somewhat traditional, evaluations of the four novels and two short-story collections in the Wolfe canon).

The wealth of Wolfe material published over the last six years may or may not indicate a "renaissance" in Wolfe studies; it does, however, without question, indicate significant renewal of interest in

cards omitted from the University of North Carolina edition for reasons of length), is, despite the editor's occasional mistranscription and garbling of Wolfe's "wild scrawl," a welcome addition to Wolfe scholarship.

The image that Wolfe sought to present to the reading public—that of a youthful and vital writer, bursting through the chains of normal human productivity to produce, on an average, three thousand words a day, a writer whose four-million-word draft of a single novel could have provided material for many novels, is best observed in the twenty-five newspaper interviews (and one reminiscence) printed in Richard Walser and Aldo P. Magi's collection, *Thomas Wolfe Interviewed: 1929-1938.* Most of these interviews, many buried in small-town newspapers, were generally inaccessible to all but the most persistent student of Wolfe's writing. Collected, however, these newspaper interviews, which liberally quote Wolfe on his life and art, create as profound a picture of the conscious

one of the great twentieth-century American novelists. Throughout this period there has been a growing fascination with the various versions of Wolfe's works and with speculations about the relationship of the author to his editors, but, in large measure, Wolfe scholars have made major strides in refining and redefining the Wolfe canon, while successfully defending it against the challenges of fraud leveled at it by sensationalists. What is left to be said about Wolfe? The answer is *plenty*—especially as the best scholar/critics increasingly avail themselves of the archival material available at Harvard and at Chapel Hill. Students of Wolfe who resist such careful, demanding work do so at their peril; as the latest crop of books demonstrates, the study of Thomas Wolfe still has much to tell us about the nature of literature and about the complexities of publishing it.

References:

Brian F. Berger, *Thomas Wolfe: The Final Journey* (West Linn, Oreg.: Willamette River Press, 1984);

Madeleine Boyd, *Thomas Wolfe: The Discovery of a Genius,* edited by Aldo P. Magi (N.p.: Thomas Wolfe Society, 1981);

Elizabeth Evans, *Thomas Wolfe* (New York: Ungar, 1984);

John Halberstadt, "The Making of Thomas Wolfe's Posthumous Novels," *Yale Review,* 70 (October 1980): 79-84;

H. G. Jones, ed., *Thomas Wolfe of North Carolina* (Chapel Hill: North Caroliniana Society and the North Carolina Collection, 1982);

Richard S. Kennedy, "The Wolfegate Affair," *Harvard Magazine,* 84 (September-October 1981): 48-53, 62;

Kennedy, ed., *Thomas Wolfe: A Harvard Perspective* (Athens, Ohio: Croissant, 1983);

Samuel Marx, *Thomas Wolfe and Hollywood* (Athens, Ohio: Croissant, 1980);

John S. Phillipson, *Critical Essays on Thomas Wolfe* (Boston: G. K. Hall, 1985).

NEW ENTRIES

Henry W. Allen (Will Henry/Clay Fisher)

(29 September 1912-   )

Keith Kroll

University of California, Riverside

BOOKS: *No Survivors,* as Will Henry (New York: Random House, 1950; London: Corgi, 1952);

Red Blizzard, as Clay Fisher (New York: Simon & Schuster, 1951; London: Boardman, 1952);

Wolf-Eye: The Bad One, as Will Henry (New York: Messner, 1951);

Santa Fe Passage, as Clay Fisher (Boston: Houghton Mifflin, 1952; London: Corgi, 1954);

To Follow a Flag, as Will Henry (New York: Random House, 1953; London: Corgi, 1955);

Yellow Hair, as Clay Fisher (Boston: Houghton Mifflin, 1953; Kingswood, Surrey: World's Work, 1956);

War Bonnet, as Clay Fisher (Boston: Houghton Mifflin, 1953; Kingswood, Surrey: World's Work, 1955);

The Fourth Horseman, as Will Henry (New York: Random House, 1954; London: Corgi, 1958);

Death of a Legend, as Will Henry (New York: Random House, 1954); republished as *Jesse James* (London: Corgi, 1957);

The Tall Men, as Clay Fisher (Boston: Houghton Mifflin, 1954; Kingswood, Surrey: World's Work, 1956);

Who Rides with Wyatt, as Will Henry (New York: Random House, 1955; London: Corgi, 1958);

The Big Pasture, as Clay Fisher (Boston: Houghton Mifflin, 1955; Kingswood, Surrey: World's Work, 1957);

The Brass Command, as Clay Fisher (Boston: Houghton Mifflin, 1955); republished as *Dull Knife* (London: Corgi, 1958);

The North Star, as Will Henry (New York: Random House, 1956);

The Blue Mustang, as Clay Fisher (Boston: Houghton Mifflin, 1956; London: Corgi, 1958);

Yellowstone Kelly, as Clay Fisher (Boston: Houghton Mifflin, 1957; London: Corgi, 1959);

The Texas Rangers, as Will Henry (New York: Random House, 1957);

Reckoning at Yankee Flat, as Will Henry (New York: Random House, 1958);

The Seven Men at Mimbres Springs, as Will Henry (New York: Random House, 1958; London: Corgi, 1960);

The Crossing, as Clay Fisher (Boston: Houghton Mifflin, 1958); republished as *River of Decision* (London: Corgi, 1960);

Orphan of the North, as Will Henry (New York: Random House, 1958);

From Where the Sun Now Stands, as Will Henry (New York: Random House, 1960; London: Hammond, 1962);

Journey to Shiloh, as Will Henry (New York: Random House, 1960; London: Hammond, 1963);

Niño: The Legend of "Apache Kid," as Clay Fisher (New York: Morrow, 1961); republished as *The Legend of Apache Kid* (London: Mills & Boon, 1964);

Return of the Tall Man, as Clay Fisher (New York: Pocket Books, 1961);

The Feleen Brand, as Will Henry (New York: Bantam, 1962; London: Mills & Boon, 1962);

The Oldest Maiden Lady in New Mexico and Other Stories, as Clay Fisher (New York: Macmillan, 1962);

San Juan Hill, as Will Henry (New York: Random House, 1962);

The Pitchfork Patrol, as Clay Fisher (New York: Macmillan, 1962; London: Mills & Boon, 1965);

The Gates of the Mountains, as Will Henry (New York: Random House, 1963; London: Hammond, 1966);

MacKenna's Gold, as Will Henry (New York: Random House, 1963; London: Hammond, 1964);

Valley of the Bear, as Clay Fisher (Boston: Houghton Mifflin, 1964);

In the Land of the Mandans, as Will Henry (Philadelphia & New York: Chilton, 1965);

The Last Warpath, as Will Henry (New York: Random House, 1966; London: Hammond, 1967);

Sons of the Western Frontier, as Will Henry (Philadelphia & New York: Chilton, 1966; London: Jenkins, 1968);

Henry Wilson Allen (Will Henry, Clay Fisher)

Custer's Last Stand, as Will Henry (Philadelphia & New York: Chilton, 1966);

Alias Butch Cassidy, as Will Henry (New York: Random House, 1967; London: Jenkins, 1969);

One More River to Cross, as Will Henry (New York: Random House, 1967; London: Barrie & Jenkins, 1968);

Maheo's Children, as Will Henry (Philadelphia & New York: Chilton, 1968);

Genesis Five (New York: Morrow, 1968);

The Day Fort Larking Fell, as Will Henry (Philadelphia & New York: Chilton, 1969);

Tayopa! (New York: Pocket Books, 1970);

See How They Run (New York: Pocket Books, 1970);

Chiricahua, as Will Henry (Philadelphia & New York: Lippincott, 1972; London: Corgi, 1973);

Outcasts of Canyon Creek, as Clay Fisher (New York: Bantam, 1972);

The Bear Paw Horses, as Will Henry (Philadelphia & New York: Lippincott, 1973; London: Corgi, 1974);

Apache Ransom, as Clay Fisher (New York: Bantam Books, 1974);

I, Tom Horn, as Will Henry (Philadelphia & New York: Lippincott, 1975; London: Corgi, 1976);

Black Apache, as Clay Fisher (New York: Bantam Books, 1976);

Summer of the Gun, as Will Henry (Philadelphia & New York: Lippincott, 1978; London: Corgi, 1980);

Nine Lives West, as Clay Fisher (New York: Bantam Books, 1978);

Seven Legends West, as Clay Fisher (New York: Bantam Books, 1983);

Will Henry's West, edited by Dale L. Walker (El Paso: Texas Western Press, 1984);

The Ballad of Billy Bonney, as Will Henry (Santa Fe: Flying Coffin Press, 1984).

OTHER: *14 Spurs,* edited by Will Henry (New York: Bantam Books, 1968).

SELECTED PERIODICAL PUBLICATIONS: "Breaking Ground for a Novel," *Roundup,* 21 (September 1973): 12-13, 15;

"Let's Tell It Like It Was," as Will Henry, *Roundup,* 24 (December 1976): 1-2, 4;

"Guarding the Packline to the Past," *Roundup,* 29 (May 1981): 5-6;

"The Far-Out West," as Will Henry, *South Dakota Quarterly,* 19 (Spring/Summer 1981): 114-125;

"Will Henry and the Indians By the Author of *From Where the Sun Now Stands* As told to Henry W. Allen," as Will Henry, *Roundup,* 31 (January 1983): 9-13;

"There Was an Old West," *Roundup,* 31 (April 1983): 9-10.

"I wrote my first 'Western' in entire ignorance of the fact that it was a 'Western,'" Henry W. Allen told an interviewer in 1982. Like many aspiring authors, Allen had planned to write the Great American Novel, but reviewers relegated his first book to the Western genre that he felt the critical media considered "lowly." Not to be dismayed, Allen decided to help "elevate the category" and kept writing Westerns (and a few non-Westerns) until thirty-five years later his reputation and accomplishments as a "Western writer" are considerable. Author and critic Brian Garfield considers Allen "unquestionably the best writer alive today who consistently turns or has turned his hand to Westerns."

Writing under the two pen names of Will Henry and Clay Fisher and his own name, Allen has had fifty-three books published, forty-six of which have been published in hardcover. Bantam Books, Allen's paperback publisher, places his sales at over fifteen million copies (roughly nine million Will Henrys and six million Clay Fishers). His books have been reprinted in England and translated into foreign languages, including French, German, Italian, Norwegian, Polish, Spanish, and Swedish. He has received five Western Writers of America Spur awards: for his novels *From Where the Sun Now Stands* (1960), *The Gates of the Mountains* (1963), and *Chiricahua* (1972) and short stories "Isley's Stranger" (1962) and "The Tallest Indian in Toltepec" (1965). He has twice received the Western Writers of America special award for "fine writing of the American west" for his novels *One More River To Cross* (1967) and *Alias Butch Cassidy* (1967). In 1972 he received the Western Heritage Wrangler Award given by the National Cowboy Hall of Fame. In addition, sixteen of his novels have been sold to Hollywood and eight have been produced to date.

While growing up in Kansas City, Missouri, Allen dreamed of becoming not a writer but a veterinarian and rancher. His father, an oral surgeon, kept a well-stocked library, in which Allen says he read widely and voraciously. After graduating from Southwest High School in 1930, he attended Kansas City Polytechnic Institute for three terms. His parents urged him to attend a four-year college, but Allen decided instead to head west. Like one of his favorite authors, Jack London, Allen did much traveling and held many jobs before finally becoming a full-time, professional writer: he caravaned cars from the Dust Bowl to California, worked in the gold fields of Colorado, and held other jobs in New Mexico, Arizona, Montana, and Wyoming. In 1932, with thirty dollars in his pocket, he arrived in California to stay.

After working briefly as a stableboy and then as a writer for the *Santa Monica Sunset Reporter*, Allen began a career as a short-subjects writer in the Hollywood studios beginning with M-G-M in 1937. That same year he married Amy Geneva Watson. He was eventually fired from his job at M-G-M for working on his first novel on company time. In 1950, with that novel, *No Survivors* (1950), completed, he returned to M-G-M on a one-year contract which stipulated that anything he wrote during that time belonged to the studio. Since Random House was about to publish *No Survivors*, Allen signed Will Henry as its author. He then wrote his

second novel, *Red Blizzard* (1951), during his year at M-G-M. Since *No Survivors* was to be published by Random House and because he needed to remain under cover at M-G-M, Allen created Clay Fisher as the author of *Red Blizzard* and sent it to Simon and Schuster. Henry W. Allen, also known as Will Henry and Clay Fisher, was off and running.

Allen's use of two pen names has attracted the attention of several critics. Anne Falke writes in *Journal of Popular Culture* that stylistically "Fisher novels [as compared to Henry novels] employ a more typical 'western' form." Historian and critic Richard Etulain writes that "in his Will Henry Westerns, Allen demonstrates an experienced hand in joining history and fiction to produce high caliber Westerns. His Clay Fisher Westerns, on the other hand, emphasize action and adventure and rarely deal with specific historical events." Finally, author and Western critic Jon Tuska considers Allen's Fisher novels to be his "more formulary efforts."

In a 1980 letter to his biographer, Robert L. Gale, Allen wrote, "I am unique among Western authors, I believe, by wide margin, in having owned and operated two authors, each working at a separate level, and successful at the two levels, for thirty years." Allen has also stated that he felt Will Henry the superior writer. Yet, in a 1981 letter to Gale, Allen wrote, "there is 'finally . . . no definable difference' in the fiction of [my] two pseudonymous selves." While Allen seems unsure about the differences in the novels written under his two pen names, he is quite sure about the effect on his career of using them. He told an interviewer: "The two-name thing was the worst mistake I ever made as a commercial artist. . . . Had I all fifty novels under one name—Will Henry—today, I would be better off professionally and commercially and historically."

Very few—at least one critic would argue none—of Allen's Westerns are what is termed traditional or formulary. Rather, most of his works are historical reconstructions, in many cases romanticized. In the traditional or formulary Western, such as those written by Louis L'Amour, the heroes, villains, and heroines are stereotypical characters, and the reader knows how the story will end—the hero will always win. In an Allen Western, the hero may be an Indian, the hero may die, or both. Allen expects the "historical Western to entertain before it educates. But once the history is brought into the story, then that history must not be violated."

Allen's fiction depicts a wide range of char-

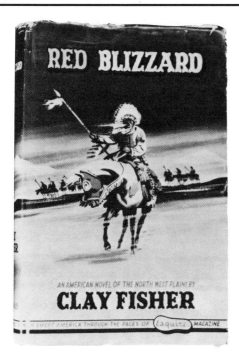

Dust jacket for the first Clay Fisher novel, an account of the 1866 Fetterman massacre in the Dakota Territory

acters and historical events. He admits to having a lifelong love for the American Indian, and twenty-three of his novels portray the fighting horseback Indian of the West. In these works, Allen set out "to render a personal tribute to the American Indian." In other works he has sought to "redraw" or revise the legendary image of a particular Western figure, such as Jesse James or Wyatt Earp. And still other Allen Westerns concern the Lewis and Clark expedition, the Civil War, the Spanish-American War, and the Gold Rush in Alaska.

No Survivors may not have been the Great American Novel Allen thought he was writing, but it is a fine Western. In the opening of the novel, Allen writes that it is "transcribed from the personal journal of Colonel John Buell Clayton, C.S.A. (1844-1878)." Clayton is an ex-Confederate officer who, after Appomattox, heads west and becomes a scout for the army. He fights under Lt. Col. William J. Fetterman's command and is injured and taken captive by Crazy Horse when Fetterman's troops are massacred near Fort Phil Kearny. Clayton is not killed because he "had shown great courage and mighty power to hurt." Crazy Horse eventually adopts Clayton and gives him the Indian name Cetan Mani (Walking Hawk). Cetan Mani marries an Indian maiden, Star of the North, and during his decade with the Sioux becomes a full

chief and Crazy Horse's constant companion. After spying on Gen. George Crook's troops before the Battle of Rosebud, Cetan Mani has a change of heart, flees the Sioux, and reports back to Custer that the army troops are in danger; but Custer only scoffs at his remarks. Cetan Mani ultimately fights beside Custer in the Battle of the Little Big Horn. After the battle, Crazy Horse, believing Cetan Mani dead, prepares his body for cremation. Here fiction gives way to fantasy as Cetan Mani escapes from his burial platform, mounts his horse Hussein, visits his dying wife, Star of the North, watches as Crazy Horse is killed, kills Crazy Horse's killer, and then meets Sitting Bull at his Canadian camp on the Red River. His skeleton and journal are found near the Slave Lake country in 1878.

In *No Survivors* Allen does a skillful job of blending the fictional account of his romantic hero, Cetan Mani (Clayton), with a partially accurate historical account of Custer's Last Stand. His sympathetic and heroic depiction of Indians in the novel was a major departure from the usual portrayal of Indians as brutal savages. His rather unsympathetic portrayal of Custer was in keeping with the numerous anti-Custer works already published. Debunking Custer began in 1934 with the publication of Frederic F. Van de Water's *Glory-Hunter*. Author Brian W. Dippie includes *No Survivors* along with Ernest Haycox's *Bugles in the Afternoon* (1944) and Thomas Berger's *Little Big Man* (1964) as the three best fictional works dealing with the Little Big Horn, although Dippie does not consider *No Survivors* as good as the last two works. Allen's interest in the "boy general" did not end with *No Survivors*. He gives an even harsher depiction of Custer in *Yellow Hair* (1953) but lessens his criticism in *Custer's Last Stand* (1966).

No Survivors is not only a good first novel; it also provides an introduction to Allen's writing. It contains many of the themes that appear throughout his Western fiction: his high regard for and sympathetic treatment of the American Indian; his depiction of the U.S. Army as inept; his creation of a fictional, oftentimes romantic, hero; his use of a framing device such as a lost journal or newly discovered manuscript on which the narrative is based; and his blending of fictional events with historical reality to create a historically accurate Western. *No Survivors* is one of his top ten sellers and personal favorites. And critically it is accepted as one of Allen's finest Westerns. Western novelist-critic Loren Estleman calls it "Will Henry's enduring 'classic.' "

Red Blizzard, another of Allen's best-sellers

and generally considered one of his better Clay Fisher novels, describes the Fetterman massacre which occurred ten years before the Little Big Horn. *Red Blizzard* is a historical reconstruction of the Fetterman massacre and the legendary ride of John "Portugee" Phillips. On 21 December 1866 Capt. William J. Fetterman and his troops stationed at Fort Phil Kearny, Dakota Territory, were ambushed and killed by Red Cloud and his Oglala warriors. In the novel, all the non-Indians are given fictional names: Fetterman becomes Major Phil Stacey; Col. Henry B. Carrington, who had never led troops in battle until taking over command of the 18th Infantry, becomes Col. Travis Clanton; and John "Portugee" Phillips becomes Allen's fictional hero, John "Pawnee" Perez, a half-breed Pawnee who had "but one ambition burning in his dark breast: to belong, by force of achievement, to the white race of his father."

In his desire to become a part of the white race, Pawnee Perez serves as an Indian scout to the soldiers stationed at Fort Will Farney (Fort Phil Kearny). His continual warnings of Red Cloud's impending attack are dismissed. Accompanying Stacy when Red Cloud attacks, he escapes as the major and his men are massacred. After being jailed for desertion, Perez is freed and begins a 236-mile, four-day ride through -50° weather and a Wasiya (blizzard) from Fort Farney to Fort Loring (Fort Laramie) to seek help for the beleaguered troops at Fort Farney. He is temporarily blinded and suffering from frostbite by the time he reaches Fort Loring. Once recovered, he is paid three $100 bills by the army for his heroic ride and leaves the fort only to be shot in the back and scalped as a traitor by another Indian.

Allen's intention in *Red Blizzard* is not so much to pay tribute to the American Indian but rather to honor the real-life but forgotten John "Portugee" Phillips. He does this by creating the fictional half-breed scout: "Had Pawnee Perez been a white man you would know his name as you do Custer's or Kit Carson's. But history has no use for half-breeds." By blending his fictional account of Pawnee Perez with historical fact, Allen attempts to revise history and acknowledge the actual feat of John "Portugee" Phillips.

Within four years of the publication of *No Survivors* and *Red Blizzard,* Allen had written and published four new Westerns and a children's book, *Wolf-Eye: The Bad One* (1951). The publication of these works and the sale of three of them to Hollywood gave Allen the opportunity to be a full-time writer.

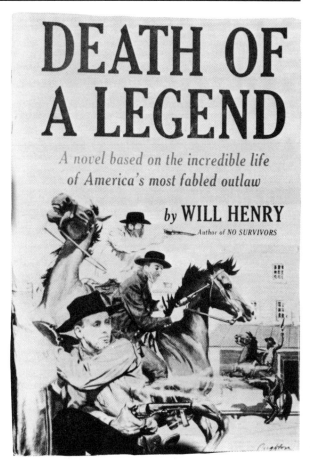

Dust jacket for Allen's revisionist treatment of Jesse James

In *The Fourth Horseman* (1954), Allen turned his attention away from depicting Indian-white conflicts to depicting an all-white feud, the Graham-Tewksbury feud—historically and ironically called the Pleasant Valley War—that arose in Arizona in the 1880s. The Grahams and Tewksburys were cattle rustlers in the Pleasant Valley before bad blood broke out between the two clans. When the Tewksburys agreed to stand guard over sheep being brought into the valley by the Daggs Brothers, the largest sheep outfit in Arizona, the Grahams, with the aid of the Blevans clan and other Pleasant Valley men, warred against the Tewksburys and anyone who sided with them. The two factions were soon engaged in a violent struggle that would ultimately claim the lives of many men.

As in *Red Blizzard* and in other Westerns, Allen fictionalizes the names of the central characters. In *The Fourth Horseman* the Tewksburys become the Fewkeses, the Grahams become the Gradens, and the Daggs Brothers become the Skaggs Brothers. He also introduces a fictional hero named Frank

Rachel, a reformed gunfighter who enters the valley looking for peace and solitude but eventually ends up fighting on the side of the Fewkeses. As one would expect from Allen's earlier Westerns, in *The Fourth Horseman* Allen sides with the underdogs, the Fewkeses. And while he fictionalizes the names of the real-life participants and invents characters, his descriptions of the valley and of the events surrounding the Graham-Tewksbury feud are historically accurate.

Along with depicting Indian-white conflicts and all-white conflicts, Allen set out in some of his Westerns to "redraw" the image of legendary Western figures. In an article titled "Jesse James and Wyatt Earp" Allen explains: "Yes, I have consciously tried to revise images we have of people of the first order of Western fame. That is to say, I am conscious that I don't agree with what is thought of the particular famed personage and I want to alter that impression to what my studies have shown me was more nearly the truth of that person. That's whether the truth made the person less or more admirable, or despicable." Two such revisionist, semifictional biographies are *Death of a Legend* (1954) and *Who Rides with Wyatt* (1955). In these two works, Allen revises the legendary images of Jesse James and Wyatt Earp respectively.

"Death" in the title *Death of a Legend* refers to both the death of the outlaw Jesse James and the "death" of the legend of Jesse James. Allen writes, "it was my conscious intention to redraw him with the darker, bloodier pen used in *Death of a Legend*." He does not let the reader down. His depiction of James is anything but the Robin Hood character that history has painted James to be. Allen begins the story by describing James as a nine-year-old boy cold-heartedly killing an old hound dog and continues to debunk the famed outlaw throughout his depiction of James's notorious career in Missouri, Iowa, and Minnesota until his death at the hands of Bob Ford.

If Allen desired to tarnish the legendary image of Jesse James, then in *Who Rides with Wyatt* he wished to polish the besmirched image that he believed historians had given Wyatt Earp. He writes at the beginning of the novel that he is retelling the story of Earp as it was told to him in 1933 by an old pioneer living in Prescott, Arizona, who had learned the story from an unnamed Tombstone outlaw. The narrative begins in 1880 as Wyatt Earp, riding to Tombstone, saves the life of a young cowboy named Johnny Ringo. The narrative ends with Ringo's mysterious death. Was he murdered? Did he commit suicide? Did Earp kill him? The

reader must decide. In between, Earp becomes involved with two heroines, Lilly Belloit, "the faded Tombstone Lilly," and Evelyn Cushman, who runs a boardinghouse; along with his brothers and Doc Holiday he shoots it out at the O.K. Corral against the Clanton and McLowry brothers and Billy Claiborne and gets revenge on the Curly Bill Brocious gang for crippling his brother Virgil and murdering his brother Morgan.

Allen believes that Earp has been characterized with "historical inaccuracy" and portrayed as a villain by historians and Western writers. Accordingly, Earp is portrayed as a hero throughout the entire story. There is no question in reading *Who Rides with Wyatt* that Allen believes Earp "the last of the great lawmen."

Who Rides with Wyatt is filled with real-life characters, such as the Clantons and the Brocious gang. The names of some fictional characters are only slightly changed from the actual names; for example, the fictional McLowrys are the real-life McLaurys. But *Who Rides with Wyatt* is more fiction than historical truth. And although it is an interesting Western, Allen's mixture of fiction and history leaves at least some critics with mixed feelings. C. L. Sonnichsen describes the novel as a "superwestern" but also writes that Allen: "on the one hand . . . has researched his subjects carefully and takes himself seriously as a historical novelist. . . . On the other hand, he likes to paint in shiny blacks and stark whites, and he gives a tremendous boost to the perpetuation of the [Wyatt Earp] legend."

In the three-year period between 1955 and 1958, Allen worked steadily—with time taken out for background reading and visiting the locales of his stories—at his Encino, California, home writing nine Western novels, his second children's book, *Orphan of the North* (1958), and his first novel concerning the Civil War, *The Crossing* (1958).

The hero of *The Crossing* is Judah "Jud" Beaumont Reeves III, a young cowboy turned Confederate scout. Armed with his Ethan Allen shotgun and a copy of *The Professional Soldier in Command: His Obligations as a Leader of Men,* written by his father, a former army general now deceased, Jud sets off "to the state capital at Austin City to join the Texas Army and drive the cursed Union troops forever from southern soil." Before ever reaching Austin, however, he kills a man who cheats him at poker and rather than face a jail sentence signs on as a special scout with Capt. John Robert Baylor. After scouting for Baylor, he joins up with Gen. Henry Hopkins Sibley, who, along with Baylor, between June 1861 and May 1862 was fighting Union troops for control of the territories of New Mexico and Arizona. During his time as a scout Reeves meets and falls in love with Estrellita "Star" Cavanaugh, the Mexican-Apache daughter of his friend and fellow scout Elkanah Cavanaugh.

The Crossing is reminiscent of Stephen Crane's *The Red Badge of Courage.* Like Crane's young hero, Henry Fleming, Jud Reeves joins the army with idealistic and glorious perceptions of war only to learn that war is anything but an idyll. "He [Jud] had seen naked war . . . and the pictures of it would not readily withdraw themselves from his weary mind." In time of battle, Jud learns that his grandfather's legend and his father's monograph fail him.

As Robert L. Gale points out, "one feature of *The Crossing* is outstanding—its hauntingly suggestive title." The final section, "The Crossing," describes the fundamental changes that Jud Reeves experiences throughout the novel. His psychological "crossings" include the transformation of his idealistic perception of war into a realistic view of human carnage, the journey from paternal dominance to independence, the transition from a socially "correct" love for a white woman to his passion for an Apache woman; and at the end Jud physically crosses the Rio Grande from Texas into Mexico.

After writing eleven novels in three years, Allen wrote and had published only two novels between 1959 and 1960, one of which is unquestionably his masterpiece, *From Where the Sun Now Stands* (1960).

"Hear me, my chiefs, my heart is sick and sad. From where the sun now stands, I will fight no more forever." The speaker of these memorable words is Chief Joseph of the Nez Percé, the real-life hero of Allen's novel. *From Where the Sun Now Stands* describes the story of the Nez Percés' attempt to flee from White Bird Canyon in Idaho and cross the border into Canada, which ended in failure with the surrender of Chief Joseph at Bear Paws in Montana on 5 October 1877. The narrator of the story is Heyets, a Nez Percé brave and nephew of Chief Joseph. He relates the story of the Nez Percés' 113-day and 1,300-mile retreat led by Chief Joseph. Along the way, Heyets grows from a fourteen-year-old boy, torn between the Christian ways of the Lapwai Missionary School and the Indian way of life, to an Indian warrior who fights bravely against the army troops led by Col. O. O. "One Hand" Howard.

In his foreword to the novel Allen writes, "May it serve . . . to dignify the Indian position and render justice to the memory of Chief Joseph and his people." What follows is Allen's finest tribute to the American Indian, a well-researched, sympathetic, and captivating description of Indian life as told from the Nez Percé point of view. Although the fictional hero Heyets acts as narrator, the great hero of this story is the real-life Chief Joseph. Gale writes that "Joseph dominates all others in this epic, is uniquely portrayed and never reduced to a stereotype, is intellectual rather than militant, and concludes that all his options will eventuate in tragedy." In contrast, and with echoes of earlier works and representative of works to come, Allen portrays the white man (in particular the army and its leaders, such as Col. O. O. Howard) as inept, rapacious Indian haters. They epitomize everything evil and represent everything that the Indian is not.

From Where the Sun Now Stands has received almost universal critical acclaim. A poll by the Western Writers of America to select the "top twenty-five best Westerns of all time" selected the novel as twenty-third. Jon Tuska considers it "a modern classic of Western American literature," and Gale calls it "an indisputable masterpiece." It also ranks among Allen's top ten best-sellers.

In *The Gates of the Mountains* (1963) Allen returned to a Northwest locale for his story. This time, however, the story concerns the Lewis and Clark expedition more than Indian-white conflicts, although Indians play a prominent part. The hero and central character is François Rivet of La Charrette, a real-life member of the expedition whose name appears on the official roster but who is rarely mentioned in Lewis and Clark's *Journals.* Taking advantage of this scarcity of information, Allen blends fiction and history to recreate Frank Rivet's story.

Rivet's first-person narrative begins on 24 May 1804 as he saves Clark's keelboat—a bit of Allen's fictionalizing—from smashing up in the Missouri River. When Captain Lewis will not allow him on the expedition, Rivet stows away on one of the expedition's boats and when finally discovered makes friends with Clark and Clark's slave, York. He serves the expedition as a boatman, a secretary to Clark, and a scout. Once in the land of the Mandans, Rivet meets and falls in love with Sacajawea, the legendary Indian woman and squaw wife of Toussaint Charbonneau, whom Clark has hired as an interpreter. When the expedition reaches Three Forks, Lewis orders Rivet bound and placed on a boat back to St. Louis; but with the help of Clark and York, Rivet is freed and trails the expedition on land. Rather than follow the party up the Columbia, however, he goes in search of his father, Achille Rivet, a captive of the Shoshone. He later rejoins the expedition as it heads back to St. Louis; but instead of returning to St. Louis and the white world, Rivet joins with Charbonneau and Sacajawea, and there his journal ends.

Allen makes extensive use of Lewis and Clark's *Journals,* quoting from them throughout the novel. The *Journals* serve as a chronological framework, and Allen pays careful attention to maintaining historical and geographical accuracy. *The Gates of the Mountains,* however, is not straight history but a romanticized version of historical events. Allen creates his story by fictionalizing the account of the real-life Rivet. Describing Rivet's friendships with Clark and York, his search for his father, and his love for Sacajawea is more important to Allen than simply retelling the story of Lewis and Clark's expedition.

In 1965 Allen made what he called "a personal choice . . . to concentrate on the Will Henry

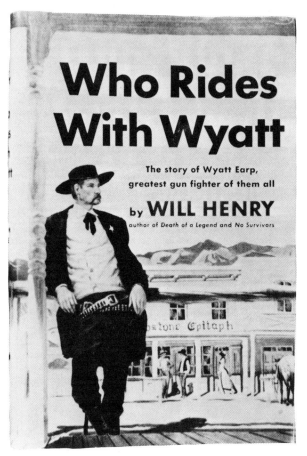

Dust jacket for Allen's semifictional biography which attempts to refurbish Earp's reputation

career and let Clay Fisher more or less bump along on his own." From 1965 to 1976 he wrote and published seventeen works, including three novels published under his own name. There are several outstanding works in this group—*Alias Butch Cassidy* (1967), which depicts George LeRoy Parker's outlaw life from age sixteen to twenty-one; *One More River to Cross* (1967), a historical reconstruction of the life of Ned Huddleston, alias Isom Dart; *Maheo's Children* (1968), a historomance involving a fictional preacher named Nehemiah Bleek; and *Apache Ransom* (1974), which concerns a Franciscan Padre, Father Nunez, and includes Ben Allison, the hero of Allen's four "Tall Man" novels. But the two outstanding works from this period are *Chiricahua* (1972) and *I, Tom Horn* (1975).

As in many other Allen novels, the plot of *Chiricahua* is tangled and complex. The various plot lines running through the work all in one way or another concern the central character, who is described as "a drifter, a drunk, and a horsethief" but remains nameless until the epilogue. One plot line concerns the Chiricahua Indian uprising that occurred in 1833. Under the command of Chatto ("Flat Nose"), the Chiricahuas fight against a cavalry unit led by the glory-seeking Lt. H. C. Kensington, who dreams of breaking the Chiricahua nation once and forever, and Peaches, Kensington's scout, who is the fictional depiction of the real-life scout Pa-nayo-tishn. Other plot lines concern a stagecoach operator, T. C. Madden, who is determined to get his stage through the Chiricahua uprising and on to Tucson; Clooney Borrum, a black stablehand; an aging sheriff, Jules Hoberman, and his vile deputy, W. K. "Pinky" Suggins, Jr.; Mrs. Carter, a pregnant woman trying to reach Fort Lowell; and Estune, a beautiful Indian woman whose baby has been killed by the army. All these characters are involved as the action moves back and forth between the Chiricahua, the cavalry, Clooney and the drifter, and the stagecoach.

Chiricahua echoes many of Allen's earlier works. Like *Red Blizzard,* it is intended to honor the Indian scout. Allen writes in an author's note: "This work is proposed in tribute to Peaches, and to the Apache Scouts of the United States Cavalry, Arizona Territory. It does not pretend to document either the history of the scouts or the territory, but rather to honor in spirit a wild, free way of life, vanished forever with Crook's conquest of the fighting Chiricahua, truly the last of the Apaches." Like *Red Blizzard,* *Chiricahua* is marked by violent action and coarse language. As in previous works,

Allen portrays the army as ineffective. And some characters—for example, Clooney Borrum and the beautiful heroine, Estune—are reminiscent of earlier Allen characters. But in spite of its complex and tangled plot, violent action and vulgar language, and excessive dependence on previous works, Gale "recommend[s] *Chiricahua* unstintingly as an ideal introduction to Allen's fiction since it is a mile-long film clip of his best special effects."

I, Tom Horn is the finest example of Allen's semifictional, revisionist novels of Western legends. In depicting Horn's life, Allen is not so depreciating as he is in *Death of a Legend* or overglamorizing as in *Who Rides with Wyatt.* The story begins with the discovery of a previously unknown manuscript, in this case the autobiographical deposition of Tom Horn written in 1903 as he awaited execution. Horn's narrative is divided chronologically into three books. The first begins in 1874 when Horn is fourteen and chronicles his adventures and misadventures from Scotland County, Missouri, to Kansas City, southwest to Sante Fe and to Prescott, Arizona. Book two describes Horn's nine years with the Apaches and adventures with Al Sieber, chief scout for the 5th Cavalry during the Apache campaign, and his marriage to Nopal, a Yaqui Indian. The action takes place during 1876-1885, but the narrative continues to the spring of 1890, when Horn heads toward Wyoming. In book three Horn briefly describes his work as a Pinkerton detective in Colorado, then chronicles the events surrounding his alleged murder of Willie Nickell in southern Wyoming on 18 July 1901, his arrest in Cheyenne on 13 January 1902, his trial and sentence on 23 October 1902, his failed jailbreak on 9 August 1903, and the moments before his execution on 20 November 1903.

It is still unknown whether or not Tom Horn killed Willie Nickell. Historians and Western critics have proposed various theories: some contend Horn murdered Nickell; others claim he was framed; while still others believe that Horn mistakenly shot Willie Nickell during an attempt to kill his father, Kels P. Nickell. Making use of Horn's own *Life of Tom Horn: A Vindication* published in 1904 and fictionalizing parts of Horn's life—such as his years with the Apaches and his marriage to Nopal—Allen's revision presents Horn as his own worst enemy: a coarse, hard-drinking, eager-to-fight gunman. But Allen clearly sides with those historians and Western critics who believe Horn innocent of the murder. *I, Tom Horn* is one of Allen's best-selling novels and also one of his personal favorites. Critically it is considered one of Allen's

best works. Jon Tuska calls it "perhaps the most successful instance of a Will Henry fictional biography."

Henry W. Allen has never achieved the reputation of Luke Short (Frederick Glidden) or Zane Grey. His works have sold remarkably well, but he has not acquired the mass following of Louis L'Amour. Allen's use of two pen names has certainly hurt his career. His reputation has suffered more, though, both critically and publicly, from the most attractive thing about his work, its uniqueness—his departure from the traditional Western format and themes. Allen takes the Indian's side, portrays the army as ineffective, and challenges the traditional views of legendary Western figures. As one critic puts it, Allen's fiction is hard to classify; "it is . . . fundamentally impossible to give him a single label." Those who read and admire his work would argue, however, that this is the very feature that makes Allen's fiction so appealing.

Several collections of Allen's short stories have been reprinted in recent years, but Allen has not published a novel since 1978, and poor health may now prevent him from writing any new works. But new and old Will Henry/Clay Fisher readers need not worry. Bantam Books, which has published Allen's Westerns for over thirty years, is committed to keeping his books in print. Indeed, several have never been out of print. "The Old West lives," Allen has written, "in untold legions of human hearts and minds"—and, he might have added, in the Western fiction of Henry W. Allen, better known as Will Henry and Clay Fisher.

Interviews:

Dale L. Walker, "Henry Allen: 'I have wandered the far Mesas,'" *El Paso Times*, 19 March 1982, pp. C1, C5;

Walker, "Wandering the Far Mesas: A Conversation with Henry Wilson Allen," *Bloomsbury Review*, 3 (November 1983): 14-15.

References:

Anne Falke, "Art of Convention: Images of Women in the Modern Western Novels of Henry Wilson Allen," *North Dakota Quarterly*, 42 (Spring 1974): 17-27;

Falke, "Clay Fisher or Will Henry? An Author's Choice of Pen Names," *Journal of Popular Culture*, 7 (1973): 692-700;

Robert L. Gale, *Will Henry/Clay Fisher* (Boise, Idaho: Boise State University Press, 1982);

Gale, *Will Henry/Clay Fisher (Henry W. Allen)* (Boston: Twayne, 1984);

Betty Rosenberg, Introduction to *From Where the Sun Now Stands* (Boston: Gregg Press, 1978);

Dale L. Walker, Introduction to *Will Henry's West* (El Paso: Texas Western Press, 1984).

Papers:

The papers of Henry Wilson Allen are held at the University Research Library, Special Collections, University of California at Los Angeles.

Frederick Barthelme
(10 October 1943-　)

Jean W. Ross

BOOKS: *Rangoon* (New York: Winter House, 1970);

War and War (New York: Doubleday, 1971);

Moon Deluxe (New York: Simon & Schuster, 1983; Harmondsworth, U.K.: Penguin, 1984);

Second Marriage (New York: Simon & Schuster, 1984; London: Dent, 1985);

Tracer (New York: Simon & Schuster, 1985; London: Dent, 1986).

OTHER: *Six Years, The Dematerialization of the Art Object*, text and illustrations by Barthelme and others (New York: Praeger, 1973);

Conceptual Art, edited by Ursula Meyer; text and illustrations by Barthelme and others (New York: Dutton, 1973);

Mississippi Review, 1977-　, edited by Barthelme.

PERIODICAL PUBLICATIONS:

FICTION

"People Were Thinking," *Works in Progress*, 5 (1972): 265-277;

"Tied to the Wagonwheel, Again," *Works in Progress*, 5 (1973): 126-130;

"The Turkey in America," *Penthouse* (December 1974): 30-33;

"The Biographer," *Transatlantic Review*, 58 (1977): 12-20;

"Table Water," *Fiction*, 6 (1980): 76-80;

"Aluminum House," *New Orleans Review*, 8 (1980): 61-63;

"Cut Glass," *North American Review*, 265 (1980): 42-44;

"Storytellers," *Chicago Review*, 32 (1980): 92-97;

"Night Class," *Denver Quarterly*, 15 (1980): 86-91;

"Parents," *New York Arts Journal*, 23 (Winter 1980): 86-91;

"The End of Magic," *Sun and Moon*, 11 (1981): 140-145;

"Architecture," *Kansas Quarterly*, 13 (1981): 77-80;

"Instructor," *New Yorker*, 59 (25 July 1983): 43-47;

"Export," *New Yorker*, 60 (23 April 1984): 42-49;

"Pupil," *New Yorker*, 61 (5 August 1985): 26-32;

"Driver," *New Yorker*, 61 (23 September 1985): 36-42;

"Cleo," *New Yorker*, 61 (18 November 1985): 48-53.

NONFICTION

"Concept Art: Idea in Statement," *Art and Language*, 2 (1970): 29-33;

"On the Alternative Press," *Texas Observer*, April 1972, pp. 28-32;

"The Will to Live: Remarks on Pacifica Radio," *Texas Observer*, July 1972, pp. 26-30.

Frederick Barthelme came to writing the long way around, after studying architecture, playing in a rock 'n' roll band, and working as an artist. He believes that these pursuits "all proceed from the same impulse—the impulse to *make*." With an interest in portraying the deepest feelings of his characters through the smallest nuances of behavior, and a sharp craftsman's eye for detail and finish, he has created a fictional landscape distinctive for its polish and immediacy.

Barthelme was born in Houston, Texas, to Donald Barthelme, an architect, and Helen Bechtold Barthelme, a teacher. He studied at Tulane University (1961-1962), the University of Houston (1962-1965, 1966-1967), and the Museum of Fine Art, Houston (1965-1966). From 1965 until 1974 his art was featured in exhibitions, primarily in Houston and New York City. As an artist, Barthelme worked with such ordinary objects as pebbled work gloves, tire tubes, and duct work, he said in a 1985 interview for *Contemporary Authors*. From found objects he went to conceptual art, then becoming "interested in books as containers, or carriers. My first two books, *Rangoon* (1970) and *War and War* (1971)," Barthelme explained, "were done in that spirit—not particularly literary containers for diverse and, in the best case, interesting ideas and entertainments."

Rangoon contains sections of surrealistic fiction (some of it featuring a character named Ollie who is given to kicking just about everything in sight, including his mother) interspersed with drawings by Barthelme's friend Mayo Thompson and photographs by Barthelme (many showing lackluster buildings and street scenes as viewed from inside a car). In *War and War*, Barthelme seems to be having a playful romp with his readers, early setting forth with great seriousness the outline

the book is to follow and then often disregarding it. *War and War* is made up of autobiographical (and pseudo-autobiographical) detail, including personal letters and stories about Barthelme's friends, photographs and funny drawings, and many remarks on fiction and the writing of fiction. Among the latter is this pronouncement: "If you don't have anything to do, or if you don't know what to do, I suggest you write a book. It is not hard. It is fairly easy. If it isn't easy you should not do it."

Barthelme's fiction gives the lie to this statement about his craft. Between the publication of the two early books and *Moon Deluxe* (1983), a collection of short stories, there was a ten-year hiatus during which he worked at writing fiction and began to get his stories published in literary magazines; in 1981 his fiction started to appear in the *New Yorker*. During part of this time he had a job in advertising in Houston. In 1977 he took an M.A. degree from Johns Hopkins University, where he studied with John Barth, and since then has been Director of the Center for Writers at the University of Southern Mississippi at Hattiesburg and editor of the *Mississippi Review*.

Barthelme's characters, like their creator, find delight and solace in the objects of popular culture, from the everyday to the extraordinary. In her review of *Moon Deluxe* for the *New York Times Book Review*, novelist Margaret Atwood credited Barthelme with "a hard, shiny, many-faceted insect's eye for the surfaces of things—seedy, greasy, plastic-coated things or lush, expensive, meretricious things—second only to Raymond Chandler's." The detailing of such objects, done to describe a physical setting, create a mood, or tell something about a character, is one of the hallmarks and strengths of Barthelme's fiction. In the title story from *Moon Deluxe*, the traffic-wearied narrator describes his rambles through the K & B Pharmacy:

> Inside you look at red jumper cables, a jigsaw puzzle of some actor's face, the tooled-leather cowboy belts, a case of cameras and calculators, the pebble-surfaced tumblers on the housewares aisle. At the medical supplies you try on several different finger splints, then stare at a drawing on a box containing some kind of shoulder harness designed to improve the posture. You look at toolboxes, opening the fatigue-green plastic ones, then the cardinal-red metal ones. You pick up a plumber's helper and try it out on the floor.... Near the stationery, you face a shelf of ceramic coin banks shaped and

Frederick Barthelme (Tommy Bennett)

painted like trays of big crinkle French fries smothered in ketchup.

In *Tracer* (1985), the arrival of a single object, a full-size statue of a horse for the beach, becomes an occasion of celebration that provides temporary distraction for the novel's troubled characters and for the reader.

"In Barthelme's modern world," wrote Joan Williams in her review of *Moon Deluxe* (*Washington Post Book World*), "women wear tool belts, have jobs once delegated to men, and are the aggressors." Though some of Barthelme's males (often either lonely or involved in uneasy intimacies, lacking meaningful work, subject to car problems, plagued with more free time than they know how to fill happily) do indeed suffer a great deal at the hands of their women, Barthelme quarrels with the critical notion that they are weak. He sees them rather as "wised-up John Waynes, able to take a hit, which they do repeatedly." Sometimes their strength lies in their ability to wait out a crisis, as is the case with Henry in *Second Marriage* (1984). But they rarely seem to be able to make or maintain real contact with the women they are attracted to.

The female characters, Barthelme says, are based on his sense that women "are now, and have always been, strong and tough." More often than not they determine the action in a story, usually by a kind of intrusion into the male character's life. *Moon Deluxe* contains stories in which this happens. In "Violet," Philip leaves his privacy and his Swanson frozen dinner to go to Shoney's with a six-foot-tall girl who has knocked on his door asking to use the telephone, adjusted his oven temperature once inside his apartment, and pointed out that his dinner is too small for the two of them. Later she insists that Philip allow their waitress's feeble-minded brother to drive his Rabbit. In "Feeders," Eddie is persuaded to let his ex-lover Iris and Iris's friend Polly move into the empty half of his duplex, and as a result finds himself, along with the two women, under surveillance by Cecil Putnam, Iris's current admirer.

"Shopgirls" portrays the man as outsider, hanging around a shopping mall to look at the young saleswomen in a department store. When one of them invites him to her apartment and tells him about a tragedy involving her father, he shies away as if frightened by the intimacy of the revelation, seeing then that "one of Andrea's eyebrows is plucked too much, and that the brows are not symmetrical with respect to the bridge of her nose. . . . You try to think of something to say about

her father, but you can't think of anything."

In other stories, such as "Grapette" and "Rain Check," age—another worry of Barthelme's males—is a distancing factor. On a blind date, the narrator of "Rain Check" tells his young companion that he will soon be forty.

> "Damn," she says. "Forty." Then she ducks her head behind the menu. "I guess that's not so bad. My dad's about forty, maybe forty-five, and he's all right."
> I smile at her menu. "It's not as bad as it's said to be. . . ."

Barthelme's characters do very little cooking, more often getting take-out food like barbequed chickens "in aluminum foil pans, wrapped in clear plastic," hanging out at Pie Country or its equivalent, or going to such believably bizarre restaurants as Red Legs, a place "with a low ceiling and, along the wall, a thirty-sheet Coppertone billboard of a very tan girl," where the waiters wear dresses. In *Tracer,* the characters get food at the Mini-Mart or their friend Turner's Pancake House or Captain Mike's Oyster Heaven, "an old red and blue tugboat propped up on railroad ties, and leaning slightly to one side. . . . "

Typical of Barthelme's characters is a kind of super-hip talk that often serves as part of a facade. In "Monster Deal," an uninvited woman explains her work to Jerry, who is housesitting for his absent friend Elliot.

> "I handle specialties, stuff you can't find ordinarily, stuff I pick up here and there. Right now it's housewares—Tupperware quality but no name, so it's cheap. Or I can go the other way, get you a thousand-dollar vacuum cleaner. Best damn vacuum cleaner you ever saw." She shakes her head and stares over her raised coffee cup out into the courtyard. "Absolutely vacuum you out of your socks— I demo'd it in Virginia and sucked up a cocker spaniel. Not the whole thing, just the tail. I got it out right away. . . ."

Barthelme's skillful use of gestures as well as language to portray a character, another characteristic of his fiction, is evident in the paragraph that continues "Monster Deal":

> She backs away from the table and takes off her shoes, using the toe of one foot on the heel of the other. "Look," she says. "It's a terrible imposition, but do you mind if I stay? That's my deal with Elliot—I stay and buy

the dinner." She picks up her shoes, putting a finger in the heel of each. "Tell you what, you check me out. Meanwhile, I'll catch some sleep."

In *Second Marriage,* a novel that had its seeds in the earlier short stories "The Browns" and "The Nile," Henry's first wife, Clare, leaves her abusive boyfriend and moves in with Henry, his second and present wife Theo, and Theo's daughter Rachel. Henry becomes odd man out of this "domestic-unit-of-the eighties" when Theo says, "I want you to move out for a while. . . . Later, maybe we can talk. Not now. Now you can get an apartment. We're keeping the house, Clare and me and Rachel."

Henry moves back to The Nile, an apartment complex where he, Theo, and Rachel had lived earlier. The Nile is one of Barthelme's most vivid and imaginative settings, with its courtyard "full of colored plastic animals, old signs, and fist-size white rocks." It also contains an Esso sign, ceramic birds, an aluminum pyramid, plastic pineapples, and a life-size papier-mâché steer, positioned by the swimming pool with its "head jutting over the water so it looked as if the steer had just quit drinking."

During the separation, Rachel acts as a kind of go-between, keeping Henry posted on things at home. Thirteen, tough and tender by turns, she is one of Barthelme's best characters. Her relationship with Henry is close, and even as she tries to comfort him, she jauntily pleads for help in understanding the odd situation they are both caught up in: "Tell me how big a deal this is. I mean, what's the correct level of anxiety for a child like me?" Henry's gloom is not much lessened by his quick intimacy with Mariana Nasser or the easy companionship with other residents of The Nile; but by resolutely staying away from his wife and Clare, he makes a happy ending possible.

Art Seidenbaum, reviewing *Second Marriage* in the *Los Angeles Times,* referred back to *Moon Deluxe*: "Frederick Barthelme produced a luminous book of short stories in 1983 . . . properly celebrated for oblique attention to such new developments as condo complexes and office parks, for their exact attention to human detail. 'Second Marriage' continues that attention, presenting new quirks among new characters and widening the lens on what passes for hip or cool or mutually consenting in modern life." Alan G. Artner, writing for the *Chicago Tribune Book World,* made a less favorable comparison, focusing on the language of Barthelme's characters. "No one constructs smart-alecky repartee better," he said. "But, in truth, his verbal interactions are more convincing when set in the framework of a short story. Their laconicism comes to sound artificial over the greater span of a novel."

In the *New York Times Book Review,* Ron Loewinsohn also compared *Moon Deluxe* and *Second Marriage.* He felt that, in some of the stories in the collection, Barthelme "got facile, occasionally gaining a gratuitous weirdness simply by detaching his incidents from any explanatory context." But in the novel, Loewinsohn wrote, "he provides the context that naturalizes these understated events." He concluded his review by saying, "Mr. Barthelme's lapses are minor. His dialogue is impeccable; his characters are fully human and engaging, rendered with unsentimental warmth. Most impressive is the thoroughness with which he has conceived his people and the complete incorporation of his themes with the plot and the method of narration."

In "Writing the Second Novel—a Symposium" in the *New York Times Book Review,* Barthelme said, "The downside of the second novel is that you're still out in the middle of nowhere doing something nobody asked you to do. . . . On the upside, second novels are easier because you're more comfortable with the form, and you have this frail tissue of confidence that maybe if you did it once, you can do it again." He did it again in *Tracer,* a stunning, moody book that contains some of his finest stretches of writing.

In *Tracer,* the triangle includes once more a male protagonist at the mercy of two women, this time sisters. Martin is in the final stages of a divorce his wife Alex wanted: she had "turned to me during one of those postcard breaks on MacNeil-Lehrer and said she thought we'd be better off if we just forgot the marriage," he explains to Alex's sister Dominica, whom he is visiting at the SeaSide, a Florida motel she manages. Dominica has "a burr haircut. She looked like somebody in boot camp, except up close she had perfect cheekbones, yellow specks in her irises, and this walking-dead makeup. She was a younger sister."

Martin and Dominica quickly begin an affair, and Martin seems to find comfort in the companionship of other residents and visitors at the SeaSide. But there are hints of trouble in mysterious, threatening occurrences that revolve around Dominica, and a visit from Alex complicates the situation by raising futile hopes. Throughout the novel, periods of activity alternate with very lonely scenes—some in which Martin is with Dominica or Alex, others involving only Martin. One of them takes place early in the story and seems to foretell the book's final sadness: "There was a mist around the pool. It moved with me, gave way around me like smoke. . . . I climbed the balcony and got on my back on the floor, listened to the mooing of the beach wind, felt my weight against the concrete."

By Dominica's arrangement, Alex and Martin meet in a ramshackle town called Odalisque, in a rented room.

> She had remarkable eyes. We sat for a minute, looking at each other, shoulders barely touching, and the shivers came again. . . . We had some kind of lovely moment, and then she smiled and started combing my hair with her fingers, watching what she was doing. That gradually turned into a kind of childlike lovemaking that I had forgotten, a catalog of affections, without urgency or awkwardness.

Dust jacket for Barthelme's second novel

Her final leaving is especially cruel in contrast to this last intimacy. In the end, Martin seems to have been bounced back and forth between the two sisters and then discarded, without any regard for his feelings.

Susan M. Dodd, in the *New York Times Book Review*, called Martin "the Unknown Soldier of the Gender War" and Dominica "a New Wave Gidget." Though she labeled Barthelme "a curator for a time capsule of the here-and-now," she also had words of praise for his "imagery and lyricism" and "shards of unexpected beauty." Writing for *People*, Campbell Geeslin said, "In Barthelme's stories collected in *Moon Deluxe*, in his first novel, *Second Marriage*, and in *Tracer*, the best moments don't come from the odd, rarely likable characters or plot (although certain incidents are marvelously original), but they come from the brilliance and beauty of the writing."

Barthelme likes the reserve of his men and women, and points out that "while they don't haul out their souls for flailing about on the page, they do have something of the full range of human intelligence and emotion, which is communicated to the reader through gesture and resonance." Writing at night (a habit that dates back to his days in advertising) in order to maintain his teaching and editing schedule, Barthelme continues to create his characters for short stories that he plans to have collected in another book, and there is a third novel in the works. Barthelme and T. D. Richter have written screenplays for *Second Marriage*, under option to 20th Century-Fox, and Barthelme is presently at work on a screenplay for *Tracer*.

References:
Margaret Atwood, Review of *Moon Deluxe, New York Times Book Review*, 31 July 1983, pp. 1, 22;

Ann Hulbert, "Welcome the Wimps," *New Republic*, 189 (31 October 1983): 35-38;

Michiko Kakutani, "Writing the Second Novel—a Symposium," *New York Times Book Review*, 17 March 1985, pp. 1, 40-41;

Ron Loewinsohn, Review of *Second Marriage, New York Times Book Review*, 30 September 1984, pp. 1, 43;

Art Seidenbaum, "New Roles in War Between the Sexes," *Los Angeles Times*, 28 September 1984, V: 14.

Alexander L. Blackburn

(6 September 1929-)

Craig Lesley
Lewis and Clark College

BOOKS: *The Cold War of Kitty Pentecost* (Athens: Swallow/Ohio University Press, 1978);
The Myth of the Picaro: Continuity and Transformation of the Picaresque Novel, 1554-1954 (Chapel Hill: University of North Carolina Press, 1979).

OTHER: *Writers' Forum,* volumes 1-11, edited by Blackburn (Colorado Springs, Col., 1974-1985);
"Faulkner and Continuance of the Southern Renaissance," in *Faulkner and the Southern Renaissance,* edited by Doreen Fowler and Ann Abadie (University: University of Mississippi Press, 1982), pp. 158-181;
"The Self as a Force for Human Survival," in *Conflict and Arms Control: An Uncertain Agenda,* edited by Paul R. Viotti (Boulder, Colo.: Westview Press, 1985);
The Interior Country: Stories of the Modern West, edited by Blackburn, Craig Lesley, and Jill Landem (Athens: Ohio University Press, forthcoming).

PERIODICAL PUBLICATIONS:
FICTION
"Sentimental Revolution," *Crosscurrents: A Quarterly,* Editor's Issue, 4 (September 1984): 119-132.
NONFICTION
"A Writer's Quest for Knowledge," *Colorado Quarterly,* 24 (Summer 1975): 67-81;
"Myth and the Picaresque Novel," *New Mexico Humanities Review,* 5 (Spring 1982): 23-35;
"Archetypal Promise from Apocalyptic Premise: The Art of Frank Waters' *The Woman at Otowi Crossing,*" *Studies in Frank Waters,* 6 (1984): 48-63.

Alexander Blackburn displays his literary talents in a variety of forms. He is a published novelist who has also written a critical study on the origins of the modern novel. For eleven years, he has edited *Writers' Forum,* a literary anthology featuring some of the newest and most talented writers in the country. His other hats include those of essayist, reviewer, critic, and teacher.

By birth and history, Blackburn is a Southerner, and he credits the South with giving him "love of language and storytelling, love of land and people from all walks of life, a sense of tragic history, a distaste amounting to scorn for Yankee materialism and puritanism, and a kind of quixotic idealism." In more recent years, Blackburn has focused his considerable energies on the West, his spiritual place. As editor and advocate for *Writers' Forum* he shows a pioneering zeal for publishing new writers from that region west of the Mississippi (although many eastern writers are included as well). Blackburn's recent essays on Frank Waters illustrate that he has been drawn into that literary titan's vision of the West, which demonstrates how the land and archetypal American Indian myths carry the human spirit forward by redeeming it from a technological wasteland.

Alexander Blackburn was born in Durham, North Carolina, in 1929. His father, William Blackburn, a professor at Duke University, taught William Styron, Anne Tyler, Reynolds Price, Mac Hyman, and Fred Chappell. The Blackburn house was filled with books. Blackburn attended Phillips Academy at Andover as a scholarship student from 1944 to 1947 and received his B.A. from Yale University in 1951, where he studied with Cleanth Brooks and William Wimsatt. Shortly after graduating, he joined the army "as an antidote to Yale" and served two years during the Korean conflict. During this time, he decided to become a writer. He was a special student in creative writing at the New School for Social Research during the spring of 1954 but then moved to the University of North Carolina, Chapel Hill, where he received an M.A. in 1956. From 1957 to 1959 he was a Cabell and Balch Fellow in American Literature at the University of Virginia, Charlottesville. He attended the

Alexander L. Blackburn

University of Cambridge from 1959 to 1963 and obtained his Ph.D. in English. Blackburn married Chilean scholar Inés Dölz Henry, a professor of Spanish, in 1975, and he now teaches, edits, and writes at the University of Colorado, Colorado Springs.

Blackburn's fiction has been profoundly affected not only by his background as a Southerner but also by an experience arising from his military service. In November 1951, he witnessed the detonation of an atomic bomb near Camp Desert Rock, Nevada. Recognizing the awesome and terrible power of that event, he faced an imperative to get at the sources of violence within the human heart, to expose them and suggest how to root them out, if possible.

The Cold War of Kitty Pentecost (1978), Blackburn's first novel, explores the effects of psychic violence upon the individual members of society, in this case the inhabitants of a small Southern university town, Poe's Hill, which bears some resemblance to Durham in the 1960s. The characters'

family histories contain incest, miscegenation, and perjury. In his essay "Faulkner and Continuance of the Southern Renaissance," Blackburn indicates that his novel is "a parable of violence, a search for its sources in history, society and self."

Max Stebbins, the protagonist, is a professor at South Atlantic University. He is a veteran who has witnessed his share of war including the death of his copilot by decapitation. A well-meaning man hampered by poor choices, including his marriage, Stebbins has returned to Poe's Hill to be near his prewar sweetheart Kitty Pentecost. Kitty has married Adam Hasbrouck, a millionaire Yankee psychiatrist who becomes Stebbins's archenemy.

Kitty dies shortly after Max returns to Poe's Hill, because her pregnancy by Hasbrouck causes her "metabolism to explode." Much of the story occurs in memories or flashbacks. The reader learns that Max's relationship with Kitty was killed in its early stages by Kitty's strong-willed mother, Kate Pentecost (neé Ball), a religious fanatic whose own background has been spoiled by rape, incest, and a child born out of wedlock.

Kate's father, Major Ball, a Confederate soldier, raped his own daughter. After this act, the two continued the incestuous relationship, which led to a child, Mary. Later, Kate and her father blamed the rape on a Black-Indian and perjured themselves to send him to jail. Their behavior taints future generations and threatens the general society of Poe's Hill.

Kate has become psychosexually disoriented as a result of her relationship with her father, and she oppresses and controls young Kitty, the offspring of her eventual marriage to the Reverend Pentecost, a missionary. The magnitude of Kate's cruelty becomes all too apparent in one of the novel's most chilling scenes, a flashback to Persia, where nine-year-old Kitty has exposed herself to an Arab boy. In a cold fury, Kate drags her daughter into the desert and digs a shallow trench. After tying up the girl, Kate threatens to bury her alive, throwing on spadeful after spadeful of sand until Kitty promises "never to marry but to be the bride of God." Much later, when Kitty turns down Max Stebbins's proposal of marriage, she sacrifices her own potential happiness to spare him her history of family violence and perversion, but Max fails to realize Kitty's sacrifice until after her death.

Before her marriage to Hasbrouck, and after Max has departed for the war, Kitty has a child out of wedlock, the result of a casual relationship with a soldier. When the son—now grown—shows up in Poe's Hill, Hasbrouck assumes he is Max's and sets out to destroy Stebbins.

Max has become mired in his own family problems. His wife Ginny, a Northerner with aspirations for the stage, leaves him and takes their son Chris. But before leaving, she cuckolds Max by sleeping with Adam Hasbrouck. Hasbrouck's perversions and manipulations are as extensive as Kate Ball's and the Major's were, but ultimately he is unable to destroy Max, even though he tries to have him fired from the university for moral turpitude and executed by corrupt government agents over drugs.

In part, Max is saved because this is no longer the "Old South." In Poe's Hill in the 1960s, truths come out eventually. Max is cleared of all charges and Hasbrouck is revealed as a schemer and pervert. The drugs he intended to plant on Max are found in his possession instead. Max's salvation is accomplished by great help from his mistress, Fanny, who unmasks Hasbrouck's intent. Max's guilt over the war and his failed love for Kitty no longer paralyze him, and he comes to understand that life with Fanny holds tremendous promise. "There is a great joy, he reflected. A great joy. Streaming from the sun. Joy abiding in the grace of the deep, wave after wave whispering us the song of life, the song of earth."

Blackburn's use of multiple restricted points of view in the novel emphasizes the theme that the individual exists in isolation, which fosters the flourishing of evil in the form of lies, violence, and oppression. The revelation of the truth is necessary to free people from their loneliness. Blackburn decided to write a novel with multiple points of view after he witnessed the atomic bomb detonation near Camp Desert Rock in Nevada. In "Faulkner and Continuance of the Southern Renaissance," he writes:

> my adoption of multiple viewpoints was the result of a vision which I can date quite precisely. In November, 1951 . . . I had the dubious privilege of participating in an atom bomb experiment in Nevada. Our dutifully radiated contingent from Georgia afterwards took a slow train east, and as it coughed and throbbed into the thin blue air of the Grand Canyon country, I was visited by a sudden realization of life as fragmentation and motion, of solitudes within the symmetries of sublimely beautiful nature. Recording the vision at once, I determined to find use for it at a future time and hence it became the structural metaphor for that novel. Out of a world fragmented by loneliness and fear and mendacity there would emerge a new society based upon personal choice and mutual acceptance.

Throughout this complex novel, Blackburn creates vivid and sharply delineated characters whose dialogue illustrates his many years of "listening" in the South. Jerry Bradley remarks in *New Mexico Humanities Review*, "Blackburn's first novel should be required reading. Although his cold war is more personal than political, it is nonetheless as dangerous as the global one, and it provides sharp insights into the personalities that thrive on frozen relationships."

The Earthly Comedy, a novel-in-progress, was influenced by Blackburn's visit during the winter of 1956-1957 to Traiskirchen, Austria, a camp for Hungarians who fled their homeland after the revolution and Soviet invasion in 1956. The image of a young boy in the camp stayed with Blackburn, who returns in this novel to themes of disintegration and isolation.

Blackburn's *The Myth of the Picaro* (1979) stands as a brave and innovative critical work. He begins by pointing out that the traditional treatment of the picaro as a kind of rogue engaged in episodic adventures "excludes the possibility of symbolic, moral and psychological coherence in the narrative." Similarly, the traditional critical focus on eighteenth-century picaresques overlooks some of the fundamental ideas behind the picaro myth and frequently ignores such picaresque masterpieces of the Spanish Golden Age as *Lazarillo de Tormes, Guzmán de Alfarache* and *El Buscón.*

Blackburn sees in these Spanish works the origins of a distinctly modern fiction, because they emphasize the dynamic interaction between an individual and his society and show the human will in action: "Differing from epic, drama, and romance, they do not present isolated human passions checked by external laws or existing in a vacuum but, instead, the unglorified will controlled by the relative contexts of psychological and sociological being actually operating within the story."

Blackburn stresses that the picaro, the "hero" of the picaresque novel, faces loneliness and isolation within a society. The culture fails, yet the picaro yearns for that society in spite of its disintegration. His exclusion from society and fear of love lead him on a restless search for meaning. This episodic journey emphasizes his fragmentation until the picaro becomes a kind of hollow man. "Creating a self that his will supports but that he knows for an illusion, the picaro evolves into a symbolic being, a confidence man, outwardly one who shares faith in existence, inwardly one reduced to spiritual nothingness."

Blackburn uses myth criticism to illustrate how these early Spanish works established a foundation that continued through the works of Le Sage, Defoe, Smollett, and Thackeray. Many modern novels contain the picaro, for Blackburn indicates that "Western Civilization as a whole could be described as 'picaresque': the picaro is modern man without a living faith . . . the lonely individual cut off from, though yearning for, community and love." His work continues with analyses of Melville's *Confidence Man* and Mann's *Felix Krull.* Perhaps one of the more surprising entries in the work is the American classic *Huckleberry Finn,* and Blackburn arrives at some startling conclusions about Huck's relationships to society and his fellowman:

We want to forget Tom Sawyer's evasion and

cherish memories of Huck and Jim on the raft, in the never-never world of the river. What we are loath to admit about Huck is his failed humanity, so we would like to believe that he escapes into freedom even at the sacrifice of love. The truth is that Huckleberry Finn has neither real freedom nor lasting love for our comfort. It is almost a nihilistic book. It is certainly a very sad book.

Yet Blackburn's analysis of the picaro myth also suggests a way out of the isolation and disintegration, a movement from the "literature of loneliness" to the "literature of love." The myth of the picaro is a kind of "negative journey into discovery," he says, one that strips away masks until the picaro faces nothing but the "millennia of his own solitude." Blackburn believes that "picaresque myth may be an ultimate kind of humanism whereby we are led to a tower or abyss from which to contemplate and accept life as it is with all its folly." Thereafter, it is possible to step back from the abyss and begin a quest for community and love.

Blackburn offers Ralph Ellison's *Invisible Man* and Joyce Cary's *The Horse's Mouth* as novels that offer variations on the picaro, suggesting that these works move toward order and toward love. In the final analysis, he claims, the picaresque novels offer "sustained inquiry into civilization and its discontents," an inquiry which has "gone all the way to chaos and back." This is where *The Myth of the Picaro* seems strongest. It warns of the abyss and encourages us toward that old imperative "Go love."

Andrew Wright notes in the *South Atlantic Quarterly:* "This is a wise and erudite book, a work of importance for students of the novel. . . ." Perhaps Gerhard Hoffmeister's review in the *German Quarterly* contains the highest praise: "What could only be outlined here is a bold and individualistic attempt to give a total concept to the picaresque genre with its individual works from the most diversified national literatures. With this work, Blackburn has shown new avenues to all further research in this subject."

In 1974, Blackburn started the literary anthology *Writers' Forum* (the first issue was called *Rocky Mountain Writers' Forum*) and has seen it through eleven volumes. While other notable literary magazines—including the *Colorado Quarterly*— have folded, *Writers' Forum* is flourishing, and the credit goes to Blackburn's editorial acumen as well as his determination to keep it going over the rough years.

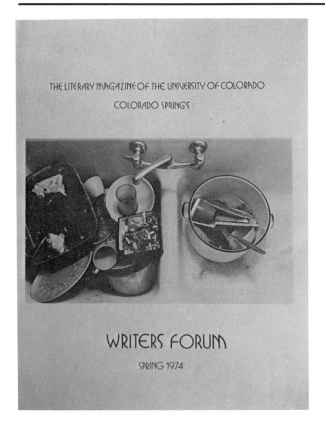

Front cover of the first issue of Writers' Forum

Although *Writers' Forum* includes writers from across the nation, Blackburn is particularly interested in publishing the best new poets and fiction writers from the West, because he feels the eastern writing establishment frequently overlooks them. While many literary quarterlies have fallen into "old-boy" networks, Blackburn encourages new writers to send in material and is proud of the number of firsts he has published, usually four or five fiction writers an issue. Even those who are not published receive a personal response and critique from Blackburn or one of the other staff members. Occasionally stories and poems are accepted after extensive revision. The anthology is now finding sound financial footing, and Blackburn has launched an endowment-fund campaign to establish a five-thousand-dollar Frank Waters Prize in Literature. His contributors have been included in the Pushcart Press Awards, and one of his firsts, Craig Lesley, has gone on to write the award-winning novel *Winterkill*. *Writer's Digest* ranked *Writers' Forum* third among the nation's top thirty nonpaying fiction markets in August 1983, and fourth in 1984.

In an interview with Jane Koerner in *Springs*

Magazine (1985), Blackburn observes, "Since the 1940s, the most vital literary region has been west of the 100th meridian, west of Lincoln, Nebraska, and Oklahoma City. The transmontane is the heart of the region. California a subregion." He lists some of the most important writers from this region, including Nobel nominee Frank Waters, and stresses that Native American writers such as Leslie Silko and Scott Momaday "lead a movement as important a record of American culture as Faulkner's southern Renaissance."

For *The Interior Country,* a forthcoming collection, Blackburn has selected fiction from important writers from the West: Frank Waters, Walter Van Tilburg Clark, Jean Stafford, William Eastlake, Raymond Carver, Joanne Greenberg, James Welch, and Wallace Stegner. Blackburn's introduction to this work indicates that the anthology should dispel some old beliefs: "To approach this interior country, we must first remove the shrubbery of capital-W, grade B Western literature and film that stands between us and the truth. . . ."

Part of the truth is not so beautiful. The West's history includes the near-extermination of the Native Americans and the exploitation of land and water resources. But Blackburn believes the West still holds great promise, "real achievements of individualism, the lingering authenticity of innocence, and the possibilities still for realizing the American dream in a land that likes to live in the shape of tomorrow."

The future of this region may depend most of all upon its mythic past. Blackburn states, "It is true to say that Ancient America has power stored up for the redemption of Modern America. Accordingly, some writers of the West, among whom again there is the genius of Frank Waters, are able to render the modern world spiritually significant and to fulfill the prime task of mythology, which is to carry the human spirit forward. Perhaps the West is the last region of the continent where the relationship of people to the land has offered, for thousands of years, myths to live by."

Today, when man and earth are threatened by nuclear annihilation, those shared myths become vital for our preservation. Blackburn hopes the rest of the nation will listen to the West, the wisdom of its mythic past and power of its mythic present. No doomsayer, he insists our salvation resides with our ability to create and preserve stories and myths that reveal our interconnectedness, our common humanity. As writer, editor, and essayist, Blackburn demonstrates his vision.

References:

Jerry Bradley, Review of *The Cold War of Kitty Pentecost, New Mexico Humanities Review,* 4 (Summer 1981): 90-91;

Margaret Carlin, "Coloradan Alexander Blackburn's Voices from the West," *Rocky Mountain News,* 19 May 1985, p. 31M;

Michael Gardner, "UCCS's Alex Blackburn: Nurturing Contemporary Western Literature,"

Colorado Springs Sun, 18 March 1979, pp. 8-9;

Frederic M. Keener, Review of *The Myth of the Picaro, Library Journal,* 103 (July 1979): 1458;

Jane Koerner, "Alex Blackburn: Making the Write Choice," *Springs Magazine,* 3 (February 1985): 14;

Andrew Wright, Review of *The Myth of Picaro, South Atlantic Quarterly,* 79 (Summer 1980): 331-332.

John Horne Burns
(7 October 1916-11 August 1953)

David G. Byrd
University of South Carolina

BOOKS: *The Gallery* (New York & London: Harper, 1947; London: Secker & Warburg, 1948);

Lucifer with a Book (New York: Harper, 1949; London: Secker & Warburg, 1949);

A Cry of Children (New York: Harper, 1952; London: Secker & Warburg, 1952).

John Horne Burns was born in Boston on 7 October 1916, the first of seven children in a Catholic family whose father was a prominent lawyer, Joseph Burns, and whose mother, Catherine Horne, was, according to Burns, "a sprightly and realistic heiress of the Boston FIF's (First Irish Families)." As John Mitzel says in his biography of Burns, this first child, his mother's favorite, was "beautiful, precocious, extraordinarily brilliant." From 1921 to 1929, he attended the convent school of the Sisters of Notre Dame. From there, he went to Andover Academy, where the school activities credited to him list only the choir and double quartet, an indication that his first love was not literature but music.

Like the heroes in his novels, Burns was a loner. Even at Harvard, he kept to himself, studying literature and finding comfort in music. Upon graduation from Harvard in 1937, he taught English at Loomis School in Windsor, Connecticut, where he was also dormitory master. In his second book, *Lucifer with a Book* (1949), he wrote a vivid

account of his experience at Loomis, expressing his disillusionment with American education.

In January 1942 he entered the army as a private in the infantry and later became a second lieutenant. He was sent to Casablanca and then to Algiers with military intelligence, censoring the mail. The war changed him. He began to question the American way of life, a theme that would later appear in his three novels.

After the war, he returned to Loomis School in the spring of 1946. When *The Gallery* was published in the summer of 1947, he had trouble with the headmaster, left the school in December 1947, and returned to Boston, working on his second novel and writing travel pieces for *Holiday.* When the critics attacked *Lucifer with a Book,* he left America and went to the country he had fallen in love with during the war, Italy. There, finding peace of mind, he began work on his third novel, *A Cry of Children* (1952). Perhaps because of the severe criticism *Lucifer with a Book* received, he labored for two and a half years on this third novel. When it appeared in 1952, the critics panned it, another devastating blow to Burns. Yet he continued to write, working feverishly on a fourth novel, which he first called "Maiden Voyages" but later changed to "The Stranger's Guise." Writing to his London publisher, Fredric Warburg, about this novel, he said that he had "never written a novel with such love and calm." But his happiness was short-lived.

John Horne Burns (Edna Douthat)

In July 1953, he received word from Secker and Warburg that the novel needed extensive revision. A few days later, he received a rejection letter from Harper in New York. In August of the same year, Burns went sailing, and a few hours later, he passed into a coma and died. The autopsy reported a cerebral hemorrhage caused by exposure to the sun, but there were suicide rumors. According to Mitzel, he had just ended a stormy affair with an Italian doctor. Although he was buried in Rome, at the insistence of his mother, his body was disinterred and reburied in Boston.

When *The Gallery* appeared in 1947, the critics applauded Burns: "Here . . . is a book by an ex-soldier that deals with the Americans in Italy and that displays unmistakable talent. . . . Mr. Burns shows the novelist's specific gift in a brilliant way" (Edmund Wilson, *New Yorker*); "With all its unevenness *Gallery* shows more promise than most U. S. novels of World War II" (*Time*). Warburg reports that in England it "received an enthusiastic reception": "a book of the highest promise" (*Times Literary Supplement*); "a raw remarkable novel" (*Evening Standard*).

Later, critics returned to this novel with respect: "It is full of strikingly brilliant figures; it is always alive with emotion; yet it is never ornate" (John W. Aldridge); "the best book of the Second War" (Gore Vidal); "What distinguishes *The Gallery* is not its 'brilliant observation' (though that is brilliant) but its imagination" (Brigid Brophy).

Although many critics called *The Gallery* a novel, it is a collection of "Portraits" and "Promenades." The "Portraits," written in the third person, are sketches of Americans, Britons, and Italians who are caught up in a war they do not understand. The "Promenades," written in the first person, are the author's reflections on the people in Casablanca, Algiers, and Naples.

In his description of the Arcade in Naples, called Galleria Umberto Primo, Burns says, "it was the unofficial heart of Naples. It was a living and subdividing cell of vermouth, Allied soldiery, and the Italian people. . . . you could walk from portrait to portrait, thinking to yourself during your promenade. . . ." The "Promenades" are reflections of a young soldier, probably Burns, who, touched by the courage of the Italians, changes the attitude he had learned in America: "I remember that at Casablanca it dawned on me that maybe I'd come overseas to die." Burns is using the word *die* to mean that his inner self as he had developed in America died in Casablanca. For the first time, he sees others, their misery, their suffering, their smiles, their stoical attitude toward life, and their love of music. He sees the Italians not as Hollywood had painted them—"movie gangsters . . . sad barbers of Brooklyn," but as proud, delicate human beings: "These carried themselves with a certain soft proudness, though I remember arrogant ones among them. A few were blond. But nearly all wore a delicacy of feature and a dignity I'd never seen before." Confronted with the fact that they were his enemies, he reflects: "Yet in those young men of Italy I'd seen something centuries old. . . . There was something abroad which we Americans couldn't or wouldn't understand. But unless we made some attempt to realize that everyone in the world isn't American, and that not every thing American is good, we'd all perish together, and in this twentieth century." Mitzel says that Burns "learned of the brutishness of the American 'civilization' he had been despatched to defend; he also got a perspective on the prig he had been on his way to becoming." Burns, "raised with orderly, disciplined and precise sensibilities," was now on his way to becoming an open human being, free perhaps for the first time to admit his homosexuality.

In the "Eighth Promenade," Burns tells that he learned in Naples that a man can cry openly and unabashedly. In America, crying "is done usually by women and babies"; but in the Mediterranean, "it's more human to weep than to laugh." He weeps because he can't "figure out the mess I and other Americans were in." He learned that music is the soul of the Italians, "the common denominator," for it comments "on the life of Naples." He learned that love is as natural as listening to music, but Americans have to "be taught how to love." The Neapolitans find love is understanding: "when history is written it will show that the Neapolitans conquered many of us. They beat us down with love. They loved love." He learned "that man is more than a physical being," that man must learn to say, "I am a human being, a citizen of the world," that "no one in himself and by himself, is much better or much worse than anybody else." Finally, he learned that "I too must die"—the old "I" of Boston, the old prudish "I."

In the "Promenades," Burns sees a world of bitterness, loneliness, death, and sometimes, hope. There are lost souls here, such as Michael Patrick, a wandering soldier, who looks for love to drive away the butterflies in his stomach. There is also Louella, a volunteer Red Cross worker, another lost soul. She is the Florence Nightingale of Naples, but she saves the spirit, not the body. Seeing human isolation around her, she exorcises her own loneliness by reaching out to all the lost American soldiers who sob inside.

The Galleria Umberto Primo does bring hope, a moment of respite from the bitter world, but it also brings death. One of the most humorous portraits is that of a Catholic chaplain and a Baptist chaplain, Father Donovan and Chaplain Bascom, two friends who try to be tolerant of each other. After a drink in the Arizona, a bar for Allied Officers, where they are accosted by a prostitute, they leave when they realize that one of the girls in front of the orchestra "is about to take off her clothes." Outside in the dark, Father Donovan is run over by an English lorry as he tries to save a young girl, and Chaplain Bascom, seeing the approaching headlights, rushes to save his buddy, only to be crushed too. The little girl stands on the curb, quietly chewing her gum, "for it wasn't the first time she'd seen the dead lying in the streets of Naples."

In the portrait of Major Motes, a censorship officer swelled with pride in being a Virginia gentleman, Burns draws upon his own position in the war. For this arrogant, ambitious man, reading letters is more important than fighting. This char-

Cover for the 1977 paperback edition of Burns's 1949 novel, set in a northeastern prep school

acterization of a pompous, misguided man who feels he is making the greatest contribution to the war effort is Burns's most biting commentary on the war—a useless entanglement of nations, sending their native sons to foreign soils to be killed, leaving them to ask, "who started this war anyway?" Becoming disgruntled too, Major Motes says, "The whole war is obscene."

But all humanity is not obscene; for some there is hope through love. Giuila, an Italian girl, falls in love with an American captain and comes to the conclusion that "the world was good after all." Although she insists on an honorable marriage, she agrees to sleep with her American captain on the night he must leave for the front "for she knew he'd be coming back to her." But for Sergeant Joe in the Eighth Portrait, entitled

"Queen Penicillin," love takes him to the Medical Center, where every three hours he feels needles puncturing his brown body. Although the chaplain tells him, "Our disease is the punishment of God for fleshly sin," like many of the others, Joe will be back: "Wait till ya get outside the barbed wire. . . . And ya meet another signorina an she shakes it at ya. That's all it takes. . . . You'll be back."

The most vivid of all the portraits is Momma, once quite poor, now a great lady for whom all merchants write on her bills "N. D. standing for nobil donna." In the midst of all the poverty in the Galleria Umberto, she has elevated her position to one of the richest women in Naples as owner of a homosexual bar. She, like Louella, is a savior of spirits, for she supplies these lost souls a haven. Into this bar come all those who were "born alone and sequestered by some deep difference from other men." But Momma's world is shattered as these forces come to blows in a melee which brings the military police. Their arrival precipitates Momma's time to faint: "almost effortless she fell out and across her cash desk. She'd been practicing mentally all evening long." Her fall from greatness closes the portrait.

Although critics have compared Burns with Norman Mailer and Irwin Shaw, *The Gallery* is not a war novel; there are no battle scenes, no long marches through battle-scarred countries, and no enemy attacks. As Aldridge says, it "expresses his faith in the power of human dignity and love to triumph even in the midst of war." The suffering and compassion of the people Burns encountered when he was in Africa and Italy awakened in him a sense of tolerance and filled a void in his soul.

Lucifer with a Book, published in 1949, is about a young veteran, Guy Hudson, who accepts a teaching position at The Academy, run by a pompous tyrant, Mr. Pilkey, "a foolish and rather dishonest old Brahmin who's been too long out of the competition of the world." A jarring book for many people of the late 1940s, it bitterly attacks the American educational system. Critics found it disturbing and controversial, yet some conceded that Burns still had the promise to be one of America's best novelists.

Atlantic said, "There are a number of biting portraits and some good scenes in the book, but too much of it consists of stereotypes and righteous indignation." *Catholic World* agreed: "He has dipped his pen too deeply in gall; his sketches are only caricatures; his sole attempts at realism are confined to the introducing of vulgar words and indecent scenes." Virginia Vaughan, writing in

Commonweal, said the book "was written too soon . . . is too long, and a few of his most acute and penetrating observations are obscured by paragraphs of unleashed fury which become rather tedious." R. D. Charques, writing in the *Spectator,* totally condemned the book as "plainly an ill-considered and immature piece of work."

Although Aldridge, writing in the *New Republic,* called the book "a disappointing successor to *The Gallery,*" he agreed that it "is at least an indication that Burns has continued to react violently and powerfully to the injustice of our time." And William du Bois, in the *New York Times,* recognized what many later critics have discovered: that *Lucifer with a Book* is indeed a novel deserving attention: "It goes without saying that there are enough flashes of brilliance here to remind us that a first-rate talent is under wraps."

Like Aldridge, the English critics saw the work as an important literary accomplishment. The *New Statesman* called him a "satirical moralist" who "has much of Henry Miller's rich comic gift, a fluency which amounts to lallomania, a passion for scatological images and strong tendency to preach," and added that it is "brilliantly funny and acutely, even poetically, perceptive." The *London Sunday Times* wrote, "His first book was bubbling with gusto. So is *Lucifer.*"

From the first gathering of the faculty, staff, and janitors, a reunion frolic "held on the lawn of Mr. Pilkey's Cape Cod House," Guy Hudson knows that The Academy is no place for a returning veteran with a Purple Heart, one who has now found American society distasteful and vulgar. He calls it "folderol," and so begins the battle between Mr. Pilkey and Guy. Guy's distaste for his situation is symbolized by a horrible scar on his face, the remnant of a wound he received in France. It is a sneer, a cold burning reminder of what he saw in the war and how he now feels toward American society: "forever now there would be a grin, hideous, when it once had been slack and amiable. Therefore when he smiled now, he seemed austere and refrigerating, like a smile smashed on a satyr centuries ago. It was a mockery and a satire on the twentieth century."

The war has changed Guy Hudson, "made him into a lone wolf." As this change begins in France, his first rebellion is through sex: "the last years in Europe had stripped him down to a lynx, a lecherous and clever lynx." Reaching over across his empty bed the morning after his first night at The Academy, he is saddened to find it empty, for "In France and Germany, whenever he was off the line, he'd never slept alone. The relief in wartime of having another body alongside his each morning had made him a resolute yet goalless satyr." Saying that he will not be "castrated" by The Academy, he retreats to New York during the Christmas holidays to rid himself of the school's taint. He promises himself that he will "cease being the priest and revert again to the satyr." And although he is attracted to the "arrowlike Beauty" of Ralph du Bouchet, who "lay open to him like a maiden," he rebuffs him and turns to Betty Blanchard, whom he seduces after a faculty party. In his little garret room on the third floor of the dormitory, he takes her with great violence.

Even before the symbolic sexual joining of these two veterans—she is an ex-WAC—the affinity between the two is explicit. Both are horrified by what they see at The Academy, and both become sacrificial goats at the altar of education. When Mr. Pilkey insists on seeing his gradebook and castigates him for giving a student a bad grade, Guy Hudson comes to grips with the hypocrisy at The Academy that taints the educational institution and in retaliation gets "sloppy-drunk." When he returns by the Girls' School, he weepingly sings to Betty Blanchard, who has opened her window, "We are poor little sheep who have lost our way." That "We" has an ominous ring for Betty, for she, too, has received a chastising for daring to accuse a student of cheating. Betty concedes that "all education is a pact with the dead." These two "lost souls," driven to each other's arms by a hypocritical faculty and a despot headmaster, find relief only in the sexual union of their bodies. Once Betty realizes she is pregnant, they feel victorious and leave The Academy triumphantly.

Writing to Warburg in 1951 from Italy, Burns said that *A Cry of Children*, his third book, published in 1952, "cost me so much blood these last two years." He felt that this book would be "way ahead of anything I've done yet." But the critics dismissed it. Whitney Balliett, in the *New Republic*, began his review, "Why John Horne Burns' third novel, *A Cry of Children*, should be such a confused, stale, and empty book is difficult to understand." John A. Lynch, in *Commonweal*, was even harsher—"One looks for something of meaning in this book, but hopelessly.... It all seems like a waste of time; Burns' writing it, Harper's publishing it, the reader's reading it"; James Bray echoed these thoughts in *Saturday Review*: "The work is strained, overblown, and obvious as a soap opera"; the *Times Literary Supplement* reviewer was kinder, but saw the flaws in the novel, "There are still a few vague

echoes of his original talent, but for the most part they are buried under a non-stop chatter of unoriginal, and now stale and petty, depravity."

A Cry of Children is the story of the incompatibility of David Murray, a concert pianist, and Isobel Joy, a flighty girl from a poor Boston Irish Catholic family. They meet, fall in love, live together, fight, and finally separate, leaving him to marry a good girl—the plot of a soap opera, causing the *Atlantic* reviewer to observe, "novelists have worked over this particular solution pretty extensively, and I failed to find anything particularly fresh or stirring about Burns' treatment of it." Although Mitzel thinks the book is not "a complete failure," even he, the champion of Burns, admits "there's too much of a change between this book and its predecessor."

While it is a poorly written book, the critics

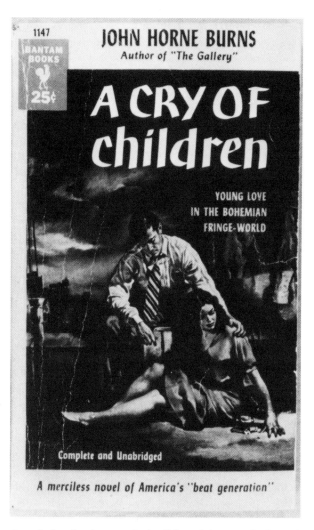

Dust jacket for the paperback edition of Burns's third novel, which received a harsh critical reception

missed Burns's purpose as they looked at the soap opera plot. It is a cry of two mismatched people who "want the freedom of kids and the responsibility of grownups." It is also about children crying out against mothers who try to smother them with overbearing love and overpossessiveness.

As the novel opens, David Murray, a thirty-year-old veteran, is living with his widowed mother, a devout Irish Catholic who spends most of her time trying to get her son to return to the church. The mother of twins, David and Teddy, the latter now dead from polio, she dominates her remaining son. Although Isobel is the same type of woman, strangling and smothering David and domineering him, she thinks, "she [Mrs. Murray] had only to will it, and he would come to her. Perhaps we should have set up housekeeping in another city, for I often felt that Mrs. Murray was in our bed."

One of the reasons the affair between Isobel and David does not work is that once Isobel has made David fall madly in love with her, she becomes like his mother and reduces him to an even greater weakling than he was with his mother. Although she expresses a love for David, she is all too quick to see him as another peg in her quest for security. Once they establish themselves in an apartment, she spends money lavishly, prettying their little love nest. Then she housebreaks him— he takes her breakfast tray to her bed, she reads his mail, and she makes him "a prisoner in this house." In one of David's sections, he says, "She had so forged my chains by now that I looked forward to these lonesome reveilles." Gradually, her ascendancy over him becomes greater; he tells her, "You have made me the typical meek American husband."

Attending a requiem mass, David hears Mary Desmond, a lovely soprano, sing "a florid *Pie Jesu.*" Talking to her afterwards, he see her as a madonna, pure and chaste: "She smelled of soap and cologne." (Now, David Murray substitutes the mother and the whore for the virgin.) But he has no recourse than to fall prey to women. Although he tells Mary, "in another forty years you'll be like my mother: a maxim for everything, with a hellish way of taking it out on our kids, by being so sweet and resigned about your sufferings," he marries this chaste woman. At the wedding, David's mother hovers behind the newly married couple while a cop says, "Nice-lookin boy. Real distinguished and spiritual. She'll break his spirit in a month. . . . When she finds her tongue, she'll give it him good and proper."

In his eternal search for the mate who will be compatible with him and his artistic sensitivity, David Murray elicits no sympathy. Mitzel says, "superficially, the lesson of David Murray is that women in any of their Christian capacities, mistress, mother, or wife are restraints and denials on some part for integrity in a creative man."

Despite the problems of his later works, John Horne Burns has a place in American literature. Many critics consider *The Gallery* the best book about World War II. As a eulogy to this novelist who wanted above everything to succeed as a writer, Brigid Brophy declared: "John Horne Burns was by far the most talented, and the most *attractively* talented, American novelist to emerge since the war."

References:

John W. Aldridge, *After the Lost Generation: A Critical Study of the Writers of Two Wars* (New York: McGraw-Hill, 1951);

Brigid Brophy, *Don't Never Forget: Collected Views and Reviews* (New York: Holt, Rinehart & Winston, 1966);

Daniel H. Edgerton, "The Ambiguous Heroes of John Horne Burns," *One* (October 1958);

John Mitzel, *John Horne Burns: An Appreciative Biography* (Dorchester, Mass.: Manifest Destiny Books, 1974);

Gore Vidal, *Homage to Daniel Shays, Collected Essays 1952-1972* (New York: Random House, 1972);

Fredric Warburg, *All Authors Are Equal, The Publishing Life of Fredric Warburg 1936-1971* (London: Hutchinson, 1973).

Edwin Corle
(7 May 1906-11 June 1956)

Carl R. Shirley
University of South Carolina

BOOKS: *Mojave: A Book of Stories* (New York: Liveright, 1934);

Fig Tree John (New York: Liveright, 1935; London: Laurie, 1936);

People on the Earth (New York: Random House, 1937);

Burro Alley (New York: Random House, 1938);

Solitaire (New York: Dutton, 1940); republished as *Virginia's Double Life* (London: Cape, 1940);

Desert Country (New York: Duell, Sloan & Pearce, 1941);

Coarse Gold (New York: Dutton, 1942; London: Cape, 1943);

Listen, Bright Angel (New York: Duell, Sloan & Pearce, 1946); republished as *The Story of the Grand Canyon* (London: Low, Marston, 1948);

Three Ways to Mecca (New York: Duell, Sloan & Pearce, 1947; London: Cape, 1948);

John Studebaker, An American Dream (New York: Dutton, 1948); republished as *John Studebaker: Story of the Grand Canyon* (London: Low, Marston, 1948);

The Royal Highway (El Camino Real) (Indianapolis: Bobbs-Merrill, 1949);

In Winter Light (New York: Duell, Sloan & Pearce, 1949);

The Gila, River of the Southwest (New York: Rinehart, 1951);

Billy the Kid (New York: Duell, Sloan & Pearce, 1953).

PERIODICAL PUBLICATIONS:
FICTION

"Amethyst," *Atlantic Monthly*, 151 (March 1933): 308-316;

"One More Hero," *Forum and the Century*, 91 (April 1934): 250-252;

"The Great Manta," *New Yorker*, 10 (5 May 1934): 23-25;

"McGuire's Kitty," *New Yorker*, 10 (4 August 1934): 15-18;

"Last Boat," *New Yorker*, 11 (7 December 1935): 38-42;

"Doing the Mud Dance," *Esquire* (December 1937): 142, 326-327;

"Good Morning Friends," *New Yorker*, 13 (11 December 1937): 28-31;

"Quejo the Killer," *American Mercury*, 52 (January 1941): 94-101;

"The Widow," *Yale Review*, 39 (December 1949): 337-343;

"Patron of the Arts: A Story," *American Mercury*, 65 (November 1951): 42-49.

NONFICTION

"Calico Days," *Yale Review*, 30 (March 1941): 549-559;

"The Ghost Town of Rhyolite," *Esquire* (May 1941): 34, 165-167;

"Seeing the Southwest," *Harper's*, 183 (October 1941): 490-500;

"Tungsten Over Darwin," *Atlantic Monthly*, 169 (May 1942): 642-644;

"There's Something About A Soldier," *Virginia Quarterly Review*, 19 (Autumn 1943): 575-592.

Edwin Corle was one of the first American writers to depict the psychological and social problems of the twentieth-century Indian attempting to cope with and adapt to white culture. His most successful novel, *Fig Tree John* (1935), is a portrayal of one man's struggle to survive in his own world as it is gradually being destroyed by another, more powerful one.

Corle, the only child of Samuel Edwin Corle and Marie Gertrude Dever Corle, was born on 7 May 1906 in Wildwood, New Jersey. He was a precocious youth, learning to read by the age of four and accumulating a library by the time he was eight. Theater was a significant influence on his childhood literary experience, as he later related memories of seeing such figures as Sarah Bernhardt, George M. Cohan, and Bert Williams.

According to his own account, he yearned to write at an early age: "My parents bought me all the books I wanted and I read day and night. At fifteen I was devouring such contrasting authors as Mark Twain, William Shakespeare, Jack London,

Henry Fielding, Sinclair Lewis, Daniel Defoe, Harry Leon Wilson, Booth Tarkington, and William Wordsworth. If anyone ever 'learned' to write at all, I learned a great deal, at an impressionable age, from those authors. Without my knowing it, I was receiving a course in authorship." An additional clue to his future vocation is provided in his admission that he once compiled a list of all the adjectives in "The Fall of the House of Usher."

In 1920, during one of his frequent trips with his parents to the West Coast, Corle got his first glimpse of the Salton Sea, a vast body of water formed when the Colorado River flooded a large portion of southern California in 1906—the same year he was born. This area was later to play a significant role in his life and art.

After his primary education in Wildwood and at the School of Practice in Philadelphia, he attended high school for three years in his hometown. The family moved to California when he was seventeen, and he finished his secondary education in Hollywood. Corle attended the University of California at Los Angeles, from which he received a

Edwin Corle

Bachelor of Arts degree in English in 1928. The next two years, as a graduate student in the College of Fine Arts at Yale University, he studied playwriting under George Pierce Baker.

Early in 1930 he returned to California, which was to become his permanent home. His first work was as a radio writer, with an occasional job at M-G-M and RKO Pictures. He once admitted that he did not like the radio business and when he finally saved enough money to launch his career in fiction, eagerly left. In 1932 Corle gave up radio writing and married Helen Freeman, whom he later divorced.

Corle's earliest publication was a short story, "Amethyst," which appeared in the March 1933 issue of the *Atlantic Monthly*. It was also included in Edward J. O'Brien's *The Best Short Stories: 1934*. The plot of "Amethyst" is reminiscent of many of the O. Henry stories in that the conclusion provides an ironic twist. It is noteworthy because it employs four narrative voices, with interior monologues documenting a miner's tale about an amethyst mine discovery and two reactions to that tale. A fourth narrator opens and closes the story with framing commentary, supplying missing facts and the irony at the conclusion.

Corle continued for several years to contribute short stories and nonfiction pieces to magazines, among them *Forum, Liberty, Scribner's*, the *New Yorker, Harper's, Esquire,* and the *Virginia Quarterly*. Some of his short stories were included in anthologies, including *Short Stories from the New Yorker* (1940).

Corle's first book, *Mojave: A Book of Stories* (1934), was well received. The *New York Times Book Review* critic stated that "these fourteen stories have a certain literary quality which is appealing. They make easy reading. In manner they recall Sherwood Anderson rather more than any of the modern writers. One discovers no 'new note'; but the tales read together give us a new background—the Mojave Desert with its heat and wastes, its oases, its history, its sunsets and loneliness, its old trails and new bare concrete highways and the American Bedouins who inhabit it." The reviewer concluded that *Mojave* "offers good entertainment. It is a first book by a young writer who has a gift for story telling and except for certain borrowed mannerisms, a way with the language."

While working on *Mojave*, Corle discovered and became interested in a local Indian character, Juanito Razon, known to area whites as "Fig Tree John." Razon was a Cahuilla Indian from southern California who had settled near the shores of the

Salton Sea, and much lore surrounded his exploits in the area. There has been so much discussion and controversy over the real versus the fictional character that Peter G. Beidler wrote a book on the subject, *Fig Tree John: An Indian in Fact and Fiction* (1977). Corle, after first seeing the name "Fig Tree John" on a signpost, grew interested in and eventually obsessed with the figure. "Bank Holiday," one of his stories in *Mojave*, contains an inchoate version of the character and provides an early attempt on the author's part at probing the Indian mind, albeit in a somewhat crude fashion. After a great deal of research, personal observations, and interviews, Corle produced his minor masterpiece, according to Walter J. Miller, "in one sustained twelve-week burst of creativity ending just before Christmas, 1934."

The fictional Fig Tree, whom Corle calls Agocho, is an Apache who leaves his reservation home in Arizona and goes west with one of his wives, Kaia. They settle near the Salton Sea and their son, N'Chai Chidn, is born. Three years later, two white outlaws attack the camp and rape Kai-a. Agocho vows revenge. Twelve years pass and whites encroach on his land. His son is near manhood, increasingly fascinated with the whites and their way of life. N'Chai Chidn gets a job on a date farm and is soon called Johnny Mack. He decides to marry Maria, a Mexican servant girl at a neighboring ranch. He also buys a Ford. Agocho soon learns of his son's actions and is furious, eventually beating and raping Maria. Matters grow worse and Johnny decides to move away. Agocho, enraged at the thought of his departure, attacks the Ford with an ax. In a furious battle scene, Johnny murders his father with the same ax. Johnny buries Agocho in the traditional Apache way, then loads his Ford and drives off to a new life in town with his wife. He has become a white man.

Fig Tree John was well received in 1935 and has been republished several times, with over 100,000 copies sold. The British edition was also successful, and Corle commented that the book got good press reaction "even from Australia and India." Oliver La Farge, author of another classic Indian novel, *Laughing Boy* (1929), commented, "Most of us who tackle Indians . . . never do more than circumscribe them," and went on to say that Corle's "two Apaches, father and son, in their amazing situation, are sometimes marked with the author's fingerprints. At other times, within the limitations of my perception, they are real Indians made clear. Mr. Corle has taken two of the great possible themes—the functioning of the intellect in savagery, and the adjustment or maladjustment of the Indian to a white world, salted them with action, spiced them with a sound love element, set them against a peculiar and most original backdrop which throws them into sharp relief, and made from the whole a sensitive and delightful story."

There have been negative reactions to *Fig Tree John*, but these have come from readers who are dissatisfied because the fictional piece does not approximate the story of the real Fig Tree John. Nina Paul Shumway and Leland Yost went so far as to label the novel a "libelous fabrication" and to publish, in retaliation, an article in *Desert Magazine* (January 1941) recounting the biography of Fig Tree John. These reactions are irrelevant, however, because Corle never attempted to present a factual portrait of a real Indian. He did attempt a "fabrication," a novel which remains a minor classic of American literature.

During the summers of 1935 and 1936, Corle spent much of his time on Indian reservations, conducting research and learning the southern Athapascan language. He admitted that he had a fair vocabulary, but added that "a white man cannot master it on less than two years' exposure." The Navajos gave him a name—Hosteen Ay Doh-Klish—which translates into "Mr. Blue Shirt."

His experiences with the Navajos led to the publication of *People on the Earth* (1937), a studied, realistic portrayal of the life of a Navajo with a "white" education and the problem of being trapped between two cultures. Red Wind's Son, the protagonist, is an eight-year-old Indian orphaned by an influenza epidemic. Walter Stratton, an Anglo minister, finds the boy, gives him his own name, places him in Indian schools, and sees to his welfare. After a white education in California, trying to return to the Navajo life-style is a disappointment for Walter, as he finds his people to be ignorant and superstitious. Moreover, they no longer accept him, some believing he is "tchindi," or evil. At the conclusion of the novel, after years of frustration and disappointment, he encounters and marries his childhood playmate, Dahiba, who has led a life parallel to his. Deep in the mountains, they begin anew. They look and act like Indians, but their minds are white. Only they know that they have become members of a third culture, an amalgam of Navajo and Anglo.

People on the Earth won a silver medal from the Commonwealth Club of San Francisco. Critics agreed that the novel is, up to a point, a realistic and carefully drawn study of a modern Navajo boy, but they found the ending marred by emotionalism and melodrama. Edna Lou Walton commented in the *New York Times Book Review* that there "is some good writing in this novel, good narrative and description. The incidents seem . . . to be rather unoriginal, but the treatment of Indian psychology is, for the most part, pretty sound." In the *Saturday Review*, Oliver La Farge again praised Corle's work as a part of the developing literature "handling the American Indian as a real human being."

People on the Earth is less well known than *Laughing Boy*, but is just as good. Both novels share strong points—for example the accurate depiction of the plight of a person trapped between two cultures—but both are somewhat melodramatic, especially by more contemporary standards. Stylistically, Corle shares a weakness with many novelists who attempt to write about people of other cultures—he slips into a simplistic narrative, especially during interior monologues, that is distracting. The protagonist, supposedly an intelligent man with a high school degree and some college experience, thinks in sentences which read as if he had barely mastered English.

With his next book, *Burro Alley* (1938), Corle delved for the first time into humor and satire in the portrayal of a town resembling Santa Fe, New Mexico, during the tourist season. The action takes place over a twelve-hour period and is roughly divided between two places: a Mexican bar called Cielo Azul and the posh La Paloma Hotel, with a third location, a roadhouse, being used as a setting for a brief time near the conclusion. A parade of characters marches through the book but, instead of Indians, Corle focuses on Mexicans and their relationships with Anglos. As La Farge points out in his review of *Burro Alley*, "the disjointed stories of a number of unlike people are held together by the dominant caricature, not of individuals, but of an entire community which has long cried aloud for such treatment."

Corle was one of the earliest novelists to recognize the blend of three cultures in the Southwest as a rich setting and a marvelous source for zany characters. John Steinbeck had already done a similar work, *Tortilla Flat* (1935), and critics were quick to draw comparisons. Edith H. Walton, in the *New York Times Book Review*, concluded that Corle was no match for Steinbeck: "He writes less well; his comedy is more labored; he gives one nothing like the same sense of knowing his natives through and through." But she called *Burro Alley* "good fun, acutely observed and suitably cockeyed," and conceded that it was "the next best thing to a first-rate comedy."

Dust jacket for Corle's 1937 novel about the tensions between Navajo ways and white civilization

Oliver La Farge was much more perceptive than his contemporaries in his criticism of Corle's depiction of Mexican-Americans: "In view of his success with Anglo-Americans and the realistic yet understanding treatment he has given to Indians in his previous books, it is deeply disappointing to see how the author handles his Spanish-Americans. One suspects the point of view of being derivative from *Tortilla Flat*, or perhaps, more reasonably, derivative from the vast mass of writing in this country which automatically uses the 'Mexican' as a butt. One does not mind a devastating handling of one's own, dominant group; but one does expect the allegedly intellectual members of our literati to give something approaching an even break to much maligned minorities."

None of the contemporary critics mentioned Corle's deft melding of structure and theme in *Burro Alley*. One of the characters, Lackland, in his continuing dialogue in the Cielo Azul, comments frequently on linear time, saying such things as

"You can walk in and out of the rain. Can you walk in and out of linear time?" or "I don't accept it as a progression of ticks of a clock or a progression of days or weeks or years." Since the action of the book takes place over a twelve-hour period, jumping from past to present at random, relating incidents in reverse order, and frequently retelling an episode from several characters' viewpoints, Corle's theme, as voiced by Lackland, is reinforced by the novel's structure.

During 1938 Corle traveled over most of Europe, contributing newspaper articles dealing with the political crises of the time, and even attended the 19th Congress of the League of Nations. These travels also provided material for later use as the setting for a large portion of *Three Ways to Mecca* (1947). While in Geneva, Corle met and was influenced by Clarence Streit, author of *Union Now* (1938), a book proposing a plan for global peace through the formation of a world government to be called the Inter-Democracy Federal Union. As a result of this encounter, Corle founded the Hollywood Committee of Inter-Democracy Federal Unionists in 1940.

For his next novel, Corle moved in an entirely different direction from all of his previous work. *Solitaire* (1940) is about a strange relationship between Virginia, a ten-year-old girl, and Ben, a simple, aged tramp. The threat of the inevitable danger of discovery and consequent destruction of the friendship in this unconventional pairing provides the suspense and interest for the reader. For most of the novel Corle matched his simple story with a simple style as he told the tale from the child's viewpoint.

Although *Solitaire* received only mild praise, Adeline Rumsey said in the *New York Times Book Review* that Corle was successful in portraying the "loneliness of the only child.... Mr. Corle has also felt keenly, and described accurately, the frightening gulf between a child and her parents. This sense of loneliness, and the injustice of the world to something it does not understand, may stay hauntingly in the mind long after the book itself is forgotten." Wallace Stegner compared Corle with John Steinbeck, Robert Nathan, and Katherine Mansfield, concluding that "there has seldom been so charming and completely convincing a child in fiction."

John Van Druten's play based on the novel, also entitled *Solitaire,* opened at the Plymouth Theatre in New York City on 27 January 1942, with Victor Kilian and Pat Hitchcock, daughter of film director Alfred Hitchcock, in the two main roles,

under the direction of Dudley Digges. Generally, the critics praised the play, although most felt that the faults of the novel—excessive sentimentality and a fantasy-like treatment—were carried over to the stage.

Corle had written a number of short nonfiction pieces during the 1930s for publication in magazines and newspapers. His first book-length nonfiction piece, *Desert Country* (1941), draws upon his love for and knowledge of the American Southwest. Here he presents a history of the people and the land of the arid regions of southern California, Nevada, Arizona, and Utah. Indians, Anglos, Mexicans, Spanish, Mormons, prospectors, miners, bartenders, and explorers are his characters. Historical events and legends provide the story line connecting them. R. L. Duffus, reviewing the book favorably for the *New York Times,* stated that Corle had included "every kind of thing that can exist or happen in a desert."

Corle resumed his efforts in fiction in this same year, as he was awarded a Guggenheim Fellowship for creative writing. He had been living and writing in a secluded area of the San Jacinto mountains above Palm Springs, but with the fellowship he gave up his hideaway and set out on a tour of Mexico and South America. On his return he published *Coarse Gold* (1942), a novel named for the ghost town which serves as its setting. After the discovery of gold in 1871 the town briefly experienced a boom, but after the gold ran out the settlement lay uninhabited, except for a single soul, for forty years. In 1942 Owen Conover, once professor of physics and now a modern prospector for a large mining corporation, arrived to search for tungsten. Corle weaves the present with the past as Conover is allied with Chris Wick, a wise and educated hermit who has been the lone inhabitant of Coarse Gold for the last thirty years. Chris's history parallels Owen's and places him at the extinction of the old town and the discovery of the new. He has spent the thirty years in between in philosophical meditation and studying physics, searching for "The Absolute."

Fred T. Marsh praised *Coarse Gold* as a "story in which past and present and intimations of immortality are skillfully interwoven in a texture of fair and candid prose." He concluded that "the book has style, has its own way with itself, bears the mark of a real story writer." This is an apt evaluation of *Coarse Gold,* which holds many charms for the reader. The initial description of the setting is rendered by using a desert jackrabbit's vision as a camera, an especially effective technique for depicting the ghost town as a physical unity stripped of human activity. Equally effective are Wick's monologue in the cemetery, which relates the history of Coarse Gold, and his "conversations" with his dog, "dialogues" that reveal his thoughts and provide the reader with additional history. The story itself is an engaging one, but the philosophical musings grow a bit tiresome. Some of the characters and events were no doubt successful in the early 1940s but are too contrived for the mid-1980s. The narrative technique, however, is splendid.

In March of 1943, Corle went into the Army Air Corps, receiving basic training at Atlantic City, New Jersey, and special training at Fort Monmouth. In 1944 he married his second wife, Jean Armstrong; his only child, Jeanne, was born in 1945.

Listen, Bright Angel (1946), which Corle had begun before going into the service, is a treatment of the history of the region of the Grand Canyon in the same style and framework as *Desert Country*. It is a guide for the visitor in that it contains geographical history, but it is also a portrait of the people—explorers and natives. A large portion of the narrative recounts the story of John Wesley Powell, a Civil War veteran who was the first to master the mighty Colorado River, during his exploration trip in 1869. This work, like all of Corle's nonfiction, was well received.

His next piece of fiction, *Three Ways to Mecca* (1947), is about a successful novelist, Oliver Walling, who insists on wearing a dog costume. This behavior is intriguing during the first and last episodes of this three-part work, where Corle focuses on Walling, his efforts to sell his latest novel to Hollywood motion picture producers, and several zany characters. The middle section, however, is a lengthy and not very interesting flashback to Paris in 1930, when Oliver met John Lackland (the same character who appeared in *Burro Alley*). Lackland also appears in the third section, visiting Walling at his Santa Barbara home some sixteen years after the Paris adventure. Reviewer B. V. Winebaum commented: "The author . . . may have had a satiric purpose in mind when he wrote *Three Ways to Mecca*. It fell by the way, smothered in hair of the dog." This novel is Edwin Corle's weakest work.

Albert Beich and William H. Wright wrote a play, *The Man in the Dog Suit*, based on *Three Ways to Mecca*. It opened on Broadway at the Coronet Theatre on 30 October 1958, starring Hume Cronyn and Jessica Tandy, under the direction of Ralph Nelson, but was not a success.

For his seventh novel, Corle returns to the people and setting of his second. *In Winter Light* (1949), like *People on the Earth*, is set on the Navajo reservation in Arizona, and Corle revives several characters from the earlier work. Thematically the new novel takes up where *People on the Earth* ended as it relates the story of a romance between a Navajo veteran of World War II, Robert Two Crows, and a worker in the reservation medical clinic, Betty Squashblossom. She lives under the protection of the Indian Agency physician, Dr. Walterhouse, and uses his surname. With the tale as framework, Corle presents the cultural contrasts between Navajos and Anglos, with the Navajos emerging as beautiful and dignified and the whites emphatically the opposite. The acculturation process is portrayed in a depressing manner, as many younger Indians who have adopted new ways are not pleasant characters. Only one white figure, Dr. Walterhouse, is in any way attractive.

Stylistically, *In Winter Light* resembles *Burro Alley:* the entire work takes place in about one day's time. The narrative consists of alternating passages of exposition by a narrator and dramatized passages. In addition, there are letters written by a radio soap opera writer to her boss in New York

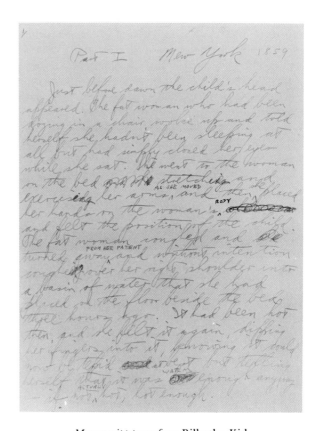

Manuscript page from Billy the Kid

concerning her research for material for a program based on Indian characters. Critic Ruth Page commented that Corle's writing is "simple, bare, almost homely, but just as his style was entirely appropriate to his attractive little novel about a child and a tramp, *Solitaire,* so it is again appropriate to his subject in the present novel." She concluded that "he succeeds in embodying a moving conflict and a resolution that, while happy, is not without humanity and pathos."

Corle's last book is a fictionalized biography. *Billy the Kid* (1953) was not very popular with contemporary critics, primarily because they had trouble classifying it. The author, a meticulous researcher (as evidenced by his nonfiction work), apparently decided with this book to join his demonstrated skills as novelist and historian. He documents the history of the creative process with a note, "From Author to Reader," included as an afterpiece. Here he reveals that he began to work on the subject as early as 1934 and names many people whom he interviewed, including A. N. Blazer, who was thirteen when he first met the historic Billy the Kid. His opinion is that the fictional work "tells the story of Billy with veracity, and is removed from fact only in the exigencies of the technique of the novel."

Critics in 1953 could not deal with the dual nature of *Billy the Kid.* Hal Borland, for example, in the *New York Times Book Review,* said that "as fiction it is second rate, and as biography it adds little to the record." William T. Pilkington, in his introduction to the 1977 University of New Mexico Press paperback edition, put the work in proper perspective as he wrote, "a number of highly acclaimed best-sellers of the last decade or so—Truman Capote's *In Cold Blood* is an outstanding example—have staked . . . claims in that uncharted territory that separates fact and fiction. Had *Billy the Kid* appeared in 1973 instead of 1953, Corle might have proclaimed the book a 'nonfiction novel' and not have been challenged on the point."

Edwin Corle spent the last years of his life at his home on Hope Ranch in Santa Barbara, California. His friend Lawrence Clark Powell had met him there in 1951 and described him as a "big, hearty, confident man and writer," as they discussed a new edition of *Fig Tree John.* An avid book collector all his life, Corle had designed his own studio/office in a cottage which contained his working library of more than 6,000 volumes. Unfortunately, he was unable to continue his work much longer, as he suffered a heart attack which claimed his life just after he turned fifty, in June of 1956. His widow donated his books and papers to the library at the University of California at Los Angeles. In 1963 she established a book collection contest held annually on the Santa Barbara campus of the University of California. After her death, their daughter took over sponsorship of the event, now called the Edwin and Jean Corle Memorial Book Collection Contests. As part of the ceremonies during National Library Week every year, there is an Edwin Corle Lecture in his memory.

Corle's fiction must be classified as sound, competent, entertaining, and frequently outstanding. His best novel, *Fig Tree John,* is a splendid treatment of the Indian. *People on the Earth* and *In Winter Light* are almost as good, but both suffer from excessive sentimentality. *Burro Alley* is excellent in places but contains the same annoying philosophical speculation that places *Solitaire, Coarse Gold,* and *Three Ways to Mecca* under the heading of mediocre.

William T. Pilkington's comments in *My Blood's Country* provide an accurate summary of Corle's contribution to American letters of the twentieth century: "Corle should not be judged by *Billy the Kid* or *Coarse Gold* or *Solitaire.* His best works are *Fig Tree John* and *People on the Earth,* and in their fields they are no small achievement. They are evidence that Corle was an unusual human being, a man who saw, truly and clearly, the configuration of the Indian's world and had no desire either to romanticize it or to re-arrange it."

In the 1930s only a few writers depicted the plight of the Indian in American society, and none did so with greater accuracy and sensitivity than Edwin Corle, especially in his masterpiece, *Fig Tree John.*

References:

Peter G. Beidler, *Fig Tree John: An Indian in Fact and Fiction* (Tucson: University of Arizona Press, 1977);

Walter James Miller, "Edwin Corle and the American Dilemma," Introduction to *Fig Tree John* (New York: Liveright, 1971);

William T. Pilkington, *My Blood's Country: Studies in Southwestern Literature* (Fort Worth: Texas Christian University Press, 1973);

Pilkington, Introduction to *Billy the Kid* (Albuquerque: University of New Mexico Press, 1977).

Mark Helprin

(28 June 1947-   )

William J. Scheick
University of Texas at Austin

BOOKS: *A Dove of the East and Other Stories* (New York: Knopf, 1975; London: Hamilton, 1976);

Refiner's Fire: The Life and Adventures of Marshall Pearl, a Foundling (New York: Knopf, 1977; London: Hamilton, 1977);

Ellis Island and Other Stories (New York: Delacorte Press/Seymour Lawrence, 1981; London: Hamilton, 1981);

Winter's Tale (New York: Harcourt Brace Jovanovich, 1983; London: Weidenfeld & Nicolson, 1983).

SELECTED PERIODICAL PUBLICATIONS:
FICTION
"Passchendaele," *New Yorker*, 58 (18 October 1982): 50-58.

NONFICTION
"American Jews in Israel," *New York Times Magazine*, 7 November 1982, pp. 34-37;

"My Father's Life," *Esquire*, 99 (March 1983): 90-92;

"Drawing the Line in Europe: The Case for Missile Deployment," *New York Times Magazine*, 4 December 1983, pp. 52-56.

Born in New York City, Mark Helprin is the son of Eleanor (Lynn) and Morris Helprin. Morris Helprin, the son of émigrés, was a movie critic for the *New York Times* who later served in the publicity department of major film companies and still later became president of London Films. Mark Helprin grew up in New York City, the Hudson River Valley, and the British West Indies. He received a B.A. from Harvard University in 1969, and it was while he was an undergraduate that, at the age of twenty-one, he sold his first story to the *New Yorker*. Although he did not feel comfortable at Harvard, Helprin nonetheless speaks well of the sort of humanistic education he encountered there as an important preparation for coping with the contradictions and paradoxes of life. In 1972 he completed his studies at the Harvard Center for Middle Eastern Studies and was awarded an M.A.

Helprin served in the Israeli army and air force in 1972-1973, after which, in 1976-1977, he did postgraduate work under the direction of Hugh Trevor-Roper at Magdalen College, Oxford University. On 28 June 1980 (his birthday) he married Lisa Kennedy, a tax lawyer and a vice-president of Chase Manhattan Bank.

Believing that his fiction speaks for itself, Helprin is very hesitant to talk about it or about himself. Nevertheless, he has described himself as Jewish by birth and by faith, although not in the orthodox tradition. He has also remarked on his determined pursuit of exceptional experiences in life; he is, for example, a skilled mountain climber. He calls himself a "Roosevelt Republican," which he believes gives his political views some latitude. He also seems to enjoy telling tall tales about himself, a fact which makes one hesitate over the credibility of some of his personal revelations, such as his claim to have never tasted coffee and his account of meeting his wife by merely showing up at her door after learning who she was from employees of a bookstore where she purchased one of his works. He now admits as fictional his account of how his father insisted that he tell an acceptable story before he was allowed to sit and eat at the dinner table.

Most of Helprin's short fiction has appeared in the *New Yorker*, and many of his stories have been anthologized—in *The O. Henry Prize Stories*, for instance. Helprin has been awarded a Guggenheim Fellowship and nominated for the PEN/Faulkner Award and the American Book Award for Fiction. In 1982 he won the National Jewish Book Award for *Ellis Island* and also received the Prix de Rome from the American Academy and Institute of Arts and Letters. Currently he is writing a novel tentatively entitled "Alessandro Giuliani: Soldier of the Alpine War." Perhaps the most important comment Helprin has made about his fiction occurred during a 1984 interview for the *New York Times Book Review*: "Everything I write is keyed and can be understood as (although very few people see it as) devotional literature" concerned with beauty.

Mark Helprin (Morris Helprin)

This concern, especially as related to the survivor, is prominent in Helprin's first book, *A Dove of the East and Other Stories* (1975), a collection of twenty short stories. In many of the stories in this book the main characters have experienced the loss of someone they loved, and they somehow learn to cope with their loss. In "A Dove of the East," for example, Leon Orlovsky loses his parents and wife during World War II. But he is a survivor, someone who has been forced by life to enter "into quiet places where [he] could only reflect," someone who develops an internal strength. Leon balances the deep pain of his loss with a survivor's equally deep appreciation of the "savage beauty" of nature, seen for example when "sharp mountains of ice and rock rise suddenly out of soft green fields," an image that objectifies his cutting losses and his vernal hope. This profound appreciation of nature's harsh loveliness—its capacity to elicit hope in the midst of despair—informs Leon's effort, even at the risk of losing his job, to care for a beautiful,

multicolored dove accidently stepped on by Leon's horse. To Leon the beauty of the dove reflects the splendor of nature and life in general. Caring for the wounded dove, Leon engages with a regenerating natural beauty which helps balance the enervating grief over his dead parents and wife.

Just as Leon offsets grief with a survivor's new strength drawn from nature's resplendent beauty, Josie in "Mountain Dancing in Truchas" finds that after the loss of her husband "she valued her own life a little less, and life itself much more." Now (like Leon tending the wounded dove) she is more devoted to her children; "she was learning to change her sadness into tenderness," as "the pain . . . withered to a point of beauty." So too the protagonist in "The Legitimacy of Medium Beauty" discovers, like Leon, "quiet moments alone" and, like Josie, "a deep and beautiful sadness": "she drew from everything she saw enough to make her life a deep cool color, a medium beauty, that full [autumn] wind which made the trees shudder, and draw breath, and seem like green water." In Helprin's survivors, sadness (loss) and beauty (regeneration) combine in the self just as they combine in the "medium" savage beauty (shuddering trees, green water) of nature, which elicits in the survivor a hope countering despair.

Helprin's survivors in *A Dove of the East* sense a majesty in nature. In "Leaving the Church" Father Michael Trelew, dying from a heart attack, fails to have the final vision he had hoped for on his death bed, but he does have a final mental recollection of nature's beauty: "The last thing he thought was how beautiful the summer rain in Rome," a hint of some sublimity in nature as comforting as the vision he had desired. The same sublimity is glimpsed whenever the protagonist of "Katherine Comes to Yellow Sky" experiences the "most sober of moments" (like Leon's quiet places in "A Dove of the East" and the protagonist's quiet moments in "The Legitimacy of Medium Beauty"): "in those mountains was the source, glancing off high lighted rock faces where no man could ever go, split into rivers eastward and westward running in little fingers to every part of the land, to the oceans where it blended with the newly turned sea foam and sun." Helprin's characters find in nature a source of strength because nature hints at a source for its own existence, as if it derived from and reflects a divine origin. In "First Russian Summer," for instance, Levi's grandfather says, "God made the forest and this clean air. And even if there were a man who couldn't see that, he could see the shape of things and how astonishing they are." Usually, however, Helprin's characters do not generalize about their sense of an intimated divinity in nature. Most often they are entranced, astonished at nature's savage beauty. The regeneration of hope that they find evoked in them through nature derives from an intuitive rather than a cognitive sense of the divine source of astonishing nature. They come to *feel*, rather than *know*, that source profoundly in their encounters with nature.

The effect of nature's majesty on Helprin's survivors in *A Dove of the East* is often expressed through whatever is artistic in them, especially in musical talent. In "The Silver Bracelet," for example, Anneka, a Dutch Jewish child orphaned tragically at the age of five, has developed a passion for music. Her mother had played the viola, and music is a way for her to create beauty out of her painful memories of her mother. In fact, "it was music which made her life a life of love." Her music is a sadly beautiful act of generosity like Leon's tending the dove or Josie's caring for her children;

Anneka especially loves to play for orphaned children, who imaginatively "could carve a mother or father" from the music. In order to attend a school where she will learn to perfect her talent, a school that "meant everything to Anneka," she must remove a silver bracelet her father gave her as a child, because the school requires that no student may wear jewelry. Like her music, evoking memories of her mother, Anneka's bracelet, evoking memories of her father, has been a source of deep comfort to her over the years. Against Anneka's will and to her grief, the bracelet is cut off by the headmistress. In a sense, the bracelet must be removed if Anneka is to perfect her musical talent; her sense of loss, her sense of being cut off from her parents and of being now indeed alone, must be complete if the potential for beauty in her music (derived from sadness) is to be realized.

The art produced by Helprin's survivors, like Anneka, reflects their view of nature as harshly beautiful. Like nature, art intimates some beautiful majesty, divinity, or meaning beyond the sorrowful human experiences in the material world. This capacity of art to hint at an ultimate divine reality informing nature is evinced aesthetically in *A Dove of the East* through Helprin's subtle correlation of the savage beauty of nature, the human self, and art.

Reviewers of this book were quick to praise its brilliant imagery, its unusual scope and power, and its taut and lyrical prose as indications of Helprin's burgeoning literary talent. Recognition was given to his ability to transmit a sense of value through the dramatic force of his immensely readable stories. Some reviewers, however, worried that the underlying idea of the intrinsic majesty of the events narrated in these stories might be more elusive for readers than Helprin has realized. These reviewers also remarked that Helprin's intense striving for a sense of loveliness sometimes caused him to lapse into archness, to permit his language to get out of his control, and to produce a sameness of tone in the stories. Questions were also raised about whether the stories were as finished as they might be and whether Helprin's refinement of atmosphere at the apparent expense of plot and characterization detracted from the effectiveness of his work.

Helprin's second book, *Refiner's Fire* (1977), is a long episodic novel somewhat in the picaresque tradition. The story opens with Marshall Pearl dying from battle wounds received on a war front in Israel in 1973; the attending doctors have no clue to Marshall's identity and predict his sure demise. Then the novel goes into a flashback in which Marshall's mother, a refugee headed for Palestine, dies aboard ship as she gives birth to her son. The commander of the ship, Paul Levy, runs the British blockade of Palestine and with newborn Marshall is taken captive. At the age of two months Marshall is adopted by an American couple. At the age of ten he attends a summer camp in Colorado, where he falls in love with a girl named Lydia; they are separated at the end of the summer. At the age of fifteen he and his adoptive father visit Jamaica, where he joins in a battle against some Rastafarians and is seriously wounded. The following year he lives in New York with the Pascaleo family, where he falls in love with the daughter. Later he goes to Harvard, where he falls in love with an organist. He and a friend abandon Harvard and hop on a train which takes them to the Midwest, where Marshall works in a slaughterhouse for seven months. After hopping on another train, he eventually stumbles upon a biology station, where he and Nancy Baker study eagles. A subsequent episode finds him the only survivor of a shipwreck off the coast of Mexico, after which he arrives in New Orleans and is told that the ship he claims to have been on really sank years earlier. For a while he stays in South Carolina with Paul Levy. There he discovers that Lydia, the girl he had met at summer camp when he was ten and whom he still loves, is Levy's sister. They marry, then visit Europe, where Marshall climbs the Alps. Lydia and Marshall settle in Israel and become citizens. Marshall is drafted, and with one day of his one-year term left, he is seriously wounded and lies dying in a hospital (the opening scene of the novel). In the hospital Marshall's birth father, who is also in the military, finds his son. In the final scene Marshall's eyes are flooded by sunbeams, as he rises as if in slow motion and pulls the tubes from his body: "Marshall arose and fixed his gaze on the hot rays of dawn. 'By God, I'm not down yet.' "

Ending *Refiner's Fire* with an image of transformative, regenerative dawning sunlight, Helprin recalls his use of nature imagery in *A Dove of the East*. Throughout *Refiner's Fire* light epitomizes the wondrous majesty of nature (beautiful, but not *sadly* or *savagely* beautiful as in *A Dove of the East*), as if creation were suffused with divinity. A flaming sky can look like "a fire from a purer place" than is the human realm. Marshall "had always been susceptible to the play of light and motion," as if they "were at every moment linked to an artful and all-powerful God."

In *Refiner's Fire* light suggests a transcendental wholeness or pattern informing the temporal realm; in the novel light contains all time in a way that certain religious mystics of the past and present and certain theoreticians of the new physics today argue that all life is a manifestation of light. As Marshall explains on a starry night to Nancy Baker, an expert on eagles, "You see, we're lying here and all time is passing through us, echoes of light from the past and future as well. The whole thing." "Nothing vanishes," and thus dreams can be "remembrances of circular time, windows into a future which has once passed"; living life in the midst of circular time is like traveling "the chambers of a nautilus." When Marshall dreams that he is a soldier dying on a Civil War battlefield, he recollects "facts in his dream as though his memory of them were real." Perhaps once he was a Union soldier and has been reborn. Marshall recalls this dream of his imminent death at midpoint in *Refiner's Fire*, which is framed by an opening and closing description of him dying from wounds received on an Israeli battlefront; this design in Helprin's narrative suggests the circularity of time, conflating past (the Civil War) and future (the Israeli battle) in a dream that is at once a memory and a prediction. In *Refiner's Fire* all time, past and future, is contained in light.

While participating in a dangerous climb, in order to observe eagles, Marshall relies on light to "save" him: "if he fell back he would be saved from the mountainous height by webs of dream-carrying light." Marshall believes that whether he should live, or die as a result of the climb, the reality of light promises a purpose or weblike design to his fate, and, since light suggests that nothing vanishes, it also promises that he will in some sense continue to live in the totality of time contained by light and perhaps even be reborn. His awareness of this divine design or force informing life makes Marshall feel as if he were "carried on a current," for "all things [are] tied into one flow." Whenever Marshall sees from a great height, he is reminded of this pattern intimated by nature, especially light, because from a "high view" he can "see the bold arrangement of things," that there is an Emersonian "balance to everything—symmetry, compensations."

Because nature suggests transcendental design, continuity, and perpetuity, Marshall revels in life—an explanation of why in the course of his youth he falls in love so often. The wondrous beauty of nature, particularly light, enkindles in him a recurrent hope in and affirmation of life in spite of encounters with loss, pain, and death; this fact is epitomized in the final scene of the novel, when dawning sunlight in Marshall's eyes causes him to rise from his deathbed. Marshall values intensely all sensations, not only during new and daring experiences resulting from "doing dangerous things all his life," but also during everyday living. Sleeping or waking, being hungry or sated, hearing noise or silence, seeing light or darkness—such mundane experiences are like poetic conductors; they are mystically infused and so connect us with the wondrous transcendental reality suffusing creation. Consider the simple act of breathing, which is routinely taken for granted: "hold . . . your breath for as long as you can and then realiz[e] how wonderful it is just to breathe; like a dry field suddenly feeling the flood." To hold one's breath is equivalent to enduring the hardships of life, like being seriously wounded in a war; from these hardships one should not remain struck down but should rise again, to breathe again, as Marshall does from his deathbed in the final scene of *Refiner's Fire*.

Marshall is a Helprin survivor, someone who rises again and again in the face of life's travail, whose internal spirit is perennially reborn. He evinces a resplendent, perpetual receptivity to the world. In a sense, he is always young and life always new to him. He cannot remain in one place too long; as he says, "All I can do is go from place to place exhausting myself as I see what there is to see." Nevertheless, in the process of these new encounters with the wondrous force suffusing creation, his "passions had been refined in fire and in ice and yet [his] love was solid and gentle and true." Marshall's sense of the transcendent in creation has been *refined* by experiences of life's extremes, and this refinement has only augmented his innocent receptivity to and appreciation of life—his love of life.

Reviewers of *Refiner's Fire* lauded Helprin's vivid imagination, his insight, and the artless grace of his style. But many critics voiced strong reservations about the success of the novel. They complained of the number of exploits without a real thread of purpose or meaning, of unresolved symbolism, of weak characterization of women, and of a pervasive dreamy romanticism in the book. Several critics, who found the novel boring, suggested that this work suffered from authorial egotism, as if it were the work of uncontrolled engagement by a prodigy showing what he can do.

"Ellis Island," in Helprin's third book, *Ellis Island and Other Stories* (1981), is very similar to *Refiner's Fire*, albeit a benign sense of humor is more prominent in the former. In the novel, refugees come to Palestine to be reborn—"they laughed, they cried, they even kissed the ground"—and in the later novella immigrants, arriving at Ellis Island in the hope of being reborn in American freedom, cry and laugh too. The protagonist of the story is a romantic survivor, like Marshall, who possesses an exuberant will to live and who falls in love very easily with women, who readily become for him symbols of life. In "Palais de Justice," an account of how an old man defeats a disrespectful youth in a boat race, we meet another survivor, whose life "had been broken and battered repeatedly—only to rise up again"; ever responsive to the "intricate and marvelously fashioned world," like Marshall, the old man "had risen each time to survive in the palace of the world by a good and just fight, by luck, by means he sometimes did not understand."

There are, as well, two nostalgic tales in *Ellis Island*, both told from the perspective of a child and both set in periods of time when an innocent receptivity to the wonder of creation was culturally more apparent in America than it is today. "Martin Bayer," set just before America's entry into World War I, recounts Martin's late-summer and life-affirming adventures as a child and his awareness of two youths "perfectly in love, innocent." Possibly reminiscent of Edith Wharton's work (but without its irony), "Martin Bayer" depicts the end of America's age of innocence: "Even looking to the ocean's horizon, he did not sense beyond the rim the haunting battles which, at other times, were felt by all as if they were the approaching storms of the hurricane season. That day was hot and blue, with a magnificent cold wind." The other nostalgic story, "A Vermont Tale," is set "many years ago, when [the narrator] was so young that each snowfall threatened to bar the door." It contains an allegorical tale within the tale that concerns the relationship of the narrator's grandparents, and in the process of being told it celebrates a time in the narrator's childhood when life seemed most wondrous, a time when "the cold outside was magical" and "the morning was so bright that it seemed like a dream."

The wonder of life, its capacity to merge magically with dream, is a feature of "The Schreuderspitze," the best story in *Ellis Island*. It is an account of Herr Wallich, a Munich photographer, who loses his wife and child in a car accident. Without saying a word to anyone, he mysteriously disappears and heads for a small town where no one will notice him. In this town he plans to put himself through a "parallel ordeal" that will intensify the strain on

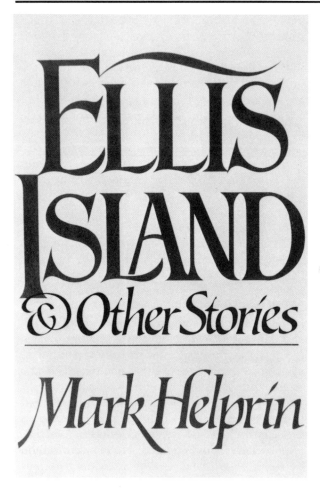

Dust jacket for Helprin's 1981 story collection, which received high critical appreciation

of his wish to die, it is also part of what amounts to a ritual of purification. Living in "a bare white room," fasting, and drinking "cold pure water," Wallich seeks "the diminution of his body" to prepare for the mountain summits, where "the air became purer and the light more direct." His ritual of purification, simulating death, is designed to reduce his attachment to the material world and his sense of loss in that world so that he can detect better, more purely, the transcendental reality intensely communicated through the direct light of the mountain summits.

"The mystery of light" figures prominently in a succession of dreams that Wallich has as a result of starving his body and mind. These dreams of scaling a mountain and witnessing the play of direct light on its summit indicate that his regimen has helped him nearly to transcend the boundaries of the material world: "Sometimes dreams could be so real that they competed with the world.... Sometimes ... when they are real and so important, they easily tip the scale and the world buckles and dreams become real. Crossing the fragile barricades, one enters his dreams."

In these dreams of climbing mountains and witnessing direct light on their summits "above time, above the world," Wallich learns that "in certain states of light he could see, he could begin to sense, things most miraculous": "that there was life after death, that the dead rose into a mischievous world of pure light, that something most mysterious lay beyond the enfolding darkness, something wonderful." His thoughts illuminated by this light, Wallich realizes, as did Marshall in *Refiner's Fire*, that time (temporal reality) is "circular and neverending," that "nothing, not one movement was lost." Light's containment of all time, light's revelation of a transcendental meaning suffusing time, and light's promise that he will again be united with his wife and child are epitomized for Wallich in the ice world of the mountain summits, an *Eiswelt* like an Emersonian Over-Soul.

Because he is still in the flesh, albeit "thinned" toward death and the spirit through his ritual of fast, he can get only a glimpse—a glance at the ridge, coast, or rim—of the supranatural ideality imaged in the icy mountain summits in his real-seeming dream experiences. Where the ice world takes fire (i.e., where light and the insight it gives are at once icily frozen and blazingly dynamic) is the edge of the mountain summit, the "sparkling *ridge* which looked like a great crystal spine"; here is "the high *rim* of things he had not seen before" (emphasis added). Witnessing this ridge or rim of

his mind and body in a way which will permit him to overcome his despair by attaining a new balance. Behind this decision is his memory of an episode in youth camp, where it was nearly impossible to carry a bucket of water up a hill until he increased the burden and carried two buckets of water at the same time: "Though it was agony, it was a better agony than the one he had had, because he had retrieved his balance, could look ahead." The ordeal he sets for himself is the discipline of his mind and body in preparation for climbing mountains, where "he would either burst on to a new life, or ... he would die." Death is certainly a real possibility, as the books on mountain climbing warn him,

and a death wish in him is a strong contender against the possibility of his becoming a survivor. Although he rigorously trains his body, he also starves it and sometimes does not eat for days.

This attack on the body is not only symbolic

icy, yet blazing light, he kneels like an explorer "claiming a coast of the New World."

The music Wallich had listened to while training in his room had hinted at this rim or ridge of insight; the music suggested "new worlds lying just off the coast, invisible and redolent." And the reader anticipates that Wallich's resolve to return to his profession, to "struggle at his craft," means that he will try to use light to make his artful photographs of nature hint, like music, at the transcendental reality (*Eiswelt*) lying just off the coast of temporal reality, at the rim of insight. Wallich is a survivor, someone who emerges from despair to reaffirm life and its manifold rich sensations because he has glimpsed in dreams and now intuitively knows of the divinity informing nature's astonishing beauty, especially light.

Of all of Helprin's books, *Ellis Island* has enjoyed the best critical reception. Reviewers were struck by the power of imagination in these stories as well as by their rich texture and their delicate and economic style. Some applauded the gnomic and artful simplicity of the stories, though a few critics thought these narratives might communicate too obliquely and might be too unfinished, as if they were in effect watercolor sketches preliminary to a more complete work. Complaints also surfaced concerning a possible absence of a coherent vision in these stories, concerning an uncertainty of focus or tone, and concerning epiphanic moments which seem more literary than felt. Whereas Pearl K. Bell specifically refuted the underlying devotional feature Helprin has claimed for his work, other critics have emphasized his fascination with the human spirit's impulse for transcendence, particularly as evinced in the frail but startling endurance of the human will. These latter reviews valued Helprin's ambitious reach and compassionate spirit in *Ellis Island*, a book which for some critics was to be ranked at the peak of literary achievement.

Winter's Tale (1983), Helprin's fourth book, is a somewhat eccentric, long allegorical fantasy, but its direction was predictable from his previous stories. Like "Martin Bayer" it is a highly nostalgic story focusing on the pre-World War I period as a time when American culture was particularly receptive to the wonder of life, a time when "things had been quieter, wilder, and more beautiful." Like "The Schreuderspitze" it mixes the dream world and the temporal realm, and like *Refiner's Fire* it has a protagonist larger than life—both characteristics of romance.

In fact, the epigraph of *Refiner's Fire* warned its readers to approach that novel as a romance,

and *Winter's Tale* belongs to that genre, as practiced by nineteenth-century American authors, even more obviously. *Winter's Tale* reflects the tradition of romance defined by Nathaniel Hawthorne, who argued (in *The Scarlet Letter*) that romance is "a neutral territory, somewhere between the real world and fairy-land, where the Actual and the Imaginary may meet, and each imbue itself with the nature of the other." Herman Melville remarked in *The Confidence-Man* that fiction "should present another world, and yet one to which we have a tie." Helprin shares both of these views, and attempts in *Winter's Tale* to integrate the actual and the imaginary, the temporal and the dream.

The story line of *Winter's Tale* is comprised of a succession of implausible incidents, but there are a plot and subplots. Athansor, a runaway milk horse that can fly and cross the barriers of time, rescues Peter Lake, who as a result of a falling-out among thieves, was about to be executed by villainous Pearly Soames. Later, after Lake falls in love with Beverly Penn (whose home he had at first tried to rob), he witnesses his lover's death and is wounded by Soames; but again he is rescued by Athansor, who flies into a cloud wall. Having fallen from the horse, Lake awakens nearly a hundred years later, in 1999, without his memory and without any signs of having aged. He is hired to tend the century-old machinery of a building in New York City where the *Sun* newspaper is published by Beverly's brother, Harry Penn, who eventually recognizes Lake and helps him regain his memory. As the twentieth century turns to the twenty-first, New York City ("deep within its new dream") becomes the locus of a golden millennium, characterized by an apocalyptic winter heralding a nascent justice that will redress the wrongs of the past century and restore a sense of beauty and wonder similar to that enjoyed by the residents of Lake of Coheeries, a place of snow and ice, forever frozen in time (1899), where stillness and motion meet. Peter Lake and Athansor are killed by Soames as if they were necessary sacrifices for the emergent new city, though they still exist in the world of light. Then comes (with a possible echo of Baruch Spinoza) the manifestation of "the metaphysical balance that inform[s] all events"—"every action and every scene has its purpose"—a balance especially evident in transformed New York City in 1999-2000 as it gives expression to the beauty and wonder typical of Lake of Coheeries in 1899-1900. New York City becomes a testament to how "all the flames and sparks of justice throughout all time reach and invigorate unseen epochs," when "the

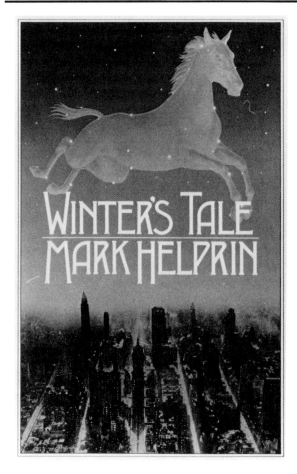

Dust jacket for Helprin's 1983 novel, his most widely read volume

reasons for everything were revealed and balances were evened."

Light in *Winter's Tale*, as in Helprin's earlier works, conveys the wonder and majesty of nature, and suggests a divinity infusing life. Particularly as reflected in "splendid ice" (where motion and stillness meet, and infinity can be glimpsed) light reveals that "the universe is still and complete. Everything that ever was, is; everything that ever will be, is. . . . Though in perceiving it we imagine that it is in motion, and unfinished, it is quite finished and quite astonishingly beautiful. . . . When all is perceived in such a way as to obviate time, justice becomes apparent not as something that will be, but as something that is." So Lake of Coheeries at the turn of the nineteenth century coalesces with New York City at the turn of the twentieth century. So human artifacts (especially rainbowlike arching bridges) and natural objects fuse in Helprin's mixed metaphors, for "nature was in the beams, girders, and engines of the city . . . ; in a still life illuminated by an electric bulb as much as in a

wheat-colored field in pure sunlight." So too Helprin uses the genre of romance to integrate the mundane (matter, motion, reason, actual event) and the eternal (spirit, stillness, imagination, dream revelation) in order to give the reader an enlightening glimpse of the essential truth of justice, balance, symmetry, design, and purpose informing life. Just as light in ice and both music and painting freeze the temporal in Helprin's narratives, "books stop time," we are told in *Winter's Tale;* Helprin's books convey a sense of the infinite stillness and eternal coalescense of all life, the sort of encounter that permits Helprin's survivors to renew their affirmation of life, the sort of intimation that in Henry James's view only romances could convey "through the beautiful circuit and subterfuge of our thought."

The language of *Winter's Tale* often flashes with beauty and evokes a sense of wonder, but its apocalyptic vision of justice remains vague; perhaps that vision can only be glimpsed in the book because Helprin believes that the metaphysical balance that informs creation can, as with Wallich in "The Schreuderspitze," only be glimpsed in life as if we were looking at a distant rim or ridge or coast. Nevertheless, *Winter's Tale*, like *Refiner's Fire*, sprawls with vaguely related, expansive (perhaps at times authorially self-indulgent) episodes. These two long works suggest that Helprin can concentrate the force of his vision better in the short story than in the novel.

Some reviewers of *Winter's Tale* were bothered by its proliferation of episode after episode as if it were an interminable bedtime tale. Others complained about a lack of a compelling story line, essential to a successful romance, and about the failure of the book's grand design, which struck some reviewers as confusing, fuzzy, vague, and unconvincing. As if in response, several critics thought that the highly imaginative, large-souled novel imparted a wider vision of the sort that permitted readers to see their time afresh and that urged upon them a sense of beauty that is as affirmative, restorative, and comforting as Walt Whitman's achievement. There was general agreement that in the novel Helprin takes risks, sometimes failing (as when his language becomes inflated and is made to carry excessive weight), sometimes succeeding (as when his assault on realism yields a life-affirming inspirational fantasy).

Winter's Tale remains a curious book. Consider Benjamin De Mott's confession: "I find myself nervous, to a degree I don't recall in my past as a reviewer, about failing the work, inadequately displaying its brilliance." *Winter's Tale* does indeed intimidate, but whether it does so because its vision is really startlingly transformative or because its vision is clouded and leaves us bewildered is not clear. Nevertheless, this novel and *Refiner's Fire*, however less satisfying than his short stories, indicate that in whatever form Helprin writes, he demonstrates a literary talent that deserves appreciation, a talent to make language evoke a sense of the beauty and wonder of majestic nature (especially light), which is apparently divinely infused.

References:

Pearl K. Bell, "New Jewish Voices," *Commentary*, 71 (June 1981): 62-66;

Christopher Buckley, "A Talk with Mark Helprin: 'I May Be an Anomaly,' " *New York Times Book Review*, 25 March 1981, p. 16;

Benjamin De Mott, "A Vision of the Just City," *New York Times Book Review,* 4 September 1983, pp. 1, 21-22;

David B. Green, "An Intimate Look at a Superb Storyteller," *Vogue*, 172 (March 1982): 430-431;

Sybil S. Steinberg, "Mark Helprin," *Publishers Weekly*, 219 (13 February 1981): 12-13, 16.

Jamake Highwater
(Piitai Sahkomaapii, tribal name)

(14 February 1942?-   )

Carl R. Shirley
University of South Carolina

BOOKS: *Rock and Other Four Letter Words*, as J Marks (New York: Bantam, 1969);

Mick Jagger: The Singer Not the Song, as J Marks (New York: Curtis, 1973);

Indian America (New York: McKay, 1975; London: Hodder & Stoughton, 1976);

Song From the Earth: American Indian Painting (Boston: Little, Brown, 1976);

Ritual of the Wind: North American Indian Ceremonies, Music and Dances (New York: Viking, 1977);

Anpao: An American Indian Odyssey (Philadelphia & New York: Lippincott, 1977);

Many Smokes, Many Moons: A Chronology of American Indian History Through Indian Art (Philadelphia & New York: Lippincott, 1978);

Dance: Rituals of Experience (New York: A & W Publications, 1978);

Journey to the Sky: A Novel About the True Adventures of Two Men in Search of the Lost Maya Kingdom (New York: Crowell, 1978);

The Sun, He Dies: A Novel About the End of the Aztec World (New York: Lippincott & Crowell, 1980);

The Sweet Grass Lives On: Fifty Contemporary North American Indian Artists (New York: Lippincott & Crowell, 1980);

The Primal Mind: Vision and Reality in Indian America (New York: Harper, 1981);

Moonsong Lullaby (New York: Lothrop, Lee & Shepard, 1981);

Arts of the Indian Americas: Leaves from the Sacred Tree (New York: Harper, 1984);

Legend Days (New York: Harper, 1984);

Words In the Blood: Contemporary Indian Writers of North and South America (New York: New American Library, 1984);

Eyes of Darkness (New York: Lothrop, Lee & Shepard, 1985);

The Ceremony of Innocence (New York: Harper, 1985).

Jamake Highwater is a storyteller whose tales of Native Americans are splendid stylistic re-creations of the oral literature of his ancestors. His novels, especially *The Sun, He Dies* (1980) and *Anpao: An American Indian Odyssey* (1977), stand as suc-

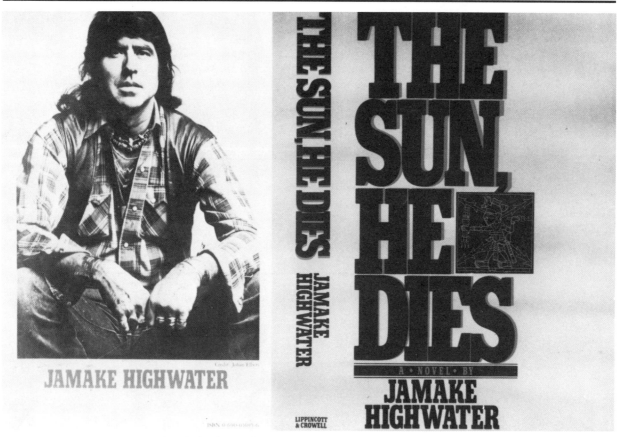

Dust jacket for Highwater's novel treating Aztec civilization

cessful examples of modern efforts to capture the Indian legender's voice that has endured the centuries—the songs, the recitals of history, the tales and the chants passed from storyteller to storyteller, from generation to generation.

Jamake (pronounced Juh-MAH-kuh) Highwater is a man of many talents. In addition to his novels, he has also compiled books (sometimes using the names J Marks or J Marks-Highwater) about music, art, dance, travel, history, and philosophy. He has published in magazines including *American Heritage, Dance, Harper's Bazaar, Esquire, Look, Saturday Review, Cosmopolitan,* and *Vogue* and has been contributing editor for *Stereo Review, Soho Weekly News,* and the *New York Arts Journal.* He was the senior editor of Fodor Travel Guides from 1971 to 1975 and has been a writer, producer, and narrator for radio and television. He has also lectured widely on world cultures.

When pressed for details about his life and education, Highwater is reluctant to reveal much because of complications concerning his adoption: "I was adopted between the age of six and ten when adoption was a highly secretive matter—to such an

extent that the state in which I was adopted permanently sealed all records of my birth and adoption. I have no original birth certificate. Since my adoption as a child I was put in the position of keeping my origins secret at my foster family's insistence. It is often difficult to know the difference between what I personally remember and what I was told. I have been silent about many details of my background because I do not possess the matter-of-fact data that supports most of the claims that other people can make. Also, in order to discuss aspects of my life and experience, I would have to make public information about my foster family that they decidedly do not wish to make public."

In July of 1984 Highwater's identity was questioned by Sioux writer Hank Adams in a detailed article entitled "The Golden Indian" in the journal *Akwesasne Notes.* Adams concludes from a large body of personal sources, physical similarities, and literary coincidences that Jamake Highwater is Gregory John Markopoulos, a filmmaker born of Greek parents on 12 March 1928 in Toledo, Ohio. *Akwesasne Notes* subsequently published, in the winter of 1985, letters from both Markopoulos and Highwater's attorney refuting Adams's claims. The editors did not print a planned second part of Adams's story, stating that it was unnecessary to "kick a dead horse."

Many biographical details published in the past are erroneous and have been used and reused by various publicists and journalists in spite of Highwater's efforts at correction. He has read and approved all the biographical information presented here. Born sometime in the winter of 1942 in Montana, California, or the Dakotas, Jamake Highwater is the son of Jamie and Amana (Bonneville) Highwater. His father, a rodeo rider and movie stuntman, was an Eastern Cherokee, intensely proud of his Indian ancestry, although not a traditional Indian, according to Highwater. He said of his father: "I am not even certain both of his parents were Native people. He was a renegade and an alcoholic—a marvelous, energetic man who helped to organize the American Indian Rodeo Association back in the 1930s and 40s. He called himself by many names during his career in circuses, carnivals and rodeos, but by the time he met my sixteen-year-old mother somewhere in the American Northwest his name was Jamie Highwater. He came from Virginia, Tennessee, or North Carolina, depending on his memory and his mood." Because of the peripatetic nature of his father's work and the fact that many Indian families had to move constantly in search of employment, Jamie Highwater left his wife at home but took Jamake with him when he went to Hollywood to begin his movie stuntwork. They lived in the back of a pickup truck for a time, with the boy "just sitting under walnut trees in the San Fernando Valley while my dad was out being killed by John Wayne."

His mother, of French Canadian and Blackfeet heritage, did much to instill in Jamake his sense of identity as an Indian. He has written about her and her beliefs, remarking that she "retained an imperturbable faith in her tribal realities which she passed along to me in a strong and constant voice. Her vivid teachings were my access to the Indian world."

Highwater's father was killed in an automobile wreck, and the boy was adopted by an Anglo family. Although he has revealed that he spent his adolescence in their San Fernando Valley home and became "J Marks," he will not give more details, he says, "to protect the privacy of my adoptive family, whose legal name was not 'Marks' though I used that name."

He began to write when he was about eight and has been a compulsive writer ever since. His grammar school teacher, Alta Black, was responsible for his deciding on a career at such a young age: "She gave me an old typewriter and a book and said I was to learn to type because I would be a writer." Other early influences were his adoptive sister and a family who befriended him, Frederick and Virginia Dorr and Frances Grigsby, Mrs. Dorr's sister. From them he learned the music of Wagner and Sibelius and what he calls the "nonlinear literature of the West." More significant than their contributions to his knowledge of music and literature, however, was the fact that they did not attempt to mold him to their ways. Highwater said: "What made these people so exceedingly important to me as a child and what has kept them close friends throughout my life is their willingness and unique capacity to grasp my reality and confirm my existence in two drastically different realities, rather than attempting to change or correct my world-view."

During the 1960s he participated in the founding and administering of the San Francisco Contemporary Theatre, which enabled him to meet some "remarkable people" and to find an "ideal outlet for (his) theatrical activities and creations." He also traveled extensively, seeing much of the United States and Canada. Traveling inspired him to visit Indian reservations and "all the great centers of ancient American civilizations." He was an eager witness to the Hippie and Rock movement in San Francisco, which he observed was "remarkably similar to Native American values in some of its viewpoints and visions." It was during the late 1960s that he began to write professionally, contributing to underground newspapers and magazines. His first book, *Rock and Other Four Letter Words*, was published under the name of J Marks in 1969. He published *Mick Jagger: The Singer Not the Song*, also using the name J Marks, in 1973. This book has subsequently appeared in translations into French, Italian, Dutch, Portuguese, and German.

The year 1969 proved to be a turning point in his life. In October, when Indians invaded Alcatraz island in San Francisco Bay and claimed it was rightfully their property, Highwater's thoughts and writings focused on his heritage. "There had always been in everything I did . . . a distinctive ritual premise. But with the Alcatraz takeover I was fired with a sense of visibility and courage. It was in 1969 that I began work on my first 'Indian' book which would bear my real name, Jamake Highwater." That book is *Indian America* (1975), one of the series of Eugene Fodor's popular travel guides.

It contains the transportation, food, and lodging information expected in such books, but it is much more. The author includes beautifully written chapters on history, traditions, legends, art, music, dress, languages, literatures, and philosophies of the Indian nations of the Americas, a treasure of information valuable long after the restaurants and motels have changed or closed.

Highwater's first foray into the genre of the novel was *Anpao: An American Indian Odyssey*, published in 1977. This book begins with the story-teller, the holy man Wasicong, sitting by the lake in the night. He addresses his listeners, telling them that his tale is of the beginnings of the world, of how Anpao was born. In Highwater's rendition, Anpao and his twin brother, Oapna, a contrary who does everything backwards, know nothing of their past. Anpao meets the incredibly beautiful Ko-ko-mik-e-is with whom he falls in love. Although she wishes to marry him, she already belongs to the

Dust jacket for the first volume in Highwater's Ghost Horse Cycle, in which Amana is the central figure

Sun. Anpao must seek the Sun's permission and, in the process, loses his brother but meets the Moon, the Morning Star, and figures such as Coyote, Buffalo, and Horse, as well as the Sun. He journeys across the face of America and across time and legend. Finally successful in his quest, Anpao returns, but with the prophecy that "sickness and death and greed are coming down upon us." Only Ko-ko-mik-e-is heeds his warning and they flee together, disappearing under the water. The novel ends with Wasicong asking his listeners, "Do you hear . . . do you hear their singing?"

Highwater includes at the end of *Anpao* "The Storyteller's Farewell," notes on his sources, and a bibliography. He explains that the book is a "personal effort to use the vast facilities of the tradition of written literature to convey the energy, uniqueness, and imagery of Indian oral tradition. I have approached it, however, not as a stenographer or as an ethnologist. . . . I have written these stories as a writer. But I have been careful to preserve the qualities unique to non-written folk history."

Anpao won the Newbery Honor Award, the Boston Globe/Horn Book Award and the Best Book for Young Adults Award from the American Library Association in 1978. Highwater has also done a reading of the novel for Folkways Records. The work was well received by the critics. Virginia Haviland, in the *Washington Post Book World*, wrote that the author "has woven across the main threads of his legendary hero's quest a significant weft of American Indian mythology, just as Homer in his famous epic of a Greek's journey homeward from Troy introduced tales of supernatural encounters. . . ." The fact that *Anpao* won the Newbery Award and has thus frequently been characterized as a children's work has probably prevented many adults from savoring the richness of its language and the magic of its story. It is a fine novel which can be enjoyed by all readers.

Highwater's work in the 1970s as an editor and writer for the Fodor's Guides to Europe provided him greater opportunities to view himself in relation to other peoples of the Western world. In that decade he lived in such cities as Paris, Brussels, and Zurich, and for a time in a small fishing village in Turkey. In 1978 he published *Journey to the Sky*, which carries the subtitle "A Novel About the True Adventures of Two Men in Search of the Lost Maya Kingdom." Highwater personally retraced the steps of New York lawyer John Lloyd Stephens and British architect/artist Frederick Catherwood in their daring and difficult mission in Honduras, Guatemala, and Mexico in 1839. In the course of researching and writing the book, he identified himself with Stephens and had so many adventures paralleling those of his protagonists that he often forgot that the tale was not his own, in spite of his insistence on historical accuracy.

Charles R. Larson in "Books in English from the Third World" in *World Literature Today* commented on *Journey,* calling it an exceptional work: "Besides reconstructing the journeys ... with painstaking detail and loving care for the matter itself, Highwater has written a first-rate adventure story which illustrates how two white men freed themselves of their own ethnocentric biases. This, I feel, is the major accomplishment of Highwater's novel: it shows that cultural blinders can be shed, that people of different racial origins can break down their stereotypic misimpressions of one another." In spite of such high praise and perhaps because of the difficulty many critics have in dealing with fiction based on actual events and people, *Journey to the Sky* has not received much attention.

On 29 March 1979 an event took place at Lethbridge University in Alberta, Canada, which Highwater called the "grand climax" of his personal and professional life. It was on that date that Ed Calf Robe, Elder of the Blood Reserve of Blackfeet Indians, a member of the Horns Society, and a descendant of the famous chief Calf Robe, conferred a new name on him "to honor my achievements on behalf of my people. It is a ceremony usually reserved for a *minipoka,* a 'favored child' of the Blackfeet Nation. My new name is Piitai Sahkomaapii, meaning 'Eagle Son.' This name-ceremony was the vindication of my mother's constant efforts to keep my heritage alive within me. Sadly, she had passed away and could not see the embrace of my people for which she had longed all her life."

Highwater's next book, *The Sun, He Dies,* was published in 1980. Hailed by Kurt Vonnegut as a "historical novel of a very high order ... a stunning revelation to all who have never before glimpsed the history of this hemisphere through a Native American's eyes," it is an epic tale with meaning on more than one level. At its simplest, it is a recounting of Hernando Cortés's conquest of Mexico between 1519 and 1521, but with a twist: it is told through the words and from the viewpoint of Nanautzin, a humble woodcutter who rose to become the chief speaker for the great Montezuma. On another level it is an allegory dealing with themes of rebirth and renewal, providence and destiny. On the moral level the narrator concludes that the great sin of the Aztecs was that they became as evil as their conquerors when they engaged in war with them.

From the first lines, "Call me Nanautzin. For I am the one who threw himself into the fire so the Sun would rise. And I am the last of my race which has fallen into a reckless night," the reader is aware of being a witness to a cultural journey through time, told from the perspective of one whose concepts of reality and history are greatly different from those of the white man. As with his two previous novels, Highwater performed extensive research, this time even learning the Nahuatl language of the Aztecs. In his twenty-five-page appendix of notes and sources, he commented on Indian storytellers and his role as one, thus providing insight into his creative process. One critic concluded that Highwater's effort to link his role as a writer to the role of teller in oral traditions was "bland, sanitized, and startlingly rootless." However, no less a critic than John Gardner said of Highwater that "one is tempted to give up the modern word, storyteller, and go back to the grand old Indian word, *legender.*" *The Sun, He Dies* has also appeared in Dutch and was very well received in Mexico in the Spanish translation by Pedro Gilbert. One critic wrote that *"El sol se muere* is a melancholy and poetic novel, written in the manner of the most exquisite Nahuatl literature ... a rich and brilliant reconstruction of the drama of the Aztec cosmos and its defeat by the conquistadores." This novel is regarded as the author's best.

Moonsong Lullaby, published in 1981, is a short book, containing only one poem of 83 lines and 16 color photographs by Marcia Keegan. It has been classified as a work for children, preschool through second grade, and characterized as dealing with themes of Indian cultures, depicting night life of animals and plants and the progress of the moon across the sky. While there is little doubt that the work appeals to children, it should not be dismissed as nothing but a poem for the very young. It is a lovely, reverent, gentle, and warm evocation of the singer's childhood, capturing the spirit of a loving people eternally linked to a wonderful landscape and appreciating that link. It is meant for anyone with the sensibility to share that evocation.

In 1984 Highwater published *Legend Days,* the first book in what he calls the Ghost Horse Cycle, named for Jamie Ghost Horse, a character who appears in *The Ceremony of Innocence* (1985), the second volume. Amana, a Northern Plains Indian, is the central figure in both books. The author's theme is the end of the legend days, the time when only the Indian roamed the land, before the in-

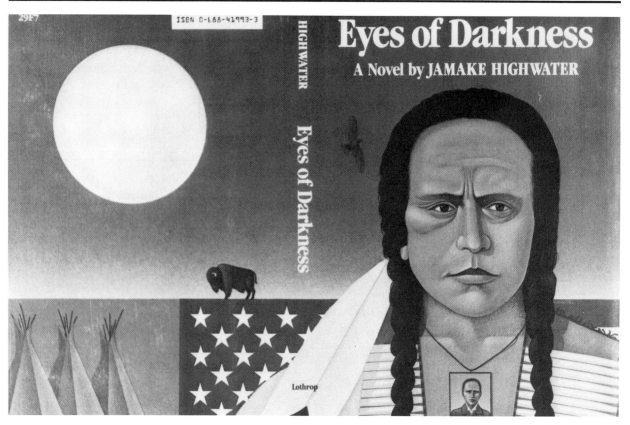

Dust jacket for Highwater's fictionalized life of Dr. Charles Alexander Eastman, a physician at the Pine Ridge Agency in South Dakota

vasion of white culture. Amana's story begins in her eleventh year, when she first sees visions of the owl of death and the fox who represents her spirit. Through her eyes the reader witnesses both the beauty and the tragedy of the Indian way of life as she gradually becomes a legend among her people because of her extraordinary strength. Disease, wars, and the decimation of the buffalo herds, all brought about by white civilization, claim more and more of her people until finally, when her husband Far Away Son is killed, Amana is left alone. Just as she is in deep despair, she sees the fox, "sniffing the dark land . . . where the ceremonial fires still burned and where we cast our tiny shadows against a gigantic sea of human dream and memory."

In *The Ceremony of Innocence* Amana is rescued by Amalia, a woman of French and Indian ancestry who has managed to bridge the gap between the diverse cultures. Amana marries a Frenchman, Jean-Pierre Bonneville, and gives birth to a daughter, Jemina. After her husband abandons them, Amana and her child move to Fort Benton, where she finally must succumb to living among the white people but never adapting to or understanding

their ways. Jemina grows up more white than Indian but eventually marries Jamie Ghost Horse, a Cherokee circus performer, rodeo rider, and movie stuntman. Through Amana's eyes the reader observes the birth of her two sons, Reno and Sitko, and her increasingly unstable marriage. Amana's strong and proud spirit grows weak as she sees her family leaving their heritage further and further behind. Sitko provides her only hope as the novel ends with the family breaking up and the children going away to boarding school. Her parting gifts to her grandson are "these memories of our people . . . these legends, these things of my life." She pleads to the Sun to give her back "the child so he can learn from the winters and the summers of my life, from the fragile traces of my people that remain beneath every day of the world!"

Critics reacted favorably to both *Legend Days* and *The Ceremony of Innocence*, with praise for the author's stark presentation in the former of the destruction of Native American society. In *School Library Journal*, Dorcas Hand complimented the poetic writing and use of mythic symbolism in the latter, and concluded that "the Indian culture lives in this book, and begins to die—although the fox's vision of Amana provides the hope that the old ways will at least be remembered." *Legend Days* was cited by the American Library Association as a "Best Book and Notable Book of 1984." The remaining two volumes of the Ghost Horse Cycle are *I Wear the Morning Star* and *Kill Hole*, to be published by Harper and Row in 1986 and 1987.

Eyes of Darkness (1985) is a fictional account of the life of Dr. Charles Alexander Eastman (1858-1939; Indian name, Ohiyesa), for three years physician at Pine Ridge Agency, South Dakota. Eastman was one of the first to view the aftermath of the Wounded Knee massacre in December of 1890. Among his writings are *The Soul of the Indian* (1911) and *From the Deep Woods to Civilization* (1916). Highwater begins and ends his tale with a depiction of his protagonist, Alexander East, a reservation physician who witnesses the slaughter of the Sioux at Wounded Knee. The horror forces him to reflect on his life and experiences, providing the reader with a flashback which constitutes the rest of the book. East spent his childhood and early years as Hakadah (later earning the name of Yesa) among his own Indian people, learning to love their ways. He thought that his father, Many Lightnings, had been killed by whites, but suddenly one day the man appeared, transformed after a decade among the Anglos into Jacob East. Jacob took his son and required him to live white. After a painful adjustment, the young Alexander graduated from mission schools and later attended Dartmouth, then Boston University to study medicine. The events at Wounded Knee forced a choice on the young doctor: to continue to live as a "white man's Indian" or return to his people. He says: "if I remain, if I continue to try to do whatever it is that I am supposed to be doing here, then I don't know what will become of me. If I do not follow the path that was given to me long ago I will become something empty and false." The book ends as Alexander East hears the voice of Yesa saying to him, "I was mistaken." *Eyes of Darkness* is a beautifully written account of a man trapped in a hazy and uncertain world between two vastly different cultures with irreconcilable realities and values.

In addition to writing both fiction and non-fiction, Highwater in recent years has been involved in many projects for television. He wrote and was host for a Public Broadcasting Service documentary, "The Primal Mind," a film based on his book by the same name. This production, which explores the basic differences between Native American and Western cultures, won the "1985 Best Film of the Year Award" of the National Educational Film Festival. Highwater's other television work includes collaboration in the production of a six-part series, "Red, White and Black: Ethnic Dance in America," and serving as moderator for "Voices of Native Americans." He was host for a series of eight programs devoted to films by and about Indians, entitled "Native Americans."

Since 1980 he has been a lecturer at New York University and was appointed assistant professor at the Graduate School of Arts and Architecture at Columbia University in 1984. His present work includes the researching of the pre-Christian heritage of Europe and the exploration of the ritual basis of sport. He is the founder and president of the Native Land Foundation, a nonprofit public trust dedicated to illuminating the "rich heritage which flows from world folk cultures and pre-Christian traditions into mainstream American and European culture." His book *The Primal Mind* (1981) was published in French in 1984, translated by Robert Tricoire, in a United States Information Agency sponsored edition intended for distribution in the emerging African nations.

His future work, in addition to the completion of the Ghost Horse Cycle, includes "Shadow Show: An Autobiographical Insinuation," a collection of profiles of famous people in his life, and "Athletes of the Gods: The Ritual Life of Sport." His fiction has already been praised by some of this country's most prominent authors and critics. As more readers and scholars of American literature become aware of the increasingly large number of excellent Native American writers—James Welch, N. Scott Momaday, Leslie Marmon Silko, and Gerald Vizenor, to name but a few—there is little doubt that Jamake Highwater's vigorous prose will continue to be highly regarded. As Dee Brown, author of *Bury My Heart at Wounded Knee*, has said, "Highwater writes in the natural poetry of his forebears, creating powerful images that are uniquely Indian. With *The Sun, He Dies*, he not only takes a leading place among American Indian writers but has surely joined the vanguard of all who write in the English language." Jamake Highwater's clean and clear voice re-creates an ancient and complex reality, translating the oral literature of his ancestors into modern printed form. He combines the old and the new, the native American and the Anglo. The result is a literature that is a joy to experience.

References:

Hank Adams, "The Golden Indian," *Akwesasne Notes*, 16 (Late Summer 1984): 10-12;

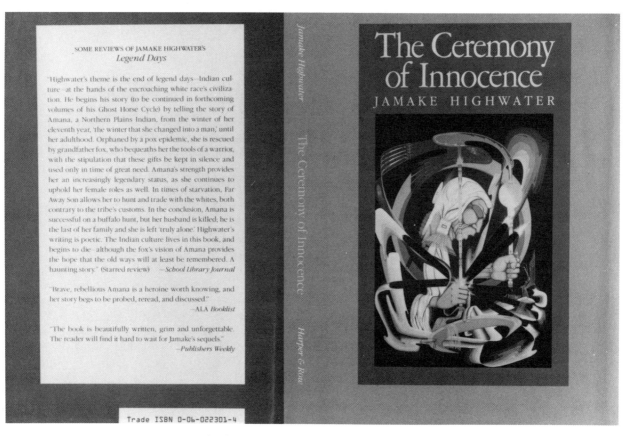

Dust jacket for the second volume in the Ghost Horse Cycle

Arnold Griese, "A New Reality in Children's Literature of the West," *Language Arts*, 60 (October 1983): 904-906;

Carol Hunter, "American Indian Literature," *MELUS*, 8 (Summer 1981): 82-85;

David Jackson, "Jamake Highwater's Native Intelligence," *Village Voice*, 3 May 1983, pp. 37-39. (This article contains several biographical inaccuracies.)

Paul Horgan

(1 August 1903-)

Brian W. Beltman

SELECTED BOOKS: *Men of Arms* (Philadelphia: David McKay, 1931);

The Fault of Angels (New York & London: Harper, 1933; London: Hamish Hamilton, 1933);

No Quarter Given (New York & London: Harper, 1935; London: Constable, 1935);

From the Royal City of the Holy Faith of St. Francis of Assisi (Santa Fe: Rydal, 1936);

The Return of the Weed (New York & London: Harper, 1936); republished as *Lingering Walls* (London: Constable, 1936);

Main Line West (New York & London: Harper, 1936; London: Constable, 1936);

A Lamp on the Plains (New York: Harper, 1937; London: Constable, 1937);

Far From Cibola (New York & London: Harper, 1938; London: Constable, 1938);

The Habit of Empire (Santa Fe: Rydal, 1939);

Figures in a Landscape (New York & London: Harper, 1940);

The Common Heart (New York & London: Harper, 1942);

The Devil in the Desert (New York: Longmans, Green, 1952);

One Red Rose for Christmas (New York: Longmans, Green, 1952);

Humble Powers (London: Macmillan, 1954; New York: Image Books, 1955);

Great River: The Rio Grande in North American History (New York: Rinehart, 1954; London: Macmillan, 1955);

The Saintmaker's Christmas Eve (New York: Farrar, Straus & Cudahy, 1955; London: Macmillan, 1956);

The Centuries of Santa Fe (New York: Dutton, 1956; London: Macmillan, 1957);

Give Me Possession (New York: Farrar, Straus & Cudahy, 1957; London: Macmillan, 1958);

Rome Eternal (New York: Farrar, Straus & Cudahy, 1959);

A Distant Trumpet (New York: Farrar, Straus & Cudahy, 1960; London: Macmillan, 1960);

One of the Quietest Things (Los Angeles: University of California School of Library Service, 1960);

Citizen of New Salem (New York: Farrar, Straus & Cudahy, 1961; London: Macmillan, 1961);

Mountain Standard Time (New York: Farrar, Straus & Cudahy, 1962; London: Macmillan, 1962)—includes *Main Line West, Far From Cibola,* and *The Common Heart;*

Conquistadors in North American History (New York: Farrar, Straus, 1963); republished as *Conquistadors in North America* (London: Macmillan, 1963);

Toby and the Nighttime (New York: Farrar, Straus, 1963; London: Macmillan, 1963);

Things As They Are (New York: Farrar, Straus, 1964; London: Bodley Head, 1965);

Peter Hurd: A Portrait Sketch From Life (Austin: University of Texas Press, 1965);

Songs After Lincoln (New York: Farrar, Straus & Giroux, 1965);

Memories of the Future (New York: Farrar, Straus & Giroux, 1966; London: Bodley Head, 1966);

The Peach Stone: Stories From Four Decades (New York: Farrar, Straus & Giroux, 1967; London: Bodley Head, 1967);

Everything to Live For (New York: Farrar, Straus & Giroux, 1968; London: Bodley Head, 1969);

The Heroic Triad: Essays in the Social Energies of Three Southwestern Cultures (New York: Holt, Rinehart & Winston, 1970; London: Heinemann, 1971);

Whitewater (New York: Farrar, Straus & Giroux, 1970; London: Bodley Head, 1971);

Encounters With Stravinsky: A Personal Record (New York: Farrar, Straus & Giroux, 1972; London: Bodley Head, 1972);

Approaches to Writing (New York: Farrar, Straus & Giroux, 1973);

Lamy of Santa Fe: His Life and Times (New York: Farrar, Straus & Giroux, 1975);

The Thin Mountain Air (New York: Farrar, Straus & Giroux, 1977);

Josiah Gregg and His Vision of the Early West (New York: Farrar, Straus & Giroux, 1979);

Henriette Wyeth (Chadds Ford, Pa.: Brandywine River Museum, 1980);

Mexico Bay (New York: Farrar, Straus & Giroux, 1982; London: Aidan Ellis, 1982);

Of America: East & West, Selections from the Writings of Paul Horgan (New York: Farrar, Straus & Giroux, 1984);

The Clerihews of Paul Horgan (Middletown, Conn.: Wesleyan University Press, 1985);

Under the Sangre de Cristo (Santa Fe: Rydal, 1985).

PLAY: *Yours, A. Lincoln*, New York, Schubert Theatre, 9 July 1942.

OTHER: Witter Bynner, *Selected Poems*, preface by Horgan (New York: Knopf, 1936);

New Mexico's Own Chronicle: Three Races in the Writings of Four Hundred Years, edited by Horgan and Maurice Garland Fulton (Dallas: Banks, Upshaw, 1937);

Maurice Baring Restored: Selections from His Work, edited by Horgan (New York: Farrar, Straus & Giroux, 1970; London: Heinemann, 1970).

Paul Horgan was born in Buffalo, New York,

Paul Horgan (© Jerry Bauer)

in 1903. His father, Edward Daniel Horgan, of Irish descent, was a prominent Buffalo resident whose primary business was a life insurance agency. He was also active in civic affairs. Horgan's mother was Rose Marie Rohr, a member of a large German Catholic family, three of whom became nuns. Horgan's parents were of the comfortable, urban middle class, prosperous enough to provide a German nurse for their three children. In addition, Horgan grew up in a religious environment of devout Catholicism. He attended elementary school at the French-Catholic Nardin Academy, excelled in German, and displayed talent for singing and for playing the violin. While family life gave Horgan a strong early interest in music, art, drama, and writing, Buffalo provided a nurturing environment with libraries, museums, and theaters.

In 1915 Horgan's relatively secure world underwent dramatic change when his father contracted tuberculosis and the family moved to Albuquerque, New Mexico, a popular health retreat for people with respiratory illnesses. Moving from the green woodlands of New York to the stark desert of New Mexico surely produced a culture shock for the twelve-year-old Horgan. But he also entered a landscape of panoramic beauty, dominated by the course of the Rio Grande; a region with a history of three cultures—native American, Hispanic, and Anglo; and a world barely a generation removed from the era of the frontier West.

Horgan became a cadet at New Mexico Military Institute (NMMI) at Roswell in 1919, continuing there until 1923, when he completed the first year of junior college. During a one-year hiatus in 1921, when his father died at the age of fifty-one and his mother grew ill with lethargic encephalitis, Horgan worked as a cub reporter for the *Albuquerque Journal*. During this time he enjoyed the friendship of the newspaper's editor, Clinton Anderson, and his family as well as close association with the Fergusson family. Of the latter, Harvey and Erna Fergusson became important regional writers of Southwestern fiction and history. At NMMI, Horgan began a lifelong friendship with Peter Hurd, who went on to become the famous Southwestern artist. As school companions they collaborated on two serial novels. (Later, Hurd illustrated two of Horgan's books, and Horgan wrote *Peter Hurd: A Portrait Sketch From Life*, 1965, in conjunction with a 1964 exhibition of Hurd's work.) As one commentator has noted, these connections continued Horgan's affiliation with the civilized world of writing, art, music, and drama that he had known growing up in Buffalo. Equally important, the circumstances within his own family undoubtedly impressed upon him the reality of illness and dying, but also surviving and coping with death, all subjects that would become powerful themes in Horgan's writing. Now, too, he had two geographical homelands upon which to let his imagination work to create literary Easts and Wests.

At the urging of friends, Horgan returned to New York in 1923, enrolling at the Eastman School of Music at Rochester as a voice student. He also got involved in the Eastman Theater as an actor, set designer, and production assistant. Here Horgan wrote a 200-page satirical novel entitled "The Furtive Saint," but it was not published.

Overwork led to exhaustion, and in 1926 Horgan went West a second time, returning to the haven of NMMI to regain his health and make a new beginning. He became the librarian there, a position he held until 1942. At NMMI Horgan also devoted himself to a regimen of writing. Making the most of a work schedule that left his mornings free for writing, he produced his first twelve books in the next sixteen years. Though none of his first five novels was published, he persevered. Simultaneously, he took his library duties seriously, reorganizing and expanding the repository's meager holdings as well as producing a newsletter entitled *The Library* through the winter and spring of 1926-1927. It was a collection of reviews, poems, and notes. In 1929 Horgan's first short story, "The Head of the House of Wattleman," appeared in the *Yale Review*. Two years later his first book, *Men of Arms*, was published. This contains twenty-seven illustrations of soldiers, from "An Egyptian Spearman" to "A War Time Aviator," sketched by Horgan with brief descriptive profiles to show the evolution of warriors and warfare. It was intended for young readers and dedicated to ten children, including Peter Hurd's older son. (Horgan's only other book for young people, *Toby and the Nighttime*, was published in 1963.)

Then in 1933 Horgan's first successful novel appeared in print. *The Fault of Angels* received the Harper Prize, and Horgan's career as a novelist was launched. This book draws on Horgan's experience in theater work in Rochester, and certain parallels to his life are obvious. The story's narrator, John O'Shaughnessy (whose last name is the same as the maiden name of Horgan's paternal grandmother), works as a production coordinator at the Dorchester Theater, a product of the city's philanthropist and wealthy industrialist Henry Ganson, modeled after George Eastman, cultural benefactor of Rochester. John previously attended a military school,

as had Horgan. The time is 1924, a year when Horgan was living in Rochester.

Horgan's story is a comic satire about theater life, artists, and society in an American city which aspires to culture after attaining wealth. The central story line follows the beautiful Russian emigrant Nina Arenkoff, wife of the newly appointed conductor of the municipal orchestra, as she tries to bring "soul" to the artistic pretensions and artificiality of Dorchester's social elite and especially to the materialistic benefactor Mr. Ganson. Nina, excessively sensitive to the point of frequent open weeping, is herself an accomplished artist in needlework and in acting. She is also a determined reformer, passionately committed to salvaging Dorchester and Mr. Ganson from mere commercial entertainment and art tainted by America's captivation with money. Nina finds allies to her cause and initially makes a dramatic impression on Dorchester's gossipy high society, even charming Mr. Ganson. Nina's heavy Russian accent makes her cute and exotic; her colorful mannerisms make her a popular party guest. But trying to infuse her cosmopolitan values into the provincial environment of the town quickly makes Nina an unwelcome reformer. After a series of unfortunate events caused by her meddling, Nina, with her husband in tow, makes a grand departure and heads for Paris—leaving America, presumably, to its undeveloped artistic sensibility. By treating the story comically, Horgan seems to say that the reformer is as pretentious as the provincial elite, that true art has much more humble and ordinary roots and expressions, devoid of unnecessary display and self-acclaim. As a writer, he would testify to this in subsequent works.

Reviewers generally approved of Horgan's debut as a novelist, several praising his powers of characterization in particular. Edward Cornelius, in the *Saturday Review of Literature*, called the novel "high comedy of a kind rarely produced by American novelists."

No Quarter Given (1935), Horgan's second published novel, centers on Edmund Abbey, a composer who is dying of tuberculosis. Part of the story is about his present life in the 1920s in Santa Fe, where he has come to rest and presumably to recuperate, as well as to produce more music; the other part, interjected in flashbacks into the former, is a reminiscing autobiographical account of Edmund's early life in New York as a child and maturing musician. Beyond the narration of Edmund's relations with family and friends and the continual specter of illness and death, the story is a tribute to one person's total dedication to his art. The true artist yields no quarter—not even to severe illness—to follow his calling. Within this thematic framework, Horgan creates a collection of people who interact to satirize certain behavior, while at the same time he proceeds toward a tragic conclusion.

At the story's beginning, Edmund is married to Georgia, a wealthy but shallow materialist who has been twice divorced and who, while absent from her husband over the winter and spring months in Florida and Bermuda, becomes very cozy with Lucien Roland, himself a married man and artist of sorts. Georgia has served as a patroness for Abbey for three years during a stage in his life when he produced a major symphony, and now provides him with a house in Santa Fe. Georgia's seventeen-year-old son, David, forms a friendship with his stepfather. In Santa Fe during Christmas break, David meets Maggie Michaelis, a twenty-seven-year-old actress from New York who is in the Southwest recovering from a broken love affair. David quickly falls in love with Maggie, but she is introduced to Edmund and becomes his lover. Nevertheless, a three-way friendship flourishes, buoyed by a mutual respect for art (Maggie has taken up sculpting, and David sees himself as a budding poet).

When Georgia learns of her husband's affair with Maggie, she returns to Santa Fe, and a confrontation ensues that results in a "civilized" resolution: Georgia and Edmund divorce; Georgia and Lucien marry after the latter divorces his wife; and Edmund and Maggie finally marry. Maggie provides Edmund with an emotional support he never had with Georgia, although in contrast with his former material comfort he now endures poverty with Maggie, as well as declining health. In spite of this, he produces a major symphony just before his death. Indeed, inspired by love, free of social distractions, and driven by determination in the face of illness, Edmund reaches his artistic zenith. In the meantime, David establishes his independence from his mother and chooses to be with his friends Maggie and Edmund.

This novel exhibits Horgan's first use of New Mexico as a setting for a book-length work and provides glimpses of his growing fascination with the land and the people of the Southwest. Reflective of Horgan's own experience, however, the settings still include the East as well. *No Quarter Given* was reviewed widely and, overall, favorably in England as well as in the United States. Sean O'Faolain, writing for the *Spectator* (London), called the novel "an admirable piece of work, and a convincing picture of sophisticated American society, told with feeling and . . . imaginative beauty." Margaret Wallace, in the *New York Times*, considered Horgan's handling of Abbey particularly satisfying in that the character remained unpredictable and slightly unrealistic, befitting an artistic genius. And, she concluded, "Mr. Horgan is even more skillful as a story-teller than as a creator of character. This is saying a good deal." The reviewer for the *Times* (London) wrote, "What is perhaps most remarkable in [Horgan's] handling of the story is that genius and disease both achieve a vivid and haunting presence all through and yet never distort its essential humanity."

Horgan's next book was in marked contrast to the two previous novels. No longer drawing exclusively on personal experience for creative material, and less concerned with art as an idea, he turned to history and the heritage of the Southwest for inspiration. He also shifted from satire to a more realistic approach. *From the Royal City of the Holy Faith of St. Francis of Assisi* (1936) contains five very short sketches of individuals who were part of the history of Santa Fe. These are not precise biographies, but interpretive vignettes of a Captain General in 1690, a Spanish woman of 1730, Catholic fathers in 1780 when the first Bishop visited Santa Fe, General Kearny and an aide in the occupied city in 1846, and territorial governor Lew Wallace and his wife in 1878. Each account provides a glimpse of life in Santa Fe to convey a sense of time and place as well as to illustrate the variety of the city's historical heritage. Moreover, each story deals with the arrival, and in some cases departure, of persons who are sojourners, not natives, to the city and who must come to grips with a new place. All are, in one way or another, absorbed by the land of the Southwest.

In a collection of six short stories published in 1936 under the title *The Return of the Weed*, Horgan dealt with the theme of decay. But, as he noted in an introductory comment, "abandoned places of human passage" are not "visible evidences of failure," but "monuments . . . inscrutable remains of aspiration wedded to tragedy." Such an observation underscores Horgan's growing appreciation of history and its suitability for literary exercises.

All the stories of this collection are set in New Mexico and touch on several centuries of time. A Spanish priest who worked thirty years among the Indians is killed in a native uprising, and the adobe mission, the physical memorial of his life's toil, is put to the torch. An old adobe ranch house, once the home of two successful brothers, weathers into ruin after the violent death of one of the brothers in a gunfight and the failure of the other brother to return from a trip east to market cattle. A land speculator and promoter of the late nineteenth-century builds an imposing mansion on a hilltop, a symbol of his wealth and his vision of the area's potential growth. But the dream falls short of reality and the dreamer dies, leaving the house to stand "empty but eloquent . . . long gone but fine with human valor." A young couple, newly married but jobless after the husband's college graduation, move from El Paso to an inherited ranch 300 miles northeast as a fallback when times get better again. When the woman can no longer endure life there, she returns with her child to her parents, while the man and the ranch go to seed. He finally sells the property to a neighbor. The ranch house, water tank, and windmill are given up to the openness and dryness of the land that "broke the substance of anything built. . . ." Old Don Elizario tells of the grand hacienda he once lived in and of how the flooding Rio Grande swept it away one year. Subsequent attempts in railroad and sawmill investments proved equally transitory, and now he is reduced to only his memories of the great house by the river. The operator of a gasoline station which was once doing a prosperous business becomes bored and melancholy with his existence on a long, lonely stretch of highway. One night, seeing an airplane fly overhead, the man abandons the station to go to California to learn how to fly. With the passage of time the deserted station takes on "the color of the land itself." Horgan's finely crafted vignettes of the reclaiming power of time and nature over what man makes testify to the author's ability to elaborate on a common theme with imagination and variety.

Mary Ross, in *Books*, called *The Return of the Weed* "a distinguished little book," and others were impressed by Horgan's vivid, almost poetic, descriptions of the desert land. But some reviewers were dismayed by the brevity of these stories.

Main Line West (1936) was Horgan's first novel set completely in the West. A melancholy and sometimes violent story threaded with a spirit of optimism, it reaffirms Horgan's growing concern with ordinary people, experiencing life's difficulties with fortitude and a moral determination to do the best they can under the circumstances. Moreover, Horgan has his main characters here resort to escapist mobility when faced with crises—they are movers one and all, whether for good or ill. Perhaps Horgan's literary migration toward realism,

clearly evidenced in this work, was fostered by the influence of the Great Depression, which so affected the nation in the 1930s and the Great Plains in particular.

In rural Kansas of the early 1900s, a quintessential traveling salesman, Daniel Milford, stops at a farmhouse for shelter during a rainstorm and meets a reserved farmgirl, Irma Gruver. A flirtatious courtship leads to a mismatched marriage and later a pregnancy. After providing her with a café in California as a source of income, Milford deserts his wife just prior to her delivery. Horgan's story focuses on mother and son thereafter, coping with mundane cares which they must meet with their own common resources.

Evangelical religion enters their lives when Irma attends a prayer meeting and concludes that the sawdust trail promises new opportunities for both of them—a mission for herself, a wholesome environment for her son, and perhaps a way back to Kansas for a new beginning. She becomes a persuasive evangelist, and her message of peace is popular during the early years of World War I when the country ascribes to neutrality. But the popular mood changes, while Irma's message does not. In the small town of Los Algodones, her peace theme stirs hostility among soldiers' mothers. Imbued with intolerant patriotism, a mob collects to force Irma to recant her pacifism and repledge her patriotism, and in the hysteria people begin throwing stones. Badly injured, Irma dies on a train and is buried in Driscoll, Arizona. Although Danny has been befriended by a kindly couple, he chooses to leave.

Most reviewers noted Horgan's fictional shifts between *Main Line West* and his earlier two novels with respect to setting, characters, and form. Generally, they echoed S. A. Lavine of the *Boston Transcript*, who praised the book as "a truly great novel" because it dealt with people "whose lives flourish directly and simply from the earth and from the heart." Some reviewers were impressed with Horgan's treatment of the theme of Americans' restlessness and mobility as well as his abhorrence for cruelty. Helen MacAffee, writing in the *Yale Review*, criticized Horgan's development of Irma and called certain dramatic incidents "illustrations rather than direct statements of the inner conflict."

In 1937 Horgan continued his interest in formal history by contributing to the production of a textbook on the state history of New Mexico. Edited by Horgan and Maurice Garland Fulton, *New Mexico's Own Chronicle: Three Races in the Writing of Four Hundred Years* is an anthology of primary source

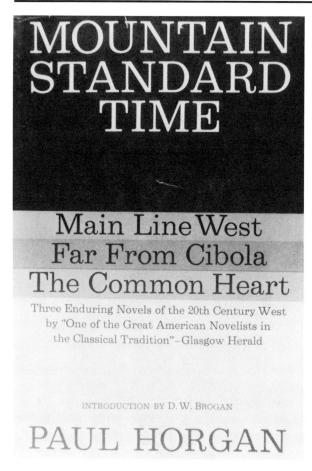

MOUNTAIN
STANDARD
TIME

Main Line West
Far From Cibola
The Common Heart

Three Enduring Novels of the 20th Century West
by "One of the Great American Novelists in
the Classical Tradition"–Glasgow Herald

INTRODUCTION BY D. W. BROGAN

PAUL HORGAN

Dust jacket for the collected edition of the novels Horgan published in 1936, 1938, and 1942

materials—reports, letters, diaries, and articles—that provides a fragmented survey of New Mexico history with particular emphasis on the life of ordinary men and women. One of the pieces in the anthology is an abbreviated version of an article Horgan had written in 1933, "About the Southwest," in which he focused on the land and people of the region and especially examined its "laminated" tricultural heritage of Indian, Hispanic, and Anglo traditions. This essay was basic to Horgan's conceptualization of Southwestern history.

A Lamp on the Plains (1937) continued Danny's story, begun in *Main Line West*. It takes place in the last months of World War I and the year thereafter. The setting is New Mexico, partly in a small backwash town named Vrain, partly on an outlying ranch, and partly in Roswell at the military academy Horgan attended. It is a story of pragmatic adjustment by a boy with no roots facing hard times. Always an outsider wherever he goes, Danny finds brief moorings, if no anchorages, during

which he experiences growth. To some extent, the novel is composed of three books, all bound together by the central figure of Danny and a few other recurring characters, but also independent of each other through new settings and different moods.

Thirteen-year-old Danny leaves the boxcar which took him out of Arizona after the death of his mother and scavenges outside the town of Vrain until he is taken in by Newt, a well-meaning but crude man who works as a mechanic in a garage. Although Newt does the best he can for Danny, the boy senses a need for more, begins attending the local school, and comes under the tutelage of W. W. Burlington, a self-styled professor and cultured gentleman who drifts from town to town impressing the local people and somehow making a living thereby. The professor introduces Danny to a kind of pompous intellectualism and gives him "the seed of beauty and knowledge." The reading room of the Santa Fe Railroad becomes Danny's lamp on the plains. But Burlington shows Danny his baser side as well: cynicism, hypocrisy, and irresponsible sexual behavior. In various ways Danny faces conflicting moral values. Eventually the professor rouses the ire of the town's philistines and jealous husbands; he is arrested on charges of theft. Although Danny recognizes the professor's weaknesses, he concludes that the jailing is unjust and with the help of Newt gets him out and onto a train leaving Vrain.

Danny's world, and his fortunes, suddenly shift when he spends a summer on a ranch. His benefactor is Wade McGraw, a widower with two sons and a daughter, and a man of decency and real kindness. Part of a family now, Danny flourishes in his new friendships, new environment, and new adventures. He performs wholesome ranch work, explores the land to discover its beauty, and shares a growing flirtation with the daughter, Kitty, that soon becomes physical. A suspicious brother, Steve, however, creates moments of discord for Danny and Kitty. When the young lovers are finally found out, Wade decrees separation. Kitty is sent to an aunt in Chicago; Danny is enrolled in the military academy where McGraw's two sons are already cadets. Nevertheless, Danny's growth now includes love and its denial.

Then begins a third phase of Danny's life, which quickly becomes a vicious torment for him. As a first-year student at the academy he must endure the infantile hazing by upperclassmen in a military atmosphere which can only be characterized as socially pathological, if not cannibalistic.

Much is made of obedience, honor, and authority, but the actions of the cadets and cadre make a mockery of these ideals through a mindless zeal to uphold them. Ultimately, the ideals are abused, perverted, or rendered hollow. Danny also faces a special tyranny from Steve, who bears a personal grudge against him and exhibits a mercurial personality that turns sadistic as he takes to "punishing" Danny with beatings. Steve's older brother, Hank, eventually intervenes, but the resolution is an officially sanctioned fight in which Steve is declared victor. More importantly, the means of attempting to secure retribution for Danny's grievances testify further to the underlying savage instincts to which the academy appeals in an effort to attain a semblance of justice. Shortly after the fight, fate brings a different kind of justice: Steve is accidentally killed while playing polo. In different ways Danny, Hank, Kitty, and Wade grapple with the reality of death. Finally, Danny's woe is mirrored in that of his old friend Newt, who is now married, impoverished, and has brought his wife to the Roswell hospital for a difficult delivery. The birth, however, provides a balance for death, and Newt and Danny provide a curious solace for one another that helps each to go on to "create his own path." The novel ends without an ending and seems to beg for a sequel to complete Danny's maturation process. Though an incomplete sequel was written, it was never offered for publication; the manuscript is now in the possession of a private collector.

Reviewers had a mixed reaction to the book. They commended *A Lamp on the Plains* for its depiction of the town of Vrain and its inhabitants. Indeed, they thought Horgan did a better job creating the characters surrounding Danny than he did on that of the hero himself; Danny appeared too conventional at times. Margaret Wallace of the *New York Times* could not judge the novel as it stood to be first-rate, for the story of Danny appeared unended.

In his fifth novel, *Far From Cibola* (1938), which had originally appeared in print in 1936 in an edited collection, Horgan reached a high point of form, symbol, and substance. It was written, he says, in a twelve-day burst of creative inspiration. The story follows the events of one day in April of 1933 as experienced by a collection of people in New Mexico, who are far from the mythical, golden city of Cibola during the era of the Great Depression. Horgan introduces several characters—widowed and impoverished Ellen Rood and her two children, the elderly Larks, the vibrant Vosz family

with three robust sons, Leo the hobo headed for California, and others—and begins an ordinary day for each of them with little or no hint of any impending crisis. Each person performs mundane tasks of life on the Great Plains such as killing a snake, greasing a windmill, and fixing a flat tire. But then Horgan assembles the people before the Courthouse for distribution of government relief, and the day becomes extraordinary in a few brief moments. When no gold is forthcoming from government representatives, the crowd becomes a mob. In an effort to quell the unrest the Sheriff fires shots into nearby cottonwood trees. The mob disperses, but Franz Vosz, who has been sitting in one of the trees is killed. Horgan follows each of his characters through the aftermath of the tragedy and onto the continuation of life.

In an afterword, Horgan notes that his is not a "proletarian novel" but a story of "human charity." Although elements of charity appear, incidents of uncharitable behavior abound—abuse of Leo, a brutal beating of a vagrant Negro, the threat of mob violence, and the responsive demonstration of power by instituted authority that results in greater violence. Nevertheless, the novel is a remarkable achievement for its brevity, the intricate intermingling of people's lives in one simple, singular day, the drama and pathos it contains, and the subtle symbolism and irony beneath the surface. Moreover, the ascending and descending crescendo of the story's form creates a profound emotional impact on the reader which makes it one of Horgan's most memorable works. It is not surprising that this story was one of those, and the only complete novel, published in the recent Horgan collection *Of America: East & West* (1984).

Reviewers greeted *Far From Cibola* with almost unanimous acclaim. S. A. Lavine of the *Boston Transcript* concluded this was Horgan at his best, and Otis Ferguson of the *New Republic* praised the author's ability to create a scene as "almost alchemic." In the *New York Times* Robert Van Gelder noted that it was "a triumph in composition, in architectural design. . . ." Most reviews recognized the beauty of Horgan's writing, a kind of "folk poetry" in this novel.

Horgan's first venture into historical fiction was *The Habit of Empire* (1939), a brief prose rendition of a firsthand account in epic verse by Captain Villagrà of Juan de Oñate's colonization of New Mexico in 1598 and the subsequent battle of Acoma. This experiment of Horgan's had its weaknesses. Although soberly written with an eye to historical fact and filled with fine description, by any measure the account reflects historical naiveté. Depending on a Spanish record, Horgan's story becomes a celebration of the Spanish intrusion into New Mexico and conquest of the Pueblos. Horgan's tone suggests an element of awe and admiration for Spanish military daring and valor even when done in the course of oppression, or worse, proselytizing. Although he recognizes ruthlessness and vengeance among the Spaniards, he glibly explains cruelty and warfare as commonplace to that time and place, failing to note that in every generation of history men have choices. Although once Horgan admits that for the Acomans "defense from invasion was another word for honour" and that their defeat was a matter of humiliation and grief, he generally depicts them as the Spaniards saw them: as pagans and savages, treacherous and barbaric. True savagery, however, is the hallmark of the invader and destroyer, regardless of rationalizations. Yet throughout the story Horgan directs little opprobrium toward the Spaniards. Indeed, he neglects to note that five hundred captured Acomans were sentenced to have one foot chopped off and to twenty years of hard labor, punishment for defending their homes, their culture, and their lives. Horgan did not return to this literary form again until the 1950s, and then with greater sophistication and success. Subsequent research seems in later works to have enlarged his sensitivities, although in books like *Conquistadors in North American History* (a 1963 reworking of some of the material in *The Habit of Empire* and *Great River*, 1954), he continued to show a Spanish bias.

During the 1930s Horgan produced many short stories for magazines and journals, some of national prominence, such as the *New Yorker, Harper's Magazine,* and *North American Review,* and others more obscure, such as *Folk-Say.* Much of his short fiction is of first-rate quality; some of his stories are his most poignant pieces of writing. *Figures in a Landscape* (1940) is a book-length collection of short stories arranged in chronological order according to the time-setting of each story, and the thirteen stories are alternatingly adjoined by brief essays which place them in some kind of context. Several of them exhibit Horgan's familiar technique of having the story's protagonist recall a past incident or relive a memory. All have subject matter relating to the Southwest.

"The Captain's Watch" takes place in Missouri on the Santa Fe Trail in the 1820s. A lieutenant, the sole survivor of a troop of soldiers killed by Indians, informs the troop's captain's widow of her loss and then leads an expedition back into Indian country to secure peace through a treaty for safe passage of commerce across the prairie. A young Indian serves as a guide to the native camp, where negotiations ensue under an uneasy truce. Part of the parley involves proving a connection between these Indians and the death of the soldiers as well as recovery of their remains or their military relics. Ingenuity and a touch of mystery aid the lieutenant, and his mission is a success. A special memento retrieved from the Indians is the captain's watch, which is returned to his son. A loss is restored, and with it a determination for settlement of the West to continue.

In "The Candy Colonel" an old officer visits a little New Mexico town where he had been in his youth as a frontier soldier. Sight of a Mexican child there stirs his memory of a violent incident in 1884, in which his Mexican lover and many of her compatriots were killed. The valley was pacified by force, but Anglo-Mexican distrust persisted. Fifty years later, the aged colonel gives candy to eager children and treasures a sad memory, but consoles himself with his sense of duty.

"The Surgeon and the Nun" is a story arising from a doctor's memory of an event thirty years earlier, in July 1905, when he was on his way by train to set up practice in a Pecos River valley town. The train was stopped by a gang of Mexican laborers, one of whom was acutely ill with appendicitis. The doctor's offer to help was opposed by the Anglo foreman, who stupidly argued his man was only shirking, and by the other workers. Amid dirt, heat, crude surroundings, and hostile people the doctor and a nun, who was also traveling west, performed a successful appendectomy. Science and faith did their duty as human need required.

These and the other stories in the collection provide a processional picture of life in the Southwest. With different characters and episodes coming briefly under focus only to be succeeded by others, *Figures in a Landscape* becomes a fictional documentary of the land and people over time. Reviewers focused on the unique structure of this collection, though some felt that the transitional essays between stories were too informative, too literary, or too elaborate, detracting from the fictional tales and causing the book to appear uneven. But individual pieces within the collection drew praise; in his *Boston Transcript* review, G. K. Smart compared "The Surgeon and the Nun" to the best of Hemingway.

Horgan's maturity as a writer capable of skillfully integrating biography and history in narrative fiction, and of gracefully asserting certain ideals, found full expression in his sixth novel. In addition, some of his dialogue began to display a philosophical cast not so apparent previously. In *The Common Heart* (1942) Horgan fashioned stories within stories, by way of memories recalled, historical incidents discussed, and personal experiences related, to reveal the novel's characters and their values.

Set in the 1920s in Albuquerque, the plot centers on Dr. Peter Rush, his wife Noonie, and their son Donald. The Rushes endure a strained marriage and family life because of Noonie's fear of intimacy after nearly dying giving birth to their son. Peter immerses himself in his work and his love of local history. Donald finds solace in the warmth of the fatherless Shoemaker family: Willa, the mother, who works as a waitress and longs for a better life for her children; her son Wayne, Donald's best friend; and her daughter Martha. Of the two families, one is materially comfortable but emotionally sterile, the other emotionally vibrant but materially subsistent.

In the book's main plot, Peter Rush acquires a new patient, Mrs. Foster, a divorced writer from the East with whom he shares literary conversations and pleasant companionship which develops into love. Noonie, learning of her husband's new interest, attempts suicide. Horgan's resolutions in the novel are, for the most part, pragmatic and moral, not romantic. Don Hilario Ascarete, a friend and elderly patient of Peter's who is near death, reminds Peter through a historical anecdote that love cannot be bought or sold, but must be paid for with life. Peter ends his relationship with Mrs. Foster and returns to renew his love with Noonie.

Although at times the novel seems to drift from one character to another with little semblance of a plot, the author argues that this story is an affirmation of life. Horgan shows appreciation here for the love of the "native earth and its human history," for the common heart of humanity, and he does so in a way that is far more positive than the tragic tales in *Main Line West* and *Far From Cibola*.

By now Horgan's reputation as a writer was established. Reviewers paid tribute to his gift for narrative and characterization. Edward Skillin, Jr., of *Commonweal* believed that the novel did not contain a strong social message; rather, it was a simple, quiet story of "sturdy people." Diana Trilling, in the *New Republic* perceived that this was a novel which argued for love. William DuBois's criticism in the *New York Times* was the most negative; he claimed that the collection of crises contained in the book did not add up to a novel. While he praised Horgan's imagery and idealism, he contended that the writer was "more the painter than the story teller . . . more poet than novelist."

With publication of *The Common Heart*, Horgan's writing career experienced a brief hiatus as a result of America's involvement in World War II. Horgan joined the army in 1942 and spent the war years in Washington as chief of the Army Information Branch of the Information and Education Division, assigned to the army's General Staff Corps. He served for three and a half years, during which time his literary production essentially stopped. However, an opera libretto written prior to Horgan's induction into the army was published in *Southwest Review* in 1943 under the title "A Tree on the Plains: Libretto of the Opera." Composed by Ernst Bacon, the opera was used frequently by small opera groups and college theaters. The play *Yours, A. Lincoln* appeared on the eve of Horgan's entrance into the army. In 1946 Horgan left the military with the rank of lieutenant colonel and resumed a life of letters. After one semester at the University of Iowa, where he taught a writers' workshop, Horgan returned to Roswell in 1947, serving as assistant to the president of NMMI for a year and a half, and lived in Roswell until 1960. He wrote eight books during this period and enjoyed subsequent accolades in the form of two Guggenheim Fellowships and both the Pulitzer Prize and Bancroft Prize for *Great River* (1954).

In 1952 Horgan's first postwar book, *The Devil in the Desert*, was published. It had initially appeared in the *Saturday Evening Post* in 1950. *The Devil in the Desert*, one of Horgan's most elegant creations, is a novella about an old priest's death by a snakebite in the Texan desert in the mid-nineteenth century. But the story is an allegory of dedication to piety and duty; of pride, vanity, forgiveness, and penance; of good and evil; and of the dignity of death. It is also one of Horgan's finest evocations of the southwestern landscape and Catholic missionary devotion. The book testified to a new religious dimension in Horgan's writing not previously exhibited so directly or strongly, although earlier stories conveyed respect for the Catholic faith and much Christian symbolism. Paul Angle, in the *Chicago Sunday Tribune*, commented that this simple novella succeeded because of its "perfectly sustained tone of language." Reviewers found little fault in this miniature masterpiece.

In the early 1950s Horgan wrote two critically acclaimed Christmas stories, *One Red Rose for Christ-*

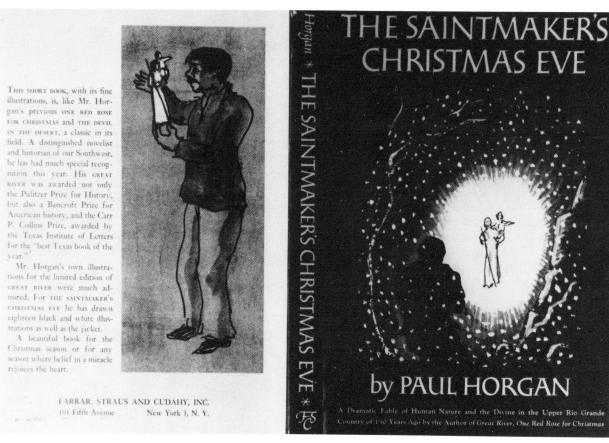

THIS SHORT BOOK, with its fine illustrations, is, like Mr. Horgan's previous ONE RED ROSE FOR CHRISTMAS and THE DEVIL IN THE DESERT, a classic in its field. A distinguished novelist and historian of our Southwest, he has had much special recognition this year. His GREAT RIVER was awarded not only the Pulitzer Prize for History, but also a Bancroft Prize for American history, and the Carr P. Collins Prize, awarded by the Texas Institute of Letters for the "best Texas book of the year."

Mr. Horgan's own illustrations for the limited edition of GREAT RIVER were much admired. For THE SAINTMAKER'S CHRISTMAS EVE he has drawn eighteen black and white illustrations as well as the jacket.

A beautiful book for the Christmas season or for any season where belief in a miracle rejoices the heart.

FARRAR, STRAUS AND CUDAHY, INC.
101 Fifth Avenue   New York 3, N. Y.

THE SAINTMAKER'S CHRISTMAS EVE

by PAUL HORGAN

A Dramatic Fable of Human Nature and the Divine in the Upper Rio Grande Country of 150 Years Ago by the Author of Great River, One Red Rose for Christmas

Dust jacket art by Horgan for the 1955 fable he wrote and illustrated

mas (1952) and *The Saintmaker's Christmas Eve* (1955).

In *One Red Rose for Christmas,* Mother Superior Mary, who heads a home for girls in New York, distrusts one forlorn child as a liar, a thief, and possibly the cause of a fire at the home, but the child becomes the instrument through which a red rose is given to the Mother Superior as a sign that her sister, Sister St. Anne, who died after the fire a year earlier, has gone to heaven. The child relates that it was Sister St. Anne who told her to give the rose. The Mother Superior is overwhelmed by the miracle and contrite for her unloving treatment of the child; she reconciles herself to the child with genuine affection and care.

The Saintmaker's Christmas Eve tells of two brothers in New Mexico in 1809 who are humble but successful woodcarvers of saints, a craft taught to them by an itinerant Franciscan father. Trying to deliver a statue of St. Christopher holding the Christ child to the remote village of San Cristobal, one brother becomes lost in a mountain snowstorm but is saved by the appearance of "the real St. Chris-

topher with the Divine Child," who guides him to the safety of the village. An injury which he receives on his leg mysteriously appears as a flaw on the carved wooden statue. Most importantly, the villagers receive their statue in time to place it in their church for celebration of midnight mass on Christmas Eve. Curiously, Horgan interjects a material element into this story by allowing the two brothers to receive extra orders for additional St. Christopher statues from grateful villagers which translates into an unexpected small fortune for the woodcarvers. Presumably good works obtain spiritual and material rewards.

These two Christmas stories were republished in *Humble Powers* (1954), along with "To the Castle," which is perhaps Horgan's best war story. Indeed, for a writer who was never personally in combat, Horgan's achievement here in terms of soldiers' emotions, psychology, and actions rivals Stephen Crane's *Red Badge of Courage.* "To the Castle" tells of a small American infantry patrol which must capture an old castle in Italy that is strategically located and securely defended by Germans, thus blocking the final Allied advance on Rome. The soldiers' reluctance to obey their lieutenant stems from exhaustion and hopelessness, but a chaplain's timely arrival restores morale and individual self-esteem. During the successful storming of the castle, he gives his life to protect one of the soldiers. In a final gesture of tribute, the lieutenant deposits the gold leaf and silver cross of the chaplain's rank and insignia in a crevice in the exterior wall of St. Peter's Basilica. In comparison, the lieutenant's receipt of a decoration for valor appears a feeble honor. Horgan's story never deteriorates into a tale of heroics and bravado; he combines realism with symbolism to create high inspirational art.

Great River: The Rio Grande in North American History, which won both Pulitzer and Bancroft prizes, was published in 1954. He had worked on this project for over a decade; its genesis lay in his historical writing of the 1930s. Horgan organized the narrative into four parts to examine the Native American, Spanish, Mexican, and United States phases of the history of the river's watershed. Eschewing any reference to archaeology or anthropology, he first describes the existence of the Pueblo Indians in the New Mexico central valley. Focusing heavily on their religious sentiments, he sketches Pueblo living arrangements, work routine, trade, and rituals. Horgan clearly respects their achievement of establishing a sense of community for survival in a harsh environment, but he is culturally myopic toward the Pueblos in some ways. For example, he judges them as less than fully mature for their failure to value individuality and monotheism, though their ability to be ecologically in harmony, rather than in competition, with nature demonstrates superiority rather than inferiority in comparison to subsequent cultures. Horgan also mistakenly depicts the Pueblos as culturally monolithic. Beyond this, he completely neglects any mention of indigenous peoples along the lower Rio Grande.

Horgan places the Spanish on a higher step of civilization in his progressive history. He begins their saga in 1519 and takes it through the eighteenth century, interweaving his account of their conquest and reign with a social history of the period. Frankly admiring of the Spanish during their Golden Age, Horgan concludes that the Spaniards on the Rio Grande fell asleep at their outposts, marking time rather than progressing, and they succumbed to the fate of the Pueblos—to live "in a fixed, traditional present," content but without growth.

To examine the Mexican phase of the region's history, Horgan shifts geographically from primary focus on the New Mexico central valley to the Texas plains, concentrating on the Austin colony of Americans in Coahuila-Texas and its growing friction with the central government of Mexico over slavery, immigration policy, trade regulations, and separate statehood. He neglects, however, the issues of Protestantism versus Catholicism, Anglo versus Hispanic legal traditions, and ethnocentrism. There is a detailed account of the Texas Revolution, after which Horgan follows the shaky years of the Lone Star Republic to the annexation of Texas by the United States. Horgan presents primarily an American view of this history with only limited analysis of Mexican actions and policies and with few criticisms of Anglo activity. Moreover, he does not offer much social history in this section; to a large extent, it is military history.

Horgan celebrates the arrival of the United States along the Rio Grande with a lengthy narrative about the American frontiersman, drawing on literary sources such as Alexis de Tocqueville and James Fenimore Cooper and echoing the frontier thesis of Frederick Jackson Turner. He characterizes the American as energetic, individualistic, democratic, and practical; a builder of communities dedicated to freedom, hard work, and neighborly communalism. But the decade of the 1840s seethed with conflict, and Horgan graphically details the military campaigns of the war with Mexico along the Rio Grande, afterward sketching such regional developments as the founding of frontier military posts, the civil war in the Southwest, campaigns against Indians, the cattle industry, silver mining, exploration of the Big Bend country, and consequences of the Mexican revolution on United States-Mexican relations. He concludes his broad survey on an optimistic note, contending that the Indian, Latin, and American ingredients of the river's history find common blending in the technological homogeneity of the mid-twentieth century and become part of the national neighborhood.

Although this work was acclaimed upon publication, it remains doubtful whether subsequent historians will make sustained use of the narrative as a guide to the past. Its scale is too encompassing, sketchy, and nonanalytical for the specialist and too long, detailed, and narrowly focused for the generalist. Still, as a regional history by a nonprofessional historian, *Great River* is deserving of respect as a literary accomplishment and undoubtedly worthy of its prizewinning status. It generally received excellent comments in literary and review journals with special commendation for its successful fusion of the novelist's craft and the historian's research. Notwithstanding the near-unanimous, superlative praise for the book, some historians and regional specialists arrived at a much more mixed evaluation of Horgan's work. J. Frank Dobie, writing for the *New York Times,* respected the prodigious research and writing that went into the two-volume study, but evaluated certain sections of it as bland and "more belletristic than realistic." He also noted Horgan's tendency to gloss the darker aspects of the Spanish record in the Southwest. Writing in the *New York Herald Tribune Review,* Oliver LaFarge, a native American specialist, weighed Horgan's treatment of the Pueblos and found it somehow analytically superficial. Walter Prescott Webb, in *Saturday Review,* chided Horgan for his cavalier disregard for footnotes but thought the result was "as good as the best" that could be done with respect to such a monumental sweep of history. Frank D. Reeve, in a thirty-page article in the *New Mexico Historical Review,* wrote the severest review of the work, citing numerous factual errors and careless description that distorted reality. On balance, however, most critics celebrated *Great River* as both art and history.

In the wake of *Great River* came another study of southwestern history. *The Centuries of Santa Fe* (1956), an elaboration of Horgan's earlier work *From the Royal City,* contains portraits of representatives of Santa Fe's society reflecting three centuries of variety and change. The sketches are a mixture of fact and fiction, for Horgan created composite characters, some of whom are identifiable as specific persons but others anonymous archetypes. In addition, some actions and quotations attributed to an individual are drawn from primary sources; other deeds and remarks are merely historically appropriate to the character. As a result, the form of this collection is closer to historical fiction than history, although the past is accurately presented. Five of the sketches are set in the years of Spanish hegemony, one during the Mexican period, and four relate to when Santa Fe fell under Anglo-American control. In sum, they convey the city's heritage.

Among the sketches of the earliest period, one tells of a priest who comes as a Franciscan missioner to the Rio Grande valley in 1635, devotes a lifetime to teaching the Indians, and becomes embroiled in the controversy between civil and secular authorities regarding treatment of the Indians. His protest finally takes him back to Spain to plead his case there, but too late. Josiah Gregg, a Missouri trader on the Santa Fe Trail from the

1820s to 1840s, is the vehicle Horgan uses to describe Santa Fe under Mexican authority. The Missourian comments on politics, society, the people, the fur trade, commerce, and growing distrust of Anglo interests in Mexican territory. This American point of view underscores the transitory tenure of Mexican rule in the city. Santa Fe developments during the 1860s and 1870s—the Civil War, Navajo and Apache incarceration, the activity of Bishop Jean Baptiste Lamy—are part of the story of the German bride of a prosperous merchant. Her world is that of local high society: military ranking officers, church prelates, and territorial governor Lew Wallace. In another sketch Horgan describes a young doctor who settles in Santa Fe in 1883 to specialize in tubercular medicine and becomes a friend of Adolph Bandelier, archaeologist, anthropologist, and historian. The two share the intellectual excitement of studying the Pueblos. The doctor also recounts the retirement and later the death of Bishop Lamy. Horgan ends his collage of Santa Fe with autobiographical observations of the city from 1915 to the time of his writing.

The Centuries of Santa Fe drew praise from critics who enjoyed its approach of fictionalized fact. Though Walter Prescott Webb and Oliver LaFarge expressed disapproval of Horgan's technique of describing anonymous personages, LaFarge, writing in the *New York Times,* pronounced the work "excellent, at once imaginative and scholarly...." He especially liked Horgan's "acid" chronicle of mid-twentieth-century Santa Fe.

In 1957 Horgan's novel *Give Me Possession* was published. A departure from earlier works dealing with eastern or western artistic crowds, with ordinary southwesterners in the routine struggle of life, or with historical material of the Southwest, *Give Me Possession* is about the impact of World War II on two lives, an attempt to personalize wartime experiences at home and on the combat field. Here Horgan focuses satirically on David and Agatha Bonbright, a young couple, both raised in comfortable affluence, members of San Francisco's social elite, preoccupied with materialism and banal frivolities until David is drafted and serves in Europe during World War II. On his return to civilian life, it seems the life of the couple will go on as before, in spite of hints that David is somehow changed by his war experience. One day David and Agatha are paid a visit by David's commander, Henry Nicholson, which triggers a memory of a wartime romance and impels David to return to France.

Here Horgan shifts the scene from civilian

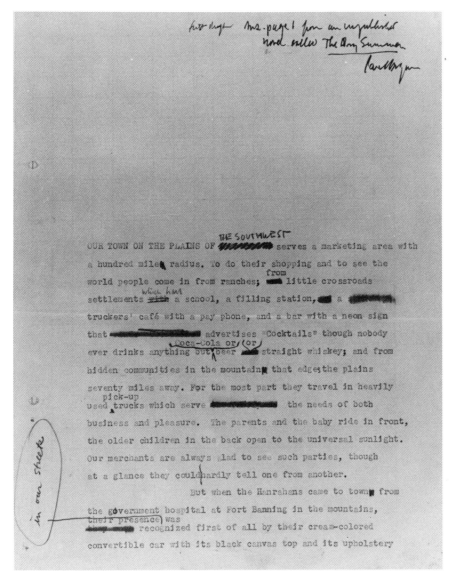

Horgan's revised typescript for an unpublished novel titled
"The Dry Summer"

back to military life, with David's arrival at a destroyed French village in September 1944, where he meets a girl named Laure among the ruins. They have a brief affair, a mutual moment of joy in a world of barbarism, and David promises to see her again someday. The promise is not kept until Nicholson's postwar visit brings about David's return to France. His trip becomes a "maturity rite." When he returns to Agatha, who is now pregnant, he is "really home again for the first time since the war."

Give Me Possession is a story of a man's reconciliation of peace and war, of personal healing. Although Horgan tries to make David real as a man

and a soldier, he is unconvincing. Moreover, the story remains only half told, for if David is at ease with himself in the end, the novel fails to develop the character of Agatha. Few reviewers were greatly taken by *Give Me Possession*. Arthur Mizener, in the *New York Times*, described the book as "an unrealized novel . . . at a level just above a cliché." William Hogan of the *San Francisco Chronicle* evaluated it as not a major Horgan novel nor a "major novel in any sense," merely pleasant reading. Gerald Walker, in *Saturday Review*, was one of the few critics who commented favorably, calling it "a graceful, witty, and lyrical book . . . a comedy of modern manners and Mammon."

In 1960 Horgan moved east once more, this time to Connecticut, becoming a fellow at Wesleyan's Center for Advanced Studies. Two years later he assumed the directorship of the Center and held this position for five years. He remained at Wesleyan as a teacher and was designated Permanent Author in Residence in 1971. He has had twenty-three books published since 1960. In addition, he has received nineteen honorary degrees, has won a second Pulitzer Prize (for *Lamy of Santa Fe)*, has served on the National Council of the Humanities, and has participated in the Aspen Institute for Humanistic Studies (becoming a member of its Council of Managers). Horgan is also a member of the board of the School of American Research and the National Institute of Arts and Letters. Never married, he still resides on the Wesleyan campus.

A Distant Trumpet (1960) is Horgan's longest novel and a successful example of Western historical fiction in its attention to historical accuracy within the flexible construct of the novel. Horgan's Fort Delivery coincides well with the actual Fort Bowie, and the fictional Maj. Gen. Alexander Quait is a reasonable facsimile of Maj. Gen. George Crook. Other characters resemble their real-life counterparts closely, as do historical events; for example, the battle at Half Moon Canyon recalls the Battle of Skull Cave in 1872, and the final campaign of Quait against the Apaches is similar to Crook's Sierra Madre operation of 1885. In minor details, however, Horgan practices author's license. Col. Nelson Miles, not General Crook (Quait), introduced the use of the heliograph, and, of course, Miles, not Crook, claimed the glory of Geronimo's final capture.

This story of military life and Apache campaigns in frontier Arizona is centered on Lt. Matthew Hazard, Capt. Hiram Prescott, and General Quait, but other military personnel including officers' wives as well as Apache warriors have a place in the story. In particular, Horgan strives to represent a nonsimplistic view of Indians and their culture conflict with whites. His novel, however, dwells more on events within people's lives in the officers' quarters and barracks and with relationships between individuals than with military action. Inspired as a boy by a visit with Lincoln, Hazard is marked for a military career, attends West Point, and receives an assignment to Fort Delivery, Arizona. There the Apache scout White Horn becomes his loyal and trusted friend; the new post commander, Captain Prescott, recognizes Hazard's abilities as a soldier; and Hazard performs his duties with professionalism and sound judgment.

After a year at Fort Delivery, Hazard goes east to marry his fiancée, Laura, and returns with her to the frontier. The massacre of a traveling party of whites by Apaches mobilizes General Quait's grand offensive to pacify the territory. The campaign is successful, although Prescott is wounded and dies and Rainbow Son, the Chiricahua Apache leader, escapes to Mexico. Hazard and White Horn serve as envoys to carry Quait's terms of surrender to the warriors. Despite exhaustive hardships, the mission succeeds, Rainbow Son surrenders, and the Chiricahuas are exiled to Florida. As a coda to the story, Horgan interjects an irony. Hazard receives the Medal of Honor, but as a protest for the imprisonment of White Horn along with the other Chiricahua captives, he rejects it and abandons his military career. Yet in the final scene he symbolically dedicates his son to a future career in the army.

A Distant Trumpet (1960) was an immeasurable improvement over Horgan's earlier attempt at historical fiction. It revealed a much more incisive understanding of history, which had come through the years of research that produced *Great River* and other historical works. But the reviewers had very mixed comments on the book, ranging from the view of Paul Engle, in the *New York Times*, who judged it the "finest novel yet on the Southwest in its setting," to that of the (London) *Times Literary Supplement* reviewer who dismissed it as "clumsy," "repetitive," and appealing to treasured American myths. Some reviewers thought the battle scenes poorly drawn and too much emphasis placed on the domesticity of fort life, but others argued that Horgan knew his subject material well, displayed great insight, and had produced an extraordinary novel of the Old West.

Citizen of New Salem, a short and highly acclaimed biography of Abraham Lincoln's early years as a resident of New Salem, Illinois, was published in 1961. Originally written for the *Saturday Evening Post* in centennial celebration of Lincoln's first inauguration, this account deals with the years 1831 to 1837, during which time Lincoln pursued a variety of occupations. It focuses on one of Horgan's favorite themes, the process of maturing. Lincoln remains a nameless resident of a rural hamlet seeking a place in the community, a vocation, and an identity. Lincoln is also the subject of Horgan's only published book of poetry, *Songs After Lincoln* (1965), which commemorates the 100th anniversary of his death.

In 1963 Horgan published another historical work entitled *Conquistadors in North American His-*

tory. Returning to his interest in southwestern history, he provided here a selective examination of the more prominent Spanish explorers and soldiers who carved imperial domains in Mexico and the valley of the Rio Grande. Beginning with an introductory sketch of Christopher Columbus, Horgan culminates his history of empire-building with the re-establishment of permanent white settlement at Santa Fe. With the exception of the material on Columbus and on Cortez and his contemporaries, much of this book repeats in abbreviated or reworked form information which Horgan covered earlier in *The Habit of Empire* or *Great River.* His analysis of the character of the conquistadors, their motivations and actions, and their historical significance reflects greater maturity than his earliest writing on Spanish empire-building. Here Horgan more fully depicts the paradoxes of the conquistadors: charm and cruelty, courage and treachery, piety and greed. He describes them as dutiful but self-serving, marveling at the resources and inhabitants of the New World but crudely wasteful of both. Despite the effort at balance, however, Horgan continues to reveal a strong basic admiration for their achievements—the act of discovery and the glory of initial settlement. Although Horgan mentions it, he does not dwell on the fact that almost every conquistador died in disgrace, poverty, or disregard. Their mark on the land and the native peoples, besides being illustrative of some of the most destructive action in New World history, was in a broader context quite transitory and far more exploitive than developmental; the real Spanish legacy in the Southwest came from the work of the humble Spanish missionaries.

Horgan leaves the reader wishing for either much more or far less in *Conquistadors in North American History.* It is not a penetrating analysis of the conquistadors, nor is it persuasive just because it is well-crafted narrative history. Few reviewers expressed enthusiasm for the book, though most found it readable and well researched. James Day took Horgan to task for sloppy homework in failing to recognize that some of the "facts" presented in the book are the stuff of scholarly dispute—for example, controversy on the precise route of explorers or on the credibility of explorers' own accounts. In Day's view, Horgan had produced "an extreme simplification of a complex historical phenomenon."

In 1964 the first book of what has become known as Horgan's Richard trilogy was published. Although *Things As They Are* is clearly an organic novel, its ten chapters can stand alone as short sto-

ries. Written in the first person as the autobiography of a mature man, the story relates Richard's boyhood from age four or five to age thirteen or fourteen, from about 1908 to 1918. Horgan successfully conveys in the book the innocence, impulsiveness, fearfulness, shyness, and aggressiveness of childhood but through the judgmental reminiscences of an older man of experience. Some of the incidents of Richard's childhood closely resemble certain developments in Horgan's life. The stories become moral lessons in such matters as aiding the defenseless; facing fear; decision-making; the lure of illusions and hypocrisy; and truth, love, and goodness as well as their opposites. Three of the stories directly introduce death into Richard's life, and a fourth hints at its possibility. But all the discovery, while experimental to Richard the boy, is meaningful primarily to Richard the man as a matter of hindsight; he sees the lessons historically, relives them in memory, and finally recognizes their true value. Thus, Horgan attains a sense of present and past simultaneously and merges action with meaning. Some stories are more effective than others, but all succeed in portraying the development of Richard's character. Almost confessional in nature, these stories contain some of Horgan's most beautiful and moving writing, and they abound with epigrammatical observations.

With few exceptions, critics were impressed with *Things As They Are.* In *Best Seller* the anonymous reviewer called it "work of rare beauty" and "a triumph of the artistic over the journalistic tendency of contemporary fiction." J. K. Hutchens of *Book Week* perceived the "universality" of the autobiographical elements in Horgan's story with which all readers could identify. Virgilia Peterson of the *New York Times Book Review* believed this was Horgan's best novel to date, and James Kraft in the *Canadian Review of American Studies* compared it to the maturation novels of Mark Twain and J. D. Salinger.

Less well received was *Memories of the Future* (1966), an account of twentieth-century military life as it affected a small group of navy families and their friends. But Horgan won the critics wholly with a 1967 collection of short fiction. *The Peach Stone: Stories from Four Decades* contains twenty stories and novellas written by Horgan over the course of thirty-six years. All but one had appeared previously in other books or in periodicals. These stories are organized under four categories: childhood, youth, maturity, and old age. Six are set in the East; fourteen have western settings. The title story, written in 1942, appears in the section related to maturity. In it a father, mother, and son are traveling on a road in New Mexico toward the mother's hometown to bury their two-year-old daughter, who died in an accidental tumbleweed fire near their house. They are isolated from each other by their grief, outwardly numb but inwardly in turmoil. A fourth person in the car is the boy's teacher, Miss Latcher, who accompanies the family out of a sense of responsibility to her student and his family but who is helpless in the presence of tragedy. Horgan creates the oppressive silence of their thoughts: the father blames himself, presuming his negligence led to the fire; the mother sees fleeting images from the car window that recall happier moments; the boy searches wistfully for a look of reassurance; Miss Latcher tries to empathize but is inadequate and even feels envy for the family's bond of sorrow. A significant memory of the mother's is a childhood belief that a peach stone, if held long enough in one's hand, would sprout. Finally the family reaches the burial ground and the grave-side rites are held. In the final moments of the story the mother reaffirms life "as if she were holding the peach stone." As her husband consoles her, the woman weeps, partly out of grief, but more for joy that in the sorrow of death she can be renewed by thoughts of life's regeneration.

The story "Old Army" was written in 1944, when Horgan was in the service, and was his first narrative about modern military life. In this collection it reflects the theme of old age. At Fort Riley, Kansas, in 1942, General Huntington is retiring from the army. It is a bittersweet occasion, complete with farewell dinner and commemorative plaque from fellow officers. On the final night before his departure, the general reminisces to close friends about his long career with pride and nostalgia, establishing a military genealogy back to the Civil War. A young lieutenant unabashedly relishes the sentiment of the moment in which symbolically a tradition of duty and honor is passed from one generation to the next. The story reflects the general patriotic feeling prevalent at the time it was written.

Everything to Live For, the second book of the Richard trilogy, appeared in 1968. Horgan had succeeded in capturing innocence and its loss in *Things As They Are*, but in *Everything to Live For*, in which he focused on Richard's seventeenth summer, he assumed far too much for Richard and his friends. They intellectualize with a kind of profundity and psychological understanding beyond their age or circumstances, and the adults' deference to young Richard as emotionally strong or

perceptually astute is inappropriate. In this novel Horgan did not sustain as successfully as before his method of melding an older narrator's perspective of a remembered past with the details of the present, and some critics found it disappointing. Others, including Granville Hicks in the *Saturday Review*, gave the book high praise. Webster Schott wrote in *Life*, "Horgan creates human beings of such authenticity, demanding a range and depth of response . . . that the novel seems to expand into its own reality." James Friend declared in the *Chicago Daily News*, "Mr. Horgan has presented . . . a series of impressions that do for the written word what Fellini has done for the motion picture. . . ."

In *Everything to Live For*, Richard visits his wealthy Chittenden cousins in Pennsylvania. As Richard is drawn into the family, he learns about the unhappiness that permeates this household, whose members act as if they were always on stage. A daughter, Lena, is an outcast because she has been involved in a scandal and married outside her family's religion and nationality. The mother has had one hand amputated, presumably the result of an accidental blow to her arm by her son Max four years earlier. Although she can be a polite hostess when the occasion demands it, she is reclusive and pours her energies into horticulture; her beautiful, healthy flowers are an ironic metaphorical reverse of her personal condition. The father is socially proper and managerially proficient but emotionally weak. Max, quick-witted and brilliant, suffers from guilt and self-hate and ultimately is killed in a suicidal car wreck at a train crossing. In contrast, Richard exudes innocence, virtue, happiness, self-acceptance, and faith. He knows "how to live with what God has given [him]." But Richard's life is not untouched by his unhappy relatives. His personality assumes complexity as he tries to sort things out. He experiences love, loses his virginity, and comes to terms with the death of a friend, even though, as he says, "death to me at that age was an obscenity." Richard enters "the kingdom of earth" and survives; his process of maturation continues but is not yet complete.

In 1970 three of Horgan's books were published: *The Heroic Triad*, which contained largely material previously published in *Great River; Maurice Baring Restored*, which Horgan edited; and the novel *Whitewater*. In *Whitewater*, Horgan used his familiar technique of flashback to tell of the adolescent life of Phillipson Durham, who is a professor when the story opens. Here again Horgan deals with the theme of a young person's coming of age. Phil and his two friends Billy Breedlove and Marilee Underwood live in Belvedere, Texas, near a reservoir which inundated a former town named Whitewater. The time is the late 1940s. A special friend of theirs is Victoria Cochran, widow of a prominent judge, who assumes a role as patroness in nurturing artistic and literary interests in the young people. The effect takes root in Phil, while Billy and Marilee are more interested in courting each other. Indeed, Phil, introspective and analytical, seems more comfortable with the past than the present.

Amid the main story line Horgan introduces elements of mystery with reference to a drowning years earlier in Whitewater Lake; of scandal in the life of Tom Bob Gately, the local banker who dallied once in adolescent homosexuality and now carries on an affair with a sales clerk at the drugstore; and of the marital unhappiness experienced by Gately, his wife, and his mistress when this affair comes to an end. Tragedy and grief take another form in the novel when Billy, attempting to paint an athletic slogan on the town water tower, falls and is killed. Phil, who was involved in the painting prank, is inadvertently responsible for Billy's fall and, along with Marilee, is devastated by Billy's death. He finds restoration, however, through unsolicited advice from Gately and even more through wise counseling from Victoria Cochran. Marilee, pregnant with Billy's child, commits suicide by drowning in Whitewater Lake. Again Victoria's support helps Phil survive the death of a friend, and she secures his future by providing a full endowment for his education. The story ends with a return to the present life of Phillipson Durham, to whom the voices of the past continue to speak, not with reassurance but in eternal question.

Reviewers expressed mixed opinions of this work. In the *Christian Science Monitor* Neil Millar highlighted its religious undertones; he saw it as a decidedly Christian novel, perceptive without sentimentality, "high-minded without intolerance." R. L. Perkin, in *Saturday Review*, thought the story substantial and found the characters authentic. Denis Donoghue, writing for the *New York Review of Books*, disagreed; he considered Billy too crude, Victoria too polished, and the author too abstract in trying to create universal types.

In the early 1970s Horgan produced two pieces of writing which varied considerably from his usual fiction or history. One was *Encounters With Stravinsky: A Personal Record* (1972), which he described as "neither a musical study nor a complete biography," but rather "a sketchbook" providing a portrait of Igor Stravinsky primarily in relationship

to Horgan. Stravinsky had been a musical hero to Horgan since his student days at NMMI and the Eastman School of Music. They met in July 1957, when Stravinsky came to Santa Fe to supervise production of his work *The Rake's Progress* by the Santa Fe Opera. They saw each other many times after that and became close friends, maintaining frequent contact until Stravinsky's death in 1971.

The book gives details of the friendship along with Horgan's perceptions about people and culture and his articulation of the underlying values which define his view of the world, of others, and of himself. It also provides a wealth of autobiographical information dealing with Horgan's student years and his involvement with Santa Fe's cultural life.

Approaches to Writing (1973), like *Encounter With Stravinsky*, defies classification. It contains Horgan's reflections about the craft of writing and provides insights about the author. In the first of the book's four parts, Horgan discusses the hard work, discipline, and faith in intuition that must go into writing. The second section consists of pages of notes—brief observations, images, epigrammatic statements, philosophical speculations—which typify the raw material from which a writer produces the finished work. A caveat which runs through many of Horgan's entries is that the writer must be aware of the "perils of fashion" and be true to his own vision. Another part of the book is a memoir of Horgan's years as an apprentice writer—between 1923 and 1933—when he wrote five unpublished novels. The last section of the book is a provisional bibliography of Horgan's writing by James Kraft, listing in six categories nearly 500 works up to 1973.

Reviewers approved of *Approaches to Writing*. P. A. Doyle of *Book Seller* declared it an "acute analysis of the mystery of writing" and appreciated Horgan's emphasis on the need for a writer to express his "own individual voice." Marshall Clinton of *Library Journal* focused on the value of the book in terms of its revelations about the author himself.

With *Lamy of Santa Fe: His Life and Times* (1975), Horgan produced a historical work of scholarly significance and originality. Although *Great River* exhibited competent research and design, in strict terms of scholarship it broke no new ground. *Lamy*, however, reflected considerable primary research. Except for Willa Cather's fictional portrait, *Death Comes for the Archbishop*, and a brief biography by Louis H. Warner, no definitive chronicle of the life of Jean Baptiste Lamy, first archbishop of Santa Fe, existed. Horgan's book tapped

Dust jacket for Horgan's biography of Archbishop Jean Baptiste Lamy, which brought his second Pulitzer Prize for history

new historical source material and enhanced understanding of the Southwest. It won Horgan his second Pulitzer Prize for history.

Born in a French village in 1814, Lamy studied for the priesthood and was ordained in 1838. He became a missionary to America, serving in northern Ohio and Kentucky until 1850, when he received appointment as vicar apostolic of New Mexico and took ecclesiastical charge of a vast new territory recently acquired by the United States. Lamy's challenges were manifold. As an American immigrant of French descent, he had to establish authority over Hispanic clerics long independent of Church supervision. Rebellion by local clergy was bitter and persistent, fed by ethnic nativism, and eventually led to excommunications. Confusion over diocesan jurisdiction required delicate diplomacy, and Lamy spent considerable time and energy achieving recognition of his bishopric from his counterpart in Durango. Lamy also had to gain the confidence and loyalty of his parishioners—Mexicans, Indians, Americans—amid intercultural distrust and within the demanding disciplines of the Church. Beyond all this, Lamy's life work centered on Church growth—securing more priests and nuns, getting financial support, directing construction efforts, traveling over his diocese and to

the East and even Rome to make reports and arrange support. The Cathedral of Santa Fe, begun under Lamy's supervision, became a monument to the man and his dedication to his work. In 1875 Santa Fe was raised to the status of archiepiscopal diocese, with Lamy as its first archbishop. In 1888 Lamy died after a life of ecclesiastical service—fifty years as a priest and thirty-eight of those as a bishop.

Horgan admiringly portrays Lamy as a builder, promoter, and civilizer who reflected the zeal and conviction of a missionary. The book documents the life of a man within the context of large events. Not an isolated story of an obscure individual, this is biographical history written with the descriptive detail and characterization of the novelist but tempered by the historian's devotion to factual truth. And Horgan is ever mindful of the importance of time and place. Interestingly, his study also becomes an examination of Church politics and bureaucratic infighting. If Horgan errs, it may be that he is occasionally not judiciously critical of Lamy, who at times was too much the Francophile when dealing with Hispanics, too much a frontier booster measuring growth quantitatively, or too much an expansionist in an age of expansion. Nevertheless, Horgan's biography is clearly a labor of love, and he conveys the strength, courage, and perseverance of Lamy as a Church leader who had to perform his duties of faith and work often as an outsider in alien places. Horgan's biography serves Lamy well.

Reviewers generally commended *Lamy of Santa Fe* for its feel for the landscape of the Southwest and its tribute to one man's life and legacy. Although *New York Times* reviewer Michael Rogin, along with others, expressed reservations about cultural biases within the work and with the author's implicit celebration of American expansionism in the mid-nineteenth century, many critics lauded the biography as an impressive achievement. Some compared it favorably to Cather's *Death Comes for the Archbishop* and felt it even more poignantly defined the man.

In *The Thin Mountain Air* (1977) Horgan concluded the Richard trilogy begun almost fifteen years earlier. The time span of this novel is the early 1920s, when Richard is nineteen or twenty, but the novel's point of view is once again that of an older Richard looking backward on formative events in his life. Richard's father, Dan, plays a major part in this story as an ethical model for Richard and as the center of another tragedy to which Richard must adjust. Richard's mother, Rose, is a source of support, trust, and love. In many ways the novel is a tribute to Richard's parents.

The story opens with Dan successfully running for lieutenant governor of New York, but after he assumes office, he is found to have tuberculosis, and the family moves from their Dorchester home to Albuquerque, New Mexico. The move is a demanding experience for Richard. Though he finds a quiet glade along the banks of the Rio Grande that becomes his refuge, circumstances press on him: his father's illness lingers, political intrigues keep the family tied to New York, and on doctor's orders Richard must strengthen himself to ward off the contagion of tuberculosis. As a result, the urban college boy, refined and highly principled, spends a summer working on a sheep ranch, where he is exposed to coarse field hands. One of them, "Buz" Rennison, eventually murders the Hispanic patron of the ranch and rapes his wife. Richard regains his moral compass in the aftermath, but is impressed by the ease of human frailty.

Returning to his family, Richard confronts a dual frailty in his father: he learns of an extramarital affair his father once had and he witnesses his father's death just when he seems to be on the brink of recovery and a renewed political career.

In the end, Richard is again the survivor, able to draw on familial love, personal growth, and tested values.

The Thin Mountain Air fared better with critics than the second Richard novel but not as well as the first. Jack Sullivan of *Saturday Review* considered Horgan's "sense of place" the strong point of the book, but did not buy the author's attempt to make readers "believe in the 'rude lyrical humanity' " of the people in the story. Others agreed that it was laden with melodrama, unfocused, and sometimes trite. But the anonymous *New Yorker* reviewer held that Horgan succeeded in delineating "sharply contrasting characters" and showed "mastery of form."

Like *The Heroic Triad,* Horgan's *Josiah Gregg and His Vision of the Early West* (1979) is a collection of previous studies of Gregg here gathered as a brief biography with a new introduction. Some of this material appeared in the 1940s as a biographical introduction to a two-volume edition of letters, diaries, and notebooks of Gregg's, edited by Maurice Garland Fulton; one part was formerly a separate article published in *Southwest Review.* Like Horgan's other biographical works, this book is as much literature as history, and Horgan focuses both on the manner of man and his symbolic importance and on the facts of Gregg's life and his accomplishments.

Gregg (1806-1849) was a figure on the moving American frontier during the early middle years of the nineteenth century. In addition to eight trips on the Santa Fe trail, he traveled to Mexico as a guide and interpreter during the military campaigns of 1846 and 1847 and eventually found his way to the gold fields of California where he died while on an exploring expedition. He established his place in history as author of *Commerce of the Prairies,* a firsthand account of mercantile trade on the Santa Fe Trail prior to the war with Mexico.

Horgan lauds Gregg's literary masterpiece as "a great work ... where poetry and truth meet. . . ." He captures Gregg's restlessness, his impressive powers of observation, his unflagging curiosity, his need to flex his mind, and his imperative to record things on paper. Gregg becomes Horgan's archetypal man of Manifest Destiny, someone who experienced and promoted the West with feeling and intelligence. If at times the biography is too laudatory and inadequately critical, too literary and insufficiently verified, too fictional and not enough factual, Horgan has found an "intellectual frontiersman" with sufficient skin and bones of history to bear the weight of fictional flesh.

Reviewers tended to focus on the form of *Josiah Gregg* more than its content. Alden Whitman, in *Books and Art*, commented that the attempt to make this a unified biography was strained and also charged that Horgan's claims about Gregg's character and "vision" lacked supporting evidence. On the other hand, William MacDonald, of *Lone Star Book Review*, was unconcerned with form and found the book increased his understanding of the Southwest.

Mexico Bay, written in 1982 when Horgan was almost eighty, was the author's fifteenth novel. It examines the relationships of four people, Howard Debler, Diana Wentworth, John Wentworth, and Benjamin Ives. Debler, a professor writing a history of the Mexican war, has family roots and an educational career in West Texas. Diana, separated from her husband John, lives with Ben, a free-spirited and self-confident painter from Iowa. Again Horgan starts his story in the present and moves to the past to reveal his characters to the reader. Moreover, he moves geographically from west to east, where Diana and Howard had first met briefly, and back west again. During the World War II years Howard had served in the navy, while Diana acted as "an ornament to position" for John, a self-centered social climber attuned to the political nuances of wartime Washington, D.C., where he worked for a war information agency. Later, John resumed a career as a playwright, and Diana left him to join Ben on the beach of Mexico Bay. While Ben paints seascapes, Diana sells refreshments. When Howard arrives there to do research for his book, he and Diana meet again.

Horgan's story takes a violent turn when Ben gets into a fight with the husband of a woman with whom he has had a casual affair. Ben kills the man and flees on a boat, which disappears at sea in a storm. Howard becomes Diana's support in the hours after the killing and Ben's disappearance, and he brings her home to West Texas. In the end, Howard and Diana marry and settle in California, where he takes a teaching position at Berkeley.

Although much of the story places Diana in center stage, Howard's appearance and reappearance, as well as his savior's role, make this novel an affirmation of a personality type dear to Horgan. Not flamboyant or overwhelming, but sober and low-key, dependable and regular, that personality reflects basic goodness and nobility in understatement. It praises honesty, diligence, and forthrightness. And in so doing it mocks others who are somehow out of balance, captivated with status-seeking or self-gratification, and who, in sum, find no real happiness. Horgan's Howard is the hero of this novel in every sense.

Critics generally applauded *Mexico Bay*, praising its characterization, narrative, and imagery. Richard James, in *Bloomsbury Review*, acclaimed Horgan's "impeccable prose," and Jonathan Yardley, of the *Washington Post Book World*, commented favorably on the novel's evocation of nostalgia and elegy. Robert O'Connell concluded, in *America*, that this book was the work of a great novelist.

In celebration of Horgan's eightieth birthday and recognition of his fifty years of productive contributions to literature, history, and art, a selection of the author's writings was published in 1984 under the title *Of America: East & West.* The title underscores the geographic duality of Horgan's settings and subject matter, and also characterizes the bipodal foundation to his personal background and sources of inspiration. *Of America: East & West* serves well as a sampling of Horgan's prodigious output and his strengths as a writer: his exquisite descriptions, the development of penetrating characterizations, the moral applications, the finely honed aphorisms, his command of language, his feeling of human nature, his romanticism and optimism tempered by realism, his Catholicism, his humanism, and his ability to say something universal for all time.

In a 1936 preface written for his friend Witter Bynner's *Selected Poems*, Horgan observed: "What people will inquire of the creative artist is: 'How did you say what you believed, how did your heart answer the world's asking, when you lived? What residue of our human feelings have you saved for us, in your own particular vessel, be it shapely or crude?' " With respect to Horgan and his work, the responses to these questions can only be made in the most affirmative manner and toward the highest level of praise.

References:

James Day, *Paul Horgan* (Austin: Steck-Vaughn, 1967);

Robert Gish, *Paul Horgan* (Boston: Twayne, 1983);

James Kraft, "A Provisional Bibliography," in Horgan's *Approaches to Writing* (New York: Farrar, Straus & Giroux, 1973);

David McCullough, "Historian, Novelist, and Much, Much More," *New York Times Book Review*, 8 April 1984.

William Kennedy

(16 January 1928-   )

Mark Busby
Texas A&M University

BOOKS: *The Ink Truck* (New York: Dial, 1969);

Legs (New York: Coward-McCann, 1975; London: Cape, 1976);

Billy Phelan's Greatest Game (New York: Viking, 1978);

Ironweed (New York: Viking, 1983; Middlesex, U.K.: Penguin, 1983);

O Albany!: An Urban Tapestry (New York: Viking, 1983).

SCREENPLAY: *The Cotton Club,* by Kennedy and Francis Ford Coppola, Orion, 1984.

At the beginning of *Billy Phelan's Greatest Game* (1978), the title character, normally a bowler with a 185 average, is working on a perfect game. Martin Daugherty, journalist, scorekeeper, and the character from whose point of view the novel is told, thinks of writing a column about this game:

> He would point out how some men moved through the daily sludge of their lives and then, with a stroke, cut away the sludge and transformed themselves. Yet what they became was not the result of a sudden act, but the culmination of all they had ever done: a triumph for self development.

Novelist William Kennedy wrote lines that have become prophetic about his own life. He too struggled through a hardworking yet unrecognized writing career until he burst upon the national scene—a new literary star at the age of fifty-five.

At age fifty Kennedy had already written three modestly reviewed novels, but the third, *Billy Phelan's Greatest Game,* had not sold well. His editor at Viking, Corlies (Cork) Smith, read the first hundred pages of Kennedy's next novel, *Ironweed* (1983), and suggested that Viking drop Kennedy, since he was still writing about the derelicts and winos knocking around the streets of Albany, New York. Afterward, Kennedy received thirteen rejections from various publishers until Saul Bellow,

who had been his teacher in Puerto Rico in 1960, sent Viking a note admonishing the company for its treatment of a promising writer. "These Albany novels will be memorable, a distinguished group of books," Bellow wrote. "That the author of *Billy Phelan* should have a manuscript kicking around looking for a publisher is disgraceful," Bellow continued.

Bellow, winner of the Nobel Prize for literature and a writer with a reputation for parsimonious praise of other writers, carried weight with Viking. The company reconsidered, accepted *Ironweed,* and set out on a plan to republish Kennedy's earlier novels and call them the "Albany cycle." Thus began a chain of events that lead to Kennedy's receiving the Pulitzer Prize and the National Book Critics Circle Award for *Ironweed;* a MacArthur Foundation grant for $264,000; contracts for the screenplay of *The Cotton Club* (1984), for a collection of essays on Albany, and for the movie rights to his novels; promotion to tenured full professor at State University of New York, Albany, after being a part-time instructor for eight years; and the 1984 republication of his first novel, *The Ink Truck,* originally published in 1969. William Kennedy's life is the stuff his books are made of.

Kennedy was born in Albany on 16 January 1928. His grandfather, "Big Jim" Carroll, was a political figure in a town known for its political maneuvering. His father was a deputy sheriff in Albany County, and as Kennedy grew up he absorbed the sights, sounds, history, and language of the area that was to become his "little postage stamp of soil" in the same way that Yoknapatawpha was for William Faulkner and Dublin was for James Joyce.

But it was not a quick and easy marriage of writer and subject. Kennedy, in fact, rejected much of his background and heritage for some time. In *O Albany!* (1983) he wrote: "I walked out of mass during narrowback sermons, refused to sing 'Too-ra-loo-ra-lo-ra,' registered to vote as an independent. . . . I believed the enemies in the world then were the goddamn Irish-Catholic Albany Demo-

Dust jacket for Kennedy's 1983 evocation of the city that inspired his fiction

crats, who were everywhere dominant, benighted, and pernicious."

Kennedy attended Albany's Christian Brothers Academy, graduated from Siena College with a major in English in 1949, and after an army tour, began a newspaper career in Glen Falls, New York. But his desire to reject his Albany Irish Catholic past took Kennedy first to Miami and then to Puerto Rico in the late 1950s, where he became founder and managing editor of the *San Juan Star;* met his wife, Dana Sosa, a former dancer; and later studied with Bellow. He also worked on a novel not about Puerto Rico but about Albany, an irony he acknowledged: "For there I was, living in San Juan, a vital city, and waking up every morning to pore through the pages of a picture book of Albany scenes from 1867 and 1842 and 1899 and other such years, trying to understand my life from these photos instead of from the bright, warm, seaspun life around me. But the fact was that the pictures, more than the Puerto Rican immediacy, were what spun my own imagination."

When he returned to Albany to care for his ailing father in the early 1960s, Kennedy took a job with the *Albany Times-Union* and wrote a series of articles about Albany neighborhoods, stories that provided details for the novels and much of the research for *O Albany!* Despite his return, Kennedy was still trying to break his ties with home and tradition through his writing style just as many of the successful writers at the time were engaged in the same exercise stylistically or thematically.

Kennedy's first novel, *The Ink Truck,* demonstrates much of the spirit of the times. Experimental and rebellious, *The Ink Truck* takes place in an unnamed city where a few strikers try to continue their strike against a newspaper in the face of all evidence that suggests the cause is lost. Kennedy's style in *The Ink Truck* recalls J. P. Donleavy and black humorists Joseph Heller, Kurt Vonnegut, and Thomas Pynchon. Like them Kennedy uses an absurd main character who ultimately fulfills the requirements of the "hero with a thousand faces."

Kennedy's hero, Bailey, demonstrates one of the elements that Kennedy has said fascinates him. He told an interviewer for the Audio Prose Library that all his books are concerned with "characters in extreme conditions." Bailey is a man who definitely lives on the edge. Part buffoon, Bailey often seems to be on a 1960s drug trip as he goes from absurd or bawdy experiences to hallucinatory fantasies. In his almost one-man strike against the newspaper, Bailey tries to sabotage the paper's ink truck. Then he sets a fire in the headquarters of the gypsies who have been retained by the newspaper bosses to break the strike. Later he is kidnapped by the gypsies; makes an underworld journey to the basement of the library; experiences an hallucinatory trip back to the past, where he faces death by plague; and ultimately returns to the present and a final challenge by Stanley, the head of the antistrike forces, who tries to engage Bailey, his wife Grace, and fellow strikers Irma and Rosenthal in group sex.

There are other connections with the turbulent times. Bailey's struggle against the powers of authority suggests the continuing battles between antiwar protesters and the Lyndon Baines Johnson/Richard Nixon figures of the Vietnam era. In fact, Kennedy presents the strikers' struggle in war imagery: "When you are in a war, even a guerilla war, even a passive war of attrition, the enemy respects only force and he shows his respect with counterforce."

Another 1960s theme that makes its presence felt is the extreme paranoia that permeates novels by writers like Pynchon, Vonnegut, and Ken Kesey. After participating in sexual fantasy requiring him to wear a bull's head for Miss Blue, one of Stanley's girlfriends, Bailey "thought of what he must look like in the bull getup and felt absurd beyond words. . . . Bailey thought: An absurd self is a hated self; and he considered the possibility of a conspiracy to reduce him to an absurd condition."

Ultimately, it is clear that Bailey is one of the 1960s heroic antiheroes who follow the pattern described by Joseph Campbell in *The Hero with a Thousand Faces*—separation, initiation, return, and related aspects of the "monomyth" such as a visit to the underworld and temptation by women. Kennedy, in fact, quotes Campbell's description of the necessity for death in an epigraph to a chapter: "When our day is come for the victory of death, death closes in; there is nothing we can do, except be crucified—and resurrected; dismembered totally, and then reborn."

In *Library Journal* Kennedy identified other major themes in *The Ink Truck:* "It is, perhaps, a metaphor for commitment, a survival handbook for failures, a study in resistance, a comedy of metaphysical lust, a report on the willful pursuit of disaster." Some early reviewers thought Kennedy had

succeeded. Shane Stevens in the *Washington Post* called it "a work of the imagination, inventive, circular and multilayered. . . . a fine debut by a writer of obvious talent and much promise." Daniel St. Albin Greene in the *National Observer* found that Bailey's "comic recalcitrance . . . throbs through the book and makes it an extraordinary achievement." Even though Stanley Reynolds in the *New Statesman* said that the "crazy, surrealistic antics serve no apparent purpose" and that the "novel has the look of something typed in dull moments around a newspaper office," he did find that "Mr. Kennedy . . . has something to say about the way American society crushes idealism."

When *The Ink Truck* was republished in 1984, Kennedy added an author's note that identified the setting and the time: "All that needs saying is that this is not a book about an anonymous city, but about Albany, N.Y., and a few of its dynamics during two centuries. . . . What pleases me most is that the political wisdom that most allowed me to survive a hostile decade has not rotted away."

But in 1969 Kennedy had not yet found his distinctive writing voice, nor had he made the peace with Albany that ultimately led to his best work. *Legs* (1975) begins the process, for it is the first book that moves fully into the Albany experience. Like E. L. Doctorow, who merged fictional and historical characters in *Ragtime*, Kennedy makes a real Albany gangster, Jack "Legs" Diamond, the central figure of his novel. The process of discovering how to tell Diamond's story was difficult. Kennedy spent three years researching Diamond's life and originally planned to write a "meticulously documented piece of fiction." He soon found that so much contradictory information exists about Diamond that facts are elusive: "What I came to eventually was a plan to assimilate all the truth, all the lies, all the fudged areas in between, and reinvent Jack . . . as a brand-new fictional character." (In *O Albany!* Kennedy includes the facts of Diamond's 1931 death in an Albany boardinghouse, as well as his speculations about the involvement of politician Dan O'Connell and the Albany police in Diamond's possible assassination.)

Kennedy rewrote *Legs* eight times, each time changing focus and style. He said that two elements converged to lead him to the final approach: "the discovery of realism and the discovery of place." When he settled on using a single narrator, Diamond's attorney Marcus Gorman, Kennedy believed he had found the appropriate technique for the novel.

Early reviewers pointed out the similarity between Kennedy's narrative technique in *Legs* and F. Scott Fitzgerald's in *The Great Gatsby*. L. J. Davis of the *Washington Post* noted that "Kennedy quite clearly finds a number of parallels between the life of Jack Diamond and the life of Jay Gatsby, and he has even gone so far as to adopt Fitzgerald's narrative strategy. That is, the story is told by a relative outsider." Peter Prescott in *Newsweek* described the novel as "cast in *The Great Gatsby* mold," saying it "is a peculiarly seductive portrait . . . a very skillful story, full of bounce and wit." The reference is appropriate, for Kennedy has Gorman mention the relationship between Gatsby and Diamond after Diamond tells him he met Fitzgerald twice and found him "like two people, a condescending young drunk the first time they met, an apologetic decent man the second time." Like Nick Carraway, Marcus Gormar tells the title character's story and is ambivalent about the man. On the one hand, he sees Diamond as an American icon, "one of the truly new American Irishmen of his day; Horatio Alger out of Finn McCool and Jesse James, shaping the dream that you could grow up in America and shoot your way to glory and riches." On the other, Gorman witnesses the cruelty of a "man for whom violence and death were the well-oiled tools of the trade."

Even more than Nick Carraway, Kennedy's Marcus Gorman recalls Jack Burden, the narrator of Robert Penn Warren's fictionalized account of the life and death of Huey Long in *All the King's Men*. Though Carraway often is a passive observer, Burden participates fully in Willie Stark's descent into corrupt politics. Thus too does Gorman find himself an ambivalent participant in Legs Diamond's underworld activity. Like Burden, Gorman is attracted to Diamond's energy, a kind of inner electricity that "lit up the world wherever he went" and "meant that he was alive, that he didn't die easily." This energy marks him as a survivor, appeals to Gorman, and suggests his connection with other Kennedy heroes.

Kennedy's presentation of Diamond is significant, for he examines carefully just how fully American ideals have been tainted, as Nick Carraway notes, by the "foul dust" that floats in the wake of our dreams. Diamond represents the American character who pursues his goals no matter what, who uses violence to regenerate himself, and whose amorality appeals to the American mind. Kennedy is keenly aware of the connection between Diamond and the American cowboy/outlaw, who for years has exerted a similar attraction for the American psyche.

Possibly because Kennedy was torn between fictionalizing the life of a larger-than-life American gangster and creating a fictional narrator who could carry the weight of his theme, *Legs* lacks the clear narrative focus that sustains interest. Kennedy, in fact, finds Gorman the more interesting character because of his "moral collapse." But if the novel is flawed by this split, it does demonstrate just how far Kennedy had moved toward finding a distinctive writing voice, one that captures the language of his hometown. As the novel begins, a barfly, Tipper Kelly, recalls Legs's death in full Irish flavor:

> So in comes big Barney Duffy with his flashlight and shines it on Bones sitting on poor Jack's chest. "Sweet mother of mine," says Barney and he grabbed Bones by the collar and elbow and lifted him off poor Jack like a dirty sock. "Haven'tcha no manners atall?" Barney says to him. "I meant no harm," says Bones. "It's a nasty thing you've done," says Barney, "sittin' on a dead man's chest." "On the grave of me mother I tripped and fell," says Bones.

Kennedy's language is also impressive. One of Diamond's enemies is called a "giant maggot, an abominable toad with twelve-ounce eyelids and an emancipated nose. . . . a globular figure of uncertain substance."

Although *Legs* marked a significant development in Kennedy's career, *Billy Phelan's Greatest Game* presents the combination of style and subject that ultimately led to critical acclaim. No longer did Kennedy work for experimentation and black humor; no longer did he concentrate on a historical figure. Rather, he used his extensive knowledge of Albany's history, language, and people to create fictional characters based on real people presented primarily in a realistic style. Through the narrator's visions, however, Kennedy tinged his work with what has been called in South American fiction "magical realism," the attempt to present, in realistic narrative prose, extrarational events as part of rational experience. He again uses a secondary figure as the narrator. Newspaperman Martin Daugherty tells the story of the kidnapping of Patsy McCall's son and the way Billy Phelan gets caught between traditional ideals of loyalty and the demands of powerful figures. Based loosely on the kidnapping of politician Dan O'Connell's nephew in 1933, *Billy Phelan's Greatest Game* recalls James Joyce's *Ulysses* in some ways, particularly the similarities between Daugherty and Joyce's erstwhile

Dust jacket for the second novel in Kennedy's Albany cycle

Ulysses, Leopold Bloom, and both novels' examination of the complex relationships between fathers and sons.

Billy Phelan's father, Francis (who is the primary character in *Ironweed*) had disappeared shortly after accidentally dropping Billy's baby brother on his head and killing him. Thus, Billy has grown up on his own, becoming a pool hustler and small-time numbers runner. Through a series of incidents he becomes a go-between in the kidnapping, but rather than giving any information, Billy chooses to remain quiet and maintain pride in his independence and integrity. In this small way, he refuses to bow to political power and breaks a spiral of deception that permeates *Billy Phelan's Greatest Game* and is one of the novel's significant themes: "We are all in a conspiracy against the next man. Duplicity."

And yet there are those with energy and integrity, such as Billy Phelan and Martin Daugherty. Both men discover the answer to their Oedipal fears, Billy by embracing his drunken father Franny, who returns to collect money for voting

illegally, and Martin by examining his relationship with his playwright father, who had been in love with the same woman Martin was. As the result of his personal search, Martin concludes: "The quest to love yourself is a moral quest."

These psychological elements provide a complexity that underpins the novel. But there are several other levels that contribute to the strength of *Billy Phelan's Greatest Game*. While Kennedy was keenly aware of the connections among the various fathers and sons and father/son figures (Martin acts as both father and son to Billy Phelan), he was also writing a political novel and wanted to demonstrate how a pervasive political machine exerts power down to the lowest levels and can control the life of even a small-time hustler.

At another level of significance is the strength of the city of Albany, which exists almost as a character in the novel. Though *Legs* led Kennedy to use Albany as one setting, that novel wandered over the countryside. In *Billy Phelan* Kennedy concentrates on Albany, and it throbs with life as Kennedy presents it in Whitmanian catalogues of details:

There was Albany's river of bright white lights, the lights on in the Famous Lunch, still open, and the dark, smoky reds of Brockley's and Becker's neon tubes, and the tubes also shaping the point over the door of the American Hotel, and the window of Louie's pool room lit up, where somebody was still getting some action, and the light on in the Waldorf restaurant, where the pimps worked out of and where you could get a baked apple right now if you need one. . . .

Kennedy's style in *Billy Phelan's Greatest Game* is something of a smorgasbord, mixing magical realism, Faulknerian flights of language, humor, and the hard-boiled language of journalists and detective writers like Raymond Chandler. When Billy's opponent, Scotty Streck, dies suddenly at the end of their bowling match, Morrie Berman is not upset, saying, "He wouldn't give a whore a hairpin."

Even though many now find *Billy Phelan's Greatest Game* most appealing of all of Kennedy's novels, the early reviewers were generally not enthusiastic about it. Peter Prescott of *Newsweek* was disappointed by Kennedy's failure to concentrate on a clear story. "We are left at the end," Prescott wrote, "with the impression of a great many glittering shards thrown carelessly before us." Jonathan Penner in the *Washington Post* thought the father/son theme too didactically presented, saying "the novel is painfully overstuffed with fathers and sons and their relationships." Both reviewers found reason to praise the novel in spite of their criticism, however. Prescott said that he would be at the "head of the line awaiting Kennedy's next novel." Penner called the dialogue "magnificent" and said the novel "creates, with total authority, a complex and interesting society."

Perhaps the tone of the reviews hurt the sales of the novel. Whatever the reason, the poor sales led Viking to drop Kennedy, and the process that makes Kennedy's story remarkable began. After Bellow's letter and Viking's reconsideration, Kennedy went from being an author without a publisher to having three novels published—and pushed. Viking's renewed enthusiasm may have created a receptive environment for *Ironweed* upon its publication in January 1983. The reviews were almost unanimously positive. George Stade in the *New York Times* was taken by Kennedy's words, which he felt "emanated from the events they described, as though the events were becoming conscious of themselves as they occurred." Prescott in *Newsweek* said that in "its refusal of sentimentality,

its freshness of language . . . *Ironweed* has a sense of permanence about it."

Indeed, it is *Ironweed*'s style that marks its distinctive quality. As the novel begins and bum, drunk, murderer-on-the-lam Francis Phelan jostles toward the cemetery, Kennedy serves notice that his novel approaches old scenes with originality. Kennedy had experimented with surrealism in *The Ink Truck,* but he had rejected it when he felt the demands for realism. Despite his attraction to realism, he believed that realistic writers ignored an important element of humanity: as he said in an interview for the American Audio Prose Library, "If you don't have that element of dream, if you don't get close to the unconscious, then you're only dealing with part of the individual." Kennedy's attraction to the possibility of a world beyond the seen comes not only from magical realism but from film. Originally surrealist filmmakers, particularly Luis Buñuel, had a major impact on Kennedy. Ingmar Bergman, another director who often goes beyond realism, was an important influence. Kennedy wrote that Bergman "transformed my vision of life and film after I saw a double bill of *Wild Strawberries* and *The Magician.*"

These references to the possibility of a transcendent world indicate another aspect of Kennedy's past: the influence of his Catholic background. Although he is by no means doctrinaire, he has given *Ironweed* elements that show his religious concerns, beginning with the epigraph from Dante's *Purgatorio:* "To course o'er better waters now hoists sail the little bark of my wit, leaving behind her a sea so cruel." The novel's time period is also important. It begins on All Hallows' Eve in 1938, (the night of Orson Welles's famous "War of the Worlds" broadcast), moves through All Saints' Day, and ends on All Souls' Day. But the most important element comes from the combination of guilt, expiation, and grace. At the beginning of the novel, when Francis Phelan returns to the cemetery where his family lies buried, he passes near the grave of Gerald Michael Phelan, the son he had dropped and killed. The headstone reads: "born April 13, 1916, died April 26, 1916. Born on the 13th, lived 13 days. An unlucky child who was much loved." The child acknowledges his father's presence and requires that Francis atone for leaving the family:

> Gerald, through an act of silent will, imposed on his father the pressing obligation to perform his final acts of expiation for abandoning the family. You will not know, the child silently said, what these acts are until you

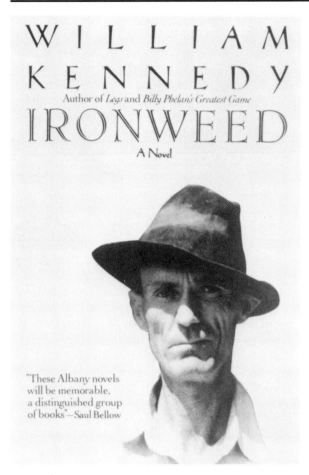

WILLIAM
KENNEDY
Author of *Legs* and *Billy Phelan's Greatest Game*
IRONWEED
A Novel

"These Albany novels
will be memorable,
a distinguished group
of books"—Saul Bellow

*Dust jacket for the third novel in Kennedy's Albany cycle, which
won the Pulitzer Prize and the National Book Critics
Circle Award*

have performed them all. And after you have
performed them you will not understand
that they were expiatory any more than you
have understood all the other expiation that
has kept you in such prolonged humiliation.

Much of the story that follows demonstrates
the way Francis Phelan, through acts of courage,
love, and will, overcomes his suffering and recognizes the healing power of guilt. Finally, touched
by learning from his son Billy that Annie, his wife,
had never told the family he had dropped Gerald,
Francis returns home carrying a turkey under his
arm. Soon he goes to the attic, where Billy had kept
his father's baseball memorabilia for twenty-two
years. Looking at himself in a photograph, Francis
reenters history:

What the camera had caught was two instants
in one: time separated and unified, the ball

in two places at once, an eventuation as
inexplicable as the Trinity itself. Francis now
took the picture to be a Trinitarian talisman
(a hand, a glove, a ball) for achieving the
impossible: for he had always believed it impossible for him, ravaged man, failed human, to reenter history under this roof.

Francis Phelan achieves grace through enduring prolonged suffering, by exerting will in the
face of suffering, and by demonstrating that even
the lowly live by a system of values that merits respect. He demonstrates compassion toward a variety of people, both living and dead, with whom
he comes in contact: for his traveling companion,
Helen, as she increasingly moves toward death
from a stomach tumor; for Rudy, a drunk dying
of stomach cancer who has taken a job shoveling
dirt in the cemetery; for Rowdy Dick Doolan,
whose head he squashed after Rowdy Dick almost
cut off Francis's hand trying to steal his shoes; for
the scab he killed with a carefully thrown rock.

Besides being compassionate, Francis demonstrates that even though he is a bum, a wino who
has drifted from flophouse to weedy field for
twenty-two years, he has other values that mark
him as worthy: courage, integrity (he *will* repay
lawyer Marcus Gorman for getting his charges
dropped), and above all endurance. As Kennedy
explains in another epigraph, tall ironweed is a
"member of the Sunflower family. . . . The name
refers to the toughness of the stem." So Francis
Phelan endures suffering to leave behind what
Dante called "a sea so cruel." The theme of return
from wandering indicates that, like *Billy Phelan's
Greatest Game, Ironweed* is strongly connected to
James Joyce's *Ulysses* and its mythic model. Francis's
wife and son await the wanderer as patiently as
Penelope and Telemachus did.

Although Kennedy's return to Albany was
clear in his fiction, he delved more deeply into the
details of his hometown shortly after *Ironweed* was
published, and resumed work on an anecdotal history of his hometown, *O Albany!* The book is of
interest to literary scholars because it provides the
factual details for much of Kennedy's fiction: the
neighborhoods of Albany, the death of Legs Diamond, the kidnapping of Dan O'Connell's nephew.
To use a word Kennedy coined, he writes "ambil-
oquently" about important historical figures who
lived on the extremes: O'Connell, boss of Albany's
Democratic machine; Nelson Rockefeller, former
governor of New York; Erastus Corning, mayor of

Albany for forty-one years. In *O Albany!* Kennedy treats those on the powerful end of the spectrum, while in his fiction he is more concerned with those at the other end.

Like the narrators in his novels, Kennedy tells Albany's story and also provides much personal information about his relationship with the city, saying:

> I write this book not as a booster of Albany, which I am, nor as an apologist for the city, which I sometimes am, but rather as a person whose imagination has become fused with a single place, and in that place finds all the elements that a man ever needs for the life of the soul.

On his birthday in 1983, Kennedy learned of the MacArthur grant. On the strength of this publicity, Francis Ford Coppola, who was behind schedule on his film *The Cotton Club* and dissatisfied with the original script, called Kennedy in as a "script doctor." Coppola, who had read and been impressed by *Legs*, thought Kennedy would be able to help salvage the script because *The Cotton Club* concerned the same time period and some of the same underworld figures that Kennedy had written about in *Legs*. Kennedy enthusiastically signed on. In the late 1960s, he had done film criticism for the *Albany Times-Union*. He saw working with Coppola as an opportunity to learn more about making movies, but he takes little credit for the film, even though his name appears jointly with Coppola's as screenwriter. He told David Thompson in an interview for *Film Comment:* "This is Francis Coppola's movie, not mine. I have a significant contribution to make to it, but that's something else entirely."

By the time he joined, much of the story had been planned and Richard Gere had been cast in the leading role as Dixie Dwyer, a young cornet player who unknowingly saves gangster Dutch Schultz's life and becomes involved with Schultz (played by James Remar) and Schultz's girlfriend Vera Cicero (played by Diane Lane). As critics later noted, Gere's part is extraneous, since the film's most interesting subject is the famous Harlem nightclub where black singers and dancers performed for white audiences. Kennedy was able to use his knowledge of the underworld of the Prohibition era to help define Gere's character, but the dialogue, which should have been Kennedy's strength, rarely rises above the usual. Nonetheless, the experience gave Kennedy the opportunity to work in film with an important director. Kennedy then began his next novel (under the working title "Quinn's Book"), set in Albany in the nineteenth century, and screenplays for his other books. Kennedy is also working with his son, Brendan Kennedy, on a children's book.

Like the weed for which his 1983 book is named, William Kennedy has endured and finally reaped many of the benefits about which struggling writers dream. His success comes primarily from his ability to write significant novels about realistic characters, in an appealing style that reflects the spirit of the times. He combines the journalist's eye and ear for details with the novelist's sense of plot, character, and language. His continuing themes—human beings on the extremes who endure; the persistence of the spirit and the possibility of grace; the attraction, power, and destructiveness of human will; the strength of roots—have found willing audiences. By adding a touch of magical realism, Kennedy lifts his work into a higher realm, one to which many writers aspire but only a few—with luck and endurance—reach.

References:

Joseph Barbato, "PW Interviews: William Kennedy," *Publishers Weekly* (9 December 1983): 52-53;

Margaret Croyden, "The Sudden Fame of William Kennedy," *New York Times Magazine*, 26 August 1984, pp. 33ff.;

William Kennedy, "How Winning the Pulitzer Has Changed One Writer's Life," *Life* (January 1985): 156-157;

David Thompson, "The Man Has Legs: William Kennedy Interviewed," *Film Comment*, 21 (March-April 1985): 54-59;

"William Kennedy Interview" [cassette] (Columbia, Mo.: American Audio Prose Library, 1984).

Florence King

(5 January 1936-   )

Lynn Felder

SELECTED BOOKS: *Southern Ladies and Gentlemen*
(New York: Stein & Day, 1975);
WASP, Where Is Thy Sting? (New York: Stein & Day,
1977);
He: An Irreverent Look at the American Male (New
York: Stein & Day, 1978);
The Barbarian Princess, as Laura Buchanan (New
York: Berkley, 1978);
When Sisterhood Was in Flower (New York: Viking,
1982);
Confessions of a Failed Southern Lady (New York: St.
Martin's/Marek, 1985).

Florence King was born and reared in Washington, D.C., the only child of Herbert Frederick
and Louise Ruding King. Her father was a well-
read, impassive English dance band musician. Her
mother was a baseball fan. King's grandmother,
Lura Upton Ruding, was a woman of tremendous
girth and ego, determined to mold Florence into
the Southern lady whom Louise refused to be.

Mrs. Ruding met with resistance, however, as
King spent an idyllic childhood and adolescence
ensconced in Washington's many libraries and
bookstores developing into the antithesis of Southern ladyhood—an intellectual. King was precocious
in kindergarten, was advanced a grade in elementary school, and was always a straight-A student.
In high school, the other students called King and
her group of friends the "Brains." She excelled in
French and determined to become a translator. But
American University, where she enrolled on full
scholarship, offered no French major, so she ended
up studying history. Her knowledge of history and
seventeenth-century French literature provide a
sound background for her trenchant criticism of
modern social foibles.

King has mastered and refined the art of the
caustic frivolity. Genuinely astute observations are
couched in one-liners, sarcasm, and extreme exaggeration. Her relentless and reckless humor has
earned her ardent fans and bitter detractors. Critics
of King's work are frequently divided against themselves and often cannot see the forest of her wisdom

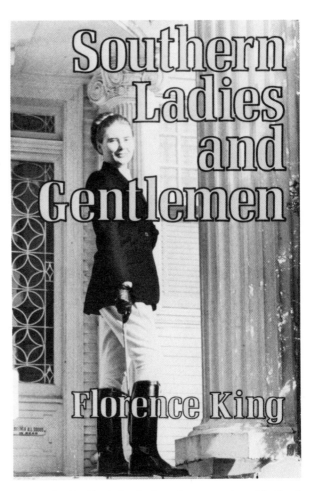

*Dust jacket for King's first book, an irreverent view of the South
and its myths*

for the trees of her sarcasm. She displays the scathing brilliance of the seventeenth-century French
salons she knows so much about. King pulls no
punches, minces no words, and insults almost
everyone eventually. Her primary targets are
Southerners, WASPs, men, and feminists—no one
is entirely safe from her scrutiny and wit.

King began writing in 1958 as an alternative
to soliciting grants and scholarships. She was working on a master's degree in history at the University
of Mississippi when she picked up a copy of *Writer's*

Market out of curiosity. On seeing that *True Confessions* paid five cents per word, she read a magazine to "study the market," and wrote a 3,500-word story in three hours. The next day she cut classes to write a second story. Her first story, "I Committed Adultery in a Diabetic Coma," was published in a true confessions magazine, as was her second, "Jilted," based on Racine's *Bérénice*.

From 1958 to 1964 she wrote for true confessions magazines while teaching school and doing temporary clerical work for Manpower. From 1964 to 1967 she wrote features for the women's page of the *Raleigh News and Observer*. King was assistant editor of *Uncensored Confessions* magazine from 1967 to 1968. From 1968 to 1972 she wrote thirty-seven pornographic novels under various pen names. Since 1972 she has been a full-time freelance writer of books, book reviews, articles, and essays. In 1965 she won the North Carolina Press Woman award for reporting.

King established herself as an observant social interpreter in her first book, *Southern Ladies and Gentlemen*, published by Stein and Day in 1975. The first sentence of the book sets its tone: "I have good reason to know that the only way to understand Southerners is to be one." King spends the next 210 pages enlightening the non-Southern and delighting the Southern with her quasipsychological explanations of what Southerners are like and how they got that way.

Southern Ladies and Gentlemen destroys, perpetuates, and invents myths about the South. King uses autobiographical information, historical background, and lively anecdotes to describe her gallery of Southern characters. According to King, Southerners are a complex blend of contradictions. Chimerical and never quite what they appear to be, they sometimes understand each other, but are almost never understood by outsiders.

From the definition of the word *trashy*, which every self-respecting Southerner knows without having to be told—"the definition of the word trashy is trashy"—to the final discussion of the pre-Copernican flirt, who imagines herself the center of the universe, this book moves swiftly from one laugh to the next. Like the very best humor, it contains a grain of truth in nearly every joke.

Assuming, as the title of the first chapter does, that if you "Build a Fence Around the South . . . You'd Have One Big Madhouse," all Southerners are insane. And King provides the perfect foil for Southern irrationality: Jonathan Latham, a northern psychiatrist come south to study the Southern mind. Latham is a Gulliver in the Land of the un-

fathomable. He encounters Southern women whose unpredictable, manipulative, and finally incomprehensible behavior leaves him baffled and babbling.

The critics were enthusiastic—with reservations. Margo Jefferson wrote in *Newsweek:* "King is an adept, clever Southern tale-teller who assigns her gallery of everyday eccentrics tags like 'The Good Ole Boy' and 'Dear Old Thing' and knows how to set up scenes in which they play out their contradictions for us. The result is amusing but suspect. . . ." She noted further that King is good on the "hypocrisies that nourish the cults of Southern Womanhood and Manhood . . . [She] is astute, but time and again she settles for entertainment."

It is the combination of shrewd perceptions and her unabashed willingness to amuse that renders King so readable. The work bears up under considerable scrutiny. Indeed, with rereading it offers up a richness and complexity that are surprising, considering its slightly rollicking, devil-may-care tone.

In *Best Seller* E. V. Sullivan wrote: "This liberated look at the underside of the Southern psyche leaves much to be desired as social criticism." But he also noted, "Some of the characterizations drawn . . . are in many respects beautifully done and reflect a real sense of humor and empathy with such personages."

WASP, Where Is Thy Sting? (1977) does for Episcopalians what *Southern Ladies and Gentlemen* does for Southerners—pins them down and pulls off their wings. The critics found it humorous but not significant. It is a very funny book about a traditionally humorless group.

R. E. Almeida in *Library Journal* sums up the book's problems and attributes: "King has a clever way with words and a critical eye for society's foibles. She blends these talents capably in this random assortment of caricatures of the WASP society with emphasis on its feminine members. Her portrayals may be a bit overdrawn for reality, but there is enough fact to stimulate empathy and provide some chuckles. . . . It is light and lively in spots and will enhance the humor section where the audience is fairly sophisticated." A sophisticated humorist could hardly do more.

He: An Irreverent Look at the American Male (1978) catalogues an assortment of male types, including the forty-niner (middle-aged conventioneer), the Liberated Man, and writers (in the chapter titled "Let Fly Poynt Blanck"). In the "Author's Note" King writes, "I am neither feminist nor Total Woman, just sick of both. I merely think that men are the funniest things since silly putty." She explains why convincingly, describing her own experiences with and without men.

In an effort to deflect the postulations of armchair psychologists she declares in the first chapter, "Virgin Spring or My Life Before Men": "When a woman writes a book critical of men . . . pseudosophisticates of the 'Aha!' persuasion . . . conclude that she is bitter because of something dreadful that happened during her childhood. . . . To nip such fabrications in the bud I shall begin by telling you the truth about my childhood. It was idyllic." The second chapter, "Too Many Parties and Too Many Pals or My Four Years in a Penile Institution," describes her undergraduate years and her graceless plunge into the world of men.

Once again the critics were divided. Writing in the *New York Times*, Jeff Greenfield succumbed to the pseudosophistication King predicted: "The sexual history is often hilarious; the assessment, by contrast, tries too hard to be witty and ends up bitter. . . . The good news is that Miss King's account of her sexual pilgrim's progress is very funny. . . . When it comes to her categorization of men, however, that humor seems to me to turn forced." The critical consensus seems to be that she is hilarious when deprecating every group except the one with which the critic aligns him- or herself. Jane Clapperton's brief assessment in *Cosmopolitan* is comprehensive: "She [King] is brisk, bawdy, inextinguishably hilarious and perceptive. . . ." King's estimate of men in *He* is, in the long run, humorous, clear-headed, and affectionate. In the end she calls for "a return to glamour and elegance in relations between the sexes."

When Sisterhood Was in Flower (1982) plays on the women's movement in the early 1970s. It is King's only novel to date, and it displays the same boisterous wit as her works of nonfiction. Political reactionary Isabel Fairfax from Virginia meets feminist activist Polly Bradshaw from New England when the wall between their apartments collapses in a bomb explosion set off by Weathermen hiding in the basement of their building. This unlikely pair journeys from Boston to California, where Polly establishes the Don't Tread on Me Women's Commune and Isabel secretly writes pornographic novels. Along the way they collect Gloria Hammond, a drugged-out medievalist who steals dimes from Kotex machines; Agnes Mulligan, a runaway wife of Wagnerian dimensions; and Isabel's Aunt Edna, who has eloped with the rector of St. Jude the Impossible, Episcopal.

Library Journal gave the book low marks: "This

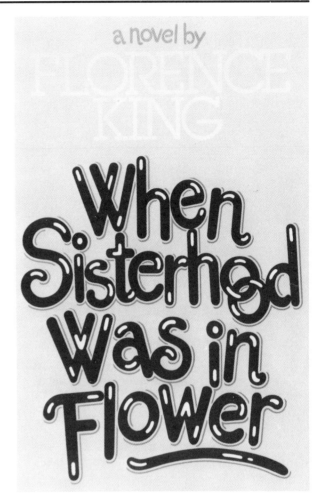

Dust jacket for King's novel spoofing the feminist movement

is satire that falls wide of the mark. Instead of pointing out the excess (feminist or conservative), King pokes fun of everything in a manner that becomes offensive when it means to be witty." *Southern Living* gave it a mixed blessing: "She can be radically funny, as in the underground hit *Southern Ladies and Gentlemen*, or she can be merely scathing, or she can be both." The *Atlantic* showered praise: "By the time she finishes the tale, women's rights lie in chaos and the reader lies half dead with laughter. Ms. King is just plain shamelessly, roaringly, outrageously funny."

Southern Ladies and Gentlemen, *WASP, Where Is Thy Sting?* and *He* have been called "pop anthropology." They all have the same basic structure: background on the subject and some loosely autobiographical information are followed by a catalogue of subgroups or types called caricatures or stereotypes by some critics. These books are humor, not pure sociology, so most of the characters employed are distillations of many people the author has known. Used to illustrate a point or characteristic, they are Everybelle, Everywasp, or Everyman. In *When Sisterhood Was in Flower*, King employs even broader stereotypes to achieve humor.

The autobiography of King's first twenty-two years, *Confessions of a Failed Southern Lady* (1985), marks a slight change of tone in King's work. While explaining the source of much of her humor, she discards her repertoire of stereotypes, and Granny, Herb, Louise, and Jensy (Granny's black counterpart) expand into their touching, funny, powerful, subtle selves. In *Confessions* King "has turned her insights on herself in this autobiography of a 'should-have-been' Southern belle gone wrong."

Confessions is just as funny as the earlier books, but with an additional control and sensitivity. Her inclusion of herself in "the shabby genteel class" strikes a chord of recognition among Southerners who may have wondered into which social class they fit. Her description of lesbian love and the integrity of the self are uncharacteristically lyrical.

Confessions has received good reviews. *Kirkus* sums it up: "With another acidulous barrage of jibes at Southern sexual mating dances and WASP ways in general, King here traces—more astringently than usual—her own rake's progress to what eventually became a satisfying lesbian persuasion." *Library Journal* concurs: "King's characters are warmly and richly drawn, and though a feminist, she is never didactic or oppressive in her approach. However, she doesn't let an opportunity for a humorous poke go by, and therein lies her skill."

In 1978 King published a historical romance, *The Barbarian Princess*, under the pen name Laura Buchanan. She refers to it as a bodice-ripper and dislikes it intensely. She says: "It is absolutely awful; I wrote it solely for the money and hated every minute of it. . . . I hated it so much that I took to drink, blossomed up to two-hundred pounds, and made so much money I bought a condo. . . . Now I have sold the condo and lost the weight and vowed never to write Cosmo Girl junk again. In short, I am happy."

King is at work on a new novel about two sisters growing up in a small Maryland town. One is a happy housewife, the other on her way to becoming a leading feminist personality. She says, "It's absolutely Greek in its onrush of tragedy, de-

cidedly unfunny, and not at all what people expect from me."

In addition to her achievements as a social anthropologist, novelist, and autobiographer, King is a discerning literary critic. She reviews regularly for *Newsday*, the *Philadelphia Inquirer*, and the *Baltimore Sun*. Her articles have appeared in *Vanity Fair, Cosmopolitan, Harper's, Penthouse, Redbook, Playgirl*, and other magazines. King lives in Fredericksburg, Virginia.

AN INTERVIEW

with FLORENCE KING

DLB: How did your family react to your choice of careers?

KING: My family didn't really react one way or the other except for my grandmother's mutterings about trashy women who read confessions magazines—but she didn't say anything about writing them. My mother simply didn't care what I did, and my father thought everything I did was wonderful, so there was no trouble.

DLB: Besides studying history at American University and the University of Mississippi, didn't you take some education courses?

KING: I majored in history at both schools and amassed eighty-three credits in it. However, I had only ten credits in education, so the year I taught tenth-grade history in Suitland, Maryland (1959-1960), I was issued an emergency certificate to indicate that I was not really qualified to teach history. This is why our schools are in such a mess. Another teacher with eighteen credits in history and thirty-six in education had a qualified certificate. He thought the Cavaliers and Roundheads were football teams.

DLB: Did you do any writing as an undergraduate in college?

KING: Never wrote anything, except the usual term papers. I had no idea what I wanted to be, but being a writer never even crossed my mind until I needed the money and realized that I was capable of doing it. As career decisions go, mine might be called the "fait accompli technique."

DLB: In *When Sisterhood Was in Flower* you write about Isabel "gathering experience." How did you gather experience or otherwise prepare yourself for a writing career?

KING: I have never done anything with the conscious intention of gathering experience so I can write about it, but the little writer's wheel is always turning somewhere in the back of my mind. When I had an affair with a psychiatrist who turned out to be a quack, I told myself that it was really worth it because I could write about it, but I think that was a rationalization to excuse my stupidity for getting into such a mess. I also had an affair with a police detective sergeant who investigated him, so you see, I needed some rationalization. It was the wildest experience I ever gathered, but I've never written about it and don't intend to. There is simply no way to make it plausible or even sane. Wild experiences tend to be useless to writers. I can get much more out of an overheard conversation on a plane or some banal but telling everyday incident. The name of the writing game is imagination, so all you really need is a trigger. I'm always filtering things that happen to me, but by the time I get through inventing and pointing up, the original incident is completely different. (The same holds true for the original person). A valuable experience, like a love affair, happens when you're not looking for it.

DLB: What took you from Mississippi to Seattle?

KING: I was bopping around the country and found myself in Phoenix. It was so hot I had to leave, so I moved to Seattle because I had heard it was cool and rainy there. I didn't plan to stay but my career hit the big time while I was there and I didn't have time to move. I ended up staying ten years, but I always planned to return to the South. Now my Seattle period seems like a dream.

DLB: Where else have you lived?

KING: I lived in Bayonne, New Jersey, while I worked for the confessions mag in New York, and for about three months in Boston. I also rented a beach house off-season in Mattapoisett, Massachusetts, a resort town near New Bedford and Fall River, from September of 1970 to June of 1971.

DLB: How does newspaper and magazine journalism fit into your book writing schedule? Do the shorter works provide relief from the grind of the longer works?

KING: Writing is never a grind; my problem is stopping. I can do ten to twelve really good pages a day, but when I get up around fifteen I start babbling and simply have to stop, though my mind keeps going and I get flashes of scenes and dialogue that I use later when I'm refreshed. I love reviewing and find that it has improved my own writing a lot. Analyzing somebody else's plot or characterization has made me more conscious of the rules of literary structure. I also enjoy doing a short op-ed piece because it's wonderful practice in tightening. My goal is a long novel that contains not one extra word.

DLB: For most writers discipline is an ongoing problem. How do you discipline yourself to work?

KING: When I wrote stuff I hated, like the porns, I had a terrible time getting started and could find any excuse for not working. But writing stuff I like is entirely different. I have no discipline problems at all now and am never tempted by TV, which I watch only for news. I don't have a stereo because music would tempt me. I love Irish tenors but that's music to get drunk by, and if I had a stereo and records I would sit here and listen and get drunk, so I don't permit myself this indulgence. I have to watch this sentimental streak of mine because I need my emotional energy for my work. Sobbing voices singing about girls named Mary would satisfy me so much that I would be drained.

DLB: How are you affected by deadlines? Do they help or hinder creativity?

KING: I don't mind deadlines in the least, but being an only child, I like to please people and be petted and loved, so I always try to get work in *before* the deadline. This is neurotic but it's constructive neurosis so I don't worry about it. I'm still trying to please "adults," but that's better than trying to displease them.

DLB: In his preface to *The New Journalism,* Tom Wolfe says that journalism is the literature of our time—that is, that fiction writers are not writing anything that compellingly describes "our time," but the journalists are. Do you agree?

KING: Most people who say, like Tom Wolfe, that journalism is superior to fiction are usually journalists who would like to write fiction but can't. Fiction is still the *crème de la crème* of writing, the thing writers aim for as they get better and better, the way status-seekers aim for the Episcopal Church. If writers would pay attention to the rules of literary structure as set down by the classicists, we would have much better novels. Most writers "just let it come," which is just vomiting, but not writing.

DLB: What is your general assessment of modern fiction?

KING: Too much "women's litter." By which I mean, bound collections of the kind of chatter one tries to tune out at the beauty shop. If I read one more amniocentesis scene I shall perish. The more women get liberated, the more they write about having babies. *The L-Shaped Room* was about a woman who had a baby, too, but it was a novel about the family of man and the brotherhood of the human race, not about sticking a needle into some woman's belly button.

DLB: Was H. L. Mencken an influence on your journalistic work?

KING: Mencken? No. And I resent his remarks about the South in "The Sahara of the Bozart." I find his style too self-conscious; he never quite learned how to demolish his enemies without raising his voice.

DLB: Who or what has most influenced your writing?

KING: The seventeenth-century French neoclassicists have influenced me the most, especially Nicolas Boileau's *L'Art poétique.* My favorite line is: "Polish, repolish, every color lay, sometimes add, but oftener take away."

DLB: How do journalism and fiction affect each other in your work?

KING: Journalism has no effect on my fiction that I know of. The idea that newspapering ruins novelists is wrong. Writing anything is beneficial in some way or other.

DLB: How do you categorize your nonfiction?

KING: I suppose my nonfiction books belong to the humorous essay category, but some reviewer called me a "pop anthropologist," which struck me as true.

DLB: You said that analyzing other writers' work helps your own. Have you written reviews that you particularly liked or regretted?

KING: My favorite review is the one I did for *Newsday,* of *Parachutes and Kisses* by Erica Jong, which I called "Diaphragms and Seatbelts." That woman is the hickey on the neck of American writing. I'm pleased with most of my reviews, except I don't think I was entirely fair to Gore Vidal in *Lincoln.* That's on my conscience.

DLB: Which of your books is your favorite?

KING: My favorite book is the new one, *Confessions of a Failed Southern Lady.* Though it's mostly funny, it also includes a bittersweet love affair, so I feel more versatile now.

DLB: What are the similarities to your experience and those described in *When Sisterhood Was in Flower?*

KING: I studied stenotype with the aim of being a court reporter, but the repetitive speed-building exercises drove me wild so I dropped it. I never roomed with a feminist, but I did room with a girl who got on my nerves because she never read a book. The only reason I stuck with her was because I got so attached to her dog. I changed him to a cat in *Sisterhood.* He got sprayed by a skunk while we were staying at a campground en route from Albuquerque to Boston. Also on this trip was a hippie girl who stole dimes from Kotex machines, so all that is true. I invented Aunt Edna, Agnes Mulligan, and Martha Bailey, as well as the Episcopal priest. They're all stereotypes, but I intended them to be, since it was a comic novel. The scrapple disaster is based on the time I decided to make scrapple from scratch. Basically, the birth bucket theme was intended as a send-up of Elizabeth Gould Davis.

DLB: How do you think physical well-being affects creativity? Do you take those long morning walks described in *He* and do you still ride horseback?

KING: I still walk because it's the only exercise available to someone who hates all sports. I no longer turn the clock around, though. Now I go to bed around midnight and get up around eight. Never seeing daylight for months on end in winter started to depress me, and also interfered with my alertness during business calls. I don't ride because I'm scared of horses, but I love riding clothes; there's something bisexual about them that turns me on. Cherubino in *The Marriage of Figaro* has the same effect on me. I melt at the sight of a woman in knee breeches.

DLB: Will you please expand on your royalist politics?

KING: My royalism is actually desperation for some escape from America's worship of the Average Person—formerly the Common Man. Politically I am a Hamiltonian elitist. I believe in a Republic of Merit in which water is allowed to find its own level, where voters, like drivers, are tested before being turned loose. Intelligence is my god. I don't care what else people are as long as they're intelligent.

DLB: What are your views on current American politics?

KING: Obviously I am a conservative, but not a God 'n' Country conservative. Those people hate me as much as I hate them. It's impossible to be a conservative in America unless you are stuffy and fearful, and I'm neither. On the other hand, I have no use for Wild 'n' Wooly liberalism. Do you know there is actually a group called the Sioux Nation Lesbian Caucus?

DLB: What, in your opinion, is the place of the writer in American life?

KING: We, not shrinks, are the proper interpreters of the human heart. We've let the boys in the white coats pull the rug out from under us.

DLB: What is your opinion of "Southern writing?"

KING: Now that the South is turning into the Sun Belt, we might finally be able to get rid of the Southern Gothic novel. Basically, Southern novels depend too heavily on child characters and the season known as That Summer, When Something Terrible Happened. The Southerner writing a first novel still feels compelled to do all this, but it's become one big cliché. So has the South's literary-industrial complex, the olfactory. Every Southern novel is full of descriptions of smells; the characters are constantly inhaling the Earth Smell, the Woman Smell, the Man Smell, the Smell Before the Rain, the Smell After the Rain, and every conceivable kind of Smoke Smell.

DLB: How do you work?

KING: With the typewriter on my lap. I use a manual portable—electrics are too heavy. I sit on the sofa; my back lasts a lot longer this way than it would at a table. It's why I can go on for so many hours. On a really heavy day I smoke three packs of cigarettes and drink one cup of coffee after another. I never booze while writing but I like a drink afterwards.

Richard C. Marius

(29 July 1933-   )

Nancy G. Anderson
Auburn University at Montgomery

BOOKS: *The Coming of Rain* (New York: Knopf, 1969; London: Barrie & Rockliffe, 1971);

Luther (Philadelphia & New York: Lippincott, 1974; London: Quartet Books, 1975);

Bound for the Promised Land (New York: Knopf, 1976);

Thomas More: A Biography (New York: Knopf, 1984; London: J. M. Dent, 1985);

A Writer's Companion (New York: Knopf, 1985);

The McGraw-Hill College Handbook, by Marius and Harvey S. Weiner (New York: McGraw-Hill, 1985).

OTHER: "Civil War Scars," in *Pioneer Spirit 76: Commemorative BicenTENNial Portrait*, edited by Dolly Berthelot (Knoxville: Pioneer Spirit 76, 1975), pp. 14-16;

A Dialogue Concerning Heresies, in volume 6 of *The Complete Works of St. Thomas More*, edited by Thomas M. C. Lawler, Germain Marc'hadour, and Marius (New Haven & London: Yale University Press, 1982);

The Confutation of Tyndale's Answer, in volume 8 of *The Yale Edition of the Complete Works of St. Thomas More*, edited by Marius and others (New Haven & London: Yale University Press, 1983).

PERIODICAL PUBLICATIONS: "Henry VIII, Thomas More, and the Bishop of Rome," *Quincentennial Essays on St. Thomas More*, edited by Michael J. Moore. Selected Papers from the Thomas More College Conference (Boone, N. C.: Albion, 1962), pp. 89-107;

"Ruleville: Reminiscence, Reflection," *Christian Century*, 81 (23 September 1964): 1169-1171;

"The Pseudonymous Patristic Text in Thomas More's *Confutation*," *Moreana*, 15-16 (1967): 253-266;

"Thomas More: Church, State, and Ecumenicity," *Christian Century*, 84 (19 July 1967): 934-936;

"Thomas More and the Early Church Fathers," *Traditio*, 24 (1968): 379-407;

"The Middle of the Journey," *Sewanee Review*, 85 (Summer 1977): 460-467;

"More the Conciliarist," *Moreana*, 64 (1980): 91-99;

"The War Between the Baptists," *Esquire*, 96 (December 1981): 46, 48-50, 53, 55;

"Unscientific Ruminations on Schools in Libertyville," *Daedalus*, 112 (Summer 1983): 161-189;

"Musings on the Mysteries of the American South," *Daedalus*, 113 (Summer 1984): 143-176;

"God Didn't Save the King from Biographers," *Boston Sunday Globe*, 4 August 1985, p. A39;

"The Precarious Opportunity: The University Writ-

Richard Marius (Margaret Byrd Adams)

ing Program," *National Forum*, 65 (Fall 1985): 16-20.

the greatest rewards of writing lie in the pleasures of designing and preserving. I remember reading once that writers remember details others do not notice—details like the fall of light after a storm on a summer afternoon, the smell of wet grass on a sunny spring morning, the gesture someone made on hearing news of a death in the family, the sound of a voice others have forgotten, the laughter of an aunt in the kitchen at Christmas long ago. Writers observe in a world of restless change. In setting their observations on paper, all writers create something—a design that makes the observations make sense, something that relates them to the rest of our thought and feeling, something that may make them memorable.

Thus Richard Marius describes the art of writing in his "informal and friendly guide for writers," *A Writer's Companion* (1985). In all of his works, as eclectic as the interests of the Renaissance which he has studied and about which he has written, Marius strives to achieve this "memorability." He claims that he writes "because I am going to die, and I don't want to perish completely from this earth." Whether the work is a scholarly article, a feature story for a popular magazine, a novel, or a biography, he wants to get the details so right and so real that the reader believes and accepts—regardless.

Richard Marius's Renaissance-like interests have developed naturally from his background and education. Marius describes these influences in the autobiographical essay "The Middle of the Journey" (a work another Thomas More scholar praised as "an essay that I wish I had written"). In this essay, Marius pays tribute to his parents and traces his literary career through the publication of his second novel, *Bound for the Promised Land* (1976), and his work on a third one, still in progress. The details in this essay are so right, so real that the reader accepts—regardless of the author's warning that "Writers are probably not the best interpreters of themselves," because, as he explains elsewhere, "I sometimes think all writers make up their past lives and get things mixed up more than they should."

Born 29 July 1933 in Martel, Tennessee, Richard Marius had an isolated but happy childhood on a farm in east Tennessee, near Lenoir City, the town that is transposed into the fictional Bourbonville of his novels. His parents, Henri and Eunice Marius, were from completely different backgrounds. His father was born in Smyrna, Turkey, educated in Ghent, Belgium, and treated for war wounds in England. He eventually came to Lenoir City as the chemist at the foundry. Here he met Eunice Henck, a journalist with the Knoxville *News*. Marius's mother traced her ancestors from the American Revolution down through her grandfather, who had been a Union soldier, and her father, who was a Methodist evangelist. After Eunice Henck married Henri Marius in 1918, they moved to northern Burma, where he worked at a silver mine. The silver market collapsed, and the Mariuses returned to Tennessee. The birth of a retarded son, Marius's elder brother, prompted the family's move to a farm outside of town. Here Richard Marius and his siblings grew up with books as entertainment, especially those read aloud by his mother. Marius acquired his love of the English language from his mother's reading and his knowledge of French from conversations with his polyglot father.

The birth of the retarded brother had another direct effect on Richard Marius: his mother promised her second son to God "to atone for her sins" that had caused this tragedy. Thus, after receiving a B.S. (summa cum laude) in journalism from the University of Tennessee (1954) and working as a journalist, Marius tried to fulfill that promise to God by first attending the New Orleans Baptist Theological Seminary and then receiving a B.D. from Southern Baptist Theological Seminary in 1958. (Marius married Gail Smith in 1955; they had two sons, Richard and Fred, before their divorce. He spent 1956-1957 studying history at the University of Strasbourg, France, on a Rotary scholarship.) These seminary experiences and the fundamentalist religious environment of his childhood are reflected in both of his novels as religious fanatics cause death and destruction.

After the unhappy seminary years, Marius attended Yale to study the ancient Near East. In four happy years there he moved from study of the Near East to sixteenth-century history for his M.A. (1959) and Thomas More for his Ph.D. (1962). From Yale, Marius went to Gettysburg College in Pennsylvania to teach history and then back to his Tennessee alma mater as a professor of history. History is a focus of Marius's scholarly publications, and attitudes toward history are also concerns in his fiction: the "conflict . . . between good history and bad history" in *The Coming of Rain* (1969) and the question of whether "writing history is even possible" in *Bound for the Promised Land*. In 1970

Marius married Lanier Smythe; they have a son, John. While at Tennessee, Marius also began teaching writing, and in 1978 President Derek C. Bok of Harvard University hired him as Director of Expository Writing.

In "The Middle of the Journey," Richard Marius discusses the three major influences on his fiction: "a love for the English language, the experiences of a vividly remembered childhood, and . . . [his] profession as a historian." These influences are reflected not only in his fiction but also in his nonfiction—feature writing, scholarly essays, and biographies.

In *A Writer's Companion,* Marius classifies both fiction and nonfiction as "creative writing" and applies the same criteria of writing to both: ideas must "make sense" and be real and "memorable." Even in his writing textbooks for students—*A Writer's Companion* and *The McGraw-Hill College Handbook* (1985) (the latter coauthored with Harvey S. Wiener)—he wants his readers to believe and accept the details. He achieves the goal through a candid, informal style that uses the first-person pronouns naturally: he is as involved in the art—and work—of writing as the student. The sources from which he draws examples of writing reflect the diversity of his background, education, and current interests. Although he draws from traditional writers such as Keats, Macaulay, Thoreau, Joyce, Orwell, and Mencken, he makes even more frequent use of contemporary writers and sources: on one page of *The McGraw-Hill College Handbook* are selections from John Fowles, Erica Jong, James Horwitz, Peter Schrag, John Houseman, and the *New York Times.* The subjects in examples range from literature and history through divorce, psychophysicists, black holes, and comedy and clowns. The handbook also covers current concerns in writing such as sexless language and the use of word processors. In general, both of the texts are being praised for their commonsensical approach to writing, their readable and even humorous style, and their use of interdisciplinary and contemporary sources for examples.

The characteristics of good writing set forth in these two textbooks are put to practice in Richard Marius's essays. A listing of essays published from 1962 through 1984 demonstrates the diversity of subjects about which Marius has written: Thomas More, memories of seminary days and a Mississippi revival, the Civil War in Tennessee, autobiography about influences on his own fiction, the Southern Baptist Convention in Los Angeles, observations on the place of the humanities in education—based on personal observations in several high schools, and thoughts about the American South. The levels of language and tone vary with the subject and audience, but readable style, use of memorable details, the sense of drama, and, when appropriate, humor persist, whether the work is published in *Esquire, Sewanee Review,* or the Yale edition of *The Complete Works of St. Thomas More.*

Developed from his graduate studies at Yale and his dissertation on Thomas More (directed by biographer and church historian Roland H. Bainton), Marius's scholarly essays are analyses of More's beliefs and his place in the political and religious developments of his day. Whether in a paper for a Thomas More conference, a section in the *Complete Works* (Marius was an editor for volumes 6 and 8), or a study of the accuracy of the movie *A Man for All Seasons,* the argument, often complex or abstract, is carefully reasoned and developed with documented evidence from primary sources—especially the works of Thomas More. The discussion also incorporates other sources from More's own day and subsequent international scholarship, including French, Swiss, Italian, and German. Quotations in these essays are in Latin, French, Hebrew, German, and Greek—and generally not translated for the layperson. For ultimate proof, Marius returns to More's own words and quotes them as originally written in Tudor English or Latin, carefully noting textual problems or errors in editing that can result in varying—or erroneous—conclusions.

Marius enlivens his scholarship with the drama of biographical and historical events, vivid imagery to convey a complex point, or a humorous aside. In a paper for the Thomas More College Conference, reprinted in *Quincentennial Essays on St. Thomas More* (1962), Marius describes a situation in which a reluctant Martin Luther, in need of friends, is "persuaded with some difficulty to write a meek letter offering apology to Henry VIII for his part in their late unpleasantness." For a historical scene provided as background in an appendix to volume 6 of the *Complete Works,* Marius captures the dramatic spectacle:

> The sack [of Rome] itself sent a shiver through Europe. Before dawn on Monday morning, May 6, 1527, mercenary soldiers of the imperial army—ragged, hungry, and unpaid for weeks—followed the Duke of Bourbon in an assault on the Eternal City. The host was made up of Spaniards, Germans, and some Italians. The attack was covered by a dense fog. Near its beginning, while he was helping to set a scal-

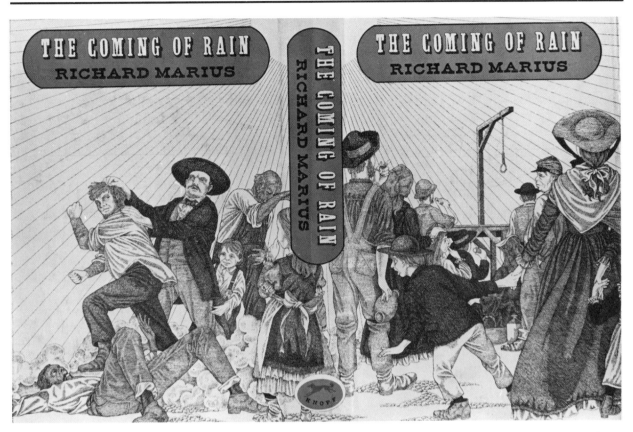

Dust jacket for Marius's first novel, covering two days in 1885 Tennessee (photo of dust jacket taken by Jerry Morgan Medley)

ing ladder in place, the duke was blasted to death by a harquebus, a primitive matchlock gun, fired down on him by one of the defenders on the wall. With him went such discipline as remained in an army that was already hardly more than a mob. Within hours the troops broke into the city, and the sack began.

This passage has a long content footnote citing a recent work that omits the "details of any atrocities" and three sources for these omitted details: a 1564 book printed in France and reprinted in Italy in 1867, a 1911 source published in Rome, and an 1875 Spanish work. After setting the scene in this introduction, Marius describes the atrocities, complete with gory details.

In a quite different endnote in "The Pseudonymous Patristic Text in Thomas More's *Confutation*," Marius comments, with a humorous twist, on Thomas More's use of Church tradition in arguing against the validity of footwashing and the Scriptural basis for its continued practice in the rural churches of East Tennessee:

these primitive congregations would have

confirmed his [More's] argument. Cut off from the outside world, these people have lived, in a sense, cut off from history and tradition. They follow a strict interpretation of Scripture because Scripture is all they have, and they not only wash feet, but they on occasion handle rattlesnakes in a literal interpretation of *Mark* 16:18—a practice which the most rigorously Biblical of the sixteenth century Reformers did not, to my knowledge, advise.

Such an irrelevant, or even irreverent, aside in formal scholarship is criticized by some traditionalists. In addition, Marius makes effective—if controversial—use of the first-person pronoun in his formal scholarship. In most essays, after careful, detailed discussions of scholars' opinions on a controversial point, Marius honestly says: "I would surmise," "my assumption," "I doubt," "I do not believe," or "I do not think for a moment." Or he specifies the basis for a conclusion: "I have examined a number of incunabula of the bible, and this [Latin quotation] is the text of all of them, so that

I think it might be presumed to be the text of any edition of the Vulgate which More might have used." When necessary, he concedes, "I clearly erred" or "I rather foolishly took More to be saying . . ." before he defends other points. Marius assumes a dogmatically personal responsibility for his interpretations.

Marius uses a personal approach effectively in less formal writings also. In his essays on the American South and on education, he combines personal experiences with scholarship adequate to found eloquent arguments about these subjects. After several discouraging days as an observer in public, parochial, and private schools in a town on the East Coast, he concluded:

> Above all, the nation must be made to understand just what is happening in the classroom and how much must be done. The glories of American education and its past accomplishments for our democracy still outshine the darkness we see now. But the darkness is there, and it is profound, and it is spreading. It remains to be seen whether this country can summon the energy, the devotion, and the money to give the same care to educating our children that it once gave to the scientific sport of landing our tiny group of pladitudinous engineers on the moon before the Russians could get there with theirs. Before we can carry out the radical reforms that are necessary in our schools, we must make our people radically aware of how bad the situation is, how threatening it is to our future as a democratic society, and how much there is to do.

The first-person singular pronoun so evident throughout the essay has become first-person plural with the shared responsibility for improvement in American education. The first-person point of view is even more evident in Marius's reminiscences about his childhood and seminary days, but these memories are often the bases for arguments for the role of the church in advocating racial change or about the responsibilities of a historian. With that firsthand perspective, he achieves an immediacy that makes his readers believe the details about his family's legends, his experiences at a revival near Ruleville, Mississippi, and the "circus" atmosphere of the Southern Baptist Convention with all of its spectacle and controversy. In these essays—scholarly, popular, and personal—Marius writes to create something that makes sense, through a carefully wrought, analyt-

ical argument, or to create something that is memorable, through a vivid description or personal experience recreated for readers. Their diversity of subjects but consistent stylistic characteristics are also evident in Marius's novels and biographies. As noted earlier, in "The Middle of the Journey" Marius explains the importance to his fiction of his memories of childhood, his love of the language, and his work as a historian. After a study of his essays, his novels, and his biographies, one must complete the list with the influence of religion. Building on these influences, Marius creates gripping stories, a Dickensian variety of characters in vivid and threatening settings, and challenging themes.

After writing and burning the manuscript of his first novel, Marius wrote *The Coming of Rain*, published in 1969. The book tells the story of two days—24-25 June 1885—in the lives of several residents of Bourbonville, Tennessee. The story opens with a hanging, which becomes almost incidental to the plot, except for the condemned man's last words—"Hey there, Sheriff, well, I see we're going to have rain by tomorrow night"—and two seemingly unrelated occurrences just before the hanging: the beating of two ex-slaves, Jackson Bourbon and his son Breckenridge, and the verbal attack on Preacher Thomas Bazely by Lawyer John Wesley Campbell and young Samuel Beckwith. Sam is the son of Sarah Crittendon Beckwith, the only member of this old Southern family to survive the War Between the States, and Samuel Beckwith, a handsome invalid soldier who happened to stop at the Crittendon place on the way home to Virginia from the war and stayed to marry the pretty owner who had nursed him back to health. Sam's father died, quite unexpectedly, about five years later, and Sam's mother has idealized him. The quiet routine of young Sam's life has been disrupted by Emilie, a German girl whose family paused briefly in Bourbonville on their journey from Germany to the American West. With this introduction to love, Sam's life has changed: "The past his mother lived to preserve became a confusion of dying echoes falling to dreamy rest beyond a haze of distance. Now, out there beyond the dull gleaming of the river he saw not his mother's past but his own, and they were more different than he ever imagined they could be." Thus Sam finally begins an odyssey to learn the truth.

Sam's wanderings lead him to a number of people: his father's friend Campbell; the one-legged Union veteran Brian Ledbetter, who is being seriously courted by Widow Weaver (who needs a man to help run the farm and rear her five children); and, fortuitously, Breckenridge Bourbon. As Sam wanders and learns, Preacher Bazely has gone mad and gone on a rampage. He yells at Breckenridge, struggling to bury his father, "I don't have all day. I have work to do—houses to burn, women to rape, devils to kill! . . . I have business with the Lord." As truth is finally revealed and the rain falls, fulfilling the hanged man's prophecy, Sam looks to the West.

Joyce Carol Oates, in the *New York Times Book Review*, and Guy Davenport, in *Life*, commented on derivative elements and formulas, especially those typical of Southern novels. However, they praised some parts of the work with phrases like "such promise," "thoroughly satisfying," "powerful," and —acknowledging the best Marius tradition—"true to life." Genuine praise came from William B. Hill, S.J., in *Best Sellers:* "This [book] almost certainly has to be the best novel of the year—not the most readable, certainly not the most popular, but quite likely the best." His prediction came true with a designation of *The Coming of Rain* as the best first novel in 1969, by the Friends of American Writers; it was also an alternate selection of the Book-of-the-Month Club in 1970.

Just as Sam Beckwith heads west at the end of *The Coming of Rain*, so, at the beginning of *Bound for the Promised Land*, the young hero, Adam Cloud, strikes out for the West in search of his father, who had run away from his home and family in Bourbonville to seek his fortune in the West. (The later novel cannot be read as a sequel since it is set in the 1850s, thirty-five years earlier than *The Coming of Rain*.) In *Bound for the Promised Land*, Marius uses a journey comparable to Chaucer's pilgrimage to bring together disparate, and desperate, characters: the likable con artist Harry Creekmore, the Jennings clan from Ohio, Shawnee Joe Mc-Moultrie, and the totally evil Ishtar Baynes and her meek husband, Clifford. The episodic plot tells the story of their move west, and, like Sam, Adam learns through experience about himself, about the discrepancy between the appearance of people and things and their reality, and about the meaning— or meaninglessness—of life. Each new hardship tests Adam and his travel companions and brings out previously unnoticed character traits in the travelers. Reasonably early in the journey, Marius removes the suspense of whether Adam survives the trip by revealing the effect of a particular event on Adam later in his life. But suspense is sustained through numerous unanswered questions: What hardships will be endured? Who else will survive?

Will Adam find his father? After the grimness and horrors of the trip, will the survivors live happily ever after?

The route that Adam and his companions take across country, with passage of time by days and weeks, can be plotted on a map. In an effort to have details so real that his readers would believe, Marius traveled the route himself, much of it on horseback. He further asserts that everything that happens on the fictional journey happened to someone: one out of twenty people who made this trip in the mid-nineteenth century kept diaries and journals, and Marius studied these personal accounts to achieve authenticity in the novel. The violence and hardships of the trip lead finally to a coda in which Adam looks back on the journey and its effects on him and others; it is, however, not a harmonious coda.

The reviewers of *Bound for the Promised Land* generally commented on the picaresque qualities of the plot and the initiation and journey motifs. The consensus was high praise for storytelling and characterization, qualities already noted in *The Coming of Rain*. John S. Reist, Jr., in his review in *Christian Century*, mentioned all of these qualities while discussing the novel's philosophical and religious undercurrents: "By choosing the journey or caravan motif, Richard Marius is able to render the narrative pace sensitively and to populate his story with a variety of characters with various backgrounds . . . we end up with a novel that is an arresting fusion of the *Bildungsroman* and the picaresque forms."

Several characteristics that *The Coming of Rain* and *Bound for the Promised Land* have in common are worth noting. Both are initiation novels with a son seeking a father: Sam wants the truth about his dead father; Adam seeks reunion with his father. The two novels present a fascinating gallery of characters from idealistic young men and young women to good-humored, tolerant men and women, disruptive foreigners, cynical people hardened by their fates, and fanatical and evil individuals who destroy those with whom they come in contact. Humor—often grim—has a solid place in each novel. The courtship of Brian Ledbetter by Mrs. Weaver begins with her son Virgil's waking Ledbetter by pecking away at his wooden leg; the hilarious episodes in this courtship provide comic relief as the tension mounts in Sam's search. In the later novel, most of the humor is in Harry Creekmore's ability to charm, and con, people, but as life becomes grimmer on the move west, there is little place for humor.

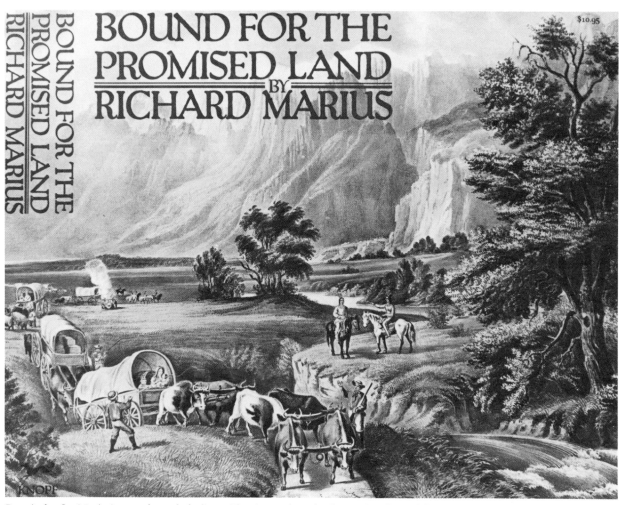

Dust jacket for Marius's second novel, dealing with a journey west in the 1850s (photo of dust jacket taken by Jerry Morgan Medley)

Marius's ability to use nature essentially as part of the plot rather than simply as a setting informs both novels. *The Coming of Rain* opens with a two-page description of a relentless drought:

> And in the early summer of 1885 there was drought. . . . The onset of summer heat came unusually early, as if to assure perfect misery, and by the twenty-fourth of June it had not rained for fifty-three days. The heat waves rolled steadily upward from the baking fields. People's eyes ached both from the cutting sunlight and from the continuous involuntary effort to focus on something sharp and clear. Day after day the wavering heat put a blur on the world. . . .
> The land was all but dead.

The tension of the weather complements the tension of suspense, until the rain precipitates the cli-

max. In the later novel, nature is a constant hazard and hardship, an opponent to be defeated, but the travelers are also in awe of the grandeur and splendor of this wild new land.

Nature is not the only threat to the characters. Evil and violence pervade both novels and are usually the result of fanaticism. In *The Coming of Rain*, Preacher Bazely, the embodiment of religious fanaticism, had ridden with Quantrill and has become a preacher to atone for his sins; the internal conflict drives him mad. His prayer over Jackson Bourbon's grave, which he believes is on a battlefield during the war instead of in the yard of a shack, is a simplified version of a belief of Martin Luther, an absurdity that is typical of Marius's grim humor:

> We may be comforted, my comrades, in knowing this one thing, that though our

fallen brother may end in hell, he will be there by the Will of God. That *is* a comfort, my friends. If we burn there, we know that there is a purpose to it. We can meditate on it forever and ever. In the fire we can think and thank God for using us and thank Him that He did not extinguish our souls in an eternal night.

Jason Jennings, the Yale-educated foundry worker in *Bound for the Promised Land,* is leading his family to California to establish Arcadia, fulfilling the dream of Ralph W. Emerson, whom Jason heard speak at Yale. His gradual disillusionment leads him to play God with the lives of others in his desperate effort to succeed, and his fanaticism enables Ishtar to use him for her evil purposes.

Ultimately, the novels are quite similar philosophically or thematically. As Marius comments in "The Middle of the Journey," "in both my novels the romantic traditions of the old South take a good beating." Also both works, as mentioned earlier, deal with the views of history. As part of this consideration, both novels are concerned with time—the past determining the present which then determines the future. Adam acknowledges, many years after his expedition, "that there must be a fatality to all the past, and you might as well resign yourself to it." Lawyer Campbell tells Sam, "And most of the time there's nothing we can do even to make ourselves *think* we can undo the past. Our past hangs on to us like a death we carry around on our backs, and we can't get away from what we did then no matter what we do—*most of the time!*" Campbell at least holds out the hope of possible change. In both novels Marius interweaves past and present through effective flashbacks to show just how interrelated past and present are. Marius has attacked the romantic traditions of the old South in these novels, but he also ponders the burden of the past, a burden that has haunted generations of Southern writers.

Characters in both novels search for meaning and purpose in life. Jason is determined that "Everything had a purpose. You followed your destiny, and you had faith that everything would always work out." But it does not, and the disasters disillusion him. Years later, disheartened by details he has learned long after the trip, Adam remembers a comment of Jason's wife, Jessica: "We are chips on the flood." And he stands at his office window looking at the ocean: "Waves were rolling in long swells against the sandy beach and the wind was blowing lines of water across the waves, so that

the pattern was crisscrossed and in such constant motion that he could not fix his tired eyes upon it." Meaninglessness removes any hint of a happy ending. In *The Coming of Rain* Sam acknowledges the lack of pattern, the lack of purpose, equally dogmatically: "There was no meaning to the universe. Things simply were as they were, and there was no reason for it, and they could be any other way, and there would be no reason for that either."

This thematic note is sounded in another, very different, work by Richard Marius. In part of the introduction to volume 8 of *The Complete Works of St. Thomas More*, Marius explains what More saw as the probable result of his acquiescing to King Henry VIII: "Then all mankind must be adrift on a vast and silent ocean where no voice altered a word of sure command and whose uncharted coasts lay beyond the horizon in a realm of eternal night." Richard Marius's fictional characters exist in a world that Thomas More could not risk; his novels can be read as fictional explorations into the philosophical ideas covered in the two biographies.

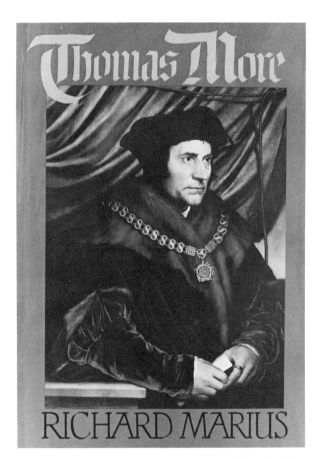

Dust jacket for Marius's biography of More, which resulted from his work on The Complete Works of St. Thomas More *(photo of dust jacket taken by Jerry Morgan Medley)*

The subjects of both biographies by Richard Marius—Martin Luther and Thomas More—are controversial and complex but admired and influential men. The goal of both of these works is to study this complexity in an effort to understand the men and their actions, to resolve the paradoxes if possible, and to consider their places in this modern, technological age.

Luther developed out of Richard Marius's opposition to the Vietnam War and his efforts at that time to teach the Reformation, "presenting Martin Luther to young men and women preoccupied with the gloom and frustration of current events." Walter Kaufmann suggested that Marius contribute to his "series of intellectual biographies," and *Luther* is the result. In his "Editor's Preface," Kaufmann states the three qualifications an author must have to write a new biography of Luther and asserts that Richard Marius has all three: he must, "know Luther's world," "know religion not only from books but firsthand," and "love language and be sensitive to its power."

The biography is basically a chronological look at Martin Luther's life, with a thematic approach when necessary. By carefully depicting Luther in the setting of his age—people, politics, religion, culture—Marius strives to understand, to explain, and, when necessary, to condemn Luther's stands. Since Marius has a general audience in mind, his approach here is less scholarly than the one used in the articles on Thomas More. Although he relies on the primary sources as the basis for his arguments, Marius translates Luther's words into English or summarizes the material. There is no formal documentation, beyond providing the title of a source in the text, but there is a seven-page, heavily annotated, topical bibliography with an introduction at the end of the book. The annotations are often personal—"I disagree mildly"—and quite candid with evaluative descriptions: "plodding," "encyclopedic study," "worshipful," "loving," "superb," "brilliant," "elegant," and "beautifully written." As with his scholarship, Marius assumes full responsibility for his interpretations: "To my mind (and here everyone must study the evidence for himself). . . ." And then he follows with the evidence for his argument.

Since Marius is trying to understand the importance of Martin Luther to the Vietnam generation, he makes extensive use of parallels between Luther's day and more recent times. These comparisons reflect Marius's historical and literary interests: Luther and Marx, Karlstadt (an ally early in Luther's career who became a foe later; his real name was Andreas Bodenstein) and Willy Loman from *Death of a Salesman,* peasants in Luther's day and modern blacks, Luther and William Faulkner—each "a genius with words, always treading to a different drummer pounding a tattoo in his own heart, able in his isolation to grow wild and true to himself." There is a Mencken-like quality in the barbs Marius pens at his age: salesmen, research and academia, modern psychology, hippie communities, Richard Nixon and Joseph McCarthy, diplomacy, bureaucracy, the Bible. His major literary tools in the narrative are the simile and metaphor: Luther's sun in the world's springtime, or the doctrine of purgatory as "a free-floating balloon drifting in the theological sky." Using the metaphor of God's Word as the sun and Scripture as "a vast and complex landscape," Marius explains the distinction Luther makes between God's Word and the Bible.

Marius's biography of Luther has a disconcerting ending. Martin Luther was a courageous leader, "one of the giants in our history, a great hulk of a name heaving itself out of our past with the insistent demand that we pay attention to him," he writes. But if the Church is dead and "Jehovah never was," Luther "perches there in the past like a great pterodactyl. . . ." Then Marius concludes on a very personal note:

> We turn from the study of Luther, the theologian of arcane lore about an arcane deity, knowing that there is no help for us but that residing in our own heads and hearts, and confessing wryly, too, that that help is feeble enough. If there is anything else that his life can teach us, it may well be that all our striving, like his, must finally be hidden in the long cold that comes for great and small alike, and that life at its best and all history, too, are but parts of a process whereby we make our own terms with the dark.

The personal style and conclusion drew attacks from critics. As Marius describes the reactions on a short vita, the book was "angrily reviewed by Lutheran scholars." Many criticized the extensive attention given to Luther's faults and excessive comments about contemporary society. In a review for the popular audience, J. S. Nelson, in *Library Journal,* praised the books as "an interesting, lively, and informative biography for the general reader." In his long analysis for *Christian Century,* Roland H. Bainton praised some points and criticized others, concluding with a personal comment: "I hear in

Marius's book the reverberations of an agonized cry of frustration because the contemporary church has let the author down."

Perhaps equally controversial in scholarly circles, but certainly Marius's most successful work to date, is his biography of Thomas More, published in 1984. The first printing of 7500 copies sold out immediately, necessitating a second printing of 4500; in the *New York Times Book Review* of 17 February 1985, Knopf proclaimed its fourth printing. By the end of the summer of 1985, the fifth printing of the American edition was sold out, and the British edition was in its second printing. The biography was nominated for the American Book Award in nonfiction for 1984.

Thomas More is the culmination of Richard Marius's research on More, the Reformation, and the sixteenth century, begun during graduate work at Yale and intensified during his work as an editor on two of the volumes in the Yale edition of *The Complete Works of St. Thomas More.* Marius summarizes his motivation to study and write about More:

> Once launched on editing More, I realized that there was almost nothing that tried to make sense of the man from the standpoint of what he wrote about religion. . . . I must say, too, that More's character has always been compelling to me. I admire the way he died, making the decision day by day to bring his death into harmony with the way he had lived. And in studying him as closely as I have, I have thought myself better acquainted with the possibilities and the limits of the human condition, and I have felt often that reading him so closely has helped me open a window onto myself.

Stylistically, the biography lies between Marius's erudite essays and his informal, personal *Luther.* The approach to More's life is thematic, with appropriate attention to chronology. The quotations are in modern English. The documentation is relegated to seventeen double-columned pages of notes and four pages of bibliography listing American and European works from 1528 through 1980. In addition, there are sixteen pages of black-and-white illustrations. As in his previous publications on Thomas More, Marius bases his conclusions on primary sources—the words of More (in modern English), correspondence to and from More, and any other relevant writings from More's time. The uniqueness of Marius's qualifications as the biographer of Thomas More is cited in Colin

Campbell's *New York Times* article on the Yale edition of the *Complete Works;* Campbell quotes Marius: "I believe I'm the only biographer of More who has actually read all of More." As Marius says about More's works, particularly his polemical writings, in *Thomas More:* "they open windows into Thomas More's soul, and they reveal an inner torment and tension that make even more imposing the stoic image of himself he presented so doggedly to the world. . . ."

The dichotomy of the public More and the private More is the essence of this biography. Marius's concern about the dual nature of More is sounded as early as 1968 in this description from his essay in *Traditio:* "the dark image standing behind the light cast by the witty, urbane, and talkative gentleman whom Henry VIII delighted to have at his dinner table." Frequently, in recounting the events in More's life, Marius reminds his readers that this division is the thesis of the biography: he refers to "the severely inner conflict of a deeply divided soul" and states that "in him the good and bad were always at war." Marius studies the paradoxes and contradictions in More's life: he personally feared death but favored execution of heretics; he never gave a statement of his reason for refusing the demand of Henry VIII, but he died publicly for the refusal; he married twice, but apparently had ambivalent feelings about marriage, at least for himself (he considered the priesthood); he was driven by pride and ambition, but desired humility ("Few people have enjoyed greater success in advertising their humility"). Furthermore, Marius captures More as the man of wit, intellect, devotion—familial and religious; the attributes are almost endless in Marius's careful portrayal: "exasperating, annoying, loving, hateful, obtuse, brilliant, witty, demanding." Ultimately, the biographer closes with a statement of honest admiration for his subject: "Yet there he stands in our history, an indomitable symbol, and few have known him well without feeling a heart lift up to what he was."

Marius wrote *Thomas More* in the same dramatic and honest style of his earlier works. Not so extensively as in *Luther,* though enough to provoke the objections of a few reviewers, he uses the first-person pronoun to state personal responsibility—"we do not know" or "we may wonder"; and "I can believe," "I have done," "I can shape," or "I can provide"—especially in the introduction and the epilogue. Frequently using the image of More as an actor on stage, Marius records his life against the rich setting of the Renaissance and the nascent Reformation, with the full drama of a fall from power and relative luxury as an official in Henry's court to the straitened existence at Chelsea and finally the hardships in the Tower. And, even for an audience that knows the ending, Marius builds to the climax of the final scene of the scaffold, where, having apparently conquered his fear of death, More gave his best performance.

Except for Robert M. Adams's scathing review in the *New Republic* attacking Marius for "blatant prejudices" and "errors" and some reviewers' concerns that the portrayal of the saint is more negative than positive, reviewers have generally praised Richard Marius for his knowledge of the man and his age and for bringing to the hagiography of Thomas More a balanced portrayal of a heroic but flawed man. As Walker Percy summarized in *USA Today*, "The delight of this splendid, carefully researched and modestly written book is that More the admirable human emerges with all his faults and despite his biographer's doubts about him." Many reviewers have been intrigued with Marius's capturing of More's wit, storytelling (an ability Marius describes as "a talent . . . unsurpassed between Chaucer and Shakespeare"), and irony (Marius discusses More's use of irony at length, to show how that has resulted in varying interpretations of More's words). Margaret Manning's unstinted praise in the *Boston Globe* is typical of the enthusiastic reviews: "Marius' book is one of unrivaled scholarship, felicitously written, and brings to life the intellectual world of the 16th century in England in an encyclopedic and fascinating way. It is a remarkable biography." In his review of *Thomas More* in the *New York Times Book Review*, Paul Johnson reiterates an evaluation applicable to all of Richard Marius's works: "it teaches us history and literature at the same time. . . ."

The three forces of language, history, and a vividly remembered childhood come together again in Marius's novel-in-progress. It builds on the Ledbetter-Weaver subplot from *The Coming of Rain* and pursues the thematic concern with the disruptive effect of an immigrant. As Marius summarized the planned novel in 1977, it tells the story of

> an immigrant who arrives in Bourbonville in the autumn of 1917. He has been wounded fighting in the Belgian army, and now he must make a new existence for himself. His coming unhinges the town. He marries a beautiful woman who is in rebellion against

her mother's stern religion. But when she gives birth to a feeble-minded son, she is driven back into the harsh old faith, and somehow the immigrant must once again remake his life.

As Marius proclaims in his opening sentence of *Luther*, "History is partly autobiography. . . ." And in "The Middle of the Journey," he warns us: "Any historian is perhaps nothing more than a weaver of glittering illusion as fragile as light and as dangerous as poison." And a memorable novelist is perhaps nothing more than a good historian with a love of the language.

References:
Robert M. Adams, "The Many Mores," *New Republic*, 192 (21 January 1985): 38-40;
Roland H. Bainton, "Luther: Builder or Destroyer," *Christian Century*, 92 (19 February 1975): 173-175;
Colin Campbell, "Yale Ends Project on Thomas More," *New York Times*, 16 June 1985, p. 48;
Guy Davenport, "A High-toned and Nutritious First Novel," *Life* (26 September 1969): 16;
G. R. Elton, "The Actor Saint," *New York Review of Books*, 31 January 1985, pp. 7-9;
William B. Hill, S. J., Review of *The Coming of Rain*, *Best Sellers*, 29 (1 November 1969): 281-282;
Paul Johnson, "A Thoroughly Modern Medieval Man," *New York Times Book Review*, 6 January 1985, p. 11;
Maria Karagianis, "Required Writing," *Boston Globe Magazine*, 11 December 1983, pp. 12, 38, 42, 44, 48, 52, 54;
Margaret Manning, "The triumph in tragedy of an uncommon man," *Boston Sunday Globe*, 11 November 1984, pp. A18, A20;
J. S. Nelson, Review of *Luther*, *Library Journal*, 99 (1 December 1974): 3128;
Joyce Carol Oates, Review of *The Coming of Rain*, *New York Times Book Review*, 21 September 1969, p. 5;
Mary O'Neill, "Marius on More: A Survey of Reviews," *Moreana*, 87-88 (1985): 75-82;
Walker Percy, "A man for all seasons in all his complexity," *USA Today*, 14 Decemeber 1984, p. 3D
John S. Reist, Jr., "Sobering Exercise," *Christian Century*, 93 (6 October 1976): 842-843;
"Writing at Harvard," *New York Times*, 20 November 1979, p. B7;
James R. Zazzali, "A man for many seasons," *Commonweal*, 112 (3 May 1985): 286-287.

V. S. Naipaul

(17 August 1932-   )

Joseph Caldwell

BOOKS: *The Mystic Masseur* (London: Deutsch, 1957; New York: Vanguard, 1959);

The Suffrage of Elvira (London: Deutsch, 1958);

Miguel Street (London: Deutsch, 1959; New York: Vanguard, 1960);

A House for Mr Biswas (London: Deutsch, 1961; New York: McGraw-Hill, 1961); republished with author's foreword (New York: Knopf, 1983);

The Middle Passage: Impressions of Five Societies—British, French and Dutch—in the West Indies and South America (London: Deutsch, 1962; New York: Macmillan, 1962);

Mr Stone and the Knights Companion (London: Deutsch, 1963; New York: Macmillan, 1964);

An Area of Darkness (London: Deutsch, 1964; New York: Macmillan, 1965);

The Mimic Men (London: Deutsch, 1967; New York: Macmillan, 1967);

A Flag on the Island (London: Deutsch, 1967; New York: Macmillan, 1967);

The Loss of El Dorado: A History (London: Deutsch, 1969; New York: Knopf, 1970);

In a Free State (London: Deutsch, 1971; New York: Knopf, 1971);

"The Overcrowded Barracoon" and Other Articles (London: Deutsch, 1972; New York: Knopf, 1973);

Guerrillas (London: Deutsch, 1975; New York: Knopf, 1975);

India: A Wounded Civilization (New York: Knopf, 1977; London: Deutsch, 1977);

A Bend in the River (London: Deutsch, 1979; New York: Knopf, 1979);

"The Return of Eva Perón" with "The Killings in Trinidad" (New York: Knopf, 1980; London: Deutsch, 1980);

Among the Believers: An Islamic Journey (New York: Knopf, 1981; London: Deutsch, 1981);

Three Novels (contains *The Mystic Masseur, The Suffrage of Elvira,* and *Miguel Street*) (New York: Knopf, 1983);

Finding the Centre (London: Deutsch, 1984); republished as *Finding the Center* (New York: Knopf, 1984).

PERIODICAL PUBLICATIONS: "Violence in Art: The Documentary Heresy," *Twentieth Century,* 173 (Winter 1964-1965): 107-108;

"A Note on a Borrowing by Conrad," *New York Review of Books,* 29 (16 December 1982): 37-38;

"An Island Betrayed," *Harper's,* 268 (March 1984): 61-72;

"Among the Republicans," *New York Review of Books,* 31 (25 October 1984): 5, 8, 10, 12, 14-17.

"Half the writer's work . . . is the discovery of his subject." With this statement, V. S. Naipaul formulates his purpose as a writer and the object of his craft—the imaginative shaping of experience into an affecting and intelligent narrative that reveals a truth to its writer. Naipaul has pursued his goal vigorously from the earliest days of his career as a writer, when, while freelancing on the BBC radio program "Caribbean Voices," he sat at a borrowed typewriter and typed out the first sentence of the first book he completed, the collection of stories he titled *Miguel Street* (1959).

In his "Prologue to an Autobiography," the first of two personal narratives that make up his latest book, *Finding the Centre* (1984), Naipaul recalls his beginner's lack of confidence that prevented him from numbering his pages and made him single-space the lines he typed to give the illusion of print. He did not want to endanger the delicate quality of feeling that had compelled him to write. That day in the BBC freelance room, Naipaul says, he was lucky; the first sentence of the story "Bogart," simple and full of promise, led to the second, to the third, and on until the story was told. With the encouragement of his colleagues, he wrote enough stories to complete a book and tried to have it published. Though he could not interest a publisher in this work and though he continued

Poster advertising Naipaul's controversial account of Islam in Iran, Pakistan, and Indonesia

to lack confidence in his ability as a writer, Naipaul wrote three novels, his confidence strengthened with each success. Since Naipaul first began writing in 1954, it has been his only profession. He has continued to write, to discover, to learn.

Vidiadhar Surajprasad Naipaul was born 17 August 1932 at the home of his mother's family, Lion House, in the central Trinidad town of Chaguanas. Vidiadhar was the first son and second child of Seepersad and Bropatie Capildeo Naipaul, who had married in 1929. The marriage was an unhappy match. At the time of his son's birth, Seepersad was estranged from his wife and was living in the neighboring town of Montrose.

Seepersad became local correspondent for the *Trinidad Guardian* in 1929. In 1934, under the strains of a public humiliation related to one of his articles written in 1933, disagreement with his wife's family on matters of religion and politics, and his resignation from the *Guardian,* Naipaul suffered a nervous breakdown from which he never fully recovered. For the next four years, he held various jobs around Chaguanas. Naipaul rejoined the *Guardian* staff in 1938 and moved to Port of Spain, where he lived for the rest of his life. He died of a heart attack in 1953.

The move to Port of Spain benefited V. S. Naipaul. There he was enrolled at Tranquility Boys School, where he began the education that eventually got him off the island of Trinidad. Naipaul was an excellent student and sat for one of the classes offering a scholarship. Scoring third highest in the 1942 island-wide competition, he won a free place at Trinidad's Queen's Royal College, where he began attendance in January 1943. Upon his graduation in April 1949, the Trinidad Education Board awarded him a special scholarship to attend college in Great Britain. In 1950 he left Trinidad to take his place at University College, Oxford, where he earned a degree in English in 1954. The death of his father the previous year and the uncertainties of his job with the BBC contributed to the sense of desperation that led him to write, from varied memories of his life on Trinidad, the story that insured his survival as a writer.

"Bogart" is the first in a series of vignettes and recollections narrated by an educated adult who looks back with bitterness upon his boyhood residence on Miguel Street, a poor Port of Spain neighborhood. The narrator reports the behavior of several characters who live on the street—such as Morgan, a pyrotechnician of genius who prefers to be thought of as a funny man; Laura, mother of eight children by seven fathers; and Man-man, the street madman, who, after a religious conversion, undergoes a mock crucifixion. He records his boyhood impressions in an ironically humorous style that gives the impression that, even as a boy, he was more mature than the adults whose behavior he observed and admired. *Miguel Street* has no continuity of plot and relies for unity on the consciousness of the narrator as he grows from awestruck child to restless young man. It chronicles his awakening need to escape from the constraints of a provincial place to the larger world. This accounts for the bitter irony with which the stories are told. The narrator, from a distant place and with the enlightened detachment of education, regrets the unstimulating background that kept him innocent for too long and made his greatest ambition to be nothing more than a man like Hat, the ignorant but charming leading citizen of Miguel Street.

Despite his bitterness the narrator does have sympathy for those who cannot escape their background. Just before he leaves the island to study abroad on scholarship, he answers his mother's charge that he is becoming too wild by saying, "Is just Trinidad. What else anybody could do here except drink?" From his vantage he understands the truth of his statement: a place devoid of possibility does not excite ambition. This knowledge prevents him from falling into a superior contempt of his fellows and helps him to realize that he is not better, but better off, than those he left behind.

Miguel Street, written in 1954 but published in 1959, was given the 1959 Somerset Maugham Award. Typical of its reception was George McMichael's statement in the *San Francisco Chronicle* that "Miguel Street is the Bowery, the Tenderloin, the Catfish Row of Trinidad's Port of Spain— its citizens a loony multitude whose knavery often rises from real kinship with pathos and tragedy. . . ." Most reviewers noted the narrator's sympathy for the poor folk he grew up with, but few commented on his ironic tone.

Ganesh, a character mentioned briefly in *Miguel Street,* became the main character of *The Mystic Masseur* (1957), one of two novels written after but published before *Miguel Street.* It chronicles Ganesh's rise from humble beginnings as a "massager" to fame as a powerful but disillusioned politician. The narrator, a student living in London, recalls his first youthful visit to Ganesh for treatment of a foot injury. Ganesh at this time was a struggling amateur, inept but friendly. As a premium Ganesh had given the boy a book he had written, *101 Questions And Answers On The Hindu Religion,* which later sparked the narrator's interest in Ganesh's career.

His book, really a pamphlet, lent legitimacy to Ganesh's claim that he was a writer. More importantly, it signaled that Ganesh had the ambition and drive to achieve fame.

From writer Ganesh progressed to mystic masseur, from healer of spiritual ills to politician. Ganesh began to eradicate the record of his past once he had won a place on the legislative council; he suppressed his autobiography, *The Years of Guilt,* which accounted for his years as a struggling healer. As his influence and importance grew, his idealism concerning fame and the application of power shriveled. When the narrator meets Ganesh again on a railroad platform in England, he has become G. Ramsay Muir, M.B.E., a man totally corrupted and wearied by his corruption. His fame and power are not what he imagined they would be, and they give him no pleasure. Though saddened that Ganesh has drifted so far from his simple dream of fame, the narrator retains sympathy and admiration for him.

The Mystic Masseur was awarded the John Llewelyn Rhys Memorial Prize in 1958. The *Times Literary Supplement* reviewer remarked, "Naipaul possesses a remarkably acute ear for dialogue and dialect, a pleasantly poker-faced sense of humor, and considerable feeling for, as well as insight into, his characters. At the moment his strength seems to lie in the presentation of individual episodes and scenes, and not to be entirely equal to the strain of a full-length novel. . . ." Naipaul later agreed with this assessment of his early work. Anthony Quinton's appraisal of the book for *New Statesman and Nation*—"Yet another piece of intuitive or slap-happy West Indian fiction as pleasant, muddled and inconsequent as the Trinidadian Hindus it describes"—represented the opinion of reviewers who felt that Naipaul's setting and characters were too exotic for the common reader, and that he was not truly testing his talent by practicing what they considered genre fiction.

The Suffrage of Elvira (1958), the story of an election in an obscure but representative district of Trinidad, offers scathing commentary on the corruption of island politics. Democracy, granted to the island in 1946, "had taken nearly everybody by surprise and it wasn't until 1950, a few months before the second general election under universal adult franchise, that people began to see the possibilities." Surujpat "Pat" Harbans seeks the support of Chittaranjan to gain the Hindu vote and of Baksh for the Muslim vote. Baksh and Chittaranjan assure Harbans that he will have their support—for a price. Harbans's worries over the mercenary

tendencies of his campaign staff are complicated by the influence of two Jehovah's Witnesses who convince the Spanish constituency not to participate in the election, the threat of *obeah* (island witchcraft) incarnated in the miserable pariah dog Tiger, and the cost of bribes to cabdrivers, who threaten to strike on the day of the election if Harbans does not raise their fee. The campaign proves expensive, but, as was expected, Harbans wins.

One episode exemplifies the corruption, absurdity, and cynicism that Naipaul claims characterized local politics in Trinidad at this time. To celebrate his victory, Harbans buys a Jaguar and drives it to the ceremonial presentation of a case of White Horse Scotch whiskey to his campaign staff. At the ceremony a crowd of disaffected (because unbribed) voters who have noted the change in Harbans's attitude toward them—accessible and friendly during his campaign, he now affects a distant and aloof manner toward his supporters—elect one of their number, Jordan, to be the recipient of a symbolic fifty-dollar bribe. "Is not something just for Jordan," Harbans is told. "You could say is a sort of thank-you present for everybody in Elvira. . . . Can't just come to a place and collect people good good vote and walk away. Don't look nice." As Harbans counts out the fifty dollars, his Jaguar is set afire and explodes.

The Suffrage of Elvira received little attention in the United States, nor is it now considered an important work in comparison with Naipaul's later fiction. All three of Naipaul's early books continue to be overshadowed by his masterpiece, *A House for Mr Biswas* (1961). Naipaul has said that his first three books are apprentice work, and, although they share an admirable stylistic proficiency, they are more important in consideration of the work they anticipate than on their own merit. In them Naipaul experiments with the possibilities of plot, character, and setting, and works out his bitterness toward the restrictiveness of Trinidadian life so that he can return to it objectively.

After making his study of shallow but successful men and their ambition, Naipaul turned his attention, in *A House for Mr Biswas,* toward the consideration of an unsuccessful man and the importance of his unremarkable ambition to own a house. "The original idea was simple . . . to tell the story of a man like my father, and . . . to tell the story of the life as the story of the simple possessions by which the man is surrounded at his death. In the writing the book changed. It became the story of a man's search for a house and all that the possession of one's own home implies. . . . The novel, once it had ceased to be an idea and had begun to exist as a novel, called up its own truth."

Naipaul added this statement about the development of his novel to a new edition in 1983. In his foreword he recalls the anxiety and the elation of writing the book. The period of four years between his graduation from University College and beginning work on *A House for Mr Biswas* in 1958 had been an active one for Naipaul. He had written three books, become a freelance editor and writer for the BBC, married Patricia Ann Hale in 1955, changed his place of residence twice, and begun, in 1957, to review fiction for *New Statesman*. Naipaul began "writing toward" the novel late in 1957 and completed it in 1961.

Mr. Biswas enters the world inauspiciously late one evening in his grandmother's house. "Six fingered, and born in the wrong way . . . Whatever you do, this boy will eat up his own mother and father," says the midwife who delivers him. The midwife's prophecy proves true. Mr. Biswas's father, Raghu, drowns while diving to rescue Mr. Biswas, who Raghu mistakenly thinks has fallen into a pool. His mother, Bipti, is forced to sell her house by neighbors who threaten her for the money they think Raghu has buried in the yard.

No longer able to support or house her family, Bipti sends her children away to live with relatives. While his brothers Prasad and Pratap and his sister Dehuti begin lives of servitude, Mr. Biswas is enrolled by his Aunt Tara in school and is later given as an apprentice to the pundit Jairam. After Mr. Biswas profanes Jairam's sacred oleander tree with night soil, Jairam releases him from the apprenticeship. Once again made homeless by people more powerful than he, Mr. Biswas begins to associate ownership of a house with power and security. The strong, he reasons, have a place to go; the weak do not. His position of weakness humiliates him but plants the seed of ambition.

Mr. Biswas returns briefly to his aunt's house to collect his few possessions and goes into the world to make his way as a signwriter. A job at the Tulsi family store in Arwacas leads to his introduction to Shama, the youngest Tulsi daughter, and results in the marriage that changes his life. Mr. Biswas quickly falls into disagreement with the Tulsis; he refuses to do what the family expects of him, though he willingly takes advantage of the amenities it offers. Shama does not appreciate his rebellion; Mr. Biswas resents the responsibilities of marriage and fatherhood. Estranged from his wife and family, he spends his next years roaming the Tulsi' holdings. In his lonely drift, Mr. Biswas re-

turns for comfort to the idea of his own house, a place of which he is master.

His first attempt to build a house leads to a nervous breakdown when the pressures to complete it become too great. Rescued by the Tulsis, he convalesces at Hanuman House, for the first time thankful for its sanctuary. Soon after his recovery, Mr. Biswas resolves to go to Port of Spain, where he intends to live with his sister Dehuti until he has found a job. His only skill is signwriting, but he has a strong desire to be a newspaper writer. One day he marches boldly into the office of the *Trinidad Sentinel* to demand a job as a reporter. The editor, Mr. Burnett, asks him to paint some signs—one of which reads "No Hands Wanted"—in the hope of discouraging him.

Finally Mr. Burnett offers Mr. Biswas a one-month trial without pay, with the understanding that when Mr. Biswas "frightens" his editor with a

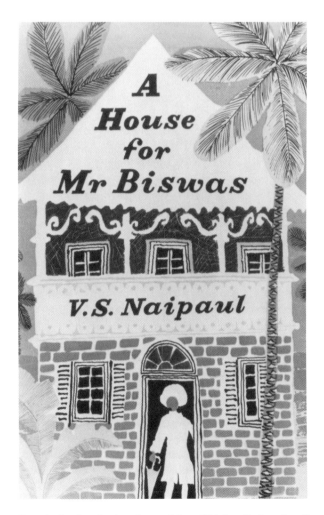

Dust jacket for the American edition of Naipaul's favorite of his novels

truly macabre and sensational story he will be given a salary. The story Mr. Biswas submits wins him the status of top reporter for the paper:

> Within twenty-four hours Mr. Biswas was notorious, the *Sentinel*, reviled on every hand, momentarily increased its circulation, and Mr. Burnett was jubilant.
>
> He said, "You have even chilled me."
>
> The story, the leading one on page three, read:
>
> DADDY COMES HOME IN A COFFIN
> *U.S. Explorer's Last Journey*
> ON ICE
> *by M. Biswas*
>
> Somewhere in America in a neat little red-roofed cottage four children ask their mother every day, "Mummy, when is Daddy coming home?"
> Less than a year ago Daddy—George Elmer Edman, the celebrated traveller and explorer—left home to explore the Amazon.
> Well. I have news for you, kiddies.
> Daddy is on his way home.
> Yesterday he passed through Trinidad. In a coffin.

His notoriety and salary give him the necessary status to return to Hanuman House and reclaim his family. Mrs. Tulsi invites him to live with her in Port of Spain while her son Owad prepares for his college entrance examinations. The strain of rebellion against the family eases, and Mr. Biswas enjoys a brief period of peace that allows him to develop a close relationship with Shama and his children, especially with his son Anand. The happiness is short-lived, however: Mr. Burnett is fired; new, conservative management takes control of the paper; Mr. Biswas is demoted from news writing to funeral coverage. World War II, with rationing, shortages, and salary reductions, brings further disruption.

The run of bad luck and hardship continues when Mr. Biswas accompanies his wife to a communal plantation Mrs. Tulsi has purchased. Here he attempts to raise a second house but fails. Defeated again, Mr. Biswas returns with the Tulsis to the misery of the now-communal Port of Spain house, strengthened in his resolve to escape.

When Owad returns from England a loud and selfish socialist, his abuse of Mr. Biswas and his family causes the final break with the Tulsis. After a particularly violent scene, Mr. Biswas acts on impulse; he borrows three thousand dollars to supplement his own meager savings and—without

first considering his needs or consulting his family—buys the first house that is cleverly presented to him:

> The very day the house was bought they began to see flaws in it. The staircase was dangerous; the upper floor sagged; there was no back door; most of the windows didn't close; one door could not be opened; the celotex panels under the eaves had fallen out and left gaps between which bats could enter the attic. They discussed these things as calmly as they could and took care not to express their disappointment openly. And it was astonishing how quickly they had accommodated themselves to every peculiarity and awkwardness of the house. And once that had happened their eyes ceased to be critical, and the house became simply their house.

Soon after Mr. Biswas moves into the house, he suffers a heart attack that prevents him from working for several months. Worry about repayment of the loan causes his condition to worsen, and a second attack makes him an invalid. Before he dies, Mr. Biswas considers the enormity of his debt and the great gift of that debt, the house: "How terrible it would have been, at this time, to be without it: to have died among the Tulsis, amid the squalor of that large, disintegrating and indifferent family; to have left Shama and the children among them, in one room; worse, to have lived without even attempting to lay claim to one's own portion of the earth; to have lived and died as one had been born, unnecessary and unaccommodated."

With sympathy and clarity, Naipaul gave his simple plot a depth of honesty and universality that won him acclaim as a major novelist. His themes—the sense of homelessness, the frustrations and humiliations of weakness, the price of dreams—are presented with humor and irony, but without bitterness. Naipaul characterizes Mr. Biswas as a simple man overwhelmed at the end of his life by the achievement of a simple dream. His success is great, for, without aid or encouragement, Mr. Biswas has taken control of his life and given his family haven against the buffetings and vagaries of a world indifferent to the weak.

Reviewers admired the work. The reviewer for the *New York Herald Tribune Books* commented that "Naipaul has a wry and an engaging sense of humor, as well as a delicate understanding of sadness and futility and a profound but unobtrusive sense of the tragi-comedy of ordinary living. He is particularly sensitive to the subtle changes which enduring relationships undergo beneath their surface continuity, particularly within a family." Louis Chapin, writing for the *Christian Science Monitor,* noted that Naipaul's style was "explicit, keen for irony, though with a realism that involves some scatological detail."

After he had finished writing *A House for Mr Biswas,* Naipaul began a seven-month, expense-paid tour of the West Indies at the invitation of the Trinidad government. From the journal of his observations in Trinidad, Surinam, British Guiana, and Jamaica, he wrote *The Middle Passage* (1962), a consideration of post-colonial decline. Middle passage was the name slave traders gave the slave-carrying voyages between Africa and the Caribbean. Naipaul used the phrase to describe the effect of three colonial cultures—British, Dutch, and French—upon the recent history of the Caribbean. These three nations established slave trades and slave-labor-based economies in their Caribbean colonies, which they abandoned when agitation, unrest, and distance made their administration impossible. This abandonment, says Naipaul, has been the cause of economic and political difficulty in the Caribbean.

Naipaul had returned to England briefly late in 1961 to write *The Middle Passage.* After its completion he left for a year-long tour of India. While in India he wrote his fourth novel, *Mr Stone and the Knights Companion* (1963), which was awarded the Hawthornden Prize in 1964. His first novel set in England, the book considers the impulse to create and the transforming quality of creation.

Mr. Stone, nearing retirement at age sixty-eight, begins to have disturbing intimations of death which disrupt the placid flow of his life. Reacting impulsively against the idea of his mortality, Mr. Stone marries and, while honeymooning in Cornwall, discovers the cause of his uneasiness. Having lunch at an inn, he and his wife encounter an old man whose retirement has robbed him of his reason to live.

Shaken, Mr. Stone returns home, where he conceives the plan for the Knights Companion, a program to ease the loneliness and spiritual decline caused by retirement. He submits his proposal to Excal, his employer, and it is quickly accepted. Mr. Whymper, a young Research and Development man, turns the proposal for giving retired Excal employees activity and companionship among themselves into a public-relations and personnel-management coup by substituting extended service in the company for retirement benefits. Whymper's

betrayal of Mr. Stone's original intention convinces Mr. Stone that his idea has no value. Concluding that "nothing that came out of the heart, nothing that was pure ought to be exposed," that "all he had done, and even the anguish he was feeling now was a betrayal of that good emotion" he had felt while working in his study to prepare his plan, Mr. Stone rejects the urge to create as disruptive and resigns himself to his approaching retirement.

Reviews of the book were mixed, but Naipaul was being given closer and more respectful reading since the success of *A House for Mr Biswas,* and reviewers appreciated his effort to gain a wider audience by writing about an English character. Naipaul had complained in his 1958 essay "London" that he felt he would have to write about sex, race, or a British or American character before he could hope to gain attention for his work, though he added that to write about sex would embarrass him, that race was too complex an issue, and that the introduction of a British character was "good business, but bad art." Compounding the difficulty of writing an English novel was the difference in temperament between the English and the Caribbeans. Wrote Naipaul, "in a warm country life is conducted out of doors. . . . In England everything goes on behind closed doors."

Naipaul did not understand the closed-door style of conducting business well enough to draw it accurately in *Mr Stone and the Knights Companion.* Walter Allen, in the *New York Review of Books,* noted that the book was "a very odd work that, despite its patent distinction, fails to satisfy. . . . What comes out . . . is the statement of a general truth rather than the vivid apprehension of a particular truth that sets up the shock of recognition in the reader."

Mr. Stone's rejection of the impulse to create marked his exhaustion with the project. Naipaul, at the time he was writing the book, was himself undergoing an exhausting ordeal of rejection. His tour of India, planned as a spiritual pilgrimage to the land of his family's heritage, proved to be a test of endurance that profoundly changed his view of himself and of the world. Naipaul's interest in India had been genealogical and sociological. His grandfather had come from India to Trinidad as an indentured laborer. By returning to India, Naipaul hoped to learn how well Indian sensibilities had survived in the rural Hindu communities of his home. He had rejected the provincial and religious values of his native Trinidad for England but had found no comfortable place for himself in English life or letters, other than his exotic value. India promised affirmation that he belonged to an older, richer culture than the colonial one that had failed to satisfy his needs.

He found instead that he could accept nothing Indian or Hindu. The poverty and squalor horrified him. The caste system, enforced by Hindu tenets of spiritual detachment and acceptance of fate, outraged him. India has not progressed, cannot progress, said Naipaul, because it limits itself too severely by absurd, outdated boundaries of tradition and religion that constrict intellectual growth. Throughout the account of his trip, *An Area of Darkness* (1964), Naipaul repeated his observation angrily, bitterly, and—after a visit to his grandfather's village, where he repudiated his kinship with India—wearily. Naipaul returned to Great Britain near the end of 1963; the trip to India, he concluded, "ought not to have been made; it had broken my life in two."

Naipaul had reached a pivotal point in his career. He had been traveling for nearly three years and had returned to England briefly while he wrote the accounts of his journeys. In London, where he had never truly felt he belonged, he came to the discomfiting realization that he was a former colonial cast adrift. Though critics considered his novels of Trinidad too exotic for the common taste, he had no genuine feeling for the English character. India had made such an overwhelming negative impression on him that he could not set his fiction there. What, then, was to be the subject of his writing? He decided once again to travel and, in 1965, left for Uganda, where he wrote *The Mimic Men* (1967), his first novel on the theme that now dominates his fiction and journalism—the rootlessness and debasing mimicry of the former colonial in a world of decaying values.

Naipaul wrote *The Mimic Men* in the style of a memoir. Ralph Singh, a Caribbean politician in exile, retires to the quiet of his hotel room to record his career. Convinced at the beginning that he can complete his memoir in a few weeks, Singh spends over four months in the writing but manages to find some order in his tumultuous past. He recalls his early days as a restless Caribbean scholarship student in London, where he met Sandra, the English girl whose rejection of her family's class and values had made her feel alien and alone. They had felt the common bond of their alienation and, at Sandra's suggestion, had married. After the wedding, they had returned to Isabella, a fictional island modeled on Trinidad.

Singh next considers the history of his childhood and learns that, as a child, he had been "sunk in the taint of fantasy." From his reading in the history of Aryan migrations, he had created an image of himself as the leader of a warrior horde sweeping on horseback across the plains and snowy steppes of central Asia. This image solaced him against the shame of his father's notoriety as Gurudeva, the charismatic leader of a short-lived political movement which espoused a Hindu pastoral way of life. Though his status as the son of Gurudeva had greatly embarrassed him in his youth, Singh later benefited from it when he entered politics.

Back on Isabella, Singh had made a fortune in real-estate speculation, built a Roman-style house, and become disaffected with the society of the island's affluent aliens. Estrangement and divorce from Sandra had followed, and Singh soon afterward became involved in politics. He notes in his memoir that his life seems to have been an uninterrupted flow of events preparing him for this last great adventure.

Singh's political career had been brief. By playing upon the same cause that his father had championed—an end to the sense of shame at personal defeat and powerlessness—Singh helped elect a Negro schoolmate to the office of minister. But Singh's wealth and Asian heritage had made him suspect to his mostly black colleagues, and, when a crisis arose, they sacrificed him. Dispatched to Great Britain to negotiate a treaty for the nationalization of Isabella's bauxite mines, Singh learned that his party had sent him to be the scapegoat for a failed campaign promise. While he dallied in England with the daughter of a lord, the party circulated rumors that he had taken bribes. Singh returned to Isabella long enough to be expelled from the country with his luggage and a small fraction of his fortune.

The Mimic Men has two themes—the frustration of the former colonial, who feels he can only mimic the example of an established culture, and the power of art to transform disorder into order. Singh discovers the common theme that has characterized his life and learns that, by knowing its cause, he can face the pain and confusion of his life. A prize-winning triumph for Naipaul—the work received the W. H. Smith Award in 1968—*The Mimic Men* impressed many critics. "Mr. Naipaul sees both the futility and the comedy in the lives he portrays. The comedy is subtle, often in the manner of Joyce Cary or Evelyn Waugh, and carefully concealed in a complex fabric of minute observation and of polished expression," wrote Arthur Curley in *Library Journal*.

The *Times Literary Supplement* reviewer called the book "commonwealth literature" and noted that it "discusses, evokes and exemplifies the situation of the former dependencies with such vigour and intensity that the vague, sometimes patronizing description is given a fresh dignity. . . ." Naipaul's reputation as a mature and important commentator on the drift of the modern world was now firmly established.

Naipaul gathered his early short stories and a screen story into the collection *A Flag on the Island* in 1967. The title story was his first attempt to write for the screen, and it was unsuccessful. Set on a nameless island in the Caribbean, "A Flag on the Island" refines the theme of colonial mimicry.

Frank, the American narrator stranded on the island by the approach of Hurricane Irene, recalls that during World War II American soldiers stationed there "brought the tropics to the island."

Dust jacket for the American collection of Naipaul's first three books, including the first publication in the United States of The Suffrage of Elvira

Frank recalls that he had imported his own illicit ideal of free enterprise to a small neighborhood whose residents had quickly turned their own quaintness into lucrative business. Feeling guilty over his responsibility in teaching the natives his American skill for turning a profit and at the same time ending the simple happiness of their lives, Frank becomes obsessed with his idea that the hurricane will destroy the island and restore it to the peace of earlier days.

Naipaul's history of Trinidad, *The Loss of El Dorado* (1969), is based on rare histories of the region and the Venezuelan Boundary Arbitration Papers in the British Museum. Focusing on two incidents from Trinidad's history—the island's use by the Spanish as the launching point for gold-hunting expeditions into South America, and the torture of a slave girl by an English governor of the island—Naipaul presents his argument that Trinidad has never recovered from the rottenness of its past and that the founding principles of greed and cruelty still operate behind the gaiety of its colorful tourist posters. The book is written in the style of a narrative and focuses on the motivation and meaning of actions taken by the Spanish and English in their administration of Trinidad as a colony.

Awarded the Booker Prize in 1971, Naipaul's next work of fiction became widely celebrated as his most brilliant work since *A House for Mr Biswas*. *In a Free State* (1971) is made up of two stories and the title novella set between two episodes from Naipaul's travel journals. This work treats exclusively with the problems of people "in a free state" who pay for their freedom with alienation, loneliness, and a loss of identity.

Santosh, in the story "One Out Of Many," is alarmed to learn that his employer has taken a diplomatic post in Washington, D.C. Although he is uncertain that his job as personal cook will be as highly esteemed in Washington as it is in Bombay, Santosh is certain that if he remains in India he will lose not only his job but his cherished sense of identity. Forsaking Bombay, he convinces his master to take him to the United States. In Washington he learns that he is one among many and that his greatest fear has come to pass; gaining his freedom comes at the cost of his idea of himself: "All that my freedom has brought me is the knowledge that I have a face and have a body, that I must feed this body and clothe this body for a certain number of years. Then it will be over."

"Tell Me Who To Kill," the story of a man who has traded the provincial limitations of his Caribbean home for the uncertainties of London life, has none of the poignant humor of "One Out Of Many." On his brother's wedding day, as he dines with the family of the English bride, he considers the dreams and disappointments of his life that have made him a bitter, ruined man.

"In a Free State," set in Africa, paints an ugly portrait of the expatriate civil servant Bobby, whose homosexuality had set him apart in London and led to a nervous breakdown. Sent to Africa for therapy, Bobby claims that the combination of service to Africa and the adventure of living in a different culture has made him a better man. When a civil war breaks out, Bobby is forced to flee across country to the safety of the consular compound with Linda, the wife of a diplomat. As he berates Linda for her reasons for coming to Africa, it becomes evident that his own motives are less than pure. He exploits Africans and Africa to assuage his guilt and confusion at being outcast because of his homosexuality. Adventure and sexual gratification are his true goals, and he feels that Africa owes him these things in payment for his service. Other expatriates encountered on the trip to the compound seem to have the same selfish notion that service entitles them to abuse Africans with impunity. Bobby's exploitation and abuse are repaid near the end of the story, just as he nears the safety of the compound, when African soldiers savagely beat him.

The prologue and epilogue to *In a Free State*, taken from journal accounts of two different trips to Egypt, serve to draw the separate stories together. The prologue records a trip to Cairo by ship, aboard which Naipaul witnessed the persecution of a graceless old English tramp by his Lebanese, Egyptian, and German bunkmates. The epilogue considers several episodes of a journey to Luxor from Milan. In both cities Naipaul encountered a Red Chinese acrobatic troupe whose presence soothed the anger and sense of futility he had experienced in his dealings with the older civilizations of Italy and Egypt.

In a Free State was followed in publication by *The Overcrowded Barracoon* (1972), a selection of Naipaul's essays and journalism written between 1958 and 1972. The overcrowded barracoon, or temporary slave-holding barracks, of the title is the former French colony of Mauritius, where overpopulation, growing unemployment, and a weak agricultural economy have created a bleak and potentially dangerous political situation for the governments of the island and of France. Other articles survey the political climate of the smaller Caribbean

islands, such as Antigua, Grenada, and St. Kitts. Naipaul also included impressions of his visit to the United States, his early consideration of his place in English letters, and previously uncollected articles about India.

Naipaul's novel *Guerrillas* (1975) is based on ugly actual events he had reported in the article "Michael X and the Black Power Killings in Trinidad," published in 1973. In the novel, Jimmy Ahmed, a Black Power revolutionary, Roche, a white South African activist, and Jane, a white, middle-aged woman caught up in the excitement of political intrigue, become involved with each other in an unsavory relationship of personal gratification and power play. None seems genuinely interested in the revolution Jimmy has started. As an epigraph to the novel, Naipaul quotes from the writing of Jimmy Ahmed: "When everybody wants to fight there's nothing to fight for. Everybody wants to fight his own little war, everybody is a guerrilla." Each character fights his battle at the expense of his professed ideal, but Jane pays the ultimate price for Jimmy's self-aggrandizement and Roche's paralyzing indecision. To regain control of his disintegrating commune, Jimmy reasserts his claim to revolutionary power and demands sacrifices to the cause. Because she is a white woman, and because Roche is considered an enemy, Jane's sexual involvement with both men makes her a convenient victim.

Naipaul wrote in his preface to *"The Return of Eva Perón" with "The Killings in Trinidad"* (1980) that the essays collected there "bridged a creative gap: from the end of 1970 to the end of 1973 no novel offered itself to me." *Guerrillas*, though well written and well made, hardly seems to have offered itself to him. By basing his work on actual events instead of memories of personal experience, as he had done in the past, Naipaul wrote what could be called a historical novel. This may account for the sterility of his presentation. Naipaul's narrative is clinical, disengaged; he expresses neither sympathy nor contempt for his characters and makes it clear that he does not wish to be associated with them in any way. His neutral prose expressed only the absurdity of the historical lesson.

The suspension of India's constitution in 1976 brought Naipaul back for a second consideration of that country the same year. The series of essays he wrote while there was collected under the title *India: A Wounded Civilization* and published in 1977. In his foreword Naipaul explained why his series has such a strong personal focus: "India is for me a difficult country. It isn't my home and cannot be my home; and yet I cannot reject it or be indifferent to it; I cannot travel only for the sights. . . . An inquiry about India . . . has to be an inquiry about attitudes; it has to be an inquiry about the civilization itself." Naipaul concluded that, because in himself there survived "phantasmal memories of old India which . . . outline a whole vanished world," the starting point of his inquiry must be himself.

Naipaul had not forgotten the lesson of his 1962-1963 tour. In *India: A Wounded Civilization*, he further elaborated upon his conclusion that the Indian traditions of caste and Hindu belief are impeding progress there when he described Indian nationalism as a return to archaism. "The sentimental conviction that India is eternal and forever revives," Naipaul contended, serves as the basis for the continuing survival of the caste system, which Indian intellectuals associate with the glories of their history. By returning to the traditions of the past, they feel, India can regain the glory of early days. Naipaul viewed this idea as the greatest failure of the Indian intellectual, for promoting a return to archaic values encourages an indifference not only to failure but to success as well.

This work aroused more controversy than Naipaul's first report, which was not as bitterly condemnatory. Many reviewers questioned the validity of his arguments and the bleakness of his outlook. L. A. Gordon, writing in *Nation*, found Naipaul's "dismissals of Indian efforts . . . much too comprehensive" and cautioned that Naipaul's "view of India is part of a larger pessimistic vision of the human condition today." Shernaz Mollinger called the work "a perceptive, humane, and moral book" after noting that Naipaul's anger seemed "the only possible honorable attitude—one certainly more moral and far healthier than either the Western observer's usual ironic detachment or the Indian's placid acceptance of the continuing human horror that constitutes his country."

An essay he wrote in 1975, "A New King for the Congo: Mobutu and the Nihilism of Africa," formed the basis for Naipaul's novel *A Bend in the River* (1979), currently favored by critics as his best book. It is set in the town of Kisangani, which is modeled on the example of Zaire, and represents the political upheaval of Central Africa. Salim, an East Indian Muslim, comes to Kisangani to open a store he has bought. In the space of the ten years he lives there, Salim watches the rise of the new Africa, personified in Ferdinand, who is taken from the bush, educated at the college called the Do-

main, and sent to the capital to participate in the building of a modern Africa.

Salim had arrived in the town not long after it had been razed by postrevolutionary violence. All reminders that European imperialists had previously built there had been pulled down and the bleak little town of Kisangani had been erected on the ruin. Salim's outlook on the success of the current government is pessimistic, and he hordes ivory for the contingency of flight. At the same time, he begins an affair with the Belgian wife of a professor at the Domain. Forced to flee Kisangani when an impending visit by the president, modeled on Mobutu, panics the incompetent officials whose lives it threatens, Salim makes his escape on a steamboat.

The reviewer in *Choice* wrote that the book "may be the most accurate available single account of what life feels like in parts of Central Africa." Irving Howe noted in the *New York Times Book Review* that *A Bend in the River* was "a much better and deeper novel" than *Guerrillas*—though it lacked the excitement of that novel—because Naipaul had "mastered the gift of creating an aura of psychic and moral tension." Other reviewers praised Naipaul as "one of the best writers now at work," and called the book "a classic dark satire," the effort of a "playful, serious mind at work on the grim stuff of modern life."

Two of the four essays collected in *"The Return of Eva Perón"* formed the bases of Naipaul's two latest novels. "The Return of Eva Perón" is a series of articles written between 1972 and 1977 when Naipaul several times toured South America. The publisher's note adequately summarizes Naipaul's view of Argentine society: "a sterile, second-hand society vandalized by inflation, corruption, and the illusion of being European, where an expensively embalmed Eva Perón is trotted out to glamorize the 'new Perónism.'" In the concluding essay of the collection, "Conrad's Darkness," Naipaul discusses the writer's purpose. He notes that "the novel as a form no longer carries conviction," that "experimentation, not aimed at the real difficulties, has corrupted response." Naipaul feels that the real difficulty for a writer is to make his fiction work, to create from his imagination and experience books that awaken "the sense of true wonder."

In 1979 Naipaul began a seven-month tour of Asia to visit the Islamic states of Pakistan, Malaysia, and Indonesia. Out of this trip came *Among the Believers: An Islamic Journey* (1981). Anecdotal and perceptive, full of sharply drawn characters and rich physical detail, *Among the Believers* nevertheless lacks the sympathy, humor, or the desire to understand different viewpoints that characterized Naipaul's earlier travel writing. His view of Islam as the religion of fanatics who substitute crude faith for reason, who destroy the benefits of Western civilization as satanic only to replace them with their own barbaric code, colors his judgment of everyone he meets and every project he visits. From the opening pages, when he expresses his unhappiness with the man who was to drive him to Qom, Naipaul's dislike and distrust grow.

Reviewers were critical of Naipaul's tone. Fred Halliday noted in *Nation* the "skepticism, which, as in his books about India, frames and sours often acute observation." Halliday added that Naipaul's pessimism caused him to miss "the role that Islam plays not just in the fantasies of intellectuals but in the idealogical consolidation of Third World states. . . . Naipaul underplays or perhaps misses the forms of foreign domination to which the Islamic revival is a deeply felt, if catastrophic, response." R. R. Harris, writing for *Saturday Review,* observed that "Naipaul is . . . a comic writer. When he keeps ironic distance, he tells wonderful, subtle stories that explain why people act the way they do. But when his sense of humor wanes, his bitterness, his impatience, his feeling of superiority become embarrassingly obvious. And this leads to quick sweeping judgments." However, Naipaul's views on Islam may have won him favor in Israel. In April 1983 he was awarded the Jerusalem Prize.

Naipaul's most recent book, *Finding the Centre* (1984), contains two personal narratives that have as their subject "the process of writing" and "seek in different ways to admit the reader to that process." Naipaul's "Prologue to an Autobiography" recounts his beginnings as a writer: "The Crocodiles of Yamoussoukro" is an account of his 1982 visit to the Ivory Coast, an African nation that has enjoyed a stable government for more than twenty years. "The Crocodiles of Yamoussoukro" also tells something about how and why Naipaul travels.

Naipaul undertook his trip to the Ivory Coast primarily to study an African political and economic system that has succeeded for nearly twenty years under black rule, and to enjoy the glamour of France, its mother country, in Africa. These professed reasons soon became secondary as Naipaul became fascinated with manifestations of African belief in the spirit world: the nighttime of power when the spirit leaves the body to accomplish all things; the totemic crocodiles of President Houphouët-Boigny, to which sacrifice is made for the assurance of power; the spirit-exorcising Celestial Christians, who saved the house of a schoolteacher

from burning; the language of ancestral drums which are the seat of tribal power. Naipaul found in this spiritual belief a completeness that he had never before thought existed in Africa and that he could relate to his knowledge of Trinidad's slave culture. His tone of good-humored fascination and openness to ideas he had previously rejected allowed him greater ease with natives and expatriates than he had previously shown and was a marked improvement over the prejudice and impatience of his Islamic tour. His bleak view that the Ivory Coast would, sometime in the future, go the same bloody way that other African nations have gone was not urgently stated and did not overshadow the upbeat spirit of his narrative. Some reviewers noted the change of tone as a mellowing of spirit and ascribed it to either weariness or age—Naipaul turned fifty in 1982.

"Prologue to an Autobiography" is, writes Naipaul, "what its title says. It is not an autobiography, a story of a life or deeds done. It is an account of something less easily seized: my literary beginnings and the imaginative promptings of my many-sided background." Naipaul cast the work in six sections, the first recreating the wretchedness and uncertainty he felt during the writing of his first important story. Included in other sections are a consideration of Naipaul's debt to his father for the desire to become a writer, a report of Naipaul's 1977 visit to the distant relative who inspired the story of Bogart, an investigation of Seepersad Naipaul's breakdown and the part his wife's family played in the humiliation that ended his newswriting career, and a brief sketch of his father's early years in Trinidad. This work is informed by a spirit of wonder that a writer could be made from a many-sided and seemingly unfavorable cultural background.

In recent years Naipaul has gained wider recognition for his work in the United States, with critics expressing great admiration for *In a Free State, Guerrillas, A Bend in the River,* and *Among the Believers.* Edward Hoagland, in his review of *Finding the Centre,* remarks that this is because Naipaul's "previously dependable flaying of the third world nations he visited has made him popular with sectors of the American intellectual community who do not ordinarily pay much attention to contemporary novelists, and he has developed here the odd celebrity of an Erskine Caldwell in Russia: brilliant local portraiture being touted for purposes of disparagement as an accurate picture of a whole continent." However fashionable Naipaul's bitterness toward Islam or the bleakness of his vision of the Third World's future may be in the United States, or however unpopular in the rest of the world, fashion is neither the purpose nor the concern of his art. His opinions are those of a curious, intelligent, apolitical outsider who cannot and will not be deluded. Hoagland notes that Naipaul often "thinks through his companions' opinions more precisely than they themselves have done," that he is "both merciless and emphatic as he watches," that he "asks the simplest questions." Naipaul travels and writes to find the center of motivation—of nations and of himself. If observation proves that bitterness and bleakness of opinion seem warranted, that is what he expresses, as clearly and concisely as he knows how.

Since 1961, when he first began to travel, Naipaul's range of interest has broadened but his world view has grown bleaker; the troubled Third World nations he has visited have taxed his sensibilities and, perhaps, worn him out with anger and frustration that the Western civilization he loves has not benefited but beleaguered these nations. He has said many times that he has become an intelligent writer rather than an emotional one because he wishes to protect himself from the violence of his reaction to what he has seen. The characters he has created in later novels, such as Roche in *Guerrillas* and Salim in *A Bend in the River,* share a weariness, a pessimism, a confusion that limits the range of their response to the tumult of their worlds. Both seem capable only of preparing for the fall of doom and waiting for their slim chance to escape ruin. And though they escape, they surrender vitality to caution and settle into restricted, joyless lives.

Naipaul's fiction after 1961 has almost inevitably become less humorous, and he regrets this. In his foreword to the 1983 edition of *A House for Mr Biswas,* a work that contains, he says, "some of my funniest writing," Naipaul admits that he has "no higher literary ambition than to write a piece of comedy that might complement or match this early book." The humor of his books prior to 1961—an emotional comment on the ironies and difficulties of his early life on Trinidad—has a vitality that allows his characters a wider, more accommodating response to hardship.

Finding the Centre reveals humor, compassion, open-hearted sympathy, and open-minded interest that have long been absent from Naipaul's writing. He seems willing, if not eager, to believe that childhood on Trinidad may have helped him more than

he thought in his ambition to be a writer, that life there gave him the special vision that characterizes his writing. He seems ready and able, after years of bleak pessimism, to write comically again. And reaching middle age has encouraged him to look back not nostalgically but thoughtfully on the influences of his past: "To write was to learn. Beginning a book, I always felt I was in possession of all the facts about myself; at the end I was always surprised." Though the surprise has not always been a pleasant one for him, it has always made worthwhile the hard half of a writer's job, the discovery of himself.

References:

Michael Gilkes, *The West Indian Novel* (Boston: G. K. Hall, 1981), pp. 91-102;

Robert Hamner, *Critical Perspectives on V. S. Naipaul* (Washington, D.C.: Three Continents Press, 1977);

Hamner, *V. S. Naipaul* (New York: Twayne, 1973);

Bruce King, "V. S. Naipaul," in *West Indian Literature,* edited by King (Hamden, Conn.: Archon Books, 1979), pp. 161-178;

Kerry McSweeny, "V. S. Naipaul: Clear-sightedness and Sensibility," in his *Four Contemporary Novelists* (Kingston & Montreal: McGill-Queen's University Press, 1983), pp. 151-195;

Karl Miller, "V. S. Naipaul and the New Order: A View of *The Mimic Men,*" in *Critics on Caribbean Literature,* edited by Edward Baugh (New York: St. Martin's Press, 1978), pp. 75-83;

Modern Fiction Studies, 30 (Autumn 1984), Naipaul number;

Robert K. Morris, *Paradoxes of Order: Some Perspectives on the Fiction of V. S. Naipaul* (Columbia: University of Missouri Press, 1975);

David Omerod, " 'Unaccommodated Man': Naipaul's B. Wordsworth and Biswas," in *Critics on Caribbean Literature,* edited by Baugh (New York: St. Martin's Press, 1978), pp. 87-92;

Kenneth Ramchand, "A House for Mr Biswas," in his *An Introduction to the Study of West Indian Literature* (Kingston: Thomas Nelson and Sons, Ltd., 1976);

Michael Thorpe, *V. S. Naipaul* (Essex: Longman Group, Ltd., 1976);

William Walsh, *V. S. Naipaul* (Edinburgh: Oliver & Boyd, 1973);

Landeg White, *V. S. Naipaul: A Critical Introduction* (London: Macmillan, 1975).

Literary Awards and Honors Announced in 1985

ACADEMY OF AMERICAN POETS AWARDS

ACADEMY OF AMERICAN POETS
FELLOWSHIP
Maxine Kumin.

LAMONT SELECTION
Cornelius Eady for *Victims of the Latest Dance Craze* (Ommation).

IVAN YOUNGER POETS AWARD
Diane Ackerman, Michael Blumenthal, Richard Kenney.

WHITMAN AWARD
Christianne Balk, for *Bindweed* (Macmillan).

AMERICAN ACADEMY AND INSTITUTE OF ARTS AND LETTERS AWARDS

AWARDS IN LITERATURE
Alan Dugan, Maria Irene Fornes, George Garrett, Carolyn Kizer, Gilbert Sorrentino, Paul West, John Williams, Paul Zimmer.

GOLD MEDAL FOR POETRY
Robert Penn Warren.

HAROLD D. VURSELL MEMORIAL AWARD
Harriett Doerr.

JEAN STEIN FICTION AWARD
George W. S. Trow.

MORTON DAUWEN ZABEL AWARD
Stanley Clavell.

RICHARD AND HINDA ROSENTHAL
FOUNDATION AWARD
Janet Kaufman.

ROME FELLOWSHIP IN LITERATURE
Oscar Hijuelos.

SUE KAUFMAN PRIZE FOR FIRST FICTION
Louise Erdrick.

WITTER BYNNER PRIZE FOR POETRY
J. D. McClatchy.

DISTINGUISHED SERVICE AWARD
Senator Claiborne Pell.

SPECIAL CITATION
William Shawn.

MERIT AWARD
Richard Stern.

AMERICAN BOOK AWARDS

FICTION
Don DeLillo, for *White Noise* (Elisabeth Sifton/Viking).

NONFICTION
J. Anthony Lukas, for *Common Ground* (Knopf).

FIRST FICTION
Bob Schacochis, for *Easy in the Islands* (Crown).

BANCROFT PRIZES IN HISTORY

Suzanne Lebstock, for *The Free Women of Petersburg* (Norton); Kenneth Silverman, for *The Life and Times of Cotton Mather* (Columbia University Press).

BANTA AWARD

Margot Peters, for *Mrs. Pat: The Life of Mrs. Patrick Campbell* (Knopf).

BAY AREA BOOK REVIEWERS ASSOCIATION AWARDS

FICTION
Harriett Doerr, for *Stones for Ibarra* (Viking).

BELLES LETTRES
Robert Hass, for *Twentieth Century Pleasures* (Ecco).

CONTEMPORARY ISSUES
Orville Schell, for *Modern Meat* (Random House).

POETRY
Czeslaw Milosz, for *The Separate Notebooks* (Ecco).

CHILDREN'S LITERATURE
Mavis Jukes, for *Like Jake and Me* (Knopf).

FRED CODY AWARD
Robert Duncan, for lifetime literary excellence and community involvement.

PUBLISHERS AWARD
Sierra Club Books.

BENNETT AWARD

Anthony Powell.

BOLLINGEN PRIZE IN POETRY

John Ashbery and Fred Chappell.

BOOKER PRIZE

Keri Hulme, for *The Bone People* (Hodder & Stoughton).

CALDECOTT MEDAL

Trina Schart Hyman, for illustrations for *Saint George and the Dragon*, as retold by Margaret Hodges (Little, Brown).

JOHN W. CAMPBELL AWARD

Lucius Shepard.

CAREY-THOMAS PUBLISHING AWARD

Vintage Books, for the Vintage Contemporary Series.

HONORS CITATIONS
E. P. Dutton, for Obelisk Books, edited by Bill Whitehead; Harcourt Brace Jovanovich, for *The Letters of Virginia Woolf* and *The Diaries of Virginia Woolf.*

COMMON WEALTH AWARD

Max Frisch.

CURTIS G. BENJAMIN AWARD

Frederick J. Ruffner, Gale Research Company.

DELMORE SCHWARTZ MEMORIAL POETRY AWARD

Edward Hirsch.

DRUE HEINZ LITERATURE PRIZE

W. D. Wetherell, for *The Man Who Loved Levittown* (University of Pittsburgh Press).

EDGAR ALLAN POE AWARDS

GRAND MASTER AWARD
Dorothy Salisbury Davis.

ELLERY QUEEN AWARD
Joan Kahn.

NOVEL
Ross Thomas, for *Briarpatch* (Simon & Schuster).

FIRST NOVEL
R. D. Rosen, for *Strike Three, You're Dead* (Walker).

FACT CRIME
    Mike Weiss, for *Double Play: The San Francisco City Hall Killings* (Addison-Wesley).

CRITICAL/BIOGRAPHICAL
    Jon L. Breen, for *Novel Verdicts: A Guide to Courtroom Fiction* (Scarecrow Press).

ORIGINAL SOFTCOVER NOVEL
    Warren Murphy and Molly Cochran, for *Grandmaster* (Pinnacle).

JUVENILE NOVEL
    Phyllis Reynolds Naylor, for *Night Cry* (Atheneum).

SHORT STORY
    Lawrence Block, for "By Dawn's Early Light," in *Playboy* and *The Eyes Have It* (Mysterious Press).

MOTION PICTURE
    Charles Fuller, for screenplay for *A Soldier's Story* (Columbia Pictures).

READER OF THE YEAR
    Eudora Welty.

HUGO AWARDS

NONFICTION BOOK
    Jack Williamson, for *Wonder's Child: My Life in Science Fiction* (Bluejay).

NOVEL
    William Gibson, for *Neuromancer* (Ace).

NOVELLA
    John Varley, for "PRESS ENTER," in *Isaac Asimov's Science Fiction Magazine*.

NOVELETTE
    Octavia E. Butler, for "Bloodchild," in *Isaac Asimov's Science Fiction Magazine*.

SHORT STORY
    David Brin, for "The Crystal Spheres," in *Analog*.

INGERSOLL PRIZES

T. S. ELIOT AWARD FOR CREATIVE WRITING
    Eugène Ionesco.

RICHARD M. WEAVER AWARD FOR SCHOLARLY LETTERS
    Robert Nisbet.

IRITA VAN DOREN AWARD

Ian and Betty Ballantine.

IRMA SIMONTON BLACK AWARD

Chris Van Allsburg, for *The Mysteries of Harris Burdick* (Houghton Mifflin).

JERUSALEM PRIZE

Milan Kundera.

JOHN DOS PASSOS PRIZE FOR LITERATURE

Russell Banks.

KENNETH B. SMILEN AWARDS

FICTION
    Saul Bellow, for *Him With His Foot in His Mouth and Other Stories* (Harper & Row).

BIOGRAPHY/AUTOBIOGRAPHY
    Primo Levi, for *The Periodic Table* (Schocken).

SOCIAL AND POLITICAL ANALYSIS
    Benjamin Pincus, for *The Soviet Government and the Jews, 1948-1967* (Cambridge University Press/Hebrew University of Jerusalem and Institute of Contemporary Jewry).

HISTORY
    Naomi W. Cohen, for *Encounter with Emancipation, the German Jews of the United States, 1830-1914* (Jewish Publication Society of America).

JEWISH RELIGIOUS THOUGHT

Rachel Biale, for *Women and Jewish Law* (Schocken).

TRANSLATION

Seymour Feldman, for *The Wars of the Lord, Book One—Immortality of the Soul* (Jewish Publication Society).

GENERAL NONFICTION

Lucjan Dobroszycki, editor, *The Chronicle of the Lodz Ghetto, 1941-1944* (Yale University Press).

JUVENILE

Kenneth Roseman, for *The Melting Pot* (Union of American Hebrew Congregations).

ART

Avram Kampf, for *Jewish Experience in the Art of the Twentieth Century* (Bergin & Garvey).

LENORE MARSHALL NATION PRIZE

John Ashbery, for *Wave* (Viking).

LOS ANGELES TIMES BOOK AWARDS

BIOGRAPHY

Michael Scammell, for *Solzhenitsyn* (Norton).

CURRENT INTEREST

Robert N. Bellah, Richard Madsen, William M. Sullivan, Ann Swidler, and Steven M. Tipton, for *Habits of the Heart* (University of California Press).

FICTION

Louise Erdrich, for *Love Medicine* (Holt, Rinehart & Winston).

HISTORY

Evan S. Connell, for *Son of the Morning Star* (North Point Press).

POETRY

X. J. Kennedy, for *Cross Ties* (University of Georgia Press).

ROBERT KIRSCH AWARD FOR BODY OF WORK

Janet Lewis.

MEDAL OF HONOR FOR LITERATURE

Joseph Campbell.

NATIONAL BOOK CRITICS CIRCLE AWARDS

FICTION

Louise Erdrich, for *Love Medicine* (Holt, Rinehart & Winston).

GENERAL NONFICTION

Freeman Dyson, for *Weapons and Hope* (Harper & Row).

POETRY

Sharon Olds, for *The Dead and the Living* (Knopf).

CRITICISM

Robert Hass, for *Twentieth Century Pleasures* (Ecco).

BIOGRAPHY

Joseph Frank, for *Dostoevsky: The Years of Ordeal 1850-1859* (Princeton University Press).

CITATION FOR EXCELLENCE IN REVIEWING

Alida Becker, *Philadelphia Inquirer and St. Petersburg Times*.

IVAN SANDROF/BOARD AWARD

Library of America, "for its ongoing publication of American classics in compact permanent editions."

NATIONAL JEWISH BOOK AWARDS

MOSES LEO GITELSON AWARD FOR BIOGRAPHY

Maurice Friedman, for *Martin Buber's Life and Work: The Later Years 1945-1965* (Dutton).

WILLIAM (ZEV) FRANK MEMORIAL AWARD FOR CHILDREN'S LITERATURE

Gary Provost and Gail Levine-Freidus, for *Good If It Goes* (Bradbury Press).

WILLIAM AND JANICE EPSTEIN AWARD FOR FICTION

Frederick Busch, for *Invisible Mending* (David R. Godine).

LEON JOLSON AWARD FOR HOLOCAUST LITERATURE

David S. Wyman, for *The Abandonment of the Jews: America and the Holocaust 1941-1945* (Pantheon).

MARCIA AND LOUIS POSNER AWARD FOR ILLUSTRATED CHILDREN'S BOOKS

Amy Schwartz, for *Mrs. Moskowitz and the Sabbath Candlesticks* (Jewish Publication Society).

MORRIS J. AND BETTY KAPLUN MEMORIAL AWARD FOR ISRAEL LITERATURE

Joan Peters, for *From Time Immemorial: The Origins of the Arab-Jewish Conflict Over Palestine* (Harper & Row).

GERRARD AND ELLA BERMAN AWARD FOR JEWISH HISTORY

Naomi W. Cohen, for *Encounter with Emancipation: The German Jews in the United States, 1830-1914* (Jewish Publication Society).

FRANK AND ETHEL S. COHEN AWARD FOR JEWISH THOUGHT

Joseph B. Soloveitchik, for *Halakhic Man*, translated by Lawrence Kaplan (Jewish Publication Society).

SARAH H. KUSHNER MEMORIAL AWARD FOR SCHOLARSHIP

Seymour Feldman, translator, for *The Wars of the Lord: Book One—Immortality of the Soul*, by Levi Ben Gershom (Gersonides).

LEON L. GILDESGAME AWARD FOR VISUAL ARTS

Evelyn M. Cohen, for *The Rothschild Mahzor: Florence, 1492* (Library/Jewish Theological Seminary of America).

THE WORKMEN'S CIRCLE AWARD FOR YIDDISH LITERATURE

Shea Tenenbaum, for *Fun Ash Un Fayer Iz Dayn Kroyn/From Ash and Fire Is Your Crown* (CYCO).

NEBULA AWARDS

NOVEL

William Gibson, for *Neuromancer* (Ace Books).

NOVELLA

John Varley, for "PRESS ENTER," in *Isaac Asimov's Science Fiction Magazine*.

NOVELETTE

Octavia E. Butler, for "Bloodchild," in *Isaac Asimov's Science Fiction Magazine*.

SHORT STORY

Gardner Dozois, for "Morning Child," in *Omni*.

NEW VOICE AWARD

Susan Kenney, for *Another Country* (Viking Penguin).

NEWBERY MEDAL

Robin McKinley, for *The Hero and the Crown* (Greenwillow).

NOBEL PRIZE IN LITERATURE

Claude Simon.

O. HENRY AWARDS

Stuart Dybek, for "Hot Ice," and Jane Smiley, for "Lily."

RITZ PARIS HEMINGWAY AWARD

Mario Vargas Llosa, for *The War of the End of the World* (Farrar, Straus & Giroux).

PEN AWARDS

PEN/FAULKNER AWARD

Tobias Wolff, for *The Barracks Thief* (Ecco).

HEMINGWAY AWARD FOR FIRST FICTION

Josephine Humphreys, for *Dreams of Sleep* (Viking Penguin).

PEN MEDAL FOR TRANSLATION
Richard Howard, for the body of his work.

PEN TRANSLATION PRIZE FOR POETRY
Seamus Heaney, for *Sweeny Astray* (Farrar, Straus & Giroux).

PEN TRANSLATION PRIZE FOR PROSE
Helen R. Lane, for *The War of the End of the World* by Mario Vargas Llosa (Farrar, Straus & Giroux).

POGGIOLI TRANSLATION AWARD FOR A WORK IN PROGRESS
Ann Snodgrass, for *Fifteen Poems of Vittorio Sereni.*

NELSON ALGREN FICTION AWARD FOR WORK IN PROGRESS
Mary Bush.

PHILIP K. DICK MEMORIAL AWARD

William Gibson, for *Neuromancer* (Ace).

PRESENT TENSE AWARDS

FICTION
A. B. Yehoshua, for *A Late Divorce* (Doubleday).

HISTORY
David S. Wyman, for *The Abandonment of the Jews: America and the Holocaust* (Pantheon).

BIOGRAPHY/AUTOBIOGRAPHY
Primo Levi, for *The Periodic Table* (Schocken).

RELIGIOUS THOUGHT
Samuel Heilman, for *The Gate Behind the Wall: A Pilgrimage to Jerusalem* (Summit).

TRANSLATION
Raymond Rosenthal, for *The Periodic Table*, by Primo Levi (Schocken).

SPECIAL CITATION
Roman Vishniac, for *A Vanished World* (Farrar, Straus & Cudahy).

PRESIDENT'S FELLOWS AWARD

Maurice Sendak.

PULITZER PRIZES

FICTION
Alison Lurie, for *Foreign Affairs* (Random House).

GENERAL NONFICTION
Studs Terkel, for *The Good War: An Oral History of World War II* (Pantheon).

HISTORY
Thomas K. McCraw, for *The Prophets of Regulation* (Belknap/Harvard University Press).

BIOGRAPHY
Kenneth Silverman, for *The Life and Times of Cotton Mather* (Harper & Row).

POETRY
Carolyn Kizer, for *Yin* (Boa Editions).

DRAMA
James Lapine and Stephen Sondheim, for *Sunday in the Park with George.*

ROBERT F. KENNEDY MEMORIAL BOOK AWARD

FIRST PRIZE
Raymond Bonner, for *Weakness and Deceit: U. S. Policy and El Salvador* (Times Books).

HONORABLE MENTION
David H. Bain, for *Sitting in Darkness: Americans in the Philippines* (Houghton Mifflin); and Joel Williamson, for *The Crucible of Race* (Oxford University Press).

WESTERN STATES BOOK AWARDS

FICTION
Alberto Alvaro Rios, for *The Iguana Killer* (Blue Moon Press).

LIFETIME ACHIEVEMENT
Eve Triem, for *New as a Wave: A Retrospective: 1937-1983* (Dragon Gate).

NONFICTION
Clyde Rice, for *A Heaven in the Eye* (Breitenbush Books).

POETRY
Nancy Mairs, for *In All the Rooms of the Yellow House* (Blue Moon Press).

WESTERN WRITERS OF AMERICA GOLDEN SPUR AWARDS

SADDLEMAN TROPHY LIFETIME
ACHIEVEMENT AWARD.
Leon C. Metz.

STIRRUP AWARD FOR BEST ROUNDUP
ARTICLE
Nellie Yost, for "The Endless Trail," in *Roundup*, March and April 1984.

MEDICINE PIPE BEARER AWARD FOR BEST
FIRST WESTERN NOVEL
Craig Lesley, for *Winterkill* (Houghton Mifflin).

BEST HISTORICAL NOVEL
Douglas C. Jones, for *Gone the Dreams and Dancing* (Holt, Rinehart & Winston).

BEST WESTERN NONFICTION
Stella Hughes, for *Hashknife Cowboy: Recollections of Mack Hughes* (University of Arizona Press).

BEST WESTERN SHORT SUBJECT/FICTION
Paul St. Pierre, for "Sale of One Small Ranch," in *Smith and Other Events* (Beaufort Books).

BEST WESTERN SHORT SUBJECT/
NONFICTION
Francis L. Fugate, for "Arbuckle's: The Coffee That Won the West," in *American West*.

SPECIAL SPUR AWARD
Dale L. Walker, for five-year editorship of the *Roundup*.

W. H. SMITH LITERARY AWARD

David Hughes, for *The Pork Butcher* (Constable).

WHITING AWARDS

Raymond Abbot, for *Death Dances* (Applewood); Douglas Crase, for *The Revisionist* (Little, Brown); Stuart Dybek, for *Childhood and Other Neighborhoods* (Viking); Jorie Graham, for *Erosion* (Princeton University Press); Linda Gregg, for *Too Bright to See* (Graywolf); Wright Morris, for *A Cloak of Light* (Harper & Row); Howard Norman, for *The Northern Lights* (Summit Books); James Robison, for *Rumor and Other Stories* (Summit Books); Austin Wright, for *The Morley Mythology* (Harper & Row).

Checklist: Contributions to Literary History and Biography, 1985

This checklist is a selection of new books on various aspects and periods of literary and cultural history; biographies, memoirs, and correspondence of literary people and their associates; and primary bibliographies. Not included are volumes in general reference series, literary criticism, and bibliographies of criticism.

Agee, James. *James Agee: Selected Journalism.* Edited by Paul Ashdown. Knoxville: University of Tennessee, 1985.

Aleichem, Sholom. *From the Fair: The Autobiography of Sholom Aleichem.* Translated and edited by Curt Leviant. New York: Viking, 1985.

Anderson, Sherwood. *Letters to Bab: Sherwood Anderson to Marietta D. Finley, 1916-33.* Edited by William A. Sutton. Urbana: University of Illinois Press, 1985.

Barnes, Melvyn. *Dick Francis.* New York: Ungar, 1985.

Bates, Milton J. *Wallace Stevens.* Berkeley: University of California Press, 1985.

Beaumont, Barbara, ed. & trans. *Flaubert and Turgenev: A Friendship in Letters.* Norton, 1985.

Bowles, Jane. *Out in the World: Selected Letters of Jane Bowles, 1935-1970.* Edited by Millicent Dillon. Santa Barbara, Cal.: Black Sparrow Press, 1985.

Boyle, Kay. *Words That Must Somehow Be Said: Selected Essays of Kay Boyle, 1927-1984.* Edited by Elizabeth S. Bell. Berkeley, Cal.: North Point, 1985.

Burgess, Anthony. *Ernest Hemingway and His World.* New York: Scribners, 1985.

Castronovo, David. *Edmund Wilson.* New York: Ungar, 1985.

Clemens, Susy. *Papa: An Intimate Biography of Mark Twain by His Daughter, Susy, Age Thirteen.* Edited by Charles Neider. Garden City: Doubleday, 1985.

Connolly, Joseph. *Modern First Editions: Their Value to Collectors.* Manchester, N.H.: Salem House, 1985.

De-la-Noy, Michael. *Denton Welch: The Making of a Writer.* New York: Viking, 1985.

Dormann, Geneviève. *Colette: A Passion for Life.* New York: Abbeville, 1985.

Eble, Kenneth E. *Old Clemens and W. D. H.: The Story of a Remarkable Friendship.* Baton Rouge: Louisiana State University Press, 1985.

Eliot, George. *Selections From George Eliot's Letters.* Edited by Gordon S. Haight. New Haven: Yale University Press, 1985.

Falk, Quentin. *Travels in Greenland: The Cinema of Graham Greene.* Salem, N.H.: Quartet Books, 1985.

Fenton, James. *You Were Marvellous: Theatre Reviews from the Sunday Times.* London: Cape, 1985.

Flanner, Janet. *Darlinghissima.* Edited by Natalia Danesi Murray. New York: Random House, 1985.

Forster, E. M. *Selected Letters of E. M. Forster, Volume Two: 1921-1970.* Edited by Mary Lago and P. N. Furbank. Cambridge: Belknap/Harvard University Press, 1985.

Frank, Elizabeth. *Louise Bogan: A Portrait.* New York: Knopf, 1985.

Garnett, Angelica. *Deceived With Kindness: A Bloomsbury Childhood.* New York & San Diego: Harcourt Brace Jovanovich, 1985.

Gilbert, Sandra M., and Susan Gubar, eds. *The Norton Anthology of Literature by Women.* New York: Norton, 1985.

Goreau, Angeline. *The Whole Duty of a Woman: Female Writers in Seventeenth-Century England.* New York: Dial/Doubleday, 1985.

Gresset, Michel. *A Faulkner Chronology.* Jackson: University of Mississippi Press, 1985.

Griffin, Peter. *Along with Youth: Hemingway, The Early Years.* New York: Oxford University Press, 1985.

Grigson, Gregory. *Recollections: Mainly of Artists and Writers.* London: Chatto & Windus, 1985.

Grobel, Lawrence. *Conversations with Capote.* New York: New American Library, 1985.

Guinness, Jonathan. *The House of Mitford.* New York: Viking, 1985.

Hart-Davis, Rupert, ed. *The Lyttelton Hart-Davis Letters, Volume 2, 1956-57.* Chicago: Academy Chicago, 1985.

Higham, Charles. *Orson Welles: The Rise and Fall of an American Genius.* New York: St. Martin's, 1985.

Hillier, Jim, ed. *Cahiers du Cinema: The 1950s: Neo-Realism, Hollywood, New Wave.* Cambridge: Harvard University Press, 1985.

Hilton, Tim. *John Ruskin: The Early Years.* New Haven: Yale University Press, 1985.

Hoopes, Roy. *Ralph Ingersoll: A Biography.* New York: Atheneum, 1985.

Hull, Gloria T., ed. *Give Us Each Day: The Diary of Alice Dunbar-Nelson.* New York: Norton, 1985.

Hurston, Zora Neale. *Dust Tracks on a Road.* Edited by Robert Hemenway. Urbana: University of Illinois, 1985.

Jarrell, Randall. *Randall Jarrell's Letters.* Edited by Mary Jarrell with Stuart Wright. Boston: Houghton Mifflin, 1985.

Koestler, Mamaine. *Living with Koestler: Mamaine Koestler's Letters 1945-51.* Edited by Celia Goodman. New York: St. Martin's, 1985.

Kohfeldt, Mary Lou. *Lady Gregory: The Woman Behind the Irish Renaissance.* New York: Atheneum, 1985.

Lauber, John. *The Making of Mark Twain.* Boston: American Heritage/Houghton Mifflin, 1985.

Lawson, Lewis A., and Victor A. Kramer. *Conversations with Walker Percy.* Jackson: University of Mississippi Press, 1985.

Levy, David W. *Herbert Croly of the* New Republic: *The Life and Thought of an American Progressive.* Princeton: Princeton University Press, 1985.

Lyndall, Gordon. *Virginia Woolf: A Writer's Life.* New York: Norton, 1985.

MacShane, Frank. *Into Eternity: James Jones, the Life of an American Writer.* Boston: Houghton Mifflin, 1985.

Manley, Frank, and Floyd C. Watkins. *Some Poems and Some Talk About Poetry.* Jackson: University Press of Mississippi, 1985.

Manso, Peter. *Mailer: His Life and Times.* New York: Simon & Schuster, 1985.

Marsh, Jan. *The Pre-Raphaelite Sisterhood.* New York: St. Martin's, 1985.

Martin, Robert Bernard. *With Friends Possessed: A Life of Edward FitzGerald.* New York: Atheneum, 1985.

Masefield, John. *John Masefield's Letters from the Front 1915-17.* Edited by Peter Vansittart. New York: Franklin Watts, 1985.

Materer, Timothy. *Pound/Lewis: The Letters of Ezra Pound and Wyndham Lewis.* New York: New Directions, 1985.

Meisel, Perry, and Walter Kendrick, eds. *Bloomsbury/Freud: The Letters of James and Alix Strachey, 1924-1925.* New York: Basic Books, 1985.

Merton, Thomas. *The Hidden Ground of Love: The Letters of Thomas Merton on Religious Experience and Social Concerns.* Edited by William H. Shannon. New York: Farrar, Straus & Giroux, 1985.

Meyers, Jeffrey. *Hemingway: A Biography.* New York: Harper & Row, 1985.

Morgan, Janet. *Agatha Christie: A Biography.* New York: Knopf, 1985.

Morris, Wright. *A Cloak of Light: Writing My Life.* New York: Harper & Row, 1985.

Munson, Gorham. *The Awakening Twenties: A Memoir-History of a Literary Period.* Edited by Elizabeth Munson. Baton Rouge: Louisiana State University Press, 1985.

Nin, Anaïs. *The Early Diary of Anais Nin: Volume Four 1927-1937.* Preface by Joachin Nin-Culmell. New York & San Diego: Harcourt Brace Jovanovich, 1985.

Nord, Deborah Epstein. *The Apprenticeship of Beatrice Webb.* Amherst: University of Massachusetts, 1985.

Oates, Joyce Carol. *The Profane Art: Essays and Reviews.* New York: Persea, 1985.

Orwell, George. *George Orwell: The Lost Writings*. Edited by W. J. West. New York: Arbor House, 1985.

Pasternak, Boris, Rainer Maria Rilke, and Marina Tsvetayeva. *Letters: Summer 1926*. Edited by Yevgeny Pasternak, Yelena Pasternak, and Konstantin M. Azadovsky. Translated by Margaret Wettlin and Walter Arndt. New York & San Diego: Harcourt Brace Jovanovich/Helen and Kurt Wolff, 1985.

Payne, Darwin. *Owen Wister: Chronicler of the West, Gentleman of the East*. Dallas: Southern Methodist University Press, 1985.

Percy, Walker. *Conversations with Walker Percy*. Edited by Lewis A. Lawson and Victor A. Kramer. Jackson: University of Mississippi Press, 1985.

Rader, Dotson. *Tennessee: Cry of the Heart*. New York: Doubleday, 1985.

Ransom, John Crowe. *Selected Letters of John Crowe Ransom*. Edited by Thomas Daniel Young and George Core. Baton Rouge: Louisiana State University Press, 1985.

Ring, Frances Kroll. *Against the Current: As I Remember F. Scott Fitzgerald*. Berkeley, Cal.: Creative Arts, 1985.

Robinson, David. *Chaplin: His Life and Art*. New York: McGraw-Hill, 1985.

Rose, Phyllis. *Writing of Women: Essays in a Renaissance*. Middletown, Conn.: Wesleyan University Press, 1985.

Ruas, Charles. *Conversations with American Writers*. New York: Knopf, 1985.

Rubin, Louis D., Jr., ed. *The History of Southern Literature*. Baton Rouge: Louisiana State University Press, 1985.

Sagan, Françoise. *With Fondest Regards*. Translated by Christine Donougher. New York: Dutton, 1985.

Saroyan, Aram. *Trio: Oona Chaplin, Gloria Vanderbilt, Carol Matthau*. New York: Linden, 1985.

Sartre, Jean-Paul. *War Diaries: November 1939-March 1940*. Translated by Quintin Hoare. New York: Pantheon, 1985.

Secrest, Meryle. *Kenneth Clark: A Biography*. New York: Holt, Rinehart & Winston, 1985.

Singer, Isaac Bashevis, and Richard Burgin. *Conversations with Isaac Bashevis Singer*. Garden City: Doubleday, 1985.

Spoto, Donald. *The Kindness of Strangers: The Life of Tennessee Williams*. Boston: Little, Brown, 1985.

Thomson, David. *Suspects*. New York: Knopf, 1985.

Watkins, Gwen. *Dylan Thomas and Vernon Watkins: Portrait of a Friendship*. Seattle: University of Washington Press, 1985.

Wilder, Thornton. *The Journals of Thornton Wilder, 1939-1961*. Edited by Donald Gallup. New Haven: Yale University Press, 1985.

Wilhelm, J. J. *The American Roots of Ezra Pound*. New York: Garland, 1985.

Necrology

Alvah Bessie—21 July 1985
Heinrich Böll—16 July 1985
Peter Bowman—12 January 1985
Carter Brown—5 May 1985
Joseph Buloff—27 February 1985
Basil Bunting—17 April 1985
Abe Burrows—17 May 1985
Taylor Caldwell—30 August 1985
James Hadley Chase—6 February 1985
Lester Cole—15 August 1985
Mary Crena de Longh—16 April 1985
David Davidson—1 November 1985
Borden Deal—22 January 1985
Margaret Fishback—25 September 1985
Robert Fitzgerald—16 January 1985
Robert Graves—7 December 1985
Merle S. Haas—7 January 1985
Gordon S. Haight—28 December 1985
James Hanley—11 November 1985
Alfred Hayes—14 August 1985
Henry Beetle Hough—6 June 1985
Ralph Ingersoll—8 March 1985

Philip Larkin—3 December 1985
Bertram Lippincott—28 April 1985
Helen MacInnes—30 September 1985
Charles A. Madison—2 February 1985
Albert Maltz—26 April 1985
David McDowell—8 April 1985
Daniel Melcher—29 July 1985
Miodrag Muntyan—27 October 1985
Shiva Naipaul—13 August 1985
Robert Nathan—25 May 1985
Melville B. Nimmer—23 November 1985
Merlo J. Pusey—22 November 1985
Morrie Ryskind—24 August 1985
Aaron Marc Stein—29 August 1985
Theodore Sturgeon—8 May 1985
John Douglass Wallop—1 April 1985
Lynd Ward—28 June 1985
John Wexley—4 February 1985
E. B. White—30 September 1985
Audrey Wood—27 December 1985
Arnold Zohn—24 May 1985

Contributors

Nancy G. Anderson .... *Auburn University at Montgomery*
John F. Andrews .... *Washington, D.C.*
Brian W. Beltman .... *Columbia, South Carolina*
Alexander Blackburn .... *University of Colorado at Colorado Springs*
Reginald Bretnor .... *Medford, Oregon*
Martin Bucco .... *Colorado State University*
Louis J. Budd .... *Duke University*
Mark Busby .... *Texas A&M University*
Tony Buttitta .... *New York, New York*
David G. Byrd .... *University of South Carolina*
Joseph Caldwell .... *Columbia, South Carolina*
Michael Collins (Dennis Lynds) .... *Santa Barbara, California*
Robert C. Conard .... *University of Dayton*
Richard Hauer Costa .... *Texas A&M University*
Mary Doll .... *Redlands, California*
John R. Douglas .... *San Jose State University*
Lynn Felder .... *Hilton Head, South Carolina*
Victor Fischer .... *University of California*
George Garrett .... *University of Virginia*
Michael Groden .... *University of Western Ontario*
David Havird .... *University of Virginia*
Carol Johnston .... *Clemson University*
Patrick J. Keane .... *LeMoyne College*
Howard Kissel .... *New York, New York*
Richard Kostelanetz .... *New York, New York*
Keith Kroll .... *University of California, Riverside*
Rena Leibovitch .... *New York, New York*
Craig Lesley .... *Lewis and Clark College*
Philippa Levine .... *Flinders University of South Australia*
Jeffrey Meyers .... *University of Colorado*
William Mould .... *University of South Carolina*
James Nagel .... *Northeastern University*
Ed Ochester .... *University of Pittsburgh*
Carl E. Rollyson, Jr. .... *Wayne State University*
Jean W. Ross .... *Columbia, South Carolina*
Stephen Sandy .... *Bennington College*
William J. Scheick .... *University of Texas at Austin*
Carl R. Shirley .... *University of South Carolina*
Morty Sklar .... *Iowa City, Iowa*
Philippa Toomey .... *London, England*
Lewis Turco .... *State University of New York at Oswego*
Robert Kean Turner .... *University of Wisconsin at Milwaukee*
Everett C. Wilkie, Jr. .... *Hartford, Connecticut*
Hal Wyss .... *Albion College*

Cumulative Index

Dictionary of Literary Biography, Volumes 1-47
Dictionary of Literary Biography Yearbook, 1980-1985
Dictionary of Literary Biography Documentary Series, Volumes 1-4

Cumulative Index

DLB before number: *Dictionary of Literary Biography,* Volumes 1-47
Y before number: *Dictionary of Literary Biography Yearbook,* 1980-1985
DS before number: *Dictionary of Literary Biography Documentary Series,* Volumes 1-4

A

B

C

E

F

G

I

J

K

Cumulative Index

L

N

O

P

Q

R

S

6655

WHAT THE LIGHT WAS LIKE
poems by
AMY CLAMPITT

DEEP
WITHIN TH
RAVIN

Lamo
Sele
for 1

Poems by Philip Schultz

SHORE GUIDE TO
FLOCKING NAMES

ROBERT HUFF

SONG
OF THE
SKY

VERSIONS OF
NATIVE AMERICAN SONGS & POE
BY BRIAN SWANN